What Makes a Marriage Last

Marlo Thomas & Phil Donahue

What Makes a Marriage Last

40

Celebrated Couples
Share with Us the Secrets
to a Happy Life

Edited by Bruce Kluger

HarperOne
An Imprint of HarperCollinsPublishers

The stories in this book were drawn from in-person interviews conducted by Marlo Thomas and Phil Donahue. The authors have edited and condensed the material for readability.

FIRST HARPERCOLLINS PAPERBACK EDITION PUBLISHED IN 2021

Designed by SBI Book Arts, LLC

Library of Congress Cataloging-in-Publication Data is available upon request.

ISBN 978-0-06-298260-5

21 22 23 24 25 LSC 10 9 8 7 6 5 4 3 2 1

For each other.

Happy Anniversary, sweetheart.

Contents

Foreword

By Marlo Thomas

So there we were on the deck of the *Mississippi Queen*, the beautiful old paddleboat that sails the river that bears her name. Phil and I had just attended the Kentucky Derby and thought the cruise would be a fun way to end the day. Sure, it was a corny attraction targeted at tourists and the hopelessly romantic, but Phil and I had just recently started dating, so we qualified on both counts.

We'd just finished our dinner when the entertainers walked on deck. They were a small band of very old gentlemen who specialized in Dixieland music—a banjo player, a pianist, and a sweet-looking little man on the clarinet. They began to play, and the crowd immediately began bopping and swaying. All three of the men were clearly having a wonderful time, but I couldn't take my eyes off that clarinetist—he was in a zone. You could see the sheer pleasure he took in making his music, submerged as he was in a personal state of bliss. I was mesmerized by him.

After a moment, Phil nudged me. "Look at the clarinet player," he whispered, "how happy he is."

"I'm already there!" I whispered back. Then I took Phil's hand.

It was just a passing moment, one of probably a billion that Phil and I have shared over the years—a warm confirmation that we'd both been moved by the same thing. And yet to this day, that little man and his clarinet remain a touchstone for us as the definition of a person who's truly in the moment. Whether it's someone delivering a passionate speech, a bustling waitress who loves her job, or a grandfather rocking a child in his

arms, one of us will nudge the other and say, "That's a real clarinet player." To us, that's the highest compliment.

This is not a huge thing, I know, but it is one more tiny connection for Phil and me, a secret code passed between two people who long ago began thinking many of the same thoughts and feeling many of the same feelings. Over a long marriage, I've noticed, there comes an unconscious agreement between two people to tuck this little moment, or that little observation, into the cupboard of shared memories they've collected over the years. That's the stuff of marriage.

Marriage. Wow. I was the girl who never wanted any part of it. That's because marriage didn't seem like a roomy enough place for me—and that's putting it nicely. In fact, I always had some cheeky remark to offer on the subject—like "Marriage is like living with a jailer you have to please," or "Marriage is like a vacuum cleaner: you stick it to your ear and it sucks out all your energy and ambition."

And now here I am, writing a book—with my husband—about marriage. Life's funny, right? In my own defense, when I was growing up I didn't see a lot of marriages that looked like a club I wanted to be a part of. Even the couples who had stayed married for a long time made me wonder, *Do they really want to?* To me, many of those couples seemed to have made a bargain, and they were just good enough people to have lived up to it. Or maybe they secretly wanted to break the deal a long time ago, but were stuck with it—and *in* it.

Others seemed basically content with one another—*but* were *they really happy?* I never believed that true happiness with another human being was sustainable forever, or even "till death do us part."

But then something happened. I went on a talk show in 1977 to promote a project, but when the host walked into the green room beforehand to say hi—that thick white hair, those killer blue eyes—it was like one of those shampoo commercials where everything suddenly goes into slow motion.

Beverly Hills, California; May 21, 1980

When we got on the air, things got a bit embarrassing. Here I was, this very strong feminist with all sorts of penetrating observations about equality and gender roles—and pretty much everything that came out of my mouth was a girlish giggle.

I'd been on a lot of talk shows by that time, but this felt more like a first date. Phil asked me more personal questions than I'd ever been asked in an interview. He dug in about the men I had dated and asked if there was "someone special." He was a man on a mission—a divorced man, I might add, raising four boys (his daughter lived with her mother)—and I was his eager accomplice.

As I look back on it now, it was not professional, but it was honest—a spontaneous, chemical reaction. People still tell us that they saw that *Donahue* episode and instantly knew something was going on.

They were right. Phil and I went to dinner the next night and married three years later. Our wedding day was everything we wanted it to be—small, just our families, thirty-five people, intimate and very private. It still feels like yesterday.

Over the decades, Phil and I have lived the sweeping landscape of marriage, and sometimes that landscape has had its valleys. But each obstacle we faced as a couple not only helped us find the solution to the challenge, but also strengthened the bond that had brought us together.

And then we got a call. It was May 2019, and Phil and I were about to celebrate our thirty-ninth wedding anniversary, when the phone rang. I picked up and heard the tearful voice of one of our dearest friends.

"We're getting a divorce," she told me, and I nearly lost my breath. She and her husband had been married twenty-eight years. They were good friends and always good company. This earthquake in their lives shook Phil and me—and many of our friends, too.

"What happened?" we kept asking each other. If it happened to them, could it happen to any of us? Where did they go wrong, we wondered—and, more to the point, where did we go right?

This heartbreaking event in the lives of two of our friends prompted Phil and me to talk about our marriage. What did we like about us as a couple? What do we still not get right? How far have we traveled since that spring day in 1980 when we made those promises to each other, and what exactly has kept us going year after year?

We started to wonder if there really is a secret sauce to a successful marriage. And that's how we came to create this book—one that would pull together the stories of many devoted couples and uncover some of the mystery of marriage in a way that could be a source of information and inspiration for other couples—from newlyweds to long-married couples like us.

This was new territory for Phil and me. For years we've been asked to write about our marriage, but we've always been reluctant. Who are we to give advice? We're not experts. And it's working, so why jinx it?

But we're living in a very negative time—a time when we're lashing out more than we're reaching out; a time in which we too often forget that we're at our best, our strongest, when we're holding the hand—and have the back—of someone we care about.

So Phil and I broke an ironclad rule of our marriage—for the first time, ever—and decided to work on a project together. Talk about putting your marriage to the test!

We began by making a list of long-married couples we admired. We thought there was so much we could learn from them about the ways they have made their marriages last.

- How has marriage made them different people, and what were they willing to change in themselves to accommodate the other?

- How did they first find each other, and what do they do today to sustain that initial attraction?

- What did they learn from their own parents' marriages that taught them what to do—or what not to do—in their own marriages?

- How do they manage their fights—and who's usually the first one to broker peace?

- Has anything slowed the momentum of their marriage—money? kids? health? career? jealousy?—and how did they get the engine humming again?

- Did anything ever threaten to blow the whole thing apart—and, if so, how did they come back from the brink?

- What advice might they give to younger couples starting out—or the already married—that they wish they had known themselves when they first took their vows?

- And what was it about their spouse that convinced them that this was someone they could spend the rest of their life with?

For Ron and Cheryl Howard (married forty-five years), it's about committing to the never-ending work of marriage. After more than four decades the couple continues to maintain domestic harmony through exercises they learned from professional counselors. "It always comes back to one important question," Ron told us: "How much value do you place in the relationship, and what are you willing to do to make it continue to work?"

For George Stephanopoulos and Ali Wentworth (nineteen years), it's about not permitting the flame of passion to flicker and grabbing romance whenever you can. "If you have the stomach flu, I get it," Ali told us. "'But otherwise, you have to make a point of having sex. We're all tired. We all have lives and careers. So push it."

For Sting and Trudie Styler (twenty-eight years), it's the recognition of a soulful, almost otherworldly connection that has pulled them together from the very start. "The moment I clapped eyes on her, I just knew who she was, instantly," Sting said. "I felt as if we had always known each other."

For Chip and Joanna Gaines (seventeen years), it was learning to trust in each other as they launched their business from the ground up. "That first year," Joanna remembered, "I started seeing the beauty of the unpredictability, and realizing what he was teaching me. It was all about learning to trust Chip. I thought, *Holy cow, we now have one life.*"

For Viola Davis and Julius Tennon (seventeen years), it's the acknowledgment that marriage is the truest of partnerships. "You can't operate separately with your own joy if it doesn't honor the big umbrella of the ultimate commitment," Viola said. "You've got to feed the good of the whole."

For Elton John and David Furnish (married for six years, domestic partners for fifteen), it's about giving a partner the benefit of the doubt when tempers flare. "Before I pass judgment," David noted, "I always try to think about what else he's dealing with. Has he just done seven shows and is exhausted? Has he just traveled through the night? Maybe a record hasn't charted the way he wants it to chart. I always try to choose my moments."

For Jimmy and Rosalynn Carter (seventy-four years), the bond is in their faith. "We read the Bible together every night," President Carter told us. "And when I'm overseas, or when Rosalynn is traveling, we still read the same chapter, even though we might be five thousand miles apart. We share the same text, and it keeps us connected."

And for Jamie Lee Curtis and Christopher Guest (thirty-six years), their philosophy of marriage included one wholly unexpected word—a word so surprising, that I actually had to ask Jamie to repeat it. I'll let you discover that word for yourself.

Phil and I set a few ground rules for this adventure. In all cases, we met with the couples in person—because nothing beats the intimacy and authenticity of a real face-to-face (to-face-to-face) double date. So even though it meant running through a lot of airports, we kept to that standard.

We also decided that longevity is the truest test of a marriage's mettle, so we wanted to speak to couples who had been married twenty years or more—though in order to hear from another generation, we thought it wise to add a few couples who have been married from fifteen to twenty years. Of course, we waived that requirement for the gay couples we interviewed. Their marriages weren't legal in the United States until 2004, and only then in select states until the historic nationwide Supreme Court ruling in 2015.

And speaking of longevity, we've included one bonus chapter at the end of the book that celebrates a couple we learned about only days before we handed in our manuscript—a charming husband and wife whose marriage earned the distinction of being in the Guinness Book of World Records. What an inspiration they are.

As wildly different as all of these stories are, they share a common plotline: that of two people joining hands and stepping up to the most challenging, invigorating, inspiring, infuriating, thrilling, terrifying, delightful, and heavenly job on earth: making a marriage last.

Foreword

By Phil Donahue

This book is the result of many airplane flights that brought Marlo and me to the homes of forty famous couples we admired who agreed to chat with us about their marriages, and what they believe contributed to their lasting unions at a time when half of us get divorced (including me, many years ago).

My first job as a journalist was in Adrian, Michigan. How powerful I was. With my microphone bearing the letters WABJ RADIO, I could stop the mayor cold on the steps of City Hall. And I was only twenty-two years old, looking more like fifteen. But I had power that surprised even me.

I was a reporter. I took no test, I did not pee in a bottle. I said I was a reporter and I was. This easy access to journalism ensures that there will always be lots of journalists (even me), making it likely that somewhere in the middle of this large crowd of reporters will be found the truth.

So it is with this book. It is our hope that readers of the stories on the following pages will find truths worth remembering, ideas that promote a marriage that lasts.

One couple shared with us their promise to say "I love you" aloud to each other every morning and night. Another told us they intentionally go to bed angry—and hope to forget the fight by morning. No two marriages are alike.

I cannot ask forty couples to share personal experiences without sharing my own. So here goes.

. . .

I've always noticed that the most important things happen when you don't look for them, and in my case, that important thing happened in Dayton, Ohio. The year was 1972, and she was on the road, promoting her TV special *Free to Be . . . You and Me.* I remembered her as very bright, articulate, Catholic—and sexy. She was also the perfect guest for my TV show, *Donahue*—famous, beautiful, popular, and very conversant on important issues about men and women, feminism and politics. She was a "hangover guest"—the kind of guest I needed on those mornings when I felt headachy and not very sharp.

I knew the moment I met her in the dressing room that here was a guest who would never, ever let me die on the air. She also had a great body, and had the year been 1953 she would have been what we Catholics called an "impure thought."

The second time I met her was in Chicago in 1977, and a lot had happened to me in the interim. I was single, trying to raise four boys (my daughter was living with their mother), and just beginning to get used to the idea of going to social events with a woman who was not my wife. When I walked into our green room at WGN in Chicago, her back was to me. She turned around and I immediately remembered the eyes, which hadn't changed since Dayton. Nor had the smile or the firm handshake.

From reading up on her, I was impressed with the things she had to say about her talented mother, who had completely turned her back on her own career so that she could be the supportive spouse of the famous Danny Thomas. I didn't realize it then, but my interest in her mother earned me her admiration and attention—and an extra-long look from those big brown eyes.

The time for the show was approaching, and we were doing something for which both of us had been disciplined in school—we were talking, aloud and with enthusiasm, and at once. We discovered similarities. Her folks, like mine, used the word "gumption" when describing people of achievement. "Gallivanting" was another oft-used word in her house and in mine. (It was what your parents said you were doing when you didn't come home on time.)

As we made our way down the hall for the start of my program, I walked behind her and wondered how this glamorous star with the bad-thought body could be so girl-next-door.

The show went very well. For both of us. When she left, I wondered if I would ever see her again. I made no indication that I wanted to, and though she was very gracious, I saw no signs that she was wondering the same thing.

All the same, that afternoon I called her Chicago hotel, prepared to offer a well-rehearsed, "Hey, you were great on my show today." She wasn't in, so I left a message.

I heard nothing from her that day. And when I retired that evening, I knew she had my message, wasn't interested, and, worse, was probably out "gallivanting" around Chicago.

The next day I met Bob Cromie in the hallway at WGN. He hosted his own show, *Book Beat*, and when I asked him who his guest was for that day's taping, he told me that it was the same woman I'd been pining for.

"She's great," I said . . . and then added, "I've got a crush on her."

Later that afternoon, Cromie stopped by my office to say, "She said she's got a crush on you." I thanked him for the report, gave the information some thought, remembered that my phoner had never been answered, and concluded firmly that for all her charm, she was capable of blarney.

Besides, Bob Cromie looked nothing like Cupid.

When I arrived home that night, a note next to the kitchen telephone, written in red ink and in my son Kevin's hand, read, "Marlo Thomas called."

. . .

Marlo made her first visit to my home in Winnetka, Illinois, during the time I was a single father raising four sons. Until then, she'd been a single woman, living contentedly on her own (two dogs, no kids), so this trip to the Donahues had to have been startling for her—first crawling over four Hondas parked in our small driveway and then entering a house that featured empty pizza boxes under every bed.

Michael, Kevin, Danny, and Jimmy extended their hands stiffly, yet politely.

Marlo soon became a resident of that house, and a very short time after her arrival, she overheard Michael say to a telephone buddy, "I'll call you back, my Dad is having a spazz."

"What's 'a spazz'?" Marlo asked.

Spazz: A sudden eruption by Dad, following a misdeed by one of the boys.

Spazzz (with three z's): A sudden *and prolonged* eruption by Dad, following a larger misdeed by one of the boys.

With the arrival of Ms. Thomas at our home, I attempted to keep my spazzes in check. Often impossible.

Like the time James Patrick Donahue, the youngest of the boys, set up a CB radio system in his bedroom and became a part of a community of "good buddies" in the neighborhood who broadcast colorful messages to each other. Apparently, some "buddy" said something that insulted somebody else, after which the insulted party exacted revenge on the Donahue's front yard.

Treed: A verb describing the act of throwing rolls of Charmin tissue high into trees of an unsuspecting neighbor, where gravity takes hold and the rolls ricochet downward through the branches, leaving a trail of toilet paper.

The "decorated" trees on the front lawn alerted me to the presence of a citizen band warrior under my own roof. I had a spazz.

Marlo does not fly back to L.A.

And then there was the boys' band. Their nightly practice sessions pierced the walls of the Pine Street homestead, making sleep in any room impossible. The entire house vibrated.

"Just ignore it," I told a sleep-deprived Marlo—who the next morning promptly ordered sound-proofing for the walls of the bedroom the boys practiced in. When that didn't work, I had a three-*z* spazzz.

Marlo stays in Winnetka.

And then new things began to happen. The young Donahues started noticing some endearing changes in their lives, thanks to the TV star in the house.

For the first time, the Donahues began having a real sit-down dinnertime, instead of the kids scattered all over the house in front of TVs.

With actual conversations, just like a real family.

And during which I learned more about my boys than I ever would have. And I saw that Marlo knew who each of them was individually, unlike most other people, who simply saw them as a flock of boys. She made an Italian dinner one night—her mom was Italian—along with a big salad, which she put down in front of Jimmy, who said, "I don't eat anything green."

Marlo? She stays in Winnetka.

Marlo Thomas was forty-two years old when she married for the first time—the time she married me! She makes every birthday and holiday a special celebration, most of all because she delights in doing it. And the presents are always thoughtful—and usually expensive.

She is an Italian-Lebanese girl filled with all the wonderful DNA of both, including an interest in closeness—hugging and kissing, verbalizing sweet nothings and the like. Imagine her disappointment, married to a man who will cuddle anywhere, anytime. But speak aloud affectionately? Not so easy.

Frank McCourt, one of the best chroniclers of all things Irish, wrote in *Angela's Ashes*: "If I were in America I could say, 'I love you, Dad,' the way they do in the films. But in Limerick they'd laugh at you. In Limerick, you are only allowed to say you love God, and babies, and horses that win. Anything else is softness in the head."

So, now, I'm smarter about my struggle against eighty-four years of an anti-intimate culture to say something truthful about me, my marriage, and my wife, who has borne the weight of a cross forced on her by a Silent Sam Irish husband who has such difficulty saying, "Thanks for not running away from Winnetka."

And finally, I promise to share more often and out loud, the comment I must have feared would make me appear soft in the head:

"I love you, Marlo."

What Makes a Marriage Last

President Jimmy and Rosalynn Carter

MARRIED IN 1946

"I fell in love with a photograph of him.
My mother said it must have been his white uniform."

As we walked up the steps of the Carter Center in Atlanta, Georgia, to interview President Jimmy and Rosalynn Carter, one question kept screaming through our minds: "Why in God's name did we decide that the first people we'd interview for this book would be a former American president and his long-admired First Lady?"

Not that we were particularly nervous about sitting down with such an historic couple. We'd both been in the presence of powerful people before, and God knows Phil had logged in six thousand hours of talk television over the course of his career—including interviews with all the presidents. But it was the bloody equipment we were worried about. We'd bought special recording devices for this literary adventure of ours—along with high-tech lapel mics—and, frankly, we were all thumbs with it. So many buttons. So many flashing lights.

As it turns out, we botched it from the get-go. Marlo assumed the red

Plains, Georgia; July 7, 1946

blinking light meant the recorder was on. It wasn't. But luckily we had brought our good old-fashioned iPhone as a backup and captured it all.

But if this first interview in our first professional project together had a bumpy start in the tech department, we couldn't have picked a better couple to begin our exploration of that grand old institution called marriage.

Jimmy and Rosalynn Carter have been married for seventy-three years—almost three-quarters of a century. When the couple wed in 1946, Eleanor Rosalynn Smith was one month shy of her nineteenth birthday and, according to President Carter, "the most timid person I'd ever met." He was a recent graduate of the Naval Academy in Annapolis, Maryland, and all of twenty-one years old.

Despite the worldwide acclaim they've earned during their time together—the years in the White House, the couple's global humanitarian work through the Carter Center, his 2002 Nobel Peace Prize—we found the Carters to be as plain and simple as Plains, Georgia, the town they grew up in and still call home. They were direct, refreshingly unguarded, and a bit feisty at times. They even bickered with each other, just like the rest of us.

President Carter, ninety-four, was the first to walk in—or should we say *bound* in. Smiling that famous toothy grin and dressed in a starched, light-blue shirt, he looked as vibrant as we'd expect of a man who still teaches Sunday school two weekends a month at the local Maranatha Baptist Church and, along with Mrs. Carter, wields a hammer and paintbrush to build houses for Habitat for Humanity. The month after this conversation took place, he became the oldest-living former president in U.S. history.

On entering, he gave us hugs and took his place opposite us at a coffee table. In one corner of the room stood the Stars and Stripes; in another, the flag of the President of the United States. One of his three Grammy awards sat atop his desk, and all around were photos of the couple's family, which includes three sons and a daughter, twelve grandchildren, and fourteen great-grandchildren.

A few minutes later, Mrs. Carter entered quietly, looking a bit more fragile than her husband, in dark slacks and a light-colored blouse. At age ninety-one, she was still the sweetly pretty woman we remembered from the days when she was our First Lady. Back then the Carters famously bucked tradition and, as her husband's most trusted confidante, Mrs. Carter sat in on Cabinet meetings.

Before we could ask a single question, President Carter, a prolific author who has written thirty-four books himself (including one coauthored with his wife, 1987's *Everything to Gain: Making the Most of the Rest of Your Life*), had a question for us: "Your book is about marriage, I presume. Do you have a deadline?"

"Yes," Marlo said. "Our book is being published in May 2020, in time for our fortieth anniversary, on May 21."

"Good. Then let's get started," he said.

Spoken like a commander-in-chief. We were off and running.

"We were both older when we got married," Marlo said. "I was forty-two and Phil was forty-four. So we wonder what it was like for you both to marry so young."

"Back then, we graduated high school at sixteen," Mrs. Carter told us in her buttery-soft Georgia drawl, "and there was nothing a woman could do except be a teacher or a librarian or a secretary or nurse. I had only fourteen people in my graduating class in Plains, and the girls were all marrying and having babies. I thought I was going to be an old maid—I literally did. Two friends who were boys would call me to go on dates, and I'd tell my mother to answer the phone and say I wasn't home. I didn't know a single boy I thought I'd want to spend my life with."

MARLO: So what was it about this guy here that made you think he was the one?

ROSALYNN: Jimmy's sister Ruth was my best friend, and I spent a lot of time at their house, though he was never there. I always said I fell in love with a photograph of him on her bedroom wall. Then Jimmy came home from the Naval Academy for the month—I was eighteen—and Ruth and I plotted to get me together with him. She'd call and say,

"Come over! He's here!" and I'd go flying over to her house, but he'd be gone again. Finally, one night he stopped by the church and asked me to go to the movies with him.

MARLO: What was it about him that attracted you?

ROSALYNN: My mother said it must have been his white uniform, but I don't know. I just wanted to meet him. Well, I knew him—everybody in Plains knew everybody else—but he's three years older than me. I first started noticing him when I was thirteen, and, I mean, there's just no relationship between a thirteen-year-old and a sixteen-year-old in that situation.

PHIL: President Carter, I've read that you knew right away that she was the one.

JIMMY: I did, yes. I had a lot of girlfriends growing up, in high school and so forth. When I went to the Naval Academy, we weren't permitted to go outside the academy much. When I was home on leave that time, I was dating a beauty queen, Miss Georgia Southwestern State.

PHIL: Whoa!

JIMMY: I would go up to see her every night on my leave, and the next to last night before I had to go back, her family had a reunion, and no outsiders were invited—so I didn't have anything to do. I was cruising around with my sister Ruth and her boyfriend, just looking for a date, and I picked up Rosalynn in front of the Methodist church.

PHIL: You picked up girls at the church!

JIMMY: Well, that's where a whole bunch of young folks would assemble at that time. Church was the center of our lives. I'd known Rosalynn since the day she was born, because we were next-door neighbors. I remember going over there with my mother, who was a nurse, to see the new baby. My mother told me later, "You peeked through the cradle bars and saw your future lifeline."

MARLO: That's precious.

JIMMY: I didn't have any ideas about romance, of course. But the morning after that first date, I told my mother that Rosalynn was the one I wanted to marry.

MARLO: Why were you so sure?

JIMMY: I just felt compatible with her. She was beautiful and innocent, and there was a resonance. We rode in the rumble seat of a Ford pickup—Ruth and her boyfriend in the front—and I kissed her on that first date. I remember that vividly. I never was doubtful about her, and that Christmas, I told her I loved her and asked her to marry me.

ROSALYNN: The proposal was actually the next Presidents' Day.

JIMMY: We disagree on this. But on Presidents' Day weekend, she and my parents came up to the Naval Academy, and I know I asked her then.

MARLO: And...?

JIMMY: She said no.

MARLO: Really?

JIMMY: So from February until May, I figured she was dating all the other available boys to find a better match. Finally, in May, she said yes.

PHIL: Why had you said no before, Mrs. Carter?

ROSALYNN: I was the oldest of four, and my father, who'd never gone to high school, died when I was thirteen. I promised him on his deathbed that I'd go to a four-year college. I graduated from junior college but never had a chance to go back.

MARLO: You got married instead.

ROSALYNN: Yes, on July 7, 1946. On our first wedding anniversary, I was in the hospital in Norfolk, having our first child, Jack.

Those navy years were a challenging time for them, the couple told us, marked by frequent separations and 1940s-era gender roles. "It was a common thing for naval couples to raise a family," President Carter explained, "and I was gone at sea most of the time. So she had full responsibility to take care of the household and whatever babies came, to shop for groceries and pay the bills. When we were first a bride and groom, I never interfered in her decision-making as far as the children were concerned or the household expenses. She had her life, and I had mine."

Mrs. Carter nodded. "I had to take care of everything," she recalled, "and this was a totally, totally different life from the one I'd had in Plains.

He was not there, so I developed a good deal of independence. I did it because I had to. I would go get groceries with the baby and get off the bus at the street corner, put the groceries down, run home with the baby, then go back and pick up the groceries. It was tough."

MARLO: Were you lonely?

ROSALYNN: Well, there were seven ensigns' wives in our complex, and everybody was having babies. Luckily, we lived upstairs from the skipper and his wife, so anytime I needed help with the new baby, she was there for me. With so many wives being pregnant and having babies, things were easier for me. We'd all get together while the men were gone.

PHIL: When Jimmy returned from sea, were you a different wife?

ROSALYNN: Not really. I was still a total housewife.

JIMMY: She was. I was completely dominant. I wouldn't interfere with her running the household, which was her life, but whenever there were major decisions to be made, I never consulted her—and she never questioned me. In fact, when I decided to resign from the navy and change our lives completely, I didn't even ask her ahead of time.

ROSALYNN: And I rebelled.

PHIL: I'm impressed that you already had a sense of your own power, Mrs. Carter. No one was going to walk all over you, and certainly not a boy. As we sit here, you don't seem like the demure wife. You don't allow your husband to talk over you.

JIMMY: That's true! But back then, after the navy, when I decided to run for the Georgia State Senate, I didn't even tell her about it. I just came home one day and changed my work clothes to a suit and tie. She asked me if I was going to a funeral, and I said, "No, I'm running for the Senate." I never even discussed that with her before I made the final decision.

MARLO: Wow.

ROSALYNN: I know. We talk about that now. We say, "How that could possibly have happened?"

JIMMY: I wouldn't dream of doing that during the last forty-five years of our marriage. Once we began working together in business, we became equal partners in almost everything. It was a transformation in our marriage.

MARLO: How did that happen?

ROSALYNN: Can I explain that?

JIMMY: Yes, if you don't get sidetracked. Go ahead.

ROSALYNN: After he came back from the navy, we had a farm supply business. We sold the farmers fertilizer and seed, and then we bought their crops when they brought them in—corn and cotton and peanuts. I kept the books for the business, so it wasn't long before I knew on paper more about the work than he did. So he'd come to ask me my advice.

JIMMY: That's true. We began to work together as equals in our business. I would defer to Rosalynn, or consult with her, before I made any major decisions. We learned how to work together.

Wearing that suit and tie, local farmer Jimmy Carter announced his candidacy for the Georgia State Senate in 1962, just fifteen days before the election. He ran on a platform of integration and racial tolerance, but carefully avoided raising the ire of segregationists. Rosalynn proved to be a savvy politico and ultimately helped her husband orchestrate a victory. Then came the governorship of Georgia in 1970, and six years later the U.S. presidency.

"It strikes me," Marlo said, "that it's not just political talent that wins office, but also a great partnership with a spouse. Look at George and Barbara Bush. The Clintons. The Obamas. But surely you can't be on the same page all the time. How do you remain friends and partners when you disagree?"

President Carter folded his hands on his lap. "We found out a long time ago that disagreements are inevitable between two strong-willed people," he said. "But we decided early on to give each other plenty of space. If Rosalynn is interested in something, she does it her own way, accepting my help when she needs it. And she gives me plenty of space to work on my own projects but helps me when I need it. We also look for things to do together."

"Such as?" Phil asked.

"We do bird-watching, fly-fishing, and tennis—and all kinds of stuff," Mrs. Carter said. "We learned to downhill ski when he was sixty-two and I was fifty-nine. Jimmy doesn't want to just learn about things, he wants to *do* them." They both had hip injuries in 2019, and, for the first time ever, Mrs. Carter noted, they had to slow down a bit. "Both of us were in bad shape for a while," she said, "but we've outgrown that now."

Over time, the Carters told us, they've learned the importance of giving each other breathing room; yet sitting across from them, it was strikingly evident that they are very, very connected. Part of that bond comes by way of their faith: they are deeply Christian.

"We read the Bible together every night," President Carter revealed, "and we have done that for fifty years. And nowadays, we both speak a little Spanish, so we read the Bible in Spanish, too."

"That's fascinating," Marlo said. "Do you go in order through the Bible or do you pick a page?"

"Well, right now we're going through the New Testament in the Spanish-English version," he said, "so one night Rosalynn will read, and the next night I'll read. And when I'm overseas, or when Rosalynn is traveling, we still read the same chapter, even though we might be five thousand miles apart. We share the same text, and it keeps us connected."

Their longevity as a couple, President Carter explained, could also be because they've tried to keep the classic promise of spouses everywhere:

"We decided quite a while ago to make sure we never go to sleep in the same bed angry with each other," he said. "We have a lot of arguments during the day, but we made up our minds that we would try to reconcile at night."

On one hand, this didn't surprise us. After all, President Carter is one of the world's most acclaimed peacemakers. As president, he masterminded the Camp David Accords between Egypt and Israel in 1978, and later, as a private citizen, he was awarded the Nobel Peace Prize for his efforts to find peaceful solutions to a range of global conflicts.

On the other hand, they're a married couple, and married couples fight. So how do they broker peace when negotiations break down?

"Well, first of all, we have a basic premise of never being deprived of an ability to communicate with each other," President Carter said. "Sometimes we get in a huff—Rosalynn or I might pout for a little while, but then we'll try to reconcile. Most of the time I take the initiative, because I realize that there are two sides to every issue or that I was wrong."

PHIL: The biggest surprise for me here, in the short time we've had to talk, is that you're a feminist, Rosalynn.

ROSALYNN: Well, Jimmy has always thought I could do anything. Always. And so I've done everything. I campaigned all over the country. I've done things I never dreamed I could do.

PHIL: And he doesn't have to win all the arguments.

ROSALYNN: That's right.

JIMMY: I don't always win.

ROSALYNN: Jimmy gave me the confidence to do things I was afraid of. I remember when we were in the Georgia governor's mansion, I used to greet tourists and talk to everybody who came through. One day, Jimmy told me I was going to have to make a speech. I was so nervous, and he said, "Why don't you just do what you do at the governor's mansion when you're talking to the tourists?" So I made the speech with no problem, ran to the telephone and called Jimmy to say, "I did it!" I did it because I had to do it.

The former president took the same bullish approach to some of the public difficulties he and his wife faced as a couple. "When you were defeated in the 1980 presidential election," Marlo asked, "did you turn to Rosalynn to help you pick yourself up, or did you go into a corner and pout?"

Mrs. Carter interrupted. "Oh, *he* had to help *me* after that loss!" she said. "I was the one who was upset. If he hadn't helped me, I don't think I ever would have gotten over it."

President Carter confirmed his wife's account of that painful time. "She was angry with the public, and with Ronald Reagan," he recalled, "so I searched for good things about not being reelected, to ease her pain. I was just fifty-six years old, I told her, and she was just fifty-three, so we had at least twenty-five years of life ahead of us. That's when the Carter Center was born. It has been a wonderful challenge."

Indeed, the center allowed the couple to continue the kind of work that had been so important to them during their years in the White House—when President Carter was dealing daily with domestic and global issues, and Mrs. Carter was busy working on mental health, immunization, and women's issues.

"Someone once told me that Jackie Kennedy labeled everything she wore in the White House and kept a record of it," Mrs. Carter said, "but I didn't have any time to fool around with a wardrobe! I did what I wanted to do and what I thought was important."

That enterprising spirit continues today. Since founding the Carter Center, the couple has tackled everything from thorny medical crises to conflict resolution in countries like North Korea and Liberia.

One thing we discovered while sitting down with the Carters is that, when you're talking to a former president, the schedule allows no wiggle room. This was confirmed by an aide who popped her head into President Carter's office and told him that his next appointment had arrived. Even so, we squeezed in one last question:

"What was the most difficult time in your marriage?" Phil asked. To our surprise, it wasn't their days as struggling farmers, nor the anguish of the Iran hostage crisis, nor even the heartbreaking election loss in 1980.

"Well, honestly," President Carter said, "the biggest challenge in our marriage was when we tried to write a book together."

We shared a glance with each other.

MARLO: What made it so hard?

JIMMY: We decided I would write one chapter and she would write the next, and then we'd swap chapters and edit each other. And I found out very quickly—this is my version of it—that Rosa's memory was very faulty. She couldn't remember details of what happened, and we also had different writing styles. I write very rapidly—I wrote thirty-four books, remember—and Rosalynn doesn't. So I would write my chapter and give it to her and say, "Here. Edit." She'd view it as a rough draft. But when *she* wrote a chapter, it was like God had handed down this precious text carved in stone, and if I so much as changed one word, it caused her serious distress. It was breaking up our marriage.

ROSALYNN: We couldn't talk about it.

JIMMY: We couldn't discuss it with each other. We just wrote ugly letters back and forth on the word processor.

MARLO: Is this your version of what happened, too, Mrs. Carter?

ROSALYNN: I don't remember my memory being faulty back then.

JIMMY: The thing is, we would agree on 97 percent of what we wrote, but then there was 3 percent we didn't agree on. Or I might have found something humorous that she thought was very serious. We had a difference of opinion about things like our first date—stories that were ancient history but important for the book.

ROSALYNN: He'd quickly write a chapter in an afternoon, so I knew that it had to be a draft. But I'd work and work on my chapters until they were perfect. I didn't want him to touch them.

MARLO: I get it.

ROSALYNN: It was hard.

MARLO: Were those the nights that you had to make up before you went to sleep?

JIMMY: No. That came a little bit later.

MARLO: That's good to know. I was feeling really intimidated by that.

PHIL: So what eventually happened with the book?

JIMMY: Our editor came down to Plains and said, "I'd hate for you to give up this book because it has such good potential." He said, "Let me work on it," and I said, "Okay." So he went through the whole book and found the paragraphs we couldn't agree on completely. He divided them up and gave half of the paragraphs to me and the other half to Rosalynn. He put an *R* by Rosalynn's paragraphs and a *J* by mine. Once I wrote a final version of a paragraph, Rosalynn couldn't change it—and vice versa. So we saved the book.

PHIL: You saved the book.

MARLO: Well, that's a relief. You saved the book, and you're still talking.

JIMMY: Yes, we're still talking. But writing a book together is tough. [*Smiling mischievously*] So y'all be careful.

John McEnroe and Patty Smyth

MARRIED IN 1997

"Women are notorious for saying, 'Oh, he's got the potential'—but potential is not good enough. Marry the person, don't marry potential."

So what would possess an edgy rock chick to marry a divorced tennis champ famous for smashing beverage carts with a tennis racket and berating penalty-imposing umpires with his signature "You cannot be serious!"? ("Thank God I wasn't with him back then," Patty told us, "I would have had a heart attack.")

And what would possess this bad boy of tennis to settle down with this much hipper, no-nonsense music moll, knowing there was a good chance she would turn him from the hothead of the court into a cool dude and loyal husband of twenty-three years?

These were just two of the questions bouncing through our heads as our cab pulled up to the home of John McEnroe and Patty Smyth on New York City's leafy Upper West Side.

Patty and John live in the one of those grand old New York buildings designed by the legendary Emery Roth. While the exterior and lobby of the building announce a chilly refinement, once you get inside the couple's apartment, things warm up pretty fast.

In person and together, Patty and John are very casual and very real, and they play off each other like jazz musicians—there's no pretense about them, no need to please; they're just themselves. They're also fun to hang with.

They live on the top floor of the building (make that *floors*—they have four of those). The very top level is "the tower," which originally didn't have any windows—it was just an open space below the water tower. But years ago, a former tenant turned it into a room, which worked out perfectly for Patty and John. They had a house full of kids in their blended family and needed every bedroom they could get.

The apartment looks out onto Central Park, where John rolled around with his kids when they were small, playing football and other games. And you know a musician lives here—a grand piano sits in the living room, and guitars are all around. "Some of them are mine," Patty said, "a lot are John's, and the girls like to play a bit, too."

John is also into art—he collects, buys, and sells it. Before we sat down to talk, he showed us an amazing piece: a beautiful, wooden clock made from a single piece of maple by Dutch designer Maarten Baas. It is the most unusual clock either of us had ever seen. In its face, you can see the upper torso of a man, as if he is sitting at a workbench behind the glass. Every sixty seconds, he reaches up and erases the minute hand of the clock, and then redraws it precisely where it goes—one minute later. And, yes, he does this *every minute*. It's a video, of course, and it's mesmerizing.

This isn't the first marriage for either for these two; both were previously married to—and had kids with—high-profile partners. John was famously wed for eight years to actress Tatum O'Neal; they had two boys and a girl. And Patty was married for two years to punk music pioneer Richard Hell, and they had a daughter.

Funny enough, John and Patty grew up about fifteen minutes apart in Queens, New York. They knew of each other through friends but had never met.

Maui, Hawaii; March 23, 1997

All of that changed in 1993. By then, John was one year into his retirement from the professional tennis tour. His first marriage was coming to an end, and he was thinking about becoming a working musician. Patty was winding down a successful fifteen-year music career—three years as frontwoman for the New Wave band Scandal and the remainder as a solo artist—and living the life of a busy single mom in L.A. At Christmastime that year, a mutual friend invited each of them to a party in Malibu with the agenda of fixing them up. Recalling that day triggered an immediate debate between them.

PATTY: My friend told me he was going to be there but then told John that I was coming there to meet him. So it was like a set-up or something.

JOHN: A blind date, in a way.

PATTY: He doesn't know what a blind date is.

JOHN: I know what a blind date is.

PATTY: What's a blind date?

JOHN: A blind date is just the two of you, and you sort of meet at a restaurant and people show up.

PATTY: No. In a blind date, you go by yourself and meet somewhere, and it's not at a party.

MARLO: You're both right. In a way it was a blind date, but it was actually more of a set-up.

PATTY: It was a set-up. But my friend was smart enough not to tell me or I wouldn't have come.

MARLO: Because?

PATTY: Because I really wasn't ready.

Whatever you want to call it, Patty and John connected that night, and he made an impression—mostly because of the way he made his entrance. "He came in the door with a kid in each arm and one wrapped around his leg," Patty said. "It was pretty funny. He could barely walk because of the weight of the kids."

John's three children—ages two, five, and six—were indeed riding the limbs of their dad as he trudged in, and according to Patty, he had her at hello. "That was his move," she recalled, "and it was really cute. I mean, come on, how can you resist that?"

"I'm not going to say if it was or wasn't my move," John countered, "but I will say it's a wonderful thing to have little kids in your arms. There's almost nothing that can top that feeling."

Smooth move or not, it got Patty's attention. "I sat and talked to him for a while," she remembered, "and then I liked him. And then I got nervous, so I started avoiding him."

For John's part, his mind was already made up. The chemistry between them convinced him to take it up a notch. "I thought we should think seriously about going out on a real date, which is why I said, 'Hey, I'm going to be here for the week. We should get together. I'm free on New Year's Eve.'"

"Do not make us tell this story," Patty said with a sigh, "because he's rewritten it so many times. What he actually said was, 'I'm not doing anything for New Year's Eve.' That was his big line."

"Well, isn't that just a way of saying, 'Hey, wouldn't it be nice...'?" John countered. "I mean, read a tiny bit between the lines."

Patty took a pass on John's New Year's invitation but agreed to a real date a full nine months later. A second date quickly followed. And then a third and fourth. But even after the relationship began to take root, Patty still had her reservations.

"You go around the world and you wind up with a guy from Queens—and I think that's awesome," Patty reflected. "But I really didn't believe in love anymore. I didn't believe in monogamy. No one around me was happily married. It all just seemed like bullshit. None of it was real, and marriage was not an attainable goal. But then there was John, trying to get me to move back to New York right away. Within six to eight weeks he was saying, 'Do you want more kids?'"

"I'm impressed with your hesitance," Phil said. "Second marriages have a pretty bad track record. You certainly didn't want to jump right in."

"I did not jump in at all," Patty agreed.

"But you were very taken with him," Marlo said. "Why?"

"I was in L.A., which is like the Viet Cong—you can't identify the enemy—who likes you, who doesn't like you. And everybody's full of shit and flirting. But when I met John, here was someone I knew. He was a guy from New York. He was very forthright. He talked a lot about his divorce and how crushed he was by it. So all of that was really endearing. And from that second date on, we were together."

John wasn't pressing for marriage either, but he was certainly amping up the relationship.

"My head was slowly starting to clear at last," he explained. "It had been two years between the end of my marriage and starting to date Patty. The toughest thing about marriage is getting out of one. That took me a couple of years, and it was horrific. Then you feel like, 'Okay, if I have any relationships, they're not going to be serious. I'll just go out with young girls who don't want anything.'"

"That sounds kind of fun," Marlo said.

"Well, that's what I thought," said John.

"And he did that for a couple of years," Patty tossed in.

"But then I realized very quickly that I needed to completely reverse course mentally," John continued. "Here was an opportunity to get a second chance that I wasn't sure I'd get again, and I'm proud of myself that I was able to make that choice. Because when you're just out of a divorce, it doesn't seem like the most sensible thing to do to get back into a very serious relationship—one that would result in two more kids and getting married again."

John did not get the chronology wrong: he agreed to table the marriage talk but lobbied for having children.

"He said, 'I don't want to get married, but I want to have a kid,'" Patty recalled, "and I didn't really want to get married either. I was thirty-seven. But somehow John saw something about us being together, and that felt very safe to me, like this weird, familiar thing. I still didn't believe in love, in monogamy, in marriage, and I was still terrified. But I had some kind of faith in him. And so I thought, *Well, I'm going to go along with him*. I called it 'stepping into the river of John.' I stepped into the river and I let him sweep me along with him until I caught up."

For months they divided their time between California and New York while Patty's daughter Ruby finished her school year. Ruby was nine years old when she first met John. After seeing mommy kiss him through the car window, Ruby laid down the law. "She said, 'I don't want you to have another kid, and I don't want you to get married,'" Patty recalled. "She'd never said that to me about anyone else I dated. So she sensed something."

"Well, that's all about the gender," Phil offered. "I'm not sure a boy would have responded the same way. I'm the expert on boys."

Phil and his first wife divorced in 1975. He met Marlo two years later, and his four sons immediately welcomed her into their lives. "I think they were craving structure and stability," Marlo explained, "and they were adorable to me."

"You're right," Patty said. "John's sons were always asking if we were going to get married. They even got anxious and upset if we had a fight."

Ruby's half-sister, Anna, was born on December 27, 1995—exactly two years and one day after that legendary Christmas party in Malibu. At this point, the subject of marriage once again reared its head. By now, Patty was pushing for it; John was thinking it through.

JOHN: Obviously, the key to success in any marriage is compromise. You also have to trust each other—and hopefully have a lot of sex.

PATTY: That's it.

JOHN: Those would be the three: compromise, trust, and sex. I think it would be impossible to have a successful marriage if you don't have all of those.

PATTY: A *monogamous* successful marriage.

PHIL: When did you first get this smart, John? When did you realize that those are the three things that any strong marriage needs?

JOHN: Probably not early enough in the first marriage, let's put it that way.

PATTY: But that's just *your* three things—your formula—no matter who it was.

JOHN: That's not what I said, but okay.

PATTY: I had to press him to get married again.

MARLO: Why is that, John? You obviously trusted and compromised with each other. And let's assume you were having sex—you did make a baby, after all.

JOHN: Well, I don't know who made this statement, but someone once said a second marriage is a triumph of hope over experience. I mean, if the first marriage was so bad, why the hell would anyone want to do that again?

PATTY: Hey, my first marriage wasn't a cakewalk either. But here I was taking his kids and my kids to the fanciest prep school in New York. I was walking four kids to school every morning with a child strapped to my chest, and I was just feeling like, *I can't take the pressure anymore.* Meanwhile, the kids kept asking us, "When are you getting married?"

The couple tied the knot in March 1997. By this time, John had been awarded custody of his three children (Kevin, Sean, and Emily) from his first marriage, and the newly mashed-up household—one retired tennis star, one former rock singer, and five stepsiblings—had relocated to New York City.

But they weren't finished.

"We were almost like the Brady Bunch," John said. "And then I had this brilliant idea. I said, 'We've got to have another kid, so that the others see how committed we are and how much we love each other.'"

Patty rolled her eyes and looked at John. "You always had that brilliant idea," she cracked. "I was your cheerleader for everything. You'd say, 'Have a kid! If I knock you up, you'll get healthier and happier!' That was your go-to move."

Apparently, the move worked. Their second child, Ava McEnroe, was born in 1999. Brady Bunch complete.

With a wedding certificate in their hands and six kids under their roof, Patty and John got down to the business of thinking about their future. To that end, Patty provided her new husband something that had been missing for a long time.

"The biggest thing that Patty did for me was to allow me to be me," John said. "She was never with me during my main career. We got together after I stopped playing, and it was the end of my first marriage. That next year was rough. I had three kids and was just trying to figure out how the hell this had happened, and coping with that feeling of failure about the marriage, and wanting the kids to be okay. So obviously there was a transitional period when you're not really sure about what's going to happen, and what you're going to do with the rest of your life."

"That's a lot of change," Phil said.

"Yeah, a lot of change, exactly," John said. "And so I was very fortunate to find Patty, who let me do my thing."

Part of John's "thing" was a brief flirtation with becoming a television personality. In 2002, he hosted an oddly conceived BBC-TV game show called *The Chair*, in which contestants had to keep their heart rates low in the face of stressful questions in order to win increasing amounts of money. Patty thought it was crazy but admired his bravery. It ran for three months.

John also hosted a talk show. In July 2004, the cable network CNBC aired *McEnroe*, an hour-long evening program with exactly one staff writer. Patty thought John's decision to step into such a demanding new role was "ballsy" and even wrote the show's theme song. It was gone before Christmas.

"I didn't even have enough time to figure it out," John said, "but I did gain an appreciation for how good people like Phil and David Letterman are. It's a lot easier to be the guy they're asking the questions to. I'd be sitting there looking at the guest, thinking, *Say something.* And he'd be looking at me like, *Are you kidding me?* It was like trying to get blood from a stone."

"Tell me about it," Phil added. "I had many of those. My hangover guests were few and far between.

"Hangover guests?" John asked.

Phil laughed. "Those are the ones that, no matter how you feel, they can carry the ball. Marlo was one of those. That's why I fell for her."

In the end, John was okay with the show's abrupt cancellation. "I wanted to be home for dinner with the kids," he said. No surprise, though, it was ultimately Patty who redirected John back to his true love: the game with the fuzzy ball.

"When I first met John, he wasn't playing," Patty said, "and I told him, 'You really don't need to do this. You've made a lot of money.' But I realize now that he needed to be busy and continue to work. Who knew we were going to have so many kids to put through school? So he actually did need to keep working and make money."

She finally persuaded him to get back in the game, both as a commentator and as a player on the ATP Champions Tour.

PATTY: But I said to him, if you're going to play, practice and get better at it.

MARLO: That's a pretty big thing to say to John McEnroe.

PATTY: Yes, it was.

JOHN: Well, there was a one-year period in there when I started playing a few events, but I wasn't really preparing that well for them.

PATTY: And I said, "Get better so you'll win." And when he did that, he beat everybody. But he just had to take it seriously. He became number one on the seniors tour.

JOHN: It was about taking it seriously and taking pride in what I was doing.

PATTY: Playing at the top of your game.

JOHN: Doing it right. I had been dabbling in music because I love music, and I was getting away from tennis. But it became fairly clear that music wouldn't be something I could pursue professionally. I love to collect, buy, and sell art, but I wouldn't say that would be my number one thing either. It's always been tennis. And then I became a commentator, which I thought I'd never do. I mean, if you'd told me I'd be a commentator and that I was going to play seniors tennis, I'd be like, "Shoot me now."

MARLO: But you're doing well as a commentator.

JOHN: I'm doing well. I'm just saying that, from where I first started, it seemed like a major step down. In the booth, they pay you a ham sandwich compared to what you could get paid if you're winning Wimbledon.

PATTY: But he also had the attitude like he hated the press. That was part of his thing. But, lo and behold, he's the greatest commentator that ever came down the pike in any sport, in my opinion. And more people now know him from talking about tennis than they do from playing tennis.

John has been a top analyst on major tennis events for more than twenty years. But even as he reunited with the thing he loved best, he couldn't help but notice that his wife was not so fortunate.

"She wasn't really playing music," John recalled. "I remember early on I was playing some music with my friends—admittedly, compared to what she does, it was bad. But one day I said, 'Hey, come on up and jam.' She said, 'I don't jam.' I said, 'But you're a singer, why don't you jam?' Jamming is like practicing to me. I don't necessarily like practicing on the court, but you've got to do it whether you like it or not. That's when I realized, at least in my mind, that she had lost the love of what she was doing."

The turning point came in the late 1990s, when John was traveling extensively on the ATP Champions Tour and was out of town for days at a time. Instead of coming home to his wife and six kids, he would stay in whatever town he was in and play concerts.

"That's when I started getting pissed," Patty said. "And then I'm like, 'You know what? You need to come home. You can't play a tennis tournament and then do a gig. Do your gigs around here.'"

John smiled. "She said, 'If anyone is going to play music, it's me.'"

And she did. In 2004, the VH1 music channel enlisted Patty and the surviving members of Scandal for an episode of its show *Bands Reunited*. That led to reunion tours followed by new albums.

At one point, John told us, he offered to be in her band. "Patty said to me, 'Yes, and we should also play mixed doubles at Wimbledon.' I said, 'But you don't play tennis.' She said, 'Exactly.' So that shut that down."

We glanced at the little man inside the clock, who painted a reminder that our time was winding down, so we asked John and Patty the same question we'd been asking everyone: How do you fight? We were almost afraid to hear the answer, given that one half of this couple is internationally famous for blowing his stack.

PATTY: It's weird, but I probably have a worse temper than he does.
JOHN: She's worse than I am. I find it somewhat bemusing that I'm the one who will be saying, "Jesus, calm down, will you?"
PHIL: But were you ever intimidated by Mount Vesuvius here? The man who became famous for ranting and raving?
PATTY: The truth is, I didn't follow tennis that much. I obviously knew who John was. I had seen the tabloids. But I never really felt intimidated

about telling him how I felt. Yeah, he would lose his temper a little bit in the beginning, maybe if I asked him to do stuff he didn't want to do. And maybe at first it probably took me a minute to really hold my own.

MARLO: John, do you ever use your signature line with her: "You cannot be serious!"?

JOHN: I'm not allowed to say that anymore. Patty won't let me use the phrase. She said, "If you say that one more time..."

PATTY: That's all he ever said. And I told him to stop saying it.

JOHN: And I said, "Look, that's what they pay me for. I mean, I have to say it. They don't give a damn about how I play. They just want me to yell, 'You can't be serious!'" My dad, God rest his soul, once told me, "Look, you don't need to go off on the umpires. You're better than them. Just play." Though he did scream it at me.

PATTY: And who else said that to you? Me.

JOHN: Right. Patty would say that because I'd lose control. Addiction to anger is like being addicted to cigarettes.

MARLO: I was a big fan of yours. I remember watching you play and yelling at the TV, "Don't do it Johnny! Don't do it!"

JOHN: The thing that people don't realize is how difficult it is. I'm amazed at how well-behaved some players are. Honestly, unbelievable. Like [Bjorn] Borg. I mean, he never changed his expression. And [Roger] Federer. Most people would be more like me, because it's a very frustrating game. You're dealing with people yelling at you—maybe because they like whoever you're playing against—and it's 95 degrees, 130 degrees on the court in Australia. Try keeping *your* composure. And then they pick two minutes out of three hours and show the times that you're a complete idiot. The reality is, they don't put microphones in the center of a football field. You don't hear the quarterback saying, "I'm going to fucking fuck you up, you motherfucker." They say that stuff. In basketball, too.

PHIL: So it was the very nature of your sport that made you stand out as temperamental.

JOHN: Yes. I mean, we were like the country club sport in a way, which it still is, and I didn't want to be treated that way. I wanted to be thought of like the other sports guys—the hockey players. They didn't have mics on them. They're fighting and trying to punch the others' lights out, and that's a legal and accepted part of the sport. But if I scream, "You suck!" to an umpire, suddenly I'm Attila the Hun. So, to me, it was always like they were making this mountain out of a molehill. And that frustrated me.

MARLO: So is that what you grew up with—screaming?

JOHN: I grew up at a loud dinner table, let's just say that. My parents were together for fifty-nine years.

PATTY: Three boys.

JOHN: Two younger brothers, living in Queens, New York. It just seemed like everywhere you turned was very loud. So loud seemed normal to me.

PHIL: So when you and Patty turn the volume down, how do you resolve an argument?

JOHN: I think you have to laugh with each other—not at each other. There will always be differences, but hopefully over time you learn to diminish things when you're having a fight. You need to learn to negotiate or defuse the disagreement. Because if you can't do that, you're doomed.

MARLO: You know, I've always had this theory about you—because I'm married to a man who seems to have this trait. Phil is very sensitive to criticism, but that's because he had a very critical mother. So I always wondered if one of your parents was critical of you.

JOHN: I don't recall it being quite that way, but I do remember being very competitive, because I was driven by them. My parents weren't nearly as bad as other tennis parents, but in retrospect, I was definitely pushed.

PATTY: They were perfectionists, his parents. They weren't critical, because his father worked all day, went to law school at night, and was second or third in his class.

JOHN: He was second. My mom would say, "Why weren't you first?" This was out of five hundred people at Fordham Law School.

PATTY: That was her response.

MARLO: That alone can make you a perfectionist.

JOHN: So I became a perfectionist, which can fuel you and push you. It certainly had an impact on what I was able to accomplish.

For all their bluster and banter, what was so interesting—and so unexpected—to us about this couple was their thoughtfulness. Here were two people whose professions had often required them to be over the top and in your face; but here in this setting, speaking about their twenty-three years together, they were effortlessly honest, in an almost mellow way. It seemed like a good moment for our final question: What advice can you pass on to young couples about to embark on this adventure called marriage?

"Marry the person, don't marry potential," Patty said. "Women are notorious for saying, 'Oh, he's got the potential'—but potential is not good enough. Have realistic expectations, and marry the *person*—not who he is going to be, but who he is."

"And don't think you can change them to the type of person you think he or she needs to be," John added. "If it happens organically, that's great. But if you go in thinking, *I can smooth the edges*, or *This is a diamond in the rough and we just have to work this through*, then it's not going to work."

"Don't marry potential," Patty repeated. "That should be the name of your book."

For any other couple, this would have been the perfect place to stop. But this was John McEnroe and Patty Smyth. They needed one last volley.

PHIL: John, you said something earlier about your wife that was lovely— that she gave you a second chance. What did you mean by that?

JOHN: The second chance was to let me be me, which is something that I greatly appreciated. And it's not just about the adulation, and me being John McEnroe the tennis player. People always ask me, "Do you love playing tennis?" And I'll say—

PATTY: —he's not answering the question, Phil. He's not answering the question.

JOHN: What was the question?

PATTY: The question is about your getting a second chance when you met me. It was a second chance at a family and happiness and having a life partner, and not only to be yourself.

JOHN: I thought I said that earlier.

PATTY: No you didn't, but I'll say it for you now. Here's your answer, Phil: John needs a best friend and a consigliere and a wife and a lover and all those things. That's what makes him thrive and be a better person. He needs that.

PHIL: Well, don't we all?

PATTY: And the thing he has said to me his whole life—and I mean, our *whole life* together—is "Don't give up on me. I'm a work in progress. Don't give up on me." And then I started saying to him, "Don't give up on *me*. I'm a work in progress, too." I grew up with only women, and I never thought I would be married. I had no idea how to be a couple, so it's been a learning curve for me. So, I think that's what you were asking about. We didn't give up on each other.

Game. Set. Match.

Ray and Anna Romano

MARRIED IN 1987

"It was like what Stallone says in *Rocky*,
when he talks about why he's dating Adrian.
He says, 'I've got gaps, she's got gaps,
together we fill gaps.'"

Ray Romano is one of those "overnight sensations" whose overnight took nearly a decade. A relative late bloomer, he spent most of his thirties knocking around comedy clubs, landing the occasional TV gig (mostly on cable), and even appearing on *Star Search* as a contestant in the standup category.

But when stardom came, it came big. On September 13, 1996, his perfectly titled sitcom *Everybody Loves Raymond* premiered on the CBS network, and it changed his life. The series—all about a sheepish Italian-American sportswriter living with his wife and kids on Long Island—was an instant audience pleaser; and if the title role seemed oddly similar to the actor himself, that was no accident, given that the character was loosely based on Ray and his home life.

When the show first aired, Ray had been married to his real wife, Anna Scarpulla, for eleven years. They were living in Queens, New York, with

Queens, New York; October 11, 1987

their three children and one more yet to come. Although they didn't know it at the time, the show would run for nine seasons and catapult Ray to the stratosphere of stardom, at one point making him the highest paid actor on television.

But a TV family, no matter how well-drawn, in not the real thing. So we couldn't wait to sit down with the real Ray and his real wife of thirty-three years.

We caught up with the Romanos on a typically sunny day near Encino, California, where the couple has lived since Ray's career took off. They prefer to do interviews at a small hotel near their home, so we got there early and booked a room on the ground floor. After setting up our equipment, we looked around and decided that the furniture in the room didn't allow us to sit across from the Romanos. Noticing more suitable furniture on the patio outside, we decided to make a swap.

We couldn't stop laughing as we lugged the heavy outdoor furniture indoors—and the indoor furniture outdoors. "Fifteen minutes ago we were just techies setting up our equipment," a breathless Marlo commented to Phil as she dragged a chair across the carpet. "Now we've graduated to stagehands!"

With everything in place, we still had time to kill, so we ordered room service. Why not? That's what you do in a hotel.

Anna and Ray soon arrived, and they were instantly familiar to us—like friendly next-door neighbors we'd known for years. We raided the mini-bar (another good thing about hotels!), passed around bottled water and sodas and M&Ms, and settled into a discussion that ranged from funny to touching to near-tragic.

Listening to these two born-and-bred New Yorkers speak about their marriage, we could immediately tell who runs the show in the Romano household and who provides the comic relief—and it's not always the one you would expect. This couple possesses a natural chemistry that can't help but make you smile.

The two met, they told us, while working as tellers at the same bank.

RAY: I was twenty-seven years old and I drove my bike to work, so I was pretty much not what you'd call the new stud-guy working at the bank.

ANNA: When he started there, I was one of a bunch of young girls at the bank and we were like, "Oooh, we can't wait to meet the new guy who's coming in today"—and then he walks in, rolling his bike.

MARLO: It doesn't sound like you were the hottest ticket in town, Ray. How soon before you asked her on a date?

RAY: Well, I worked there for two years and didn't have the guts to ask her out until I left. At that point, I'd started doing standup comedy and I wasn't making a living from it. I was just doing it at night and working with my friend who owns a futon mattress company during the day. I never had the idea that standup would be my career when we started dating. I just loved doing it. I always tell Anna that she took a gamble because she went out with a guy who lived at home and rode a bike to work.

MARLO: Forget the bike. I don't know many women who would want to go out with a twenty-seven-year-old guy living at home. You obviously saw something in this guy.

ANNA: I don't know. Working at the bank we got to know each other, and the friendship grew into a relationship. And he was funny and kind and sweet.

RAY: I haven't heard the word sexy yet.

ANNA: We didn't have any expectations when we were dating. Kids today, they have this idea of what they're looking for in their future.

RAY: Right. They start dating with a goal in mind, like "This is a guy I could marry and start a family with."

ANNA: We didn't think everything through. We were happy. So we just took it day by day.

RAY: It was like what Stallone says in *Rocky*, when he talks about why he's dating Adrian. He says, "I've got gaps, she's got gaps, together we fill gaps."

ANNA: I think that's true with us. We fill gaps.

Ray and Anna dated for two years before she finally brought up the subject of marriage. Then he proposed to her at a dinner with his family by holding up a fake newspaper he had made with a headline that read, ANNA GETS A ROCK!—which was especially funny, because Anna had already picked out her ring. They were both living with their parents at the time. She was in her early twenties, and he was closing in on thirty.

"I think everyone in our neighborhood stayed home until they were married," Anna told us. "I'd say 95 percent of them did."

"A lot of my buddies really didn't move out until they got married," Ray added. "I lived at home until I was twenty-nine. I just happened to get married later than the rest. But also, my career wasn't going anywhere. I had dropped out of college and was in nowhere land."

Amazingly, the first time either of them lived with anyone other than their immediate families was when they were finally married. Anna took to it faster than Ray.

"I loved it," she said. "For me, it felt like I was running the show. I took charge of all the household things. I became *the household person.*"

Ray smiled. "I used to talk about that in my standup," he said. "Like, day one—when you move in with someone—is a crucial day because there are decisions to be made that you don't think are important when you're living on your own, but they really are when you're living with someone."

"Like what?" Phil asked.

"Like what side of the bed do you get?" Ray said. "I thought that was trivial—and then I realized, 'That's her side *for life*, right there, and I blew the call. I didn't look at the TV angles."

While Anna-the-household-person adapted to domestication, Ray, not so much. Not at first, anyway. Anna thinks she knows why.

"We were brought up the same way," she noted. "His mom took care of the men in the house. My mother, very Italian, took care of the men in our house, too. So, I think, we had a lot of the same background and we just kind of fell into our roles."

Before Ray could reply to his wife, Anna finished her thought. "Which I wish we hadn't fallen into, because I do *everything.*"

We looked at Ray. Ray looked at us.

"I'm not proud of this," he began, "but the first load of laundry I ever did in my life was when I got the TV show and had to come out to California by myself. And I remember having to call Anna and say, 'Where do I put the thing and the soap and the whatever?' All of a sudden I'm living on my own—but I was still being taken care of."

To hear Anna tell it, the wedding, with her hand-picked ring and all, almost didn't happen, at least not in a Catholic church. To get married in that particularly devout setting, couples were required to take part in a consultation session called Pre-Cana, a course that advises young couples on the responsibilities and challenges of marriage.

It's important, it's compulsory, and you need to be on time.

ANNA: So Ray was supposed to pick me up for Pre-Cana at, like, let's say 9 a.m., and he's always late. So, I warned him, "You better be on time. I don't want to be late." I'm the opposite of him—I'm very punctual. So, does he show up when he's supposed to show up?

PHIL: I'm going to guess no.

ANNA: *He freakin' overslept!* So, I get into my car and I drive to his house. His parents aren't home—they were away—and I'm ringing the bell and knocking on the door and screaming at the side of the house. And he's asleep in his room. With the fan on. He can't hear, and I was furious!

RAY: But the thing is—

ANNA: —so we went to this class. I was pissed off the whole day. I was like, "I don't know why I'm here. Why are we here, Ray?"

Ray and Anna are both Italian American, and Italians are known for their shows of temper.

"I get a little loud," Anna admitted.

"She yells at me," Ray said. "I don't really return it."

He looked at his wife. "Nothing really sets me off that I start yelling at you, right? But I think that's because I'm always the one in trouble. I usually don't have the right to yell at you."

"I'm glad you feel that way," Anna replied. "I'll get mad because I don't think things through, and he'll say, 'Okay, okay, calm down for a second.' And then it gets kind of quiet and everything just calms down."

"So who's the one who makes everything better?" Marlo asked. "Who's the first to apologize?"

"No one," Anna said. "We don't apologize to each other. I mean, it has to be a *big* fight for an apology. If it's a stupid little fight, no, we don't really apologize. We just get over it and that's that."

We looked at Ray.

"Not to go back to my act again," he said, "but it's like, guys are always trying to score points with their wives, but we're always behind. Anna never feels like she has to score points with me because—"

"—because I guess I don't do anything wrong," Anna said.

"No, no" Ray said. "It's not that you don't do anything wrong—it's that you do so much good. You do so much more good."

To make up for his deficit in points, Ray said, he does little things that, in his mind, help him catch up—like bringing her flowers.

"I'll be in my car, and I'll see this guy selling flowers on the corner. And I'll think, *Okay, let me get some flowers for her and take them home. That'll be sure to score some points.* And so I come home and give them to her, and she says—"

"—thanks for rolling down the window," Anna said.

When Ray's TV career was just getting off the ground with *Raymond*, no one was sure if the show would be a hit—or canceled. So, rather than uproot the family from their hometown, the couple decided that Anna would stay back in Queens with the kids, and Ray would head west solo.

ANNA: So he became this Hollywood star, and I was like the stay-at-home mom. I didn't have a career. I was not in this business. So I stayed in Queens for the first season, and he moved out to L.A. He was living with his single friend, who was always looking for girls. So I told the friend, "You're not allowed to bring girls up there. We're paying for the apartment, and you are *not* having girlfriends up there." Because, you know, Ray's a new celebrity—and girls out there are looking for the next best thing. But I knew he was loyal.

RAY: Because you were with me. You knew who I was.

ANNA: It was the other women I worried about.

RAY: Because they might hold me at gun point?

ANNA: Yes, they may force you to sleep with them, I don't know. And then you'd say, "But I *had* to." So anyway, yeah, maybe I was a little worried. But I trusted him. I really trusted him.

RAY: I could tell a story, but it's got a bad word in it.

MARLO: Go ahead—I'm sure we've heard it.

ANNA: Which story is this?

RAY: About being in a threesome.

ANNA: Oh, right.

RAY: So I had to do a threesome on this show, *Vinyl*, that I did on HBO. Martin Scorsese directing, Mick Jagger producing, I play this music producer, whatever. It was about rock-and-roll in the seventies. So in this scene I do a threesome—

ANNA: —with two young girls. Are you going to tell them that part, about how young they are? Young *naked* girls.

RAY: We're shooting in New York. So, after I do the scene, I talk to Anna, and she goes, "So what was it like?"

PHIL: Who's asking you this?

RAY: My wife.

ANNA: I asked a lot of details. I needed to hear the details, which I didn't get.

RAY: Are you sure I can tell this story? I don't want to be inappropriate.

MARLO: Go ahead. You got us hooked.

RAY: So I tell her, "Well, it's really horrible—there's the guy over there on the camera, and there's a boom mic up here, and we're all wearing protective stuff, and this actress is sitting on my lap.

ANNA: Right! And I ask, "Where was her hand? Where was *your* hand?"

RAY: But it was so unromantic! Anyway, that ends, and Anna has to fly back to L.A. I call her after her plane lands and I say, "How was your flight?" She says, "It was good. I sat next to this actor, this young Latino actor…"

ANNA: Well, wannabe actor…

RAY: "And he found out you were my husband, and so we were talking and he gave me his card." So, right away, I'm jealous! "What do you mean, he gave you his card?!"

ANNA: A thousand questions.

RAY: And she's like, "What are you talking about? He gave me his card because he knows I'm married to you." And I say, "But why would he give you his card?" And I kept going on and on and getting annoyed. And I'm saying, "What was his name? What was his name?" And she stops me cold and goes, "I don't know, Ray. What was the name of the girl who sat on your cock?"

Here is a marriage that has endured it all: family separation, relocation to Hollywood, sudden celebrity, the occasional fictitious sex scene, lots of yelling—and yet none of that, or perhaps all of that, prepared them for what was to come next. And it came in the guise of a life-threatening disease.

In February 2010, Anna was diagnosed with stage 1 breast cancer, a highly treatable but no less frightening condition that can be fatal if allowed to spread. A lump in her breast was found by her gynecologist, who didn't think much of it—but Anna did, and she had it checked out with a mammogram. That's when she called Ray to tell him the news.

"When I picked up the phone, you were crying," Ray said to Anna, "and I immediately thought you were calling about my father—because my father was close to leaving us."

"Yes," Anna said softly. "He was ill at the time."

"But you were calling to tell me that the doctor had found something," Ray continued.

"Yes," Anna said. "I was very upset."

"And then we went in for the biopsy," Ray said.

"Yes, you came with me for the biopsy," Anna said, "because honestly, you don't get any results, but it's nice to have somebody with you."

Waiting for the results was, in fact, nerve-wracking, especially since Anna felt she knew for certain that there was something very wrong—despite assurances from the surgeon.

"He was like, 'Nine times out of ten these are nothing,'" Anna remembered, "and I said, 'Okay, I hope so.'"

Worse for the couple, while they were waiting for a verdict from the doctor, they had to host a Super Bowl party at their home. It had been planned long before Anna's diagnosis.

"We had at least fifty people over," Ray said, "but every time I started to have fun, it kind of popped back in my head."

"We just wanted to get through that day," Anna said. "It was very scary."

"It's like the elephant in the room, isn't it?" said Phil.

"Yes, it is," Anna agreed.

And soon enough, the elephant was confirmed—it was cancer, and it needed to be treated.

"First, we kind of got emotional," Ray said, "but we didn't want to waste any time. It's a blow. All weekend I was just trying to convince myself, *Well, it's not going to be that.* So when you actually hear it, it's a blow."

Ray called his manager to cancel a show he was going to film in Pebble Beach, "and it kind of hit me when I was talking to him—when I had to tell him why. I remember I was standing in the closet, and then I got a little . . . it overtook me a little bit."

We all got quiet. Anna broke the mood.

"Mind you, Ray is such a hypochondriac," she told us. "He's always like, 'I think I have stomach cancer. I think I have this other cancer.' And it's funny—well, it's not funny—but I said to him, 'You're the one who always thinks you have cancer, and now I'm the one who gets it.'"

In a way, Anna said, she was relieved it was her and not Ray with a potentially fatal disease. "There were plenty of times when I thought, *Not that I want to have this, but I'm glad it was me and not you because at least I know how to handle it*—because with him, he's so emotional."

"I was emotional anyway," Ray said.

"I guess I'm stronger, maybe, in that sense."

"You are," Ray said. "You are."

As if things weren't alarming enough, while Anna and Ray were consulting on the extent of the treatment—radical mastectomy, lumpectomy, chemo, or radiation—the doctors discovered that Anna had cancer in not one, but both breasts. Now she was looking at double mastectomy or double lumpectomy.

In the end, she chose the lumpectomies, followed by chemotherapy and radiation. During all of this, Ray developed irritable bowel syndrome, most likely caused by the stress.

It turns out that the doctors who reassured Anna and Ray that everything would turn out all right were correct—and Anna has the scars to show for it. She calls her breasts her "war room," because "I went through war and came out of it somehow." Her chemo-ravaged hair grew back, the radiation "suntan" on her breasts is gone, and Ray's bowels are under control.

And as a result of living through this frightening ordeal, Ray learned to say "I love you."

"I learned how strong she is," Ray said, "and I learned, you know, that I'm not the most demonstrative man—and Anna knows this about me. But when something like this happens and you face the fact that you may lose someone, it shines a light on how much you love this person. And that I should say so."

"Yes, you should," said Anna, with a soft smile. "Every day."

PHIL: Why do you think it was hard for you to say "I love you"?

RAY: My father was undemonstrative—it was hard for him to show anything like that. He never said "I love you" to me. Never. So I go out of my way to make sure my kids don't feel that. But even when I do, it doesn't roll off the tongue. I feel self-conscious doing it, so they pick up on that a little bit.

ANNA: It doesn't come natural.

PHIL: So after her surgery, did you start telling her that you loved her?

ANNA: No.

RAY: Well, I did—then.

ANNA: You probably said it a couple more times after that.

MARLO: Are you saying it wore off over the years?

RAY: It didn't wear off—but I think I've said this before: the reason this marriage works is because, thankfully, she knows that I love her, and for women who have to hear it out loud, it's not going to go that well when you're married to a guy like me. But one little interesting tidbit was the day you had your—it was a very emotional period, because the day you had your surgery was the day my father passed away.

MARLO: Oh, no.

ANNA: Yes. We were driving to the hospital at 6 a.m. and my mother-in-law called us to say, "They think today is going to be the day that he passes."

RAY: And you went in to get prepped, and while you were getting prepped my mother called me and told me he passed away. And then I saw you before you went in—but I didn't tell you. You asked, 'How's your father?' and I didn't want to tell you at that moment. But then, I had a feeling that my father kind of went to a place where he could look over you...

[*Ray took a breath.*]

RAY: Now I'm getting emotional.

[*Ray paused and took another breath.*]

RAY: And that he'd make sure everything goes well for you.

MARLO: That's a lovely thought.

ANNA: That's the religion in us. That's about all the religion we have in us.

"It's good to have the same outlook, the same values," Ray said. "But then it's also—I'm just speaking for ourselves—it's also that we're compatible. She's *that* person; I'm *this* person. I'm *this* person who performs and needs attention. She's *that* person, who doesn't feel neglected by *this* person. So, I mean, especially in this business, the pieces have to fit that way."

"He needs that attention from other people, not just his family," Anna added. "I don't. For me, all I want is the attention from my family."

"And she doesn't even get it from me as much as she should," said Ray, with a self-conscious laugh.

"Yes," Anna added.

"And yet she accepts that," Ray said.

Before we began to break down our equipment (and return the hotel's furniture to its proper places), we asked Ray and Anna one final question: What do you think you get from each other that you can't get from anyone else?

Anna went first.

"I think it's his loyalty and just being who he is that fulfills me," she said. "I just love that I am safe with him. I know that he will always be there for—maybe not always in the way I want him to be there, but he's there. And he tries. I know that's hard for him. I'm okay with sometimes having to take a backseat to the other parts of his life—I don't mind being in the background—because I know, in the end, he's going to come home. And that's where I need him to be present the most—at home."

Then Ray.

"Anna knows that my career makes me happy," he said, "and that a lot of my life is about the next show or the next thing. Is there a touch of narcissism there? Yes. But she's given to me the space to do that because she knows that she and the kids are still the most important things to me— even though it's sometimes hard for me to say it. I also get the truth from Anna. In this business, where everyone is either phony or kissing your ass, I know that's not going to happen with Anna. Whether it's showbiz related or anything else, she's going to tell me the truth and not be mean about it—and it's exactly what I want."

PHIL: So she's your reality check.

RAY: Yeah—like the day that *Everybody Loves Raymond* premiered. I was in L.A. and Anna was home in New York with the kids. And so to celebrate, my buddies and I decided to go to Las Vegas. I call Anna to tell her that, and she says, "Oh you're going to Vegas and I'm home with the kids?" I say, "But do you understand what is happening right now?" I was being kind of mockingly cocky. I said, "My show is about to premiere. Right now, I'm about to be broadcast in front of the whole United States. Thirty million people are going to see me tonight. And tomorrow *I am going to be a star!*" To which she replied, "Yeah, well, you're still the dick I married."

You gotta love these two.

Viola Davis and Julius Tennon

MARRIED IN 2003

"I always thought marriage was 50/50,
but it's 100/100."

For the past few years, Viola Davis and Julius Tennon have lived in Toluca Lake, a Spanish-style enclave of Los Angeles in the San Fernando Valley. When we drove up searching for their house number, we saw a man in a pale gray shirt standing in the street. It was Julius, waiting in front of his house for us. We told him he must be psychic to be there at the exact time of our arrival. It was also warm and hospitable—very him, as we would soon find out.

Julius guided us into a beautiful stone courtyard with a tranquil, cascading waterfall. A mahogany door swung open to reveal a barefoot Viola, looking young and soft in a white, gauzy minidress. Their nine-year-old daughter, Genesis—an adorable, bright-eyed girl, her hair piled high on her head—glided in to meet us. Her manner was as sweet as her face.

Julius gave us a tour, showing us the room he had put together to honor Viola's accomplishments. He said she had put everything away in boxes, but he unpacked it all to create this room. There they all were: her Oscar, Emmy, Tony, Golden Globe, and BAFTA awards, plus numerous other

Los Angeles, California; June 23, 2003

citations and photographs celebrating her amazing work. The shiny and impressive display was matched only by Julius's pride in his wife.

When we sat down at their dining room table, which was encircled by comfy, padded white chairs, we were immediately struck by Viola's lightheartedness. We're accustomed to seeing her bold performances on screen, and her formidable strength when she is accepting an award. But across the table from us she was gentle and low-key.

Julius is an actor, too. In fact, he and Viola met when they were both cast in the pilot episode of Steven Bochco's *City of Angels*.

"My mama always said if you want to date a girl, don't ask for her phone number," Julius said. "Give her *your* number, and if she's interested she'll call."

Julius did as his mother recommended, handing Viola one of his professional postcards with his photo on it.

"You know those cards for actors?" Viola said. "They usually have their shirts off."

"Of course, I did have it together," Julius added, "but I had my shirt on."

"That's so funny," Marlo said.

But Viola was nervous—it took her six weeks to make that call. At the time, she felt she was a "horrible judge of character" and wasn't ready to start another relationship.

"I was in therapy because I was having anxiety attacks about living in L.A.," she said. "I just didn't know how to connect with people. I felt like my funky look, my funky ways, me not really caring about being thin or cute—I felt like I didn't fit in. New York was my city. I was a journeyman actor with no delusions of becoming a star. Before Julius, I was not a great girlfriend and I had a lot of bad boyfriends, but I was attracted to them for a reason. I remember a friend of mine said, 'Viola, why do you keep meeting assholes? Did you ever stop to think it might be you?' That was my big 'aha!' moment."

MARLO: So when you were thirty-five, I'm told, you prayed for a husband.

VIOLA: I did, because I realized I was lonely and couldn't even get a good boyfriend. I was like, okay, this is not working. This is not the fantasy I envisioned.

PHIL: So how did the praying come about?

VIOLA: I was doing *A Raisin in the Sun* at the Williamstown Theatre Festival, and a friend of mine said, "Why are you alone?" And I almost started crying. He said, "Is there a reason you don't have a relationship?" I said, "I guess I just never found anyone who loved me." So he said, "Go into your room. I want you to get onto your knees and ask God for what you want." And I thought, *Oh God, is this an "on fire for Jesus" person?*

MARLO: But you did what he told you to do.

VIOLA: I did—and he told me to be very specific. So when I prayed, I said, "This is what I want: He doesn't have to be black, but I would like him to be black. I want him to look like a football player because I love football players. And I want him to be from the South, because I love country men. And I would appreciate it if he's already been married, and he already has kids, because I don't want that pressure. And I want him to be spiritual, churchgoing, funny, and maybe someone who's an artist, so he's got that artistic sensibility."

Three and a half weeks later she met Julius, who fit all of those requirements. Still, given her past misfires with men, she had reservations. So she spoke to her therapist about Julius, mentioning how he was good-looking, how he had politely given her his card, and how he had invited her to church. "There must be something wrong with him," she worried.

"There's something wrong with everyone, Viola," her therapist replied. "There's something wrong with you. Call him." By the time Viola finally worked up the courage, she was afraid Julius had forgotten her.

He hadn't. "In fact, he invited me to where he worked, and I immediately saw his emotional openness, his emotional availability—that's one of the things I prayed for. I'd never had that before. With men, I was usually like, 'Okay, how do you feel about me? Do you love me? Do you not love me? Do you want to be with me or not?' With Julius, I never had to guess."

Julius was equally love-struck—and he got an immediate crash course in the things that make Viola Viola.

"I remember the very first time she stayed with me," he recalled. "I went into the bathroom after she left to go to work, and the tops of the bottles—the moisturizer, the creams, everything—they were all off. It seemed like that bathroom had been blown up. I cleaned up like I always do, and when she came back, she said, 'Why'd you do that? Why'd you put everything back?' I said, 'Listen, honey, don't worry about it. Just do what you do and I'll do what I do.' And that's the way we've rolled ever since."

VIOLA: I'm much tidier now.

MARLO: That's Phil and me. I always say, "He's a brilliant man who doesn't know the meaning of the word 'hamper.'"

JULIUS: She's gotten better over the years. It took her a while, but I still do my thing and she doesn't question it anymore.

VIOLA: He's a little OCD. It's like, "Vee, there's all this mess on the floor," and I'm like, "Oh, my God"—it'll be two little crumbs!

MARLO: I'm a bit of a neat freak, too.

PHIL: Marlo will walk into my study, talking like crazy about everything the whole time, and she'll be straightening up a book or moving this magazine over there where it belongs—because I set things down and that's where they stay. You can tell where I've been in the house.

MARLO: I know he had orange juice over *here*, because that little orange cap is over *there*. And I know he had a piece of toast, because the butter knife and crumbs are by the sink. I know exactly what he did and when he did it. And then, of course, there's a cabinet door open so you know he took a glass from there. If he ever murdered anybody, I would know exactly where he'd been and what he was thinking when he did it.

Julius's neatness came from his mother, who also taught him to cook, do laundry, and iron. He knows how to clean baseboards and wash blinds. One of his brothers was also influential, urging him to stay organized by immediately hanging up his clothes and keeping shoehorns in his shoes to maintain their shape. His father was more of a wild card, a trucker who drove an eighteen-wheeler.

"He moved people all over the United States," Julius remembered, "so when I was a kid—in the summer when school was out—I used to travel with my father everywhere. I loved it."

"And they moved Jackie Kennedy," Viola said.

"That's right, we did," Julius said. "We moved Jackie Kennedy out of the White House to New York. I remember it was a lot of fun—like an adventure."

Julius also remembered his father's womanizing ways.

"I used to find him in those juke joints," Julius said. "My mom would say, 'Go get your dad, and tell him to bring some money home to buy some food.' So I'd go in—you know, kids weren't supposed to be in there—and my dad would see me and say, 'Come on over here, boy,' and he'd scoop the woman off his lap. He would never say, 'Don't tell your mom,' but I knew not to do that because I wanted to keep the peace. Sometimes there wasn't peace. I love my mom, but she was kind of the meanie. She would be the one who would get it going. One thing I appreciated about my father was that he would never strike out at my mom the way she did. And sometimes it got a little rough."

"What did you do when that happened?" Phil asked.

"You know, kids," Julius said softly. "You kind of cry, and they say, 'Well, go to the other room, dah, dah, dah.' But you hear the argument anyway. And when you hear stuff starting to get thrown around, you can only imagine what might be going on."

Julius was one of eight children, not all from the same mother and father, and grew up in Austin, Texas. His biological parents weren't married even though they were together for nineteen years.

"I never questioned it," Julius said, "but I just wanted them to get along. That's all I ever really cared about."

Julius was divorced twice before he got together with Viola, raising his two elder children as a single parent. In Austin, he worked as a juvenile probation officer and took whatever acting jobs he could find to support them.

Viola is from Central Falls, Rhode Island. Her mother was only fifteen and her father was twenty-two when the two got married. They had six children and stayed together for forty-eight years. Among other jobs, her father groomed horses, including the legendary Triple Crown winner Secretariat, at a South Carolina racetrack. When he was dying of pancreatic cancer in 2006, she thought to ask him whether that had been his greatest job. It turned out he hated grooming horses, saying his best job was being a paperboy. Her mother often worked in a chocolate factory.

MARLO: It sounds like a pretty stable childhood.

VIOLA: Not really—not in terms of food, in terms of finances, in terms of good housing, in terms of just a lot of strife in the house. My father was an alcoholic, although I loved him. Some people feel you can't love a parent who is troubled, but I did. And there was also a lot of domestic violence. But within all of that, I will say this: they allowed us to use our imaginations. Whenever we would write skits, my parents would let us take whatever clothes and shoes we wanted from their closet. They thought everything we did was great.

MARLO: It was pretty bold of you to get married, given the struggles you witnessed as a kid.

VIOLA: Listen, I did not want to get married. I never had any visions of walking down the aisle in a white dress. I admired every woman who was alone and happy and had a lot of boyfriends, women who were independent. I was a narcissistic artist.

But all of that changed when she met Julius, even though they had very different personalities.

"I am an introvert," Viola said, "maybe a step away from being a straight-up loner. I love my time alone. I love getting lost. I could drive to a theater, watch a foreign movie, eat sushi by myself with my book, and that's it. To have to answer to someone was very difficult for me. I didn't want to give up my independence or my name."

Julius, on the other hand, is an extrovert who strikes up conversations with strangers. "I'm the mayor of everywhere," he confessed with a laugh. "I can just walk into a room—even the subway station—and start having a conversation." But he didn't make any demands on Viola to change her manner to match his.

"When I met her, I was just excited about the possibility of what the relationship could be," he said.

Within three months of that meeting, they were living together in a two-bedroom apartment in Van Nuys, California.

"Relationships are an act of faith," Viola said. "My life got better as soon as we got together. I had someone who had my back. My car broke down on the 405 on my way to work, and I didn't call AAA, I called Julius. He was there in ten minutes and gave me his car and stayed with my car so I could go to work. And we had so much fun. When he first brought his clothes to my apartment, I loved it. There was nothing about it that I questioned. It was easy. It was right. It was perfect. I was coming from New York after having three or four roommates, and before that living at Juilliard in the dorms. And here I finally was with an apartment in Los Angeles and a Christmas tree, which I hadn't had in years."

As comfortable as the relationship was, however—and before they could take the next big step—Julius and Viola had to confront a hard reality that hangs a weight on many relationships: they both had money problems.

"I had bad credit," Viola confessed, "and I didn't know what to do about it. I was holding on to my apartment in New York because it was rent-stabilized, but the ceiling was caving in and the pipes had burst, and I wasn't able to sublet it. So I was here doing a TV show, paying rent and sending my family money. I was all over the place. I'm not saying I was completely irresponsible. I wasn't. I just didn't have any structure.

"Then Julius came in," she continued, "and it was all about two becoming one—that person appearing and making your life easier. That's what it was. He said, 'Vee, this is what we can do. You and I can share the rent. This is how you build up your credit.' And I was like, 'Oh, really?' And suddenly I started saving money and my credit got better. I even got my first car because of Julius—an '86 Volvo that I bought for $2,500."

Julius's money issue was a lot simpler: he was in debt. "I'd said to her, 'Baby, don't worry about it—I've got good credit. But I want to be free of all of my debt, so when we get married, we can start off on equal footing.' So Viola just put me to task. She said, 'You're doing all this stuff, talking about how you want to get married, so you're either going to put up or shut up. So your debt is my debt. We're going to do this together.' I remember not really saying anything that night, but the next day I told her, 'You know what—you're the girl for me.' I told her she was putting me up against the wall, but that wasn't a bad thing."

Viola and Julius made it official on June 23, 2003—a full four years after they'd met—with just sixteen people at the ceremony. They wore pink shirts and white pants that they'd bought at Express.

For two people who are so in sync, we wondered, what are Viola and Julius like when they're not on the same page?

VIOLA: I'm the door-slammer.

JULIUS: I'm the guy who just goes away.

MARLO: I'm the chaser. I follow Phil around till I get him to hear me.

PHIL: And now I let her catch me.

MARLO: What about jealousy? Do either of you have a green streak?

JULIUS: Not really. I think it's good to have a little jealousy, but not overly.

PHIL: What about you, Viola? Here you've got this good-looking husband—he's friendly, he's gregarious...

VIOLA: I do have a little jealousy. And I can always pinpoint those women who are very questionable. They may come off really nice, but I have a radar for them. I don't think men have that radar. So I'm very, very articulate about that.

MARLO: Right. So what do you say?

VIOLA: I say, "She can't come to the house no more."

MARLO: Statistics say that half of married couples divorce. We're among the survivors, thankfully. Is there something that you can get only from each other that's part of the bond?

JULIUS: One of the big things I get from her is a captive audience. I can tell her anything.

PHIL: She listens.

JULIUS: Yes, she listens. She takes it in and always has something to say to keep the conversation going. She's interested in my well-being and happiness, and I think that's huge when you're going through something. And she's smart as a whip. I love that in her. You have to really listen, let it land, take it in. Sometimes you don't have to answer right away, but you have to listen to each other. It's so huge in a relationship because once you stop listening, you're not there, you're not in it.

MARLO: Somebody once said that a good marriage is when both people don't go crazy at the same time.

VIOLA: That's the first thing Julius told me. "Vee, two people can't be down at the same time." He is definitely less stressed out than I am.

JULIUS: I'm always just reminding her that it's not as bad as it may seem. Allow yourself to breathe. And then let's talk through it. The stress she has with her career and the publicity and everybody wanting something, pulling at her, sometimes you feel like an octopus.

VIOLA: For me, that one thing about Julius that you're talking about is his capacity to love. Not everyone has that. It's like the Toni Morrison line—love is only as good as the lover. That person who has a capacity to love also has the capacity to stand by you during all the ugly, messy but beautiful things that can happen to you. That's what you need in life. That's the elixir, as far as I'm concerned.

For someone who initially had no interest in getting married, Viola ended up holding two more ceremonies with Julius, wearing a white dress both times. "There was never any tension, never anything but joy planning each of them," she said.

The second wedding was back East in Rhode Island, attended by 135 people. "My mom was inviting everyone in the city of Central Falls," Viola recalled, laughing. "She'd go into the grocery store and say, 'Viola's having a wedding. You want to go?'" The third ceremony—a vow renewal—was in Santa Monica, with a bountiful buffet of sushi, barbecued chicken, corn on the cob, and a guest list that included the cast from *How to Get Away with Murder*, plus Oprah Winfrey, Stedman Graham, and Gayle King.

"I said, 'I want all of it!'" Viola recalled. "I was like that little kid in Central Falls hollering, 'This is the life I want. This is the fantasy. I want it all.'"

"And I went along with it," Julius added. "I said, 'Okay, I'll be there. What time?'"

In her mid-forties, Viola made another big decision: she wanted a child. Julius was in his fifties, his children grown up enough to be giving him grandchildren. Still, he listened.

"I had to think about it for a little bit because I'd been on that horse before," he said. "My first wife is where my two elder kids are from. I got custody of them when they were three-and-a-half and one-and-a-half years old. So I knew what it was about. I knew the discipline and all that stuff. I raised them by myself as a single guy in Texas for seventeen years."

"Phil's four boys lived with him," Marlo said. "You two have that in common."

"Yes, we do," Phil said. "And the Downy goes in the rinse cycle."

"That's right!" Julius said, laughing. "And I wouldn't trade that experience for anything in my life. It helped shape me in a way. It made me realize the responsibility that my mom had taught me from a young age."

So Julius signed on for another round of fatherhood. "I decided I could get back on that horse again," he said, "and, you know, 'Happy wife, happy life.'" He calls adopting Genesis the "joy of our lives."

As a first-time mom, Viola felt the same conflict that many working mothers feel, as career and home life tugged at each other.

"But it wasn't about interrupting my career," Viola said. "It wasn't anything like that. I just thought, *I don't want to fail at this!* It was really, really hard to have another role in life that required so much of me. I didn't want to be a shallow actress and say, 'I'd rather be on a set than be at home changing diapers.' That wasn't me. I just wanted to do everything great. I wanted to be superwoman."

Luckily, their career success meant they could hire a nanny and a housekeeper, easing the transition into parenthood. They also have a personal trainer who puts them through workouts three times a week. Their production company, JuVee, employs another eleven people, which they find invigorating as well as stressful. To help them stay calm and keep the romance alive, they settle into a hot tub together every morning. Sometimes they'll go off to Santa Barbara for a weekend or book a hotel somewhere for a night just to enjoy a little privacy. They appreciate being able to afford such niceties, not forgetting where they came from.

They also love to celebrate. "We have the best parties," Viola said. "And we're both cooks, too."

"I'll show you my turkey before you leave," Julius crowed. "I made a video of it."

"He's so proud of his turkey," Viola said with a laugh.

"Smoke that sucker, then cook it for ten hours," Julius confirmed.

Yet even as they enjoy the good life, they are both mindful of the work that a marriage requires.

"I always thought marriage was 50/50," Viola said, "but it's 100/100. When the stress is really, really high, I just go to therapy because I feel there are answers I need that I can't put on Julius. There's certain work I have to do on my own. Julius is great with everything because he'll listen and say, 'Vee, stop thinking about a month from now. We're not there yet. Think about today.' And that helps me a lot. But when I feel this anxiety coming on from insecurity—things that are deep-seated and connected to my past—I know I need to go to therapy.

"The best thing I brought into my marriage," she continues, "is the ability to ask myself, 'What am I contributing to it?' Or 'What am I doing to destroy it?' That's been my personal responsibility, not to put everything on him. Not to say, 'Make me happy, Julius. Make the marriage good, Julius. Be the great husband, Julius.' I also have to step up."

"It's always about keeping our marriage at the forefront," Julius said. "I've told her, 'Honey, whatever you want, I'm doing it.'"

Viola said she deeply believes in keeping the promise they made to each other through ups and downs. She also recalled someone once telling her that when couples marry, they experience "a sort of dying" of their old lives.

"What does that mean?" Marlo asked.

"That your joy and your happiness are important," Viola explained. "And that your husband's joy and happiness are important. But you can't operate separately with your own joy and go on your own path if it doesn't honor the big umbrella of the ultimate commitment. And I see people doing that a lot. They go off on their own tangent because it serves their own needs, a life choice that can literally affect the marriage. You've got to feed the good of the whole.

"But I will say this, and then I'll leave it alone," Viola concluded. "My big thing about marriage—and it's advice I give to all of my friends—is that marriage does not start when you walk down the aisle. Your marriage starts when you look over at a person who you love more than anything, and there's something about him—just one character trait that makes you say to yourself, 'Oh man, that's going to drive me crazy, I don't know if I can deal with this.' And then the next minute you say, 'But you know what? I love him.' That's when your marriage starts."

Sting and Trudie Styler

MARRIED IN 1992

"We still have a pretty intense sexual charge between us.
When she walks in, she lights up the room."

The modern yet very warm home of Trudie Styler and Sting occupies an entire floor of a building in the Chelsea neighborhood of New York City. It was designed by the late Zaha Hadid, the celebrated Iraqi-born British architect who is often called "the queen of the curve." Lined with windows that overlook Manhattan, the bright, smoothly contoured space includes a large terrace that holds a statue of a naked man, which was modeled on the sculptor himself, Sir Antony Gormley. Sting said he loved living in the apartment because it's "so female, no sharp corners."

When we walked in, Sting was nestled on a sofa, peacefully reading. He told us to make ourselves at home, adding, "The boss will be here in a moment."

Almost on cue, Trudie glided in like a lovely, blonde sprite. She wore a sweater with "Friday" embroidered on it—the day it was—while Sting wore jeans and a T-shirt that said "1993." They've been together since long before that—1982—and between them they have six children and seven grandchildren. And yet, throughout our interview, they seemed like newlyweds, Sting gently touching Trudie several times—her hair, her shoulder, even picking lint off her sweater.

55

At sixty-eight, Sting shows no loss of sex appeal, and the connection between them felt electric. We settled in at a long, wooden dining table with cheerful, multicolored chairs, eagerly anticipating the lunch to come, which was being prepared with organic vegetables. "Even the stock is from scratch," Trudie told us.

First things first, though. How did they meet?

"Well, we were neighbors," Trudie began.

"Yes, we were neighbors," Sting quietly echoed.

At the time, she was dating Peter O'Toole. Sting was married, with two young children. Born Gordon Sumner, he's from Wallsend, in northern England, and was a schoolteacher before he moved to London, where he soon soared to superstardom as principal front man for the progressive rock band The Police. She had moved from Bromsgrove to London to pursue acting, via Stratford and the Royal Shakespeare Company.

"Neighbors?" Phil asked. "So how did you first connect?"

"Well, you know when you meet somebody and you recognize them?" Sting said. "The moment I clapped eyes on her, I just knew who she was, instantly. I felt as if we had always known each other."

"Well, that must have been kind of hard if you were neighbors," Marlo said.

"It was very difficult at first, because it wasn't in either of our plans to meet someone new who would change the course of our lives," Sting responded. "So, we tried to ignore the instinct for a couple of years."

Marlo turned to Trudie. "And did you know right away who he was, too?"

"It's like a recognition of somebody who you feel you know, even though you actually don't," Trudie said, finishing Sting's thought. "There's something very compelling, drawing you closer to someone. And of course, it was the least ideal situation that you can imagine. And when it happens to you, it's like a storm coming at you."

"A tidal wave," Sting finished back.

Wiltshire, England; August 20, 1992

Over time they understood that the connection was very real. They laughed at the same things, had similar backgrounds, and shared a fondness for nostalgia. When they eventually moved in together, the media attention was intense and invasive and unkind to all parties, turning an already complicated situation chaotic.

"It was a painful time and best left in the past," Trudie said. "The good news is that our six children have always been real siblings to one another, and we're really happy about that."

MARLO: So how did you learn to trust each other? It started as an unexpected collision, and then things tore apart. Finding trust is like going off a precipice. When we first met, Phil had never been with an actress before, so he was concerned about how he'd know if I was acting or telling the truth.

STING: I have the same problem, Phil. I never know when she's pretending. She's a good actor.

MARLO: But, in essence, aren't we all? Even when I cried, I could tell he wasn't sure if I was crying for real. Of course, we've been together a long time now, so he knows. But I'm wondering: At what point did you begin to feel comfortable and trusting?

STING: There was a chapter in our history that was us against the world. We were in a foxhole, and you have to trust that person because you're surrounded by danger. I was a mess and she protected me. That was very formative.

TRUDIE: A lot gets sacrificed when a relationship ends and a new one begins—and I was very mindful of my responsibility to Sting's children. I never had the role of stepmom. I've always just aimed to be a low-key friend to his kids, to be there if they needed me. And I think, bit by bit, as the years went by, we built up a real love for each other, and that mattered hugely to me.

When I hear questions about, "Oh, you're madly in love and passionate," and all that, I admit that, yes, it's true. But I also think that friendship needs to be part of the discussion about the longevity of a marriage or a relationship. Without that foundation, I don't think we could have survived the complicated circumstances of coming together.

PHIL: Falling in love with a rock star is a very dangerous thing, isn't it?

TRUDIE: You mean lots of women—

PHIL: —throwing their underwear.

STING: It's a stereotype. It's only partially true.

TRUDIE: Well, it used to be really difficult for me, feeling so jealous all the time. I had to sort of look at where my jealousy came from. And growing up as one of three girls vying for our mother's attention was something that happened a lot in our household. We were feisty—the three sisters—and we would clobber each other just to say, "Shut up and let me tell the story."

So what about fighting? As loving and connected as the couple appeared, there's no such thing as nonstop bliss, not in any marriage.

"I tried fighting with Sting early on," Trudie said, "because I used to be a very volatile person. But he doesn't deal very well with people yelling at him. When I did my shouting and yelling thirty-something years ago—for whatever reason was upsetting me—the veil would come down."

She turned to her husband to remind him. "You would just look at me, and I'd think, *I'm being met with silence. What a waste of my energy.*"

Sting surmised that the reason he doesn't engage in yelling matches is because he didn't want to be like his parents, who were very volatile, always fighting. "So I never wanted that in my life. It was too toxic for me." His mother was twenty years old when he was born, and his father about twenty-four.

"So, you were instructed to behave in an opposite way," Phil said.

"Yeah, I suppose they were educating me without meaning to," Sting said. "Trudie and I can disagree about things—not hugely important things—but we will have a conversation rather than an argument. It's a daily negotiation, sort of like a treaty. And I don't lose my temper."

Trudie eventually learned that she had to switch her strategy to make changes happen, or to resolve whatever was frustrating her.

TRUDIE: And so began the long journey of, "How can we do this better? How do we resolve conflict better?" Well, obviously, you can only learn to listen to somebody if you're not being yelled at or yelling at someone in return. Good communication can only come from sitting down and having meaningful, warts-and-all talks, and not turning them into accusations.

MARLO: That's hard to do. When you get angry, it's almost impossible to say, "Okay, let's have a nice talk where we don't accuse each other of anything." Sometimes our tempers take us to places we shouldn't go. I had an aunt and uncle who used to threaten divorce every time they fought.

STING: Well, that's an ultimatum. That's a threat. And it's not actually part of our vocabulary.

TRUDIE: I would never play the divorce card in an argument. That's a heinous idea to me.

"So did you learn how to communicate rationally from your parents?" Phil asked Trudie.

"I think there wasn't much space in their lives for being in love in the romantic sense, not by the time they had three daughters growing up in the house," Trudie answered. "I think they just got on with it. And they didn't have much money—no one did where we lived. My father was a quiet man, the classic man of few words. Later on, after I met Sting, Harry would see him and say, 'You're up, then.' And Sting would say, 'Yes, Harry, I'm up.' And we'd leave the room and he'd say, 'You're off, then,' And we'd say, 'Yes, Harry, we're off now.' And when we'd return: 'You're back, then.' 'Yes, Harry, we're back.'"

The lack of deeper communication led to a lonely life for Trudie's mother, who was by nature vivacious and outgoing. Trudie sensed that her mom envied women who had more gregarious husbands, so she'd perform little songs and dances with her sister, Heather, to make her mom laugh. That delight in cheering up her mother sparked Trudie's interest in acting, which led to training at the Bristol Old Vic. She is now also a producer and a director.

So given what they witnessed from their own parents, Sting and Trudie were left to figure out on their own how to create a healthy, satisfying marriage. But there were hurdles. Like most couples, they both have busy lives, so it's not always easy to find time to talk, particularly when Sting is on tour.

Which raises another issue: He doesn't like cell phones.

"They're an addiction," Sting said. "I'll make a call on mine and then I'll turn it off."

"That's a problem for me," Trudie said. "When Sting's on the road and he makes his call to me and I miss it and try to call him back, his phone is off." She turned to Sting. "So basically I can only speak to you on your terms. You can call me anytime you want, but when I call you, your phone is off."

Sting surrendered a sheepish smile. "You're not easy to get ahold of either," he said.

"Well, the big accommodation is absolutely no phones when we eat," Trudie told us.

"Unless it's yours," Sting teased.

Trudie parried that her life as a producer means constant communication, a 24/7 gig she likens to being a parent. Things go wrong on film and television sets all the time, she said, and she has to be available to put out fires. "Every time I pick up the phone, it's like, 'Mom, something else has gone wrong!'"

Cell phone quibbles aside, Sting is fairly Zen about the other mundanities of married life. "I'll go into the bathroom and see that Trudie left the top off the toothpaste again, or that she left the lights on in every room. There was a time when that sort of thing bothered me, but now I think, *That's my Trudie*. So I put the top back on the toothpaste and turn the lights out after her. I like who she is. And as flawed as I am, she actually still likes me. We're not here to change each other."

One thing Trudie has worked hard to change on her own, however, is her jealousy, something that still lingers from the early days of their relationship. Back then, when she saw women throwing themselves at her boyfriend, she would swallow her pride and try to build up her confidence. "I'd think, 'Well, I'm pretty too, and I'm the girlfriend now!'" Occasionally, when young women would ask her "Do you know how lucky you are?," she'd shoot back, "He's the fucking lucky one."

But the trickiest part of being out together, Trudie remembers, was simply trying to keep up with Sting as he walked ahead of her—partly to get away from the hordes besieging him and partly because he tends to walk "unreasonably fast."

"With me invariably in high heels and tight Azzedine Alaïa dresses it was even harder to keep up with him," Trudie said.

But fending off Sting's female admirers was something Trudie became very attuned to. "As soon as I came into a room I could kind of pick them out," she said. "*Oh yeah, this one. Note to self: I'll keep my eye on her.*"

Trudie also fiercely guarded her territory when it came to protecting their children. Sometimes when the couple would be pushing a stroller along a sidewalk, total strangers, spotting Sting, would practically whack her and the stroller aside just to get near him.

"I have seen women who pay me far too much attention crumple to the ground in a heap," Sting joked.

Gradually, however, Trudie began to relax about all the attention Sting got when she came to terms with how his public image had nothing to do with his private persona. Even so, after ten years together—and three children—marriage was not on the agenda.

We asked Trudie why they waited so long to marry, but rather than respond to either of us, she turned to her husband.

"What I remember you saying is that the biggest failure you ever felt was your marriage and that you never wanted to fail again," she said. "I respected that and was okay with it for a few years. I was also worried that, having been the catalyst for the breakup, I didn't want to be rushed into the new institution and create a vacancy for another woman."

They eventually moved their family from London to the English countryside and found themselves surrounded by a much more conservative community, Trudie said. "Not being married and having three children going to school became an issue. One of the kids came back from school one day and said to me, 'Somebody said I'm a bastard today. Is it true?' And I said, 'No, that's your dad.' " Sting laughed.

That fleeting moment essentially motivated Sting and Trudie to make it official on August 20, 1992. They celebrated the event two days later at their Elizabethan estate along with 250 guests. A fourth child arrived a few years later.

Marriage, the couple quickly discovered, had more benefits than just legal codification or silencing school bullies.

"People gave Trudie more respect and deference than they did before," Sting said. "I was proud to say 'This is my wife.' "

Case in point: In the years before the marriage, party invitations would read "Sting and Guest."

"It would really smash my feelings," she recalled. "I would often decline or have somebody call and say, 'Sting *and Trudie* would be delighted to accept.' I remember the first invitation that came to 'Mr. and Mrs. Sumner.' I liked how that felt. After that, I didn't have to try so bloody hard."

That's not to say that she takes being married for granted.

"I always feel great excitement when Sting has been away and I know he's coming home today," Trudie said. "I'll pretty myself up for his return. I'll have my hair done and my makeup on and my heart will beat faster. I'll be as giddy as a young girl."

TRUDIE: For somebody in my sixties, when my husband says I look pretty
   or he admires the dress I'm wearing or tells me my eyes are beautiful,
   I feel like I start to walk on air again, just like I did when I was thirty.
STING: However, if I don't like what she's wearing, I say that, too.
MARLO: So does my husband.
STING: I say, "Look, if you want to believe me when I say I like something

you're wearing, then it's the same when I say I don't like something. I'm telling the truth, so you make the choice."

TRUDIE: It still hurts my feelings.

MARLO: I know. Sometimes Phil tells me on the way down in the elevator, and I go, "Oh, God, it's too late." I'll make the stupid mistake of asking, "Do you like what I'm wearing?" And he'll say, "You have better things than that." And then I know I shouldn't have asked him because he's going to tell me the truth.

Trudie said she still gets out her fancy lingerie when the couple stays at hotels. "There's a decadence about a hotel room that, even after thirty-something years, I'll still feel like, 'Oooh, we're in a hotel! And there're no kids!'"

This seemed like as good a time as any to address a story that has dogged this couple for thirty years. In 1990, Sting gave an interview in which he casually tossed off a comment that he and Trudie practiced tantric sex. The remark stuck like a tattoo and became wildly embellished.

"I know it's been crazily exaggerated," Marlo said, "but what is tantric sex anyway?"

"Really?" Sting said with a brief sigh, then patiently dove in. The tantric sex, he explained, evolved from the couple's decades-long study of yoga—the spirituality, the physicality, the celebration of existing. "It's got nothing to do with how long you make love for," he said, "that's just silly talk. It's actually about being conscious of what you're doing.

"We still have a pretty intense sexual charge between us," he continued, "but what's important is that I really like this woman and she really likes me. The sexual thing can cool off. It doesn't have to be super-charged the whole time. But when she walks in, she lights up the room. And it's got nothing to do with sex, actually. For me, it's all to do with liking how she presents herself to the world, liking the decisions she makes, the comments she makes, the observations she makes. I enjoy her company."

"The tabloid version is that we have sex for five or six hours," Trudie added. "If only we had the time! It's really about intimacy on many levels.

We could go to one of our favorite restaurants in cities all over the world and I could order exactly what he would want to eat, because I know what pleases him. It can be as everyday as that. Or it can be about giving each other our full attention. The fun is in the time that we give to each other, reminding us of all the ways we hold each other precious—kissing and holding each other, being very much in the moment together. It's just about feeling that you're at one with your love."

Connection. That word pretty much defines what we witnessed up close during our afternoon with this wonderfully earthy couple. Now grandparents, Trudie and Sting have become more conscious than ever of the passage of time.

"We've had so many years together that are now behind us," Trudie said, touching Sting's hand. "And so when we look to the future, and we look at our friends who are starting to get sick, I sometimes say to Sting, 'I love you in the in-between moments of life.' And then I'll take his face in my hands and look into his eyes and think, 'Please, God, let us be together for as long as we can possibly be. Please let us be well and have these moments forever.'"

I never made promises lightly
and there have been some that I've broken
But I swear in the days still left
we'll walk in fields of gold

—"Fields of Gold," Sting

Alan and Arlene Alda

MARRIED IN 1957

"We are often asked the secret to a long marriage, and
I say, 'The secret to a long marriage is a short memory.'"

I always love coming here," Phil said as we entered the beautiful home of Alan and Arlene Alda, high up on the fifty-first floor of a modern New York City high-rise. "It's amazing what you can buy on a taxi driver's salary. Wasn't it just yesterday that you were a cabbie?"

"Yup," said Alan, "if you consider fifty or sixty years ago yesterday."

Arlene laughed. "Time flies," she said.

If it's true that friendships—like wine—improve with age, then Alan and Arlene are a treasured vintage to us. Marlo and Alan first met while making the film *Jenny* in 1970; and as with any strong friendship, the good times multiplied once the spouses joined in. At this point we've lost count of the dinner tables where we've sat across from each other, the holiday parties we've attended together, the nonstop laughs we've shared.

"We're doing a book on couples who have been married since forever," Marlo wrote to Alan in an email. "Know anyone interesting we can talk to?"

Alan's email back was three words: "Come on over."

The Aldas' sunny apartment is, of course, very familiar to us, with its magnificent views of this magnificent city: the Empire State Building, Riverside Park, the twinkling bridges of the Hudson River—and, just to

Arlene and her niece, Beverly, in Houston, Texas; March 15, 1957

the north, the Bronx, the borough where Arlene grew up, and which she immortalized in her 2015 book *Just Kids from the Bronx*.

Two items in the living room tell you a lot about the apartment's occupants: Near one window stands a professional telescope, which Alan—a passionate science geek—uses to gaze at the stars. And nearby is a beautiful piano made of walnut. In addition to being an award-winning photographer, Arlene is a trained musician—the clarinet is her instrument, but she plays piano every day, "for both the challenge and the pleasure." She's not alone when she plays: photos of their three daughters—Eve, Elizabeth, and Beatrice—and seven grandchildren keep her company.

Science and art and love. It's a nice combination.

If ever a couple had humble beginnings, it's Alan and Arlene. They met at a party thrown by a mutual friend, which would have been uneventful had a rum cake not fallen from the top of the refrigerator and landed with a splat on the floor. The two strangers, feeling sympathy for the embarrassed hostess, both had the same instinct. They each grabbed a fork, dove to the floor on all fours, and began digging into the cake, prompting peals of laughter in the room.

A couple was born. They spent the next three weeks seeing each other every day and were married eleven months later. That was sixty-three years ago.

But, boy, were those first years tough. Alan was a struggling actor, so he drove a cab at night to keep food on the table for his wife and first daughter.

"In those days, you didn't automatically get a cab to drive," Alan recalled. "I'd show up at nine or ten at night and have to sit on a bench for a couple hours until they finally gave me a taxi. I remember the first night, I was sitting there behind two old-timers, and I overheard one of them saying to the other, 'Yeah, I knew it was a holdup as soon as he got into my cab.' The other guy says, 'How did you know?' The first guy says, 'Well, he puts this gun to my temple and says "Take me to 42nd Street." That's when I knew.'"

The cabbie gig soon became a way of life, Alan said. He'd drive all night, trying to stay awake, then get home at four in the morning, leave the money he'd made on the kitchen counter, and collapse into bed. The following day, Arlene would portion out the cash into envelopes she had labeled.

"The envelopes were my obsessive-compulsive way of dealing with money we didn't have," explained Arlene. "Each envelope had a purpose—rent, food, gas and electric, phone, extras. That's how I organized our finances."

MARLO: Sounds like a pretty tight budget.
ALAN: It was—and each dollar meant a lot to us. At the time I liked to drink a can of beer at dinner, so I would buy a brand called Fox Head that sold for $1.05 a six-pack. I remember one time not having any beer for a whole week because that $1.05 was needed for rent.

ARLENE: And remember, you could actually buy a whole box of spaghetti at the market for 11 cents. It was great. We could have two full meals of spaghetti for under a quarter.

ALAN: Of course, I'd have to work overtime if we wanted sauce.

PHIL: When you think about it, living that way took such nerve. Looking back, do you ever wonder what made you two think you could be married and become parents with no money?

ALAN: We were stupid.

ARLENE: Well, our thought was, we were two college-educated kids who were both smart and both had talent. I had a teacher's license, and I did teach. Alan was very industrious, and he didn't mind driving a cab.

ALAN: I was also a doorman, I colored baby pictures...

MARLO: You were living the gig economy before there was such a thing. But what about the stress factor of living such a hand-to-mouth existence? That would take its toll on most couples.

ALAN: We both had a positive attitude. It never occurred to me or Arlene that I should quit acting. I never heard from my partner, "Are you sure you want to keep trying to find work as an actor? We have a future to think about." We both had this irrational idea that we would survive and do okay. And surviving was all I had in mind. At the time, I couldn't even imagine what having money was like. I would walk the streets of New York, trying to get into casting offices, and I'd pass luncheonettes and hamburger joints, and more than once, the thought occurred to me, "I guess being rich is to be able to walk into any of these places and order anything you want."

ARLENE: But we had optimism.

ALAN: It was more than optimism. I was aware that I would try to get what I wanted, but I knew I would want what I eventually got. And that's better than optimism.

MARLO: That's very Zen.

ARLENE: What he had was something special. He didn't go to acting school, but he was on the stage with his father when he was very young.

He'd watched his father acting, and the confidence he had in himself was evident.

Indeed, Alan had the best theatrical mentor a kid could want. His dad, Robert, was an acclaimed film and stage actor, a singer and dancer, and a veteran of vaudeville and burlesque. As a little boy, Alan enjoyed going to work with his father, where he was surrounded by chorus girls and strippers. That alone gave him an insiders' view of show business.

"The strippers were not as friendly as the chorus girls," Alan recalled with a grin. "The chorus girls mothered me and took me up to their dressing rooms, combed my hair, patted me on the head and called me Alfie."

"Sounds like our marriage—pat you on the head, comb your hair," said Arlene. "But it was that confidence that drew me in. We were in this together. We wanted something and we were willing to work for it. It never occurred to me that it might not work out. We knew what we wanted, but we were very flexible in case it didn't work out."

"Do you think that was a generational thing?" asked Phil.

"Could be," said Arlene. "It's shocking to hear kids talk today. They measure everything in terms of dollars and cents. We didn't think that way. It was not such a monetary society. Of course, everything was more affordable. At one point, we could live in New York with three little kids. But then came the eighties and Reagan and condos, and affordable housing began to disappear."

Even though the couple agreed that they would take whatever life offered, they never stopped trying to fulfill their dreams. But the work came slowly. For nine full years, Alan struggled to find traction as an actor; so Arlene supplemented the household income by teaching music and performing with a local orchestra and a chamber music group. The couple also made an important decision: they relocated to Leonia, New Jersey, across the Hudson River.

"Until the move, we'd been living in an apartment across from Columbia University," Alan recalled, "but we wanted a real house with a real yard, where the kids could go outside and play."

"There was also a practical reason for this," Arlene noted. "This was the 1960s and the city was a mess—it was bankrupt. Our oldest daughter was starting school, and private school wasn't even on our radar. I was brought up in public schools and I believed in that system. Unfortunately, our neighborhood school in New York wasn't good enough, and we didn't have the money for private school, even if that had been our choice. We wanted the kids to have a community where they could walk to good schools, walk to shops, and have playmates. We found that community."

Then in 1972, everything—*everything*—changed.

MARLO: So there you are, just another typical suburban family, putting down roots in New Jersey, and Alan, you land the starring role of Dr. Hawkeye Pierce in a new TV show called *M*A*S*H*. What did that mean to you at the time?

ALAN: It meant that from 1972 to 1983, I had a steady job.

PHIL: And it wasn't driving a cab.

ALAN: That's right. I mean, most actors have to change jobs every couple of weeks. If you're in a play, maybe you'll run a year, if you're lucky. I used to be amused at people who would say, "I've been in this job ten years and now I have to find a new job." For the first time, I had steady work.

PHIL: Steady work that would make TV history. And you didn't just act in it. You wrote and directed many of the episodes. But the show filmed in L.A., and you famously "commuted" to work. What was that like?

ALAN: The first couple of weeks I would talk on the phone to Arlene and the girls several times a day and then fly home every three weeks. But I found that I was missing the life that was taking place every day at home. So, for about four years, I'd fly home every time I had two days off—including every weekend. The more time I spent at home, the more connected I was. One week I remember I flew home three times in one week.

MARLO: Oh, my God. You were the king of the redeye.

ARLENE: He loved those girls so much, and the girls missed him. But as they got older, it became sort of a sad joke. I would get up at 4 a.m. and go to pick him up when the redeye landed. That sounds like a sacrifice, but it wasn't, because we'd have this whole hour in the car together. That was important. Then we'd get home and he'd fall asleep—and when he woke up at noon, he'd look around and say, "Hey, where are the girls?" They were teenagers—one had an appointment, another one had a lesson. I liked that he got to see me, but sometimes he didn't get to see the kids.

ALAN: Arlene realized that our job at the time was to be the ones in the rocking chairs when the kids left, saying, "See you later," and not the other way around.

During the summer, when school wasn't in session, the entire family would decamp to Los Angeles, but as the girls grew and started college, it became increasingly difficult to get them to leave their own lives.

Meanwhile, Alan's star was growing brighter. In his various capacities as actor, writer, and director of *M*A*S*H*, he earned twenty-one Emmy nominations, winning five times, becoming the only person to have won Emmys in all three categories.

The kind of success Alan was experiencing can sometimes attract uninvited admirers. We asked Arlene how she handled that.

ARLENE: You mean jealousy?

MARLO: Yes, for both of you. He's in L.A., you're in Jersey. Surely some thoughts are going through your heads. Like, "I wonder if he's enjoying the company of some young woman on the set," or "I wonder if she's enjoying the neighborhood butcher back home?"

ALAN: The butcher—I didn't worry about.

ARLENE: The baker, maybe.

MARLO: So you have no jealousy bone at all?

ARLENE: No. The only time I feel jealous is when something interferes with the time I spend with him. I'm jealous of the phone calls. I'm jealous of the computer.

ALAN: The computer means nothing to me. It's just physical.

ARLENE: I mean, it's not that I don't understand what jealousy is, but I'm just not prone to thinking about who he's with and what he's doing.

MARLO: Even if you're at a party and some woman is hanging all over him?

ARLENE: Oh, well, I've seen that. To me that's hilarious. I'll say to him, "Did you see the way she was hanging on you?"

ALAN: And I'll say, "I thought that was appropriate."

ARLENE: It doesn't even register with him.

ALAN: You know what comes to mind is the story of me shooting that shower scene...

ARLENE: Oh, in Canada. He was directing and acting in a movie with this beautiful young actress, Veronica Hamel.

PHIL: I remember that movie. It was *A New Life*.

ALAN: Right. Veronica and I had a shower scene, but we couldn't find the right location to shoot it, so we shot it in the shower of the apartment Arlene and I had rented in Toronto. So we're in the shower half-naked—or almost naked—and the camera is rolling. At the very end of the scene, Arlene comes home early, walks by the bathroom, sees us in the shower stall, and says, "What time are we going to lunch?"

MARLO: You're a far better woman that I am, Arlene.

ALAN: I mean, there was a full crew crowded into this bathroom with us, but I think it shows Arlene's complete sangfroid about movie kisses.

ARLENE: I mean, maybe it's stupidity on my part, but things like that just didn't bother me.

Starlets in your shower or not, it all comes down to trust, the couple noted.

"But trust is an earned thing," Marlo said. "It takes time to trust people."

Arlene nodded. "I guess it goes back to the days we grew up in, and being young," she pointed out. "That's when we learned to trust each other. It was a simpler time, and we weren't wrapped up in technology. Communication was person-to-person. That helped."

"We're both lucky to have found each other," Alan agreed. "We enjoy the time we spend together. And we do simple and simple-minded things.

We play cards together. We've been playing the same card game for about forty years."

"What's the game?," asked Phil.

"Spite and Malice," answered Alan, naming a traditional double-solitaire game.

Marlo laughed. "It completely defines who you are."

"Perfect name for a game," agreed Alan. "I'm going to teach it to you. It's really fun. It takes one hour to play one game, and by the end you're screaming and cursing at each other."

"Screaming and cursing," Phil said. "Is that how the Aldas deal with stressful situations?"

"You mean real fights?" Alan asked. "It's funny, we never had arguments about money—either when we had no money or when we had some. And money is a common problem for most couples. Some people may come from families that take everyone's viewpoints into consideration and not yell, but maybe more people are like us. We're passionate. We have strong ideas. I remember one time we made a business mistake because we both panicked each other, but nowadays one of us will temper the other's fear. I think as time has gone by, we've gotten better at figuring out how to work things out."

ARLENE: You get pretty good at these things after sixty-three years. It makes me laugh because we are often asked the secret to a long marriage, and I say, in my liveliest voice, "The secret to a long marriage is a short memory." And there's some truth to that. I can honestly say I can't remember the details of any of the stresses. At some moments, it seemed like the sky was going to fall in any second—but two days later, we were asking, "What was that all about? Why were we stressing?" The only issue I remember us having is that my style of handling the kids was different from Alan's.

PHIL: In what way?

ARLENE: I was more organizational and he was more playful. My tendency was to look at my watch and say, "We have to get to school, we have to get dressed, we have to get the food on the table." Well, now I've learned that we didn't have to do any of that. It was the rule I set up for myself that caused the stress. Alan's way of dealing with the kids was to play with them. He loved that he could make them laugh. I loved that he could make me laugh. But at the time, I felt he was overindulgent, and he felt I was too strict. Eventually we worked it out.

ALAN: Listen, you can't avoid disagreements about things—sometimes sharp disagreements—but it's always important to remember that the person you're disagreeing with is someone you love. Remembering that one thing colors the interaction in a significant way.

ARLENE: It's fine to argue. It's fine to disagree. That's life and that's good. It's good energy. But when you start denigrating a person by calling them names, that is not okay, and you can't take those words back. They stick.

ALAN: I think that's what I'm saying. Even before you utter a denigrating word, you have to step back and ask yourself, "Who is that person over there? What stranger am I faced with?" Well, it's not a stranger. It's the one you love. And if you can remember that in the midst of a heated disagreement, it makes things much easier.

PHIL: You can do that in the middle of a heated disagreement? What extraordinary control.

MARLO: You both appear to be so in sync. When aren't you?

ALAN: Well, this is such a small thing, but Arlene doesn't have the same sense of spatial relationships that I do. So when we walk into a room, she'll enter and then stop right after the doorway, and I'll knock her over.

ARLENE: It gets dangerous. It happens mostly in department stores, right? I'll walk in and I have to see where I am, but he's behind me saying, "Move!"

ALAN: But, again, that's an example of a very little thing that could grow into a big thing if you don't remember who this person is. You have to remind yourself that this lump in front of you is the person you love.

ARLENE: Hey, wait a minute . . .

While Alan's ascent to stardom had been relatively conventional—small roles led to larger roles, which led to M*A*S*H and beyond—Arlene's photography career came about in a far more personal way. It began back in the mid-sixties, after the couple's third daughter was born and Alan's career was just starting to take off. Although Arlene's work as a musician and teacher had been satisfying, her role as a loving spouse and parent started to feel limiting. The move to Leonia had solved many problems—especially for the kids—but she began to sense that she'd left a bit of herself behind.

"I had a deep-seated conflict when the children were little," Arlene recalled. "Alan was busy and I was home alone with the three kids. Like a lot of women with young children, I felt stuck. I wasn't developing my intellect. I wasn't growing. It wasn't as if I didn't love being with those kids. I did. I was like a lioness—I wouldn't leave them with a stranger. Only my mother, my sister, or Alan could be the babysitters. But I had this sense that Alan was growing and I wasn't. I remember feeling, *I'm going to dissolve into nothing if I don't take care of myself.* I went to a psychologist who helped clarify that there was turmoil."

"How great that you dealt with it head-on," Marlo said. "You could have been the woman who walked away. You could have been the miserable wife who stayed and began picking at her husband and children."

"I realized that this is not good," Arlene said. "It wasn't working for me."

"How old were the girls at this point?" Marlo asked.

"They were little," Arlene said. "They were six, four, and three, something like that. So when Beatrice, who's our youngest, went off to kindergarten, I realized I had three more hours in the day. I'd always loved photography. My father loved photography. My brother loved it. So I took a photography class. At that point, my life took off. Photography became an obsession. It was just so wonderful. I felt like I was soaring into a creative new way of looking at things."

Arlene was so consumed by this new passion, Alan remembered, that their day-to-day life changed noticeably. "I would knock on her darkroom door and say, 'The kids are asking about dinner,' and she'd say, 'Send out for pizza' or 'Call Chicken Delight.'"

"That must have been a big change for you, Alan," said Phil. "Did you ask yourself, 'How am I going to be able to accommodate this new woman?'"

Arlene answered for Alan. "He loved it," she said. "The first thing he said was, 'You need a new camera.' So we went out and I got a Nikon. It was funny. He'd say, 'Now get this lens,' and 'Get this lens, too.' And I'd say, 'I don't want all these lenses. I don't know what they do yet. When I need that lens, I'll buy that lens.'"

"I would be her grip when she'd go out shooting," Alan added. "There was a lot of equipment, so I carried it."

Arlene's "obsession" blossomed into a thriving career—one that eventually produced twenty books, many for children, as well as features in *Vogue, People,* and *Good Housekeeping.* And one-person art shows in prestigious galleries. "I'm not a person who has hobbies," Arlene explained. "If I get interested in something, it becomes full-blown—something I want to do very well."

It was around this time that Alan began teaching himself to be a movie director, shooting short films on 16-millimeter or Super 8 film, then putting up posters around their town, inviting neighbors to attend mini–Alan Alda film festivals.

ARLENE: He drove me crazy. He would shoot these little movies and do dangerous things. God, it still makes me sick to think about it.

ALAN: They were all little sketches or abstract films, and one was a story about a little girl who finds car keys hanging on a hook in her home and decides to drive the family car around the block—which is an interesting and scary little movie. What was even scarier was the way I shot it. Our daughter Eve, who was, what, eight?

ARLENE: I forget how old she was. It still gives me a stomachache.

ALAN: She was actually at the wheel of the car, and a friend of mine was just out of the frame so he could take over the wheel.

ARLENE: And the brakes.

ALAN: I was on the hood of the car with the camera, shooting through the windshield.

ARLENE: Can you imagine?

ALAN: So, the car is moving, and I'm getting a shot of Eve driving. And I say, "Now put on the brakes." So, she had to almost slide out of the shot to pretend to put her foot to the brake. And the brake goes on, and the car had just been waxed so I slid right off the hood.

ARLENE: He could have been run over! I mean, I kept saying, "This is your idea! I don't like your idea!" But I couldn't stop him. You ask about accommodations? There are certain things I'll accommodate, but I had to look the other way because I didn't want to watch.

ALAN: I don't know if you're like this, but I have this totally irrational idea that when the camera is turning, I can't get hurt.

MARLO: I think that, too. It's make-believe, for God's sake.

As Arlene's photography became increasingly recognized, Alan was there to support her work, just as she had supported his. After all the challenges they'd faced as a couple—from the 11-cent pasta to the ups and downs of raising a family to the constant separations—it was as if they were finally coasting on the life they'd long ago dreamed of, and the seas ahead were clear and calm.

And then, in an instant, that life was threatened in a terrifying and un-expected way. It was the fall of 2003, and Alan was in Chile taping an epi-sode of his popular PBS documentary series *Scientific American Frontiers*. He was gazing though a telescope at the Andromeda galaxy when he suddenly became doubled over with abdominal pain, and his stomach ballooned to twice its size.

He was rushed to an emergency room, where doctors diagnosed an intestinal obstruction and told him that he could die without immediate surgery.

"So you're going to do an end-to-end anastomosis," he said as surgeons prepped him for the knife.

"Yes, how did you know that?" the doctors asked Alan.

"I did many of them on *M*A*S*H*," he said.

Alan would later admit that going for the laugh in the midst of a life-threatening situation was instinctual, but there was little about his condition that was funny. Back in the States, Arlene received the 1 a.m. phone call—the kind every spouse or parent dreads—reporting on Alan's crisis. It took her a day and a half of connecting flights to get to her husband's bedside.

"She walked into the hospital room and saw me on the bed," Alan recalled, "and even though by then I was sitting up and cracking jokes, she fell down on her knees, grabbed my hand, and kissed it. It was a moment of genuine feeling and affection that was so powerful it made me remember the hundreds of times that I'd experienced her real and simple, unforced expressions of love. As time goes on, it's still unforced. We express our love for each other a lot. Sometimes I wonder if other people do that."

"It made me realize how precious life is," Arlene reflected. "You know, there are so many ways we're very fortunate. There's a simplicity to our lives that I just love and Alan just loves. Like, if we're home, I don't need to cook something elaborate. He has a favorite dish. It's pasta, any kind of pasta. And I can make that very easily. One night recently we were home and about to binge on some series, and I said, 'How about rigatoni with just oil and garlic and some little peas?' And he loved it."

"I can taste it now," said Alan.

"You see?" said Arlene. "The appreciation that he shows for this simple thing—it just warms my heart."

We never want an evening with Arlene and Alan to end, but it was getting late, so we began to make our way out. Before we got to the door, we paused to look at our favorite piece of art in the Alda home—a floor-to-ceiling frame that holds a blue lace dress. It's an heirloom that perfectly depicts the durability of the couple's marriage.

We already knew the story behind the dress, but we asked Arlene to tell it again—for the record.

"This was my wedding dress on March 15, 1957," she began. "I was in Texas, playing the clarinet with the Houston Symphony. It was mid-calf length and white at the time, and it was just right for the very simple wedding we wanted. We had only eighteen guests, which was perfect for

The dress—once white, now blue

us. We didn't have a photographer at the wedding, so this dress—and one tiny photograph of me wearing it, along with my sister's five-and-a-half-year-old daughter, Beverly, who was our flower girl—are the only real mementos we have of that joyous day. Later on, two of our daughters, Eve and Beatrice, wanted to wear the dress to their rehearsal dinners before their own weddings. Beatrice dyed it blue. And when our fiftieth anniversary came around, all three girls surprised us by having it framed as our gift."

Simplicity and humility have been a constant in Arlene and Alan's marriage. And there is no doubt in our minds that they could lose all of their material possessions and barely notice, as long as they had each other. And pasta.

Arlene ran her hand along the frame. "This dress has never shredded or fallen apart in any way during these sixty-three years. I wish I could claim that I carefully put it away in an heirloom box after the wedding. Not so. Maybe that's why our marriage has lasted. Benign neglect. Things were made to last in those days."

"Is that your advice to young newlyweds?" asked Marlo. "Benign neglect?"

Arlene shook her head. "No, it's this," she said. "What you think is important may not be so important. Just relax, laugh, and have fun. Together."

Capt. Chesley "Sully" and Lorrie Sullenberger

MARRIED IN 1989

"Whenever he gets asked to do too much, my constant refrain to him is, 'Landing in the river was enough.'"

A mere ninety seconds—that's all it took to forever change the lives of Lorrie and Chesley Sullenberger.

The date was January 15, 2009, and it began like any other normal working day for Capt. Sullenberger, a respected and experienced pilot for US Airways who had logged roughly twenty thousand hours of flight time. He and his copilot, Jeffrey Skiles, were strapped into their seats aboard Flight 1549 at New York's LaGuardia Airport, headed for Charlotte, North Carolina, for what should have been a routine, two-hour flight. Including the crew, 155 people were on board.

Broken clouds hung over Manhattan when the screaming engines of the Airbus A320 lifted the nose of the jet into the sky at 3:24 p.m. The wind was nine knots, coming in from the northwest.

"What a view of the Hudson today," Captain Sullenberger said to Skiles as the jet reached three thousand feet above the Bronx, traveling at 213 miles per hour. And then suddenly, a bang. A flock of Canada geese slammed into both engines of the aircraft, instantly crippling it. Within

three seconds, Sully began to take remedial action. Without engine thrust, he made the fast decision to use gravity for forward motion; and, unable to return to LaGuardia or reach any other airport in neighboring New Jersey, he glided the lifeless jet onto the surface of the frigid waters of the Hudson River. All 155 souls survived and were rescued from the wings of the plane by a flotilla of boats.

To this day, the raw numbers remain staggering: three seconds to make the life-saving decision; one-and-a-half minutes to execute the plan; 155 lives saved.

Flight 1549 immediately became known as the "Miracle on the Hudson," an iconic, uplifting moment in aviation history that transfixed the world and made Captain Sullenberger a hero and instant celebrity.

And for those of us in New York, it was an astonishing event that had taken place in our own backyards. Like many New Yorkers, we can see a piece of the Hudson from our apartment. Not since 9/11 had we felt such an intimate connection—and proximity—to an event of such magnitude.

Overnight, the nickname "Sully" became synonymous with intelligence, bravery, preparedness, quick-mindedness, and coolness under pressure. President Barack Obama invited him to his first inauguration the following week; Tom Hanks portrayed him in the inevitable blockbuster motion picture, directed by Clint Eastwood.

In the frantic moments after the water landing—once Sully was sure everyone was safely off the plane—he called the airline from the deck of a rescue ferry to report the incident to his superiors. Then, even before he had reached dry land, he placed a second call—this one to his wife in San Francisco.

Lorrie had not been watching the news. She is a fitness expert, writer, and local television personality who frequently speaks on women's health issues and how to prepare for life's challenges. In other words, she is precisely the kind of woman who could grapple with the dramatic turn the couple's lives took that day.

Hillsborough, California; June 17, 1989

When Sully tried to reach her, however, it became a classic marital moment. Lorrie was on a business call with a colleague and ignored the beep of her husband's calls. He continued to dial the couple's two landlines—and her cell phone—eventually hanging up after three or four rings, then trying another line. He never left a message.

SULLY: It was like, *I need to talk to you.*

LORRIE: The third time he did it I was really irritated with him. I was thinking, *Why are you being such a pest?* And so I said to this producer I was talking to, "Sully wants something, so let me get rid of him and I'll call you right back." And so I hung up with her and answered Sully's call by saying, *"What?!"* Sully tells that part in his speeches, and people in the audience love it.

MARLO: So you were expecting more of the typical husband check-in call.

LORRIE: Yes. He would usually call and say, "I'm on the way," or something like that, so when he said, "I just wanted you to know that I'm okay," I thought that meant, *Okay, he's on the flight.* I didn't keep track of his exact schedule, so I wouldn't have known exactly where he was supposed to be at that time. I mean, often with their kind of schedule they will fly four or five legs in a day. And then he said, "No, no, there's been an incident."

MARLO: "Incident" is a better word than "accident."

LORRIE: I guess I wasn't picking it up right away. And then, when I really listened to him—his voice sounded raspy and kind of breathy—he didn't sound normal to me. I don't know why, but that's when I turned on the television.

SULLY: I'd asked you if you were watching TV.

LORRIE: He said, "I hit a flock of birds." Even though I was looking at the pictures on the screen, I was still like, *"You what?!"*

SULLY: It's too much to take in all at once. And she said, "Are you *okay* okay?" I said, "Yes, I'm okay. Not a scratch, not a bump, not a mark, not a bruise."

In truth, Sully had suffered some physical manifestations from his ordeal, and he was not able to return home to San Francisco for two-and-a-half days. When he finally did, his wife was speechless.

"I was stunned," Lorrie said of his appearance when they were reunited. "He had lost thirteen pounds and had barely slept. When you lose weight that rapidly from that kind of shock, well, he looked like he'd been in a car accident. His eyes were really dark and sunken and he was gaunt, like something was wrong. I think that's when I fully appreciated why Americans were celebrating, because even though it had been a successful outcome, for everyone on that airplane it was still an accident."

"Traumatic," Sully said.

"And then he became kind of aloof from me and he couldn't quite connect," Lorrie recalled. "His first words to me were, 'I hope they all know I did the best I could.' I realized that he was reliving it all, over and over and over."

Normally Sully had low blood pressure and a low pulse, but both remained very high for the next ten weeks, even with medication. It took him months to get back to sleeping soundly through the night. He wasn't allowed to pilot a plane until his normal sleep pattern improved.

We met with the couple at our home while they were in Manhattan on business. We went into our interview fully aware of how exhausting it must be for them to relive that day over and over. And even though our conversation was going to be about their marriage, it would be revealing to learn how their twenty-year partnership had been instrumental in helping them navigate the rough waters that lay ahead after the incident. The actual water landing was one thing, but then came the unexpected: the media onslaught, a protracted investigation by the National Transportation Safety Board, an influx of money and book offers, and an exhausting demand of their time.

"Everybody wanted a piece of me," Sully told us. "This was not my natural temperament—to want to be in the spotlight. We had these opportunities that were coming in fast and furious, amazing opportunities that wouldn't have happened in a hundred normal lifetimes."

Lorrie nodded. "I felt protective of him," she said, "and I also knew that it was contrary to his personality to be so public about it. In the early days—and early years—after the incident, I used to say I felt like these people were piranhas and would have picked the meat off his bones. But I also knew that he felt a great civic duty and calling to do the right thing, and so he was going to rise above it all to do whatever he had to do."

Within five days, the couple was at the Obama inauguration. Sully, along with the crew, was seated on the risers behind the new president, framed in the camera shot with him. That night, they attended the inaugural ball where the Obamas had their first dance.

"And our whole crew met the president and First Lady behind the scenes at the inaugural ball," Sully said. "And then the next month I was at the State of the Union address and was acknowledged by the president in the room. Then a few months later we went to Buckingham Palace where Prince Philip gave me an award."

Sully was also awarded the French Legion of Honour and ranked second in *Time* magazine's "Top 100 Most Influential Heroes and Icons of 2009." At the end of the year, he was named the 2010 Grand Marshal of the Tournament of Roses, and he and Lorrie led the parade in an open-roofed vintage car, waving to the crowds in Pasadena.

Throughout it all, Sully and Lorrie kept reminding themselves to keep their priorities straight and put the needs of their family first. At the time, their daughters, Kate and Kelly, were teenagers.

"With each new thing we would say, 'This is a once-in-a-lifetime opportunity,'" Lorrie explained. "Of course, being typical teenagers—wonderfully self-absorbed, as teenagers can be—they would say, 'We've heard that before.'"

Sully laughed. "Well, actually, at first we did think that these were once-in-a-lifetime opportunities, and some of them probably were," he said. "But with time, we got more selective and didn't just say yes to everything. That made things not quite so crazy. We realized it was going to be a marathon and not a sprint."

"These things take on a life of their own," Phil said. "Did you see any end in sight?"

"At first we had no idea how long it would last," Sully answered. "Would it be something that would last six months or a year and then we're done? Well, it turns out that we have been fortunate enough—or good enough at what we have done—to make it sustainable. Here we are ten-years-plus on, and I'm still staying busy."

"I know you're very modest, but a hero is a hero," Marlo pointed out, "and that can last a lifetime. Neil Armstrong landed on the moon fifty years ago, and nobody has forgotten that."

Sully had to agree. "We've had our colleagues tell us that if they had to choose someone to be on that flight that day—knowing what the challenges were going to be—I would be one of the ones that they would want to do it. But I also seem to be particularly suited—just by chance—to be in the public eye in the aftermath. So I think we've done a good job of doing the second part, as well. And that's what's made it last a while."

MARLO: It's interesting. People do have things happen to them that they don't expect. But how you cope with the aftermath makes all the difference. Some marriages shatter in the wake of something this enormous. I wonder how many of those astronauts' marriages survived.

LORRIE: John Glenn's, for sure.

MARLO: There must be enormous pressure living with a giant hero.

SULLY: Well, it was hard for Lorrie professionally.

MARLO: In what way?

SULLY: She was the one who was already on television before this all happened.

LORRIE: What bothered me in the beginning was how demeaning people would be. We would go to a big event, and Sully was determined, by gosh, he was going to introduce me to everyone. I can't tell you how many times he would say, "And this is my wife." For whatever reason, one sticks out in my head. It was an event we did for the Olympics in

Vancouver. Sully said, "This is my wife, Lorrie," and the guy he was talking to literally got this frown on his face, like, *I don't care about her.* Then I would tell Sully, "Don't introduce me at all." A few thousand times of that is kind of painful. And now, I guess, I've just kind of gotten over it, and I don't really care anymore.

SULLY: Oh, I think you do still care—and you're entitled to that. For a long time, people would approach you just to get to me, and that was also really offensive.

MARLO: My mother lived with that. She was Danny Thomas's wife. But for her, it was a gradual trajectory—from him being an unknown comedian doing small clubs to becoming a Las Vegas headliner and then a national television star. People would walk right over her to get to my father, and she felt bad about it. It hurt her confidence. But that took decades to play out. For you, it was so sudden.

LORRIE: These days if something like that happens, I try to think, *Well, this says far more about them than it does about me.*

PHIL: Give us an example.

LORRIE: We had gone to some event, and we were going to be seated at a table of ten. We were among the guests coming in, and so everyone else was already seated at the table, and there weren't place cards. When we got to the table, we saw our empty chairs, and the two people sitting on either side of us didn't know exactly where we were going to sit down. So when we finally sat, the man who was going to be on my side realized that he "got" me, not Sully, and the disappointment on his face was so powerful. It actually made me laugh out loud. I leaned down to him and said, "I know you don't know this yet, but really, I'm the fun one."

MARLO: Oh, that's fantastic.

LORRIE: It didn't seem to make him feel any better.

SULLY: But it's actually true—she *is* the fun one.

Since the first day they met in 1986, Sully has always found the blond and vivacious Lorrie (born Lorraine Mary Henry) interesting and fun to be with. At the time, they were both working for the now-defunct Pacific Southwest Airlines. She was in the marketing department and helping to promote the fiftieth anniversary of the air traffic control center in Fremont, California. The public was invited to watch the controllers on the radar scope and see how the system worked. Sully was the "token pilot" chosen to meet the crowds. The plans called for a management representative to stand alongside Sully for the event, and Lorrie happened to be on call that day.

"How fortuitous," Marlo said. "Was there an immediate attraction when you two first saw each other?"

"Actually, I thought he looked tired," Lorrie said.

"That's because I was," said Sully.

"Well, that's true—he had flown in on the redeye," Lorrie explained.

But there was something about his name that stuck for Lorrie. Sort of.

"It's funny," Lorrie remembered, "the guy told me there was a crew member who was going to speak and his name was Sully Sullenberger. I remember thinking, *I don't care, whatever. I'll never remember that name.* Meanwhile, Sully had gone off with another pilot friend to look at something, and I remember thinking, *I need to get that guy back here—but damn, what's his name? It has a lot of S's in it.* Anyway, I went over to Sully and said, 'Excuse me, could you please come back over here?'"

The event went off as planned, and afterwards, Sully suggested that they have a drink. The idea that Sully was asking her on an impromptu date didn't register with Lorrie. At first, she thought he was suggesting that they go to the commissary down the hall. There was a reason for the misunderstanding. By then, Lorrie was almost thirty years old and had basically had it with dating, after being so discouraged by the men she was meeting.

"My description of myself before I met Sully," Lorrie said, "was that you could put me in a room with three hundred nice guys and an asshole, and I'd find the asshole every time." All the same, Lorrie agreed to have a drink with Sully the following week.

Their relationship was a slow boil. They lived fifty miles apart in the Bay Area. Once a week, usually on a Monday, Lorrie would be near Sully's town for sales meetings. He was thirty-five then and didn't have seniority, so he worked weekends; Mondays were often their only mutually free day.

Yet even with such relatively limited face time with each other, Sully began to warm to the airline marketing suit. One of the things that most impressed him about Lorrie was her participation in the local Big Sisters organization and how she'd bonded with a four-year-old girl named Sara. Not long after they started dating, Lorrie introduced Sully to Sara at a taqueria. When Sully began asking her questions, she matter-of-factly told him that her father was in prison.

Sully was enormously moved by that. "I kept telling Lorrie, 'You're the only stable influence in Sara's entire life, and if she comes out of this okay, it will be because of you.' And she has. Sara is forty now, with a family of her own. So that, along with our daughters, I think, is one of the crowning achievements of Lorrie's life."

After two years of dating—sometimes with Sara in tow—Lorrie moved in with Sully. The following year, on June 17, 1989, they were married in Hillsborough, California.

The decision to marry took a bit of time, Lorrie told us, as she needed some persuading. After all, they came from such different backgrounds. Sully's parents were married for almost fifty years, and he was politically conservative, embodying military-like precision from his years flying fighter jets in the Air Force.

"When we first started dating," Lorrie began, "if I asked him what time it was, he'd say—"

"—it's 8:37 and a half," Sully finished. "Nowadays, I say, 'Oh, it's just past 8:30."

Lorrie had never been that precise. She was more of a "tornado," she confessed, a child of divorce with an alcoholic father. "A lot of children of alcoholics will sabotage a relationship," she explained, "even a good relationship. I watched other young women get swept away with lust that served no one. I didn't want to mess this up. I didn't want to repeat what

I had witnessed from my own parents. I just wanted to know that I could be a good partner, and I wanted to find a good partner."

Sully proved to be the man she was looking for.

PHIL: The media depiction of you is this almost perfect, all-American couple—a marriage that is totally in sync. What are some of the things we don't know about you two?

LORRIE: Well, since Sully landed in the river, he's become a fabulous public speaker—

SULLY: I had to learn how to be one.

LORRIE: But my joke before all this—and even now—is that Sully says about twenty-five words a day. At the end of that twenty-five, he's pretty much done.

SULLY: That's an exaggeration.

LORRIE: We would go to an event, and people would start talking to him, and I'd say, "No, no, no, you're using up his twenty-five words, and when we get back home there's going to be none left." His parents loved when I said that.

PHIL: Is he that way when you're talking about personal things, just the two of you?

LORRIE: Well, sometimes—and I don't do this much anymore—if I'm talking to him and he's being quiet, I'll say, "This is where you say, 'Uh-huh.'"

MARLO: Right. Like, "Just grunt and let me know that you're listening— or at least alive."

SULLY: Then there are other times when she's telling me something that she wants to share—something that I should actively listen to, but not feel like she's asking me to fix it for her. But my initial inclination for too many years would be to try to fix it for her.

LORRIE: Or offer me advice on how to fix it, when I knew all those options going in. I was just musing out loud.

MARLO: I have the same problem, but in reverse. I'm the fixer. Did you ask him to stop doing that?

LORRIE: I did.

SULLY: Yes, she did. So I've gotten better at listening.

LORRIE: I think this is kind of the old male-female joke, because when I think he's not listening I'll say, "You're not listening to me," and he can repeat back, verbatim, what I've just said, even though he's not looking at me and not really paying attention. But in his intellectual brain he can remember those words and spit them back out. And I would say, "I don't need you just to hear. I need you to *listen* to me."

SULLY: And have that emotional connection.

LORRIE: And that means you need to look at me, and you need to listen to what I'm saying.

MARLO: Not just hear it.

LORRIE: Not just hear it.

SULLY: And I get that now.

LORRIE: Obviously, everyone's marriage is different—we know that's the case—but I don't know if people have been so influenced by the commercialization of marriage that they expect it to be easy and simple all the time. I never thought that going in, so maybe that was a benefit for us.

One of the early challenges Lorrie and Sully faced in their marriage was that they couldn't have children naturally. They tried in vitro fertilization, but the attempt wasn't successful. Consistent with their dispositions—his exactitude, her energy—the couple did not permit that disappointment to interfere with their plans to start a family.

"At the end of the day," Lorrie said, "when the doctor told us we could do this again, but that it was really a crapshoot, we decided to move straight to adoption."

"And we actually verbalized that," Sully explained. "It's not about having a child, it's about having a family. And there are a lot of ways to do that. It always surprises me now when we talk to people who are going through some of these same challenges, and often they are so are locked onto having their own biological children, exclusively, that they don't really consider that other option as a good one for them, too. But we were able to go there right away."

Lorrie laughed. "We actually joked about it," she said. "We said that having a biological child would have been a bit of genetics roulette, anyway, what with my father's alcoholism—

"—and my father's temperament," Sully added. "We might have created a Frankenchild."

Their daughter Kate arrived in 1993, and her little sister Kelly joined the family in 1995. Lorrie stopped working in order to be with them full time.

With the doubling of their family's size, Sully worried about the financial changes in the airline industry—bankruptcies, mergers, pay cuts, pilots' pensions being gutted. The opportunities born from the Miracle on the Hudson spurred Sully to use his newfound celebrity to advocate for his fellow pilots.

"I felt an intense obligation not to walk away," he said. "To pass up this chance to have a greater voice about promoting the flying profession—or things I care about, like safety—would have been a dereliction of duty. I knew I had to use this bully pulpit for good."

Sully testified before Congress about airline safety and the state of the piloting profession.

"Your testimony was pretty rough," Phil noted.

"Yes," Sully confirmed. "I said that the airline industry was morally bankrupt as well as financially bankrupt. I said that they were using their employees as ATM machines instead of respecting us and paying us what we were worth; that they were enriching themselves at our expense; and that what we did and how we did it mattered, because we literally held our passengers' lives in our hands."

"Using your celebrity status like that didn't exactly endear you to airline management or the industry at large," Phil said.

"Correct," Sully said, "but I felt like I owed it to everybody else— all my colleagues still flying and facing all these challenges—to be their spokesperson and to try to advocate for better safety, and for better pay for all of us. We'd taken huge pay cuts to try to raise the status of our profession, which had been degraded over many years."

Sully returned to flying as soon as he could and said it felt comfortable, like putting on an old pair of jeans. After a year and a half, the National Transportation Safety Board fully exonerated him for the incident on the Hudson, deeming that landing the plane in the river was the correct, most expedient solution, rather than trying to reach a nearby airport.

Aviation had always been Sully's passion, but after a few months he decided to step away from the profession. Part of the reason is because, by his own account, he had become a distraction.

"I would make the announcement, 'This is Captain Sullenberger,' and then it was a big deal and so much of a distraction that it kind of disrupted the operation. Also, after my testimony before Congress, some people were happy to see me leave as soon as I wanted."

Sully's new life afforded him the freedom to pursue public speaking opportunities and to write books. His 2009 book *Highest Duty: My Search for What Really Matters* was a No. 1 New York Times Best Seller, and it was adapted into the Clint Eastwood–Tom Hanks film, in which Laura Linney played Lorrie.

The couple eventually accepted the idea that Sully's fame—for better and worse—was not going away. As always, Lorrie remains protective of her overtaxed husband. "As recently as a year ago," she told us, "whenever he gets asked to do too much, my constant refrain to him is, 'Landing in the river was enough.'"

Sully looked at his wife and back to us. "Even now, nobody else can understand," he said. "Some of our friends that we had for a long time, prior to this event, would behave in such a way as if they were thinking, *Oh, come on. That flight was how many years ago? And they're still talking about it? Get over it.* Well, we can't because everybody else is still telling us about it. They can't really see the people that we have grown to be because we *had* to. It's interesting to see how some friends could never quite make the same transition that we had to make."

"And the new friends you've made?" Marlo asked.

"They know us only as the people we are now. Not that we've changed. We haven't really changed who we are."

When we asked the couple what advice they might pass on to their daughters about marriage, Lorrie drew from her own experience of watching her and Sully's lives explode onto the world stage, and how they clung to each other for support. "We always say we're each other's best friend," she said, "but sometimes we revise that and say, 'No, we're our *only* friends.'"

We turned to Sully.

"Well, my advice is that not every problem is a ten," he said. "Most things are probably a two or three."

"Of course, this is a Sullenberger scale," Lorrie quipped.

Sully elaborated. "Don't fight about every little thing. Don't sweat every little thing. Don't be irresponsible. Plan ahead."

"Sully is a bit of a perfectionist," Lorrie noted.

"Oh, I wouldn't say just a bit," Sully said. "I'm very much a perfectionist, absolutely. I've learned to cope with it. I've learned to moderate it, but it's still my absolute focus."

"But isn't perfectionism what saved 155 lives on that day in 2009?" Phil asked.

"Well, those are wonderful traits for landing in the river," Lorrie said, "but that's not necessarily what you want on a date night."

Just before they got up to leave, Lorrie told us that they had gone to see Bruce Springsteen's movie *Western Stars* and how she was struck by how Springsteen characterized his twenty-nine-year marriage to Patti Scialfa as "broken pieces fitting broken pieces."

"I leaned over to Sully in the movie theater and said, 'Oh, my God, that's the perfect saying about how people stay married.'"

"Is that how you feel about your own marriage?" Marlo asked.

"I think our whole marriage—our whole relationship—has been one of meeting each other halfway or more than halfway," Sully said. "My way of describing it from the very outset was that I felt like we were complementary, that we filled in each other's little paint-by-numbers lives. She's good at things that I'm not good at, and vice versa."

"But I bet the thing you're best at," Marlo said, "is staying calm and centered when things get rough for you two. A lot of husbands don't have that cool."

"Yes, he is great at some things, but he's not great at everything," Lorrie said. "As I've often said: he landed on water, he doesn't walk on water."

Elton John and David Furnish

MARRIED IN 2014

"Going from Stonewall to being able to actually
get married to your partner—in the space
of fifty years, what an achievement."

T he last thing on my mind was looking for someone to love," Sir
Elton John recalled. "Absolutely, it was the last thing on my mind.
I just wanted to meet some new people."

It was October 1993, and Elton was "rattling around" his house in
Windsor, England, looking for company, not romance.

"I'd been sober for three years, and I hadn't really met anybody outside
of AA for a long time," he told us. "I phoned up a friend at two in the afternoon and said, 'Can you invite some people for dinner? I know it's late.
If you can't do it, that's fine.'"

The pal came through and rounded up a handful of guests for the impromptu Saturday night dinner party. Ad executive David Furnish was
among the invitees. Like Elton, he harbored no romantic fantasies about
how the night might turn out. Indeed, the last-minute invitation had come
through a friend of a friend.

And then they saw each other.

"He walked through the front door and was dressed impeccably in a beautiful Armani waistcoat," Elton remembered. "And he had a lovely smile."

For his part, David was similarly thrown by his first encounter with the living legend. "I was just part of a group," he explained. "I thought I would walk into this rock star's house and meet a big ego, someone who would sit on his sofa and regale us with stories of his great life and great accomplishments. He wasn't at all what I expected."

Part of that surprise, David noted, was Elton's kindness, and the genuine interest he took in his guests. "I was taken aback," he recalled. "He didn't want to talk about himself at all. He wanted to hear about our lives, our careers, our families, our interests, and our friends. I think that's the thing that really attracted me to Elton: he's very, very masculine and he's very strong, but he's also incredibly kind. I find that an unbeatable combination."

At one point in the evening, Elton took David on a tour of his house, where he keeps many of his famous collections—art deco posters, lamps, china, and a massive library of records and books. He learned that he and David shared a passion for film and photography, so they thumbed through a few photography books together. After dinner, the guests headed off to a Halloween party, but not before Elton got David's telephone number.

"The other guys teased him about that the rest of the night," Elton explained, "but all I was thinking was, *I must see him again*."

The next morning, Elton white-knuckled it until 11 a.m., when he finally buckled under and placed the call. The conversation was straight to the point: Elton invited David to dinner at his house in London. This time it would be just the two of them, he said. David accepted.

Aside from the Armani threads and the winning smile, David had other assets that attracted Elton: "He had a job. He had his own car. He owned

Civil ceremony: Windsor, Britain; December 21, 2005.
The couple was legally married at their home in Windsor on December 21, 2014.

his own apartment. He was so intelligent. It was like, 'Oh, my God, an independent person!'" Elton exulted. "I'd never been out with an independent person before—I mean, a couple of people, maybe, but that came as a real bonus. It was just *Wow, this is incredible!*"

At the time, Elton was forty-six years old and David had just turned thirty-one. A native Canadian, David had a business degree and a prestigious position at the advertising giant Ogilvy & Mather. A few years earlier, he had been transferred to London and been promoted to the firm's board of directors. Celebrities did not intimidate him.

Over Chinese takeout from Mr. Chow, Elton and David got to know each other. "We talked and talked and talked—we just hit it off straight away," Elton said. "And thus began the relationship that has now lasted for twenty-six years. It must have been kismet. What made me make that phone call to meet some new people? If I hadn't made it, he wouldn't be in my life. This is a very romantic story."

To get that story, we flew to Toronto and met up with the couple in their luxury suite at the St. Regis hotel. Elton was on the third leg of his worldwide Farewell Yellow Brick Road tour, so planning the get-together was like a game of Follow the Tour Bus—first it was supposed to be Vancouver, then Los Angeles, then Vancouver again, and finally we landed them in Toronto, David's hometown.

But then Elton's assistant told us the news: the tour was exhausting, so Elton and David could give us only thirty minutes.

On hearing that, we each went into our signature modes: Marlo began doing damage control, crunching her research notes into ten rapid-fire questions that would fill precisely thirty minutes of interview time, and not a second more.

Phil turned on the TV and propped up his feet.

"Why aren't you helping me with this?" Marlo asked Phil.

"Because they're not going to stop us at thirty minutes," he said in that unflappable way of his. "Trust me."

Phil was right: we arrived at their suite, said our hellos, and talked for ninety minutes.

And we can't lie: there's something about sitting across from a music legend that brings out the excited teen in all of us—his infectious songs dancing in our heads. But the couple instantly put us at ease with their warmth and authenticity. Elton wore a powder-blue suit with a rose appliqué on the front pocket (and rose-colored glasses to match), and David sported a navy turtleneck. Only moments into the talk, we'd forgotten that we were in the presence of rock royalty. We were just two couples talking about something dear to us.

David and Elton actually had two weddings. The first was a civil ceremony at Guildhall in Windsor, Britain, on December 21, 2005—the first day civil unions were legal in England.

"It was a great step forward," Elton said. "We wanted to make a statement as a gay couple, a famous gay couple. We wanted it to be on the first day."

David concurred. "Prior to that we'd always said, 'We don't need a piece of paper to validate who we are,' but I think we were a little naïve. If anything was to happen to Elton, I would have had no rights at all—so there was the financial security side of it. But we also felt that, symbolically, it was a very important message to send to the rest of the world."

Indeed, the international media turned up for the event outside Guildhall, and the couple posed for the crush of photographers and waved to the throngs that had gathered to celebrate them. Afterwards, David and Elton threw a party for six hundred of their friends and family.

But it was the days that followed that David remembered best. "About a week or two after all the hubbub died down," he recalled, "we were in Italy, and at one point we both looked at each other. I said to Elton, 'It feels different. It feels better.' There is something about having society validate your relationship. I know some people will think that's incredibly bourgeois, but it means something, particularly for a gay couple. In Italy, I was always known as the *ragazzo*—the boyfriend—or "Signore David." I felt like I was kind of an appendage or an accessory. But after the civil partnership I would go into a restaurant and they would say, 'Oh, how nice to have the husband of Elton John here.' It's society saying it supports and respects your union."

When same-sex marriage was legalized in Britain in 2014, the groom and groom had another ceremony, also on December 21, at the home in Windsor where they met. In addition to guests like David and Victoria Beckham, Hugh Grant, and Ed Sheeran were their two small sons: Zachary, who was about to turn four years old, and Elijah, almost two. The boys acted as ring-bearers.

DAVID: We gave them little stuffed bunnies, and we took our relationship rings—which we'd had since six weeks after meeting—and put them on ribbons around the rabbits' necks, and each little boy held a rabbit. When it was time to exchange rings, they handed us the bunnies and we pulled on the ribbons and the rings came off. We wanted the boys to be a part of this.

MARLO: That's adorable. Did the actual marriage mean more to you than the civil ceremony?

ELTON: It meant more to me. The civil partnership was moving, but the marriage was even more moving. I think it's because we had the children there. And going from Stonewall to being able to actually get married to your partner—that's incredible. I mean, in the space of fifty years, what an achievement. It didn't happen all over the world, but it certainly happened in our country, in England, and we both thought it was a real opportunity to show our commitment and to demonstrate that we love each other.

PHIL: Most people mark the Stonewall riots in New York as the turning point for gay rights. It has been an incredible journey.

MARLO: And that's why your marriage is so important to young people everywhere. Kids look up to you, and it's meaningful that you recognized that trajectory from Stonewall to the legalization of same-sex marriage.

ELTON: Yes, as a gay couple of fame, it's necessary to say, "This is incredible legislation." We must do this to make sure people feel comfortable doing it.

DAVID: We are more protected societally. We are protected more financially.

Our children are more protected financially. Society supports marriage, and everybody going through life needs support.

PHIL: David, you're fifteen years younger than Elton, but surely you still felt discrimination growing up, yes?

DAVID: I tried to come out to my mother when I was twenty-one, and she sat at the kitchen table for a week and cried—but not because she rejected me. She said, "I'm frightened for you. My greatest joy in life is being married to your father and having children, and none of these things will be available to you. You'll never have a lasting relationship. You'll be discriminated against in your job and never have a career. You could catch this thing, this gay plague, called AIDS." And there were no role models. There was no Tim Cook. There was no David Geffen. The only person my mother had heard of who was gay was Boy George. And so to find myself all these years later at my wedding, marrying the man I'd been with for more than twenty years—and with our two sons by our side—was like a dream. [David's dear mother died just three days after this interview.]

Although both ceremonies took place on the same day of the year, David and Elton do not wait until December 21 to commemorate their anniversaries. Instead, they honor their bond every Saturday, paying tribute to that fateful dinner party many years ago. No matter where they are in the world, they send each other handwritten cards.

"And so we have twenty-six years' worth of cards," Elton said, smiling.

"Twenty-six times fifty-two," David chimed in. "Do the math." (We did—that's 1,352 love notes.) And though Elton's punishing tour schedule often forces the couple to rely on FaceTime in order to see each other, when it comes to their Saturday ritual, they have never once resorted to digital communication.

"There's something very spiritual and real about handwriting," David said, "and the cards are a chance to reflect on the week that's passed and talk about the week that's coming—to celebrate the victories, mourn the defeats, acknowledge what's important to you. We talk on the phone probably five to ten times a day—what I call sound bite conversations, because Elton doesn't like the phone very much—but with that card and that handwriting, you feel the soul of the other person."

When Elton and David are together, the cards go on the table next to the bed. When they're not, they send them by courier.

"It's part of the success, I think, of a lasting relationship," Elton reflected. "Communication is the most important thing. Talking the issues over. David has a very rational way of dealing with things. I go from naught to one hundred in a second. I have an atomic temper, which I inherited from my dad."

It was not surprising to hear Elton refer to his parents during our conversation. Indeed, his painful childhood made up a significant portion of his poignant, brutally honest, and often hilarious memoir, *Me*, which was released just days before we met with the couple. He was born Reginald Dwight to "parents who never should have got married in the first place," he wrote. His upbringing in suburban London included constant criticism and sometimes physical abuse from his mother. His unaffectionate father, a flight lieutenant in the Royal Air Force, disciplined Elton for trifles like crunching his celery too loudly or taking off his school blazer incorrectly. When his parents fought, Elton would run to his bedroom and lock the door, escaping the confrontations he hated. As an only child, he had no sibling to share his anxiety with; so he found serenity in the things that calmed him—primarily playing the piano and listening to his collection of records.

"Thank God there was music ever since I grew up," he said. "I found solace in my music and my objects, my books, my records, my toys. And that's why I've always loved things—because things could never answer back or tell me off."

But even as he discovered that material objects made him content, a much more personal possession—his sexuality—remained a mystery to him until he was in his twenties.

"I didn't know anybody in our family who was gay," he told us. "I didn't even know about gay people. And at the time it was illegal to be gay in England anyway."

"It was illegal here, too," Marlo noted, "but where I grew up—Beverly Hills, which was an artistic community—I knew a lot of gay people, though many were closeted.

"Tell them what they used to say back then," Phil prodded.

"In Hollywood there was a saying that just because a man is married and has three children doesn't necessarily mean he's gay."

"A lavender marriage," David said.

"It was a terrible way to live," Marlo noted.

Elton was engaged to a woman, a secretary, when he was in his twenties and then wed a different woman when he was thirty-six. This took place during the sixteen years he was addicted to drugs and alcohol, he revealed, and the marriage ended after just four years, though they remain friends.

David, on the other hand, grew up in a largely stable and loving—though conservative—Canadian household. Although he ultimately disproved his mother's dire predictions about his future, he eventually clammed up about his sexual orientation, hiding it even from his colleagues in London. Consequently, when he and Elton began seeing each other, he worried about being outed by the paparazzi, so the couple kept a low profile at first. They officially became boyfriends after just six weeks of dating, but they took things nice and slow before moving in together.

DAVID: We've never lived in each other's pockets. As close as we were before we had the kids, I was always respectful of Elton's career, what drove him, and what he was passionate about. I didn't want to go on the road and follow him around the world. It was very important for me to pursue projects and do things in my own right. He was like, "Listen, you have your work to do. You go and do it. Come and see me on the road as much as you can, whenever you can."

ELTON: Which was new for me because, in all of my other relationships— apart from my first one—I took hostages.

PHIL: What do you mean by that?

ELTON: Well, when I met someone, I gave them a Versace shirt, a Cartier watch, I sort of—

DAVID: —took their identity. Took their life. Took everything.

ELTON: I used to like younger people, so I would father them. With David I had an equal. Although he's younger than me, I don't *feel* like he's that much younger because, mentally, we're the same age. I've never had to fuss over him.

MARLO: Did you eventually tire of your hostages?

ELTON: Oh, they tired of me. They resented me in the end. They had no life of their own. When you take away someone's personality and their original identity, they always become resentful. And why not? The thing is, David had an independence before me and that independence was fantastic. It was always 50/50—always—which I'd never had before.

PHIL: So in such a new kind of relationship, how did you handle conflict?

ELTON: Usually with me, it's the little things that set off the big issue. My habit was to run away and lock the door so no one could get near me. Childhood stuff again. With David, I learned not to do that. Communication is everything. Getting your feelings out. Getting rid of your resentments. He's great with me.

MARLO: Give us an example.

ELTON: When we first got together, I did that same behavior a couple of times, and then I thought, *This is ridiculous. This is the same thing I've been through.* When I got sober, it gave me the tools to communicate. David knows how to deal with me because artists, you know, can be a nightmare. We all have this diva-ish thing, and we can go to the dark side pretty quickly. I honestly think that our relationship—and we've been through a lot of backstabbing, people betraying us, having children, the career—is stronger than it's ever been, without question. And now he's my manager as well as my husband.

PHIL: David, when Elton goes from zero to one hundred, what do you do?

DAVID: Well, the worst thing I can do is go from zero to one hundred, too, because that feeds into his fury. He goes prefrontal cortex, and you just have to give him his moment to wind it back in. Before I pass judgment on a difficult situation, I always try to think about what else he's dealing with at that moment. Has he just done seven shows and is exhausted? Has he just traveled through the night? Maybe a record hasn't charted the way he wants it to chart.

MARLO: Oh, David, that is so smart and sensitive. Elton, when you're in this place, do you come back and say you're sorry?

ELTON: Oh, yes.

PHIL: How long does that take?

ELTON: Not very long. I will always own up to my behavior.

DAVID: He's a perfectionist-artist, and success is very important to him, so he keeps a pretty high bar. Nothing makes an excuse, though, for insensitive or inappropriate behavior. So what I do is store something away temporarily—take it off the table, if he's just having a bad day. I always try to choose my moments, and wait until he's out of whatever other storm he was dealing with.

MARLO: How did you learn to do this?

DAVID: I kind of learned it on the job, more by instinct than anything. I mean, after we had the kids, we needed some couples therapy. We needed support. I went into treatment and got sober. I've been sober coming up on six years.

For all the positive ways David and Elton are alike, they also share a history of substance abuse, though Elton's was a decidedly more public battle. Even as he soared to superstardom in the 1970s and 1980s, he was chronically dogged by a variety of dependencies—alcohol, weed, cocaine, you name it—and it wasn't until 1990 that he actively sought help.

He chronicled this struggle in his memoir and has been equally forthcoming about his sobriety. "Twenty-nine years ago today, I was a broken man," Elton announced on social media on July 19, 2019. "I finally summoned up the courage to say three words that would change my life: 'I need help.'"

For David, the demons were more private.

"He was away so much, and I was on my own a lot," David said, "so I think I turned to the bottle for solace, to comfort me—even though we stayed connected with the anniversary cards and phone calls. I'm fortunate that my drinking was very much sitting at home alone at night with a bottle of red wine at the kitchen table or in front of the computer."

Phil turned to Elton. "It must have been painful witnessing David go through the same hell you'd endured. Was there ever a point that you said to yourself, *Okay, that's it, I've got to bail on this*?"

"No," Elton said emphatically.

"That's a big deal," Marlo said.

"Well, when you love somebody that much, you can't do that," Elton replied. "I knew that sooner or later he would get it. But I hated watching him. I would go down to the kitchen and find him asleep at the table, and I'd think, *Oh, God*. And then I would say, 'You're drunk,' and he'd go, 'No, I'm not.' And that really annoyed me."

David ultimately recognized his dangerous descent and decided to do something about it. "I just felt I wanted the clarity, particularly with the children," he noted. "I thought, *I'm not the person I used to be*, and I wanted to hit the reset button. So I picked up the phone and called my doctor and asked for help. Once I got sober—and because of the kids—I felt that we needed help. Everybody needs help. We each had a counselor who worked with us."

Elton jumped in. "At first, I resisted that because I didn't want a bloody therapist. And then we had them come over to the house in England—one for him and one for me. We did them separately, we did them together. It was great. But I was afraid. The fear of rejection. The fear of being criticized."

MARLO: David, by the time you were going through this, Elton had already been through rehab, right?

DAVID: Yes. He'd been sober twenty-three years. Talk about making concessions. You know, he was never, *ever*, like, "You can't drink around me, you can't drink in the house." Instead, he told me, "As long as you enjoy it responsibly, I'm happy for you to have wine."

ELTON: But I was worried about him because I knew from my own addiction and alcoholism, you cannot tell someone to do something. When he did it on his own, I was there for him. It was extremely raw. I was in Brazil when he was in treatment. It was hard on both of us, probably the hardest point of our relationship. He was coming out of a fog. He had lots of resentments. He had lots of anger.

MARLO: He reminded you of yourself, right?

ELTON: Yes.

MARLO: Were you worried when he was drinking that you might drink again?

ELTON: Never—but I was worried stiff about him, and I couldn't do anything.

PHIL: David, Elton said you were resentful. At what?

DAVID: Well, before I took the business over, everybody used to come to me when Elton was extended beyond the boundaries of wise fiscal responsibility. They'd say, "You have to talk to Elton about the spending. It's really getting out of control." I wasn't controlling the business at the time. I wasn't doing the spending. So, it was a horrible position to put me in. He resented it and I resented it.

ELTON: I said, "You know, I've never worried about business things before. I promise that I will now look at finances with you." I'd never wanted to learn that before. So, I had to bring myself to the party as far as business matters were concerned, because I just left everything to him. And in a relationship, you just can't do that.

PHIL: And you went to AA, David.

DAVID: Yes. We're both in AA now—we go to meetings together, which is really nice. I'd never really understood Elton's program of recovery before that. It's very personal. In fact, you're supposed to keep it all confidential. So when I went into treatment, a lot of things about Elton's behavior became abundantly clear to me. Clean house, trust God, help others. Those are the three principles of AA.

Helping others is something Elton knows a lot about. The Elton John AIDS Foundation has raised nearly half a billion dollars to help prevent the spread of HIV and provide treatment and services to people around the world impacted by the epidemic. He founded the U.S.-based organization in 1992 and the United Kingdom base in 1993, motivating governments around the world to beat AIDS. David is the charity's chairman.

"That's something we've always done together," David noted, "and I think those things helped stop my addiction from becoming dysfunctionally desperate. My bottom was relatively high compared to other people's, and I believe that's because I'd done a lot of work with the charity. I think if people put those three principles—clean house, trust God, help others—into their everyday lives, it takes you out of yourself."

This notion of giving back—especially for this couple—resonates deeply when it comes to gay and questioning youth.

"As two very public, happily married gay men," Marlo said, "what would you want to say to gay or questioning kids who see the example you've set as a couple and wonder whether they could ever find someone to love and marry as you've done?"

David glanced at his husband and rested a hand on his arm. "The first thing I'd say is learn about yourself before you give yourself," he said. "Your own identity and your own self-worth are the greatest things you can bring to a relationship. If you don't learn to love yourself, you can end up in a relationship with the wrong person, being whipped about or taken for granted or pulled down paths that aren't the real you."

"That's something that didn't happen when you met Elton," Marlo said. "Why?"

"I met Elton when I was thirty-one," David answered, "and I'd achieved a lot in my own right, you know? I had a strong sense of myself and my abilities, my strengths and weaknesses. A lot of people tried to bring me down. A lot of people thought I would be with him only for a year or two—that I'd get my watch or my car or my whatever, and then I'd move along and the next one would come down the conveyor belt. But because I came from a long, loving relationship with my parents, I believed in the sanctity of marriage, and I saw the strength and the support you get from building a life with the right person. I always fundamentally believed in that as something to achieve."

We turned to Elton. "My advice would be: do not get into a relationship too soon," he said. "Travel. See for yourself what the world is like. Don't just stay in America. The greatest things I've learned in my life came from seeing other cultures and seeing how lovely people are all over the world. You have plenty of time for relationships."

"You waited forty-six years before settling down with David," Phil said.

"But I wanted a relationship as soon as I could have one," Elton responded, "because I didn't have one as a child, really. Not a tactile one. That's why the first person I slept with was the person I wanted to be with, because there was tactile love there. So I say, find out who you are. Be comfortable with that person. And if you're not sure who you are, then take the time to find out."

MARLO: How are you both with third-party admirers? Are either of you the jealous type?

ELTON: I've been a little jealous sometimes when people show him attention.

MARLO: Do you say it?

ELTON: Yes. I just say, "I'm uncomfortable." I think in a gay relationship you have to have freedom sometimes. Men are very flirty. I think it's different with men than with a woman and a guy.

MARLO: I don't think so. The feeling is the same. It's territorial.

DAVID: Sometimes it's important in a relationship to acknowledge that someone else finding your partner attractive isn't a bad thing. If someone finds me attractive it's good for my self-esteem. It doesn't mean I'm going to suddenly run out the door. Just because you're on a diet doesn't mean you can't look at the menu.

MARLO: That's funny.

ELTON: There are other people I find incredibly attractive, and I'll tell him. He'll do the same thing. We don't like the same kind of people. But we just saw someone—

DAVID: —in the elevator. A professional hockey player.

ELTON: He's a Toronto Maple Leaf, and we both went, "God, almighty!"

MARLO: Did having the first child disrupt your relationship?

ELTON: Oh, not at all.

DAVID: It brought us closer together. We'd been independent adults for such a long time that the responsibility of raising a child meant we both hit the same learning curve at the same time. And because we were able to take the boys with us, we did it together.

PHIL: What things did you learn on this learning curve?

DAVID: When Elton was doing his residency in Vegas, we had a very wise, experienced nanny who said, "You both have pretty bonkers lives with lots of things going on, so if you can do one thing together as parents, consistently, do bath time and story time. Those are really important moments in a child's day."

MARLO: Did the advice work?

DAVID: Oh, the boys got great solace from it. There we were at Caesar's Palace in Vegas, and Elton goes onstage at 7:30. Bath time is 6:30. So the boys come over and we blow up an inflatable duck-tub right there in his Caesar's Palace dressing room. We fill it with water and, between 6:30 and 7:00, do story time and bath time with the boys right there.

MARLO: That's so sweet!

DAVID: We kiss the boys goodnight, they get in their pajamas, go back to the hotel, go to bed, Elton goes onstage and does his show.

ELTON: We still do that.

Elton and David were in the delivery room when Zachary was born in 2010 and then Elijah, in 2013, both children to the same surrogate. Lady

Gaga is godmother to both of them. After a few years, the couple realized the boys weren't always going to be portable enough to go on worldwide tours.

Then came the big change. "I always thought I was going to die on the road," Elton explained. "We were two gay people going around the world, living a lovely life, and then the children came into our lives and David sat me down in the house in France, on the terrace, and said, 'What do you want to do now?' I said, 'What do you mean?' He said, 'Do you still want to die on the road?' I said, 'No, I don't. I want to spend time with my children.'"

So David placed the boys' school schedule in front of Elton. He explained that because they needed to be in school full time—to forge identities of their own and develop their own communities—that either David or Elton had to be home with them at all times.

So the two dads spit-balled the options. "Elton said, 'Well, I don't want to miss out. I want to be there to watch my sons grow up,'" David recalled. "So I said, 'That's great'—but we had a life that was financially structured on him doing a hundred shows a year, and that meant him touring around the world all the time. That's when I decided to take control of the business."

Removing his Daddy cap and putting on his accountant's visor, David hammered a five-year business plan to put money in the bank while putting Elton on the stage—one last time.

"Elton had never had a business plan in the history of his career," David said, "so I told him, 'We need to get you off the road. We need to do a farewell tour. We can do a series of activities to celebrate your legacy and get the record sales out. We have to grow our passive income streams, because records don't do as well as they used to, and the touring income will disappear.'"

"And you signed on to that?" Phil asked Elton.

"I told him, 'Let's do it,'" Elton said.

On September 8, 2018, Elton launched his final Farewell Yellow Brick Road tour, a three-year, three-hundred-concert blitz across five continents.

At the time of our meeting, the tour had already grossed more than $200 million.

PHIL: How on earth were you able to grab the reins like this, David?

DAVID: When I first started seeing Elton, he wasn't that interested in the running of his business, and I, a conservative Canadian boy who'd worked for a global advertising firm, was very well-schooled in all of that stuff. A lot of people took advantage of Elton's trust and good nature and kindness. So I bided my time. You don't get into a relationship with someone who is essentially a corporation in their own right and say, "Well, I think your manager is not doing this right," or "This seems off to me." I've always found with Elton that the best thing to do is drop seeds, make observations, say things like, "I think it's very strange that this person seems to have a lifestyle that's very close to yours, yet they're only making a small percentage of what you earn.'"

MARLO: So, you try not to scare him.

DAVID: I try not to make it a confrontation because he's been so badly programmed by his mom in particular. His response to confrontation is always to run away and shout at you or leave the room.

ELTON: It's fear.

DAVID: Yes, and the feeling that you've done something wrong. So I just have to be patient. And then the moment arrives. He is a good listener.

ELTON: David is very annoyingly wise and it's like having a great record producer. You write a song, you record it, they criticize it, you go nuts because it's your little baby, but they're usually right.

DAVID: A good friend of mine gave me some fantastic advice very early in my relationship with Elton, and it always flies into my head. He said, "You're going to be living in the public eye now, and the people who know you the least will judge you the most."

MARLO: Yes, that is so true.

DAVID: So, when I got sober and decided to take the reins of the business, I said to Elton, "Look, you make the majority of the money and you spend the majority of the money. If you and I sit down at least once a month and we look at a spreadsheet of what's come in, what's gone out, and how we're doing, that will give me all the information I need to give you the accountability you don't have." People in the past who were rewarded by commission were able to culture him in a way that the more they kept him working, the more money they made. Of course, they all talked a good game and said, "Oh, we're worried about Elton's spending." But the reality was, they loved his spending because the more he had to make to pay his bills, the more they made. I had to break that cycle.

ELTON: I never had any doubt that this was an honest, lovely, kind, beautiful man. And I've never had anybody in my life like that before. Even when he was drinking, we still had an open, honest relationship, and he came through on everything he said.

DAVID: Life isn't about pleasing everybody. I mean, the most important thing is: you pull together.

MARLO: And how do you do that?

DAVID: In a crisis or in a non-crisis, as long as you're looking at each other in the eye and you're all right with each other, that is all you need. You have to treat each other and the relationship with respect. We don't always get it right, but we do try our best. We never say we are the perfect couple, nor do we see ourselves as role models. There are a lot of things in our relationship that are extremely personal, and we insist on keeping those things private from the outside world.

They've weathered so much together—addiction, separations, anger issues, money worries, tabloid snooping, judgmental friends, and, yes, a portion of the world that still seems hell-bent on telling people of the same gender that they are not allowed to love each other, wed each other, spend the rest of their lives together.

To that end, we can only imagine the blissful harmony they'll experience when Elton is off the road and the world spins a little slower on its axis for them. Perhaps then they'll have the time and space to celebrate once again the instant connection they felt at that dinner party so long ago. Only now, they won't have to wait for Saturday to do it.

And you can tell everybody this is your song
It may be quite simple but now that it's done
I hope you don't mind, I hope you don't mind
That I put down in words
How wonderful life is while you're in the world

—"Your Song," words by Bernie Taupin, music by Elton John

James Carville and Mary Matalin

MARRIED IN 1993

"I'm a big believer in kicking the can down the road.
Behind every successful marriage there's a collection of cans."

It would be easy to call James Carville and Mary Matalin an "unlikely couple," and why not? Everyone else does. But frankly, that would be a little lazy. Because after spending some time with this colorful, engaged, weird, unique, and staggeringly smart twosome, we think a better term might be "a match made in heaven."

They burst onto the national scene in 1992 as the respective brains behind the rival presidential campaigns of that year. In this corner was James Carville, the bald-headed, twang-talking Louisianan who'd burnished his creds as a statewide campaign consultant before cementing his rep as the "Ragin' Cajun"—Bill Clinton's field marshal who famously distilled the White House cage match that year to four simple words: "It's the economy, stupid." Staring him down from the opposing corner was the Chicago-born politico Mary Matalin, who, like her future husband, had worked her way up from local ballot boxes to riding shotgun on national campaigns, this time with President George H. W. Bush, who was seeking a second term.

Clinton ultimately slam-dunked Bush in that election, but to the dropped jaws of the world, Mary and James wed one year later. Diehard liberals wondered aloud, "How could he marry *her*?" Rabid conservatives mumbled, "What the hell does she see in *him*?" But Mary and James got the last laugh, parlaying their odd-couple profile into a lucrative brand that landed them on talk shows, magazine covers, and bookshelves (their 2014 book *Love & War: Twenty Years, Three Presidents, Two Daughters and One Louisiana Home* is a must-read for anyone interested in the definitive he said/she said narrative)—and, best of all, a robust marriage of twenty-seven years.

That they were perfect for this book was a given.

Catching up with this couple was as complicated and surprising as they are. We set a date for four o'clock on a late summer afternoon. James showed up at our New York apartment—at 4 p.m., on the dot—wearing a matching sweatshirt and baseball cap, both bearing the logo of LSU, where he teaches political communication. Mary—who had agreed to meet us there as well—sent a message a few hours earlier, telling us that she was stuck in D.C. but would join us by phone at the appointed time. As instructed, we called her on her cell after James's arrival—and got her voicemail. We tried a few more times, and still no answer.

Marlo was unraveled; Phil was unrattled; James was laughing. Apparently, he'd seen this dilemma play out many times before.

So we decided to conduct the interview with James alone. The next day, we finally tracked down Mary, and, at her request, supplied her with our questions (via email), securing her promise to return her rebuttals in writing.

She did promptly—and, as it turns out, this is the way Mary and James prefer to be interviewed. "We don't like to be pitted against each other in an interview setting," one of them told us (we'll never reveal which one). "We need our own space to answer the questions honestly."

So, what you read below is a joint interview conducted separately—the only one of this type in the book. We began our conversation by addressing

New Orleans, Louisiana; November 26, 1993

the odd situation we'd found ourselves in: talking to a famous couple one spouse at a time.

Okay, so here we are. Mary, you've gone AWOL, James is laughing, and we're getting the distinct impression that the two of you have totally different concepts of time. Are we right?

JAMES: I am, by nature, very punctual—and Mary, well, that's just not one of her values. You either get used to things and accept them or you're going to be chronically irritated. Sometimes I get a separate car to go to the airport because I'm not going to wait until the last minute. She'll say, "What time are we going to the airport? What time do we have to walk out the door?" Well it's the same thing as we always do—an hour and a half before it leaves. Give ourselves time to get there, get through security, get a bottle of designer water and a couple of newspapers and whatever the hell else. Then board the airplane. But she'll keep asking me the same thing. I've learned not to snap.

For social events, I tend to show up relatively early and leave relatively early. She likes to show up late and leave late. I'll say, "Okay, fine. I'll use Uber or Lyft." I think Uber and Lyft are great instruments of domestic tranquility, because you can go when you want to go. Some people look at a clock and see one thing, and other people look at a clock and see another.

MARY: Hmm. I wouldn't put it exactly that way, although we do experience time differently. James was likely laughing because I rarely answer my phone—for the following legit reasons:

1. I don't like talking on the phone.

2. I have trouble tethering to inanimate objects, such as devices, batteries, chargers, outlets, etc.

3. At any given time, my phones are either dead, broken, or lost.

4. Anyone who needs or wants to get ahold of me can track me down.

5. I am plagued with a monkey mind and prefer communiqués in writing. Perhaps forty years in politics has rewired my synaptic connections, because I surely loved talking on the phone as a teenager.

So, to the heart of your question, yes, we march to the beat of different drummers. He is relentlessly peripatetic—like a shark, he would drown if he slowed down to take a breath. I accept his need to *move, move, move, soldier*; and I respect how well it works for him. When I am in a *move, move, move, soldier* state of mind, it works for me, too. But only if it's regularly interspersed with episodes of solemn, off-the-clock space-cadeting. Which James also excels at, by the way, only he doesn't indulge as often as I do. He works too hard. But it works for him. And me. If he couldn't get his pantyhose all up in a knot over my untimeliness, we'd probably have to talk about politics.

By the way, we've never missed a plane. But two cars is fine with me.

Obviously, you don't agree on a lot of things, yet you made clear in your book and in interviews that you're not going to stop loving each other or get a divorce. What is it about your bond that makes you so confident, given your political differences?

JAMES: I tell people I'm not changing political parties or my sexual orientation. I'm pretty much the way I am. If I had to say one thing—and I think you and Phil know this—when you become famous for something, people think that's all you are. Everybody looks at athletes and sees them as just athletes, because they can hit a ball or throw it. But in reality, they're complex people. People look at me and Mary, and they say, "We saw you on *Meet the Press*." They think those two people on TV are all about politics and politics only. But there's so much more about our life than that. We have feelings and relationships and family and kids and friends. We have things we're interested in and places we want to go. Politics are what we do for a living.

Everyone is defined by many things. Look at the troubles that marriages can have. You can have financial issues. You can have health issues. You can have in-law issues. You can have religious differences. We've never had to deal with those. Political differences are just one thing. If you look at my cell phone today, you'll see that I've had probably twenty political conversations—but when I see Mary tomorrow in Virginia, I won't be that excited to talk about politics. I'll sit in my chair and we'll talk about what the kids are up to. Our life is a lot more complicated than the politics part of it. It's the other stuff that binds us.

MARY: What is it about our bond? Stubbornness? Weirdness? Faith? Love? He makes me laugh? He's good in bed? He makes a mean cheese omelet? I love his family? He's an incredible dad? If you can find someone who has the definitive answer to what makes a marriage work, let me know. All I know is that he's my total package.

Every couple we talk to has their own way of dealing with disagreements. But very few of the couples have been as deliciously different as you two. When there's a problem, how do you cope?

JAMES: I'm a big believer in kicking the can down the road. Of avoiding the thing. I think behind every successful marriage there's a collection of cans—of unresolved issues—a long way down the road somewhere. In most marriages there's too much need to have a discussion. It's counterintuitive, but some things you've just got to let go of. Because if you bring them up, you're not going to end in a good place. People like to say, "We need to get this on the table! We need to land this ball!" No we don't—*just leave the ball where it is.* Give it enough time and it'll go away.

I think in every marriage, you have to let some things fester. It's not that easy, and obviously there are some things you can't do that with. But many others will just get better with time. So if I was to give advice to a young couple about this, I'd said, "Get yourself a foot, get yourself a can, and give that can a kick." It doesn't work for everything, but that is the preferred solution.

MARY: "Kick the can" is James's latest iteration of "it takes two to fight," a marital tool he's deployed since the Iraq War. I understand the theory, and I agree with it when an immediate solution is unavailable.

However, I firmly oppose a "kick-the-can" strategy when it's meant to cover for denial, or even simple nondiligence. In life, as in policy, I lean toward "a stitch in time saves nine." Patience is not my strong suit. If a ready solution is obvious, experience suggests taking it, moving on, and not permitting perfection to be the enemy of good.

We are both horrible fighters. The only way to make peace is to agree to an avoidance strategy for areas of irreconcilable incompatibility. I am moody and emotional but hate drama. He is a drama queen but never moody, except when he's hungry or in any physical need—then he is focused and relentless until he gets what he wants. Which is always amusing and frequently amazing to witness.

As James says—with which I heartily agree—the trick is to get the big things right and the little ones will take care of themselves. He's a good life coach.

The story in your book about September 11 was very touching. Although both of you spent that day apart, you were very much in each other's heads. As a couple, how did you two find that kind of instinctive trust in each other?

JAMES: I remember it was a beautiful day. I was having breakfast with Bob Shrum at the Sheraton Hotel in Washington. Bob looked at his cell phone and got a message that said a plane had just crashed into the World Trade Center in New York. And I just looked at the sky and said, "Airplanes don't crash into buildings anymore." Within minutes, we knew it was more than that.

I had to figure out where my kids were. I had one child in the first grade—maybe it was kindergarten—and another who was in a Montessori school. I knew that this guy who was working there would get my youngest out. I got my oldest. But Mary was with Vice President Cheney. There was no way I was going to find her. I mean, I had enough sense to know that.

Then forty-eight hours later, by God, I got a phone call and a voice said, "Mr. Carville, this is Commander So-and-So, United States naval attaché to the vice president, and I'm authorized to tell you that your wife is safe and okay, and I can't tell you anymore." I said, "Well, thank you very much. I appreciate that." I told the kids, "I don't know where your mother is, but I know she's safe."

MARY: I think about that a lot, because it was, as you say, instinctive. We may have myriad blind spots, but the well-being of our daughters always takes primacy. Also, he is a man's man and knows how to bend the world to his needs one way or the other. Finally, he is a Marine—true, brave, strong, and loyal. And clever.

We also have an inexplicably intertwined mind-meld when either is in a precarious position. When we first moved to New Orleans, the girls and I got caught under the live oaks in a tsunami storm with ferocious lightning. Naturally, I didn't have my phone, but I knew he would find us. And he did, even though he had no idea where we had set out. He's like a homing pigeon for his family.

Finally, I figured he would figure out I was alive, would anticipate I was a tad busy, and would pick up the slack. And if anything had happened to me, he would feel it. Either way, I knew he would know my only wish would be for him to secure himself and the girls.

What changes have you made to accommodate each other? Mary's move to New Orleans—which is a whole different culture—is a perfect example of accommodation. You're both such strong individuals. What others can you cite?

JAMES: Well, I think what I've sort of learned—and it took me a long time to do this—is that, with my wife, it is less important that you agree with her and more important that you understand her. I think that's true of a lot of people. It's probably sexist to say this, but I think it's maybe truer of females that they really want to be understood.

I also understand that, instinctively, she's a person who likes to slide into the flow of life. I'm more abrupt. I'm a person who jumps in—*Let's go! Boom! Get going!*—so I had to learn the difference between jumping and sliding.

I also try not to sound impatient about things. She likes a well-done steak. The wrong thing to say is, "How do you eat that? You're ruining a good piece of meat!" I've tried that. It does not work. If she wants a well-done steak, then that's it. I accept the sliding in, and I accept the well-done steak.

MARY: I think we've been quite accommodating to each other. He has his own bathroom, closet, man cave. He has no travel restrictions. I very, very, very rarely require a command appearance from him and no domestic chores to speak of. He goes to bed at 9:30 p.m. and is up with the sunrise; I stay up all night and head to bed when the sun comes up.

I think our best accommodation to marriage is requiring so few accommodations from each other. We just fit. We probably make way more accommodations for the girls.

But, if I had to name a difficult accommodation—and I am not kidding when I say this has been the most difficult for me—we really have different relationships with animals and plants. Also, he talks out loud to no one when he's driving, which is fine. We love to just float off to our own wavelengths. Together. Sometimes we are simply parallel riders, and that's a good feeling.

By the way, I loved New Orleans before I even knew James Carville existed. It was I who wanted to marry there, and I who wanted to move there. He actually accommodated me in that instance by agreeing to the house I wanted. We call that move a "win-win" in our "Good Decision/Bad Decision" game.

What have you learned from each other, and what do you feel the other has learned from you?

JAMES: I've learned to appreciate beauty more. I've never seen a person like fabric more than Mary does. You should see her in a fabric store. She found a fabric store in a little town we went to that was just a few blocks away, and she couldn't have been happier. I've learned a lot about beauty and space. I never paid attention to colors before, and she's very much of a mix-and-match person.

She also has a very good spatial sense—kind of an instinct for interior design and arranging things and deciding where stuff goes. Our youngest daughter has inherited that from her. If there is such a thing as heaven, I can tell you exactly what's going to happen: She's going to get there and St. Peter will say, "The Man wants you to rearrange the furniture in the hereafter," and she will be there in heaven doing nothing but rearranging furniture. She'll make it perfect.

MARY: Let me give you a list:

- He suffers fools gladly.

- He is kind to a fault.

- He finds humor in almost all circumstances.

- There is much value to his relentless need for structure.

- He tends to run to the sound of a gun but can prioritize problems and direct his energy efficiently.

- He always keeps the gas tanks full.

- He reads everything and is not discomfited by skipping to the end of a book first.

- He has an astounding, almost unlimited mental library of interesting (if not necessarily useful) tidbits and stories. Many of them are true.

- What you see is what you get with James.

- He is *never, never* boring.

- He hates trash talk.

- He loves to help people help themselves.

- He's the best college teacher ever.

- He's relentlessly curious.

- He is a world-class traveler, hotel snob, wine mini-master.

- He has world-class friends, on every continent of the globe.

- He thinks I don't know when he's spinning me.

- He's a living kaleidoscope. There is no one more interesting than him, and no one can make me as mad or as happy as he does.

What he learned from me is how to do his hair. We are working hard on how to tie a bow tie.

You mentioned the Iraq War earlier, on which you famously disagreed. How do you remember that time, politically and as a spouse?

JAMES: We were not together on that. She was working for Vice President Cheney and obviously thought it was something that was a good idea. I served in the Marine Corps during the Vietnam conflict and, for complicated reasons and mostly just pure, stupid luck, I didn't have to see combat. But when I saw people coming back and began hearing what they were saying, I was like, *Jesus, thank God.*

But you get over your differences. Life goes on. It wasn't like a fundamental difference. I'm sure that they believed in it, but I just couldn't. Most stuff I could get over. That took a little longer, but I still did.

MARY: I try not to classify political issues as marriage issues. I am an outcome/results/show-me kind of personality; and although those forensics can apply to domestic tranquility, too, emotion is pretty hard to extricate from the marriage and raising kids environment. So maybe there was some emotional bleed-over in my memories of that time.

But in *all* times, James is knee-jerk competitive. I took his point then, and do now, as well-meaning people did disagree with the policy. Perhaps being in the middle of it gave me something between a myopic and magnified view of the problem, which in any event, was way more informed than his.

I have, do, and always will listen to all points of view supported by data. In that case, despite the herculean efforts of James and his ilk to revise history, we all were working off the same data, were all fully aware of the need for major global and domestic security adjustments to an asymmetrical threat, and we all supported the necessity of acting before all the "knowns could be known," to paraphrase Donald Rumsfeld.

James's people voted for the policy they subsequently decided to oppose for personal political power purposes, though they have yet been able to formulate a contemporary security strategy. But I digress.

What would you say you're especially proud of each other for?

JAMES: She served her country. She was in the White House at a very trying time in American history. She was chief of staff for the vice president. She was a pioneering woman in Republican politics. (Women didn't have an easy time with Democrats back then either.) She's very talented. She's a very good writer.

MARY: His tenacity; authenticity; manliness, loyalty, strategic mind, steadfastness, ability to compartmentalize, synthesize, clarify. He is the smartest person I've ever known in the most unique way. He is never unkind. He is truly patriotic. I'm especially proud of his boundless energy and his impatience for whining. He is never intimidated or jealous. He takes care of his people. He puts up with me.

Tell us about the moment you first realized that this was the right person for you?

JAMES: It was pretty early. We met in January and we went to Louisiana that Easter. Every Easter, my family would have a reunion, and I warned her about them. I said, "Look, I'm just telling you that they're all going to be gathering up and saying, 'James has got a girlfriend,' and all that." So we get there and, of course, people are eating crawfish and sucking heads and slurping oysters, and kids are running around. She was in this Easter sundress—more dressed than anybody else, but that's all right, they liked that. So we get in this boat and we're rowing across this little pond, and at one point she stands up and the boat tips over. We fell in the water and got all wet and muddy. Everybody was laughing at us, and my uncle looked at these two young, damn idiots and said, "And to think, one of them is going to elect the next president." That's when I knew.

MARY: The first night we met. Almost instantly. He's electric.

Are you ever jealous when someone flirts with your spouse—or when your spouse does the flirting?

JAMES: She knows how to flirt a little bit, which is good. I kind of like that. Some people don't, but there's nothing nefarious about it. She's very charming in that sense. So I say enjoy it. Enjoy the fact that your wife has some presence about her and that people like that. I know I like it.

Also—and I know this is not politically correct, but who cares at my age—she takes care of herself. That counts for something. Maybe this is a southern thing, but I like to walk in a room with my wife and have her command attention. I'm going to be honest about that. And I like it when she wears colorful clothes. People notice her. She has a kind of presence about her. It's a skill that's gone out of fashion, and Mary has it.

MARY: No, I love it. He's a great flirt. I love to watch a master at work. I have confidence in my position as his favorite flirt.

James has revealed that he has attention-deficit/hyperactivity disorder [ADHD] and that Mary is "the opposite of that." How do you two live with the yin and yang of that?

JAMES: Yes, I have ADHD. It was kind of an issue. We actually went to a high-end guy in Washington, and he put me through some test. And he said there are some things, meds, that he could give me. I said I didn't want to take meds to change my head. I like how I think. I was fortunate enough that I built an infrastructure around me that made me able to deal with it. Mary completely agreed. It's hardly debilitating, particularly if you have resources and you have somebody to send you a text to remind you of things. I think this condition sometimes makes the people who have it more creative, too. They creatively know they have to get around things.

MARY: It has its moments. It can be lonely if you don't take care to carefully listen and watch and see what he is really trying to convey, or to mindfully consider when and why he is completely not getting me. I am *not* "the opposite of that." I am also hyper and wacky on a kind of ADHD spectrum, but it manifests differently in women.

The trick for me is to recognize when we are speaking different languages. It can be frustrating, but it incentivizes yoga practice! Our priest once sent me an article about what it's like to be inside a mind like his. Fascinating. He channels his monkey mind to large strategic thinking. I channel mine to tactile creative projects—sewing, drawing, designing, making music or mechanical distractions, like fixing running toilets or taking apart machines. He wouldn't know a screwdriver from a circular saw but likes when I get out my power tools. I see the leaves on each tree; he sees the forest.

There is not one person I love or have ever loved who wasn't somewhere on the spectrum. It's an interesting ride. And an acquired taste.

You're in a profession of winners and losers. When one of you is victorious and the other is suffering a loss, how do you celebrate and commiserate at the same time?

JAMES: I used to love doing campaigns. But one day you're running a campaign and everybody is calling you. Everybody wants something. Every reporter wants to talk to you. You walk out at a debate and there's a gaggle of reporters and TV cameras and everything. And then the day after, it's thundering silence. Just like that. Even when you've won, it's like, *Damn, I was just this guy who was the center of the universe, and now no one cares anymore.* Around Thanksgiving, I always get depressed. And when you've lost, it's really depressing. One minute you're here and the next you're gone. It's like someone's hit the light switch, but they didn't use the dimmer. It's just... *boom!*

MARY: We quietly lick our own wounds and try to be happy for the guy. James likens it to having sons on different high school football teams. When politics is an honest, hard-fought debate, it is easy to respect the victor. When it's all emotionally BS, name-calling, I just shut down. As a general rule, I hate to lose, so he can get on my last nerve. He is a far more gracious loser, and a truly modest winner.

Among the many issues where you two differ, climate change has to be high on the list.

JAMES: I have a real passion for the whole coastline and climate. I've become, like, obsessed. But the thing I'm thinking about is how every movement, good or ill, always has emotion and art behind it. The most important movement in the history of the earth—climate—has none. This was a revelation I had, and I know I'm right.

How do I tell you that I am desperate about this issue? There's no lapel pin. There's no bumper sticker. There's no flag. There's no song. We need to understand that tidal tables and temperature charts and algorithms are not what move people at the end of the day. They need symbols. They need music. If I show you a crucifix or a crescent, you'd know exactly what I'm talking about.

My daughter reminded me that Harvey Milk designed the rainbow flag before he was assassinated. I can put a rainbow flag in my window and communicate very effectively. Or I can put a confederate flag in the back of my pickup truck and tell you everything you need to know about me. When I was for the civil rights movement, we had "We Shall Overcome." Earth Day was a good try. But how can we communicate in an *emotional* way?

MARY: I support adaptation to climate change, which has been a staple of existence since the Big Bang. I am a staunch conservationist, coastal restoration advocate, antipollution freak, steward-of-the-earth person.

I loathe with every fiber of my being enviro-terrorism group-think hypocrisy, based on manipulated models in pursuit of political power.

I loathe stupidity, ignorance, and trendy, data-dearth causes—like electric car showoffs who don't understand how electricity is made.

In the metaphysical sense, what kind of conceit supports a worldview with a central concept that man can defeat God's creation?

But my greater moral objection to climate change kooks is the unthinkable inhumanity that would result should their relentless, idiotic, cult brainwash enough millennials to legislate their "fix" to this multi-millennial recurring phenomena: KILL ALL HYDROCARBONS!, which would disrupt the world's greatest source of economic mobility, sci-fi innovations, life-giving miracles.

Although I agree with James's theory of emotional subtext for message penetration, in general, in the case of climate kooks, I don't think it's the absence of emotion. It's the massive, force-fed presence of their propaganda.

In truth, I do not know what issues James is focusing on. He's partnering with people, I trust, so maybe it's coastal restoration, in which case, I will write him a song.

In most cases, our parents' marriages dictate our own, whether we're copying the things we admired about them or avoiding the things we didn't. What were your mom and dad like, individually and as a couple?

JAMES: I'm very fortunate. Literally we have, like, no divorce in my family. We were very Catholic, very stationary people. Everybody stays pretty much in the same place. I like to say that everyone in my family has the same zip code.

My dad was a postmaster and had a general store. Relative to other kids I grew up around, I would be considered affluent. If your dad owned a store and was the postmaster, that was a big deal. But really, I grew up with more reputation than money.

My mother had eight children, and when I was about thirteen or fourteen, she decided she was going to sell encyclopedias. She was a great salesman, and she taught me a lot. She'd say, "Okay, let's drive around the neighborhood and look for a yard and a garage"—many people had carports back then—"that has a boat and a bicycle." I'd say, "Okay, why are we doing that?" She'd say, "Because that's going to tell us that they have disposable income and a child." She knew the demographic. She knew what she was looking for.

So we'd get to the door and she'd start talking with these ladies about these World Book encyclopedias. She'd turn to me and say, "By the way, son, what's the capital of Vermont?" I'd say, "Montpelier." She'd say, "What's the capital of Argentina?" I'd say, "Buenos Aries." The ladies would say, "That kid is a genius." My mother would say, "Yes, that's because he's got these World Books!"

And so these ladies would say, "To tell you the truth, they sound good, but I've got to check with my husband." This is 1960 in Louisiana. Her poor husband would come in and say, "Mrs. Carville, I'm sure they're good, but we've got big expenditures coming up. Come back and we'll talk about it." She would answer, "I find it interesting, sir, that you can afford a Bass boat for yourself, but not educational materials for your children." And, boom, the guy was just silent while his wife looked at him. It was the greatest sales-closing, haymaker punch I've ever seen thrown in my life—and I saw her throw it any number of times. And every time it produced a sale.

I learned a lot from my mother. What she did to sell those encyclopedias could be applied to voters—like, "Well, let's see, this group of voters has these characteristics..." And she did this without computers.

MARY: My parents were astounding individuals and a fairytale couple. They were madly in love and never fought in front of us kids. So I really don't know how to have a healthy marital fight.

The times and circumstances of our respective marriages are so disparate; and James's and my personalities are so alike—unlike those of our respective parents', who shared the same marriage model: one diva per couple—that it's hard to draw any meaningful comparative conclusions.

We are both blessed with parents who loved each other and their kids unconditionally. Some think in long marriages, "He married his mother" or "She married her daddy." But I think it's more like: in long marriages, you *become* your mothers and fathers.

A very cool part of long marriage is watching your kids become their own special unique beings—with little pockets of the two of you mashed together, emerging episodically, going through the same insane growing-up events that you both did, only in incredibly less dangerous times. And you can say to each other with such clarity, "Man, I wish I knew then what I know now." I always wanted to know what that really felt like, and to reflect on all the times I did not take my parents' advice. It's a humbling experience.

You two are now empty nesters. How has that changed you emotionally, and your day-to-day married life?

JAMES: So much of your life revolves around, "Oh, we've got to go get the kids" and whatever. And then all of a sudden you're there and they're gone. My kids are now at school, and I'm thinking, *I'm going to go there every week so I can spend time with them.* And then I realize, *You're kidding me. How dumb was that*? I mean, they probably want to spend as much time with me as I wanted to spend with my own parents when I was that age.

I think Mary's and my lives have become more separate and more together at the same time. And now, weirdly enough, we're more married than we've ever been. We probably spend less time together than we used to, but it's better time together. So much of the time we used to talk about the kids, and now it's just a different phase, a better phase, I think.

Life is always different cycles.

MARY: Our family is a bit of "a movable feast," a work in progress. I have never felt empty, as the family makes joy that sizzles your heart and is always with you. Also, our family is so extended—and our threshold for throwing a party so minimal—that we aren't often long apart. My default mode is following the curiosity of the day, which is so available in New Orleans, so I often lose track of time. But it's either terrain we've all crossed together or will. They are always in my heart. Truly present.

If there were a young couple here with us now, what wisdom have you learned about marriage that you would want to pass on to them—either what to do, or what not to do?

JAMES: At the end of the day, this thing is more about the heart than the head. Inside, you know if this is the person you should be with, and if that person is really compelling and attractive. The basic chemistry of humanity is going to be the same. Your life does not change so much from the day before you got married to the day after. Nothing changes. Most people are living together when they get married anyway.

What changes is when a child is born. When you have a child, you have to understand that the power equation in that marriage is going to change dramatically as soon as that baby is born. Because the female has to carry it, the female nurses it. You come home and you're not in any way going to argue about chores. I mean, those are the real things that are going to affect people as they go forward. The idea of "marriage" doesn't hold the same meaning.

I believe in the institution of marriage and the changing definitions of it, and all of that. You can call it marriage or anything you want. When you're in a relationship, it has consequences. And when you have children, it has *huge* consequences. Let's say I've got two young kids. I'm out with a friend and he says, "Let's go out to dinner, let's make a night of it." And I would answer, "Are you kidding me? My wife would kill me if I'm going to sit here and not help with the kids." And of course, I understand her completely.

The other thing is, don't expect people to change. Divorce courts are littered with people who thought they could go off and just marry, believing he'll stop gambling or she'll stop drinking. Generally, that is a poor way to start.

MARY: One more list:

- Pick the hill you want to die on.

- Listen before you speak.

- Breathe before you think.

- Think before you plant your flag down.

- Communicate with clarity.

- Choose your words with care. Less is more.

- Have a joint church/neighborhood/community project.

- Water your plants and rescue animals.

- See many great works of art together; share books and music.

- Take care of yourself, so you are at your best for caretaking.

- Keep an eye open for growth—your partner's and your own.

- Laugh together at something every day.

- Savor good chocolate.

- Take and give space with joy.

- Hold hands.

When Mary sent us her answers to our questions, we were so pleased with them that Marlo dashed off a thank-you email to her.

"For a woman who was such a pain in the ass," Marlo wrote, "I have to say I love you."

Mary's answer was both instant and perfectly Mary:

"Ass-pain-giving is the least of my irritating traits."

Tony Shalhoub and Brooke Adams

MARRIED IN 1992

*"The bottom line is—and I say this as a woman—
women are impossible and men are annoying."*

You wanna hear something funny?" Tony Shalhoub said, dipping his carrot stick into the hummus. "Just before you got here, Brooke and I were rushing around, getting ready, and fighting like crazy. I mean, we were really wailing away at each other, screaming like, *'Ah-hhhh!'* And then we started to laugh. I said to Brooke, 'This is hilarious. In a couple minutes, we're supposed to be talking about our wonderful marriage. We need to shut this fight down!' "

Marlo glanced across the table at Phil. "Wanna hear something even funnier?" she said to Tony and Brooke. "We were doing the same thing on the cab ride over because we were late. The driver almost threw us out of the car."

We knew this was going to be fun.

They may have been fighting before we arrived, but you'd never know it from the warmth and hospitality actors Tony Shalhoub and Brooke Adams showed us when we entered their very homey Manhattan apartment. Just a few days earlier, they'd celebrated their twenty-seventh wedding anniversary.

We settled in at the dining room table, where they'd laid out a generous spread for us on a large lazy Susan ("Brooke went to one Trader Joe's and I went to another," Tony revealed), which was, of course, piled high with way more food than we could all eat—though we tried.

"This is so Lebanese of you!" Marlo said to Tony, in a nod to their shared heritage. "Our grandmothers would be very proud of you."

Like many acting couples, Brooke and Tony met while doing a play together. The year was 1990, and Brooke was knocking 'em dead every night on Broadway in the title role of Wendy Wasserstein's landmark comedy *The Heidi Chronicles*. Tony was costarring as Heidi's lifelong best friend, Scoop—a name that now belongs to the couple's adorable Goldendoodle.

"It was kind of a *showmance*," Tony said of their backstage relationship.

"Without the '-mance,'" Brooke ribbed.

"Okay, so it was a working relationship," Tony conceded, "but there was an attraction, too."

At the time, Brooke—like Heidi—was a single mother, and her adopted one-year-old daughter, Josie, "sort of picked Tony" to play a larger role in her mom's life. "I had a nanny who brought her to the theater every Saturday when we had a matinee," Brooke recalled, "and the first thing she would do when she came in the stage door was scream, 'Nony!' and climb upstairs to his dressing room. He would lift her in his arms, put her in his makeup chair, and make her up."

The costars went their separate ways when the play ended; and a year later, Tony was in Seattle, appearing in another production.

"I followed him," Brooke admitted. "I pretended I was in Seattle visiting a friend, but I knew he had broken up with his girlfriend. So I went to see him in this play and I met his sister, Amy, who was visiting. I knew I'd already wowed Tony, so I thought, *I've absolutely got to wow this woman.*"

"I didn't know any of this at the time," Tony said. "I wish I'd known."

"You would have been a little more aggressive?" Marlo asked.

"I would have been a little more confident," said Tony.

Snedens Landing, New York; April 27, 1992

They started dating after the play ended. By then, they were both living in Los Angeles.

TONY: We were both terrified of marriage and commitment. Each of us had been engaged before we met, and we avoided marriage like the plague.

MARLO: I ran from the same plague. I was forty-two when Phil and I got married.

BROOKE: I was forty-two, too.

TONY: And I was thirty-eight. Even though I'd waited a long time, I was very certain once I met Brooke that this would be it for me. So very shortly after we started dating, I proposed. She said, "Can I think about it?" But I knew it was a great decision for me. For one thing, I knew I'd be marrying up.

MARLO: In what way?

TONY: You know, she was someone way out of my league—a wonderful, talented person, a success, a mother, and a beauty. I just felt like there would never be...

BROOKE: A better opportunity...

TONY: ... that I would never want or need any other person. It just felt like the right thing for me. I had that certainty, that absolute certainty.

BROOKE: I was not as certain.

TONY: She still isn't.

BROOKE: I'm certain now. But back then, I was already prepared to be a single mother, do you know what I mean? I thought, *I have the child, I don't need a man.* But Tony was just so nice and sweet and romantic and talented.

TONY: Desperate, I think, is the word she's reaching for.

BROOKE: I knew this would be a very smart choice. But what is being in love, anyway? What is love? I just find all of that stuff so hard.

You think love is hard? Add to that the challenge of both spouses trying to survive in what is a very mercurial profession.

"You just have to be thick-skinned," Tony offered about the actor's life. "There is a line I love that is credited to Walter Matthau: 'All it takes in this business is forty big breaks.'"

"But still," Phil commented, "what an exciting life you both have led. I mean, it's not like either of you were starving actors."

"But we *were* starving actors," Tony said. "We were just starving at different times."

After decades of hopping from one acting job to the next, Tony found A-list stardom in 2002 when he began his Emmy-winning run in the TV series *Monk*, playing a San Francisco Police Department detective who suffered from obsessive-compulsive disorder. From there, he parlayed his popularity into a series of acclaimed roles, from his Tony-winning turn as an Egyptian colonel in the Broadway musical *The Band's Visit*, to his flat-out brilliant portrayal of a tightly wound 1950s dad in TV's *The Marvelous Mrs. Maisel*.

Still, for all his success, he's the first to acknowledge having his heart broken by the business.

"There were a number of times when I didn't get the thing that I thought I should have gotten," he said, "or something I thought would catapult me that didn't really click. So for most of my thirties, I was a journeyman actor—working steadily but just scraping by. If a job came up, I would throw some clothes in a suitcase, close my apartment door, and go."

Tony touched Brooke's hand. "But it would take Brooke to convince me that I could have a real, actual life," he continued. "I remember when she showed me pictures of her house in the Hollywood Hills. I was like, 'Wow, an actor with a house!' She really gave me the confidence and the stability to have faith in myself and the knowledge that things could improve."

When they first met, Brooke was an established star who'd made her mark in such popular films as *Cuba*, *Key Exchange*, *Invasion of the Body Snatchers*, and, notably, Terrence Malick's *Days of Heaven*, which was one of the defining films of the New Hollywood in the 1970s. Of the two of them, Brooke was the bigger name.

"Fans recognized her all the time when we went out," Tony said, smiling.

"And now the tables have turned," Brooke added.

Indeed, as often happens in the turbulent waters of Hollywood, after a fast start, Brooke found it increasingly difficult to catch wind in her sails. By then, she was the mother of two (after she and Tony married, he formally adopted Josie; then together they adopted a second child, Sophie), and getting traction proved to be difficult.

BROOKE: I had to start letting go of my career as an actress, which was very hard for me. I'd been in it since I was six years old. I had to give up stardom—well, I didn't have to, but I did.

MARLO: Why?

BROOKE: Having the kids, certainly, but also nobody seemed to want to hire me. I went kicking and screaming. I pursued it for a while, but then at a certain point I stopped, because it was just so painful. But I didn't let go easily. I would say, "Okay, that's it. I'm just not going to do it anymore!"—as if anybody cared, other than me. I think I was expecting somebody to step forward and say, "No, you can't quit! You're too fabulous!" But nobody did. So the end came slowly. I still struggle with it.

TONY: But also, she reinvented her creative side by learning to paint.

BROOKE: That's true. Tony has given me this amazing opportunity to do that because he keeps working.

TONY: She started to paint when the kids were little, because it was something she could do at home. She's developed her talent over the past quarter century, and it's been amazing to watch.

Tony wasn't just being a supportive husband. Brooke is a commissioned artist who regularly sells her work, and many of her paintings grace the walls of their home. We took a private peek at the collection, and we were wowed. Among our favorites were lovely portraits of their wedding and of their two daughters. She also created a haunting series of images she painted from photos of her and Richard Gere in *Days of Heaven*.

And yet, her days in front of the camera still occasionally play in her head.

"Letting go of that career was very hard on my ego," she told us, "but it's definitely been a learning experience. In a way, it's been good training for other things in life."

Like most couples, Tony and Brooke took their cues on marriage from their parents. Neither of them had the best role models, they said. Brooke grew up in New York, where her father was an actor, theater producer, and at one point, vice president of CBS. Her mom had been an actress. She has one sister—actress Lynne Adams—and both of them became "theater rats" who attended the famed High School of Performing Arts. Every summer, they would appear with their parents in plays.

"But they drank a lot," Brooke candidly revealed about her mom and dad, "my mother in particular. That really destroyed her life. And my father had affairs."

"How do you know about that?" Phil asked.

"She was so upset that she would tell us," Brooke said. "And then we found out many years later that she did, too. I mean, they were theater people."

"No wonder you didn't want to get married," Marlo said.

"We never had any money," Brooke said. "My fathers' theaters were always in the red, and my mother was a beauty—really lovely—but she had this problem. Still, they never divorced. They stuck with it, but I don't think either of them was very happy."

Tony grew up in Michigan, the second youngest of ten children. His was a raucous household in which his mother deferred to his immigrant father, who was the family disciplinarian. "He was gregarious," Tony recalled. "I wouldn't say he was super-macho as he was very family-oriented. He was all about reaching out and being part of the larger clan."

"I know about the Lebanese household," Marlo said. "My childhood home was very noisy, very loud. Lots of expressing—of everything."

"Ours, too," Tony said with a laugh. "I think that was not so much a function of our ethnicity, but rather just the sheer number of people. It was a chaotic house, with big personalities all around, and everyone vying to be noticed, being understood, and being *right*."

It was because of this volatile upbringing, Brooke revealed, that she actually had to instruct Tony how to fight when the two of them are caught in their own tempests. He was quick to confirm that.

"Brooke really did teach me to fight," Tony said, "because I didn't know how. Growing up, I was taught not to express anger, and I now realize how screwed up that is. But there were just too many of us; and if everybody got to express their anger, it would have been bedlam. How do you deescalate twelve people screaming at each other? And then my dad had this other thing: every six or seven months he would just blow."

"Out of the blue?" Phil asked.

"Yes," Tony said. "He was fine, fine, fine, fine, fine—and then suddenly one day he would blow for a day or two. He'd go down the line of children and go, 'By the way, and by the way, and you and you and you.' He wasn't violent, but he was so big and so loud, just a big presence."

In those moments, Tony said, his mother would wait for the storm to blow over. "But afterwards, everybody was walking on eggshells until the dust settled. The damage, at least in my eyes, was not easy to recover from. And so that's why it was hard for me when Brooke and I would fight. I didn't want it to go so far that I would break the marriage."

BROOKE: But it never got broken in your house. Your parents stayed together—nobody left.

TONY: They stayed together because that's what people did back then. By the time I was an adolescent and teenager, it was pretty rough between my parents—like a tense truce. So when Brooke and I would argue at the beginning, it was hard for me to fully express my anger.

PHIL: Is that a fair assessment, Brooke?

BROOKE: Yes. He would get angry, and then I would get really angry, and he'd say, "Well, you told me to get angry." And I'd say, "Yeah, but that doesn't mean I don't get to be angry back."

TONY: That's because I was afraid it would go too far and not be recoverable. But she would say, "No, we can duke it out. You'll yell and I'll yell, and then everything will be fine—we'll move on." It took me a while to be able to trust that we could unleash everything and still come out okay on the other side.

MARLO: I don't blame you for feeling that way. If you grow up thinking you can never get angry, you must have thought anger was a forbidden land.

TONY: Right. I thought, *Well what happens if I do?* Until Brooke, I was never able to see fighting as a productive way of expressing what needs to be said. And now we've gotten really good at fighting.

PHIL: As a child I remember never having a grievance validated. If you said, "I'm tired," my mother would say, "We're *all* tired."

TONY: Exactly. Exactly.

BROOKE: For some reason, I knew that Tony and I had to learn to fight it out with each other, or I wouldn't be able to be in our marriage— and probably, neither would he. That said, Tony doesn't escalate fights, which is a very good thing. He now knows how to fight, but he doesn't escalate it—and that's probably the secret of our relationship.

TONY: What do you mean I don't escalate it?

BROOKE: You don't take it to a higher place.

TONY: I resent that!

BROOKE: But the bottom line is—and I say this as a woman—women are impossible and men are annoying.

TONY: That's Brooke's philosophy.

BROOKE: But it's true. And I think you have to appreciate a spouse for the ways they aren't like you. Because women really *are* impossible. They're fantastic, but they're complicated—and men are a little simpler, usually. They're—

TONY: —stupid, I think, is the word she's looking for.

The conversation turned to the subject of accommodation and how giving up old habits—particularly bothersome ones—can dramatically improve the health of a marriage. Marlo noted that the biggest of her accommodations was learning to rein in her need to be "a fixer."

"After about ten years together," Marlo said, "Phil wanted to discuss some problem he was dealing with, but he started off by saying, 'I want to tell you something and I don't want you to *say* anything and I don't want you to *do* anything. I just want you to listen.' I was a chronic fixer, and it was extremely hard for me to change that part of my personality. At first I would manipulate behind the scenes to fix things, but then I realized that was a betrayal, so I stopped doing that, too. That was like a huge sea change for me; and, truthfully, I don't do that with anybody else. If you told me you had a problem, by the time I got to the elevator I would have made three calls to get it fixed."

Phil's accommodation to Marlo was a lot simpler: he stopped "going bananas" on her.

"When we first got together," he said, "my Irish temper used to go from zero to seventy. It took some years, but I finally learned to take a moment to breathe and not spontaneously combust. I'd just say to myself, 'What's the payoff? I'm getting nothing from this. And she sure isn't.'"

BROOKE: That's huge. I guess what I would say is that I had to learn how to not get irritated by Tony's controlling ways—those little things, where everything has to be done a certain way.

MARLO: Like?

BROOKE: Like putting dishes in the dishwasher in a precise way. I mean, if I put them in, he actually rearranges them.

MARLO: So he really is Monk?

BROOKE: He knows how everything should be done, and he doesn't trust anyone else to do anything. And the truth is, I'm fine with that once I allow my passive nature to kick in—and I've finally learned to do that. So, that's an accommodation, I guess, because the alternative—trying to get him to stop being so controlling—is impossible.

MARLO: What about you, dishwasher boy?

TONY: Well, I don't know that I would call this an accommodation, but Brooke has made me less fearful and more confident about what was possible in our lives. Money, for example, is an impossible thing for me to figure out, understand, and manage. But Brooke's whole thing is that, yes, we can afford something if it's worth investing in, or donating to charity, or just giving to family and friends. Or even just buying and enjoying something for ourselves. I grew up with not a lot of money, and I was always worried that it was somehow going to run out. It was a hard thing for me to embrace.

MARLO: That's a really big thing, Tony. Letting go of a fear like that isn't easy. Some people just can't do that.

BROOKE: He also had to let go of being jealous.

TONY: She's right. I used to be horribly jealous.

MARLO: Really?

BROOKE: Oh, my God, this is so cute. Tony still thinks that any man I meet is going to fall in love with me. And I don't want anyone to tell him any differently, so, of course, I play it up. I'm like an old invisible woman, but he still thinks I'm everybody's dream date.

TONY: She thinks I'm imagining this, but I'm not completely blind. I see how men respond to her. I'm not making this up.

PHIL: And that just kills you, right?

TONY: It's torture. It's torture.

BROOKE: And for me it's just fun that he actually thinks this. It's ludicrous but flattering.

MARLO: My husband is very jealous, too.

TONY: Really? Oh, good. I'm not alone out there.

PHIL: Nope, not alone.

BROOKE: How about you, Marlo?

MARLO: Oh, sure. I'm Lebanese and Sicilian. Women would just fall all over Phil. I think it was Erma Bombeck who once wrote that Phil is every woman's fantasy of a husband.

BROOKE: That's true!

MARLO: Women wrote me letters when we got married telling me just how despondent they were about it. One woman said that every day at 9 a.m., after her kids had gone to school and her husband had gone to work, she'd put on lipstick and sit down and watch Phil. Women just loved him because what they saw on television was a man who completely understood women. I mean, he didn't really at home any more than any other guy, but he understood the issues that women cared about, and he treated women as if they had a brain—because he believed they did. But at home, he was still the guy who didn't put his clothes in the hamper.

As our conversation wound down, we asked Brooke and Tony to name the one thing they get from each other and no one else. Actors are great at exercises like this, because acting is all about articulating feelings that are often difficult to reach. Neither of them disappointed.

"My life," Brooke said immediately. "I totally get my life from Tony."

"I feel that way, too," Tony said. "Brooke is responsible for my life. Take a look around you—everything you see. This is all Brooke. That's why I talked earlier about marrying up. But mostly what I get from her is a level of trust and honesty and intimacy, and the knowledge that we can really let our flaws, our vulnerabilities, and our shortcomings be revealed without permanent judgment or too much of a cost. There's a feeling of constancy I get that tells me, no matter what, Brooke will be there."

Brooke smiled and glanced at her husband. "Let's face it, marriage is hard," she said, "but Tony and I get to have everything we want, really. We fight, we laugh, we hate each other, we love each other. And it's amazing, really. I sometimes go from thinking 'I'm the greatest thing in the world' to 'I'm the biggest piece of shit,' but when I'm feeling like I'm shit, he doesn't think so—and that's what I really love about this marriage."

"Whereas, when I feel like I'm a piece of shit, she validates it," Tony said.

Brooke laughed and turned back to us.

"I think the answer to your question is pretty simple," she said. "We like each other."

Michael J. Fox and
Tracy Pollan

"In marriage, you have to take it all—
the good with the bad. If you love somebody,
you deal with whatever it is they're dealing
with. Their issues become your issues."

Gratitude. That is the prevailing feeling you get from Michael J. Fox and Tracy Pollan.

These two have been married for thirty-two years, and for twenty-eight of them, they've lived with Michael's diagnosis of Parkinson's disease. But not for one second does that overshadow the good fortune of their lives: a strong marriage, healthy kids, and flourishing work. And it is their ability to stare down that uninvited presence in their home and carry on with buoyancy and hope that is their greatest fortune of all.

I met them at the Fifth Avenue apartment where they've lived since 1995. It was the first time I'd interviewed a couple for this book without Phil, who was down with the flu. We could have tried to reschedule; but because Michael and Tracy were about to leave for a trip, we thought it best to keep the date, and that I would try to fly solo with the conversation.

Nina, the couple's warm assistant, welcomed me into their home and, along with their dog—Gus, "part Great Dane, hound, and Chow"—led me to the dining room, which has beautiful park views from each window and a forest of American elms just below. "It's like living in a tree house," Michael said. A very beautifully furnished one, I might add: the living room is awash in serene, pale colors, and it houses the piano the kids practiced on when they were younger. Michael favors his guitars, which he keeps in his study.

We hadn't even sat down before Michael, Tracy, and I discovered one of those "small world" things unique to Manhattanites. Turns out that many years ago, Phil and I lived on the Upper West Side in the very same apartment that Michael and Tracy rented shortly thereafter. Now we all live across Central Park on the same street. On a good day, Phil could probably launch a golf ball onto their balcony. Or maybe not.

As the three of us settled in at their dining table, I was struck by how young and fresh they looked—not many years removed from that moment in 1985 when they first met on the set of the TV sitcom *Family Ties*. Tracy, primarily a New York theater actress at the time, had been cast to play Michael's girlfriend on the show; Michael was a megastar—or as he likes to say, the "idiot clown prince of Hollywood"—thanks to both his hit series and the 1985 big-screen blockbuster *Back to the Future*.

It has been twenty-nine years since Michael first detected the symptoms of his illness, but the burden of his condition didn't show on either of their faces, nor in their demeanor. In fact, what they talked about most was the joy they take in each other's company and their mutual commitment to their family.

"We keep each other laughing," Tracy said. "In marriage, you have to take it all—the good with the bad. If you love somebody, as I love Michael, you deal with whatever it is they're dealing with. Their issues become your issues."

And that's when the thankfulness comes in. "I deal with this health thing," Michael says, "and what keeps me balanced is gratitude. I have

gratitude for my family—first and foremost Tracy—but also our kids [Sam, thirty; twins Aquinnah and Schuyler, twenty-five; and Esmé, eighteen]. They are really great—perfect, in fact. I know everyone says that about their children, but ours are so nonjudgmental and undemanding. Tracy and I often look at them and say, 'What a great life we have. This is beautiful what we've done.' So for me, being in this place of gratitude is like being in a place of acceptance. If you accept something, it doesn't mean you're resigned to it; it just means that you're honest about it. Acceptance is so much a part of life and marriage. You accept your partner and your family for who they are."

That acceptance—the clear knowledge that they love each other and are there for each other 100 percent—pervaded our conversation. "There are times when I just want to fall into her," Michael said, "because after thirty years, Tracy is my best friend in the world, the first person I think of when I think of anything. It's automatic. It's nice."

Besides having lived in the same apartment, Phil and I share one other similarity with Tracy and Michael: their first moments together were caught on film, just as ours were. I was a guest on Phil's show, after which we immediately started dating. And Michael and Tracy met on *Family Ties*, a hit series that ultimately earned Michael three Emmys. I will always remember his character, Alex Keaton, a diehard Republican living with his liberal family in Reagan-era America. He was hilarious, winning, and adorable. Tracy was cast to play his girlfriend, a "brainy dancer" named Ellen.

While Tracy once told *People* magazine that she initially found Michael "funny, but cocky," he found her intriguing. "There was such a dignity about her, and a thoughtfulness," he told me. "At the time, I never considered anything carefully; I just jumped into whatever situation I was in and took over. But when I met Tracy, I thought, *Wow, she really has poise.*"

They shared their first kiss onscreen, but that's as far as things went. Off camera, Michael was dating actress Nancy McKeon, and Tracy was going back to New York and her longtime live-in boyfriend Kevin Bacon.

Three years later, however, the two of them—by then both unattached—

were cast together again in the 1988 movie *Bright Lights, Big City*. This time, sparks flew.

MARLO: So it took two times for you to click. What made you realize this was the right person?

MICHAEL: It's interesting you should ask that. When you're younger, you have relationships with people but you kind of know instantly that it's not the right person, even though you might go a fair distance with them. You think, *This is fun—now how do I get out of it?* But then you meet someone else and you think, *This is fun—I don't ever want to get out of this.*

TRACY: There was also a leap of faith at that point because we were so young. It's funny, when you're that age, you all make these huge decisions you're too young to be making. Like, I look at my daughter now deciding on colleges, and I think *What does she know? How does she know which school is right?* Same thing with us. We were in our early twenties—that's still kids—but we both had this very strong feeling and we just jumped into it.

MICHAEL: I wouldn't do anything differently—our lives have turned out fantastically—but we had our son, Sam, really early in our marriage, so that was a quick adjustment. We were never really traditional newlyweds; we were parents within a year of our wedding.

MARLO: So in just four years, your partner had become your spouse, and then your co-parent.

TRACY: Exactly. Also, when we got married, Michael's life was very large. He had a lot going on—job after job, movie after movie. We would walk down the street and everybody would say hello. "Hey, Mike!" "Hi, Mike!" I called him Mr. Mayor. He had that kind of persona where everyone wanted to talk to him and be with him. So for me, I had to figure out how to accommodate room for that big life while maintaining my own independence.

MARLO: That's tough. Did you recognize that accommodation, Michael?

MICHAEL: Yes. And at the same time that she was finding that space for herself, she found space for me. I didn't realize how much sensory overload I was dealing with until Tracy told me, in so many words, "This is going to kill you. You don't have any room for *yourself* in your life. You don't have any room for relationships that are real and are based on something other than business or mutual benefit." And I thought, *Wow, she's right.* All of a sudden, I started to crave privacy and to go where no one would give us special attention.

TRACY: Michael had so many people working for him—agents and assistants—and when we'd argue, he'd say, "Nobody else in my life says that to me!" And I'd be like, "Yeah, that's because you pay all of them! I'm the only person who isn't worried about being fired." Right?

MICHAEL: Absolutely.

Although they came from different parts of the world, their family lives were remarkably similar. Tracy grew up in a Jewish family in New York, and her parents were married sixty-four years, until her father's death in 2018. Michael hails from an Irish-Canadian army family from the west coast of the country. His dad died from a heart attack in 1990, after a marriage of forty years.

Both Tracy and Michael were lucky enough to witness strong, loving relationships.

"We had a fun, large family, and we were taught that family was everything," Tracy said. "My parents had a wonderful marriage, and having that foundation was everything for me and my siblings. Our goal in life was to have that solid family relationship for ourselves, knowing that everything falls into place after that."

"And it's really weird that I had the same family," Michael added. "My parents and Tracy's are exactly the same age and grew up at the same time. I had three sisters and a brother, though my mother would say she had six kids because she lost a son before I was born. But in terms of closeness, our family was like Tracy's. My mom and dad were really devoted to each other. We traveled across Canada quite a few times, with everybody loaded into the Pontiac and brothers and sisters overlapping each other and hitting each other in the head with their seatbelts."

"Were your parents affectionate with each other?" I asked. "I could always tell when my mom and dad headed off to their room for private time, but Phil says he never saw his parents show any kind of sexual attraction, or even a kiss on the mouth. Did you ever see any of that?"

"I did when they were younger," Michael said. "Even when they got older, after my dad got heavy, my mom would go in and wash his back when he was in the bathtub. She'd say, 'Dad's in the tub—I'm going to go do his back.'"

Tracy recalled her own parents' relationship. "I definitely saw love and affection, but I feel like I saw even more of it in their later years when their bond got stronger. They would always hold hands—*always*—whether they were walking down the street or watching a movie. My dad in particular was quite affectionate with my mother."

"He loved her so much," Michael said softly. "He worshipped her."

"They both felt that way," said Tracy.

That Tracy and Michael brought that same durability—and harmony—to their own marriage was apparent. But I wondered what it was like when one of them is down.

MARLO: I'm usually a pretty optimistic person, but when I'm blue, Phil is the only person who can do a reality check with me. If it's about an acting job I didn't feel confident about, he'll say to me, "I don't know why you feel that way—you were so good." Or if I feel I made a faux pas with someone, he'll say, "You didn't say anything wrong—I thought you were charming." He pulls me up. He's my cheerleader.

MICHAEL: I'm like you. I'm supposed to be Mr. Sunshine, and I tend to go along and get along and have a good time. But sometimes, when stuff is hard to deal with, Tracy has just the right thing to say that makes me look at it another way. She can take big things and make them the right size so that the bad stuff doesn't take up too much room.

TRACY: For me, the problem is that I often get too affected by arguments with friends or family members. When that happens and I'm upset, the only person I ever want to talk to is Michael. He'll put it all into perspective. He'll tell me, "It's just one day, and you're not going to feel the same way tomorrow. And it doesn't matter what anybody else says or thinks—all that matters is what you know."

MARLO: It's hard to picture the two of you fighting—and I'm not just saying that. You both seem so connected.

MICHAEL: Tracy and I don't pick scabs. In some marriages, people look at their partner and see vulnerability and they just can't help but go after that vulnerability, like it's a sport or something. We don't do that. We love each other and respect each other. I really am interested in what she has to say. I'm not just giving her space to talk; what she says is valuable to me. Hers is the best advice I could get from anybody.

MARLO: When you do get into an argument, how do you push the reset button?

MICHAEL: If I've said something stupid, I have a tendency to want to take it back and make it all okay. But that doesn't really work. Things have to be discussed and resolved. So if we have a disagreement, I'm now more likely to give it some air, to allow things to settle and let Tracy think about it.

MARLO: When you say "give it some air," do you mean that you don't get into a confrontation about it?

MICHAEL: I don't do what I really want to do, which is keep coming in the room every five seconds and saying, "Are we okay now?"

TRACY: I also find no benefit in having to hash through every single thing. Sometimes you just have to say to yourself, "You know what? He said something schmucky and it made me feel bad. But he's a good person and I'm going to give him the benefit of the doubt that he didn't realize that what he said hurt my feelings." And he does the same with me. We'll just look at each other and say, "I know you didn't mean it. Let's move on." You don't have to get mired in the negative when you could be celebrating the positive.

MICHAEL: At a certain point, if you know you're a good person—and Tracy is a fantastic person—you just have to trust yourself. She's not going to leave the baby on the street corner or betray a friend or do something damaging to her family. She is always going to do the right thing.

Michael was first told about his condition in 1992. He was twenty-nine years old.

"The diagnosis came very, very early in our marriage," Tracy recalled. "I didn't even go to the doctor with him because we didn't think it was going to be anything big. At that point, he had very few symptoms."

The first sign had come the year before, when he was on location in Florida, filming the romantic comedy *Doc Hollywood*. He woke up one morning to discover a disturbing twitch in his left pinky. At first he wrote off the tremor as a "goofy injury" he'd perhaps sustained the night before, when he'd had a couple of beers with his costar Woody Harrelson. "Maybe we'd gotten into a slap-fight," Michael mused in his memoir. But the symptoms quickly spread to his arm, and subsequent examinations confirmed the worst: that Michael had Parkinson's—a disease he has sardonically dubbed "the gift that keeps on taking."

It was all so fast.

MICHAEL: Four things happened in a really short amount of time. Tracy and I got married. My father passed away. Our son was born. And I got diagnosed. Then I quit drinking, which was a fifth thing. These were massive changes, and I became a different person. But I had to become that person to survive and go on with my life. I needed to own my diagnosis, own what that meant to my family, and be prepared to do what I needed to do to make that okay. That was a big test early in our marriage.

MARLO: A huge test. Tracy, how did you deal with this?

TRACY: It's interesting—we got this big piece of news, but then nothing really changed in the day-to-day. You're told that everything is going to be the same for a while, but not so in ten years. It's a hard thing to have to grapple with as a newly married couple. We had a very young child, so it was definitely something to process and deal with. But for a while, our lives stayed the same.

MICHAEL: I remember the moment I told her, after I got the diagnosis from the neurologist. We were in the hallway leading to the bedroom in our old apartment. I told her and we just held each other. As Tracy has said, it was like a bus was coming at us, and it was going to hit us one day—but we didn't know when. What should I do? Go to bed? Take an aspirin? I felt like I'd brought an elephant to the party and it wasn't invited—how were we going to accommodate it?

MARLO: Did you ever worry that she might bail on you?

MICHAEL: I worried that I might be bailable, that I might not deal with it well. And initially I didn't deal with it very well.

MARLO: In what way?

MICHAEL: I kind of ignored it, and then I overmedicated—or wrongly medicated—by drinking a bit more than I had been. That all lasted for about a year and a half. Then I got serious about it. But Tracy had to deal with all of that. So, no, I wasn't worried about Tracy bailing on me. I was worried that this was my thing, and that I had to find a way not to let it become something that separated me from my family, but instead, use it as something that connected me with my family.

MARLO: Tracy, were there ever moments when, in the back of your mind, you were thinking, *Oh, my God, I can't do this*?

TRACY: Not in a big-picture way. There have definitely been moments when I've thought I couldn't handle some particular thing, but I never thought, *I'm out for good*. That's not how I live my life. It's not how I was raised.

MARLO: How did you get through the days when it all became too much?

TRACY: I'm a very, very independent person, and I need my time alone. I need time to exercise and time to spend with my friends. As long as I'm able to carve out time for myself—especially when things feel overwhelming—I can regenerate and come back into a situation feeling stronger and more whole.

Listening to Tracy speak about integrating her husband's illness into her own life reminded me of just how complex marriage is. We promise love and devotion after we take that short walk down the aisle, but no wedding vow can prepare us for the unexpected.

"I remember when Phil and I first got married," I told Tracy and Michael. "He had five children from his previous marriage. His four boys lived with him, and they became a part of my life. I loved this man, and so I loved them. Then one year into our marriage, one of his boys developed an emotional problem and began doing harmful things. I dug in as if he were my own child and began searching for ways I could help. It was a rough time, but we eventually all pulled through it. Years later, Phil said to me, 'You know, I thought you might bail on me back then,' and that surprised me. Yes, I was scared to death—I'd even had frightening dreams—because I'd never known anything like this. But there was never a question that Phil's challenge wasn't also my challenge."

As I related this story to Michael and Tracy, they both nodded.

"As a couple, you're *always* dealing with something," Tracy said, "whether it's the death of a parent, or an illness, or an issue with the kids, and all of those things can seem so difficult and insurmountable. But once you've gone through them together—once you've gotten to the other end—it makes your marriage stronger. You realize, 'Okay, we handled that. We can handle the next thing.' It gives you fortitude together and a feeling of a united front."

MARLO: How are you facing the physical challenges, Michael?

MICHAEL: I do my physical therapy. It used to be exercises, and now it's physical therapy. It's tough. I'm going through a transition right now because I can't walk as well as I once did. I used to walk my dog over to the Museum of Natural History, and then go to the dog park, then walk back through the park. I can't do that anymore. I may be able to do that in my future, but not right now. It's a change.

MARLO: You all went on a safari in the Serengeti recently, yes?

MICHAEL: Yes.

MARLO: How did you do?

MICHAEL: Did great. At first I didn't want to go. I knew I wouldn't be able to get out of the car and track the animals. But Tracy said, "You'll sit in the Jeep and look at the elephants. You'll have a good time."

TRACY: What he actually said was, "If one of those animals starts coming for us, he'll know I'm the one who can't run."

MICHAEL: Right. I'm the one by the watering hole who's sick and lame and old. So, yeah, Tracy is always encouraging me to get involved and not to project where I might be. I probably tend to take on things a bit more than is advisable, but I do that because I figure I'll just meet the day. And Tracy gives me the encouragement to meet the day. She told me, "When we get there, we'll deal with it."

MARLO: I think that's great. Did you enjoy the safari?

MICHAEL: Loved it.

TRACY: It was amazing.

MICHAEL: I just stayed in the Jeep.

It was time to wind down our conversation, and I reflexively turned to my left, which is where Phil usually sits, to ask him if he had any other questions. Funny, right? I felt a quick sting of sadness that he wasn't there—just one more telltale reminder of how intimately we depend on our spouses. I turned back to Tracy and Michael and asked them the question Phil usually likes to wrap up with: What advice would you give to a young couple contemplating marriage? It seemed an especially apt question to ask a couple who got married when they were in their twenties.

Tracy's response was both simple and profound: "I would say, number one, give each other the benefit of the doubt. Know that you love this person and they love you, so assume the best, not the worst. And number two, carve out time together, even when you have kids—but also carve out time for yourself, because it will inform the time you have together."

I turned to Michael.

"Always remember that marriage is a new thing, a different thing, for the two of you," he began. "It's you plus another person making a new life. Your socks may not end up in the same place where you used to put them, and things might not always be the way you like them, but embrace the newness."

And above all, Michael added, be there for each other. "People always say, 'Oh, you have these health issues,' and I reply, 'There are worse issues. There are people who have pancreatic cancer or who lost their kids. There's horrible stuff in this world, and I'm doing okay.' But every once in a while, I'll tell Tracy, 'I haven't got it today. I don't know how to get beyond this.' And she'll say, 'You will. You feel this way today, in this moment, but tomorrow you will feel different; new things will show up, and they will change how you feel.' And she'll be right.

"And so when I hit a wall—when I just need someone to get underneath me and get me up over that wall—she's always that person. Always. Every time."

Michael and Tracy showed me to the door, and I began the short walk home. I hadn't taken more than a few steps before I began to cry. What I'd witnessed for the past ninety minutes was the very heart of the marital bond. It was uncanny to me—and remains so today—that love and pain, joy and sadness, the best and the worst, can coexist so closely, and yet with such grace.

Michael's illness is always there. The movement he has little control over is there. His disease is in their marriage, and their marriage is in his disease. They are braided as a given, and that braid is made of love and commitment and steel. It filled me with love for them. And it filled me with love for my own husband.

This is marriage.

Neil Patrick Harris and David Burtka

MARRIED IN 2014

"Next time I saw her, I said, 'Who was that guy that you're dating?' and she said, 'David? Oh no, he's totally gay.' I said, '*Reeaally*?' And then I started stalking him."

Neil Patrick Harris and David Burtka are a fairly decisive couple. But one thing they couldn't settle on was what to call themselves.

"Once we started dating, we never really stopped," Neil said. "But same-sex marriage wasn't legal at that time. So we were conscientious of what wording we used when we introduced each other. I just didn't like the word *partner*. It eliminates any sense of romance. 'This is my *partner*.'"

"Agreed," David said. "And then there's *lover*."

"*Lover* sounds only romantic," Neil said.

"Right—very 1980s," David said. "And *boyfriend* just sounds juvenile."

"Juvenile and short-lived," added Neil. "My *boyfriend* and I have been together for two months!"

"Exactly," said David.

"So after we'd been together for a few years," Neil concluded, "I

Perugia, Italy; September 6, 2014

started saying *my better half*. And then once the whole Proposition 8 thing happened—and it happened very quickly—we didn't want to get married straight away just because we were suddenly allowed to get married in California. We wanted to get married because we wanted to get married."

So that's what David and Neil did on September 6, 2014—three full years after New York's Marriage Equality Act legally permitted them to be husband and husband in New York State, and nine months before the United States Supreme Court expanded that right to same-sex couples from coast to coast.

The ceremony was small—just forty-seven family and friends in attendance—in an enchantingly pretty villa in Perugia, Italy. "The nice thing about an Italian wedding is that everything is so delicious there," Neil remembered. "Like the white wine, or the red wine *della casa*, or the pasta with fresh herbs and tomatoes. And then there were the flowers and the views..."

Food. Love. Passion. These are recurring themes when you sit down to talk with this smart and funny couple.

Phil was still down with the flu but feeling much better—he'd even offered to join me on my trip uptown to meet them. But it's never a good idea to bring cold germs into a house with kids, so I made the journey alone.

Neil and David live with their children, nine-year-old twins Gideon Scott and Harper Grace, and a fluffy little who-knows-what rescue dog, Gidget, in a restored 1905 brownstone in the Harlem neighborhood of New York City. They bought the townhouse in 2014, after spending nearly a decade in Los Angeles. The five-story building has a rich history—it's been a speakeasy for mill workers, a music school for girls, a bed-and-breakfast, and...

"I think it was a brothel," Neil said in his usual deadpan, one that David knows well.

"No, it wasn't," David replied, drily.

"It wasn't?" Neil said. "Maybe that's just wishful thinking."

Brothel or not, they've done a top-to-bottom renovation to turn it into an elegantly festive house for two young children, a dog, and two active men coming into the prime of their suddenly divergent careers—with a fitness area, a playroom for the kids, a movie screening room, a chef's garden (David grows tomatoes, cucumbers, carrots, beets, lettuce, and herbs), and a top-notch professional kitchen.

"When you're married to a chef person who is also an actor," Neil noted, "your place is always filled with good times and food." David's first cookbook, *Life Is a Party*, was released in 2019.

After touring their home, we settled into the plush, red velvet chairs in their old-Hollywood-style screening room on the first floor. I was told I'd just missed the kiddies, who were out on a scheduled play date. Gidget more than made up for their absence by panting her affection.

When they first met in New York in 2003, David and Neil were both performing on Broadway. David was appearing in the revival of the musical *Gypsy*, starring Bernadette Peters. It was his Broadway debut, and he'd landed the plum role of Tulsa—a grueling song-and-dance assignment that Neil calls "the role that every young male actor from the ages of eighteen to thirty covets." Neil was starring just ten blocks away as the Emcee in a revival of *Cabaret*. Fittingly, Neil first laid eyes on his future husband while strolling through the theater district. He recalled the moment vividly.

"My friend Kate Reinders, who was also in *Gypsy*, was walking down the street with this very studly dancer guy in a leather jacket with, like, amazing hair, so I just figured she had a boyfriend who was really hot. Next time I saw her, I said, 'Who's that guy you're dating?' and she said, 'David? Oh no, he's totally gay.' I said, '*Reeaally?*' And then I started stalking him."

Because of their similar Broadway schedules, Neil—in coordination with Kate, presumably—would just happen to show up at the same bar or restaurant after their respective performances.

DAVID: I'd go to meet Kate, and Neil would be there at the bar. I'd think, *What is going on with this guy?*

NEIL: I was circling him like some sort of—

MARLO: —vulture. Were you looking at him, too, David?

DAVID: I had a boyfriend at the time and things weren't going so well. He was in Los Angeles, and because long-distance relationships don't really work, we finally broke up. And then I gave this guy a date.

MARLO: Were you as physically attracted to him as he was to you? He's kind of cute, you know.

DAVID: When I first met him, he looked very strange. He had jet black hair and he was very white with bright blue eyes, so he didn't necessarily look like Neil. I mean, he was still handsome, but it wasn't like...

NEIL: I was in the character of the Emcee. My hair was dyed black, my eyebrows were dyed black, my armpits were dyed black, and my skin color is pretty pale, so I looked a little bit like a vampire. But then I had David come to my show with Kate. That was a very sexy version of *Cabaret*, if you remember, and there was a lot of walking around the audience and sitting in people's laps and making out with the other cast members.

MARLO: Was that a turn-on?

DAVID: Yeah. It was.

MARLO: Talent is always a turn-on.

NEIL: I played the whole show to him.

MARLO: I bet you did. I bet you did.

NEIL: And look where it got me.

MARLO: You got yourself a mate. And then it started.

DAVID: And then it started. We lived in New York for a couple of months, and then we made the move to Los Angeles. It was nine years in L.A.

Neil was already a big star—an award-winning actor, comedian, and singer who easily toggled among movies, stage, and TV. His career had launched into the stratosphere when he was a child actor starring in the TV series *Doogie Howser, M.D.*, in 1989, and he'd charted a steady course ever since.

David, on the other hand, was feeling adrift. One moment, he and Neil had been fellow actors on Broadway—working the same schedule and spending all of their free time together—and the next, they'd relocated to a different coast, where Neil was insanely busy. When he wasn't starring on TV in *How I Met Your Mother*, he was also appearing in a hot web series (*Dr. Horrible's Sing-Along Blog*) and taking the spotlight in just about any room he walked into with his charm and celebrity.

David grew depressed. Deprived of meaningful acting work and away from his friends and family, he felt torn between love and resentment for his boyfriend. "I wasn't having the best time in L.A., but we stuck it out because he was doing a job there," David explained. "But I was an actor, too, so I was feeling that jealousy, like, 'Hey, what about me?' Because he gets a lot of attention. A lot of attention all the time."

"Do you still feel that way?" I asked.

"I feel two ways," David said. "Sometimes I say, 'Behind every great man is a great partner,' and I should feel happy and honored that he's sharing his time with me. And then other times I'm super upset and annoyed and just sort of stomp my feet and say, 'Hey, I need some attention here, too.'"

Neil completely understood. "What made it even more challenging is that, as actors, we both wear our emotions on the sleeve," he said. "So sometimes I'll be sharing good news with him about some new job opportunity for me, and because he's in the same field, he's wishing that opportunity was his own. I get that."

"And we're two guys," David added.

"Yes," said Neil. "We're the same sex, which amplifies it as well."

On top of feeling isolated in a town where he had few friends, David suffered a huge blow: his mother was dying of cancer. "It was fast," he recalled. "Twenty days in the hospital—leukemia—and I thought, *I can't be in Los Angeles and be depressed and go out for auditions that I don't want to do.*"

That was the moment that David decided to dive feet-first into a monumental career change: "I walked into Le Cordon Bleu and became a chef and started working right away."

Enrolling at the famed culinary academy felt comfortable to David. When he was growing up, his parents enjoyed entertaining, and David and his sister were often enlisted in food preparation and cleanup chores for cocktail parties. Being in the kitchen was also therapeutic for David. "Cooking makes me happy," he said.

It also made him more content in his relationship. "He was able to get the attention that anyone wants," Neil observed, "because hunger is such a basic desire. And because David is so skilled as an actor and a chef, he can combine his passion for both. So he's often getting more attention than I am, in certain ways. He's able to provide an experience for people on the daily—his kids, his husband, his friends."

"I never thought about it like that," David said. "I just thought, 'Everybody has to eat, so why not eat well?'"

Although they both grew up with sturdy marital role models—David's parents were married thirty-nine years, and Neil's have been together more than fifty—they entered into their relationship from entirely different places. For David, marriage and kids was always a forgone conclusion.

"Once I was living in New York," he recalled, "I saw lots of different relationships and men having babies together and starting a family, and I always knew in my gut that that was going to be me. I was going to find someone and settle down with that someone and stay with that someone and start a family and grow."

For Neil, things were uniquely different. "I was on a television show when I was fifteen years old," he explained, "and so all through prepuberty to puberty—that time when you're figuring out what turns you on—I felt like I was under the microscope of the television lens, so I didn't have the freedom to randomly hit on somebody or go to a bar. I was by myself a lot. I had a fantastic group of friends in Los Angeles, but I wasn't dating. So I just figured I was going to be alone or single for most of my adult life. I never even showered with another person until I was in my late twenties. So all of this was new to me."

But there in L.A., reeling from the death of David's mom, their visions of what their futures might look like began to converge. At the time, gay marriage wasn't legal, but that didn't stop them from thinking about kids.

"His mom passes away very suddenly and you think, *What are we here for?*" Neil said. "Random shit happens all the time—and that changes everything—so why wait for someone else to get leukemia? Having kids is a real game-changer, so why not move it to the next step?"

"My mom really wanted grandkids," David added softly, "and after she died, Neil and I looked at each other and said, 'Life is too short. Let's do this. Let's start the surrogate process.'"

Which is exactly what they did. Thankfully for the couple, they could afford the price tag of baby-making, given Neil's steady employment. But the procedure was complex—and it involved two women. The first was an anonymous donor who provided two eggs for the couple; then Neil and David contributed their own genetics ("two of our best guys," David said); nature did its thing; and then both fertilized ova were implanted in the second woman, who carried the babies to term.

From Neil's perspective, the experience spoke to the difference between heterosexual and same-sex couples when it comes to starting a family. "When same-sex couples want to have kids, it's because they've really thought it through," he observed, "because you can't do it accidentally—"

"—as much as we tried," David interjected.

"We say that in jest," Neil continued, "but there's a lot of truth to it. David and I had many conversations about family and its importance, and the timing was right. And so when we had our kids, we were ready for them."

David nodded. "I always find it funny when someone says gay people shouldn't have kids," he said. "I mean, they have gone through so many hoops and they really want to have kids so badly. They've been invested in it, they've thought about it, and they've taken the time to do it."

Gideon Scott Burtka-Harris, and Harper Grace Burtka-Harris—fraternal twins—arrived on October 12, 2010.

"Babies!!" Neil announced on Twitter three days later. "On 10/12, Gideon Scott and Harper Grace entered the Burtka-Harris fold. All of us are happy, healthy, tired, and a little pukey."

MARLO: Okay, so what did this do to the love nest?

DAVID: Oh, my gosh—I mean, I'm sure you and Phil have heard lots of stories about what happens. It was rough. And I have to say, for the first five years, I wasn't sure it was going to work out. I thought we were on a really rocky road. I didn't know if I could—

MARLO: —be a dad?

DAVID: Be a dad and be a husband at the same time. It pulled us apart. And it's so universal.

NEIL: And yet it also brings you together, because you're constantly having to do things. Once you have kids, it's much harder to say, "That's it! I'm out of here!" because there's so much responsibility. And yet you also have no time to say, "Let's stay up all night and drink and have sex."

MARLO: That was my next thought. Without prying, how do you find that time and stay romantic when you have little children?

NEIL: I'd like to know.

DAVID: Me, too. We'll read your book and find out.

NEIL: Actually, we do make a concerted effort to connect. We'll have date nights.

DAVID: Date nights or staycations, or we'll go on vacations with each other. And sometimes if we're traveling for business, we'll try to parlay a couple of days for ourselves, either before or after.

NEIL: And, by the way, afternoon sex is underrated.

DAVID: Right—especially when the kids aren't home from school yet. "Hurry up! You've got ten minutes!"

MARLO: So nighttime is out of the question?

NEIL: Well, if you're waiting until the kids go to sleep to have sex, you're going to be asleep yourself.

DAVID: Exactly. It's like you're really excited during the day. "This is really going to happen..."

NEIL: "Tonight your world is going to be rocked!" Cut to snoring.

For all their well-honed banter about being tired and sex-deprived spouses, both Neil and David concede that real intimacy runs a lot deeper than a stolen roll in the hay before the kids come home. "We respect each other's needs," Neil said, "and it's not just a carnal need that must be fulfilled. I really like it when we're sometimes watching TV and then going to sleep and cuddling—I feel like that's as intimate as having sex with each other. We don't have to quantify how many days it's been since we had sex, because we spend a lot of time together anyway, and we connect. We'll go see a show and have dinner, and then we come home and go to bed. I don't feel like we've missed out on part of the night just because we didn't get off, do you know what I mean?"

"No," David said.

"How dare you!" Neil shot back.

Watching these two go back and forth, I was struck by how gregarious and appealing they are, and wondered if that ever led to problems.

MARLO: There's a prevailing myth that gay men are promiscuous, even if they're in relationships. Is there any truth to that? And, if so, is that something the two of you put on the table and discussed?

DAVID: We know other couples who have open relationships, and it just wouldn't work for us. I'm more of a jealous person, so I wouldn't be able to do that. I would be worried all the time, like *Who is he with?* and *Am I not good enough?* So, I think I'd go crazy if we had an open relationship. I'd drive myself nuts. I'd tap his phone and hire a private detective and figure out where he was going.

MARLO: Are you Sicilian?

NEIL: Well, honestly, when we started dating, our sex life was so strong and it maintained itself. We spent all of our time together, so it wasn't some relationship of convenience. I would also happily disagree with the conceit that gay guys are known for being promiscuous with each other. That is disappearing as the culture is changing.

MARLO: So where did the myth come from?

NEIL: It comes from the time when gay guys weren't able to be out publicly and stand so tall and be so proud of who they were. Back then they had to pretend that they were someone else, and so promiscuity was understood because they weren't able to tell anyone that they were having sex on the sly. But now there's a normalization. Guys cheating on each other is no different from the old story about the man who has a wife at home and a mistress on the side. Historically, cheating is not unique to two gentlemen.

DAVID: We're so out of the loop, anyway. I mean, now there's Grindr and Bumble and all these hookup apps where you swipe left and swipe right...

NEIL: We started dating before any of that stuff.

DAVID: Right, we missed that whole generation. I was out the other night with a friend of mine. We were in a gay bar watching a drag show, and he was literally looking at his app while all these people were around him in the bar. That's how people date now. You go to gay bars and you see people on their phones. Screens everywhere. There's no human connection.

MARLO: Well, from a personal perspective, I wondered whether you had conversations about boundaries when it comes to other people. I know my husband and I had that conversation. I always needed my guy to be my guy.

NEIL: We've had boundary conversations, but they've been fluid. I think one of the things that's kept us together all of these years is that we both define a relationship as something that's relatively indefinable. Marriage never stays the same. When you have sex with the same person over and over, it gets redundant, and so you try different things. Then one day you don't like each other, and suddenly you're not attracted to each other, so you have to figure out how to be *reattracted* to them—but in a different way because you're aging. Then suddenly you're in love with their soul more than their body, but then you get in love with their body again. It all keeps morphing. So in a weird way, we keep falling in love with each other in different ways, over and over, and I think that keeps our sex life alive, because we're not trying to continue doing what we used to do.

DAVID: And if something ever happened and he sort of, you know, strayed, I think that would be okay.

NEIL: This is so good to hear!

DAVID: Don't even.

I was starting to miss Phil. These guys were clearly funny, and I knew he would have loved listening to them. But their sassy repartee also made me wonder what they sound like when they're having a fight.

"We tend to blurt out the things we want to say," David confessed, "and that's not always the best way to express yourself. But I also think that's a good thing because we don't hold anything in. We share our feelings— we're actors, too, remember—so we want to know 'where you're coming from' or 'how you're feeling,' and we're always reading each other's faces. Like, if there's something wrong with him, I know immediately what's going on."

Neil agreed. "If you don't communicate," he said, "you're going to build up assumptions, and those can turn into resentments, and I think that's more corrosive than anything. So the lines of communication deserve to be open. Can things get fiery and messy? Of course. But we don't throw slanderous comments or insults. We don't call each other a piece of shit or put each other down. That doesn't accomplish anything."

"So your arguments are constructive and rational?" I asked.

"We'll just try to get our points across," Neil said. "I'd rather overcommunicate and overshare and at least know where we're standing. We know couples who pretend everything is fine when it's really not, and then this chasm exists with so much left unsaid; and when it gets so bad that they need to start communicating, there's so much to say that they don't even know where to begin."

David and Neil see a couples counselor weekly and have been doing so for nearly their entire fifteen years together. They both stress that they seek counseling together not as "a last resort" but, as Neil says, in "an overarching desire to maintain and continue our relationship."

DAVID: If we're dealing with a really touchy subject and it's not going anywhere, we'll table it until we see our therapist. And that's been really helpful because we know that, for that hour or two, we're there to work. It's a work session.

MARLO: When you're not with your therapist, how do you deescalate mid-argument?

NEIL: It's good to take a moment during a conflict to go to your corners and cool down—the truth is always kind of somewhere in the middle. Because when you're in the heat of it and you're fighting and you're stressed and the dopamine is pouring in your brain and you're seeing red, you're not in the headspace to say, "You know what? I'm overreacting. You're right." But if you walk away, or go exercise . . .

DAVID: I usually need twenty minutes . . .

NEIL: Then you come back together and say, "What are we doing? Why are we fighting?"

DAVID: And it's really important to remember that in moments of heartache or turmoil, neither of us means harm. We don't wish any ill on each other. We're together and we're in love and the trust is there. It's not a malicious thing—it's usually just about two big, bossy personalities wanting to be right.

MARLO: You both seem to have the same spirit. How are you different?

NEIL: I would say that one of the differences in us is that David is an everexpanding heart. He operates from an emotional core, which is bright and beautiful and pure. But he's often emotion-based more than logic-based, and I, in turn, logicize things and tend to miss the opportunity to really feel things in the moment—because I'm always processing potential outcomes or reimagining what has just happened. My brain works a little too fast, and his heart works a little too fast. Sometimes we balance each other out in that way, but sometimes we don't.

According to David, the efforts he and Neil have made at resolving conflict are having positive results. "I think that we communicate a lot better now," he offered. "Now that the kids are more self-sufficient, we're cuddlier and want to be around each other and are being more tactile with each other. I've also been sober for the past three years, so I don't drink any alcohol. That's helped a lot."

I was surprised by the sudden mention of an alcohol issue; but like everything else with this couple, they addressed the topic with candor and honesty. "I was upset a lot," David explained. "I was depressed in L.A., so what did I do when I was depressed? I drank more." He also took prescription medicines, he said, without telling Neil—and Neil never noticed. "Addicts are great actors," David said.

"Was the drinking starting to affect your relationship?" I asked.

"Yes," David replied. "It not only made me more depressed, but it also made me more apt to start a fight, or be more right, or be more headstrong."

Neil leaned forward. "For whatever reason," he said, "when David chose to drink with a capital D—as opposed to just a glass or two of wine at dinner—a switch would flip that would turn him into an almost different version of himself, and it was a little out of control. And if we'd both been drinking, it became very *Who's Afraid of Virginia Woolf*–y, as we'd try to get our points across, and the conversation would elevate with no real resolution. And then we'd kind of rinse and repeat every day: you'd wake up, you'd try again, your day would be weird, and then you'd go out and drink again."

Significantly, it was not Neil's idea for David to stop drinking—indeed, he commented, it wouldn't have worked if he'd laid down the law with David. "It's such a personal decision," he said, "that if I were to tell David that he needed to stop drinking, it would be met with resistance more than acceptance."

"So what made you stop, David?" I asked.

"I'm better without it," he allowed. "I owed it to myself and I owed it to my kids that I shouldn't be in an altered state. And I didn't like waking up feeling crappy. I was also taking things for granted. There are a lot of demons inside my head that I'm still working out, so I think that it's better if I'm clear. It was a decision I completely made, and he supported me."

"And it's one of the things I'm most deeply proud of about David,"

Neil said. "His determination to do that—it's a very hard and complicated decision."

The kids were due home any minute, and I didn't want to intrude on that busy part of their day. I packed up my equipment, and the guys walked me to the door. But in all honesty, I really didn't want to leave. Speaking to these two felt like hanging out with old friends.

When I got home, Phil was in the kitchen, getting a glass of juice. He was in his sweats and looking better. Our conversation went something like this:

PHIL: So, how did it go?

MARLO: Oh, you know, the usual.

PHIL: What's "the usual" mean?

MARLO: Just your typical married couple—two guys who survived one case of career envy, a death in the family, depression, a bout with alcohol, a career change, a hit TV show, a hit cookbook, two cross-country moves, two surrogate births, two kids, and a year-long renovation of a gorgeous old building in Harlem.

PHIL: Anything else?

MARLO: Yes, a country whose laws have finally caught up with the human heart.

PHIL: Wow. I'm sorry I missed that.

MARLO: Me too. You would've loved them. So what do you want for dinner?

PHIL: Up to you.

MARLO: Let's do Italian. I've been thinking about pasta and fresh vegetables, and maybe a nice della casa wine....

LL COOL J and Simone I. Smith

MARRIED IN 1995

"My mother said to me, 'Let him go. He's going to come back within the next two and a half years, and when he comes back he's going to come back correct.'"

We have to admit, we're not rap music aficionados. But one of the things we do know is that to call LL COOL J simply a "rapper" is to miss the enormous impact of his artistry. More than just a garden-variety performer who strings together clever, edgy rhymes, he is a pioneering hip-hop artist, record producer, actor, and entrepreneur who has done what pioneers do best: reshaped the cultural landscape.

There's a reason that the words "bold genius" and "boundless contribution to the human spirit" were used to describe him when he became the first rap artist to receive the prestigious Kennedy Center Honors in 2017. And there's a reason that he coined the term G.O.A.T. (Greatest of All Time), in part, to describe himself. He is the Muhammad Ali of hip-hop.

And his songs are not filled with violence—okay, maybe a few: "Mama Said Knock You Out" and "Rock the Bells"—but there's no hate or misogyny in his work. No violence to women. No "bitch." No N-word.

But sexy? Oh, yes.

Our big question was: What do we call him? LL? COOL? J? We asked his assistant, and she said, "Oh, just call him Todd." Todd? Yep. He was born James Todd Smith in Queens, New York, in 1968. But when he exploded onto the rap music scene in 1984, he stepped into the spotlight as LL COOL J—which was short for Ladies Love Cool James.

And they do. Especially Simone I. Smith, his wife of twenty-five years.

This is the story of two city kids, both of them raised by their grandparents, who taught them to be forthright and decent, stick by each other, and approach life with a sense of responsibility. Devoted parents of four, they are a pair who passionately believe in friendship, faith, and the good manners they learned as children.

It all began one Easter Sunday, when an acquaintance asked Todd—then a rising star with one record under his belt—if he'd like to meet his cousin, Simone.

"I said, 'Nah, nah, nah,'" Todd recalled, "and then I looked over and saw Simone and I was like, 'All right, I'll meet your cousin. Bring her over.' So, I said hello to her and then we kind of vibed—we had a nice moment of eye contact. I said, 'You should come around.' She said, '*You* come around.'"

The burly six-foot-two rapper stood chatting with the diminutive high schooler (Simone stands all of five feet two inches), and he eventually got around to asking for her number. Simone was skeptical.

"I said to him, 'Well, you're probably going to take my number and throw it in the corner with a bunch of other numbers,'" she recalled. "And he was like, 'No, Shorty, I'm going to call you.'"

Todd did more than just call. Two days later, he dropped by Simone's house with a friend and suggested they go out for a bite. Simone asked her sister to join them, and the four Queens teens did what any kids would do on an impromptu double date: they got take-out Chinese and brought it back to Simone's house.

"That was our first date, and pretty much the rest is history," Simone

said. "We hung out almost every day until Todd had to go back out on tour. That's when he tried to break up with me. I remember saying to him, 'Why do you want to break up with me?'"

"I was going to ask the same thing," Marlo said.

"He said, 'I don't know what you're going to be doing while I'm on tour,'" Simone continued. "He thought I might start dating someone else while he was away. So I said to him, 'What do you think I'm going to do, get a boyfriend while you're gone?' I told him we weren't going to break up, and we stayed together."

We made a date with Simone and Todd while we were in L.A. on yet another West Coast swing of our great couples crusade. We met with them at the hotel where we were staying in Beverly Hills. Todd was dressed in head-to-toe black, including a wool ski cap and aviator shades. But not even his hip urban attire could conceal that sweet smile of his.

Simone, two years Todd's junior, looked great in an oversized jacket with the words GOD SAVE AMERICA across the back. She wore a wide-brimmed fedora, with a fountain of beautiful boxed braids—called "goddess locks"—cascading out of it, along with a pair of huge hoop earrings. She's also got a killer smile.

As LL COOL J, Todd virtually put hip-hop music on the map when he was barely twenty years old. As of 2020, he has released fifteen albums (eight of them platinum) and won two Grammys. He is also an in-demand actor, who has appeared on the CBS crime show evergreen *NCIS: Los Angeles* since 2009.

As we were to discover, nothing about this couple is conventional—including the trajectory of their relationship, which runs almost parallel to that of Todd's career.

MARLO: Simone, you were in eleventh grade when you met Todd, as his career was just taking off. Weren't you worried about all those girls he'd meet on the road?

SIMONE: Absolutely, absolutely. And back in those days we didn't have cell phones, so I'd be home waiting for Todd to call, and if he called and I wasn't home, he would be mad because he couldn't reach me.

MARLO: He was jealous?

SIMONE: Yeah, I would say that. But dating someone like him at that time—I saw how the girls reacted, whether we were going to Red Lobster or to a movie.

MARLO: That must have been hard.

SIMONE: It was very hard. But I'm pretty confident with who I am. I have always been that way, and that's what I think I bring to the table as a wife—or at that time, as a girlfriend. The difference is, when you're a girlfriend, you're a little unsure, because you don't particularly know where you stand.

PHIL: How long was it before you got married?

SIMONE: Well, we had two children first—Najee and Italia—they're sixteen months apart. I was nineteen when I got pregnant with our first child. We got married when I was pregnant with our third.

PHIL: Why didn't you two get married once you had a baby?

TODD: I mean, personally, I wasn't ready, to be honest. Everything kind of happened a little quickly, do you know what I'm saying? I was still finding myself, and I just wasn't ready for that. That's the truth.

MARLO: Did you live together?

SIMONE: We had a condo.

MARLO: So as young as you were, you were both stepping up to the life you'd started together. You'd made a nest.

TODD: I believe you have to be responsible—you've got to take care of your kids and the mother of your children. That's just how I was raised.

PHIL: Did you get that from your grandmother?

TODD: From my grandfather and the family I was raised in. You just don't abandon ship when it comes to kids. I know that seems simple, but it's just basic manners. These are your kids. You're never *not* going to take care of your kids.

MARLO: A lot of black men take heat for not being there for their children.

TODD: I think some of that is true and some of it is marketing. But for me, trying to shirk my responsibility wasn't even an option. At the same time, I wasn't ready to do the Brady Bunch, either. I mean, they were my kids and I was going to take care of them, but this was moving at light speed.

SIMONE: But we were living together with the children, and then Todd was on the road.

PHIL: And you trusted him, it sounds like.

SIMONE: I trusted him for the most part, but there was a time that we split up for two years. We weren't married yet, but we had two children.

TODD: It wasn't like I walked out or abandoned her. We broke up.

SIMONE: I don't know if I ever told you this, Todd, but I remember when I was pregnant with Tali, and my mother had gotten sick; we were on the phone and she was telling me that I needed to let you go out and sow your wild oats, as they say. This was, maybe, two or three weeks before she died. But what she said to me on the call was, "Let him go. I won't be here, but he's going to come back within the next two and a half years, and when he comes back he's going to come back correct."

MARLO: Wow. And this was before it happened?

SIMONE: Yes. And I was like, "Ma, you sound crazy." And it didn't dawn on me then, but to this day I believe that God was speaking to her prophetically. Because everything that my mother said actually happened. She told me that when Tali was around six or seven months, Todd and I would break up, and that he'd come back within two-and-a-half years. "You just have to let him be," she said.

PHIL: So your religion must have played a role here?

SIMONE: My religion played a big role in my childhood, in our marriage, and in raising our children. Absolutely.

Leading up to the breakup, Todd was busy building a music career that would separate him from his family for long stretches. "It wasn't like I was this guy going to work from nine to five and coming home every day," he explained. "I was away a lot because of the touring."

Simone accepted absences as part of the deal. "Todd was an artist," she recalled. "He was LL COOL J, so he was working on music, recording, touring. When he was in town, of course, he saw the kids, and I had a great relationship with his grandmother and my mother-in-law. The kids actually went to school in Queens, right across the street from the house that Todd grew up in."

Marlo turned to Todd. "So it sounds like Simone was holding down the fort while you built a career," she said. "My mother did that, too, as my father worked his way up from small clubs to headlining in Las Vegas. But I think Dad missed his kids and worried that he couldn't be home with us. When you and Simone were broken up, did you struggle with that, too?"

Todd paused. "I mean, the real answer is, I was just focused on my career, focused on my purpose," he said. "You've got to do that if you want to be successful. It doesn't mean you don't care about somebody, but you have to focus on your progress. That's what I was singing about. I knew I wasn't going to be the worst guy in the world. I knew I was not going to *not* pay child support, or fall behind. I knew I'd do the right thing."

"So even during your breakup," Marlo said, "you were able to come back to be with your kids."

"Right," Todd said. "I think it's important that children have their father in the household. And it may sound a little cliché, but just leaving her with the kids wasn't the thing to do."

Given that they had broken up, Todd would occasionally bring a girlfriend with him when he visited Simone and the kids. And Simone dated, too. It helped that Todd's grandmother was available to babysit the kids, and she also frequently lobbied for the couple to get back together.

MARLO: Reconciliations can be awkward, because there are a lot of hurt feelings. Were you willing to take Todd back right away?
TODD: Oh, please. She was absolutely willing.
SIMONE: We became friends first.
TODD: I was the father of your children first. But, yes, at first it was a cordial relationship.

SIMONE: One night, Todd came over to the house, and we were talking, then the doorbell rings. It was this guy I had been dating. We'd broken up two months earlier—he thought that I was breaking up with him because I was back together with Todd, but that wasn't true. Anyway, he starts to come into the house, and Todd winds up beating him up.

MARLO: Really?

SIMONE: So, I always say that Todd came back and got his girl—that he had to beat this guy up to get his girl back.

PHIL: Did you really beat him up, Todd?

TODD: No, I didn't.

SIMONE: Yes, he did.

MARLO: This sounds like a movie. What really happened?

SIMONE: He beat him up.

TODD: No, I took him out for hot chocolate.

MARLO: Come on...

TODD: I mean, we got into a—

SIMONE: —he beat him up.

MARLO: Why?

SIMONE: Because the guy tried to push his way into the house, and Todd wasn't having it.

PHIL: So, there was an actual physical encounter.

MARLO: Phil calls this an "Irish-type activity."

SIMONE: It was cute, though. It was cute.

MARLO: Come on Todd, details.

SIMONE: Loosen up some, Todd.

MARLO: You were staking your claim to the woman you loved.

TODD: Well, I mean, it was odd the way he tried to go about doing it. And that didn't work for me.

MARLO: I see. So, you were annoyed that he tried to walk in and take over.

TODD: Well, it was a little deeper than that. He tried to come through the window.

PHIL: Literally? Through the window?

SIMONE: Well, the way the condo was, the windows were right there. And when Todd wouldn't let him in, he was tall enough to go through the window.

MARLO: Why was your ex-boyfriend so mad?

SIMONE: He saw Todd's car parked outside, and he was like, "I knew you was getting back together with him." But it wasn't really like that, because at that time Todd and I weren't back together.

With the exception of the window-crasher, Todd largely kept rough stuff out of his life and out of his songs. When we asked him about the relatively nonaggressive tone of his music, he credited his upbringing, particularly by his grandfather, who was an Army Medical Corps veteran.

"I was raised by a Catholic World War II veteran," Todd explained. "He was a guy who would go to the Masonic Lodge on weekends. He was in block patrol and a very responsible citizen. This was a guy who fixed his own cars and washed his hands up to his elbows. So, instead of me being raised by the Vietnam generation, I was raised by the World War II generation. The values are a little different. The thinking is a little different."

It was also his grandfather who encouraged his musicality. When Todd was eleven, his grandpa gave him two turntables and a sound mixer, primarily to keep young Todd off the streets.

"I had wanted a mini-bike," Todd recalled. "All the kids in the neighborhood had them, but then I got hit by a car while I was riding one. My grandfather didn't want me outside anymore, and he didn't want to put a basketball court at the house, because he didn't want a whole bunch of guys over there. That causes trouble. So he finally said, 'Look, you like this rap stuff, you like to deejay. I'm going to get you two turntables and a mixer.'"

At the same time and just a few blocks away ("maybe three or four minutes, if you hit no lights," Simone said), Todd's future wife was also being raised by her grandparents, whose marriage would ultimately last sixty-one years. Her parents had divorced when she was five; and as a child, she divided her time among bowling leagues, church choir, and the Girl

Scouts. Her neighborhood was no less rough than Todd's, but that didn't intimidate this Queens girl.

"Growing up," she began, "it wasn't the way it is now. Like if guys fought—"

Todd interrupted. "I've got to jump in here," he said. "It was tough, but when you grow up like that, it's different from how you see it as a visitor. You grow up in it. Maybe there's a difference between the male and the female experience, but I grew up with guys carrying guns and selling drugs. A lot of my buddies, my friends, got killed."

"How did both of you manage to stay out of that?" Marlo asked.

Todd leaned forward. "A friend of mine once said to me, 'Yo man, let's go up the block and sell some drugs for the guy up there. We can make money,'" he said. "I thought about it for a second, because I would have loved to have some money. But then I said to him, 'Nah, nah.' He said, 'Why not?' I said, 'Because I'm going to have to kill people.' I was sixteen, fifteen. He said, 'What do you mean?' I said, 'Because there's no way you can be successful doing that if you're not willing to go all the way, and that's not a road I want to go down.'"

"How did you know what you wanted?" Phil asked.

"I knew I wanted to live a life where I was contributing," Todd continued, "not a life where I was involved in that kind of stuff. You have to remember that in these neighborhoods, no one is sitting around talking about the stock market. No one is talking about annuities. No one is talking about grad school. No one is saying, 'Bonnie's kid went to grad school, and this other one is going to Brown or Cornell or Duke or Yale.' Like, nobody is talking about that. The conversations are about who got shot, who stayed out of trouble, and who you don't go near. You're learning the rules of engagement, not the rules of success."

Todd and Simone nodded their heads simultaneously. "My kids didn't grow up the way I did, at all," Todd said. "Period. Especially the two younger ones—they didn't even get a taste of it. The oldest one might have gotten, like, fifteen minutes of fame in Queens, and then he was out. But when you look at the differences in their conversations—they're hearing about school, they're hearing about college, they're hearing about generational wealth, they're hearing about words and ideas and concepts and family trusts. I never even heard the word 'college,' really. Even though I had cousins who were school principals and math teachers and detectives—and uncles who were actually cops—it was a very blue-collar and you-get-out-of-high-school-and-you-go-to-work type deal. So when you're in that type of an environment, it takes a lot to navigate through that. Does that make sense?"

MARLO: Yes. Like your children, my siblings and I didn't grow up in tough neighborhoods like our parents did, either. We were Beverly Hills kids. Still, my father would tell us never to run away from a policeman, and my mother would warn us, "Whenever you walk down the street at night, walk down the middle of the road—that way you can run in either direction."

TODD: That's good advice, though. I used to do that.

MARLO: It *is* good advice. But we never felt that kind of danger in our neighborhood.

SIMONE: But you know what? Just because it's less likely to happen in Beverly Hills, you can never say never, because anything can happen anywhere.

TODD: That's right. You have to remember that, in America there's dirty laundry everywhere. Now, you guys, obviously—where you are in life—you've seen it all. And the reality is, people live along a spectrum in our country, and you can apply that spectrum to various things—whether it's policing or law enforcement. And the way people get treated is really based on where they are perceived to be on that spectrum, and that is just the absolute truth, as much as we don't want to believe it. I mean, us sitting here is an unlikely conversation, right?

I'll give you an example. There are some things that you, Marlo, as a woman, can tell Phil and me that we can't relate to, even though I'm black and he's white. There are certain things that neither of us can really relate to when women say them. But that doesn't mean we can't empathize. That doesn't mean that we can't lock in and be open to what you say and believe you.

But the thing is, there are a lot of people who, because of implicit bias, don't believe certain things. They don't believe women are being harassed; they don't believe that the black guy got harassed by a police officer. That confirmation bias, that conditioning, makes it hard for some people to believe things because they've never experienced them. Like, I've never been afraid walking in a parking lot at night.

MARLO: But you're a big man.

TODD: I know, but I'm telling you I've never been afraid walking in a parking lot at night. I feel like you should be afraid of me—I ain't afraid of you. Do you know what I mean? That's what I'm talking about—those are the differences. So okay, the first time I got my new car and was riding around, a cop saw me in Queens with my brand new car—

SIMONE: —they used to stop Todd all the time.

TODD: The first time a cop saw me—the *first* interaction with the police—he said, "Oh, the crack business is doing great isn't it?" That's the first comment I heard. They thought I was selling crack. Immediately. Immediately.

MARLO: How awful.

SIMONE: Because that's what it was like growing up in Queens.

TODD: Or the first time I got a Mercedes-Benz in L.A. I bought it in California and got it shipped out to Queens. It was a convertible. I was driving on the south side of Queens, and twenty cop cars surrounded me. Guns drawn.

MARLO: My God. You must have been terrified.

TODD: Not really. We're used to it. That's expected.

SIMONE: But back then, they weren't shooting black men the way they're shooting them now.

TODD: Well, they were. It just wasn't in the media. It wasn't on the internet. But they were. A lot of guys I know got killed by the police.

Although their similar life experiences are surely part of their bond, the world they've made together has its own unique challenges and necessary accommodations. We asked Simone about that.

"I would say that being married to Todd requires a lot of compromise," Simone said. "I mean, in any marriage there's a lot of compromise, but in our marriage, one person compromises more than the other."

"So you're saying that you accommodate him more than he accommodates you?" Phil asked.

"I would probably say yes, because of who he is," Simone agreed. "There are a lot of things that go on that, if I wasn't built the way I was built mentally, I probably wouldn't last in a relationship being married to somebody who was a sex symbol. Do you know what I'm saying?"

"I totally get that," Marlo said. "I'm sure it's hard."

"It comes with the territory," Simone said. "There are women who come up to me and say, 'Oh my God, your husband is so gorgeous,' and I just say, 'Yeah, he is.' Some of them are fans, and they genuinely mean that. But then there's that smaller group of women who are disrespectful—they'll disrespect you, they'll push you out of the way. It doesn't happen often, but it has happened several times since we've been married."

Todd nodded as Simone spoke. "I think you have a better chance of keeping things intact if you just relax a little bit and be confident in the relationship," he said. "If you don't get too caught up in this stuff, I think you have a better chance of things lasting. I might do a music video tomorrow that has twenty girls in it because that's just the nature of what I do. But you don't want to make it all about that. Your relationship can't just be about those interactions—that's not healthy."

MARLO: I saw a very sexy video of Todd's in which a beautiful girl was literally all over him. I mean she was on top of him and under him and behind him. At one point, I think she even licked his face. What was that song?

SIMONE: "Doin' It." Now, *that* was a video—and it caused problems for us, because Todd came home every day talking about it. "Oh, yeah, you're going to love this video!" And I was like, "Okay, good." They filmed it for, like, three days. And every day, it was, "I really think you're going to love this video, Simone. I did a construction scene today." I don't think that scene even made it into the final cut.

MARLO: But it's a good song. Great lyrics.

SIMONE: And I loved the song, too, when Todd first recorded it. But that video! We were living in California by then. We had just gotten back from vacation and we were at the house. Everyone was there—my grandmother, his grandmother, his aunt. And Todd was like, "Oh, the video is here!" And when he put that video on, I just went off. I said to him, "What about this video did you actually think I was going to like? *You've got girls licking you on your face!*"

MARLO: But it's okay that he did it, right? It's his job. It's—

SIMONE: No. Now, wait a second. It may have been his job, but it was also a video that, at every interview Todd went on, everybody always asked him the same question: "How does Simone feel about this video?"

PHIL: Did you understand how she might feel, Todd?

TODD: Yes. But the thing I've learned is, I respect Simone but I can't compromise the art. I have to be true to the art. I'm not going to try to be an artist and not do certain things just to make her happy, because then I won't be happy. And if I'm not happy, she ain't going to be happy anyway.

SIMONE: Again, there's that compromise. And it's a compromise that I just have to deal with, because it's something that he's not able to compromise about.

TODD: Right. And my response to that is: the life that you live is based on that compromise. So those full bellies and those cozy lit fires and those glasses of wine are being provided by that compromise, so it's one of those things. You know, unfortunately I'm not a playwright, do you know what I'm saying? You didn't marry a playwright. You didn't marry a novelist.

MARLO: That's a perfect answer. I get it.

TODD: Well, it's the truth. And I'm just being sincere.

"You impress me as such a strong woman, Simone," Phil said. "Confident and strong."

"You've got to be," Simone said. "You've got to be strong."

"Where do you think that strength comes from?" Marlo asked.

"I think it comes from my faith in God," Simone said. "I think that's how I was built. It's in my DNA. My grandparents raised me, and, like Todd's grandfather, my grandfather was in World War II. He worked for Eastern Airlines for twenty-five years; and after that, he worked at a senior citizen center. My grandmother did private nursing and catered parties all my life, up until she was maybe seventy-five years old. So, I had a really solid spiritual foundation from both of them, and I just think it's the way God made me. I can deal with a lot. I'm a tough cookie."

Todd cut in. "She is a tough cookie," he concurred, "and, you know, my intention is never to be disrespectful. That's not the goal. But you also want to be true to what it is that you're doing, so that it can work from your spirit. So I've tried to keep that in mind. I've tried to keep true to my spirit. And I know, Simone, you don't want me to be a shell of who I should be by making compromises that won't allow me to be my authentic self. Because if I did, then I wouldn't be the best *me* I can be for *you*."

"So you have your dream and you follow it," Marlo said. "Then what kinds of accommodations do you make for Simone?"

"Well, she does a lot of shopping," Todd said with a laugh, "but beyond that, I give her a lot of freedom. I'm not a person who's on her neck every five minutes about everything. I allow her to live her life while being supportive of her dreams and goals."

One of those dreams turned into reality in 2009, when Simone launched her own line of jewelry. A self-described "hoop girl" and "accessories queen" ("I've been known to wear funky hoop earrings on the red carpet with a to-the-floor gown"), she converted her passion for all things sparkly into her own company—Simone I. Smith—that offers the full gamut of jewelry, from earrings and necklaces to bracelets and her signature "Lollipop" line—bejeweled pendants that look like tiny Tootsie Pops with a bite taken out. Among the celebrities who have worn Simone's creations on the red carpet are Rihanna, Mary J. Blige, and Missy Elliott.

And her husband has been behind her, 100 percent. "I lent my support to that not just by default," noted Todd, who bought Simone her first pair of "door-knocker" earrings when she was just seventeen years old. "I put my money where my mouth is and put action behind it, and actually tried to make things happen."

Visitors to Simone's website will note that a portion of the proceeds from each piece sold is donated to the American Cancer Society—a philanthropic effort promoted with the words "Beat cancer like a boss." That slogan came from Simone's own harrowing experience: In 2004, at age thirty-four, she was diagnosed with chondrosarcoma, a rare form of cancer that had developed into a tumor in the tibia bone of her right leg. The resulting surgery required the removal of the entire right tibia and replacing it with the fibula from her left leg, along with a steel rod and screws.

MARLO: You must have been scared to death.

SIMONE: Out of my mind. People can tell you all day long, "I know how you feel, I know how you feel," but you *do not* know how it feels when a doctor tells you that you have cancer, because your mind automatically starts going crazy.

TODD: We found out about it together. We faced the challenge, and I tried to be as supportive as I could be. As crazy as I am in all the videos and the music and all of that, I am equally supportive in other areas. I try to provide a buffer and make sure that the right energy is around.

PHIL: Did you get off the road while she was sick?

TODD: Oh yeah. An album had just dropped and I didn't even go out on the road to promote it.

MARLO: God bless you, Todd. Your grandma taught you right.

SIMONE: But he still wound up having good hits off that album. I tried to get him to go out and promote it because we were in New York and I had family around, but Todd wouldn't leave until I was out of the hospital. He wanted to be there with me. He has a little mushy side to him—he actually offered to give me his tibia bone.

MARLO: He did? And what happened?

TODD: It was too big.

MARLO: Still, that's quite a gift. Better than any piece of jewelry a husband could give his wife. Phil never once offered me his tibia.

Time and again throughout our conversation, both Simone and Todd channeled their grandparents' wisdom in response to our questions, so we weren't surprised to hear a few more pearls when we asked the two of them what advice they'd pass on to young couples starting out.

"One day," Simone recalled, "my grandfather said to me, 'If you don't want to talk to him for a week or two, don't talk to him, but make sure you take care of home.' That's what he told me. 'Make sure the kids are good. Make sure dinner is cooked. Make sure you take care of home.' That's advice I would give to any new wife."

"That's very practical," Marlo said. "Keep your own world steady, and you're better prepared to take on other challenges. I like your grandfather."

"Well, another thing that I learned early on came from my grandmother," Simone added. "She told me that no matter how mad I get at Todd, to never stop praying for him. He may be on my last nerve, but when I get down on my knees, I pray for him. That's good advice, too."

Phil turned to Todd. "That wisdom is tough to beat, big fella," he said. "What advice would you give to a budding young couple?"

Todd thought for a long while before he answered.

"Well, first I would say, always be supportive of your spouse," he began, "regardless of the ebbs and flows of emotions. Always be protective. It's like they tell you to do on airplanes. Always put your oxygen mask on first in order to properly put the oxygen mask on your family. I think that that's very important. When you go after your dream and make it a reality, you will be able to be there for your family. In other words, you can still attend that daddy-daughter dance and still go to that soccer game, but don't give up all of your own potential to do that. I see a lot of twenty-eight-year-old guys rushing home when they should be going out and trying to make things happen. Yes, they're family men—and that's a beautiful thing—but sometimes they give up their entire lives to be present at every single moment with their kids and their wives, and then when they're forty they feel like everything is behind them, and all because they thought they'd be a bad guy for going after their dream. So my advice is: by maximizing your own potential, you can take care of the people around you."

"So you're saying it's important to be a little selfish," Marlo said.

"Yes," Todd said, "but it's the right kind of selfishness. It's the kind of selfishness that would help this country. It doesn't mean to ignore your family, and I'm not implying that you should do that. I'm just saying to put your oxygen mask on first and then help the person next to you. If I take care of me, I can contribute to you. An old hustler in Queens once told me, 'When you come to me, come with something in your hand, not with your hand out.' And that's true."

Simone turned to her husband. "I have some girlfriends who aren't looking for that in a guy. They don't understand about maximizing potential."

"And they're going to end up with a loser," Todd said. "*Where we going, baby? What's for dinner, baby?* They're losing all day long. But if you want to be with a winner, you've got to understand this: just focus on your dream, and you can help your family's dreams come true."

Rob and Michele Reiner

"I'm thinking, *Jesus, what a bitch!*
But I'm also really attracted to her."

As far as Rob Reiner was concerned, professional photographer Michele Singer was not the girl of his dreams. In fact, Rob almost ended it with Michele before they even met. If that sounds like something out of a romantic comedy, there's a good reason for that: their thirty-one-year marriage has been the perfect blend of laughter and love. This is Rob's second marriage, Michele's first.

We met up with the couple on a warm spring day at their home in Brentwood, a quiet neighborhood in Los Angeles. They live in a country house, all wood and stone with a shingle roof. The moment we entered the property's white wooden gate, we felt like we were back at our old house in rustic Connecticut.

Rob and Michele greeted us inside the yard, along with their beloved Goldendoodles, Chipper and Zuzu. As we walked to the house, they showed us the beautiful rose garden that screen legend Henry Fonda, who was also an avid horticulturist, had seeded and maintained when he'd lived there. The garden is still in bloom today.

Fonda was just the beginning of the house's sterling Hollywood lineage. He lived in it for ten years (both Jane and Peter were born there). Then it

was sold to screen star Paul Henreid, he of lighting-two-cigarettes-at-once fame—one for him, the other for Bette Davis—in *Now, Voyager.* Twenty years later, it was bought by Norman Lear, who made it his home for eighteen years. Rob spent a lot of time there during the run of Lear's series *All in the Family,* in which he played Archie Bunker's long-haired, liberal son-in-law Michael Stivic ("Meathead").

"I always used to say, 'If I ever make any money, I'd love to own a house like this,'" Rob told us. Well, he did and now he does.

Rob and Michele have lived in this comfortable home for twenty-eight of their thirty-one married years. Those decades encompassed most of Rob's directing career, which stands as one of Hollywood's most creative and commercially successful runs, with movies like *Stand by Me, The Princess Bride, When Harry Met Sally...,* and *A Few Good Men.*

As we made our way around the grounds, we saw mementos of the life the couple has forged there. The swings, jungle gym, slide, and trampoline that their three children played on are still standing. Rob and Michele hope to see their grandchildren play on them one day, but for now they're enjoyed by the kids of friends who tag along when their parents come to visit.

And there's one more feature whose continued existence is a testament to the big-hearted couple's sentimentality: Henry Fonda's nearly century-old potting shed, left as it was when the actor puttered inside of it—rusty sink, broken slats, lopsided cabinet doors and all. The structure is clearly falling down, but Rob didn't have the heart to put it out of its misery. "We just couldn't remove it," he told us.

Once inside, we got down to talking with Rob and Michele about their marriage. It reminded us of those delightful vignettes in *When Harry Met Sally...,* as a couple talks into the camera and shares the story of how they met and fell in love. Moviegoers can thank this real-life love story for that film's happy ending. Rob was originally going to go in a different direction, but... well, let's let them tell it *Harry-Sally* style:

The Big Island of Hawaii; May 19, 1989

MICHELE: The beginning didn't start out so well because we were going to meet each other and then it didn't happen. And then I met him on the set of *When Harry Met Sally*.... We got married seven months later.

ROB: It's a really good story. I had been single for ten years. My romantic life was an utter mess. I was in and out of different relationships. That really became the basis for *When Harry Met Sally*...—the whole question of, *How do men and women get together?* We were in preproduction on *Sally.* I was sitting with Barry Sonnenfeld, my director of photography. I look at this magazine on a table and Michelle Pfeiffer is on the cover. I'd had lunch with her six months earlier on a professional thing, and I said to Barry, "I heard she's getting divorced. Maybe I'll give her a call." And Barry says, "You're not going to call her. I have a friend in New York. Her name is Michele Singer, and she's a photographer. You're going to marry her." And I said, "Does she smoke?" That's really what I said, because Penny [Marshall, his former wife] smoked four packs a day, and I couldn't stand it. And he said, "Yes." I said, "I don't want to meet her." And that was that.

Well, not quite. When *Sally* was about three-quarters of the way through production, Rob was filming an outdoor scene on New York's Upper West Side. During a break, he was standing on the set with Barry when he looked across the street and spotted Barry's girlfriend, Susan (who ultimately became Barry's wife) talking with "a very attractive woman."

"I asked Barry, 'Who is that woman?'" Rob recalled. "Barry said, 'That's Michele Singer.' I said, 'That's Michele Singer?'"

"Uh-oh, *the smoker*," Marlo said.

"Yup," Rob confirmed. "But Barry, Susan, and Michele were heading to lunch, so I wormed my way in, along with Billy Crystal, Carrie Fisher, Nora Ephron, and Bruno Kirby. So we're all sitting at a table in this place called Docks. Michele is next to Nora, and I hear her say, 'Well, I can make better vichyssoise than *this.*' And I'm thinking, *Jesus, what a bitch!* But I'm also really attracted to her. And so we walk back to the set and I chat her up a bit. We make a date to go to Cafe Luxembourg."

By then, Michele had heard from Barry about Rob's earlier veto of her as dating material on account of her smoking. Her comment at the time was short and sweet: "Okay, then fuck it," she had said.

Now they wind up across the table from each other at Cafe Luxembourg.

"The first thing she says," Rob recalled, "is 'Look, if this doesn't work out I don't want it to hurt your friendship with Barry.' And I'm thinking, *We haven't even ordered drinks, and this is already not working out.* I'm also sweating because I'm so nervous. And she's running to the bathroom every fifteen minutes to smoke because she knows I don't like smoking. So it's this crazy back-and-forth the whole night. But we got through it and started seeing each other a bit."

Their subsequent dates were more relaxed, though Michele quickly learned that her new romantic interest wasn't exactly seasoned in the bar scene.

MICHELE: One night after he finished shooting for the day, I said "Let's go to this bar I know on Canal Street." We get there and I realize that this forty-one-year-old guy has never ordered a drink in his life, and he doesn't know what to get. And I'm thinking, *What's going on here?* So he orders a port.

PHIL: A port?

ROB: I ordered a port. I didn't know what to do. I mean, I've been to bars before, but I don't drink.

MARLO: That's hilarious. So when did you know things were getting serious?

ROB: *Harry/Sally* finished shooting and I went back to L.A. I said to her, "So you'll come and visit." She came out around Thanksgiving, and I just knew. It was weird, because we talked on the phone every day and every night, but the minute she walked off the plane, I was madly in love.

PHIL: And you felt the same way, Michele?

MICHELE: Yes—it just clicked. I can't explain it. I'd had terrible relationships before that, and I was already thirty-three years old, so it wasn't looking good for me. But, seriously, I never had any doubts about him. We just fell in love and that was that.

ROB: You know, *Harry and Sally* was originally going to end with them not getting together, because I couldn't figure out how people ever get together with anybody. But once Michele and I started getting closer, I changed the ending so they'd wind up together.

Rob and Michele got married just seven months after they'd begun dating. If the courtship was brisk, the "wedding" was even brisker: a spur-of-the-moment elopement while on vacation in Hawaii.

"Seven months is a pretty short time to know each other," Phil said. "How did you know this was the right next step?"

"I was married for ten years, and I had been single for ten years," Rob explained, "and it just felt right."

"It just felt right," Michele echoed.

"We were standing around in Hawaii and we said, 'Okay, let's do this,'" Rob recalled. "And, of course, then I got a terrible stomachache and I had to drink a lot of Pepto-Bismol. That calmed me down. But then we said, 'Wait, don't we need witnesses or something?' And just as I said that, this elderly woman in a motorized cart rolls up to us and says to me, '*The Princess Bride* was a delight from start to finish!' I said, 'Thanks. Do you want to witness a wedding?' We recruited her on the spot."

Rob and Michele grew up in very different households. Michele's mother had lived through the Holocaust—she was the only one in her family to survive Auschwitz. She married Michele's father shortly after they met. All Michele would allow is that "it was a terrible marriage."

Rob is the son of comedy legend Carl Reiner, who was married to the Bronx-born Estelle Lebost—whom he'd met in the Catskills—for almost sixty-five years. They were an adorable couple. Carl drew on their loving and supportive relationship in creating Rob and Laura Petrie in his landmark TV comedy *The Dick Van Dyke Show*. And, of course, Estelle won the hearts of movie fans everywhere when her son cast her in a tiny role in *When Harry Met Sally* . . . .

The scene is now a classic: While having lunch in a busy deli, Sally attempts to prove to Harry that most women fake orgasms, and she makes her point by faking one of her own—right there in the restaurant. Moaning, panting, thrashing her arms, and slamming her hands onto the table, Sally reaches a perfectly convincing climax, right over her turkey on rye. Cut to Estelle in the next booth, who summons a waitress and gestures to Sally: "I'll have what she's having," she says. Five words and a star was born.

Estelle and Carl remain to Rob the very embodiment of a strong marriage. When Estelle, at the age of sixty-five, wanted to revive her teenage dream of being a singer, Carl's encouragement propelled her onto nightclub and cabaret stages. We remember attending one of those engagements and watching with delight as Carl set up her music stand. You had to love him just for that.

"On my parents' sixtieth anniversary," Rob recalled, "someone asked my mother the secret to her long marriage. She said, 'Find someone who can stand you.' I think that's the key."

PHIL: I remember having [acting couple] Joe Bologna and Renee Taylor on my show once, and a woman in the audience asked, "Renee, how did you know you're with the right person?" And Renee said, "Well, I thought about it and I finally came to the conclusion that I'm not going to do any better than this." I never forgot that moment.

ROB: Right. They seem so different, those two, and yet it worked.

MARLO: They actually wrote a television special for me—just a wonderful show—but, oh my God, they fought so much. They would do these long, wet kisses, and pat each other on the butt, but when they yelled and screamed, it was terrifying. Chuck Grodin—who directed the show—said to me, "What do they do when they go home? Kill each other?" But it worked. They were married for fifty-two years—until the day he died.

Rob and Michele maintain that they don't fight often, but when they do, it gets "loud, very loud," according to Michele.

"Yeah, two loud Jews can go at it pretty good," Rob agreed. "And there's a fast escalation. It goes from zero to sixty very, very quickly."

MARLO: If you have a marriage, a real marriage, you fight. And when you fight, what do you learn from that? Alan Alda told us that in the middle of a fight—when his temper rises—he has to stop and remind himself, "Wait a minute, I actually love this person; I have to cool this down."

ROB: During the fight he does this? I can't do that.

MICHELE: That's pretty admirable. I usually walk out of the room. That's how I cool off. Then I come back in.

ROB: Once I'm set off, that's it—and then I feel horrible afterwards. That misnomer "Love means never having to say you're sorry"? Bullshit. Love is *always* having to say you're sorry—if you are.

PHIL: I'm impressed with how self-aware both of you are.

ROB: Lots and lots of therapy. We've done some together, but ultimately it's up to each of us to work on our issues and neuroses that we bring to the marriage. The only way you can improve things is to work your side of the street. You know what your failings are—work on those and try to make the relationship better by bettering yourself.

Fundamental to a marriage's success is the ability to change something about yourself in order to accommodate your spouse. In Michele's case, that change was profoundly difficult: she quit smoking.

"I'd been a smoker for twenty years," she told us. "It was the hardest thing I've ever done."

"Did Rob give you an ultimatum?" Marlo asked.

"No, no," Michele said, "it was a totally virtuous thing on my part. But I also wanted to get pregnant, so I knew I needed to quit. It was better that I quit, actually, because I was always hiding it from him. When we first met, I'd have to go outside to smoke, and when I'd come back in, I'd brush my teeth and wash my hair and my face. And I couldn't smoke in the car. I hate the freeway anyway, but all of a sudden I'm driving and I'm a nervous wreck and I couldn't smoke in the car because you don't smoke in the car. And nobody smoked in L.A. and I couldn't smoke in the house and I couldn't smoke in the car so there was nowhere to go!"

"Even when we eloped in Hawaii," Michele continued, "I was running out back having a cigarette while he was drinking the Pepto. I had to quit."

While accommodation is a good thing in a marriage, Rob noted, sometimes the best thing you can do for your spouse is give them the freedom to be themselves.

"You get a lot of strength from someone letting you be who you are," Rob said. "You have to accept the person, and if you can, just that fact makes that other person feel better."

"He can sit on the couch all day and not move," Michele explained, "and I have to move constantly and be busy all the time. That's what I like to do. So while he's lumping out on the couch, I'm running around. He never says, 'Come sit with me. Where are you going? What are you doing?' We let each other be."

MARLO: We're like that, too.

PHIL: Well, not entirely. Marlo walks into my study—no matter what time, or how long it's been since she's been there—and she immediately starts fixing things. I mean, putting this here, putting this away, talking all the time about something else. I mean, she really is a control freak that way—total OCD.

MARLO: I call it OCO.

ROB: Obsessive compulsive...

MARLO: Order. Obsessive compulsive *order*. If we're in a hotel room for more than two days, I've already done things to it. I've put nuts in a bowl, I've put flowers in a vase, I've laid out the magazines...

ROB: It's nesting.

MARLO: I mean, if I see a man in a terrycloth robe, I start squeezing orange juice.

PHIL: I put something down on my desk, it's there for four-and-a-half years...

ROB: And you know where it is—

PHIL: —and I know where it is. It's not bothering anybody. But she wants to tidy it up.

ROB: Well, Michele is right. She likes to keep moving, and I live a lot in my head. I can be comfortable just sitting and thinking about stuff.

MICHELE: There's a divot in the couch where he sits.

MARLO: That's so funny. I'm going to have to send you some foam.

ROB: But she's great because sometimes she'll push me to go out, and I'm always happy I did.

Michele recalled the couple's thirtieth anniversary.

"We were heading to New York, and he said, 'I have a great idea. Let's get that room at the Carlyle where we used to stay when we first met. We'll order room service and that will be our anniversary.' We're not usually very romantic, so I liked that idea. But the plane was delayed for three-and-a-half hours, and we didn't get in until around 11:30 at night. We're in the car on the way to the hotel, and I suggest going to this place in Soho that stays open until four in the morning. He's like, 'Forget it, I really don't want to go.' And I'm saying, 'C'mon, it'll be fun.' And this goes on, back and forth in the car, and finally, the driver says, 'You're better off just saying yes, because if you say yes, you'll have a good time. If you say no, it'll take her hours to get over it.' So we went and it was fine."

ROB: I think what the driver said is true: that women hold on to stuff more than men.

MARLO: The hurt, you mean.

MICHELE: Anything.

MARLO: Well, that's because a lot of times men are only half-present.

ROB: That's true. I mean, sometimes it's even just an eighth or a twelfth present.

MICHELE: I was coming home from the Lower East Side once. I texted him to get some coffee and said I'd be home in a couple of minutes. I walked into the apartment and asked, "Did you get the coffee?" He said, "No, I thought we were going together." *They're just not paying attention.* My sister calls it domestic ADD. But I don't get mad about it anymore. We coexist very well together. He lets me be, I let him be, then we get together at three in the morning and start yelling and screaming about stuff. There's a synchronicity about it.

And what is the "stuff" that causes them to yell and scream the most? In a word, politics. The couple's bedroom is just below their daughter's, and according to Michele, on one particular evening, when hollering pundits were filling the airwaves, she had to come downstairs and plead with her parents to pipe down.

"'Can you two please stop screaming?' she said to us. I mean, she can hear it through the vents! But this is what we do. We wake up at three in the morning and start yelling about these things. We get on Twitter and scream, 'Oh my God, have you seen this?!' There are not that many people I can do that with—or vice versa."

"We have exactly the same political take on things," Rob agreed, "but she's more of the driving force than me. She is an irate citizen, basically. She understands that there's too much injustice in the world, and she wants to fix it all."

While the two are clearly on the same page politically, Rob and Michele often find themselves at odds over their approach to disciplining their children. They have three kids—Jake, twenty-eight; Nick, twenty-five; and Romy (named after Rob and Michele), twenty-one—and over the years, Michele has been more apt to "lay down the law" with them, while Rob has been at the other extreme: he's hands-off.

ROB: I'm like the grandfather. I'm the guy who says, "Whatever you want to do is okay with me." That's something I got from my parents. They didn't discipline me either. So my thinking is: you love your kids and you hope they do the right thing.

MARLO: So, you're saying you just don't understand why discipline is needed.

MICHELE: Exactly. And I'll give you the perfect example. When the boys were little, I said to Rob, "We really need to teach them how to make a bed." Our eldest said, "But Daddy, you don't make your bed." And

Rob said, "You know, he's right. That's it—we're not talking about it anymore." And that is the history of this household. Even the kids complain that there aren't enough boundaries and that they weren't disciplined enough.

MARLO: Are your boys slobs?

ROB: No. They're really not.

MARLO: Phil is a bit challenged in this area.

ROB: What—the towel doesn't get picked up off the floor?

PHIL: No, I'm better at that.

ROB: I'm pretty neat, but Michele says to me, "Fold the towel and put it back on the thing." So, I do that. And when I read the newspaper, she'll remind me to put the sections back together so the next person can read it. She teaches me those things.

MICHELE: Rob's parents would come into the house and never say hello, never say goodbye. They were in their own little world. I had to teach Rob how to say hello and goodbye. I had to teach him to tip.

ROB: I tip a lot, but sometimes I forget. So it's true: she basically helped raise me.

MARLO: That's such a nice thing to say.

ROB: She did. They say that girls mature faster than boys, but I think the truth of the matter is that girls are just more mature than boys. And the reason for that, I think, is because they're more in touch with their feelings. Men can never understand what it would be like to have an actual physical human being growing inside you. That means women are going to respect life more. They're going to care about life more than a man.

Like any couple, Rob and Michele have faced their share of challenges, but like everything else they do, they don't shy from the work of tending to the marriage. "We've had some difficult years," Michele explained, "but we talk things through a lot, and I think that's really helpful."

"It's a cliché," Rob added, "that what doesn't kill you makes you stronger. Either a problem is going to drive you apart or it's going to bond you together. It's about staying focused with each other and picking up where the other one drops down.

"One of the doctors I used to go to said it's like two horses pulling a cart," he continued. "The two horses are the mother and father and the children are in the cart. If one of the horses falls down, the cart goes in circles, so you need both. Now, sometimes, one of the horses may not pull so hard, and the other one has to pull harder. So they take turns pulling the load. We do a lot of that."

From a courtship that almost ended before it began, to a real-life montage of work and play, laughter and hollering, politics and Pepto-Bismol, this most engaging pair has somehow become each other's "sure thing."

"I was thirty-four years old," Michele reflected. "I'd never had a good relationship, ever. I didn't have decent role models—not my grandparents, not my parents, no one. Rob had been divorced already and was having a miserable time. It's not like anything was working right. And then . . . it just so happened that we met. There's no explaining it."

Despite the challenges—or "bumps," as Rob calls them—the couple has confronted over three decades, Michele rejects the notion that marriage is hard work.

"What's so hard?" she said. "It's not that hard. The point is, I don't think there are any secrets to a good marriage. I don't think there's any template to go by. We both worked on ourselves, and we met at an opportune moment. And that almost didn't happen. I very easily could have been a struggling photographer right now, living in a studio apartment in New York."

PHIL: And so if you were to pass on one piece of advice to a young person contemplating marriage, what would that be?
ROB: Find a best friend you can have sex with.
MICHELE: Works for me.

Jamie Lee Curtis and Christopher Guest

MARRIED IN 1984

"It has been a challenge to live in a marriage
which is born from people who are very,
very, very, very, very different."

Life is joyful. We're here to manifest our destinies and have some laughs. It's like that old Sheryl Crow line: all I want to do is have a little fun before I die. For me, it comes down to laughter. There's no fight we have ever had, even in my ragiest rage, that he can't drop me to the ground making me laugh."

Jamie Lee Curtis is talking about her husband, Christopher Guest, as she proclaims that humor in marriage is "foundational" for her. We were not surprised that humor came up almost immediately when talking about marriage with Chris and Jamie.

Chris, one of the great comedy minds of his generation, was a writer for *Saturday Night Live* and an ensemble member in Rob Reiner's *This Is Spinal Tap*. He directed, cowrote (with Eugene Levy), and costarred in, among others, the classic faux documentaries *Waiting for Guffman* and *Best in Show*.

Brentwood, California; December 18, 1984

Jamie, an accomplished dramatic actress and horror "scream queen" (in 2018, she resurrected her iconic role as Laurie Strode in *Halloween*), is also deft at comedy. Who can forget how she schooled Kevin Kline's character in all the ways he is stupid in *A Fish Called Wanda* or channeled her inner teenager to shred a guitar like a rock star in *Freaky Friday*?

In one of the couple's bathrooms hangs an original *New Yorker* cartoon, one of many they've collected over the years. It depicts a newly betrothed couple driving away from the church. The woman is still in her bridal gown and the groom is saying, "Do you mind if I put the game on?" The cartoon is called "The First Straw." You can't help but laugh at it.

Chris and Jamie's Spanish-style home, nestled in the Hollywood Hills, was built in the 1920s. Like Jamie herself—whose parents were legendary actors Janet Leigh and Tony Curtis—it has an impressive Hollywood pedigree. Luise Rainer, the first actress to win back-to-back Academy Awards, was a former owner.

We sat down with the couple at their rustic dining table, the lush outside greenery brushing against the windows.

MARLO: We've really been looking forward to talking with you two. Just so you know, if there's a question you don't want to answer, just say so. So, let's start with a basic question: What would you say is the foundation of a good marriage?

CHRIS: I don't answer that question.

MARLO: Okay.

CHRIS: What's the next question?

MARLO: What about the other question?

CHRIS: What happened? Oh, I forgot the question.

Marlo was in her element going around in circles with Chris. As he reminded us, forty years ago he had costarred with her in a made-for-TV movie, of which she was also the producer.

"This one day during the shooting you were having a difficult time," he recalled. "The director said maybe I should tell you a joke. I was just a person playing your brother. We're on the set and I told you a joke. It's a tool for some people. You had other things on your mind, but I remember you laughed and said, 'Yes, that's good.'"

"I'm sure I really appreciated it," Marlo said. "There's nothing better when you're having a bad day than someone making you laugh."

Chris and Jamie are fun to talk to, and the story of how they met would be perfect material for any romantic comedy screenwriter.

JAMIE: I saw his photo in a magazine and said out loud to my girlfriend, "I'm going to marry that guy." I'd never seen his picture before—it was him with Harry Shearer and Michael McKean from *Spinal Tap*, just looking like a regular guy. They were not in character. My girlfriend said, "Oh, that's Chris Guest—I tried to put him in a movie once. He's with your agency." So I called my agency the next day, and when the agent picked up the phone, I said, "I think this guy is cute. I'm single. Here's my number"—but he didn't call me. So I started dating somebody else, a nice guy, but it wasn't a romance for me. Ultimately, I took that person to the airport to send him off, and then I picked up two friends of mine in West Hollywood, and we went to Hugo's restaurant and sat down. Chris was facing me at another table.

CHRIS: I didn't know who she was.

JAMIE: So then he waved at me, and I waved at him. We didn't say anything to each other, and then five minutes later he got up. He stood at his table and waved again, I waved back and he left. We didn't speak. But then he called me. That was June 28.

MARLO: That's so sweet that you know the dates.

CHRIS: July 2 was our first date and we were married in December.

MARLO: Wow.

CHRIS: I knew right away, and I think you knew right away. It was very clear to me. It's hard to say exactly what it was, but I knew. It wasn't even a question.

PHIL: It's a feeling.

CHRIS: It's a feeling that you can't really articulate. We'd both had relationships in our lives, and this was just immediate.

PHIL: So there was a bit of pure lust.

CHRIS: It was definitely passion. It was different—that first realization for me was, *Oh, yes, this is the person.*

JAMIE: We went out July 2, but Chris left on August 8 to go to New York to do *Saturday Night Live* for a year. And I was in Los Angeles making the movie *Perfect.* We got engaged in September. We got married on December 18.

Chris and Jamie have been married for thirty-six years. To listen to their easy banter, one might think their household would be like living in a Noël Coward play. But their short engagement introduced a significant challenge into their relationship and marriage. Unlike their daughter Annie, who recently got married after knowing her fiancé for more than three years, there was no getting-to-know-you phase.

Phil could relate. "Early in Marlo's and my relationship, I told her that I had never dated an actress before," he said. "At that point, I had dated mostly journalists and other professionals. So the one thing that worried me was, How would I know when she was acting, and how would I know when she was telling the truth?"

"I was so touched by that," Marlo recalled. "I was raised among actors, so that concern never came up with the people I dated. But when he said that, I realized it was something he would be dealing with."

"We didn't know each other at all," Jamie said. "We had never spent more than thirty-six hours together at one time before we got married. We once did a weekend around Thanksgiving and my birthday, when we went to an inn in East Hampton and spent three days there, but that was it."

While some might consider it a gamble to make this huge commitment knowing so little about each other, Jamie reasoned that their marriage was instead "an ongoing education in who we are." And who they are, she continued, is "wildly different people—and I would say it has been a challenge to live in a marriage which is born from people who are very, very, very, very, very different."

MARLO: So what's the big difference?

JAMIE: Everything.

CHRIS: We formed a company pretty soon after we got married, and the name of that company is Syzygy—s-y-z-y-g-y. It's a strange word. And it means—

JAMIE: —a pair of opposites.

PHIL: Opposites in what ways?

JAMIE: Chris and I do everything very differently. Chris is very technical. He studies. He plays golf. I wake up in the middle of the night and he's standing there in the shadow, practicing his swing in the dark. I don't practice at all. I just walk out there and slam the ball. It causes friction because I don't do it the way Chris does it, and he doesn't do it the way I do it. So again, the split of who we are doesn't make us good golf partners, but somehow the fundamental connective tissue for me is humor, because there's nobody funnier in the universe than my husband.

PHIL: How else are you different?

CHRIS: She's outgoing, I'm ingoing. I think what happens is: you grow. Socially, I now do more things than I used to. Hopefully I'm doing things differently than I would have then.

JAMIE: I'm doing things differently now, too. I've gotten more ingoing.

CHRIS: I think it starts to move toward a center place.

JAMIE: I'm much happier being by myself than I ever was. But I think a lesson for young people who may read this book is to see how I did subsume myself, very much like I watched my mother do. When she married Bob Brandt, she subsumed herself into Bob's life and gave up a lot of Janet. And without Chris asking me to do so—I was not a feminist—I took his name originally. It was Mr. and Mrs. Christopher Guest. I wanted that traditional role. And what has occurred, I think, in the metamorphosis of our relationship is that I have taken myself into account. And it's challenging when you take something back. As I took on my own being through a lot of work—that we've both done—I had to reclaim Jamie.

MARLO: How did you do that?

JAMIE: An example is when we named our two children. We named them Guest. Even the middle name was Chris's family name, because that was a tradition in Chris's family. Both of our kids are adopted, and I didn't feel I even had the voice to be able to say, "What about my family?" But my family, as you know, is made up of show business people with fake names. Many years later, I did change our children's names legally to include my name. So for me the goal has been to actually find out who I am in the marriage and not lose the marriage.

CHRIS: I think the idea is: in life, apart from a marriage, you want to find out who you are. And in our case, we were doing it at the same time. I kept my name by the way.

MARLO: I'll make note of that. Is there something that you changed about yourself to accommodate the other? For example, at the beginning, Phil and I were in a power struggle. I'm a type-A, he's a type-A. I was used to running the show, as was he. We had to let go.

JAMIE: We're not those people.

PHIL: I went to war very fast with Marlo, early on. I mean real mad. And I don't do that as much anymore.

CHRIS: Well, it's still early in the day.

PHIL: That's true.

MARLO: So how do you fight?

JAMIE: Cold War.

CHRIS: It's mostly...

JAMIE: Quiet.

CHRIS: We've had some fights where we raise our voices, but we're not, you know, screaming people banging on the walls. My dad was English and very reserved. I guess I'm more like him.

MARLO: Cold War is an interesting comment. I've never heard anybody say that.

JAMIE: It's... you withhold.

MARLO: And when you have your cold war, how long can it last?

CHRIS: Tops, five years.

MARLO: "Tops, five years." I love you, Chris.

JAMIE: A few days. You know how you get over it? There's always just a moment when there's a gesture. It's silent, the physical act of touching each other. I swear, it's nothing more than just a silent contact.

PHIL: Like, "I'm good, are you good?"

JAMIE: Yes. And there isn't in that moment the need for, "I'm really sorry I said that" or "I'm really sorry that happened." Within an hour from that moment, the whole thing is over.

CHRIS: And there's an attorney there, just to mediate.

MARLO: I think there's a lesson to be learned from that: that you don't have to have a big brouhaha to come to the end of it. Just one person touching the other one and saying, "Are you okay? I'm okay," is a lovely thing to pass on.

Trust is another bedrock of an enduring marriage, and we wondered if there was ever a moment in which Chris and Jamie first recognized that they'd built that trust.

"I don't think it ever suddenly occurred to me, 'Oh, now I trust her,'" Chris said.

"But there was a moment at around the seven-year mark," Jamie recalled. "There was a woman with whom we were friends who lived in Sun Valley, Idaho, where we lived at the time. I remember I went over to her house one day and I was particularly mad at Chris about God-knows-what. I was bitching a little bit, and she asked how long I had been married. I told her seven years, and she said, 'Oh, you're just starting to get to know each other.' I wanted to punch her in the teeth, but she was absolutely right. By that time we had a daughter, and we were still working on all of the things that every mother and father tries to figure out about how to live their lives. At seven years, we were just starting to say, 'Oh.'"

"It never really stops, hopefully," Chris added. "But I tend to want to do things that are difficult, to try to test myself to get past—whether it's practicing, which I do every day—"

"—practicing?" Phil asked.

"Practicing instruments," Chris said. "I play the mandolin, the guitar, a bunch of instruments. It's something you have to do. In a relationship, people get to a point and say, 'This is just too hard—see you later.' And many times you see people with five marriages, and it's always the same thing: they bail out for the same reasons, and they just keep doing that. And it's because they've never learned anything from the original relationship."

"By the way," Jamie said, "I have thirteen marriages in my family of origin—between Tony, Janet, and my stepmother Barbara. *Thirteen*."

"Wow," said Marlo. "Well, I was never going to get married. In fact, when I guested on Phil's show, he asked me why I hadn't. I said it just wasn't for me. One of the reasons was that my father was one of ten children—nine boys and a girl. Nine Lebanese men who were not so nice to their wives. They weren't physically abusive, but they were very dismissive. My mother, meanwhile, was one of five on the Italian side—four girls and a boy. And all of these marriages were dominated by the men. I didn't want that. I wanted to run my own life. With my first money, I bought a house on Angelo Drive in Beverly Hills. I bought myself china and silver and crystal patterns. I was staking my claim. I didn't need a husband to have any of those things. And that was it—until Phil and I met."

"How old were you at that point?" Jamie asked.

"I was thirty-eight and he was forty," Marlo said. "And all of my girl-friends were married—some were even on their second marriages and had kids from this one and that one. It all looked like a mess, and I wanted no part of it. But somehow something happened—and it happened, as you said, right away."

"But that doesn't mean it's easy and great," Jamie said.

"Relationships evolve continuously," Chris added. "It never stops, and there's no shortcut to doing any kind of work—and there never will be. You need to put in the time. And with a relationship, there's no school for that. Some guy is seventeen and a woman is sixteen, they graduate high school, and they get married. How are they supposed to know anything?"

Jamie maintained that when she and Chris have gone through difficult times, it brought them together rather than pushed them apart. Perhaps the most significant challenge was her battle to overcome an addiction to Vicodin and alcohol, which she previously revealed to *People* magazine. She is now twenty years sober and reflective on how her addiction arrested her evolution of finding her own self.

JAMIE: I hid it very, very well. No one in my family knew.

MARLO: Well, obviously. You're a brilliant actress.

JAMIE: I was a very good drug addict.

MARLO: And you never got fed up, Chris? You never said, "I won't live with this"?

CHRIS: No, it was a gradual thing.

JAMIE: And we're not those people. I'm not proud of that, because I actually think it's healthy when people flip the gasket and say what's really on their mind.

CHRIS: It was not a blatant thing. It was not the cartoon of someone crashing around and falling down. I *gradually* noticed it. And, yes, it did bother me. I didn't know what to do. I had never been around that.

JAMIE: And, again, it was subtle. I'm not going to minimize it because, I'm very proud of being twenty years sober, but I've referred to myself as a very high bottom.

PHIL: How long did it take you to talk about it?

JAMIE: I remember very clearly Chris mentioning a couple of times that he noticed I was drinking more. And, you know, when someone self-medicates, you can't talk about it to them because the wall goes up. I do remember he tried very gently. Chris is a gentle human being.

PHIL: Did it ever get to the point, Chris, that in the back of your mind you thought you might leave?

CHRIS: No.

PHIL: Do you think you could influence her to acknowledge the problem?

CHRIS: No. I've learned through Jamie's meetings with various people who have gone through this that the other person can't influence that. I have friends who do things that are not good for them. They could be smoking cigars, and you say, "I don't know that it's healthy for you to smoke four cigars a day," and they put up the wall. So there's nothing you can do. You don't have the power, and once you realize that, you have to back off. Back then, I didn't know anything about any of this.

JAMIE: And, as I said, I hid it really, really well. I was an opiate addict and no one knew. But my terrible time wasn't terrible. Giving it up was terrible.

Chris and Jamie are loath to offer marriage advice (he: "It would be a little presumptuous"; she: "I don't think we're those people"); but Jamie did allow that if she were in the company of newlyweds, the one thing she would advise them is to tell the truth.

"That's a big thing," Chris agreed. "And that's not being glib—that's a big thing. But no one really has the information. In life you've been brought up without the knowledge of any of this stuff. So you're stumbling into this blind and there is no other reference point about what you're supposed to do. How do you handle the adversity? The challenge of this? How do you do all that?"

"So you have to figure it out yourselves," Marlo said.

"Well, yes, if you're lucky," Chris responded.

"And, by the way," Jamie added, "I want to acknowledge that we were not by ourselves. We actually had a lot of help."

"How do people know how to do any of this?" Chris said. "How do people know about having a child? You can read all the books you want to read, but that's not going to explain to people how to deal with this different presence in their house. You just have to figure it out. I remember when our daughter was at that age that she didn't want to go to bed—the crying stage. In one of these books it said, well, you just let them cry. And I remember the two of us sitting on the floor outside the door of her bedroom—she was one and a half or something—and we were there together, next to each other, and we're hearing these screams and holding this book, thinking, *Are you crazy?* We're supposed to just have this little person screaming, 'Mommy, Mommy'? But it didn't push us apart. It made us realize that we didn't know what the hell was going on."

"Neither did the book," said Marlo.

"Right," Jamie said. "Bob Iger recently called social media one of today's great evils because of the assumptions that are made, based on what people post. The Instagram life. The Instagram parents documenting every moment—"

"—and how perfect it all is," Marlo interjected.

"How can you live up to any of it?" Jamie asked in exasperation.

It was at this moment that Jamie stepped into a territory that no one else we'd spoken with had addressed.

JAMIE: This woman who has helped me figure out a little bit of who I am once said to me, "The secret to marriage is: How much hatred can your marriage actually survive?"

MARLO: Hatred?

JAMIE: Yes. The idea that you wouldn't hate the other person is crazy. I think what happens is that people have an idealized agreement. They go into this thing with all the best intentions; and at some point, I think, they start hating some things—and then they get really terrified and they leave. And what I'm saying is, if our contribution to your book about marriage is the word "hatred," then both of us, I think, will feel really good.

I'm not saying that we have a perfect marriage. We don't. I don't think there is one. But I think what people want to know is that other people struggle, that life is hard. It's the reason that quote from *The Princess Bride* is so profound: "Life is pain, Highness. Anyone who says differently is selling something." And so I think people actually want to know that other people have struggled.

CHRIS: And that they're not alone.

JAMIE: There's another quote I learned from recovery: "If you stay on the bus, the scenery will change." That basically means that feelings come and go—they can change from one day to the next. You may hate your spouse one day, and the next day you don't hate them. But you wake up and it's a new day and a fresh start. The scenery has changed.

CHRIS: The key, ultimately, is to work on stuff. People get married, and at the first sign of some kind of struggle or difficulty, what do they do? A lot of people leave. It's like people ask me, "What's the easiest instrument to learn?" I say, "I have bad news: There's no instrument that's easy to learn."

JAMIE: Nothing's easy.

CHRIS: And relationships evolve continuously. It never stops.

JAMIE: You know the hackneyed question, "What's the secret to staying married?" Don't leave.

Chip and Joanna Gaines

MARRIED IN 2003

"I call him names. He actually likes it.
He'll say, 'Good punch!'"

All Joanna Gaines wanted to do was a quick on-camera wrap-up of that day's episode. The problem was, her husband, Chip—standing, as always, directly to her right—was in a goofy mood. Again.

"The thing about this house..." Joanna began.

Chip interrupted. "How far do you think I can stick this nail up my nose?" he said, before demonstrating with a real three-inch nail that he could, in fact, insert the entire thing up his right nostril.

"Baby, look, it's all the way to my brain," Chip said, as Joanna stepped out of frame, shaking her head and murmuring, "You're a weirdo."

Cut!

But Chip was just beginning, blessed as he is with an unending arsenal of bits, all of them designed to crack his wife up on camera. And he's always successful. As Joanna tried to begin again, Chip pretended to take a call from his mother on his cell, complaining to her that Joanna was being mean to him.

"You're a child," Joanna said wearily. Cut!

Next Chip blew into her ear and asked her if she was distracted, think-

Waco, Texas; May 31, 2003

ing about him in a Speedo. She dropped her head and shook it. "Having Chip is like having a whole set of triplets," she said to the camera. Cut!

Then he rolled up his sleeves and began flexing his triceps. She rolled his sleeves back down maternally, then wrinkled her nose. "Whew, you really need a bath, big boy," she said. Cut!

And on and on it went.

But if being held hostage to the guy's nutty behavior cost the couple a few extra moments on the set every episode, it was worth the price. That's because, over the course of nearly two decades, Chip and Joanna Gaines managed to parlay a small-town home renovation business into a hugely successful TV and retail empire that has made them the darlings of both celebrity and business press.

"Farmhouse Fever Sweeps City Homes!" crowed *The Wall Street Journal*, pointing to the Gaineses as the inspiration behind the real estate phenomenon. *People* magazine has featured the couple on its cover—together or singly—nine times.

We'd been looking forward to our trek out to Waco, Texas, home to Magnolia, the couple's home decor and construction corporation, and the forty-acre farm they share with their five kids and a menagerie of animals (including dogs, cats, horses, cows, goats, pigs, chickens, and the occasional turkey). Marlo even dug up an old pair of cowboy boots for the journey. But at the last minute, Chip and Joanna's breakneck schedule found them in Boston—not exactly tumbleweed country—so Marlo put on her city boots, and we caught the shuttle from New York and met them at their hotel in Beantown.

In person, Joanna—who is German, Korean, and Lebanese—is just as lovely and serene as she is on television. And Chip is 100 percent country boy, with his toothy smile, unruly red-blond hair, and signature baseball cap—as always, worn backwards. It's their differences that make them such fun to watch. Think Sonny and Cher, *countrified*. He's restless, she's centered; he's goofy, she's pragmatic; he's down-home, she's sophisticated. And together they are guileless and completely authentic—qualities that have endeared them to their vast American TV audience.

Their hit show *Fixer Upper* aired from 2014 to 2017, and from the get-go, it was catnip for homeowners across the nation. Part reality show, part makeover contest (think *Queer Eye*, only dustier), its premise was relatively simple: A couple is shown three houses for sale in central Texas, all of which require some measure of repair. After they make their selection, the action bounces over to the Gaineses, who turn the ramshackle dwelling into a stylish dream home. Even for viewers who knew squat about home renovation, it was forty-five minutes of vicarious thrills and dry-wall-to-dry-wall fun.

But the show's real magic generated from the partnership of its costars. She is the design brains behind their operation and has often been credited as being the godmother of "farmhouse chic," an interior design style that relies on such timeless touches as clawfoot bathtubs, wainscoting, and, of course, her beloved shiplap. And he is the resident brawn, a self-described "chubby forty-five-year-old" in a T-shirt and tool belt who loves to tear down the walls in beat-up houses ("Demo day!") and watch his wife turn them into gems.

He's the green light, always coming up with crazy new schemes; she's the yellow light—cautious, thoughtful, patient.

They seem as if they've always been together, but they actually didn't meet until several years after college, in 2001, when they bumped into each other, literally, at the Waco tire shop owned by Joanna's father.

"One day, I was walking out of my dad's store," Joanna recalled, "and Chip was walking in, so we kind of hit each other. He said, 'Hey, you're that girl in the tire commercials.' And I thought to myself, *Oh, no, this is one of* those *guys*."

At the time, Joanna was doing local TV spots for her father's business and was known in town as "the Firestone Girl."

Chip cringed. "It's kind of sad and embarrassing to remember that now," he said. "It was so unoriginal."

While the encounter was not exactly love at first bump, Chip followed Joanna outside and struck up a conversation. "I was super introverted and quiet at the time, like a closed book," Joanna confessed. "But even though he kept asking me all these questions—'Why are you staying in Waco?' 'Tell me your story'—it was the first time I'd ever sat with a guy without questioning his motives. We talked for about an hour, and he was a wonderful listener."

The next day, Chip called the store and asked Joanna out on their first date. She said yes—though a bit warily. "I was twenty-four, grew up with two sisters, and had only really dated one-and-a-half guys," she said. "I'd always thought I would be attracted to someone like my father, who is quiet and stoic and a bit mysterious."

"Your dad is half Lebanese and half German, right?" Marlo asked.

"Yes," Joanna said, "and I thought I would end up with a guy who even looked like him, with dark, strong features. So when Chip and I went on our first date, I thought *Holy cow, this guy can talk! This isn't what I had in mind at all...*"

Chip was not exactly what Joanna's parents had in mind for her, either. "They thought he might be a risky bet because he was outside the box," Joanna said. "He was a bit of a playboy and a charmer. But I told them it wasn't a male-female thing—that Chip genuinely loves people. They said, 'Well, just make sure he's not a sweet-talker.'"

Chip nodded. "I'd always been a salesman," he confessed, "even before studying marketing in college. I was the type of guy who could sell ice cream to Eskimos. And when we started dating, I was twenty-seven or twenty-eight and not a mature person. Back then, marriage and kids and family were not on my radar, even though this was a conservative part of Texas, where some people got married straight out of high school."

"But you clearly hit it off on that first date," Phil said. "Did your heart go pitter-patter, Joanna?"

"Yes, I had the pitter-patter," Joanna said. "I never told him this until later, but on that first date as he was talking, everything kind of went away and I just saw his mouth moving. And I remember having this internal dialogue: 'This is the guy I'm going to marry?' 'Nope, it's not. He's a talker and you always wanted a quiet guy.' 'No, this is the guy!' And I kind of held on to that last one. I'd never had that instinct before."

Joanna recalled a night four or five months into their relationship. "We were playing basketball, and as he was leaving he said, 'I love you, Joanna.' And I said, 'Thank you.' Chip said, 'Thank you? *That's* nice!' And I was like, I am not going to say, 'I love you' back. I'm not just going to give that away. I held everything so tight. I didn't want to get hurt."

Despite his declaration of love, Chip was not beyond playing his own little games, he said, "like trying to not call for a while to shake things up."

"How did that work out?" Phil asked.

"She would never call me!" Chip said. "So then I would call her and say, 'Didn't we have this great date? Why don't you ever call me?' And she'd say, 'If you're waiting for me to call, you're going to wait until the cows come home.'"

Joanna laughed at the memory. "Well, that's because my dad taught me, 'You don't call the boy!'"

It wasn't as if Joanna held all the cards, however, as Chip's family had their own reservations about her.

"My family's history is kind of trailer-park white trash," Chip explained, "like *Deliverance* meets *The Last Picture Show*. We're also super competitive—my sister makes me look like a lapdog—and whenever we'd get together for family outings, Jo wouldn't say anything. My family would say, 'She's beautiful and all, but what about a personality?' And I was like, 'Just you wait. It's there. It just takes her a second to unpack it.'"

That turning point came, Chip recalled, when he and Joanna tagged along on a trip to Mexico with his family.

"We got into this contest on the beach where you had to spin around three times, chug beer, then run a relay race," Chip explained. "By the end, about thirty women had been eliminated and it was just Jo and this other woman, neck-and-neck. Jo scratched and clawed and fought all the way to the end—the poor other woman passed out—and Jo won. It was like a collective moment when the Gaines family looked at her and said, 'She's a keeper.'"

"Because she won?" Phil asked.

"Because she didn't quit," Chip said. "She was a quiet assassin."

By then, Chip was already working in real estate, flipping houses—a profession that didn't really qualify as gainful employment to Joanna's family.

"Her dad would take me on these cute little dates," Chip recalled, "and he would say to me, 'So I was just thinking about you. How's the job hunt going?' And I was like, 'I'm not hunting. I've got a job.'"

About a year after they began dating, Chip decided to pop the question; but, typically, he did it his own way. He duped Joanna into believing they were going to a concert, but instead, he shanghaied her to a jewelry store, where he dropped to a knee and proposed to her, then took her inside to design her ring: a modest round diamond in a platinum setting. Despite Chip's offer in subsequent years to upgrade the ring, Joanna has always demurred. "My ring is part of our story," she said.

Chip and Joanna were married on May 31, 2003, at the historic Earle-Harrison House, a white-columned antebellum estate in Waco. The ceremony was beautiful, but their first year together was not. That's because these two started out not only as husband and wife but also as business partners.

PHIL: When I read that you had a difficult first year, it reminded me of Marlo and me. Our first year was hard, too. We fought a lot.

MARLO: We weren't used to anybody telling us what to do. I had my own show, he had his own show. We'd fight, and then I'd cry.

JOANNA: Oh, that is so me! Our worlds collided. When we were dating, Chip would buy these super-cheap little houses and flip them, then rent them out to college students, so I knew that was his business. But after we married and finally settled into our new house, he came home one day and said, "Hey, I just bought this house and we're going to move." He was so spontaneous, and I was used to having everything scheduled.

MARLO: So he did things without telling you.

JOANNA: Yes. He was twenty-nine and had never heard anyone say, "How about we wait six months?"

PHIL: Is that a fair description, Chip?

CHIP: Well, I was buying these places...

MARLO: They must have been pretty crummy houses...

JOANNA: They were the crummiest...

CHIP: So I was buying the crummiest places and saying, "I can make these worth something," and she was saying, "I don't care what you think you can make them—right now they're terrible!" But I was brought up in an entrepreneurial family. We just *did* stuff. Of course, my decisions *were* affecting her financially...

MARLO: In other words, you don't believe marriage is a democracy.

CHIP: Well, it wasn't a "my way or the highway" kind of thing. If she had come home and told me, "Hey, I decided to buy this product because we can sell it for twice what I paid for it," I would have said, "You're a genius!" I would have been enthralled.

MARLO: But you're the kind of guy who does something and then talks about it later. That would drive me right up the wall.

JOANNA: In fairness, he has gotten better. He had to learn to walk me through something. And it must have been hard for him, because every time he drove me past a property he wanted to buy, I'd say no. I said no to everything.

CHIP: A hundred percent. And at that point, if I had gone ahead and bought the properties, it would have been defiant because I would have been doing what she specifically asked me not to do. So I would try to get her to a maybe, and then I'd say, "Just watch it play out and maybe you'll have more confidence the next time."

PHIL: So the tears came because . . .

JOANNA: Because I loved comfort and predictability, and he was stretching me. I loved *safe*, and everything Chip did was the opposite of that.

MARLO: But it sounds like you came around.

JOANNA: Yes, because as it turns out, I needed someone to pull me out of the box I was planning to stay in for my entire life. That first year, I started seeing the beauty of the unpredictability, and realizing what he was teaching me. It was all about learning to trust Chip. I thought, *Holy cow, we now have one life*. I began to see the rewards of saying yes, and it tasted good. It was fun. And the next time, I would say yes quicker. I realized that Chip had great instincts and I could either hold him back or say, "Hey, I trust you here."

PHIL: And how about today? Can you hold him back now?

JOANNA: Let's just say I know when to fight.

The two started out doing small remodels, which was all new for Joanna (she'd majored in broadcast journalism, even interning for Dan Rather at *48 Hours* in 2000). "I'd never done renovations. I didn't get it," she said.

"I didn't get that new paint plus new flooring equals a house that looks and smells better. I remember these proud moments when the same house that made my family and friends say, 'Why is he investing in *that*?' would suddenly become something they wanted to buy. Chip taught me how to find the beauty in these $30,000 homes and then draw that beauty out."

"It sounds like you were becoming a team," Phil said.

"We were," said Chip. "And what made this such a match made in heaven is that I was used to getting the sale paint from the paint store, knowing that no matter what color it was, it would look better than the dog turd khaki white that was there before. But Jo would say, 'Hey, did you ever think about this color or that color?' I didn't care—it was the same amount of effort for me, no matter what the color—but she started falling in love with the actual aesthetics."

Before long, Chip and Joanna found their groove: They'd buy a house, fix it up, sell it, buy another, flip that, and keep going. It was a precarious, labor-intensive first few years of marriage. "We didn't have a lot of money," Joanna said, "so after every project, we'd say to each other, 'Okay, we have to get this one rented or this one sold...'"

"Every one of them was a life-or-death deal," said Chip.

The pressure began to crank up even more within a year of their wedding, when Joanna became pregnant with their first child, son Drake. "It's one thing to run over a landmine by yourself," Joanna said, "but once you've got a wife or husband on one side and a toddler on the other, things change. We had a lot going on: I also opened up my little retail shop, Magnolia, which I never would have done without Chip."

That came about, Chip said, because "I found this journal of hers where she had written down all these really creative, thoughtful business plans for either a retail store, a bakery, or a spa that she would like to own or operate at some point in her life, and she was like, 'Why are you reading this journal of mine?'"

"I would have said the same thing!" Marlo said.

"Of course," Chip said, "because it was a private thing. But I certainly wasn't being snoopy."

"Well, I think most wives might have thought you were," Marlo said. "So what did your plans say, Joanna?"

"I had drawn out what I wanted, including the building," Joanna said, "but writing it out was as far as I'd gone. The second I realized I would need to borrow money to make this dream happen, I thought, *Well, I don't know how to do that. That's hard.* But when Chip saw the journal, he said, 'Why would you just leave this here? Why not really go for it?'"

"She never would have done it," Chip confirmed. "She just dreamed about things in a hypothetical way. I said, 'Pick one of the three—the retail store, the bakery, or the spa—and let's do it.'"

Thanks to Joanna's great eye—and Chip's encouragement—that first store did very well, but she closed it after two years to focus on the house flipping and her burgeoning interior design business, which included a design blog. There was also a new tenant on the premises: daughter Ella Rose arrived in 2006.

Six years later, everything changed. In 2012, a TV producer who had read Joanna's blog approached her about bringing the couple's real-life business to a reality TV show on the HGTV cable channel, which focused primarily on real estate and home improvement. Chip was sure the pitch was a scam—but Joanna returned the call and found out it was the real deal. Although the two admit they were not initially naturals on camera (they didn't even own a TV), *Fixer Upper* was a hit, and Chip and Joanna headlined it for five straight seasons, eventually capitalizing on its popularity to spin out a line of home goods, shops, a market, a construction business, a quarterly magazine, books, and ultimately a new media company that will include their own TV network. Along the way, they added three new members to TV's favorite fabled family: Duke in 2008, Emmie Kay in 2010, and baby Crew in 2018.

Chatting with this enterprising couple, it was easy to see how their chemistry has made them so well-liked on TV. But those wildly different personalities can often combust. Chip remembered one particular encounter early on in the marriage.

CHIP: We were having some knock-down, drag-out debate, and she slammed this can of white primer down, and it splashed all over her face. Now, I'm looking at her with this primer all over her face—and I'm not talking about a little sprinkle, it was literally dripping off her eyes and cheeks—and I was like, "In my family, this would call for a timeout." But not Mama. Mama barked through the whole thing, wiping herself off as she did so. And it was like a wah-wah moment—I couldn't hear a word she was saying. I was just literally thinking, *Boy, I love this woman. She is so passionate.* Anybody else would say, "Hold on a second, we'll get back to this argument in a minute." Not her. She just kept going.

MARLO: That's so great.

CHIP: Well, we can both go at it. I've got a fiery personality, and early on, I would bark at her. She once said to me, "Just because you're the loudest doesn't make you right." But a year or two into our marriage, I thought, *I don't want to raise my voice like that.* And we both asked ourselves, "Do we want to pull against each other like this, or do we want to be pulling together?" So Jo and I had a subconscious little handshake that said we would never pull against each other no matter what—because life is so hard. We can't be fighting each other and the world simultaneously.

PHIL: That's a healthy approach, but how did you do that?

JOANNA: For my part, I've always told myself, "I don't ever want to change Chip Gaines." Because if my job as a wife was to change him, I would fail miserably. The whole point of marriage is not to change each other—it's to grow together. I always wanted to let Chip be Chip and trust that, as I was growing, he was growing, too, so that we're growing together.

MARLO: How did that trust develop?

CHIP: I just realized that if I jumped into something, she was going to catch me.

PHIL: And did you figure this out instinctively or need to talk it through?

JOANNA: We didn't really talk about it. I think we both realized pretty quickly that we weren't fighting about who was right and who was wrong; it was more about, "Hey, you're not trusting me right now."

And when I learned to trust him, my life turned from black-and-white to color.

MARLO: Did you set any ground rules?

CHIP: We made a pact early on that we would never talk about divorce.

PHIL: That's a good rule.

CHIP: So if neither of us is ever going to leave, then how are we going to figure out a problem that seems impossible? And then you figure out impossible things.

MARLO: Some people have the rule that they never call each other names.

JOANNA: I call him names.

CHIP: But I'm such an idiot that I always find them funny.

JOANNA: He actually likes it. He'll say, "Good punch!"

Most couples would be at each other's throats inside of a week if they had to manage a family and a business under the same roof.

"There's a reason this book is the first and only professional project Phil and I have worked on together in forty years of marriage," Marlo noted. "We weren't sure we were cut out for that kind of double-duty."

Joanna nodded. "Well, working together isn't for everyone," she said. "But for us, what's been so special is that we've been together for every high and every low. We've never known it any other way. It's not all roses, for sure, but overall, working together has been a gift."

"But how do you turn off the business talk when you're on personal time?" Marlo asked.

"It's funny you should ask," Chip said. "About five or six years ago, we challenged each other to go on a date and not talk about business at all. I love our business relationship, but I want a romantic partner, too. And I swear, it was like the most awkward first date ever. We were like, 'So, how's the weather?'"

Being in business together, of course, also means talking money—a lot—and that's a subject that amps up tension for most couples. "Finances are the hardest thing," Joanna said, "especially when you don't have a lot of means, which we didn't at the beginning. Chip never did anything secretly, but sometimes he wanted to do things with our money that I didn't think we should do right then."

Chip cut in. "She'd be thinking about retirement or college funds, and I would say, 'Babe, we've got a lot of problems right now, but college funds are not one of them. We need this money right now. We are going to just scrape by forever if I don't have access to all of the money.'"

"He makes a good point," Phil said.

"Right," said Joanna. "He knew how to grow the money. If it had been up to me, the money would have been hidden underneath my mattress. It wouldn't grow."

"So he essentially told you, 'You have to trust me with all the money,'" Phil said.

"Yes, he did," Joanna replied. "But I love the details, so I'd sit with all of the receipts and divide them up—expenses, assets, whatever. I started realizing that was my gift. And that made him a better businessman."

"She would say, 'You can't take all the money, because we need to pay certain bills,'" Chip explained. "I was comfortable robbing Peter to pay Paul, but she knocked that completely out of me. So if we had $10, she'd say she needed $3 to pay bills and I would take the remaining $7 and try to roll it into $14."

MARLO: And what happened with the college funds?

CHIP: Jo and I want to give our money away. We want our kids to have their college funds, but we're not looking to make them the next Paris Hilton multimillionaires by the time they graduate from high school.

MARLO: So what was the biggest scare you ever had, and how did you deal with it?

JOANNA: I would say when we did this development of about thirty-six homes and then the housing crisis hit in 2008.

CHIP: We had all of our eggs in one basket.

PHIL: Good God. So what happened?

JOANNA: We literally built one house at a time, sold it, and then built another one. Our plan had been to build them all at once.

MARLO: You must have been terrified.

JOANNA: We *were* terrified. We would look at each other on a Friday and say, "Hey, should we just shut our doors?"

PHIL: And go bankrupt. How did you get through it?

JOANNA: We definitely prayed together. I felt like I was on my knees more than I was not at that time. I said, "God, I trust you." I felt like every Friday, God got us through.

CHIP: We would get through a Friday and be like, "Hey, let's go out to a nice dinner."

MARLO: Along with your success and wealth, you're both good looking and probably attract a lot of attention. Do either of you ever get jealous?

CHIP: I don't have a jealous bone in my body. And Jo is just so freaking confident and stubborn that if I ever messed around, she would be like, "Well, good for you. Adios."

JOANNA: I'm a nice person, but I don't give off a "Hey, come talk to me" vibe.

CHIP: Jo gives off the "I am closed for business" vibe, and I give off the "I am open for business" vibe.

JOANNA: At first, I struggled with whether Chip just charmed everyone. But the more I got to know him, the more I realized that his heart is pure gold. I trust him.

CHIP: And I'm the most loyal person in the world. Even if the most beautiful woman on the planet were interested in me, I can't imagine violating Jo's trust like that. I wouldn't trade some temporary hypothetical thing for what I know to be the most valuable thing on the planet. I mean that from the bottom of my heart.

JOANNA: Every woman wonders whether her guy will be faithful, but I realized early in our relationship that Chip stuck with things: He had one dog for eighteen years that was his favorite. He wears a white T-shirt every day. He's worn the same boots since college. He's always worn the same brand of jeans. He drives the same kind of truck. He is loyal to everything in his life.

MARLO: Any guy who wouldn't trade in his truck certainly wouldn't trade in his wife.

We typically ended our conversations by asking our couples what advice they'd give young-marrieds just starting out. To our surprise, it turns out that before they were married, Chip and Joanna actually *sought* the kind of advice we were talking about.

"It was a formal thing called premarital counseling," Chip said, "and it was an actual couple who gave us a kind of personality test."

"And what did you learn?" Phil asked.

"There were some simple, sweet things they suggested," Joanna said, "like going on a date night every week. So when we were first married, we'd get dressed up and go out on Tuesday night, and now, five kids later, we still go out on Tuesday night. Another bit of advice was not to get a TV for the first six months and instead do something that let us focus on each other. Play cards. Play a game. Go on a walk. So we did that, and seventeen years later, we still don't have a TV."

"Those are great ideas," Marlo said. "What about the bigger-picture issues?"

"Support each other," Joanna said, "because when you feel supported by your spouse, anything seems possible. Look at each other as equals who both have something very valuable to bring to the table."

"What has Chip brought to you?" Marlo asked.

"Well, the thing I carry with me the most is that Chip sees beauty in everything. When we were just dating, I would notice how he'd talk to the banker and the homeless guy the same way—he saw the value in both of them as human beings. He digs deeper and finds the gold. And so what he's taught me is that behind everything there's beauty, and now that's one of my greatest passions in life: to find that beauty in everything."

While Chip was often the comic relief on *Fixer Upper*, he took this moment to swap laughs for honesty—but, as always, with that Chip Gaines spin.

"I'd advise someone to pursue the person they love like a hornet," he said. "It's easy to say you're always going to love somebody when you're dating them, but after five or ten years, you're tired. You're older. Jo and I don't look the same way we once did in our bathing suits. Whatever. But I know that if I woke up tomorrow, I'd still pursue her the way I did when I was hoping she'd go on that second date with me. I'm not saying she'd never cheat on me, but it's not going to be because I never told her I loved her or because I didn't send her flowers or I forgot our anniversary.

"I viewed marriage as forever even before I knew whether Jo and I would make it for five minutes," Chip concluded. "Joanna talks about my dog and my jeans and my truck, and it's true—I don't take those things lightly. If I tell her we're in it for life, she can take that to the bank."

George Stephanopoulos and Ali Wentworth

MARRIED IN 2001

*"If you're married and not having sex,
something is wrong. Red flag!"*

Anyone who doesn't believe that opposites attract should meet Ali Wentworth and George Stephanopoulos.

Here is George: discreet, prudent, thoughtful, almost statesmanlike—exactly what you'd expect of someone who was salutatorian of his Columbia University class, a Rhodes Scholar, and a White House advisor to President Bill Clinton before becoming chief anchor at ABC News. This is a man who spends his days interviewing presidents, generals, and former FBI directors.

And here is Ali: actress, comedian, author, producer, and the yin to his yang. Unguarded and hilarious, she is the woman who pops open her blouse to a studio audience—and a shocked host Jimmy Kimmel—wearing only star-shaped pasties (and looked great, by the way); who not only admits to having plastic surgery but video-blogs every unflattering step; and who has confessed that one of their daughters has walked in on her and George *in flagrante delicto.*

But together, they're perfect. He's the Abbott to her Costello, the Rowan to her Martin, the Desi to her Lucy: she wisecracks, and he looks at her with a knowing, proud smile. It's clear that George is in—*way* in—on her jokes. She makes him more playful; he is, she says with no pun intended, her "anchor."

They met in 2001, got engaged two months later, and married five months after that. Even then, friends were scratching their heads over this odd coupling. "People in the back row of our wedding were making bets about how long we'd last," Ali told us, "but I always say, 'It's like a good melon—you just know if it's right.'" And to this day, she says, "When he walks in the door after work, I'm just as attracted to him as I was the week we met. I go, 'Look at that sexy man!' I really do."

The feeling is mutual: George said that Ali "brings all of life into the house—everything."

They live near New York's Madison Avenue where things are buzzing. The home they've made for themselves, their two daughters (sixteen-year-old Elliott and fourteen-year-old Harper), and their hound dog, Cooper, is stylish, homey, and warm.

When we arrived at their apartment, we were first greeted by the woman of the house. There's something about Ali—just seeing her made us smile. She has a certain fairyland feel about her—all spontaneous, like a kid—and best of all, she's not guarded. What's she got to be guarded about? Life doesn't seem to be that scary to Ali. She takes it all on with an Earth Mother sensibility.

George arrived a moment later. Watching him do the news on TV, we never would have fixed them up. But seeing them side by side, you get it. They are closely attuned to each other. They're also very sexy.

Which was easily our first topic of conversation. Any interview with this pair *has* to start with a discussion about sex because, well, Ali is an expert on the subject. (Google her, and see what pops to the top: "Ali Wentworth is proud of her hot sex life," "Ali Wentworth loses friends over sex life with George," "Ali Wentworth would give up her phone before giving up sex.") Yes, Ali sees her sizzling home life as a high priority, and yet . . .

New York, New York; November 20, 2001

ALI: I talk too much about sex.

MARLO: But that's what makes it fun to interview you.

PHIL: It's not naughty!

ALI: Especially when you're married.

MARLO: Let's talk about that. In your books, like *How to Make It Last*, you often discuss sex and marriage. What is your best advice for married couples?

ALI: It's simple: have it. And have it on a regular basis. I've learned in talking to a great many women that if you're married and not having sex, something is wrong. Red flag! The next thing you know, a few years have gone by and someone is cheating or asking for a divorce. I may have four-hour talks with my girlfriends, but the one thing I have with my husband—and only with my husband—is a physical relationship. I tell my friends, "If you have the stomach flu, I get it, but otherwise, you have to make a point of having sex." We're all tired. We all have lives and careers. So push it.

GEORGE: Ali makes fun of me because I'm skeptical whenever I hear about married couples not having sex. I sort of don't understand the point…

ALI: Well, there are a *lot* of sexless marriages. I don't want to name names, but more than you think, George.

GEORGE: Maybe.

MARLO: And then do these couples split?

ALI: Yes. They break up, or they have affairs. It's amazing how many couples tolerate no sex—and how long they tolerate it.

PHIL: George, guys don't really talk about not having sex, do they?

GEORGE: Not really. No.

ALI: But women talk about everything! We not only say, "Are you having it or not having it?," we talk about menopause and vaginal lubricants. Right now among my girlfriends, the hot topic is coconut oil, coconut oil, coconut oil. And I don't think sex should be hidden from the kids, either. On weekends, George and I will say to the girls, "Okay, we're going to go take a nap," and in unison they'll say, *"Ewwww! Gross!"* But I want my daughters to see that after eighteen years of marriage, we still like to fool around on a Saturday afternoon. It's healthy.

Sex is just one of the crucial ingredients in a marriage, Ali and George told us. Another is trust.

GEORGE: I don't think we've ever had a big trust issue. Maybe little, tiny things, but never something big, like worrying about an affair.

ALI: If someone came up to me and said, "Your husband is cheating on you," I would actually laugh. Absolutely not! No way! It's just not in his nature.

MARLO: I feel the same way about Phil. One of his producers once told me that when a woman comes on to Phil, he doesn't even realize it.

ALI: George realizes it; he just shuts it down. I'm an actress, so if someone flirts with me, I think, "Great!" I get upset when construction workers don't whistle. I remember one time this rock star was flirting with me, and when I told George, he wasn't upset, like, "Who? Which guy?" He just laughed.

PHIL: So, George, what do *you* do when someone comes on to you?

GEORGE: There is no part of me that invites it. And, despite what Ali said about flirting, it's hard for me—impossible, really—to imagine either one of us having an affair. I don't want to tempt fate here, but...

ALI: Yeah, don't appeal to my rebellious nature.

PHIL: In our case, Marlo bought me a wedding band. It's six feet wide and—

ALI: —it's actually a choke collar...

PHIL: —and if a woman gets too close to me, there's a *beep, beep, beep.*

MARLO: Yes, and when he was on the air, I loved that he would hold the microphone in his left hand with this huge gold ring showing. Hello!

For George and Ali, trust was there from the beginning—even if the match didn't seem exactly written in the stars. "When we met, I had just had a torrid love affair with a British actor, and I was ready to get serious," Ali recalled. "A friend said, 'Let me introduce you to my old friend George Stephanopoulos,' and I said, 'No, no, no. Thank you very much, but I'm from Washington, D.C., and I grew up around journalists and politicians—that's the last thing I want.' I was aiming for Matthew Perry or Hugh Grant. But a few weeks later, I was coming to New York from L.A. and decided to call him. I figured that if nothing else, it would make a great dinner party story: 'My Date with George Stephanopoulos.' He was not my type, and I wasn't his."

The two decided to meet at Barneys for lunch (a compromise—she'd suggested coffee, he'd suggested dinner). "I figured that if it was a complete disaster," Ali told us, "I could at least pick up some Kiehl's body scrub in the store." She didn't bother dressing for seduction—she wore a black suit and put her hair up ("I don't think I even showered")—but the two ended up talking for hours. Something was definitely happening. "When I left lunch that day, I knew I was attracted to him," Ali said. "I couldn't believe it."

Having already booked a trip that weekend to Canyon Ranch with her mom and sisters, Ali spent the entire time at the spa talking on the phone with George. "My mother or sister would come into my room and say, 'We have yoga,' and I'd say, 'Go.' I talked to him the whole time. I didn't lose one pound."

GEORGE: It was as close to immediate as can possibly be.

ALI: And you had dated the island of Manhattan, too.

MARLO: Is that true, George?

GEORGE: I'd dated a fair amount. But now I was forty, and I knew this was someone I could be with forever and be happy. It's partly faith, partly intuition, partly attraction—but it's nothing I've ever questioned from the very first. It was never even close to not happening.

MARLO: That's so interesting. Everybody always says, "When you know, you know." So did we. We knew, and that was it.

ALI: It was the same for us. When I met him, I felt like I'd met somebody from my tribe. I just understood him. With every other man I'd dated, I was so concerned with performing—you know how in the movies, the girl will get up in the morning and put on her face and do her hair and get back into bed and pretend she's asleep? I did versions of that with everybody, but I didn't feel I had to do that with George. I wasn't going, "Does my breath smell?" or "Oh, my God, my cellulite." I wasn't pretending to be in this relationship.

PHIL: You weren't auditioning.

ALI: No. I had gotten the part.

GEORGE: We got married quickly, and after that, the babies came fast.

PHIL: Did that affect your sex life?

GEORGE: No. We still wanted it.

ALI: We were newlyweds in every sense of the word—although I do recall that a few weeks into the first pregnancy, I felt like I was no longer the sexy wife. I had hyperemesis, so I threw up a lot. I remember George coming home from work one day in his business suit, and I was on all fours, naked, throwing up on the living room rug. Even the dog was disgusted with me.

MARLO: Oh, my God.

ALI: And I remember thinking, *Well, here is your new life—vomiting everywhere.*

PHIL: What were your thoughts, George?

GEORGE: I just felt bad for her. The thing is, when you get married and have kids, you can't be afraid of it disrupting your life. By definition, it's going to. You need to be open to the changes that being married and having kids are going to bring you every single day. You have to let the chaos in.

Let's make that *happy* chaos. In this household, the family—all four of them—make a point of eating dinner together every night, starting off by holding hands and talking about what they are grateful for that day. "There's a lot of hard stuff that happens in life, and you have to celebrate the good stuff," said Ali. "If George's contract gets renewed, let's celebrate it! We don't have to be obnoxious about it, but let me make a cake and have the kids stick some M&Ms on it and say, 'Good for you!' And on our anniversary, I don't want a diamond necklace; I want the two of us to write letters to each other: 'Hey, it's year eighteen! Look at us! I still love you!' Those moments are not to be tossed aside; they are to be savored."

"We savor, too," Marlo said. "We have this code word we made up years ago called 'PHM.' We look at each other at certain moments and say—"

"—a Perfectly Happy Moment," Phil filled in.

"Ali is great at celebrating moments," said George. "But I also think we're not in dreamland. Every single day there are these little hills that we have to figure out how to navigate—our kids have a setback or we have a fight—but if you accept that and still say, 'Boy, this is worth fighting for, working through, and enjoying,' then it's even better in a way."

ALI: There are times when we'll get overly upset about work, but then we go, "Wait a minute, wait a minute. We have a great marriage, great kids, we're all healthy." And if he's upset, say, over a job thing—I can always tell because this vein on the side of his head gets really big—I know to quiet it down at home. I'll tell the kids, "Put all your bitchiness in a box and go be nice to Daddy."

PHIL: Is that how you were raised?

ALI: No. My parents divorced when I was one, then remarried and started new families, and I was sort of tossed in between. They both worked—he was at *The Washington Post*, and my mother was in the Reagan White House—so you bet I put on tap shoes and said, "Look at me! Look at me!" But because of that, I make a point of being very present with my kids and my marriage. My mother and her second husband slept in separate bedrooms toward the end and had completely different lives. I thought, *That is not going to be my marriage or the way I am with my kids.* I try never to miss a lacrosse game.

GEORGE: When you have kids when you're older, you're ready to make that investment. When I come home for dinner at six, I know that is exactly where I want to be—I'd rather be talking to my family than anyone else.

They are a lucky couple—and they know it. But even "meant to be" couples have to make compromises. We asked them what they had done over the years to accommodate each other.

"Despite my job, I am definitely an introvert," George said, "and being out socially completely drains me. But she gets energy from being around people."

"You and I should have gotten married, Ali," Marlo said.

"I know," said Ali. "We would have been the life of the party."

"But we learned how to accommodate, respect, and change with each other," George continued. "It has opened up a different side of myself, and I think Ali has gotten more in touch with her introverted side. Our kids have a mix of both."

However, those adjustments took some time, Ali revealed. "When we were first married, we'd argue because we'd go to a party, and George would want to leave, and I'd go, 'Hold on a second—I'm just saying good-bye,' then twenty minutes would go by. And then another twenty minutes. I would talk and talk and talk, and George would be sweating by the front door with the 'got to go's.' Now, not only do I completely understand that, but I even know when he looks at me a certain way that we're out that door—no discussion. I don't even say goodbye.

"As it turns out," Ali added, "it's actually the right time for me to leave, too, so it has benefited both of us. And sometimes we go solo; we don't need to be joined at the hip."

GEORGE: That's true. If I don't want to go to something with Ali, it's not a reflection on her.

ALI: We don't need to perform out in the world as a couple.

MARLO: I get it. Phil doesn't want to go to every fundraiser for St. Jude Children's Research Hospital—I do, like, a zillion a year—but at first I'd say, "You have to come." After a while I thought, *Why does he have to? Really, it's my commitment.*

PHIL: When I married Marlo, I married a hospital. During our wedding reception, Danny, my new father-in-law—who founded St. Jude—stood up and said, "I haven't lost a daughter; I've gained a fundraiser."

MARLO: And he did.

That reminded us of another issue we had in common with Ali and George: when both halves of a couple are celebrities, things can get tricky. How do they deal with that?

"I'm very honest about my life," Ali said, "and when we met, I was used to turning everything into comedy. So years ago, the *New York Post* did a story that said George and I were getting a divorce, and a *Washington Post* reporter somehow got my cell phone number and called to ask me about it. I'd never before had to worry over publicity about my personal life, so I told the reporter, 'You tell me how many people who have sex twice a day are getting divorced.' I thought it was a great way to combat gossip by saying something truthful but funny. But this story had legs! It was repeated everywhere, and George was upset with me. He's a lot more private, and he said, 'Don't talk about our sex life.' I told him that I was my own person and could do whatever I wanted, and back then I could be a mean fighter."

GEORGE: That's true. But we figured out how to navigate that, as well. One thing we've learned about fights is how important it is to take time to cool down. And even though Ali might be a louder fighter—even today—I'm a little more persistent. I want to make sure the conversation is done and truly resolved.

PHIL: So you know how to come back from a fight. That's a big thing.

GEORGE: To come back, you actually have to go through it. You have to finish it. You have to communicate everything you need to communicate. That's the only way. You can't just push it down.

ALI: Early on, we'd have a fight and go to bed and lie there in silence, pretending to be asleep but waiting for the other person to say something. Eventually, we'd start talking again. We had fights that we didn't resolve until the sun came up.

GEORGE: Needless to say, it wasn't good for the guy I was interviewing in the morning.

ALI: Now we nip 'em in the bud. Because we've heard from couples who've split up that, over time, the little battles became a war in which they spent days not speaking to each other, and pretty soon that became the norm.

GEORGE: I cannot imagine that.

PHIL: I can't either.

ALI: Can I also add that we always end our fights by having sex?

PHIL: Well, that's perfect.

GEORGE: It's essential.

ALI: It's essential.

MARLO: It does make the problem go away. You kind of ask yourselves, "What was that all about, anyway?"

This was something that all four of us agreed on: that the petty skirmishes that happen in any marriage—over whose turn it is to walk the dog or whether the toilet seat should be up or down—fade away if there is a real sense of commitment. "A friend recently got married and asked for advice," Ali said. "Besides telling him to have lots of sex, I said, 'Go into your marriage with the belief that it is forever.' Too many people go into marriage and think, 'I'll try it . . .' "

"And that those vows have a kind of escape clause," George interjected, "and it just doesn't work. You have to believe in it and think, 'This is it.' On the other hand, if you have any hesitation in your gut before you get married, listen to it."

PHIL: If you're Catholic like me, divorce is not an option. It never occurred to me during my first marriage that I would get a divorce.

GEORGE: You were young when you got married the first time?

PHIL: I had just graduated from Notre Dame.

MARLO: And I had gone to Marymount. When we started going together and we were having a wonderful time, he said to me, "Do you think the fact that we were raised Catholic has made this even hotter?" And I said, "I sure do." But I also remember asking Phil, "What would have happened if we'd met when you were married?" And he said, "Well, with all due respect, nothing. Nothing would have taken me away from my wife and kids." And I thought, *I can love this man. He is not bullshitting me.*

ALI: It meant he wouldn't cheat on you, either.

MARLO: I knew he wouldn't, even though I had grown up in Hollywood, where people weren't so trustworthy and were pretty cavalier about marriage. All my father's friends were having affairs and breaking up—or threatening to.

ALI: I feel fortunate that way. When I married George, I got an anchor, someone who is my moral compass. There is nobody else I go to for advice. I question myself a lot; he doesn't question himself. He has more integrity than anybody I've ever met. And for me that's incredibly grounding because I can do the fun and the funny and bring color into the house, but he's the gravity, which is important.

MARLO: How do you think you've changed since getting married?

ALI: I think I'm a richer, fuller person for marrying him. I'm definitely better for marrying him.

GEORGE: I am, too.

ALI: I'm *more* better. You just have a better sense of humor.

Judges Judy and Jerry Sheindlin

MARRIED FROM 1978 TO 1990; REMARRIED IN 1991

"Don't marry someone thinking you're going to
change them. Don't try to teach a pig to sing.
It doesn't work, and it just annoys the pig."

Well, let's just say it's not what we expected.

Who is sassier, tougher, and more down to earth than Judge Judy? Nobody. So when we drove up to the home she shares with her husband of forty-one years in coastal Connecticut, we had to double-check the address. This was a palace!

First came the enormous iron gate at the foot of the long gravel driveway. Next, the towering pillars, with big marble flower urns on top. And once we were buzzed onto the grounds, we rolled up to an enormous—and beautiful—stone mansion. Think Royal Family, American style.

Judges Judy and Jerry greeted us at the door. "Who designed this knockout?" asked Phil. "It's Custom by Judy," Jerry said with a laugh, adding that they'd built the house eight years ago, tearing down a one-hundred-year-old home to clear the way.

We both love houses, so Judy and Jerry graciously gave us a quick tour. The couple's adorable Shih Tzu, Scout, happily trailed us, her hair so long

249

that she dust-mopped the floor with every step. Room after room, the place was magnificent—homey and bright and beautifully decorated. Framed pictures of their large and blended family hung everywhere. We also couldn't help but notice that the home includes three separate dining rooms: one of them seats thirty, for larger events; a second serves eight comfortably; and the third one—which the Sheindlins affectionately call "the nook"—is smaller and more intimate, offering a lovely view of the garden. So if you ate three meals a day at Casa Sheindlin for two straight weeks, you could effectively sit in a different chair in any of the dining rooms for every meal, and that would still leave a handful of the chairs untouched!

We briskly finished our tour, peeking into the couple's bedroom (Judy's closet would make Cher fall over with envy) and their old-style screening room, a glamorous red velvet theater dominated by two seven-foot statues of Dan Aykroyd and John Belushi as the Blues Brothers, which Jerry and Judy picked up at a warehouse sale in Stamford.

And here's the kicker about this marvelous homestead: the Sheindlins live in it only six weeks a year. The rest of the time they're at their residences in either Florida or Los Angeles, the latter where the missus tapes *Judge Judy*, her iconic courtroom reality show, which is now in its twenty-fourth season.

We chose the nook for our sit-down, and as we were setting up our equipment, Judy glided in, carrying a tray of sumptuous goodies—cheeses, sausage, crackers, and fruit. "Prepared by my own non-cooking hands," she announced in that unmistakable voice.

"This is quite the spread you have," commented Marlo. "You must do a lot of entertaining."

"We do. See that patio out there?" she said, gesturing to an expansive terrace near the pool. "The last party we did was for one of the grandchildren's fifteenth or sixteenth birthday, so we turned the whole thing into an eighteen-hole miniature golf course."

First wedding (*top*): New York, New York; June 14, 1978.
Second wedding (*bottom*): New York, New York; September 8, 1991.

"We've also done three weddings," Jerry chimed in.

"Excuse me," Judy swiftly corrected. "We did three weddings, but only two have lasted so far. So that's just two and a half."

"Well, the first thing I have to do is to congratulate you, Judy," Phil began. "I know a little bit about daytime TV, and you've dominated your time slot for years. You may be the most successful living person on television right now."

"It's an interesting achievement," Judy pointed out, "because I didn't start until I was fifty-two years old. It took courage on the part of a TV producer to say, 'I see something in her, and maybe others will see it, too,' because I had absolutely no experience."

"You certainly knew the law," Phil said. "You were legitimately credentialed."

"I was legitimately credentialed," nodded Judy, "but I don't think that's what made it successful."

"So what was the secret?" Marlo asked.

"Oh, I just love talking about me," Judy said with a laugh. "I think that Americans between the coasts have a certain frustration with the judicial system. It takes so long, and there's never a satisfying result. Too many judges, especially in civil cases, don't make a judgment. They want everyone to be a little happy but a little unhappy, too. But you're supposed to make judgments. I understood that's my job. I'm a judge. You know if you won or lost when you leave my courtroom."

That seemed the perfect spot to begin our cross-examination.

MARLO: Winning and losing is a big part of marriage, as is negotiating. I was talking to Phil in the car, and I wondered, how do two judges not become too judgmental with each other? Also, when you're having a disagreement, how do you go about pleading your case to each other?

JERRY: I am terrific at pleading my case. However, I'm constantly being overruled. I have learned my place.

PHIL: I know you're joking, but I have a feeling there's some truth behind that.

JERRY: As a couple, we tend to do the right thing. As soon as one of us gets to the point where someone says, "You know, you're right," then we're together. But if we can't get to that point, we argue and argue until someone finally gives up. And that someone is usually me.

JUDY: That's true because you're usually wrong. The fact is, we're different. I'm a very linear thinker. Things, to me, are logical. If something doesn't make sense to me, it's not going to end up well. And for Jerry... how can I phrase this in a way that's not going to end up in an argument?

MARLO: Give it a try.

JUDY: Jerry is a linear thinker, too, but at the end of his thought process is what will satisfy him, not necessarily what's correct. So I'm the one who always has to say, "Jerry, this might make you happy, but it's not the right thing to do."

PHIL: So what happens then?

JUDY: Sometimes we get to an agreement, and sometimes we have a blowout—and then he says, "You win. I give up."

MARLO: Oh, come on, Judy, are you ever wrong?

JUDY: Rarely.

JERRY: I believe she was wrong once when she was twelve years old.

JUDY: Am I ever wrong? I'm sure I am—but not with him. Women are nurturers, at least that's been my experience. My mother was that way. She took care of everything—the house, my father, the children, her friends. And it wasn't until she died—and she died very young, at fifty-seven—that we realized that my father, this wonderful giant of a man, didn't even know how to cash a check at a bank. She made my father look like a giant. He always had the right gift to give because she bought it. She would hand him the card to sign. She made everything work.

PHIL: So you've taken on the same role with Jerry?

JUDY: Yes. We have a big family, so there's always lots of maneuvering. And when the children grow up and get married, their mates become part of the negotiation. And then they have children, and they get older, too, so there's a lot of juggling to do. Take Father's Day. Someone has to coordinate where the family should go while taking into consideration that some people like one thing and other people like something else. I don't know if Phil is very good at this, but Jerry is not. Would that be a fair statement?

JERRY: I think so.

It was interesting to hear Judy mention blowouts, as we could actually picture her facing off with Jerry, given her pull-no-punches persona on television. Phil chased that down.

"Tell us about a typical blowup," he said. "How long does one last? And which one of you is more likely to be the peacemaker?"

"That has fluctuated over the years," Judy answered. "I would say that for the first fifteen years I was the peacemaker. Jerry was a difficult person for a while."

Jerry nodded. "I was unreasonable," he admitted. "I wouldn't listen to what she was saying. I would insist that I was correct. But as the years went on, I began to accept that she simply has better ideas than me. So now it's not really necessary to argue about some things. Remember, we've been married for some forty-odd years, and at this age, some things aren't all that important to fight about. Luckily, Judy has a terrific sense of humor and the capacity to make me laugh. That helps a lot."

Judy and Jerry had both been married before—Judy to a doctor for a dozen years; Jerry for roughly the same amount of time to a financial planner—and those marriages produced a total of five children. The two of them married in 1978, but twelve years later their marriage reached a critical crossroads. According to Judy, her husband had become "a project," and that project was failing.

MARLO: What do you mean by "project"?

JUDY: Let me back up. Jerry had a relatively short-term first marriage, which produced three terrific kids. And I think he had a lot of guilt with regard to leaving his wife and children—this was before he met me. And, I don't know, that was a lot of a baggage to bring to our relationship. A lot of baggage. So let me put it to you honestly. You want honesty in this chapter, correct?

MARLO: I'd like it.

JERRY: I'm not so sure I do.

JUDY: I am a girl who always needs a project—whether it's building a house, decorating a home, cleaning a bathroom. I am a project girl. And with Jerry, I knew I was getting a project that was going to be... not easy. After twelve years, the highs of our marriage had been very high, and the lows had been low—but it was never boring. So for those first years I was really trying to make up for everything he'd been through.

MARLO: And that's how he became your project?

JUDY: Yes. I just knew that there was lots of turmoil that he probably couldn't pinpoint in his brain, but he knew it was not making him feel content. And I felt it was my job to make it all better. But then my father died. And my father was my champion.

MARLO: Yep, I had one of those.

JUDY: Right—I know you did. And when you lose that, you have every right to say, "All right—somebody has to take care of me."

PHIL: And that's what you told him?

JUDY: Yes. I said, "I've been taking care of you for twelve years, now it's your turn to take care of me." And he was totally unaccustomed to that role. I wasn't asking for anything unreasonable, and he wasn't being unreasonable saying that he really didn't know how to do that. He was fifty-five and had lived a certain way all his life. He couldn't even conceptualize taking over that role. He just couldn't.

MARLO: So you said to him...

JERRY: "I'm changing the rules."

JUDY: "I'm changing the rules." It wasn't an argument. I didn't say, "You do it my way." I just said, "I'm changing the rules."

JERRY: What she said was, "Unless you change, we can't stay together." I said, "Tell me what you want me to do. You can't just say 'take care of me.'" What does that mean? Do you want me to carry you from place to place? Do you want me to buy you things? Do you want me to feed you? Do you want me to keep you warm? What you have to do is tell me—use your words and tell me what you want me to do to take care of you." She said, "Just take care of me." And I said, "I don't know how to do that."

PHIL: And so . . .

JERRY: And so she said to me, "If you can't maneuver this, I'm going to divorce you." And I said, "Oh, yeah? I dare you." And the next day I got divorce papers. The next day. So, that was the end of that.

Because they were both judges in the same courthouse—Jerry a state supreme court judge, Judy a family court judge—the wheels turned fast. "The papers were all signed expeditiously because we were two judges getting a divorce," Jerry explained. "The judge signed them immediately."

After thirteen years of marriage, Judy and Jerry were no longer husband and wife.

"He didn't think I would do it," recalled Judy.

"I never thought she would do it," Jerry said, shaking his head. "Divorce is serious business."

Although, by profession, judges are supposed to exhibit a cool restraint, the sudden split sent both of them reeling.

"We were angry," said Judy. "And I think Jerry was the angrier of the two of us, because I was breaking up the family. And our family unit had become extremely important to the children. They cared for each other."

"We had five children," Jerry added, "three from my first marriage, two from her first marriage, and they all got along tremendously well. It was a true family."

Jerry moved into Manhattan with his kids, and Judy stayed in the family home. But circumstance threw them together often. There were the kids' birthdays to celebrate—and, of course, the rather odd kismet of working in the same building.

"Even so," Jerry said, "I missed her presence the very first week that we were separated. It was the first time in years that we didn't get to see each other every single day. It was such a strange experience."

Judy felt the same way. "When you have feelings for a person that you can't quantify or even describe—even if you're not talking to each other because you're pissed off—it's still nice to know they're in the other room. Do you know what I mean?"

Working in the same court system as his ex-wife, Jerry had the luxury of knowing where and when to reach her. So one morning about a year after their divorce, he picked up the phone and called Judy. When she answered, he cut right to the chase.

"I said, 'What are you doing tonight? Do you want to have dinner?'" Jerry recalled. "Much to my surprise, she said yes. So we had dinner, and then gradually grew closer during the year. I missed her terribly, and I couldn't stand the fact that somebody had already fixed her up with another guy. That drove me crazy. I would call her up and demand, 'Did he kiss you?' She said no. And then she told me about the date."

That story, as Jerry recounted it, is classic Judge Judy. She'd been asked on a date by a gentleman who was somewhat portly, and he took her to a restaurant. When the waiter approached their table, the date said, "I'll have the roast beef and the potatoes, and also some French fries and a big glass of Cabernet." As the waiter wrote down the order, Judy held up her hand. "That's what he *wants* to eat," she said emphatically. "But what he's *going* to have is"—and then she placed a much healthier order for him.

"She never heard from the guy again," Jerry recounted with a satisfied laugh. "That was it!"

"Well, he was overweight," Judy explained, "and he ordered this monster dinner!"

Jerry beamed. "I was so pleased hearing her tell me that story because, at that moment, I knew she eventually had to come back to me."

MARLO: Is that true, Judy? Did you miss him too?

JUDY: I missed him. I missed him.

MARLO: And so you got remarried, which is really interesting to me. You'd been through a very rough patch, and now you'd reconciled. Why not just start seeing each other? Why did you have to get married again?

JUDY: I like being married. I actually had to drag him to the altar the first time. He had no intention of getting married. He had no intention of divorcing his wife, even though they had been separated for three or four years. After we were together for about a year, I said, "I want to see your divorce in the newspaper or don't bother calling again."

JERRY: And I said to her, "What do we need a paper from the government for? Let's just live together." She said, "Okay, you go and ask my father if we can live together." I said, "I'm not going to do that." So she whipped out a calendar and said, "Pick a date. Now."

PHIL: So how did you two decide to retie the knot?

JERRY: Interestingly enough, I picked her up from work at family court one day, and we were walking through downtown Manhattan. Suddenly I said to her, "This is silly. I'm uncomfortable being with you all the time and not being married to you. Let's get married again." She said, "Well, how are we going to do that?" I said, "The clerk's office is right up the street. We can go in and get a license…"

JUDY: And they'll waive the twenty-four hours.

JERRY: Which is what they did. As soon as they saw us, they accommodated us. We're both judges. We got the license immediately.

MARLO: And you were emotionally ready for this, Judy? After all, you'd been so determined when you'd ended the marriage.

JUDY: During the year we weren't together, I did a little growing myself. I realized certain things were important, and I decided I wasn't going to eliminate them.

PHIL: So who did the ceremony?

JERRY: My ex–law partner, Herbie, was a supreme court judge. I called him up and said, "Are you busy?" He said, "No." I said, "Well, we're coming up to get married again." Then I called my oldest son, who had a law practice in Lower Manhattan. He was my best man. And Judy called her girlfriend of forty years to be her maid of honor.

PHIL: This is fantastic—like a romantic comedy.

JERRY: So we go up to Herbie's chambers, and he performs the following ceremony. To me he says, "Do you take this woman to be your lawfully wedded wife forever—in good times and bad, in sickness and in health?" I said, "Yes." He looks at Judy and says, "Do you take this man to be your husband?" She says, "Yes." He says, "In good times or bad?" And she looks right at him and says, "In good times or forget it."

MARLO: You said that? You are so funny!

JUDY: It's true. And then Herbie says, "Oh, this is a real tearjerker."

And just like that, the divorcees were newly married. But things had changed between the couple. For one thing, Judy came to grips with the reason Jerry had been difficult the first time around and why she had so easily adapted to the caretaker role.

"I came from a mother and father who liked each other," Judy explained. "My father adored me so I had a good feeling about myself. Jerry didn't have that kind of upbringing. His parents were more dysfunctional than mine. He was a middle child, not very well behaved, and his mother didn't know how to deal with that."

Then Jerry sat forward. "My mother and father were born in Europe," he began, "where parents believed in corporal punishment. They would beat the children. So when they came to this country, they thought the way to bring up children was to abuse them, to hurt them, to hit them. They didn't understand what that does to a child. And it's hard to get over that, because here are two people who supposedly love you, and yet they apparently get pleasure out of hitting you, hurting you, bruising you, making you cry. It's something that stays with you for a long time."

"Did this abuse spill over into other parts of your life?" Phil asked.

"Yes," Jerry said. "My disciplinary record in high school was so bad I couldn't get into a college. So I went into the navy, which straightened out my thinking process and made me want to make something of myself. Finally, when I got out of the service—I was nineteen years old—I applied to colleges again, and one school said, 'Well, you're a veteran, so we'll admit you, but only on the condition that you maintain a C average and stay out of trouble.'"

"You are exhibit A of an abused child," Phil observed. "You acted out in school what was happening at home. How did you feel about your parents after you grew up?"

"I didn't like them," said Jerry quietly. "They were not nice people, and it's hard to like someone who's not a nice person, even if they are your parent. So this is baggage that you carry with you. I don't even like to talk about my upbringing. My kids say, 'You know, Dad, you never talk about your parents.' I just shrug and say, 'I don't remember much about them.'"

"How did this affect the way you raised your kids?" asked Phil.

"I never laid a hand on any of them," said Jerry. "It took a negative point of view to give me a positive sense of how to bring up children. The five children between us were never abused. I rarely even raised my voice to them."

"Was Jerry a changed man when he came back, Judy?" Marlo asked.

"He didn't change," Judy said, "but he did learn to use a calendar better. He learned to write down: 'October 21, Judy's birthday. Buy present, card.'"

"Wasn't he more inclined to take care of you, given your ultimatum?" Phil asked.

"No, he wasn't," said Judy, as if it were the most obvious thing in the world. "But I think we both had a realization that we were better as a couple than we were separately. I did date during the year we were divorced, and I realized that most men are alike—only mine had hair. I know that sounds flip, but it's really not. I think women enter a relationship thinking that they can modify or change whatever behavior is annoying to them, but that's not going to happen. I used to sweat the small stuff. I had to give that up."

"But certainly some compromise was necessary," said Marlo.

"Every relationship is different," Judy said, "but there is a common thread of unhappiness, and that unhappiness comes from trying to make another person different from who they are. You can try, but they're always going to resent it. I tried to accommodate Jerry and learn how to ski because his first wife was a skier. I bought myself ski clothes and went to the top of the mountain. And you know what? I hate the cold. I just despise cold weather. So it didn't work out. I don't think you should marry anyone with the expectation of changing who they are."

MARLO: So what do you think is the foundation of a long-lasting marriage?

JERRY: A deep love for your mate. A devotion. If it's anything less than that—if it gets to be shallow—it's at great risk of being destroyed. That's why 50 percent of marriages fail. It's this deep love that is missing.

JUDY: I believe that men's brains and women's brains are different. Women will accommodate men from the beginning, and after they get married they say, "All right, you start accommodating me. You start changing." I remember when one of our kids was getting married, she complained to me that her fiancé cleaned the bathroom with a sponge, then tried to clean the kitchen with the same sponge. She told me, "I don't know if I can deal with this." And I said, "Sweetheart, this is as good as it gets. The truth is, you're not going to be able to modify that behavior, and if you're not prepared to live with that, then don't do it. Otherwise, buy a dozen sponges." And they're still married, almost twenty-five years.

PHIL: And do you feel the same way, Jerry?

JERRY: Yes. And the truth of the matter is: no matter how you slice it— no matter how many sponges you buy—it's all irrelevant unless there's a special feeling when you speak to her, when you hug her and tell her you can't do without her. If you love your mate, it all works out. The little irritations fall into place. But you can't replace the hug, the kiss, the making love. And in my case, she has a tremendous ability to make me laugh.

As one would expect, Judy wanted to get the last word in.

"Here's what's important," she said. "Accept that men and women are different, and don't marry someone thinking you're going to change them. I did that. Like they say, don't try to teach a pig to sing. It doesn't work, and it just annoys the pig."

"And so if a young couple was in front of your bench," Marlo said, "and you had to give them your personal verdict about whether or not they should marry, what would you tell them?"

"I'd tell them they had to have that intangible feeling of looking across the room and saying, 'I've got to have me one of those,'" Judy said. "My father once told me that the first time he saw my mother was at a dance at the Jewish center when she was just eighteen. She was so pretty. My father was with his best friend, and he looked at him and said, 'You see that pretty girl over there? I'm going to knock that halo off of her head.' And he did. But he loved her from the first minute he looked at her. He saw her and he said, 'I've got to have it.'

"That's how I felt when I saw Jerry. I said, 'I have to have that forever.'"

Lily Tomlin and Jane Wagner

MARRIED IN 2013

Lily: We didn't really care about getting married.

Jane: Don't say that. It doesn't fit the book.

F or some, it's the eyes; for others, it's the smile. For Lily Tomlin, it was the outfit.

"She came into the party and she was wearing a little navy blue suede suit," Lily remembered.

"Don't describe that," interrupted Lily's life partner, Jane Wagner. "I was designing clothes back then because I thought I was never going to make it any other way. And I had a flair for designing, and what she describes is so awful—"

"—it had hot pants and those stretchy boots they used to make that came up to the knee," Lily interrupted back. "And instead of a purse, she wore a little backpack."

"Well, no wonder you were smitten," Marlo said.

"So when she was leaving," Lily said, "I put a little note in the backpack with my phone number on it, and I said, 'Call me.'"

We were sitting with Lily and Jane in their suite at the Regency Hotel in Manhattan. They were in the city to attend a retrospective of their work together at Lincoln Center, so we swung by to meet with them.

"You are so perfect for our book," we'd told them on the phone earlier that week. "You've been together forever, you work together, you play together, and you love each other."

And they do. Lily and Jane have been romantic and creative partners for more than forty years. Both are exquisitely talented, but only one has gotten most of the glory.

"It just makes me furious," Lily told us—and who can blame her? After all, the parade of endearing characters and brilliant oddballs Lily's given voice to over the decades were largely authored by Jane.

Part of the problem is that they met when Lily was already famous, a breakout star on *Rowan & Martin's Laugh-In*. At the time, the fast-paced sketch comedy show (1967–1973) was a forerunner of *Saturday Night Live* and a cultural phenomenon. Lily joined the cast at the end of 1969, creating indelible characters like Edith Ann, a five-year-old philosopher who sat in an oversized chair and dead-panned hilarious commentary; and Ernestine, a snorting, nosy telephone operator who coined the catchphrase "one ringy-dingy."

Jane's debut as a critically acclaimed writer also happened in 1969. *J.T.*, her compassionate teleplay about a boy and a stray cat in Harlem, won her a Peabody Award.

"Although *J.T.* was a big success, I had no idea what I was going to do afterwards," Jane told us. "And at that point I had only dated—who was the newscaster?"

"Chet Huntley," Lily supplied, with mock chagrin. "But that was hardly the 'only one' of anything you had dated. And I don't know why you want to tell that part, anyway."

"Well, because meeting you certainly changed my life around," Jane countered.

Back then, Jane was living in New York and Lily was holed up in a Malibu beach shack, but they had similar southern backgrounds. Jane was

Los Angeles, California; December 31, 2013

from a small town in Tennessee and Lily from Detroit, although her parents were Kentuckians and she spent many a vacation there.

In 1971, Lily traveled to New York to promote a comedy album she'd made of Ernestine's monologues (it went on to win a Grammy), and a mutual friend brought Jane by Lily's hotel to introduce them to each other.

"Was it love at first sight?" Phil asked.

"Well, I'm not sure Jane fell for me as hard and as fast as I fell for her," Lily said, "but when I saw her, I was gobsmacked. I had heard about her for years from friends—how beautiful she was, how brilliant, how talented. I was getting ready to leave for a meeting that afternoon, so I knew I had to get her attention. Before I left, I took her in my arms and kissed her full on the lips. It was so impulsive, but I believe it got both of our attentions."

This friend turned out to be quite the matchmaker.

"It was Betty Beaird," Jane said. "She's always mad that we don't give her credit."

"We'll give her credit now," Marlo said.

"My record label was giving me a party," Lily explained, "and I said to Betty, 'Tell Jane to come to the party tonight,' and she did."

It was at that shindig that Lily caught that first glimpse of Jane's little boots-and-backpack ensemble and slipped her her number.

"All evening, we exchanged a lot of steamy looks across a crowded room," Lily recalled, "and then I had to go to Chicago. I had a phobia of flying in those days—so many of my friends had OD'd and I just got plagued by the thought of death—so, I took a train to Chicago the next morning."

Jane sighed. "They died of drug overdoses, not flying."

"But I had a day to settle in Chicago and I wanted to spend it with Jane," Lily continued, "so I actually flew back to New York. When I landed, I phoned her, 'I don't have much time, I have to see you.' So much for my phobia."

When it came time for Lily to return to Chicago, Jane insisted on accompanying her back to the airport as a form of therapy, to watch planes take off, one after the other.

"Don't you see how narcissistic it is for you to think your plane is going to go down?" Jane challenged her. "It did help you, didn't it?"

These days, people continue to be more familiar with Lily's work than Jane's, including her binge-worthy Netflix series *Grace and Frankie*, costarring Jane Fonda, and movies like *Grandma* and *I Heart Huckabees*. And of course there are all those wonderful earlier films—*9 to 5*, *All of Me*, and *The Incredible Shrinking Woman* (which Jane wrote), all of which have become cinematic chestnuts.

But even if the writer on a project was someone else, Lily has often relied on Jane for that special touch. "Jane always wrote lines for me that

I would try to get in to my movies," Lily explained. "They would always sharpen a scene."

Arguably, the couple's most memorable collaboration goes back to 1985 and the blockbusting one-woman Broadway show *The Search for Signs of Intelligent Life in the Universe*. Written by Jane, it is a rumination on American society as told through a series of mind-bending monologues. Lily's deft embodiment of the play's thirteen characters—from a bag lady to a teenage punk rock chick to a philandering, bodybuilding dude—cemented Lily's rep as a captivating solo artist and earned her a Tony for Best Performance by a Leading Actress in a Play.

Many of our favorite lines from Jane's script continue to live on in our minds (and online) for their originality and absurd hilarity.

I worry if peanut oil comes from peanuts, and olive oil comes from olives, where does baby oil come from?

All my life I've wanted to be somebody.
But I see now I should have been more specific.

No matter how cynical you become, it's never enough to keep up.

Although the scale of fame tips in favor of Lily, it became apparent during our conversation that there is not a whiff of rivalry between them. Their rapport is fun, funny, and infectious, and they seemed to be held together by a cosmic kind of glue. We quickly grasped that talking to the two of them was going to be freewheeling and footloose. And never boring. All we had to do was hold on for the ride.

Both women were in their thirties when they met. Lily was out as gay among her friends, but the press tiptoed around the subject. For her part, Lily never denied being gay publicly, but she didn't directly address it either. Back then, there was her burgeoning career to consider, as well as protecting the feelings of her mother, a fundamentalist Christian.

Jane had a circle of gay friends but felt somewhat adrift. "I kind of fell in with that group, but I was very anxious at first because after a while

I realized that I was in deep. I was staying at the Y—$10 a night plus breakfast—where everything seemed so southern and so religious. I had these new friends now, but I didn't want them to find that I was living at the Y. That was a little embarrassing to me."

After that brief trip to New York—and her return trip from Chicago—Lily was a woman on a mission. Soon, she persuaded Jane to come out to Los Angeles for an extended stay to help her with a comedy album devoted to Edith Ann.

LILY: Oh, I absolutely pursued her. I was madly in love with her. It was only after knowing her that I happened to see *J.T.*—the first thing she ever wrote—because they played it every year on CBS at holiday time. Originally, Jane had planned to be a song writer. She is so gifted—she plays piano by ear—and I so adored her writing and convinced her she could write anything. And she did.

JANE: But *J.T.* wasn't funny at all, so I never understood why you thought—

LILY: —I wasn't looking for comedy. I was always looking for the material to be a wondrous thing, like an epiphany, something washing over you. At first, she sent me a bunch of pages for Edith Ann with annotations and scribblings in the margins and cross-outs, but I had no trouble reading it, and I have been doing it ever since.

PHIL: Was writing comedy material easy for you, Jane?

JANE: I didn't know I could be funny. Well, I was mildly witty at dinner parties, but I didn't know I was going to write that way. She brought it out in me.

LILY: I'm not sure that's correct. Everything Jane writes is based on the truth, so you couldn't help but feel uproarious laughter; or it would be filled with so much resonance and humanity that you would chuckle in recognition, if nothing else.

JANE: We had a great time. That's where we bonded, over Edith Ann.

MARLO: And Jane, did you have a crush on her right away too, or no?

LILY: Not so much.

JANE: I think I did. But I was a little cooler about it.

LILY: She had an old apartment on Washington Square that was rent-controlled, and the outside front door was always unlocked. I would be frantic back in L.A., worrying about her going home late at night. Pretty soon we became a couple in my mind, and I was just worried sick about her because she didn't care a thing about locking that door or looking over her shoulder if somebody ran up behind her on the street. She had to walk up two flights to get to her apartment, and I would be so worried until I could get her on the phone. I had her come to L.A. to put me out of my misery.

PHIL: Sounds like you two knew this was it.

LILY: Yeah.

JANE: I stayed even though that shack in Malibu was pretty horrible. That was all I was questioning about her.

LILY: Jane is exaggerating about the house—although, it did roll out into the ocean shortly after I gave it up.

Lily eventually bought a house in Los Angeles, and she and Jane officially moved in together, along with their menagerie of cats, dogs, and later, a goat. Not everybody in Hollywood was accepting of their relationship. In the early to mid-1970s, Lily starred in TV specials written by Jane—who was tapped as head writer of a staff—and they drove to the studio together.

"A couple people—one was a writer—said to us, 'Why can't you come in different cars?'" Lily explained. "The writer was a friend, but we knew she was just trying to protect us from any blowback we'd get for being gay. There was no social media in those days, but it could feel like it if you were gay. Needless to say, we did not change our driving habits or our living style. I have forgotten half of this, but I do remember that some friends would say to me, 'People are talking.'"

Still, the couple dismissed the gossipy commentary and attended events together as dates. In 1975, *Time* magazine offered Lily the cover if she would officially come out.

"I was conflicted over the decision," Lily recalled. "I realized that *Time* was making me that offer not for my work but simply for being gay, and that jarred me. Jane and I both wanted to be recognized as artists, and I was more than a little scared of the possible career fall-out—and, maybe more so, how it might affect my mother."

"I get that," Marlo said. "This was about twenty years before Ellen DeGeneres appeared on *Time*'s cover, declaring that she was gay—and even then, that stirred up controversy for her."

"That's right," Jane said, "but looking back, I regret our decision. I'd be proud of it now the way I imagine Ellen DeGeneres must feel proud—and rightfully so. If Lily and I had been the first, we would have been proud of ourselves, too."

"I also remember when you were on *The View*, Lily," Marlo said, "and Barbara Walters said to you something like, 'So Lil, you never married. Is it that you just never found the right guy?' And you said, 'Barbara, you and I both know that's not the reason'—and Barbara just got quiet. That was so brave of you."

"It wasn't so brave," Lily replied. "But I couldn't lie. Jane and I were not secretive. We just weren't ready to hold a press conference about our lives together. From our behavior—and the content of many projects we did— our hardcore fans knew that we were gay. I just walked a tightrope those first few years, because I felt I had to, which was so stupid. I wish I'd been more of an activist."

Lily's career continued to soar. For her first movie, Robert Altman's *Nashville*, she was nominated for an Oscar for Best Supporting Actress. Then in 1977, Jane compiled and wrote new material for Lily's first one-woman Broadway show, *Appearing Nitely*, which Jane also co-produced and directed.

Lily's mother came to the show and stood in the aisle after it was over, Lily remembered. She shook everyone's hand as they exited, thanking them for coming to Lily's show, as if she'd invited them personally.

Telling this story again jogged a memory for Lily about her mom.

"I once said to her, 'Mother, you're so witty, you're so engaging, you're such a good storyteller—people just so love you.'" Lily recalled. "And my mother said, 'Well, to be honest, sometimes I think it up ahead of time.' Isn't that great?"

"I just love that," Marlo said. "My mother was like that, too. I remember once she was about to have a pretty serious operation. I was in her hospital room beforehand, combing her hair and meditating with her and doing everything I could to keep her calm and get her ready. Suddenly, she said, 'Do you think this is funny?' Then she tells me this joke about a woman who goes to her doctor and says, 'Doctor, all day long I'm having these silent little farts. In fact, as I'm talking to you now, I've had two or three silent little farts. What do you think?' And the doctor says, 'I think you need to get your hearing examined.' Well, I laughed really hard at the joke, and my mom said, 'Oh, good. I want to tell it when I get in there.' She actually wanted to go in the operating room and entertain them—you know, like, warm up the room."

Lily was born Mary Jean but took her mother's name—Lillie—and re-spelled it as her professional name. Her mom died in 2005, eight years before Lily and Jane married in a backyard New Year's Eve ceremony at a friend's house in Los Angeles. But Lillie knew that her daughter and Jane were in a deep relationship. "My mom really loved Jane," Lily said.

"Lily, you wrote a story about your childhood for my memoir about comedy," Marlo said, "and I love your stories from when you were a little girl. Tell us a memory you have of your mom from that time."

"Well, I swear we were the only family in Detroit who never had a car," Lily said. "So my mother would have to walk three really long blocks to the supermarket, then we would jump on the streetcar for the ride back, because my mom's arms would be heavy with huge bags of groceries. I was about seven and my brother, Richard, was about four, and we were no help at all, so we would follow Mom as she headed toward the back of the streetcar. My brother sucked his thumb in those days, and as we passed a seated woman, she said, 'You're too big a boy to suck your thumb!' My brother pulled his thumb out long enough to say, 'Oh, you shut up!' And I began to read her out, 'You're not his mother. Mind your own business!'

We heard ding, ding, ding. We looked up to see our mom getting off...
a stop early."

"That's so funny," Marlo said. "What about you, Jane?"

"I was the first child born in my mom's generation," Jane said, "and when the time came for my mother to go to the hospital, all the sisters and brothers were piling into the cars and peeling out—and my mom was left standing on the porch. When I was born, my head was pointed, and everyone said that I was such an ugly baby I shouldn't be shown to my mother until she was well enough. I had a wet nurse, Emma Coleman—part Cherokee part African American—who molded my head back to a more normal shape. But there's still a trace of a point, which only Lily knows about."

PHIL: What made you two decide to get married?

LILY: There was always a fellow on the red carpet who would ask us, "When are you going to get married?"

JANE: That wasn't the reason we got married. At least I hope not.

LILY: No, but it was an impetus. I mean, we didn't really care about getting married. We don't like to say that because so many gay people think it's important to get married.

JANE: Then don't say it. That doesn't fit the book.

PHIL: Try not to argue. It makes me nervous.

LILY: It wasn't that I didn't want to. It's just that we'd been together, like, forty-two or forty-three years, and I also had a distinct rejection of the concept of marriage. I think gay people can come up with something better than marriage, because it doesn't always work out so great for heterosexuals.

JANE: That's it. Squareness.

LILY: I say there's no excuse for a square gay person.

MARLO: You guys are a hoot.

LILY: No, don't print that. I was just being—

JANE: —no, leave it in. [*To Lily*] She's going to do exactly what she wants to do, anyway.

LILY: The truth is, we don't like dismissing marriage. So many gay people have struggled, and marriage is extremely important to attaining equality.

JANE: And what is more important than family? I mean, you've got to have an institution that protects the family, and marriage does that, maybe badly, but still for the most part good.

PHIL: Did you both consciously decide not to have children?

LILY: We flirted with the idea of having kids. The family from which Jane is descended were all quite intelligent; and Jeffrey, Jane's nephew, was incredibly good looking. So in our romanticism, we were going to approach Jeffrey to harvest his sperm and donate it to us for a baster baby. Luckily, Jeffrey turned up married and became the father of a brilliant little boy before our plan could be realized.

JANE: Jeff knew nothing about our plans—so, Jeff, if you're reading this, sorry for the shock and awe. But, it's nothing compared to the shock and awe our whole southern family would have felt if our plans had panned out.

MARLO: Speaking of kids, what would Edith Ann say—in her own words—about the two of you and your marriage?

JANE: Let her tell you herself:

EDITH ANN: Jane and Lily are so much fun to live with. We go to bed really late and then we get up really late. And, by then, hey, I've missed school. Again! Jane lets a kid do whatever I want, and Lily tries to make me eat healthy food and stuff, like, that I hate. Lily won't let me have coffee ice cream at bedtime, because she says it keeps me up all night. But Jane and I don't see what's wrong with being up all night. They keep a Christmas tree in the dining room the whole year. Sometimes, at night, we lie on big pillows and look up at the tree with beautiful lights. They cover me with tinsel and a star on my forehead on Christmas Eve. Mostly we have fun, and I learn so much stuff from them, you'd think I'd get better grades.

In addition to her talent and versatility, Lily has a reputation for being a fighter, primarily against bureaucratic authority. Throughout her career, she has resisted producers, directors, and censors telling her what to do, what to cut, or where she had to throw in a laugh track.

We'd read about Lily's temper on film sets, especially during the making of *I Heart Huckabees* when she reportedly went toe-to-toe with her director, David O. Russell. Lily said she adored him and simply had a meltdown—"as did he"—as she sometimes does with Jane.

"I'm the one with the temper," Lily confessed. "Jane becomes recessive. Usually, I'm the one who apologizes. It's not hard because I love her and can't bear for her to feel lonely for even five minutes. Sometimes, I withhold the apology when I feel especially misjudged—but I'm not able to hold out for very long, no matter how wrong she is."

"It's best to just let her have the meltdown," Jane said.

Lily nodded. "I just get stressed out and crazy," she said, "and then when I try to make up, she makes me feel guilty."

"I think anger management would be a good idea for people," Jane countered. "She's never done it."

We asked them what they typically fight about and inadvertently reopened an old battle.

JANE: Okay, so I like to read magazines, and I can hardly read one magazine without getting more tear sheets and research—

LILY: What she's saying is that she's accumulative and inquisitive—which means, she collects stuff and then thinks about it. Now, I'm not a tidy person, but I'm sort of neat. I'll keep the main part of my life cleared of as much clutter as I can, which is not doing a lot.

JANE: There. You said it. "Clutter"—the operative word.

MARLO: So, you're the clutterer.

JANE: Well, I wasn't going to use that word. I didn't use it. I think that's a pejorative word.

LILY: But she is a voracious reader—books and magazines—and she watches two television shows at the same time.

MARLO: And so . . .

LILY: I just tolerate it. I can live with it.

MARLO: So you've learned to tolerate someone who's messier than you are, without complaining.

JANE: I don't like the word "clutterer" and I don't like the word "messy." Brilliant articles is not clutter.

MARLO: But to Lily it looks like clutter, and she's learned to tolerate it.

JANE: Tolerate. Tolerate.

LILY: But I'm also trying to learn. I've tried to...

JANE: Who brought this subject up?

LILY: I've tried to express this to her in ways that would help her have access to it more. Because the stuff piles up so hugely.

JANE: Oh no, now it's getting really bad.

MARLO: Honestly, what word do you want me to say instead of "clutter"?

JANE: There's no better word, I guess. I wish we hadn't brought up the subject. There are so many other things in the world we could talk about. The climate crisis, for instance.

MARLO: Okay, we'll drop the subject. It's not worth getting divorced over.

JANE: Well, I've never thought she was going to divorce me over anything like that, so obviously the clutter wasn't that *clutterous*.

Despite the tension of the great clutter debate, it incited a moment of reflection from both women on the art of marital harmony. "You can't impose what you want on the other person," Lily noted. "In terms of, say, neatness, you can't expect the other person to be like you or to reflect your chosen behavior."

Jane agreed. "All those millions of things you do behaviorally that seem so negative—it's much more positive if you could just catch yourself and not do them. If those behaviorisms are negative, it's not worth doing them just to irritate her. There's got to be more wisdom in relationships. They don't have to be so reactive."

"And if a young couple was here with us right now," Phil asked, "what wisdom would you give them on this topic?"

"When you're critical," Jane said, "soft pedal that criticism—because who knows when you're right. Patience!"

"That's fantastic," Phil said. "What else?"

"Remember," Jane continued, "when you're angry at your partner and say something hurtful, you will be more angry at yourself later for having said hurtful things to the person you love. You'll feel angry twice. Not good for your blood pressure, and certainly not good for your relationship."

The flip slide to their arguing, Jane was quick to note, is when she and Lily are truly there for each other.

JANE: There was a time when I had a really bad review for something I'd written, and she stuck by me in such a wonderful way.

MARLO: Wow. So you've learned to bring each other back. The important thing is not so much what happens in your careers, it's how you get through a bad thing. People need ways of coping.

JANE: I can only answer in my case. When you stood by me and you were there for me when the bad reviews happened, I thought maybe I would never write again. Maybe I would be too fragile. And I don't have the resources. Lily always seemed much stronger to me. She was much more dynamic. I was more introverted and shy.

PHIL: Well, watching you, I'm tempted to conclude—

JANE: —that I'm dumb and she's dumber.

PHIL: That you're two alpha females. Do you agree?

JANE: I've always thought she was the alpha.

LILY: No. I'm just more demonstrative, but she's the alpha. I may be an alpha career-wise or something.

JANE: Diva, actually. I never thought of myself as an alpha, but maybe I had to be to live with her. I think our sense of humor is the thing that saves us, basically.

LILY: Our sensibilities are what drew us together, really. She was somebody who expressed what I felt so deeply that we just understood each other that way.

MARLO: Oh my, what a thing to say—Jane expresses what you feel. That's huge. No wonder you love each other.

LILY: In literature. Words. But I didn't know that when I first met her.

MARLO: But to be that in tune that you can express what she feels. Wow. That makes me cry, it's so strong. I don't think Phil and I express what the other one feels. That's a beautiful thing, very unique.

LILY: Jane is very much an empath. She's so much more sensitive to other people. I'm more chatty. I see somebody more as a character. I see mannerisms. When you leave here, she'll tell me all about you.

MARLO: I can't wait. I'm going to leave your microphone on.

JANE: By the way, are you going to have chapter titles for this book?

MARLO: Of course, why?

JANE: You should call ours "Dumb and Dumber."

MARLO: I promise you it won't be called that. If anything, it would be called "Alpha and Alpha."

JANE: I also think the book should have a theme song. Use Al Green's "Let's Stay Together." That's one of our favorite songs, and it's beautiful.

PHIL: Remind us how it goes.

LILY: " 'Cause you make me feel so brand new..."

JANE: "And I want to spend my life with you."

PHIL: Perfect.

Bryan Cranston and Robin Dearden

MARRIED IN 1989

"If the red light on your car says 'Engine Trouble,'
would you open the hood and start tinkering?
Of course not. So what makes you think that you
can fix your marriage if that warning light is on?"

B ryan Cranston met his future bride Robin Dearden while holding her at gunpoint. But that was just their day job. When we first met the couple, things were decidedly less tense.

We were at a mutual friend's Super Bowl party, and Bryan was on "voice rest," tending to a sore throat. His hit Broadway show, *Network*, was dark that evening, and Bryan was giving his vocal chords the night off. He was portraying unhinged news anchor Howard Beale, and he needed the extra day to recover from the challenges of raving like a madman for hours at a time.

Meaning, he wasn't speaking. At all. To anybody.

So instead of hearing that familiar, mellifluous voice in person—the one that made Walter White such a complex and damaged human in the revolutionary television show *Breaking Bad*, the one that made us laugh out loud as the hapless dad Hal in the Fox TV comedy *Malcolm in the*

Los Angeles, California; July 8, 1989

Middle—he communicated in pantomime and by writing short messages on a notepad.

Bryan and Robin agreed to tell us their marriage story, and by then his voice had recovered. We met them at their New York City apartment in the late afternoon, giving us all enough time to talk before he was due at the theater for that night's performance.

So wouldn't you know that our Uber took us to the wrong address? Panicked, we checked our phones, discovered our error, and shouted the proper address to the driver. "Can you get us there right away?" we begged. "We're already late for an appointment."

"Sorry," he shot back over his shoulder. "You have to get out and reorder a new ride. That's the way Uber works."

We hurriedly climbed out of the car and tried to hail a taxi. It was rush hour. In Manhattan. Good luck.

We finally arrived at the Cranstons a full hour late, frazzled, embarrassed, and babbling apologies. They couldn't have been more gracious about our tardiness, which was a clear first sign of their genuine warmth and kindness.

Robin helped us as we hurriedly set up our equipment at their cozy dining banquette, next to a large window that overlooks the park and the colorful horse-drawn carriages on the street below. The couple calls Los Angeles home, but they bought these New York digs a few years ago, as Bryan frequently works in the city.

After a few moments, Bryan entered, dressed in the comfortable clothes he would wear on his walk to the theater—a nightly routine, he said, that gets his energy going. He slid into the booth next to his wife, and we easily began talking.

PHIL: The more couples we speak to, the more we discover how influenced they were by their parents' marriages. What kind of marriages do you two come from?

BRYAN: All seven of my parents' marriages were wonderful.

PHIL: What?

ROBIN: He's not kidding.

BRYAN: My mom was married four times, my dad three times, and they had numerous boyfriends and girlfriends in between. So marriage was an institution—meaning, as Groucho Marx once said, if you went into it, you belonged in an institution.

PHIL: But, really, seven marriages? Not ideal role-modeling for you.

BRYAN: It wasn't the best representation of what marriage is, but in many ways my parents taught me what not to do.

PHIL: What was the biggest lesson?

BRYAN: That this laissez-faire attitude about marriage didn't work.

MARLO: And what about your family, Robin?

ROBIN: Mine was the complete opposite of his. I had a *Leave It to Beaver* childhood. I'm a native Californian like Bryan, but I was raised in Whittier, which is a tiny town—Nixon's hometown. My parents were married for more than forty-seven years, until my dad passed away. But they never instilled in me the need to be married. They never said, "We can't wait for grandchildren!" Some parents do that.

PHIL: The Catholics do. If you're Catholic and not married by the time you're twenty-four, your mother would start a novena.

ROBIN: Or you'd be a priest.

MARLO: So by the time you were out of the house, you weren't really on the lookout for a husband.

ROBIN: That's right. I never wanted to get married—it wasn't high on my list. And then when I met Bryan, I thought, *Oh, I guess I* do *want to get married.*

Bryan was born and raised in Los Angeles; his parents were in show business and, in fact, met in an acting class shortly after World War II. Their first child, Bryan's older brother Kyle, arrived shortly after they were married. His mother never pursued acting as a career, Bryan said, because in those days, "becoming a housewife and mother is what you did."

Despite the spousal revolving door Bryan witnessed as a child, he got married at age twenty-one. In fact, it might be because his parents had made getting married look so easy, so casual, that he took the plunge without ample consideration.

"It was just the wrong time, and I wasn't in love with her," Bryan admitted. "It wasn't fair to her and it wasn't fair to me. Sometimes you hear young men say, 'I guess it's time to get married.' Well, the minute you hear someone say, 'it's time,' that should be a caution flag."

Bryan surmised that the times they lived in had much to do with his headlong rush into the doomed marriage. "Our formative years were during the sexual revolution of the sixties and the seventies," he said, "which celebrated a kind of looseness in relationships. It was easy to get waylaid by—"

"—by the fun," Marlo said.

"Yes, by the fun. And freedom. And convincing yourself you may be in love with someone when you're really not. You may not even have that much in common with them. So now you're in pretty deep and thinking, *How do I extract myself?* That was the situation I found myself in. But I got married anyway, very young."

"But if you didn't love her..." Phil said.

"I really liked this woman," Bryan said, "and, in fact, I loved her on *some* level. But I was not *in love* with her—at least not to an extent where I could see myself committed to her for the rest of my life. And yet, that's what I said when I stood at the altar."

Luckily, the marriage ended before children came along, Bryan reflected. "That's when I realized that, if I ever got married again, I had to be in love and really know what I was doing. I needed to know, not wonder."

That opportunity first presented itself two years later when Bryan was cast as the "villain of the week" on the 1986 CBS-TV show *Airwolf*, in which Robin—then an already seasoned actress—had also landed a role. The show starred Ernest Borgnine, Jan Michael Vincent, and a high-tech helicopter. "It was a really terrible show," Bryan said, "and the characters mirrored marriage in those days: the men were either good guys or bad guys, and the women were victims or femme fatales. I was the bad guy on this episode, and Robin was the victim of the week. I kidnapped her and held her for ransom."

"Along with a few other women," Robin added.

"So you had a gun on her?" Phil asked.

"I threatened to kill her or date her, whichever she chose," Bryan joked.

The two did not start dating after *Airwolf*, however, but they continued to cross paths—enough to suspect that, perhaps, something was stirring in the cosmos. A year later they ran into each other in an improv comedy class. At the time, they were both involved with other people, so they just became friends.

Then came the trip to England.

ROBIN: I was in Oxford for a summer theater program with the British American Drama Academy. He'd already planned a trip to Scotland and England, so while he was there, he decided to stop by Oxford to see me.

MARLO: Like, "I just happened to be in the neighborhood... here in Great Britain." So he drops in and... what happened?

ROBIN: I thought, *Oh, it's you.*

MARLO: Really?

ROBIN: I'd never felt that way in my life.

PHIL: Let me catch up. What does "Oh, it's you," mean?

ROBIN: It just means... I can't explain it. It was this reaction that said, "Oh, I guess I *do* want to get married. And I want to marry *you.*"

MARLO: Did you feel the same way, Bryan?

BRYAN: I was very keen on this. But I think we were lucky. I think we were guided to this. At the time, we were both seeing someone else, so there wasn't any of that tension: *Should I make a move and ask her out?*

ROBIN: Right. We could "fun flirt."

MARLO: So when did things move from fun to something more?

BRYAN: We had the most romantic date along the river at Stratford-upon-Avon. It was a beautiful day. I rented a punt and we had sandwiches and a bottle of wine. At one point, we were punting along and we found a shady little spot under a tree...

MARLO: And?

BRYAN: And we kissed like bandits.

ROBIN: We *made out* like bandits.

The simmering passion suited them—for the time being, at least. They both knew the fire was there, but more than anything, Bryan, wary of making the same matrimonial mistake twice, wanted to "slow it down and allow it to be romantic," as opposed to pushing things physically.

"Making that commitment and then having to backtrack to figure out who this person is—the one you just had relations with—is an easy trap to fall into, young or old," Bryan said.

So they took things slow—until they didn't. Bryan proposed to Robin about eighteen months later, and he did it in typical Bryan fashion. It was during a getaway to a rustic cabin on Big Bear Mountain in Southern California that Bryan popped the question to his beloved. In the bathtub.

Things began nicely enough: a warm bubble bath in a remote cabin in the woods, music playing softly in the background, a bottle of champagne nearby. But what began as a romantic idea quickly turned into a slapstick routine.

"The bathtub was a standard-sized tub in a crampy cabin in the mountains," Robin recalled, "so there wasn't any room for me to face him. It was not a beautiful tub and we weren't looking at each other. I'm facing the spout."

"Well, otherwise," Bryan explained, "the faucet would be right in the middle of her back. I orchestrated the whole thing this way, because I knew if she was facing me, I would crack. The only real way to do it was for me to straddle her, like we're both on horseback. So we're taking this nice bubble bath, I had the champagne, I had a little music going..."

"And I'm thinking, *What the hell is this?*" Robin said.

"But every time I start to talk," Bryan continued, "she tries to turn around to look at me, and I turn her face back toward the wall so I can get the lines out."

Since they were naked—as a couple might be in a bubble bath—offering the engagement ring presented a challenge. Bryan's brainstorm was to put the ring on his baby toe and hide it underwater. At the appointed time, he would ask The Question, then lift his leg out of the water. Only snag: the ring was way down there at the other end of the tub.

"So he asks me to marry him, and suddenly this foot comes up out of the water with the ring on his toe," Robin said.

"And, of course, I couldn't reach it," Bryan noted, "so I say, 'Here—take the ring off my toe.'"

"Is this a horror movie?" Phil asked.

"It sounds like an improv," Marlo said.

What it was, actually, was a moment that was both romantic and hilarious.

"I especially liked the idea that he would cry if he looked at me," Robin said tenderly.

"I know," Marlo said, "that's so sweet."

"And it *worked*," Phil said.

"Work" is an apt word to describe the Cranstons' marriage, in that this is a couple who confront challenges with tender care. Problems that arise are handled professionally through couples counseling—something both Robin and Bryan firmly believe in. And it doesn't take much to get them into a session, either. In fact, if only one of them needs it on a particular day, the other is obligated to go, no questions asked. They've been going to a therapist, apparently successfully, since even before the marriage.

Robin explained: "Bryan used to say to me, 'I love you, I know I want to marry you, I just don't know when.' But I was thirty-four, so there was a part of me that was thinking, *But you're assuming I'll still be here.* And that made me mad."

"It is a little bit offensive," Marlo noted.

"I was just being honest," Bryan said. "I wasn't ready. So what else should I say?"

"No, no, you're lucky that she cared enough," said Marlo.

"Isn't it amazing that the timing of *any* couple can work out?" Bryan asked. " 'You're ready.' 'Oh, I'm not ready.' 'Oh, I've got a girlfriend.' 'Oh, I've got a boyfriend.' How do we ever find each other?"

Bryan noted that couples therapy carries a stigma—that people who go into counseling are often considered weak or even "sick." But he and Robin have taken to it naturally, referring to their sessions in, of all things, automotive terms.

"People say all the time, 'Oh, you go to therapy,' as if your character is in question," Bryan said. "And I say to them, 'You drive a car, right? If the red light on your car says "Engine Trouble," would you stop, open up the hood, and start tinkering? Of course not. You don't touch it.' So I ask, 'Do you actually think you can fix your car? No, you don't. So what makes you think that you can fix your marriage if that warning light is on?' And that's all it is. Just a caution light saying, 'Pay attention.' "

"Or, 'You might want to look into this,' " Robin added.

"So we say, 'Let's just go get a tune-up,' " Bryan continued. "And because, early on, we both wanted it to work, I came up with the rule that would take the decision-making out of it. If either one of us said, 'I want us to go in to see the therapist,' there was no discussion to it. The signal was to say, 'It's really important to me.' We agreed that if one of us throws that trump card, the other one backs off."

Both Robin and Bryan find that they are open-minded during their sessions and that problems actually get solved, even when it's Robin's idea and Bryan doesn't feel he'll have anything to offer.

"We'll get in there and we'll be holding hands," he said, "and just the idea of being in that environment and offering up a thought invariably makes us feel closer."

"It's all about having somebody who's impartial and looking at both sides," adds Robin, "looking at how I receive information, how he receives information, and then offering, 'Well, what I think you're both trying to say is this...' "

"An interpreter," Phil said.

"Yes," Robin agreed. "An interpreter."

MARLO: That sounds perfect. But most therapists don't make house calls, so how do you two work through challenges when you're on your own? You're both headstrong, you're both funny, so your disagreements must be interesting. First of all, are you Scottish, Bryan?

BRYAN: Mostly Irish and German.

MARLO: And you, Robin?

ROBIN: Me too. Irish and German.

MARLO: I ask because I'm Italian and Lebanese, and Phil is Irish. So we have very different ways of arguing. We've actually had to learn over forty years how to deal with confrontation. I used to say to him, "Someday there'll be nothing left but an eyelash and a patch of white hair on the ground. And people will say, 'They were here.'"

BRYAN: Shreds—there's Phil and there's Marlo!

MARLO: So how would you describe your style of combat?

BRYAN: I would first say that I'm the moodier of the two of us.

ROBIN: He's crankier than I am—

BRYAN: —and she is much steadier in her comportment and personality than I am. If I have an issue or a problem, I go inside my head and, like most men, I want to be left alone. I don't want to talk about it and get a hug. I'm just like, *Let me work this out. Let me fight my way out of the cave.*

PHIL: And where does that take the two of you as a couple?

BRYAN: When I get in those moods, we're most susceptible to the disconnect. And it's mostly because I've said something or done something that hurt her feelings.

ROBIN: I think this is true generally for women.

MARLO: I agree. So how do you come back?

BRYAN: She realizes that she was wrong and apologizes and all is forgiven.

MARLO: Funny. But the truth is, if you don't know how to come back from a fight, the marriage will suffer.

ROBIN: For me, it's about letting things go. If you harbor these feelings—if you hang on to stuff all the time, which I do more than he does—it's not good. It took me years to learn to let things go.

PHIL: So he explodes—

Bryan Cranston and Robin Dearden

ROBIN: —and I pout.

BRYAN: But she's learning to not take things so seriously, including a fight. I've never felt like, "That's it—that's the final straw! I'm out of here!" I've learned how to apologize, how to recognize that I'm at fault or have overstepped. I've learned to identify when the train is going down the wrong track, and we're not so far down the road that I can't say, "I've made a mistake and I'm sorry. Now we need to get the train back on the right track." The quest is in identifying the switcher at that moment of fight-or-flight. That's when you need to say, "Ah, that's the switch. Start making adjustments now, and don't go too far down the road."

MARLO: That's such a great visual—a switch that you can pull to stop this now.

PHIL: What about thoughts of divorce? I once asked Billy Graham, "Have you ever considered divorce?" He said, "Divorce, never. Murder, yes." Have you guys ever thrown around the D-word?

ROBIN: No.

BRYAN: No, because then you're holding a threat over someone.

ROBIN: Right, that's a threat.

BRYAN: And if you're really thinking about that, then there's a problem.

The couple's daughter, actress Taylor Dearden, was born in 1993, four years into the marriage. As with many Hollywood couples, Bryan's extended periods away from home stirred some resentment in the spouse he left back home.

"My tradeoff in our marriage was him being gone all the time," Robin said. "That's always been hard for me, but those are just the logistics of what he does. I mean, he wasn't in the Bahamas on vacation. He was working, so there's that. But, again, what I've learned most from marriage is what to keep and what to let go of. I like this person. I mean, besides loving him, I *like* him. He's a really, really good man."

But even as Robin managed to reconcile her husband's itinerant career, his frequent absences led to one decision that is perhaps the marriage's most sensitive topic: Bryan wanted to have more children, but Robin did not.

"With Bryan being gone as much as he was, I think I really would have resented having two kids when he would be off on a movie somewhere for six months," she said.

Co-parenting hadn't been a problem early on, when Taylor was small. "*Malcolm in the Middle* taped just down the street from us," Robin said, "which is amazing—nobody gets a chance to do that in show business. And he was total hands-on all the time." But Bryan landed the starring role in *Breaking Bad* just as Taylor was entering her teen years. The series was filmed in New Mexico; and after its five-year run, the movie offers followed, requiring that Bryan travel to distant locations for long periods of time.

"By then, Taylor was like my best friend," Robin said. "And having her—and not having to deal with all the parenting that's involved with a younger child for those long periods that he was gone—was, selfishly, exactly what I wanted.

"This was a big therapy thing for us," Robin continued softly. "I was one-and-done. I was also forty, though I don't know that it would have been any different if I'd been thirty. I was good."

PHIL: So how did you get through that?

BRYAN: Well, as a progressive enlightened male I said to her, "I think it's only fair that, because of the biological issues, you should have two votes and I'll have one vote."

ROBIN: We talked it out for a long time.

BRYAN: I thought that maybe when Taylor was one year old, I'd bring it up. And when she was two, I'd bring it up. And after that, I wouldn't bring it up again. I think that's what we did.

ROBIN: But we did go to therapy for that, and I learned something really interesting about him. When we were getting deep into the conversation about him wanting more children so much—and me being fine without them—the therapist asked Bryan, "Why do you think this is so important?" And he had this epiphany. Because he has two siblings, and because his parents were so fractured, he thought that one child and two parents is not a family. I didn't think that way because I didn't have a fractured family.

BRYAN: I really relied on my brother—who's two years older than me—during the fracture of our family. He was, like, running defense for me, and blocking for me, and figuring things out. And we were very close for a long time. I really needed my brother, and in many ways I think he needed me, too. And our little sister needed both of us to take care of her, to babysit when Mom was drinking too much. And so that's what I kept thinking. *It's not for me—it's for Taylor. It's better for Taylor to have a sibling.*

As difficult as the decision was for both of them, Robin's investment in Bryan's happiness spoke to what Bryan refers to as the "character" of a spouse. "Looks fade," he said, "abilities come and go. So does money. But the character of a person is what you hitch your wagon to. Character, to me, is determined by the choices we make under pressure. Not the easy ones, but the ones we make when times are tough."

Robin turned to us. "You know when I fell even more in love with him?" she said. "It was when his grandmother had dementia and was in a nursing home and had to go to the bathroom. He said, 'I'll help you, Grandma.' And she said, 'Oh, no, no, no!' because she wasn't really sure who he was, and she said she'd be too embarrassed. So Bryan said, 'Oh, Grandma, don't you know? I'm a doctor now.' And she said, 'Oh, okay.' I just thought that was the dearest thing."

Bryan listened to his wife's recollection and returned with a memory of his own—this one from one of their first dates, at the Huntington Botanical Gardens in San Marino, California.

"We came up to a bunch of flowers," he recalled, "and she said, 'Oh, look at the roses!' with such enthusiasm. I realized, I would never gush like that. Maybe I'd say, 'Yeah, those are pretty,' and I'd probably smell them. But she gets so excited—she has this positive outlook that isn't at all cynical or sarcastic. Even now, she gets excited when we're walking at night in the summer and she sees fireflies. It's such a joyous, childlike appreciation of simple things—to be able to exhale and to take in your surroundings and appreciate life and be in the moment *at that moment*, and say, 'Things are good.' And to be able to count your blessings."

We left the apartment sooner than we wanted to—we were having such a good time—but we had to let Bryan get to the theater. We'd seen the play when it first opened, and the part was indeed a grueling one. And all that hard work paid off. Three weeks later, Bryan won the Tony Award, Broadway's highest honor, for his spectacularly angry performance in *Network*. We watched the awards broadcast from home. Halfway through his thanks, Bryan looked down into the audience and caught the eye of his life partner.

"And to my lovely wife, Robin," he said to the world, "who told me, 'Go out there and be mad as hell every night—just don't bring it home.'" And it's clear he didn't.

Gloria and Emilio Estefan

MARRIED IN 1978

"I told him, 'Babe, I promise you I'm not going to break up the band.' Then I gave him back the engagement ring, went home, and told my mom, 'I hope you're happy now.'"

Here's the rule of thumb if you want to get together with Gloria and Emilio Estefan: you've got to catch them on the fly—because, boy, are they busy. The day we caught up with them, they'd just flown into New York from their home in Miami Beach for a day and a half so that Gloria could perform at a big gala, celebrating the opening of the new Statue of Liberty Museum. Between rehearsals for the show, the couple still found time to drop by our apartment to talk. Not wanting to waste a minute, we swiftly seated them at our dining room table, where we had set out a platter of snacks.

In the afternoon, the sunlight in our home streams brightly through our dining room windows. Harsh light is never flattering to anyone; but in Gloria's case, the sun gave her a radiant glow. Though pressed for time, they were easy and relaxed, as if they had all the time in the world.

Which is hard to fathom, given the pace this couple has been keeping for more than four decades. The day we met, their hit autobiographical Broadway show, *On Your Feet,* was set to open in London. They

Miami, Florida; September 2, 1978

simultaneously oversee a multimedia entertainment company, a recording facility, restaurants, hotels, and a charitable foundation. Separately, they are success stories; together, they're a dynamo—over the years, Gloria has won seven Grammys and Emilio nineteen. And in addition to his work with his wife, Emilio has produced, managed, or guided the careers of a who's who of recording icons, including Jennifer Lopez, Ricky Martin, Jon Secada, and Madonna.

Within a few minutes of being with Gloria and Emilio, you pick up their rhythm as a couple, and you can't help but feel they were made for each other. Their road hasn't been an easy one, but they've shared every bump of it with the will and determination of two people who have never doubted for a minute where that road would take them.

They met in Miami, both part of the Cuban expat community. He played accordion and percussion in a band, the Miami Latin Boys, specializing in nostalgic songs that expressed longing for their homeland. Gloria's parents brought her to the United States as a toddler and Emilio left Cuba at age fourteen, first living in Spain before landing in Florida. Fate brought them together at a church fundraiser, where his band performed along with a youth ensemble. Gloria was seventeen and Emilio was twenty-two.

"I heard her sing and I told her, 'What a beautiful voice you have on you,'" Emilio said. "But I also noticed that she was extremely shy."

"When I would sing for my mom, I would stare at the floor," Gloria confirmed. "She was the diva, the all-powerful force. I didn't think I had it in me to be good enough to be on a stage."

Mom was nicknamed Big Gloria and had been a child star in Cuba, even winning a worldwide contest in the 1940s to go to Hollywood and dub Shirley Temple's musical numbers in Spanish. Ultimately, Big Gloria's father didn't allow her to leave Cuba, refusing to split up the family. He also didn't think highly of the entertainment business, so Big Gloria missed out on her shot at fame. But by singing lullabies to her daughter, she became Gloria's earliest musical influence.

About three months after performing at the church, the Miami Latin Boys had a wedding gig. Gloria was in the crowd, and Emilio saw her pass by.

"I said, 'Hey, aren't you that girl from the church thing?'" Emilio recalled. "'Why don't you come on up and do a song with me and the adults in the band?' Gloria said, 'Oh no, no, I don't want to do that.' But her mom said, 'Yes, yes, sing a song.'" Gloria did as instructed and the crowd loved her, giving her a rousing standing ovation.

Emilio instantly recognized how the band could benefit by having a female lead singer and possibly move in a new direction—one that fused their traditional Cuban roots with a modern Miami sound. "I told her, 'Oh, my God, this would be fantastic!'" Emilio explained. "'We'll do this for a living. We don't make a lot of money, but it's fun.'"

Gloria demurred. "I told him, no, I couldn't do this because I knew my mom would kill me." And with that, she disappeared back into the crowd without leaving her phone number.

"I wasn't even supposed to go to that wedding, but my mom had guilted me into it," Gloria told us. It was something she had to do for her father, who was an old army buddy of the father of the bride. Years before, back in Cuba, Gloria's dad had been a political prisoner who was jailed by the Fidel Castro regime; he then immigrated to the United States, where he joined the U.S. Army and was sent to Vietnam. There, in his mid-thirties, he was poisoned by the defoliant Agent Orange. After that he developed multiple sclerosis and became an invalid. Gloria had attended the wedding to represent him.

A couple of weeks later, Emilio successfully tracked down Gloria and asked her one more time if she'd like to join the band. She again declined.

"In my mother's mind, it was college, college, college," said Gloria, who was studying psychology at the University of Miami at the time and had two part-time jobs—one as an interpreter at the Miami airport (she's fluent in Spanish and French), the other giving guitar lessons two nights a week. Since the age of fourteen, she also had been her father's caregiver and her younger sister's babysitter while her mother went to night school to secure her credentials to teach school in the United States. Still, Gloria was torn by Emilio's offer, especially given the pull music had on her.

"Music saved my life," she told us. "I would come home from school and take care of my dad and my little sister until my mom came home later in the night. So, music was my catharsis. I would lock myself in my room and just play songs on my guitar and sing and cry."

But Emilio was a man on a mission, and he eventually persuaded Gloria to give his band a try.

GLORIA: I brought my mom, my grandma, and my sister with me to a rehearsal.

MARLO: What a hot date!

GLORIA: Oh, yeah, but he had a girlfriend at the time who was thirty-six. I always found him very cute, but for a while he was just my boss. And he seemed to be a lot older because he was very responsible.

PHIL: He was already a mover and shaker at twenty-two.

GLORIA: Actually, when I started in the band, he wasn't there for the first month. His father had won the lottery, and Emilio took a bunch of the money off the table and bought a clothing factory. He knew that otherwise, within two months his dad wouldn't have any left.

PHIL: Was he a spendthrift?

GLORIA: He just loved to give people money. He once tipped someone $100 for a Coca-Cola.

EMILIO: My dad won the lottery twenty-seven times, but he died with one pair of shoes and one suit because he gave all the money away.

PHIL: How much was in each lottery?

EMILIO: Sometimes about a quarter-million, and one time about $800,000.

PHIL: That's a lot of money to go through!

MARLO: So, were you attracted to Gloria from the start?

EMILIO: I don't believe in love at first sight. But I loved her eyes. I loved her personality, and I knew she'd gone through a lot in her life.

It wasn't long before Gloria's father had to be permanently hospitalized, his disease progressing to the point that he could no longer be nursed at home. Gloria stayed in college, managing to sandwich in rehearsals and performances with the band, which was now called the Miami Sound Machine. Unbeknownst to her, Emilio had broken up with his older girlfriend.

On July 4, 1976—America's bicentennial—the band was performing in a rough area of Miami, and Emilio suggested that Gloria leave her car at his apartment and go with him in his van. On the way, he turned to her and said, "You know, I bet we'd get along great if we got married."

GLORIA: I looked at him like 'What the hell?' We hadn't even been on a date. And then I laughed because I figured he must have been kidding.

I'd never gone out with anybody because I was taking care of my dad, so there was no social life for me. I didn't think I would get married, period, to tell you the truth. I was going to be a psychologist, and I wanted to go to Paris and study international law and diplomacy at the Sorbonne.

MARLO: I think it's amazing that you were considering being a psychologist with that voice. How could you think that?

GLORIA: Because I'm an immigrant and needed a job. Being a singer wasn't in my nature. I don't like being the center of attention. I wanted to *live*, to go out and *do* and *be* and get my career together.

In the van, Emilio let the subject of marriage drop and drove on to their Fourth of July gig. Later that night, during the band's third break, he asked Gloria to go outside for some fresh air. They were standing on the third-floor deck of the venue in the middle of the water between Miami and Miami Beach, fireworks going off all around them. The setting couldn't have been more romantic.

"So we're out there getting air," Gloria remembered, "and he says, 'You know, today is my birthday.' I say, 'Wow, what a coincidence! The bicentennial is on your birthday?' He goes, 'Yeah, why don't you give me a birthday kiss on the cheek?' I say, 'I'll get you a present.' He says, 'Sure, I'll take a present, but come on, it's just a little kiss on the cheek.' So I go, 'All right, fine.'"

And just as Gloria moved in on Emilio's cheek, he turned his head and their lips locked.

"The sneak," Gloria said with a laugh. "He lied."

"Well, the fourth *is* my birthday," Emilio said. "But it's in March, not July."

MARLO: What a con man!

PHIL: But you knew he was a good boy and that you weren't falling for some shady guy.

GLORIA: Yes. And I knew his family. He had a lot of cousins, whom I'd met at rehearsals and family get-togethers. I loved his parents. I thought they were wonderful.

MARLO: So once he stole the kiss, what happened?

GLORIA: He asked me out that night, but I said no.

EMILIO: It was little by little. That's why I say I don't believe in love at first sight. A commitment, friendships, relationships—they all take a longer time.

PHIL: Was there one moment that clicked for you, Gloria?

GLORIA: Yes. I'm a huge Mel Brooks fan, so for our first date we went to see *Young Frankenstein*. As we're coming out of the theater, he looks at me and says, "That wasn't that scary." I said, "You do know it's a comedy, right? It's not supposed to be scary." I knew at that moment that I was going to marry this man.

Emilio continues to make Gloria laugh every day, she says, saying things without realizing they're funny. "He changes people's names, for some reason making them more difficult than the original," Gloria said. "He called Aretha Franklin—who loved him, by the way—Urethra Franklin. He's got these amazing business neurons and won't forget one detail of anything, but he is very absent-minded about normal stuff. We were once riding in the car after we got married and the radio was on, and I started singing along. He said, 'You know, you sing really well.' I said, 'I'm the lead singer in your band, remember?' He said, 'Oh, right, for a minute I thought you were just my wife.'"

Two years after Emilio's spontaneous marriage proposal in the van, he gave Gloria an engagement ring. The date was February 12. He had intended to spring it on her on Valentine's Day, but he was too excited to wait. They were married on September 2, 1978. Emilio's parents lived with them for the first two years, which Gloria said she loved since they were so helpful and warm.

Big Gloria was another story.

"She gave him hell after we got serious," Gloria said of her mother. "She freaked out and tortured him, shutting the door in his face when he came to pick me up. She was mean to him. *Mean.* She was worried that he was a musician, not a doctor or a lawyer. I would keep telling her, 'Mom, he's a great guy,' but she wasn't having any of it."

"Didn't your engagement help demonstrate that he was serious?" asked Phil.

"No, she got even more difficult with him after that," Gloria said. "He never disrespected her, he never trash-talked her to me, but he did start thinking, *Uh-oh*, because you marry the family as well, right? So, one day he said to me, 'You know, I don't think I can handle your mom.'"

"Wow. Your mother was that bad?" Marlo asked.

"She was always feisty," Gloria said, "but in that instance, I think she was afraid."

Rather than get angry at Emilio, Gloria was sympathetic. "I told him, 'Babe, I wish I could tell you differently, but I understand where you're coming from. I promise you that I'm not going to break up the band.' And then I gave him back the engagement ring, went home, and told my mom, 'Okay, I hope you're happy now.'"

Within a week they were back together.

And yet even the couple's marriage didn't thaw relations with Gloria's mother, nor the birth of their son, Nayib, in 1980. Gloria's father died that same year—he was just forty-seven—causing her mother even more grief. And when Gloria and Emilio went on tour, they took along her younger sister. As far as Big Gloria was concerned, that was the final straw.

"She didn't talk to me for two years," Gloria said. "I don't want to make her seem like a devil—she was an amazing woman. She raised us, she put me through school, took care of my dad. It's just that when it came to this love relationship and this guy, she thought he would pull us away. I kept trying to call her, but she was a very hardheaded woman."

Although Big Gloria stood firm on her excommunication of her daughter, one thing would force her to break the stalemate: thinking that Gloria was dead.

The date was March 20, 1990. By then Gloria was a massive star with four gold and platinum albums, nearly a dozen top ten hits (three of them number one), and two Grammy nominations. And Emilio was rapidly gaining a reputation as a chart-busting music impresario whose influence spanned the Latin and pop universes. That afternoon, Big Gloria was holding a meeting at the public school where she was an educator when an announcement flashed across the TV screen: Gloria Estefan had been killed in a bus crash.

"She collapsed right there in the teacher's lounge," Gloria told us. "Her friend rushed in a minute later and said, 'Don't pay attention to the news—they were wrong! They're now reporting that she's not dead. She's very hurt, but she's not dead.'"

Gloria and Emilio had been on a sold-out world tour to promote their bestselling album *Cuts Both Ways*, when a freak snowstorm hit near Scranton, Pennsylvania. A truck was jackknifed across the road, halting traffic. Gloria was taking a nap on the bus's couch, resting up for a show that night. When the bus stopped, she opened her eyes, thinking they'd arrived at the venue. At that moment there was an explosion. The bus was rear-ended by a speeding eighteen-wheeler, slamming them into the flatbed truck in front.

Gloria found herself on the floor of the bus, Emilio standing over her covered in blood. The front of the bus had been sliced off and it was snowing inside, the temperature freezing. Their son Nayib, nine at the time, suffered a broken collarbone. Gloria was in enormous pain and couldn't get up. She knew her back was broken. A nurse from a nearby vehicle came on board and ordered her not to move, bracing Gloria's head until paramedics arrived ninety minutes later. The hospital in Scranton wasn't equipped to deal with her injuries, so she and Emilio—whose ribs had been broken—were air-lifted to New York City.

Gloria's surgeon stabilized her spinal cord with two eight-inch titanium rods, and after she recovered from surgery, Gloria poured herself into rehab, six to seven hours a day. As part of her regimen, she spent three months floating in a pool. "And I couldn't walk," she told us. "My exercise was lifting my foot an inch off the ground."

Gloria's doctor delivered the hard truth about what to expect, explaining that while she might be able to walk again—given time—she'd probably never get back onstage or have more children.

"But then he said to me, 'Look, this is just what medicine tells us—and it is going to be rough, because everything in there got thrown around. But I've also seen things that you can't explain medically, and I'm telling you, it's up to you.' So I told him, 'Well, if it's up to me, I'm going to be okay.'"

"What about Emilio?" Phil asked.

"Emilio would walk into the room and look at me and start crying, thinking I was in denial, and I would say, 'Babe, I'm going to be okay. I promise you, I'm going to be okay.'"

MARLO: So, how did you get through that? That's a big hit.

EMILIO: I have a picture that was taken two days before the accident when we were getting an award and I had no white hair. Three months later I'd gone totally white.

GLORIA: Yeah, he went gray in like two months. My mom was sure he was going to leave me because she didn't think he could handle it.

MARLO: Did you get scared that he would do that?

GLORIA: No. I knew he wasn't going to leave me.

EMILIO: The real truth is, when her mother came to the hospital, she gave me a hug. She went to open the door, thinking it was the bathroom, and she saw me in the closet crying, kneeling down and praying, and I think that really impacted her. She said, 'I'm so sorry, I'm so sorry.' She realized how much we had as a family.

PHIL: This must have been so disorienting for you, Gloria. You hadn't spoken to her in two years.

GLORIA: I remember her coming into my hospital room, and how she grabbed my hand. All I said was, "Wow, Mom, I don't remember your hands being this small." And that was it. We never mentioned anything again.

EMILIO: You know, after the accident she spoke to me so many times and said, "Emilio, you have to realize I lost my husband. I lost my house. I was separated from my family. My daughter was the main thing in my life, and I was afraid of you being in the music business and taking her away, and I would never see you again." And I understood a lot of that. She was an incredible woman. I became closer to her that day.

MARLO: Did the accident change your relationship with each other?

GLORIA: These things either tear you apart or you become very, very close. He had to bathe me, and I'm so independent. He would have to set me up, lay me down. I couldn't sleep for more than forty-five minutes at a time because the pain was so excruciating—which, by the way, I took a lot of hope from when I was on the floor of that bus. Having spent so much time with my dad being injured and in a wheelchair, I knew a lot about the workings of the spine and that if I was in pain, I hadn't severed the cord. The only thing that would alleviate my pain was changing position, so Emilio would get me up every forty-five minutes and help me walk a few steps. He was like that around the clock and never complained.

MARLO: Did you think that she would get back onstage?

EMILIO: I didn't care. I just wanted her to walk.

Getting there wasn't easy. Over the next few months, Gloria endured bouts of depression and crying jags, "wallowing" in her condition, she told us. At one point, Emilio reminded her that, even if she never walked again, she could still write and sing. And then he showed her a wrinkled piece of paper with the words "coming out of the dark" written on it. He explained to her that during the airlift from Scranton to New York, a ray of sunlight kept hitting him in the eye, no matter which way the helicopter turned. So he'd written down those five words, put the paper back in his pocket, and had forgotten about it. It had even been washed a few times with the pants.

"And then he says, 'Look, Jon Secada is in the studio right now—I asked him to come in," Gloria recalled. "He said, 'I'd really love it if you came with me. You can just come in and sit.' He hadn't left my side for three months, so I figured, *You know what? I'm going to go.*"

When the couple arrived at the studio—Gloria in her back brace—Jon Secada was already there. He began singing a melody; and with Emilio's and Jon's help, the song "Coming Out of the Dark" poured out of Gloria. "It just came *through* me," Gloria remembered. "It was a thank you." The song would ultimately soar to number one on the charts.

On January 28, 1991—ten full months after the accident—Gloria walked onto the stage at the American Music Awards in Los Angeles to a thunderous standing ovation. Clenching her fist and gazing into the audience at her husband, she performed "Coming Out of the Dark," less as a hit song than as an anthem of triumph.

"Everybody had sent me prayers and cards," she said of her long recuperation period. "I had people in the hospital on their knees praying the entire time I was there, and for the first time I really understood prayer because I could feel it as a physical presence. I felt like I was juiced, plugged in. And I thought, *I'm going to put the love these people are sending me right into my body.* So that song was a thank you to everybody who took time out of their life. The words are *Why be afraid if I'm not alone. Life is never easy, the rest is unknown.*"

Gloria's dire prognosis was wrong in one other way: her second child, Emily, was born in 1994 and is now a singer and musician.

"We call her our miracle baby," Gloria told us, beaming. "And she *is* a miracle. She is the best musician of all of us—she plays percussion and sings beautifully."

The sunlight was no longer blazing into the dining room, and our conversation was drawing to a close. "We've kept you a long time," Marlo said, "and we're loving it, but tell us one last thing. You've experienced so much together—personally and professionally—that you must have discovered some secret to your longevity. What would that secret be?"

"Keep shaving your legs," Gloria said.

"Beg pardon?" Phil said.

Gloria laughed. "That's what I say when I'm joking around with young girls who ask me that question. I say, 'Keep shaving your legs,' which in a nutshell—for both men and women—means, 'This is your lover, and always remember that.' Because when life comes and hits you with parenthood or economic issues, you have to remember that you're still each other's loved one. You still have to make the effort to keep the love alive, keep it fresh. Emilio has been a dream because he's always considerate and always put together. To me, love is a drug. We fall in love because that's what nature wants us to do, for the human race to continue. But a marriage takes a lot more than physical attraction to survive. You have to be on the same page, have the same values, the same priorities. That's what's going to carry you through."

We turned to Emilio. Ever the businessman, he likened his long marital journey to a kind of contract.

"Marriage is a piece of paper," he said. "Love is a commitment of respect and communication. For me, I'm always thinking, 'How can I make her happy?' And I never want to lose a moment of that happiness for an argument or a discussion that's not worth it—because your life can change in a minute. When I go to sleep at night, I tell her how much I love her, because you can never be sure that you're going to wake up in the morning. And now..."

"And now?" Marlo said.

"And now we're going to go back to rehearsal."

Why be afraid if I'm not alone
Life is never easy, the rest is unknown
Up to now for me it's been hands against stone
Spent each and every moment
Searching for what to believe

—"Coming Out of the Dark"

Jesse and Jacqueline Jackson

MARRIED IN 1962

---

*"He can never, never, never call me a name.
That's disrespectful. When I call him names,
that's not disrespect, because he knows all of
the names I'm calling him are accurate."*

November in Chicago. We should have remembered—after all, we lived there for ten years. But somehow we forgot.

It was just after dawn on a cold morning in New York, and we had a 1:30 p.m. appointment with the Reverend Jesse and Jacqueline Jackson at their Rainbow/PUSH offices in Chicago. We'd planned well, arriving at La Guardia Airport at 8:30 a.m. for a 9:30 departure. But the Windy City had other plans: delay after delay after delay. Three hours later, we wondered whether we'd ever get out or should we just go home. But this was to be one of our last interviews. "We're on the ten-yard line," Phil kept saying. So we stuck it out. We finally took off at 3:30 p.m.—a mere seven hours after we'd gotten to the airport.

It was a bitter night in Chicago—11 degrees and windy. We arrived at the Jacksons' office at 7:30 p.m. They were kind enough to have waited, so we had a warm reunion. Phil and Jesse were old friends from the *Donahue*

days (Jesse appeared on Phil's show more than twenty times), and the years just melted away. Jackie introduced us to their staff and two of their children—daughter Santita and son Jonathan—and filled us in about the progress of their other children, Jesse Jr., Yusef, and Jackie Jr.

But the day had taken its toll on all of us, so we decided to get some sleep and meet again in the morning at 9:30 sharp.

And sharp we were. As we set up our recorder and mics, we noticed that the Jacksons' assistant, Alanna, was also preparing to record our session. The only other couple to double-tape us had been Bob and Elsa Woodward. But given the questionable luck we'd had getting to Chicago, having a backup didn't seem like a bad idea. Doubly covered, we began to chat.

"We've been friends a long time," said Phil. "And you two have been married fifty-eight years. But I've never heard the story of how you met."

"I first met Jackie when we were in college," Jesse began. "She was into modern dance and was a heavy user of the library. And she was just beautiful beyond measure. A mutual friend told me I had to meet her."

"Which appealed to you more," asked Marlo, "the fact that she was a knockout or that she was a heavy user of the library?"

Jesse laughed. "Maybe at the early stages in a relationship, we're attracted by what we see. But there were a lot of beautiful girls on campus. You move beyond what you see. One day I was talking to Jackie and I said, 'Let's go to the library.' I was a sophomore and she was a freshman, and I was doing my little show-off thing. I said, 'I can help you with your homework.' She said, 'I'm working on a term paper.'"

"About China and the U.N.," Jackie added.

"I said, *What?*" Jesse recalled. "This was out of my zone. I mean, I was in college, but China and the U.N. were a big deal intellectually. But it was her values that ultimately appealed to me, even at twenty years old—church values, academic passion, and her resentment of segregation. Early on in our relationship, we demonstrated and marched together. We

Greenville, South Carolina; December 31, 1962

had that foundation in common, because if you do not have that much in common, you should never marry. You marry shared commonality."

"So you were both activists from the start?" asked Marlo.

"Oh yes," Jackie said. "I'm from a military family. My stepfather was in the military and he taught us to fold the flag for fun. I knew how to fit the sheets on a bed. But when it came to marriage, I am progressively old-fashioned. Church was important to me, as was the knowledge that there is something greater than myself that has plunged us into this world. I believe in divine intervention in life, and when I first met my husband-to-be, I wasn't interested in a boyfriend. I was looking for shared values, a shared vision."

For Jackie and Jesse, that shared vision revolved around three core convictions: faith, education, and racial justice. They were married in Jesse's parents' home in Greenville, South Carolina, on December 31, 1962. Jackie was eighteen, and Jesse was twenty-one.

"I think many marriages don't last long because they have no roots," Jesse said. "They cannot withstand the fierce winds that blow in our lives. And if you don't have a foundation and shared values, that's when the tree topples."

"And what tree grows without roots?" added Jackie. "Without roots, a tree cannot grow."

"When does that foundation appear?" Phil asked.

"When you grow beyond the emotional and physical stage to shared interest," Jesse explained. "That's where children come in. Your caring for them must exceed your caring for yourself. Some say, 'I left my marriage because I wasn't happy.' Happy? Marriage is about fulfillment, not just happiness. It's about an obligation to the relationship and to other people."

PHIL: It's interesting that your first conversation with Jackie was about a library. By the time you met her, you'd already made national news because of a library, right?

JESSE: Yes. I was in college and I had to do a speech, so I needed to look at biographies. I came home to the colored library and they didn't have enough books, so the librarian sent me to the central library—the white library. When I arrived, the police were there. The librarian said, "We'll give you the books in seven days." I said, "I need them now." It was my Christmas visit, and I had to get back to school, so I didn't have seven days. The police said, "You heard what she said." It was so casual—I couldn't believe it. I went in the back and I cried. That summer seven of my classmates and I went to the library together and we were arrested. That's when I lost my fear of death and jail, frankly. It was the first time I went to jail. [*Jackson and his fellow students, all African American, conducted a sit-in at the Greenville Public Library on July 16, 1960. They were arrested for disorderly conduct and became known as the Greenville Eight.*]

PHIL: So did the fact that you and Jackie were both activists—and shared such deep religious beliefs—make life easier at the beginning? A lot of marriages get off to shaky starts.

JACKIE: I believe that a marriage is a corporation, really, fashioned for families, and that a lot of the lack of success today is due to high expectation of a big wedding. I got married at eighteen, and boy, was I naïve coming into this institution! I have a wonderful little story to tell about my husband.

MARLO: We're all ears.

JACKIE: That first year of our marriage Jesse was traveling a lot, and I was unhappy. I went to him and I said, "Reverend, you're supposed to make me happy," because I really felt a man was supposed to make you happy. That was his job. And he looked at me and said, "I can't do that. That's your responsibility to you."

MARLO: How did that make you feel?

JACKIE: I hated him. I was depressed for months. Isn't that why I got married, to be made happy by my husband?

JESSE: You need to make your partner secure—

JACKIE: —I'm going to finish my story, Reverend. After hating him for a full year—after planning to run away and get a divorce—I figured it out. He was helping me to grow. There are things he enjoys that I don't. He likes sports, and earlier in our relationship, I loved theater. I'd take him to a show and he would go to sleep and snore, and it was very embarrassing for me. But it finally occurred to me that I shouldn't humiliate him by imposing things that I enjoy that made him miserable. He was open to me calling my friends and going to the theater with them.

PHIL: So you learned that marriage was about growth.

JACKIE: Yes. Reverend was talking before about the need for a foundation to the marriage, and I think it's so important that, as Americans, we think about the expectations of a marriage. Initially, it involves this wedding that is so big and so expensive, but with what in return? The gifts are not so magnificent—the sterling silver this, and the china that—but after that, then what? After the sex, then what?

JESSE: In retrospect, what we had in common was that we demonstrated together. We resented the barbarianism of racist institutions. We had a desire to achieve academically. We wanted to make provisions for our children. And there was a certain church expectation. At the end of the day, it's about mutuality and mutual security and fulfillment. That's important. Love has to mature. At first, it's like a puppy dog. It's exciting, it's young, it's fresh, it's sexy. Then responsibility comes in and you have to share your responsibilities and resources. For example, I don't have a checking account. Jackie has all the money.

JACKIE: You're the CEO. I'm the COO and the CFO.

JESSE: My point is, if I can't trust her with my money—if I have my money and she has her money—well, that's a burden on a relationship right there. You have to share and you have to have trust on the important things. And Jackie has never let me down on making mature decisions.

Jesse Jackson was born out of wedlock in Greenville, South Carolina, in 1941, the child of a sixteen-year-old high school girl and her neighbor, a married professional boxer. A year after his birth, his mother married a post office janitor, who adopted him. Throughout his youth, Jesse was active in school and local politics. He attended college on a football scholarship; and after graduation, he attended the Chicago Theological Seminary.

Although he left the seminary three classes short of earning his degree, he was ordained a minister in 1968.

Having grown up in the south, Jesse experienced the atrocity of Jim Crow segregation firsthand, and he was barely in his twenties when he began participating in high-profile civil rights demonstrations of that era—from the lunch counter sit-ins to the Selma-to-Montgomery marches. But it was his association with the Rev. Dr. Martin Luther King Jr. that cemented his reputation as an electrifying orator and a tireless soldier in the fight for racial justice.

Although King was wary of the young firebrand's ego, he tapped Jesse to lead the Chicago branch of the Southern Christian Leadership Conference (SCLC), where the twenty-five-year-old activist dug in for the fight.

"While your work on the front lines was a bonding experience for you two," Phil said, "it extracted a toll on your lives. Huge sacrifices. You've been arrested. You had two grueling presidential campaigns. Both of you constantly traveled and were targets for white supremacists. And, basically, you both gave up everything to work with Martin Luther King."

Jesse remembered it vividly. "Dr. King said, 'I want you to leave the seminary and work with me full time,' but I was determined to finish. I said, 'I have only six months left,' and Dr. King said, 'You come with me and we'll see what you learn on the road.' I said, 'But Dr. King, you have a PhD. You already have your degree.' And that's when Jackie said, 'You should go work with that man.'"

Jackie jumped in. "Reverend was vacillating about whether or not to keep his scholarship at the Chicago Theological Seminary through the Rockefeller Foundation, and our housing and everything was included in that package. When it came time for Reverend to make the decision, he was trying to balance what might happen to his family if he went with Dr. King full time."

"So from the start," Marlo said, "your passion for your marriage and the movement went hand in hand. What decision did you ultimately make as a couple?"

"I took the risk of going with Dr. King," Jesse said, "and Jackie applauded it as opposed to resenting it. Had I been married to a different woman, I'm not sure she would have let me make that decision. Some of my friends were working for the Urban League, and they made more money and faced less risk. They had stable administrative jobs. With Dr. King, there was no insurance. You may go to jail or you might not come home."

"I loved Dr. King," Jackie said. "I was loyal. I was on the team. I didn't just assist the Reverend Jesse Jackson. I worked with Dr. King."

"So what happened to the scholarship?" Phil asked.

"He lost it," said Jackie, "and wound up making $37 a week."

"And you supported that?" Marlo asked.

"Oh, absolutely," said Jackie.

The couple's life became a whirlwind of activism, a steady drumbeat of boycotts and protests and marches that reached a horrifying crescendo with King's assassination in Memphis, Tennessee, on the evening of April 4, 1968. Jesse was on the floor below King at the Lorraine Motel when the gunshots cut through the air. Three years later Jesse launched Operation PUSH (People United to Save Humanity) as an activist organization to promote civil rights and social justice, and in 1984 he founded the similarly activist National Rainbow Coalition. That same year, Jesse launched his first bid for the U.S. presidency, a race against Democrats Walter Mondale and Gary Hart in which he captured enough interest to be considered a real force. But even that was a struggle. The media simply didn't cover many of his rallies, even though the candidate produced huge turnouts.

"We were out in Iowa working really hard and drawing big crowds, but getting little press," Jesse recalled. "The media had determined that our run didn't make any sense and that I couldn't win. They were marginalizing us. I said to Jackie, 'It's tough out here.' I hit a low point and began wondering if it was worth it. But Jackie was blunt. She said, 'You're going to get through all of this. You're going to fight. You can't let people down. Now, you get some rest and you keep fighting. Do not let your people down.'"

Jackie nodded. "We were being ignored by the media," she said, "and he felt it. But I knew that once people see that you have a movement—and you keep on with it—the establishment will notice. And that's what happened." Indeed, Jesse captured 21 percent of the primary vote.

During this time, the Jacksons traveled the world to pursue their fight for human rights. In the process, his celebrity began to compromise his family life.

"Whenever I came home after an absence," Jesse recalled, "I couldn't take the children out in public. I had to retreat to the backyard and play basketball with them. If I went to the movies with them, they became the star's children, even though they didn't think of themselves as such. I regret that. I remember one time Jesse Jr. had a basketball game at school and I didn't go, because I wanted to avoid the Jesse Jackson factor. Jesse Jr. said to me, 'I appreciate all that you've done but there's nothing like my mother coming to my games to see me play ball.' I felt bad about it. There was a tension in my soul. *Both* parents should go to PTA meetings, but I didn't attend them because, how do you negotiate this high-profile stuff? So my wife stepped in and filled the gap."

"I stepped into the gap," Jackie echoed.

"Did you have security around the house?" asked Phil.

"Oh yes," said Jackie. "Once, one of the security men left a gun on the radiator. That morning we woke up and came downstairs, and there was Jesse Jr. with the gun."

"How frightening for you!" Marlo said. "How old was he?"

"He was, I don't know, maybe nine," said Jackie, "and he was holding the gun the way he saw on television. He was holding it out to shoot it. So I said to him, 'Point the gun to the floor,' and he did."

Beyond ensuring the physical safety of their children, the Jacksons were also mindful of allowing them to experience as normal a childhood as possible. But because of Jesse's frequent absences, a lot of the critical decisions fell to Jackie.

JESSE: I once came home from the road, and Jackie told me she'd decided that Jesse Jr. should transfer to the LeMans Academy [boarding school]. He was doing well in school, but he had my name and my friends and my enemies. Jackie saw that and decided to move him to LeMans. Jonathan went, too. And when Santita was a junior in high school, some kids said to her, "Are you Jesse Jackson's daughter?" She said, "Yes," and they said, "You're lying." Santita said, "He's my father!" and almost got into fisticuffs with them. She should not have had to bear the burden of Jesse Jacksonism.

JACKIE: They all did. But you said it so clearly, Reverend. Our children inherit our friends and our foes. So we needed to juggle them and protect them so that they could have a fair chance. As I said, marriage is an institution, and it has many parts, especially when you have a family.

JESSE: And you have to trust your spouse to make decisions that are important to you. One of the properties of love is trust. Love and trust matter.

MARLO: It's so interesting to me how you integrated your family life into your work and your work into your family life. The two were tightly bound.

JESSE: Yes, they were. Someone once asked Santita, "Why is your father always absent?" and she said, "He's helping to feed the hungry for our sake." She had been taught that. She'd been taught that I was out doing something meaningful. Jackie taught our children to respect my work and to respect me. When I went to Syria, I took Jesse Jr. with me. I took them with me when I went to Cuba and South Africa. But in those in-between times, their mother was cultivating them for her long game.

MARLO: And you trusted her to pass these values on to the children.

JESSE: Yes. And now in their adult years, we see the imitation of our work in their lives. Santita is an activist and journalist. Jesse Jr. is a lawyer and former congressman. Yusef is a lawyer. Jonathan has an MBA in business. Jacqueline Jr. has a PhD and is now a university professor. This academic aspiration came out of our house.

JACKIE: And we're so very proud of all of them.

While the Jackson children clearly learned about political activism from their parents, Jesse recalls a similar education from his own parenting, only more chilling.

"Oh, my God, I learned so much about politics from my father," Jesse told us. "He had three jobs as a janitor, one of them at the bank. On Sunday afternoons, we'd go there and buff the floors and empty the cans. Occasionally he would see $5 lying out on a desk or on the floor and he'd say to me, 'You see that $5? Don't touch it. They put that money there to test our honesty.' Then he would write a note saying that he found the $5, so that they would know he did not touch it or steal it."

Jesse was referring to his stepfather, though he typically uses the term "father" when talking about both his biological and adoptive dads. "People say I had a father deficit when in truth I had a father surplus," he once told a reporter. He has also spoken of how both men played a role in his activism.

"One time, my father was working one of his jobs," Jesse recalled, "and the man who was in charge had been drinking with two of his friends. They were red in the face. One of them said to my father, "Charlie, come here." At that moment my father was buffing the floors. I was watching this and, even at seven, I was very aware of the tone in the man's voice and what it meant. My father had been in the Second World War, and when he came back home, he'd told us how badly blacks were treated in the war."

"So what happened when the boss told him to come over?" Phil asked.

"The man said it again: 'Charlie, if you don't come here right now, I'm going to kick you.' Dad stopped the buffing machine and took his keys out of his pocket. He walked over to the man, handed him the keys, and said, 'I cannot be responsible for what happens to the leg that does the kicking.'"

"Wow," Phil said. "He quit rather than be patronized?"

"Yes," Jesse said. "So, it was actually my father who introduced me early on to this struggle."

Throughout our conversation, Jackie hung on to every word her husband said, often agreeing with him, sometimes correcting him, occasionally encouraging him to clarify a particular memory ("take your time," she said at one point). It was apparent just how deeply her husband's life and work were also her own.

"When you agreed to marry this guy, did you realize what you were signing on to?" Phil asked Jackie. "Have you ever imagined what it would be like to have a less public existence?"

"I don't know any other life," Jackie explained. "But I have never been a celebrity. I am a what-you-see-is-what-you-get personality. You ask me a question and there's no powder-puffing. I'm going to be as candid as I possibly can."

"She's never had First Lady–itis," Jesse confirmed with a smile.

"I never *wanted* to be a celebrity," Jackie added. "When someone says, 'Aren't you Jesse Jackson's wife?' I say, 'No. I left her at home.' I have lost my identity many times. Sometimes I'm Santita's mother. Other times I'm the mother of Congressman Jesse Jackson Jr. And I've traveled on my own and done my work for the cause."

Jesse was quick to amplify the details of his wife's global activism. "There's an international dimension to her life," he said, "like her meetings with Fidel Castro and Yasser Arafat and Daniel Ortega. She also led the first [civil rights] delegation in Lebanon. That's when I was most afraid, because she was there when the bombs were falling. It was Christmastime and I was home with the kids. I watched the bombing on television and I panicked—I told her to come back. She said, 'I can take care of myself.' I just couldn't imagine her being over there and me being home. When I went to Lebanon, I was greeted as Jackie Jackson's husband."

PHIL: You have both led such purposeful lives, and the way you inspire each other is extraordinary. Are you always like this?

JACKIE: Most of the time. But that doesn't mean we don't fight. I have to fight with him to keep him sharp, and I do that every morning. We have our exercise.

MARLO: Really? What kind of exercise?

JACKIE: I shout at him and call him names.

MARLO: Well, that's a first. No other couple we've spoken to intentionally fights. What names do you call him?

JACKIE: I'm not telling you. It's our little secret.

MARLO: Does he call you names back?

JACKIE: No, no, no. Absolutely never.

MARLO: Oh, I see. So, the woman can call the man a name, but the man can't call a woman—

JACKIE: —he can never, never, never call me a name. That's disrespectful. When I call him names, that's not disrespect, because he knows all of the names I'm calling him are accurate.

JESSE: And if I call her one name in return, she'll remember it thirty years later.

JACKIE: That's something I appreciate about marriage. I think women have the right to say things because men are all those things. And if they are not those things now, they're going to be them in the future.

PHIL: What kinds of things?

JACKIE: Self-absorbed, for one. See, there's a difference between being self-absorbed and self-centered. Self-centered means you're focused, you're straight ahead, and you're clear about yourself. Self-absorbed means you're selfish. Men are hunters—they get their little bows and arrows and guns and go off into the darkness and lie in the dirt and sneak up on little animals. That's men. Women are gatherers. We pick fruit and vegetables in the sunshine. I think women are essential in holding a marriage together. If a woman wants to keep the marriage, she will keep it. And if she's finished, it's done.

PHIL: I have a feeling you can yell at your husband and he's not going to run out the door.

JACKIE: He won't run out the door, no. He takes punches. Oh, he's good. He can take a punch.

PHIL: It seems to me that you never get jealous about him.

JACKIE: I'm not jealous about him. No, no.

PHIL: Never?

JACKIE: Let me tell you a story. We went out one night and this lady was so stunned to see Reverend that she ran right past me and grabbed him by his neck and just swung and swung and swung. And Reverend kept saying, "This is my wife, this is my wife!" And I kept moving farther back. It was like, "I'm not getting the hell beat out of me—*you* deal with this woman." And he kept saying, "This is my wife. Jackie, come here!"

PHIL: Understood. There's no denying he's a tall, good-looking man.

JACKIE: Good looking, good looking…

PHIL: But you're not worried about him?

JACKIE: I am not worried about him.

As we talked about jealousy and fidelity, topics we'd broached with every couple, the conversation veered into territory that was arguably the most sensitive chapter in the Jackson's fifty-eight-year marriage.

"So, when we were in Atlanta," Jackie began.

"I was in—" Jesse interrupted.

"No, no—let me tell it," Jackie said, "because you'll just tell pieces. We were in Atlanta and some other woman walked up to me. My God, she was gorgeous. She had her camera and said, 'I want to take a picture,' and I said, 'Okay, you can.' She said, 'And who are you?' I said, 'I'm his wife, and you cannot stay around him too long because you're too good looking. This one is mine and he's taken. Now take your picture and leave.' And she said, 'How can you stay with him after he went out there and had that baby?'"

"Did you know what she was talking about?" Marlo asked.

"The Reverend had a child," Jackie said matter-of-factly. "I have five children. Reverend has six."

We'd actually heard bits of the story Jackie was referring to. In the mid-1990s, Jesse had an affair with a political scientist who was writing about his foreign policy record. The relationship produced a daughter, and by 2001, the indiscretion had become public. In a statement, Jesse expressed his love for the child and his remorse for his infidelity. He asked for his family's—and God's—forgiveness and pledged "emotional and financial support" for the baby and her mother.

It was a shocking turn of events that could have blown most marriages apart, especially for such a high-profile couple.

MARLO: This is a tough story for you, I realize. Do you mind discussing it?

JACKIE: I don't discuss it because it's something that I dealt with and that I now feel comfortable with. The young lady, Ashley, is now about twenty, and I'm very comfortable with this.

MARLO: Did you get mad at him? Did you throw him out?

JACKIE: Of course I was mad, because, as you know, as a wife you feel you're the sexiest, the best. But that's something you have to get over, because women are very bold in our society today. We promote and applaud bad behavior from women.

JESSE: Let me just say—

JACKIE: —no, no, let me finish my conversation. We promote the behavior of women, and women today can be very intrusive, and very insulting to their sisters. You can't keep this up and be my sister as a woman and a feminist and a womanist.

JESSE: There are days when there is sunshine and the wind is behind your back, and on others, some rain must fall.

JACKIE: I think there are some realities here. We are people. Nobody in this world today is perfect. If you're looking for a perfect person, be perfect yourself. Don't put that responsibility on me and my family. We're not perfect. We have a lot of flaws, and I personally don't like to discuss the problems of anybody. Tell me how you got out of it. Tell me how you moved forward. That I'm happy to discuss.

MARLO: So you decided that this incident was not going to destroy your marriage.

JACKIE: I promised in sickness and in health, in good times and in bad, through triumphs and sorrows. This marriage is a test of my character. I learned this from my mother. Every time I received my report card, the first thing she looked at was my character—what my conduct was like. I don't try to look for good people—I try to *be* good. That's a test of my character.

MARLO: All the same, most other women would have thrown their husbands out. It's to be admired that you stuck it out.

JACKIE: Oh no, I'm not to be admired. We have to be very careful; I am proud to be a woman—if I have another chance to come back, I want to be a woman again, and I love being an African-American woman. But I want women to be the very best people. I do not want to see women imitate the behavior of men. Yes, my husband had many years of being movie-star glamorous. But give me a break. I'm not going to sit back as a woman and say, "Oh, these poor innocent women just fall for his charisma." Why are you there with my husband? Why do you have so much breast revealed? And I'm not supposed to address you and ask, "Aren't you cold?" This is embarrassing and it's insulting. I'm very sad that women act this way because I take such pride in being a woman. Character counts, and this is something I want women to understand. I want women to have the same respect they are demanding from men.

PHIL: And Jesse is still here.

JACKIE: Oh, I don't worry about him. He's not going anywhere.

MARLO: He never was.

JACKIE: And I don't worry because I'm a good woman, and I don't have any woman to fear. I do respect women because I am one, but I have some expectations of them. I haven't lowered my expectations.

PHIL: Still, you must have been hurt when you found out about the child.

JACKIE: I was disappointed, but I wasn't disappointed in my husband. And I'm not disappointed in men, because I feel men don't have certain skills or capabilities. I know that society makes men feel like they're all that and a bag of chips, but I feel that women are so necessary for men and that's why women were created last. The Lord thought about it, the Lord stopped and rested, and he looked at that man he created and said, "This man needs a little help." And all of the finest ingredients that God may have missed when men were being composed went to women.

MARLO: A second draft.

JACKIE: And that's why I call him Reverend. I don't call him Jesse. I call him Reverend so that it reminds him of who he should be.

MARLO: I don't know a lot of couples who would speak so openly about something so personal.

JACKIE: Reverend and I are like comrades. We've been in a war. We don't get badges. Nobody gives us some huge prize for trying to maintain ethics, character, honesty, and our service to our country. There's no reward for what we do or have done.

PHIL: So what advice would you offer to a young couple about to be married?

JACKIE: That I still believe in the little farm that is the entire family. Today, this generation is moving forward without advice from the elders, so I would encourage them to listen. Oftentimes, older people can see things. As they say, new brooms sweep clean, but old brooms remember the corners.

Jesse remained largely silent through this part of the conversation. But when he spoke, he did so softly.

"If you live long enough, you're going to have some tough times in life," he began. "But as someone once said, tough times don't last but tough people do. Part of what Jackie's done for me down through the years is to help give me balance and protect me and protect our family's interests. Look at us. We were in college together and church together and demonstrations together and raising a family together. And we're still present together. I'm more married now than I was forty years ago. I wouldn't know what to do without my wife. I pray to God that he takes me first. Otherwise, I'd be lost. I couldn't survive."

And then the long-time minister couldn't resist one final metaphor.

"Life is like a rocket," he said, "and there are three stages to that rocket. The first stage is very exciting—you're taking off. The second stage is for leveling off. And the third stage of that rocket is for the children. It's for legacy. There is no atmosphere at that level. There's no adversary at that level. Your life is above the clouds."

Melissa McCarthy and Ben Falcone

MARRIED IN 2005

"I get mooned a lot."

W hat is learned with laughter is learned well." If that age-old credo is true, then speaking with actress Melissa McCarthy and director Ben Falcone about their marriage qualifies as a master class.

The joy they take from each other is palpable, and the howls they incite in others is their obsession. And that makes sense: comedy brought them together; and laughter, they firmly believe, is a life-enhancing elixir.

"She makes me laugh very hard," Ben told us. "I think whatever life force I drain from myself with my constant anxiety and worry, she gives years back to me by laughing."

Ben isn't being figurative. He and Melissa actually believe laughter leads to longevity. "Whenever we have a good laugh," Melissa explained, "especially a crazy one, when you're like, *Oh, my God*, and you're almost dizzy—we always assign it a specific amount of time that it added to our lives. And I'm always adding it up. I'll say, 'Okay, that was like two months—I just got two more months to live!'"

Los Angeles, California; October 8, 2005

BEN: We had a really big one a couple of weeks ago.

PHIL: Tell us.

MELISSA: We were reading Judy Blume's *Tales of a Fourth Grade Nothing* to our daughter Georgie.

BEN: The material is dryer than I remember.

MELISSA: There's a lot of talk about poster board.

BEN: At one point, Jimmy and Sheila are doing a group project, and Sheila wants to use yellow poster board and Jimmy wants to use blue. This particular section was not interesting to Georgie.

323

MELISSA: I was nodding off.

BEN: So I decided that I would try to add a little color to the book. Sheila and Jimmy were having this argument, so I read it literally. I screamed every piece of dialogue—like, *"I want the yellow paper!"*

MELISSA: All the words were very bland, but he just kept screaming them in the angriest voice—*"Yellow is a much brighter color! Blue is too dull!"*—and Georgie and I were lying on the bed, crying with laughter.

BEN: I was really going for it. I was committed to the bit and almost threw out my voice.

MELISSA: That was like a six-monther, right there. Six more months to live.

MARLO: What a great way to think about time.

MELISSA: I love hearing someone laughing like that in a restaurant—like they're losing their mind. There's a certain sound to laughter that you can't control.

BEN: Because it's cathartic, absolutely. It's like a good cry.

MARLO: When you laugh so hard and can't stop, and you have to hold yourself not to pee. My favorite kind of laughter.

MELISSA: That's what I always think of with couples. You don't have to be a comedian to get this. But if there's never any laughter in a relationship, how do you get through someone being sick or something? Without a little goofiness, I think it would be hard to be in a relationship. You need those silly moments.

We spoke with Melissa and Ben at the home they keep in Atlanta, Georgia, which serves as a base when they are shooting one of their joint projects: Ben directs, Melissa stars, and often they collaborate on the script. Beyond earning a tax break for filming in the Peach State, the couple wanted "something that felt like home" for their two preteen daughters, Vivian and Georgette.

"We kind of live like gypsies," Melissa explained. "We do uproot them from Los Angeles, whether we're working together, or only one of us is working. We all go. We don't separate. So this house feels familiar for the girls."

Not that Melissa and Ben are hung up on their home's pedigree.

"I don't know what you'd call this house," Melissa said.

"Traditional with a neoclassical contemporary flair," Ben offered.

"*Oh, Daddy,*" Melissa purred, with a southern swoon.

"It's actually postmodern," Phil concluded.

"I like that," Melissa said. "That makes us seem edgier."

Whatever the house is, it's beautiful. We were sitting on the porch out-fitted with swinging sofas. Nearby were two golden retrievers—the petite Betty and the barking Harper—and out in the backyard was Habersham, a big, yellow plastic horse knocked on its side by a recent windstorm. Right-ing Habersham was on Ben's to-do list that day.

Melissa and Ben met in Los Angeles at the Groundlings, which, along with Chicago's Second City and the coastal Upright Citizens Brigade, is one of the country's premier improv and sketch comedy troupes. Its alumni roster reads like a Comedy Hall of Fame roll call—from Will Ferrell and Lisa Kudrow, to Jon Lovitz and Maya Rudolph.

"He was always my favorite person to write with," Melissa recalled, adding that they spent the better part of a decade making each other laugh.

"So how does it happen that suddenly you turn from writing partners into something a little more than that?" Phil asked.

Ben explained that the transformation was pretty organic. "After re-hearsal, a lot of us would go out to a dive bar on Melrose Avenue called the Snake Pit," he said. "Melissa and I would end up staying the latest together because we wanted to hang out. Then we realized that we had to make a choice: to either start dating or become alcoholics."

"Everybody else would leave and I'd say, 'If you're going to have an-other one, I'll stay with you,'" Melissa recalled. "Eventually, we truly thought that we should date because we were just drinking."

So when the boozy buzz wore off, were there genuine feelings there?

"Well, I knew I liked him right away," Melissa said. "We sat next to each other the first day in class at the Groundlings. We all did monologues and different characters, myself included. Everybody tried to do the most outrageous thing—loud, crazy characters—but when Ben went up, he did this very quiet, very strange character. He was pleasant but creepy. Turns out he was talking to his new cellmate in prison. And I thought, *How interesting.* Everyone in class was leaning forward to listen."

It wasn't just Ben's comedic technique or spontaneity that won Melissa over. It was his moxie.

"I've told this story to people before, and they're like, 'You found him creepy and that's why you liked him?' Maybe—I don't know. It's just that he was doing something so *different.*"

For Ben, the attraction was much more basic: "She was the funniest one," he said. "She was very pretty, and she seemed to like me."

"Funny, pretty, she likes me," Marlo said. "That covers all the bases."

"Exactly," Ben said. "And I thought, *I'll take it.*"

Perhaps one of the reasons Melissa and Ben seem so attuned to each other is that they share the same midwestern roots. She is from Plainfield, Illinois, and he is from Carbondale, home of Southern Illinois University, which Melissa attended. Their origin story has a nice little *Twilight Zone* twist. Melissa is three years older than Ben, and she used to listen to music in her friend's basement in the house across the street from Ben's. This was seven years before they met, when Melissa was eighteen years old and in her punk phase.

"I knew of her because she and her friends dressed very aggressively," Ben said.

"Forgive me, but I'm ancient," Phil said. "What does 'dressed aggressively' mean?"

"Blue hair and a full-length black outfit," Melissa said.

"Aha," Phil said. "That *is* aggressive."

"We weren't trying to be menacing," Melissa explained. "It was more like a competition to see what would make the weirdest outfit. I was a terrible punk. Yes, I did look menacing, but that wasn't the goal."

Melissa and Ben married while they were with the Groundlings. They confess to not being entirely sure when they started getting romantic ("We struggle with years—I think we met in 1996," Ben said), but to their best estimation they dated for roughly six years and then married in 2005. Their career breakthroughs were many years away.

"My first regular job was *The Gilmore Girls* [as chef Sookie St. James]," Melissa recalls, "and I couldn't believe it. That was the first time that I had a long-term job. It was a big deal if I even got a line in something."

Ben was equally thrilled to land a small break, noting that an "under-five" (the actors' union contract term for a character with five or fewer lines of dialogue) was fine with him. "I was the guy who walked in and gave the governor a cup of coffee," he noted. " 'Here's your coffee, governor.' "

"I had a few of those when I was starting out," Marlo said. " 'You can go in now, Mr. Addison.' "

"You still remember it!" Ben said, genuinely impressed.

"How could I ever forget?" Marlo said.

Raised on a farm, Melissa hails from a large, Catholic family (her grandparents emigrated from Cork to Chicago at the turn of the twentieth century), and she caught the acting bug early. She cut her teeth with walk-on roles on both the big screen (a waitress in Disney's *The Kid*) and small screen (a saleswoman in *Curb Your Enthusiasm*) before knocking audiences sideways in 2011 with her hilarious turn in *Bridesmaids*, an in-your-face performance so bold and bawdy that it earned her an Oscar nomination. Ben played her romantic interest in the film.

So quick was their subsequent show business ascent that it was common to think of them as overnight successes—but that is a rarity in this business, as they both pointed out.

MELISSA: We starved for a long, long time.

BEN: Yes, we did.

MELISSA: I think that's why we appreciate our careers so much. I started at twenty. We both worked nine hundred other jobs because we were always doing shows. At the Groundlings, you pay for the classes, and even when you get into the main company there's no pay. It's a great place to learn, but you're not making a dime so everybody has to have real jobs.

PHIL: Like what?

MELISSA: I was a nanny, I waited tables, and then I pretty much started working as a production assistant when I got out to L.A.

BEN: I worked at CPK—California Pizza Kitchen—and was fired. There was a secret shopper, a spy, somebody who comes in and reports if the server doesn't offer everything in the proper amount of time and in the correct sequence of service. There are eight steps. I could talk all day just about this.

MARLO: Oh, a spy. How awful.

BEN: It was the one in Brentwood, near a movie theater. We didn't get a lot of business, but everyone who went to a 7 p.m. movie would be in a hurry. The spies asked me detailed questions about the scampi pizza, and I think my answer was, "It's really good." I got a 36 out of 100.

MELISSA: Way to go.

BEN: In my defense, I'd once gotten a 90.

MARLO: Atta boy.

MELISSA: I hate when people upsell. I don't need the spiel.

BEN: "Would you like some delicious spinach artichoke dip with that?"

MELISSA: No.

BEN: "Would you like a Long Island iced tea for lunch?"

MELISSA: You could always go back. You've still got it.

BEN: I do still have it.

Strange town, Hollywood. After years of struggle and modest successes, *Bridesmaids* earned the couple some serious attention. Toby Emmerich, then an executive producer with New Line, called asking whether the couple had anything they wanted to do.

"How did it feel to suddenly be a player?" Phil asked.

"Insane," Ben said.

Melissa jumped in. "I just remember not being sure what he even meant, because no one had ever said that," Melissa remembered. "All we had was this weird script Ben had written about a woman going on a road trip with her grandma who's an alcoholic." That film was the dark comedy *Tammy*—Ben's directorial debut—which earned more than $100 million worldwide against a $20 million budget. Melissa eventually shared a co-writer screen credit on it.

"This is what I find so interesting about married couples who work together," Phil noted. "Often the success of the relationship contributes to the success of the project."

Ben nodded. "I wrote the script basically to show people the full range of what Melissa could do," he said. "At that point, she was getting type-cast as the fast-talking friend. And after *Bridesmaids*, people said she was raunchy, which is not true at all. So I wrote this thing to show what Melissa could do, and the irony is we never would have gotten to make it unless her role in *Bridesmaids* hadn't already shown people what she could do."

There on their porch it was hard not to notice that Melissa and Ben are tuned to the same frequency. Their banter was so breezy and their manner so laid back that we began to wonder what things look like when they don't get along.

PHIL: Did you fight before you got married?

BEN: Sure.

MELISSA: Yes. But he's much more mellow. He's even-steven all the time; I'll go crazy and then calm down.

PHIL: Some people fight as a way to connect.

MELISSA: Fighting is not excitement. I think sometimes those are confused—that you're feeling some kind of rush from fighting. I just don't think that's a foundation you can build a relationship on. That's the wrong rush.

BEN: Our biggest fight was because I was eating grapes too loudly. It really spiraled out of control.

PHIL: So you're the volatile one, Melissa?

MELISSA: Yes.

PHIL: And you adjust to her volcano, Ben?

BEN: Yes, I'm dull.

MELISSA: Steady is not dull.

BEN: I think it's healthier to be like she is. My dad is like that. He'll let it out, but then his blood pressure goes back to normal. Whereas my mother isn't as volatile and the blood pressure just spikes inside.

MELISSA: You probably worry more than I do. It's a good balance, though.

BEN: It's a really good balance because she's funny and fun, and if I get into a place where I'm like, "Oh, my God, I've got bird flu," she's like, "You don't have bird flu. Let's go have a sandwich."

MARLO: I go right to brain damage.

BEN: Sure. I got that one, too.

MARLO: Really, I lean toward hypochondria. Yesterday, I had a bad headache from this head cold that went from my eye all the way up my forehead, and I asked Phil if it was possible to get a stroke from having the wrong cold medication. He said, "No, that's not possible." I said, "But it really hurts. Are you sure it couldn't be an aneurysm?" He went back to his crossword puzzle. My whole family is like this. Whatever we read about, we think we have it. We've had everything but beriberi.

Okay, so back to fighting. Who's the one who makes up?

MELISSA: It's pretty even. I usually cause it.

MARLO: That's good to know.

MELISSA: I do know that I've gotten calmer as the years have gone on. Don't you think?

BEN: I think so, for sure. And hopefully I'm a little less worryish—but having kids makes you worry more, so she's got her hands full with me right now.

MELISSA: When he's really worried about something, I lean into it. He always thinks he's being poisoned, so I just tell him I've been poisoning him. I'll say, "You don't have to worry about being poisoned because you're definitely being poisoned. I'm telling you, it's really happening."

BEN: Like, I'm insane, but she lets it be. Do you know what I mean? Instead of trying to fix me, she tries to help me, which I think is good.

MARLO: What's the difference between fixing and helping?

BEN: Well, instead of saying, "You can't be anxious anymore. You better go talk to somebody and figure it out," she's like, "Hey, why don't you stop doing that right now and we'll go do something else?" And I'm like, "Oh, what a great idea." We don't try to fix each other very much, which I think is important.

MARLO: That's sort of like an improv, isn't it?

MELISSA: Yes, you kind of go with it

PHIL: I'll have to try that at home.

MELISSA: But we also talk things out if we're frustrated or something is irritating. We don't have to pretend we're not irritated or pretend something isn't bugging us. I can say, "Stop eating your grapes so loud, you're driving me crazy," and he'll say, "Stop being so sound-sensitive. No one should care how loud I'm eating grapes."

BEN: How funny would it be if this conversation revived the great grape argument? But this brings up a mistake I made in taking a piece of marriage advice: don't go to bed mad.

PHIL: A lot of couples we've spoken to live by that advice. Jimmy and Rosalynn Carter, to name one.

BEN: Well, I thought, *Let me just see what happens if I actually go to bed mad.* I tried it once, and I realized that in the morning I had forgotten what I was mad about. You're not getting any answers if you're parsing out an argument when everybody is tired and possibly had a drink or two. I've never had the thing where you're having an argument at ten o'clock at night, and then you say, "Well, that was good. I'm glad we got to the bottom of that. We agree. Truce signed." I think there's something to be said for revisiting an argument in the morning. Because then it's just, "Yes, it would be good for you to put the clothes that are going to the dry cleaner in the correct hamper, because you do keep forgetting to do that."

MELISSA: I love that your motto is, "Go to bed mad."

BEN: I say, go to bed pissed. Just be pissed and go to sleep.

Grape-chomping and hamper-skipping aside, Melissa and Ben do tend to get along, and both credit their respective parents as stable—and very funny—role models. Melissa's folks have been married for just over half a century. Dad worked for the railroad; Mom was a secretary at World Book Encyclopedia and then at a bank.

"They are truly each other's best friends," Melissa reports. "They still hold hands and they still make each other laugh. They're really funny, and I think that's the key. My father will do weird things just to make her laugh. I was once on the phone with my mom—this wasn't that many years ago—and she started laughing. I asked what was so funny. She said that my father had gotten up from his chair in the den and left the room. Two seconds later, he just slid by the open door in his socks, wearing only his underwear and T-shirt, then he put his clothes back on, came back in and sat down. He did it clearly just to make her laugh."

Ben's parents recently celebrated their fiftieth anniversary. He was an English teacher; she's a social worker. Both, he said, are also very funny—his mom especially. Just as Ben went all in with his Judy Blume rage routine, his mother is all about committing to a bit.

"To this day," Ben said with a certain awe, "she tells me she's an alien. Growing up, she would tell us not to make her angry because she would have to take off her Peggy suit and reveal that she was a Martian. She'd play it very straight. *'I do not want to have to take off my Peggy suit.'* It would scare us to death. Finally, I got pretty upset about it and I said, 'Mom, please just say that you're not an alien,' and she said, 'You're making everything less fun right now.' That was the closest I could get to it. I'm sure if she was here right now, she'd say, 'No, I'm a Martian.' She's not going to quit on it. I admire how committed she is to the bit."

MARLO: Do you two have bits you do all the time?

BEN: I have a sea of bad bits that she tolerates.

MELISSA: I get mooned a lot. It's always done the same way. We'll both be in the kitchen. He's always reaching to adjust something, and then he'll say something to make me turn around—and there it is.

BEN: It's only the top. I'm very tasteful about it.

PHIL: That's the tail of a whale, isn't it?

MELISSA: Oh my God, I've never heard that.

BEN: That's what you're going to start hearing now. I've got other material I'm working on.

MARLO: What's one of your other bits? I've now found a topic I really want to explore.

MELISSA: He does a lot of high pants.

BEN: It's the inverse.

MELISSA: You just walk into a room and his pants are—

BEN: —as high as I can get them without hurting myself. And I do dinosaur hands. Also, the kids have discovered Lizzo—she's a really good rap singer and artist. Her lyrics tend to be explicit and we're bad parents, so we let them listen to her songs.

MELISSA: Not all of them.

BEN: But some of them. So I've started doing super-wholesome versions of her songs for the kids—that they hate. So that means you've got to go back to it hard.

MELISSA: The girls are like, "Stop!"

BEN: And we're like, "Ooh, that struck a nerve, so let's hit it again." And then she's Marbles.

PHIL: What does that mean?

MELISSA: It's this character I did eons ago. Ben and I would make these videos—they're on YouTube. Marbles is this incredibly brilliant woman who is socially strange and very extreme looking. Sometimes, if we're eating breakfast, the girls will ask, "Marbles, do you like your breakfast?' and I'll just start saying absolute nonsense.

BEN: And if ever I need a laugh, I'll just ask Marbles a question.

MELISSA: It's all pretty weird.

One common assumption about funny people—especially those in show business—is that they avoid serious topics. Not this duo. We asked them if they ever find themselves looking at each other and thinking, *Wow, I really did the right thing marrying this person.*

"I must think that twenty times a day," Melissa said. "It's his actions. It's his kindness. He makes me laugh all day long, which is great—but it's the kindness and the way he is with our girls, and how he is with everybody, really. He leads with kindness at all times."

"I totally get that," Marlo said. "That's Phil, and I'll give you the perfect example. We didn't want to be late today because we knew you two had limited time, and we had to get here and set up the recorder and the mics. So I'm saying to Phil, 'Come on, let's go, let's move.' And the reason I say that is because I know there is no way that we can get out of a hotel or any public place without him making everybody feel good, all the way out the building."

"Which is great!" Ben said.

"But I mean *everyone*," Marlo continued. "The woman in the elevator. The guy at the front desk. The doorman. I've got blinders on—I'm running out the door to find the car, and he's back there going, 'Nini, what a lovely name.' So, yes, there's a part of me that gets so annoyed by it because I'm always in a rush. But the other part of that is, 'What a nice man.' He's just a much nicer person than I am."

"That's what I think all the time," Melissa said. "Ben is just nicer."

"But it's a good mix, Marlo," Ben interjected, "because from the sound of things, he might never get anywhere if you weren't around. He would just be fluttering around some hotel lobby. He would never get to lunch."

Not all has been laughs for this couple, however. We asked them to name a time in their marriage when an unexpected challenge arose. Ben revealed that the scariest thing their family had to face was when Melissa suffered a pulmonary edema following the birth of their eldest daughter and had to be admitted to the ICU.

PHIL: That had to be terrifying. How did you deal with it?

BEN: By getting shingles.

MARLO: Did you really?

BEN: Yes, apparently if you get stressed out enough, you can get shingles.

MARLO: Oh, my God.

BEN: I bravely got shingles.

MELISSA: Yep, he bravely got shingles.

BEN: She was in the hospital for three to four days, and then she had to take it easy after that. And, of course, we had a new baby at home.

MELISSA: Thank God that both of our moms were there.

BEN: And that's when one of the fires came. We had just gotten a new house—her water broke the day the contractor left. Vivi was born. What a great day. We get home and she starts feeling really, really sick. Back to the hospital. Meanwhile, while we're at the hospital, the hill behind our house is on fire.

MELISSA: One canyon over.

BEN: I hosed down the house like a lunatic—that thing you do when you say, "What does that do? Nothing." But I tried. But, yeah, health-related stuff is always hard. I couldn't do much except just try to pitch in. Thank goodness she was all right.

PHIL: Melissa, same question. What's been your scariest moment of the marriage?

MELISSA: Luckily, nothing health-related with him. But my biggest fear is that I'll blow it—that I'll make him so irritated that he'll leave. I mean, I'd still follow him if he did. I always tell him, "It's okay to leave me, but I'll come with you like it doesn't matter."

BEN: Tell them about the dream.

MELISSA: I don't have a lot of bad dreams, but I have a recurring one—probably like twice a year—where I walk in and all of our friends are there, and everything seems great, and then I see Ben's girlfriend is sitting on his lap, and they're all laughing and having a great time. I'm shocked and horrified and crying, and I say, "You guys all know that he's dating someone, and nobody told me?" And they say, "See how you're acting—that's why he had to date Donna. Donna doesn't act like that."

PHIL: You actually have a name for this dream woman?

MELISSA: I think it's Donna.

BEN: I hope it changes.

MELISSA: Who knows? But it's the only dream I have where, after I wake up, I'm still rattled for about fifteen minutes.

MARLO: Wow. That's kind of sweet, in a way.

MELISSA: And then I'll try to talk to him about it, and he'll start with the jokes. He'll say, "Well, I think you'd like Donna if you just gave her a chance."

As we began packing up our equipment, we caught a glimpse of Vivi and Georgie running through the house. "You two are such fun that it's easy to forget that you're also grown-up, responsible parents," Phil said. "Do you ever find yourself consciously setting an example for your kids the way your parents did for you?"

Melissa collected her thoughts. "I think our girls have a better shot at getting a good partner if they've been able to watch their parents be great partners," she said. "In our case, I think they know what a good man is. They see how Ben treats me and they see how I have a voice. That's pretty huge. That's a great thing to be able to show your kids."

Ben jumped in. "And they know that they have a baller mom," he said. "Sometimes Melissa feels bad. She'll say, 'I'm working so much—I should be home more.' And I say, 'Isn't it kind of cool to show our girls that mom's a boss?' It's not like what we do is surgery or anything, but there are a hundred people all waiting for Melissa, and she's great to work with. She takes it all seriously, and she does the work so that *everyone* can go home and be with their own kids. I think that's a good way to be a role model."

"And what advice will you give your girls when it's their turn to walk down the aisle?" Phil asked.

"Just be who you are," Melissa said. "I always use the example of people posting pictures of their vacation on social media, as if they're asking, 'Do you think it was a good enough vacation?' Well, did you have a good time? What do you care what everybody else thinks? It's a weird thing that people now need to be validated about their choices instead of just making the choice—and that they try to show themselves in a way that's not really who they are.

"So I tell my daughters they should not go into a marriage thinking they can change the other person's personality quirks," Melissa concluded. "Part ways before you walk down that aisle because you can't change people in that way."

And just when we thought we were getting serious:

BEN: So, yes, you want someone who fills your tank, not someone who depletes it. Oh, my God, that's a saying.

MARLO: That's going to be the name of our book.

BEN: It is?

MARLO: It's got to be.

MELISSA: "Fill Your Tank."

BEN: No, wait: "Go to Bed Mad and Fill Your Tank."

PHIL: Scene.

Kevin Bacon and Kyra Sedgwick

MARRIED IN 1988

"There is no Plan B. No matter what,
we want to work it out."

I t took some persuading to get Kevin Bacon and Kyra Sedgwick on board to talk about the success of their thirty-one-year marriage. As Kevin told us on the phone, "My first piece of advice is not to take advice from celebrities."

We laughed. But like all good jokes, it rang true. For many of the couples we spoke with, their marriages are a safe haven from the media gossip mill, and they were hell-bent on protecting them. But in this case, in spite of their reservations—and after a man-to-man between Phil and Kevin— they invited us to their home on the Upper West Side of Manhattan.

Tucked inside a wonderful old relic of a building, their apartment over-looks the reservoir in Central Park. We had the same gorgeous view years ago when we lived up the street, and we loved the way the lights of the city's buildings danced on the water at night.

Built in 1906, the building is fronted at street level by a wonderful porte cochere that's wide enough to admit horse-drawn carriages but too narrow for today's cars. We took the elevator to the Bacon-Sedgwick apartment;

Sharon, Connecticut; September 4, 1988

the door was unlocked and we were greeted by Kevin, who was dressed in an unbuttoned, short-sleeved blue shirt, his hair sandy and loose. Their sweet little dog, Lily, jumped on us, paying no attention to Kevin's commands not to. We love dogs, so we didn't mind the enthusiastic hello one bit, and we happily returned her affection.

Phil fell in love with the large, open living room, with matching black fireplaces occupying each end, books everywhere, and a twelve-foot-long wooden table at the center. Sunlight flooded through the windows, offering that great vista of the park. It was warm and inviting—just like the couple, as we soon discovered.

Kyra, blonde hair thick with bouncy curls, entered the room carrying a pitcher of water and four glasses. She dove right in.

"I never want to come off like a celebrity who knows more than anybody else in the world," she said. "I would never feel comfortable saying, 'Eat the way I eat' or 'Do the things I do.' What the hell do I know? Who am I to say that what works for me works for somebody else?"

Kevin agreed. "From the beginning, we had very specific rules about what we would talk about in public or on a red carpet," he said. "And one of those rules was that we didn't do interviews together or try to cash in on our Kyra-and-Kev cute thing. I don't even really like reading articles about actors. So often you see these idyllic couples on the cover of *People* magazine, and six months later they're divorced. So, whenever people asked us how we've stayed married, I started saying, 'Keep the fights clean and the sex dirty.' I felt like that would just end the conversation."

"And it does," Kyra added.

Even after just a few moments with them, it was obvious how in sync they are—the way they talk, the way they gesture—so it's no wonder their public image is that of a very tight-knit couple. But surely they must have ups and downs like everybody else. We started with that.

"We fight very rarely," Kyra said, musing. "I don't know. Sometimes I think, 'Is that bad?' But honestly, we don't like to fight, so when we actually are in an argument, we're both looking for a solution. For the most part we're struggling to get back to everything being okay, because it sucks to fight."

The longest fight of their marriage, it turns out, was in the 1990s when they were living in rural Connecticut with their two young children. Kyra is a born-and-bred New Yorker, and she felt like she was losing her mind. She missed the pulse of the city, while Kevin was content in the countryside. They argued about it for six months.

"It was really, really bad," Kyra said, even though Kevin eventually came around to her side. "Kicking and screaming" is how she described their move back to New York.

"I felt a lot of financial pressure," Kevin said, explaining how difficult and expensive it is to find an apartment big enough for a family in New York City. "I always think that every job I do is my last job."

He then turned to his wife and said the words that every spouse on the planet likes to hear. "Boy, were you right in so many ways."

Actors' incomes are often insecure, of course, but the idea that Kevin Bacon worries about his next job seemed inconceivable to us. He's been in sixty-some movies and on countless TV shows, working steadily since he was a teenager. He's also produced and directed a number of projects and has been in so many ensemble casts (*Animal House, Diner, Footloose, JFK, Apollo 13*) that a party game was named in his honor—"Six Degrees of Kevin Bacon." The "Bacon number" in the game is derived from how many actors it takes to connect him to any other randomly selected actor, basically making him the center of the entertainment universe.

Tension over money has been many a couple's downfall, and we knew we'd eventually have to address how Kyra and Kevin lost millions by investing with the notoriously crooked financier Bernie Madoff. But before we moved on to that delicate subject, we wanted to learn about their foundation as a couple, and what made them solid enough to weather such a shocking betrayal.

They met in Cambridge, Massachusetts, while filming a Lanford Wilson play, *Lemon Sky*, and had a "little fling." Kyra was seeing somebody else, and Kevin had just come off a long-term relationship with actress Tracy Pollan. Kyra didn't expect their on-set romance to go anywhere. But Kevin had other ideas, leaving her several phone messages after she finished filming and returned to New York. They didn't see each other for another couple weeks, but they spoke on the phone—a lot. Then he visited her in Los Angeles, where she was on another job.

That was it. They moved in together—along with their two big dogs.

"I was thinking the other day about how, with our dogs, we were immediately a family, whether we knew it or not," Kevin mused. "We were sharing responsibilities: dog walking, who's going on the road, how long will you be gone, who's going to take care of the dogs? I mean, I know dogs aren't kids, but it was a nice transition."

So what made him decide Kyra was the one?

"She was gorgeous and super-independent and the right amount of different from me," he said. Kevin is the youngest of six and grew up in Philadelphia. His father was a city planner, which is perhaps what led him to become someone who likes to make a plan and stick to it. Kyra, he would quickly find out, will make a plan and then change it—several times.

"She has a more mercurial kind of approach to life," Kevin said, "with really big heights of joy and then super, super sadness on bad days. She comes from a world where everybody—pretty much on both sides of her family—was into thoughts and feelings. It's an emotional honesty. My upbringing was much more held in, so I've had to learn how to be more open and comfortable expressing doubts and fears and pain and anxiety and all those things."

"I've been scratching at Phil for forty years to tell me how he feels," Marlo said. "I'll say, 'Phil, how do you feel?' and he'll say, 'Fine.' I say, 'Fine? There's no information in *fine*. What does *fine* mean? Give me any other adjective. Are you sick? Happy? Hungry? Anything but *fine*.' I remember Phil once said on one of his shows, 'Women lead men to their feelings,' and I thought, *Whoa, he gets it. Yes, women do that. They need to.* There are very few men who say, 'I can't get my wife to tell me how she feels.'"

"On the flip side of that," Kevin said, "Kyra has gotten to an understanding that, for me, it's not always about getting to my feelings. I'll play my guitar or walk around or go for a run and be in my own head for a while. It's what I call 'going into the cave.' I can work it out that way and come out the other side, and the result will still be what she wants: to get me out of my mood."

Kyra was only twenty-three when the couple married in 1988. Kevin was thirty. Their son Travis was born the following year.

"We were like kids with a kid," Kyra said. "The night after I got home from the hospital, we went out for dinner and stuck him in a little baby carrier under the table. And then we went to see *Batman*." Their daughter, Sosie, arrived in 1992.

Kevin added: "Nobody ever told us this—and we didn't read it in a book—but I think we felt it was more important for the kids that *our thing* stayed good. I always knew that I was going to fuck up as a parent somewhere along the way, because everybody does. Anyone can sit on the couch in a therapist's office and think of the ways their mommy and daddy damaged them. I don't think there's any way around that. I'm going to be told that I worked too hard or wasn't there enough or was too judgmental, but the one thing I always remembered"—he looked at Kyra—"was that if we could stay good, that would be a good message for them."

PHIL: That's a lot of insight for a first-time parent.

KEVIN: It was just a guess, really.

KYRA: The thing is, there is no Plan B. No matter what, we want to work it out. I come from divorce, and I think that we both knew that we had to stay strong and that our thing had to come first. It really did. Yes, when the kids needed to be attended to, they did come first; but we knew they were going to go away at some point and we were going to be left together. Since my parents had an unhappy marriage, I wanted to make sure that we were modeling a good marriage for the children— that we could quibble about things and get over it, and that it's not too scary. No one gets too loud.

MARLO: Did you witness that when you were younger? Your parents were loud?

KYRA: Oh, yes. Well, not my mother's first husband—my dad. He wasn't loud, but he left very, very early on. But my stepfather and my mother, they had a complicated relationship.

MARLO: What about your parents, Kevin?

KEVIN: They were married until they died. Although I have to say that there were a lot of things about that marriage that made me think, *Oh, that's not the way I want to be married.* But overall, I think that, yes, theirs was definitely a good model for staying in a marriage.

PHIL: Kyra, you were a young girl from a divorced marriage. How did you dive into marriage without reservation?

KYRA: When I fell in love with him, there was no question in my mind. Not for one single, solitary second did I think, *What am I doing? Why am I rushing into this? Why are we having children so quickly?* I didn't know anything else, but this, I knew.

KEVIN: We don't do a lot of looking in the rearview mirror.

MARLO: But you also must know, as we do, that there's some foundation of your coupledom. What is it? What is that foundation?

KYRA: I think the foundation is that we really fucking love hanging out together, and we really love each other, and we really want to spend time together.

They had a small wedding on September 4, 1988, witnessed by thirty-five people, which happened to be the exact number of guests we had at our wedding. Their ceremony lasted just ten minutes or so, followed by a big party.

"I think people should put as little focus on the wedding as possible," Kevin offered. "Some couples think of the wedding as the marriage, and boy, it is not. If you put the wedding in a pie chart, it's just a four-hour window over the course of thirty years, and yet there's so much emphasis put on it. Sure, it's nice if you have a good time, but the rest of it is garbage. I mean, people get so freaked out about the wedding. Ours definitely didn't define our lives together."

"Also," Kyra added, "the person you marry is not necessarily going to be the same during the whole trajectory of the marriage. Let each other grow. Let each other change. If you don't, that's when trouble happens."

We couldn't help but notice how Kyra and Kevin's guard was gradually coming down, as they warmed to talking with us about their marriage. And we warmed to them. This was becoming a shared conversation about real, lived experiences—it felt nothing at all like red-carpet talking points.

This seemed especially true when Kevin offered his thoughts about starting a new family and how that affects the relationship with the families that the couple came from.

"The new family we created has to come first," he said. "And that can be tough because families want to hold on to everybody as strongly as they can. You still love your brothers and sisters and parents and cousins and aunts and uncles, but our family is first. Then again, there are a lot of places in the world that it's completely the opposite, culturally."

Given that Kyra and Kevin are both actors—leading man and leading lady types—we wondered whether jealousy ever reared its head in the relationship. After all, they frequently find themselves on separate film sets, forming close bonds and surrounded by beautiful people.

"Perhaps foolishly, I have not been jealous," Kyra said. "I remember one time during our marriage I watched him caressing an actress's breasts in a movie, and I leaned over and said, 'That must have been fun.' Maybe I'm deluding myself, but I don't get jealous. He doesn't have a wandering eye. I know what that looks like."

"I think I'm a more jealous person than she is," Kevin said.

MARLO: I remember once when Phil was doing the *Donahue* show, he had Sophia Loren on as a guest. The next day, she called him and asked him out to lunch. Phil called and asked me what I thought. Well, what I thought was, "Are you kidding me?" I mean, if she'd wanted to have lunch the day *before* she was going on the show, I would have understood that she wanted to get to know him, to warm him up for her interview. But she wants to go out to lunch *after* the show? That seemed a little odd. So I said to Phil, "No, I don't think it's a good idea to go to lunch with Sophia Loren." And he said, 'Yeah, that's what I thought."

KYRA: Good answer.

PHIL: I may be clueless, but I'm not stupid.

KYRA: If you do things to make the other person jealous—little things, things that you know aren't cool—then that person is going to be jealous.

KEVIN: Some people like that, though. It's not quite jealousy, but for me, when you're married to a well-known actress, at times you have to share her with the world.

PHIL: I know what you mean. Marlo was the first woman I ever knew who had an interest in so many things other than me.

KEVIN: I wrote a song lyric about that once: her going off into the public eye, and you really have to share her. I've had trouble with that in the past.

MARLO: What's the lyric of the song?

KEVIN: It's called "Arm Wrestling Woman," and it's kind of a metaphor for being with a famous person. In the song she's an arm wrestling star.

MARLO: Really? How does it go?

KYRA: "And I will love her ever more. And I will rub her—"

KEVIN: "—feet when she's sore. And I'll share her with the world. That's just the way it is with an arm wrestling girl."

MARLO: That's great!

KEVIN: I'll tell you one thing we're never jealous of is each other's career. I've never felt any sense of competition with Kyra.

PHIL: Kyra, you made a real accommodation in your marriage. You stopped working when you were raising your babies.

KYRA: He worked more than me, so by that math, I gave up things for sure. I said no to things that weren't going to work out in terms of location and being away.

KEVIN: I think you always put your children in front of your career. I looked at my career as necessary because I had to take care of my family. It's easier for a guy that way. I was a good dad, I think. I was there as much as I could have been.

KYRA: You were.

KEVIN: For a very long time, Kyra was conflicted about work. She would look at a job with trepidation because it meant going away.

KYRA: I also think it took me a long time to embrace my ambition—that didn't happen until I was into my forties.

That's when Kyra starred for seven seasons in *The Closer*, a TNT series that filmed in Los Angeles. By then their kids were teenagers, and they didn't want to relocate; so Kyra took off for the coast, and Kevin stayed behind with the kids in New York. They all flew to visit each other on weekends whenever they could.

"I have some regrets about that," Kyra said softly. "I missed a lot. But financially it was really good for us when we needed that help."

It was in the midst of *The Closer*—which ran from 2005 to 2012—that the news hit about the arrest of Bernie Madoff, the fraudulent financier and asset manager who operated the biggest Ponzi scheme in history. Kyra and Kevin had invested their entire pensions in his firm—and lost all of it.

"We found out when the world found out," Kyra said. "We had both been working professionally—Kev since he was seventeen and me since I was fifteen—and it was our savings, all the money we had. My sister called me because she was invested in it too—our stepfather had suggested it— and she said, 'Are you sitting down?' It was all over the news, about five o'clock on a winter day, just before Christmas. It was a hard day."

"But we're so privileged in about a bazillion ways," Kevin said. "And you can't take it with you. He's a bad man, but we were dumb to—"

"—trust him," Kyra finished, adding that they had never met Madoff. "We were both in shock at first. But then you do a really quick body scan to get some perspective—you have to; otherwise, you just freak out: our children were safe, we were still working, we could make the money back."

"So, yeah, it felt awful and scary for a long time," she continued, "but we knew we were going to get through it. And so many people had it so much worse—people who were old and no longer employable. I remember Kevin saying, 'Look, we're artists and we're not money people. We got screwed. I don't fault us tremendously for not being money people.'"

What was so striking about their memories of the Madoff trauma was not about how much money the couple lost, but how the strength of their bond got them through it.

"This is a pretty strong example of how a couple faces a big challenge," Marlo noted. "It shows that you don't have to lose each other. And you don't have to blame each other, either."

"No, no," Kyra said. "If anything, he could have blamed me because it was my family that got us into it. But he's not like that."

"The first thing I thought," Kevin said, "was, *Holy shit. Let's—I don't know—let's have sex or something. It's free!* But no, it didn't challenge the marriage. In fact, the marriage was what made it easy. The money was gone, but we still had each other."

Dr. Mehmet and Lisa Oz

MARRIED IN 1985

"When we argue about the dog, it's not really about
the dog. It's about me not feeling heard, or Mehmet
feeling too controlled. When you acknowledge
your actual feelings, it's uncomfortable."

The thing about Mehmet Oz is that it's virtually impossible for him to say something that isn't trenchant and immediately relatable. He's an aha moment kind of guy. And the thing about Lisa, his wife of thirty-five years, is that she's even smarter—something Mehmet will be the first to admit.

But get them into a room together to talk about marriage—the surprising ways it has changed them both, why a hyper-busy life can translate into hot sex, how infidelity is like marshmallows—and the brain wattage practically crackles. Here is a couple who not only made a life together—along with four kids—but also created a TV show, viewed by millions every day, that has become iconic for demystifying everything from fitness to broccoli. He's the star, she's a producer and frequent cohost, and that exquisite alchemy is very much what we witnessed when we paid our visit to their home.

349

Bryn Athyn, Pennsylvania; June 29, 1985

The Oz family lives in what Lisa calls a "nice, normal" New Jersey neighborhood that used to be entirely Italian. Well, it might be nice and normal now, but there was a time, Lisa told us, when Al Capone's driver and bodyguard lived next door. Yet that never stopped her from dreaming about building an Italian villa with lots of land for their four kids—Daphne, Arabella, Zoe, and Oliver, all now grown. Mehmet imagined living on the water, so they found the perfect site for both fantasies on the Hudson River, with breathtaking views of both Manhattan and the Lady of the Harbor, the Statue of Liberty.

When we walked through the couple's large mahogany front door, we could see everything—the water views, the city skyline—through the French doors ahead. The beautiful unpolished, natural stone from Turkey in the entryway is a nod to Mehmet's heritage. And the home basketball court in the basement—with its seventeen-foot ceilings—is perfect evidence of his focus on fitness. No wonder he stays so slim.

Lisa greeted us in that way some people do that says, "I'm so glad you're here!"—and you know they really mean it. Then Mehmet bounced in, dressed in one of his signature colorful shirts—this one hot pink—followed by Khaleesi, their yellow Lab, and Baby Cat, their Siberian of the exact same shade. We chose to sit just off the entrance, a room filled with streaming sunlight. Somewhere in the middle of our visit, Mehmet opened a bottle of red wine. How Italian!

Sitting with these two, we couldn't help but feel that their relationship was somehow preordained. And in a way, it was: Lisa says Mehmet was literally the man of her dreams.

"Six months before I met him, I had these recurring dreams about this person I was going to marry," she told us. "He was a young man with dark hair and green eyes, and I knew he would be my husband. This really frustrated me because I had been dating this amazing guy for three years who was a great friend, and who *didn't* have those features. And then the dreams went away. Six months later I walked into a restaurant in Philadelphia to meet my father for dinner and suddenly I saw Mehmet. I assumed he was a waiter at first because he offered to take my coat, but then I instantly recognized him as the man I had dreamed about. Turns out he was having dinner with my father, too. I thought, *Oh, my gosh, that's the guy I'm going to marry.* I went home that night and broke up with my boyfriend, which was not very nice.

PHIL: Just like that?

LISA: Yes. Over the phone. Because I thought, *Now I know I'm not supposed to be with him. I'm marrying this other guy.*

PHIL: Why was he having dinner with your father?

LISA: Let me back up. It had been a business dinner at this restaurant between our fathers—they were surgeons who worked together. His father called my father and said, "I'm bringing my son to dinner. You have four daughters—bring one of them to entertain my son." Typical old-school Turkish man. What was I supposed to do? Belly dance or something?

MARLO: Did you resent that?

LISA: No. I was at college and wanted to see my parents. I just didn't realize I was going to be on the chopping block! After that night, Mehmet called and we started dating.

MEHMET: Well, we actually dated secretly at first.

LISA: Not exactly. We just didn't tell his father. My parents knew. I was nineteen.

PHIL: Why didn't you want your father to know?

MEHMET: I didn't want him to have the satisfaction of thinking he had set us up.

Though Mehmet says he wasn't looking for marriage ("I was voted the last guy to get married because I was so ambitious," he told us), the chemistry was instantaneous. "Lisa was physically very attractive to me," he recalled. "Beyond that, she cared about emotion and sensuousness in ways I'd never even thought of. It's like someone took off the blinders that I had worn for the first twenty-two years of my life."

Up until then, Mehmet had lived a carefully circumscribed life, even turning his meals into an exercise in self-discipline and efficacy. "He had no appreciation for food," Lisa said, "so he ate the same thing every day. Literally."

Yes, Mehmet acknowledged—all true. "I had a whole system: I'd go to the grocery store, buy a bunch of chicken legs, put spices on them, and stack them in the freezer. When I got home from a long day at med school, I'd throw the chicken into the oven, exercise, come back after forty minutes, eat the chicken, and study."

"Wait—no vegetable, no potato?" Marlo asked.

"Nothing," Mehmet said. "It was the most ridiculous thing. We laugh about it now, but back then, I mean, who had time for food?"

Lisa opened Mehmet's eyes not only to a world beyond chicken legs but to many other things. "I didn't realize how important a wife would be for me to be emotionally healthy enough to do the things I wanted to do," Mehmet said. "If you're a very logical person, like me, there's no emotional overlay—there's no color to the world you're building. It's just lines. Then, all of a sudden, in the middle of all the plans I was making, I met her and started to see the world in Technicolor instead of black and white."

After two years of dating, Mehmet and Lisa married in 1985, while he was still in med school and long before he became famous as Dr. Oz, everyone's favorite life guru. Though their dads were both heart doctors, Mehmet and Lisa had grown up in very different cultures—he's Turkish American, and she's a self-described "American mutt," with an Irish-Italian dad and a Swedish-English mom.

"It was a perfect match of two immigrant cultures," Mehmet said, "different sides of the same coin." But life together took some adjustment.

MARLO: How did marriage change both of you?

LISA: He's a different person.

MARLO: In what way?

LISA: In that every value he grew up with was different from the ones I grew up with. He acts more like my family now.

PHIL: Can you give us an example?

MEHMET: Yes. In Lisa's family, everyone is brutally honest. They say exactly what needs to be said. I come from a culture where you don't do that. You skirt around issues. I'm a salesman—good at motivating you to do what I want—but I'll bend the truth along the way. In her family, you just blurt out the truth, and that became a fundamental building block of our family.

LISA: His family will tell you what they *think* you want to hear. Here's an example: We always want Mehmet's mom to come visit us. We'll plan a great trip and then call her, and she'll say, "Yes, of course I'm coming."

MEHMET: No, she'll say, "I'm thinking of coming" or "It's worth looking into." That means there's no way she's coming.

LISA: Exactly. It gets frustrating. My family is very honest. They're polite—they never talk about sex or religion or politics—but they insist that people mean what they say and say what they mean.

MEHMET: There's also a quality of fidelity.

LISA: But it's not just about the values we came from, but that, as a couple, we established our own set of values. That was important because we also come from very different traditions. I'm Christian, he's Muslim.

PHIL: Did that difference in religion matter at all?

MEHMET: No. Lisa had a strong spiritual foundation. Her mother is a minister, and their faith is very important to them. My family had strong sentiments about faith, but it wasn't a powerful influence in my personal life, in part because I grew up in Wilmington, Delaware, and didn't know any Muslims. My grandmother taught me the prayers, which I can still recite.

LISA: But we got married in my faith, which is called Swedenborgian, and it's very inclusive. It's based on the writings of an eighteenth-century Swedish philosopher and theologian named Emanuel Swedenborg.

PHIL: You solved that difference so smoothly. Are you that successful solving other differences?

MEHMET: In marriage, you adapt to each other. As much as I've changed to be in sync with Lisa's values, she's actually changed quite a bit, too—mostly in how she thinks about her life goals. When we were first married, I would study, study, study at night. And Lisa would put her book under her pillow and fall asleep on it. She said it was the Edgar Cayce approach. He saw the Dead Sea Scrolls in his dreams, and she figured she'd do the same thing.

LISA: Mehmet always had an incredible work ethic. I had my own bizarre philosophy, which roughly translated to, "If you have to work, you aren't as smart as you thought you were." I was trying to learn by osmosis, sucking the knowledge through the pillow.

MEHMET: And I kept saying to her, "As bright as you are"—and Lisa is Mensa, she crushes me in board games—"that's not enough to succeed, because in life you actually have to deliver on tasks." Trust is about two things: being competent to do the right thing, and then doing it. So early on, I would give her homework assignments...

LISA: Homework assignments? What are you talking about?

MEHMET: They weren't really homework assignments. I'm talking metaphorically.

LISA: Example, please. I'm confused.

MEHMET: Like, "Write ten more pages of your screenplay. If you don't actually write the screenplay, then you're not a screenplay writer."

LISA: Well, okay, yeah. I'm a procrastinator.

MARLO: That's what my acting teacher always used to say: it's not in the thinking, it's in the doing.

Hearing the two of them speak about their differences, we were immediately struck by two things: their refreshing honesty about their feelings for their partner, and the ease with which they fessed up to their own shortcomings. We explored that a little further.

"Let's talk about openness," Marlo said. "Are you in sync that way? With Phil, I sometimes have to drag information out of him."

"I think that might be a universally male thing," Lisa said.

Mehmet leaned back in his seat. "This is a natural tendency in a lot of relationships," he said. "The feminine energy will ask the extra question. If one of the kids calls and says they'll be home late, I'll say, 'Good. See you later.' But Lisa will say, 'Where are you going? Who are you with? Why are you going to be late? How late?' Fifteen questions later, she'll know everything that's going down. Whereas for me, they're going to be late—okay, see you later."

"Do you fight about that?" Phil asked.

"Oh, yeah," Mehmet said. "Early on in our marriage, my leaving the hospital at the end of the day was a classic situation like this."

Lisa shook her head. "Okay, he'd call at 8:30 and say he was leaving and would be home in a half-hour," she said. "It was dark, and he was riding a bicycle. Cut to three-and-a-half hours later, and he still isn't home. This was before cell phones, and I'd think he had either been hit by a car or been mugged. He must be dead."

"I'd go right to dead, too," Marlo said.

"She was calling the morgue," Mehmet said with a smile. "But the thing is, I would run into someone at the hospital, or a patient would get sick, so I wouldn't even think about the fact that I had made a commitment to leave. Plus, there's a cultural barrier. Not to blame it only on this, but in Islamic cultures, time is relative. If you say, 'I'll see you in the morning after the morning prayer,' that could be anytime. Whereas in the U.S., if you say you'll meet someone at 7:30, you'd better be there five minutes early or you're already late."

A lot has changed since those med school days. Today, the two not only run Mehmet's daytime TV show and website, but together or separately, they have written eight *New York Times* bestsellers. Mehmet still practices surgery at New York–Presbyterian Hospital, Lisa has her own *Lisa Oz Show* on radio and a podcast, and she runs a production company specializing in family-friendly media.

We wanted to know whether this frenetic lifestyle—being pulled in so many directions—had been a boon to their marriage or an impediment. Lisa turned quickly to a scientific explanation.

LISA: Well, studies have shown that physical attraction is heightened by danger or excitement. So the more varied experiences you have in your life, the more interesting the marriage stays. And as individuals, if you're not growing separately, you've got nothing to bring to the relationship when you're together. It doesn't have to be a career, but you have to have something that keeps you interesting and interested. Otherwise, people get bored and take each other for granted.

MARLO: On the other hand, when Phil and I were first together, our lives were crazy—he was living in Chicago, I was living in L.A.—and we were arguing all the time. He had the responsibility of a show every day, and I was making movies for TV, and we'd get together on the weekends. It was a chaotic life. For some reason, we fought a lot on Sundays—I would get on the plane crying, and think, *How could we have such a beautiful, sexy, loving time and then have a fight?* It took a while to realize it, but the fights were about the pain of separating after having such a loving time.

MEHMET: But craziness and having busy lives also builds respect. I chose medicine because I wanted a profession in which I could never know it all. Knowing that your curiosity will be perpetually challenged makes the job fun. So I wanted to marry someone who would complement me, who would challenge me all the time. I think part of what makes marriage work is recognition that you have to reinvent yourself and let the other person reinvent herself as well. I doubt that you two are the exact same people you were when you got married.

MARLO: Oh, God no.

MEHMET: You don't always go in the same direction. You have to give your spouse permission to evolve in a different way—it's her life, after all—and then still love her. You can't take her for granted, or things fall apart.

PHIL: You speak about marriage in terms of evolution, but isn't there also a biology to marriage?

MEHMET: Yes, and those fundamental hormones govern us. The one that made me fall in love with Lisa when I saw her in the restaurant was dopamine. That's the titillating excitement. And then there's serotonin, which makes you feel good, too. And oxytocin, which comes into play with the pair-bonding, cuddling, and loving. But these chemical hand-cuffs fall off after five, six, seven years, and you start to become ordinary to each other.

PHIL: You're talking about the seven-year itch . . .

MEHMET: Exactly. And once those handcuffs are off, you have to evolve into something more than basic biology. Now your minds have to keep you together, and that's more of a challenge.

MARLO: Right. But your heart is always in it.

LISA: Sometimes. But sometimes you just want to strangle your spouse.

MARLO: What is that thing you said to me the other day about your marriage, Mehmet? That the "prosecution never rests"? That was the funniest.

MEHMET: I didn't think you were going to say that in front of Lisa.

LISA: Don't worry. I hear that all the time.

MEHMET: But it's true. It's how Lisa shows her love—she pecks. She pecks, pecks, pecks, pecks, pecks. She wants to make sure I love her, so peck, peck, peck, peck, and I have to react to the pecking. She's just kicking the tires, making sure they work.

PHIL: So how does that manifest itself?

MEHMET: She'll say, "So why are you late? What are you doing right now? What are you thinking?" She's just checking to make sure things are thoughtful and constructive. I'll give you the best example: our dog, Khaleesi. There is not a single day that I wake up and come downstairs that she doesn't remind me to take Khaleesi out and feed her.

LISA: But even after three years, he still doesn't do it properly, and it drives me crazy! Khaleesi is so beta that she will not poop unless you're standing next to her and tell her to. Mehmet thinks he's doing his duty by shoving her out the door, closing the door, waiting for five minutes, and bringing her back in. You know this is true, right?

MEHMET: Yes. But I'm not going to stand out there in the pouring rain so a dog can go poop!

PHIL: It's easier to train the dog than the dog owner.

LISA: I'll come downstairs and he's sitting at the kitchen table typing away.

He's left the dog outside for, like, fifteen minutes. So I go outside, and the dog runs over to the grass and poops. That's what he means by pecking. It's following up. Quality control.

MEHMET: It reminds me of this couple who came in to see me. The wife is yelling everything at him because he's deaf. She leaves to go to the bathroom, and I start yelling my questions at him, and he says, "Shhh. I can hear just fine. It's just that if she has to yell, she won't talk as much."

MARLO: That's so good.

MEHMET: True story.

With all their success, fame—and, let's face it, their flat-out physical attractiveness—we had to wonder about how they've managed to resist what must be constant temptations.

"Are you ever concerned about other women, Lisa?" Phil asked. "I mean, he's a surgeon and a TV star. He's surrounded by women all day long…"

"Keep going, keep going," Mehmet said. "Really pretty women. Attractive, intelligent, charismatic women…"

"I'm a very jealous person," Lisa admitted. "I don't even like him talking to other women. But I was more jealous when I was younger. And he's built trust by now. He's got a good track record, in spite of all the women. I was way more concerned when he was a doctor in the hospital because there is an intimacy there that doesn't exist in the entertainment world. However, one thing is central to our marriage: I will stay true-blue to Mehmet—no matter what—but if he cheats on me or lies consistently, I'm gone."

"No second chance," Marlo said.

"Right," said Lisa. "I used to have a contract that said if he cheated on me I could perform a—"

"—Bobbitt operation," Mehmet said with a smile.

"Yes, the Lorena Bobbitt operation," Lisa continued. "But instead of throwing it out the window, it would go into the garbage disposal, so there would be no reattachment. He signed it and said, 'Fine.'"

"Phil was jealous when we first started going out," Marlo said. "I remember once at a beach party I was talking to this guy, whom I did not find one bit attractive, and Phil said, 'You were talking to him all night!' I said, "Who? *That guy?* I would never think anything about him!'"

Lisa turned to Phil. "How about you? Did you flirt with your fans?"

Phil shrugged. "I don't think so," he said.

"Not even Sophia Loren," Marlo confirmed. "He had her on his show and the next day she invited him to lunch. Sophia Loren, for God's sake. But he didn't go."

"A toast to Sophia Loren!" Mehmet said, raising his glass.

"A toast to Phil!" Lisa said, clinking her glass with her husband's. "Mehmet has had situations like that," she said, "and his go-to response was always to invite me to lunch, too. The woman would show up and there would be three of us."

"That avoids the awkwardness," Mehmet added. "You can't create a vibe that there might be the possibility of an affair."

"Right," Phil said. "You're not sending out a message that says, 'I'm available.'"

Mehmet leaned in. "Let's also remember that infidelity often happens because you don't respect yourself," he said. "If I'm not worthy as a man, then you're obviously not worthy as a woman—because, otherwise, why would you have married me? If I'm a loser and you married me, then you must be a *big-time* loser. But if I'm a winner, I picked the best person out there, and how can I possibly cheat on her?"

In true brainiac fashion, Lisa compared extramarital affairs to "the marshmallow test," a Stanford University study that explored the delayed gratification skills of children: Could they resist eating a plump marshmallow placed before them if they were told they would get two marshmallows by waiting a short period of time?

"Are you able to resist the urge?" Lisa asked about the temptation of cheating. "A lot of people cannot. But what marriage teaches you is that what you feel like in the moment is not necessarily the most important thing. There's something bigger."

On and on they went like this, each one topping the other with one funny, whip-smart comment after another. And then suddenly Mehmet couldn't resist an urge of his own: unable to bear being just an interviewee any longer, he suddenly turned into Dr. Oz, the interviewer.

"What would you tell the younger version of yourself about marriage that you wished you'd known?" he asked. We'd been prepared to ask them that very question, but he beat us to the punch.

MARLO: Well, I never wanted to marry.

MEHMET: Why?

MARLO: I didn't see any marriages that I wanted to emulate. My father was one of nine boys. I saw eight uncles who were condescending to their wives. They'd say things like, "What does she know?" Or if she was unhappy, they'd say, "Where's she gonna go?"

MEHMET: That's the worst.

MARLO: So I had it in my mind as a young girl that *I* would always have a place to go. I was ambitious and determined to be independent. I would make my own money and take care of myself.

MEHMET: Were there other reasons you were gun-shy about marriage?

MARLO: Well, I felt that my mother had given up everything for my father. She'd had a singing career—her own radio show in Detroit—but left it behind to follow his dream. She was a great mother and raised good, decent kids—she was always there to say, "What time are you coming home?" or "You can't stay at that girl's house if her parents aren't there." But she lived with a lot of conflict. She wanted to be there for her children, but she couldn't bear being away from my father. When I grew up and had a husband of my own, I realized how heartbreaking it was for her. After Dad died, she told me, "I left you kids often because your father mattered to me more than anything in the world." I was very touched that she confided that to me. You have to remember, he was often in Las Vegas, Miami, and other club towns, where there were chorus girls and a whole different life, and she wanted to be there with him. I remember one time when we were very little, we were crying because she was leaving, and she said, "Mommy has to go because we girls are here together, but you have to go to school and Daddy needs a girl, and I'm the only one who can go."

MEHMET: You should tell *their* story in your book.

MARLO: They loved each other and that was the good part. The not-so-great part was that my father was definitely the dominant figure, which was another feature of marriage that troubled me.

MEHMET: It may have appeared that way, but was that true in every decision?

MARLO: Well, actually no. My father would always say, "Rosie runs the house," and he often demonstrated that. We had a house in Palm Springs that we went to on the weekends, and it was next door to Frank Sinatra's house. Our families were close—my dad was Frank Jr.'s godfather. One time, John Kennedy was supposed to stay at the Sinatra compound, and Sinatra wanted Bobby Kennedy's family to stay in our house. My dad said, "I've got to ask Rosie." He did—and she said no. Her actual words were, "I don't want those shanties in my house."

LISA: Oh, my God.

MARLO: I know. My mother had a thing about Irish people. She grew up in a Detroit neighborhood where the melting pot wasn't always so melty or friendly. When I fell in love with Phil Donahue, I thought, *Oh God, how am I going to tell her this?* But once she met him, she was whistling "When Irish Eyes Are Smiling." She adored him. But anyway, when the Kennedy thing happened, my father said to Frank, "This isn't worth the trouble to me. She doesn't want it. I'm sorry."

LISA: That must have been such a wild childhood. So what ultimately changed your mind about marriage?

MARLO: This man. This man right here. Before Phil, the men I dated were lovely, but I always dated a couple at a time. One would be sexy, another would be someone smart who I could learn from, which I loved. But I could never find someone who had it all. Then I met Phil, and he was so good and decent and loving and sexy and smart. And safe.

That mention of safety struck a chord with Lisa. "My primary identity is as Mehmet's wife," she said, "and that's a scary place to be because it makes you vulnerable. But we're both willing to be vulnerable. So when we argue about the dog, it's not really about the dog. It's about me not feeling heard, or Mehmet feeling too controlled. When you acknowledge your actual feelings, it's uncomfortable, but we're both at a place where we feel safe enough in the relationship to take it to that level."

We were just about finished with our bottle of wine and it was time to wrap up. So we asked Lisa and Mehmet our million-dollar question: What makes a marriage last?

"Marriage is a priority for both of us," Lisa began. "And that means that we act on that and refocus when we've lost sight of the ball."

"It's so easy to hold grudges, especially on foolish things," Mehmet added. "It's important in marriage to remember that it is *all* small stuff except for the really, really important things."

"So you see marriage through a big-picture lens," Phil observed.

"I do," said Mehmet. "Marriage is the building block of our species. Think about it: You put me in a cage with a baboon, I don't stand a chance, but if you put me and Phil in a cage with two baboons, we'll almost always win because we'll connect. Marriage is that ultimate bond that allowed our species to thrive—it elevates us. These days, when we fight with our kids about whether they should live with their partners before marrying, we cite statistics showing that people who do that don't succeed as often in marriage. They say, 'Why not give it a test drive?' And we say because if there are things you need to work on, you might not work as hard."

"If you don't have other options, you have to figure it out," Lisa concluded. "Part of making marriage work is approaching it with a mindset that this *is* going to work."

"And 'I will do my part in making it work,'" Marlo said.

"Exactly," said Lisa. "And when people say love is blind, I disagree. I think lust is blind, and when you're overwhelmed by chemistry, you don't see any issues. Once you get married, you start to do the real work—and marriage is work, it absolutely is—and to pretend that it's just going to be smooth sailing is naïve. In marriage, if you focus on how your spouse annoys you, or never pays attention to you, or doesn't worship you, your marriage will fail. You have to look for what you love in your husband, even when you're annoyed by him."

MEHMET: And don't forget makeup sex.

PHIL: You're not the first couple to use that as a way back.

MEHMET: You're right. But the bottom line is this: I would do anything for her. Climb any mountain, take any bullet—in the chest, too, by the way. I might do things that justifiably make her really angry at me, but I would never let anything block me from delivering my love to her. I always tell people: "You deserve your marriage, and you deserve to win every battle that comes along to protect it. If you appreciate how valuable it is to your long-term happiness, you will never let anyone touch it."

MARLO: So you're an optimist about marriage. That's so hopeful.

MEHMET: Well, a lot of people think of marriage as a hindrance—that it brings you joy and love but will get in the way of where you need to go. And it's just the opposite. It's a nuclear reactor that continually generates energy to allow you to do things you never could have imagined doing otherwise. I definitely would not be where I am today if I hadn't married Lisa when I did. Many people don't realize that by not committing to a relationship earlier in life, they give up what would have taken them to the promised land.

LISA: The marriage bond will give you peace in your most desperate times. When something bad happens in my life, I get to lie in bed with the person I love and put my head on his chest, and suddenly everything is okay. I think our marriage changed the arithmetic of our lives; the synergy we have brought us things that neither one of us could have come close to on our own. When you're willing to sacrifice for the benefit of the union, then what you get is not one plus one equals two, but one plus one equals infinity.

Billy and Janice Crystal

MARRIED IN 1970

"She was saying to me, 'We're a team, and I
believe in you. You'll become the comedian who
I know you can be. I trust you with this.'"

Nineteen sixty-six was not a banner year for the New York Mets.
The team finished a dismal ninth in the National League, just
one notch up from their bottom-of-the cellar finish the previous
season. But July 30 was a very good day for the team—they beat the visiting Chicago Cubs 6–3—and for one particular baseball fan in the stands:
Billy Crystal, who was on his first date with Janice Goldfinger. They still
have the ticket stubs.

"We've been together all this time and it still feels like yesterday," Janice
remembered. "Sometimes people are just meant to be together."

Cupid really knocked it out of the park when these two first laid eyes
on each other that long-ago July. Billy, then an eighteen-year-old summer
day camp counselor, home from his first year at college, was playing catch
on the beach with a good friend. Suddenly, a seventeen-year-old fellow
counselor strolled by. She was wearing a pink bikini. Billy looked—and
looked again.

West Hempstead, New York; June 4, 1970

"It wasn't just that it was a sexy walk," Billy shared. "There was a determination to it that was very positive."

"I was a dancer, so I just walked a certain way, I guess," Janice reminisced with the tiniest trace of a blush. "And he seemed to like it. I don't think I can walk like that anymore."

Whatever it was about her gait, Billy said, it hit him like a line drive to the chest. "I turned to my friend and said, 'I'm going to marry that girl.'"

And marry that girl he did, four years later. A full half-century on, they're still side by side, with two children and four grandchildren.

We were supposed to meet with Billy and Janice at their Pacific Palisades home while we were in L.A., but they got tied up with business in New York. So when we got back to the city, we invited them to our place. Marlo had previously interviewed Billy for her books. The first time, he had talked to her about the words that guided him during his early days as a young comedian; and for her memoir—which included interviews with comedians she admired—they discussed their shared, lifelong love affair with laughter.

But this conversation was going to be more personal. And it would include spouses. Whole different kettle.

The Crystals are known for being a very in-sync couple—five decades will do that to you—so we couldn't wait to talk to them and find out about the glue that kept them together, while so many other show business marriages fall apart. We put out an easy buffet of munchies for our conversation—dips, chips, veggies, tea, and coffee—and you could see the New York deli kid in Billy, who went for it all. Cleveland Philly had no trouble digging in either.

"So what's your big secret?" Marlo asked. "Fifty years. There's got to be something you can tell us."

"We're Jack and Mary Benny," Billy said, paying homage to one of his favorite comedians. "I still feel like we're dating and I think that's a great thing. It doesn't get old. If we're going out for the evening, it's always like asking her out on a date. I'm seventy-one now, but in many ways I still feel like I'm eighteen."

Perhaps it's hereditary; both came from homes in which their folks treasured each other's company.

"My parents were never embarrassed to show their affection in front of us," Billy said. "In any home movie I have, they're always kissing, or my mom has her hand affectionately on my father's shoulder, or he's touching her in some way. My dad died when I was a teenager, but I'll always remember how romantic they were together. He worked so hard during the week, and he was gone until Sunday. But on Sunday mornings, my mom would wake up, and there would always be a single red rose in a bud vase, waiting for her. That meant that somewhere, during his drive home from the Lower East Side where he did his jazz concerts, he stopped to get her a rose. I love that about him."

Janice's parents, too, remained together until her father's death in 2013. They were married in 1948. "They always had fun together," Janice remembered. "I haven't thought about this in a long time, but I can still see him picking her up over his shoulder and carrying her around the kitchen to make me and my two siblings laugh."

"He was a big presence," Billy confirmed with a broad smile, "like Jackie Gleason. When I first met him, I was a little intimidated by him, but he was filled with joy."

"Was he funny?" Marlo asked.

"He was funny," Janice said. "We have home movies—silent, of course—of them doing all kinds of crazy things with masks and coats, parading through the living room. It wasn't like a show business family or anything. He just liked to goof around."

PHIL: I still can't get over how long you've been together.
BILLY: I didn't even drive when we first started dating.
JANICE: Oh, that's a great story.
BILLY: Go ahead...
JANICE: He didn't drive, but when he finally got his license, he borrowed his mom's car and we went to Green Acres Shopping Center in Valley Stream. We squeezed into a very tight parking spot, and neither of us

could get out of our car doors. We were locked in. And then the car stalled and we couldn't get it started.

MARLO: You're kidding!

BILLY: I don't know how I got into that spot—and we couldn't get out! But it forced conversation. It was hilarious. I remember when we left your mother's house, she whispered to you—so I could hear—"Don't make him nervous."

Billy and Janice were very young when they walked down the aisle; he was twenty-two years old and she was just twenty-one and a half. But despite their youth, Janice maintains, the trust was immediately there.

"I saw his character from the very moment I met him," she explained. "I mean, here's an eighteen-year-old kid and he was able to do an impression of Jack Benny! I went, 'No, seriously? Where did you come from?' We might as well have been on Mars, because that was not our background at all on Long Island. I didn't know anybody in show business or even anyone who performed."

But Janice would soon become very well-acquainted with life behind the footlights. Just a few years after their wedding, Billy began forging a career in comedy—he was part of a sketch troupe with two of his best friends. "But we just couldn't bust it," Billy explained. "We couldn't get through. We did a *Mike Douglas Show* and the colleges, but it's hard for three guys to make any money in comedy. At most, I made $4,200 one year, and most of that was from substitute teaching at the same junior high school that I had gone to."

That's when Billy made the decision to go solo. He began doing standup at the legendary New York comedy club Catch a Rising Star, a launching pad for such comedy icons as Ray Romano, Elayne Boosler, and Jerry Seinfeld. It was an exciting time for the up-and-coming comic, but it was hard on the young couple's schedule.

BILLY: We lived an hour outside of Manhattan, so that meant that I would have to leave home at nine o'clock at night with the hope of getting on stage by midnight. Then it would take me an hour to get back home. By this point, we had a baby who was six months old, and I wasn't making any money. So Janice said to me, "Listen, I'm going to go back to work. We really need the money. I'll be the hunter-gatherer right now, and you'll take care of Jenny all day. I'll be home around five o'clock. You'll hand her off to me, do whatever you have to do—take a nap, get ready, write material—and then go. That's what we have to do right now."

PHIL: That's really impressive.

JANICE: Well, I was making $10,000 a year—which was a lot of money at that time—in the theater department of Nassau Community College.

BILLY: With health benefits. That was the big deal.

MARLO: Against $4,200 for teaching. And what did you make as a comedian at Catch a Rising Star?

BILLY: Nothing at first. Later on I got $25 a night on weekends.

MARLO: Wow. My dad did the same grind when he was a young comic. He worked for $12 a night.

BILLY: So, yeah, this was the most selfless thing ever: a young mother with a six-month-old baby saying, "I've got to go back to work. We need the money. You'll do this. You'll be great." And this was hilarious: we had the worst apartment in this high-rise building in Long Beach. It was directly over the garage, which had one of those big entrance doors. Every time somebody came in and out of the building, the apartment would shake. So, when I would leave at 9 p.m., I would stand on the roof of our Volkswagen and unplug the electric eye on the garage door so it wouldn't wake them up whenever somebody wanted to come in.

PHIL: That's an act of love right there.

BILLY: I wouldn't get home until two or three in the morning and then the baby was up at 6 a.m. and Janice would leave by seven. That was my day. I was the only man in the playgroup, the only man at the playground, the only man in art class. We did that for about a year and a half.

JANICE: He was the first "house husband," as they used to call it. We don't say that anymore. Erase that!

BILLY: But it really tells you about Janice's selfless attitude. She was saying to me, "Yes, I'm the mother, but *we're* the parents. We're a team, and I believe in you so much. You'll become the comedian who I know you can be. I trust you with this." That was the lesson.

MARLO: You know, trust in each other is such an important thing. I was thirty-eight years old when I met Phil. I had never wanted to be married; he'd been married before and wasn't all that eager to marry again. We met in January, and that August we went to Italy together. It was his only two weeks off all year. At the time, I was working on a movie script with Elaine May. She called me in Rome one morning—I took the call in the lobby—and said, "You have to come home immediately. I think Mike Nichols can direct our movie—something of his just fell through and he's available." I said, "My God, Elaine, I can't come home! I'm with this guy and I'm crazy about him. It's the only time off he has all year. If I leave here now I'll lose him." She said, "You've got to come." I said, "Oh, Lord, let me think about it." So, I go up to our room. Phil is just getting up, and I say to him, "So, you know, Mike Nichols is the biggest thing in the movie world, right?" And so I tell him about Elaine's call. He says, "Oh, for God's sake, it's not a funeral. You have to go back now? You can't wait a week?"

At this point, he's looking at me like I'm a completely disposable human being. So, I say to him, "Look, I don't know your business, but is there any interview you really want—one that, if you could get it right now, you'd leave Italy immediately?" He says, "Yeah, Jimmy Carter." And I thought to myself, *Okay, I can love this guy.* He didn't say, "No, there's no way I could rip myself from this sexy, fabulous thing." He didn't bullshit me with some romantic con job. He's honest. He's not going to fool me. He's not going to screw with my head. I can trust him.

And, by the way, I did not leave Rome and we did not get Mike Nichols. But as it turned out, it wouldn't have happened anyway.

BILLY: But I think you're right. When he said, "Jimmy Carter," something clicked for you and told you to go for it. It's about knowing yourself and what you need and what makes you feel happy and safe. And if this man or this woman feels the same way, you can grow together.

Billy and Janice indeed grew together—they had a second child—and as Billy's career took off, the couple remained conscientious about keeping their family intact. Billy credits Janice with leading the charge on that.

"You have to wear blinders if you want to do your work well," Billy reflected, "and I remember one time when I was on the road a lot, doing standup mostly, Janice sat me down and said, 'We should really think about less work. I don't want you to become Uncle Daddy.' So I said, 'I get it,' and I got off the road for a while."

Even when Billy landed an irresistible role—the part of the Emcee in a summer stock production of the stage musical *Cabaret*—the two of them figured out a way to keep their own connection strong: Janice—who had danced in high school and college—joined him in the cast.

JANICE: He wanted me to go with him, and I said, "I can't be on the road with you for three weeks—what am I going to do there?" And he said, "Well, then dance again and be in it." So I became a professional dancer. I was the lead dancer in the chorus.

MARLO: And the kids?

BILLY: They went to her folks' in Florida while we went on the road together with the show. It was great.

PHIL: No guilt?

JANICE: No, because my parents were great with them. I had no worries. They even came to see us at one point, but they were terrified of the makeup that we had on. I mean, my three-year-old daughter, Lindsay, didn't even recognize me as her mom!

BILLY: It was funny. They arrived backstage, mid-matinee. The second act opens with the Emcee dancing with the chorus girls in a kick-line, and he's in drag, wearing fishnets and a wig. Our little one is in the wings, looking at me in my high heels. She must have been thinking, *What the fuck?*

JANICE: But all of this goes back to the issue of trust, because at the time I was really questioning if it was a good idea for me to do this. After two performances everything was hurting. But I trusted Billy when he told me, "Of course you can do this!" and that everything would be okay. I believed him and I did it. We did a week in each city and had a blast.

MARLO: So the bottom line is: the two of you kept your connection to each other, and that was as important as your connection to the family.

JANICE: Yes. Even when the kids got older, if Billy had to go on the road—like performing for two weeks in Tahoe—he would do it when the kids were on vacation; or we would take them out of school and go there together. We grew up together and not apart. We grew together and played together and worked together and did it all together.

Their mutual trust—and respect—notwithstanding, Billy and Janice, like every married couple, do fight. But even in the throes of battle, they've developed a synchronicity. For one thing, they don't buy that old saw "Never go to bed angry."

"I never held to that," Janice said. "I think it's important when you are so sure of your point of view that you give the other person the night to think about where you're coming from. It's okay to do that. Marriage is not always a bed of roses, and, yes, on occasion we have gone to sleep mad at each other. It's a lot easier now, because you can binge on lots of TV shows."

"Paddy Chayefsky once said a funny thing to me," Marlo said. "'I can't sleep unless I know I'm making somebody angry.' So when the two of you *do* fight, who's the volatile one?"

Billy and Janice looked at each other, and then Janice raised her hand. "I am," she confessed.

"But volatile isn't exactly the right word," Billy quickly interjected. "She has a short attention span for getting into a discussion if there's a disagreement. She'll say, 'I'm not talking about it!' and then it ends. So I'll just throw up my hands and say, 'Okay, then I'll wait.' I've learned to be patient."

"Well, that's because I sometimes feel like I've made my point and I can't make it any stronger," Janice countered. "He'll say, 'You're not hearing what I'm saying,' and I'll say, 'No I *am* hearing it. And that's the problem—I'm

hearing it but you're not *understanding* what I'm saying and here's why…'
And then it goes back and forth and back and forth, until we finally say,
'What are we fighting about? This is now silly, right?'"

MARLO: When you're in mid-fight, are either of you screamers?

BILLY: No.

JANICE: No.

MARLO: Phil and I used to scream, until somebody decided that they
didn't want to do that anymore.

PHIL: Was that you?

MARLO: That was *you*.

PHIL: Yeah, well, I guess in the beginning I did go off on Marlo a bit, but
then I thought, *What is this getting me? What's the point? She feels bad. I
feel bad.* So I just stopped it.

JANICE: Well, Billy's definitely not a screamer. And the one or two times
he *has* screamed, I thought, *Wow, I must have gone over the line, because this
is a new him.*

MARLO: So who's the first to come back from a fight?

JANICE: We both do. I think we've become better communicators. We
just give ourselves a little breathing time, and when we come back, we
come back honestly. We'll say, "Look, let's talk about this, let's move on,
and then let's go to a movie."

Movies are, of course, a very big part of the Crystals' lives. Following
his breakout stardom as a headline comedian, and his memorable gigs on
TV—notably the soap opera spoof *Soap* and a season on *Saturday Night
Live*—Billy carved out a string of signature roles in some of Hollywood's
most beloved screen comedies, including *City Slickers*, *When Harry Met
Sally…*, and *Analyze This*. Even in that regard, Janice has not only been a
supportive spouse, she's been his leading lady—in a sense.

"Whenever I get my scripts and have to learn my part," Billy said,
"she runs lines with me. Seriously—she's been my costar in every movie
I've done. She was Sally in *When Harry Met Sally…*, she was Curly in

City Slickers, and she played Hamlet when I was the gravedigger in Ken Branagh's *Hamlet*. She's also my sounding board in every speech I give. She'll say, 'Can I see your speech?' I'll shrug. She'll say, 'What, you don't trust me? I just want to look.' I'll say okay, and then we'll go over my jokes and she'll comment, 'You know, maybe you shouldn't say that…' And I listen."

For all his on-screen success, however, Billy has held fast to that decades-old promise he made to Janice not to become an Uncle Daddy. To paraphrase the immortal song "It Had to Be You"—a tune amply sampled in *When Harry Met Sally*—he had "wandered around and finally found" the life he and Janice had always dreamed about, and that meant it was up to him to keep that connection strong, even when he was three thousand miles away.

JANICE: When he was filming *When Harry Met Sally* . . . in New York, he called and said he was coming home for the weekend to surprise our daughter Lindsay on her birthday.

BILLY: It was a Friday, and her actual birthday was that day. So I finished shooting at noon and I asked, "Can I leave and be back Monday?" They said, "Yeah. Go." So, I raced to the airport and called Lindsay. She hated that I was gone. I wished her happy birthday and told her, "There's going to be a big box coming for you. It's from me. We're shooting now—I've got to go!" I hung up and ran to the plane.

JANICE: So, I get this giant box. When he gets there, I put it at the front door and he gets under it. I ring the bell—and, of course, in the background he can hear me going, "Oh, I wonder who that is!"

BILLY: Like really bad summer stock acting.

JANICE: Awful. Awful. Intentionally bad. So Lindsay comes to the door and says, "Oh my God, look at this box." And I say, "I wonder what's in it? Let's open it." She lifts it up and Billy comes out.

BILLY: And do you remember what she said when I came out? "Somebody pinch me."

MARLO: "Somebody pinch me."

PHIL: What a lovely story.

BILLY: So, that's how we've been. Not to get too psychological, but my father died when I was fifteen. It's been so important for me not to miss anything, because it could happen to any of us at any point. I think I've been very conscious of being there when I'm supposed to be there and even when I'm not supposed to be there.

JANICE: Not missing a birthday, not missing a volleyball game with our daughters. And we're doing the same thing with our grandkids. We have a baseball game tomorrow, and a play tomorrow night, the minute we get off the plane. It's a conscious effort. No, it's not even an effort. It's just being there for each other.

In 2004, Billy wrote and starred in his Tony Award–winning, one-man Broadway show *700 Sundays*, a laughter-and-tears journey through his childhood on Long Island and those precious days that he shared with his father, jazz impresario Jack Crystal. An intensely personal project, it required Billy to hire the most trustworthy coproducer he could find. Not surprisingly, he chose Janice for the job.

"I told her it would be a great adventure for us," he said. "And it was. She did an amazing job with it. Every night, either she would be at the theater or we would meet right afterwards, and that was our life. It was no different from the Catch a Rising Star days, because it was still all about 'I believe in you.' And this time we did it together."

More important than giving the couple another way to connect, *700 Sundays* permitted Billy to do something both profound and unexpected: it helped him draw a line from the family he came from to the family he and Janice had built.

"The great thing about the show," he said, "was that it was time to let go of all of this pain that I had been carrying—to put the suitcases down, because they were so heavy—and to make the air more breathable. And now, our kids are grown and our grandchildren are sixteen, thirteen, soon-to-be-ten, and six. The girls are the teenagers and the boys are the bear cubs. And sometimes Janice and I just look at them and say, 'When did this happen?' And whenever I see them, I still think about my father and say, 'Damn, he would have loved these kids.'"

For such a sentimental guy, Billy chose a partner who, he says, is not as sappy as he is. "I'm very romantic," he told us, "and I have to add, a little more than Janice."

"Well, outwardly," Janice admitted. "I don't care as much now, but twenty years ago, if he wanted to give me a kiss on the street, I'd say, 'Honey, there are people around!'"

So where does her husband's extra dose of amorousness come from?

BILLY: I guess I got it from the single red rose.

JANICE: I still have the letters he would write me in college class...

BILLY: ... and we have every Mother's Day and Father's Day card each of us has ever gotten. Now we just write a number on them: 48, 49, 50. The numbers are getting higher. And, yeah, the little things—a trinket, a little gift, a little something—I do that a lot.

JANICE: He really is a romantic. When I look in his eyes, I still see the eighteen-year-old boy who I first met. That's still there.

BILLY: Even now?

JANICE: Even now. That spark has never gone out.

Dr. Sanjay and Rebecca Gupta

MARRIED IN 2004

"Big arguments never really end. He's still mad at me
for buying him a ham sandwich fifteen years ago!
Those fights are still there, like a splinter in your skin."

Most of us remember that one moment from our wedding that captured the day's magic in a single burst. For some, it's walking down the aisle on your dad's arm. For others, it's catching that first glimpse of your bride as she steps toward you. And for many, it's that first special dance. These moments stand out.

For Rebecca and Sanjay Gupta, it had to have been the horse. Because, well, let's face it, when's the last time you saw a horse at a wedding? And a white one, at that. With the groom riding on top of it.

Sanjay is a first-generation American whose parents emigrated from northern India in the 1960s, prior to their own marriage. So when it came time for Sanjay and Rebecca to plan the details of their 2004 wedding in Charleston, South Carolina, they decided to honor his heritage by going full-throttle Hindu. The grounds of the outdoor venue were storybook perfect, a glorious landscape of roses and delphinium draped in rich red velvet, all cast in a soft golden glow. Sanjay trotted in atop that snowy steed, a tradition that harkens back to the days when families traveled far for a wedding. He was dressed in a crisp white tunic, his head swaddled in a gold-trimmed red turban, and he was accompanied by the entire wedding party, playing music and dancing. A joyous procession if ever there was one.

Rebecca, though a lass of Swedish descent, made a grand Hindu entrance, too, carried by her brothers on an elaborately decorated chair. She wore a silk, hand-beaded *lehenga* (a two-piece dress with exposed midriff) and a patterned *choli* (scarf) on her head. Both bride and groom wore lavish flower garlands around their necks.

Rebecca joined her betrothed on a *mandap*—an elevated platform with a fire burning at its center—where they sat atop colorful pillows like royalty. At one point they were literally tied together by cloth (talk about bonding!) and then participated in the *mangal pheras*, a ritual in which they walked around the holy fire four times to symbolize the most important qualities of marriage: duty, love, fidelity, and respect.

All these years later, Rebecca's memories of that day were vivid and moving.

"Hindu weddings are very interactive," she said, "so near the end of our ceremony, all of our guests brought flowers up and sprinkled them on our bowed heads. It gave everyone a chance to bless our marriage. It was joyful."

It all sounded magical, but it also made us wonder about the challenges of a marriage when the two halves of a couple come from different cultures—and particularly one in which arranged marriages have been the norm for centuries.

"It's interesting," Sanjay noted, "I think there is a deep desire, especially for immigrants, to have their children marry within the same culture. But my parents were a little different. My mom was from what is now Pakistan; she fled during the 1947 partition [when British-ruled India was divided into India and Pakistan], so she was a refugee child for the first twelve-and-a-half years of her life. My dad was also from India, but from a very different part—it was like a completely different country. So my mom and

Charleston, South Carolina; May 15, 2004

dad immigrated here, but when they got married, neither of their parents attended the wedding. They didn't support it."

"Because?" Phil asked.

"Because it was a love marriage, not an arranged one," Sanjay said. "That was unusual and unacceptable in their world."

"And a big deal in the sixties," Rebecca added.

That willingness by Sanjay's parents to buck tradition also paved the way for Rebecca and Sanjay's marriage. "While they probably wanted me to marry somebody Indian," Sanjay said, "they were much more open because of what they had lived through themselves."

Although Sanjay had dated Indian women before Rebecca, he'd never had a serious romance, and certainly had not met anyone he would bring home to meet the parents. "My dad was funny," Sanjay recalled. "He'd say, 'I don't want to meet any girls unless you're going to marry them,' and my mom would follow along. They are not frivolous people—they're engineers, mathematicians—and if I were to have brought home a girlfriend, they would have felt like, 'So if you're not going to marry her, why are we meeting her?' They're loving, but not emotional in this regard."

Unlike with many of the other couples we met, Sanjay and Rebecca's marriage wasn't remotely whirlwind. From the time they met until their wedding day, fourteen years had passed. Theirs is that rare kind of union—one that grew out of a slow-and-steady-wins-the-race courtship, in which the relationship was given time to breathe, to take root, to grow.

"At the heart of our marriage is trust," Sanjay told us. "I don't trust anybody more than I trust Rebecca to have my best interests at heart. And I have respect—genuine respect—for her, too. You can like someone, you can even *love* someone, but if you don't have respect for that person, a marriage won't work."

Even when this couple has disagreements—and they've had their fair share, they said—that same trust and respect, along with their deep, abiding friendship, remain intact. "When I get angry at Sanjay," Rebecca said, "I always remember that he is my best friend in the whole world."

The two met in 1990, when Sanjay was in his first year of medical school and Rebecca was an undergrad at the University of Michigan. "It was a classic American story," Sanjay told us, laughing. "Mutual friends introduced us at a bar." Though both were dating others at the time, there was an instant connection—as friends. And that's how they remained for the next three years: good, possibly even great, friends. "We had a lot in common," Rebecca remembered, "so one of us would say, 'Hey, do you want to get together for coffee or to talk about science class?' We started out by meeting every few months, then every couple of weeks, and then every couple of days. It was a natural progression."

Sanjay agreed. "We sort of eased into it. It was a long ramp-up period, so we had a lot of time to get to know each other."

Once they became romantic, the couple's relationship was often long-distance, with Sanjay finishing medical school and completing his hundred-hours-a-week neurosurgical residency in Michigan and serving as a White House Fellow—primarily under Hillary Clinton—in Washington, D.C., while Rebecca earned her law degree in South Carolina.

The Guptas now live in Atlanta, where Sanjay practices neurosurgery at Grady Memorial Hospital and is on the faculty at Emory University—jobs he balances with his Emmy-winning career as senior medical correspondent at CNN. We met them at a health-care event in Atlanta that Mehmet Oz had invited us all to. After chatting with them for just a bit, we knew they'd be a great couple for this book. They were spirited and fun to talk to, and it was clear how much pleasure they took in each other's company.

They told us they would soon be in New York on business, so we invited them to drop by our place when they arrived. They took us up on the offer, bringing along their ten-year-old daughter Soleil, a dark-eyed beauty who is a striking combination of her Indian dad and Scandinavian mom. (The couple also have two other daughters, Sage, fourteen, and Sky, twelve.) Like any preteen, Soleil said her polite hellos and then took off for the living room to watch the Disney Channel as the four grown-ups sat down for what quickly became a warm and soulful conversation. But it was clear from the way they looked at Soleil how much these two value their family life.

"These are the wonder years with our three girls," Sanjay said at one point, "the best years of our lives."

We began our conversation talking about the way marriage has transformed over the past two generations of the Gupta family.

PHIL: Your parents were cutting-edge to marry for love, and you two took the baton from them. Is this becoming the norm now in India?

SANJAY: I must say I've met tons of Indian people—my contemporaries—whose parents had arranged marriages, but no one whose parents married the way mine did. So when my friends are thinking about getting married, they often turn to my parents to ask, "You weren't from the same part of India, the same caste, the same background—how did it work?"

MARLO: Sanjay mentioned that his dad told him not to bother bringing anyone home to meet him unless he had serious intentions. So, Rebecca, how did you feel when you walked through that door the first time? What was their reaction?

REBECCA: Well, in my family, if you meet somebody who comes to your home, you give them a hug. Sanjay's parents were never like that. They'd say, "Nice to see you," but they were never big huggers.

SANJAY: My dad still shook my hand—no hugs.

REBECCA: Until I came along! It was sweet how they've warmed up to the changes. These days, if I don't hug them when I walk in the door, his dad is like, "Where's my hug?"

PHIL: That was a big change, wasn't it?

REBECCA: It definitely wasn't their way, and it definitely wasn't his dad's family's way. We've gone back to India to spend time with his dad's family, and there's not a whole lot of affection going on around the house. But we're all hugging. Our daughters are all over their grandfather, running in and hugging him, holding his hand and jumping on his lap. And you can see that he loves it.

MARLO: That's lovely how he adapted to a new way of life, and then embraced it.

SANJAY: Well, part of that difference stems from the tension over my parents' marriage. My dad's parents never fully accepted my mom. They had the same religion, but my dad's mom was the most devout Hindu of my four grandparents.

MARLO: And your mom's parents?

SANJAY: I think that, because they fled persecution, religion for them was a bit of an indulgence.

MARLO: You both grew up in small towns in Michigan, but your cultures were very different. Rebecca, how did your parents feel about your marrying a Hindu?

REBECCA: My dad had passed away long before Sanjay and I started dating, but my mom just loves him. She's a big sweetheart, and she thinks he's so smart and fascinating. She always wants to know where he's traveling because she worries about him so much.

PHIL: Mothers worry, no matter their culture. Had you been apprehensive about how she'd welcome Sanjay into her family?

REBECCA: Not really. All my life, I've never thought about those kinds of differences. He's the person I care about, and I don't see him being any different, other than the fact that he brings this wonderful culture into my life. It's really Sanjay who notices the differences. He'll be the one who points out that he is the only nonwhite in a room, or the only guy. Those things never crossed my mind, but being around him and his family has made me much more sensitive to how immigrants feel—or how Sanjay feels when he's the only Indian in a crowd of a thousand people.

SANJAY: That's true. Where I grew up—especially if you're the only person who looks like me—you tend to take on the characteristic in other people's minds of every sort of fringe group. I was ten years old during the Iran hostage crisis in 1979, and suddenly I was somebody else—an outsider. It didn't make sense for me to remind people that I wasn't Iranian, because that was missing the point. I was the outsider. I remember that being a really hard time for me.

MARLO: I've seen that dynamic of "the other" up close. My mother was Italian, and my father was Lebanese, and they were both children of arranged marriages. My mother grew up lower middle class in Detroit. Her father was the stereotypical Italian male in the fruit-and-vegetable business. He owned two produce trucks, and that was considered a big success. In those poor neighborhoods, the Italians had their area, the Jews had their area, and the Irish had their area—and the Irish were considered lower class than all of them. I think that's why my mother had a thing about Irish people.

PHIL: "There's those shanty Irish again!"

MARLO: Right. But Phil changed her thinking about all Irish people once she fell for his charms.

Getting along with the in-laws is, of course, an art form that requires patience, skill, and a whole lot of diplomacy. But what about getting along with a spouse? Most couples we spoke with agreed that apart from the big issues—money, career, children—it's the little day-to-day annoyances that send both spouses into separate foxholes.

"Perfect example," Phil said. "In our house it's football. Marlo gets annoyed if I'm watching a simple little NFL game on the weekends. Can you imagine that?"

"Hold on," Marlo countered. "I actually like football, and if it was one simple little game, I wouldn't mind. But you turn Sunday into an all-day marathon—no lunch, no dinner, just football. As Erma Bombeck once said, 'Any man who watches three football games in a row should be declared legally dead.'"

Sanjay laughed with recognition. "Well, for Rebecca and me," he said, "the main issue is about neatness. I'm a really neat person and she's not."

Rebecca shook her head. "It's not that I'm not a neatnik," she explained. "It's just that there's only so much time in the day to get everything in order. In our house, we share a closet and a bathroom—we don't have his-and-hers this and that—but we do have separate offices. In his office, there is nothing on his desk but one little computer. Maybe a glass of water, too. That's it. My office is a constant mess, with boxes and stacks of paper everywhere. Everybody who comes into the room trips over stuff. Then Sanjay walks in, and he's like, 'I'm going to lose it.'"

Sanjay winced. "I get an almost visceral pain when I look at it," he said. "She'll say, 'I can't find that document,' and I'll go, 'Really? I wonder why?'"

Rebecca's solution is simple: "I tell him: 'Just shut the door.'"

"I'm like Sanjay!" Marlo said. "I try to sneak in and organize Phil's study, but he hates that because then he can't find anything."

"And what about you, Rebecca?" Phil asked. "Are there similar small things that get under your skin?"

"When small things drive me crazy, I try to take a bigger view of the situation," Rebecca said. "For instance, when his mom and dad come to visit, they like to make tea in a pot, and they don't clean it every time because they know they'll make tea again. It used to drive me crazy, but I realized it was more important that I have a good relationship with them— this is just some stupid little pot."

"So you recognize that you have control over being annoyed and adjust your reaction to it," Marlo said.

"Exactly," said Rebecca. "Here's another example: I can't stand how the dishwasher is packed unless it's done a certain way. So if I see that someone else is packing the dishwasher, and the dishes are all crazy, I know I'll have to repack it the way I like. I'll say, 'Please don't be offended. I'm not saying that you're not doing it correctly'—well, in a certain respect that is exactly what I'm saying—but I know that it's really my issue. I'm the one being bothered by it. It's my problem to overcome."

Just as he does on television, Sanjay put the facts together in a coherent, logical way. "After fifteen years," he concluded, "I've come to realize that things like neatness are all about mindset. Rebecca has a ton of things going on and three kids to manage, and it's hard to keep all of that organized. She has painted a vision of life for me that made me realize I shouldn't worry so much about things like neatness."

For the Guptas, as with so many couples, one big issue has been finances—but on this front, they are more aligned.

"It's not so much about spending," Sanjay said, "because we both come from frugal backgrounds and neither of us is a big spender. It's more about staying on top of finances."

"Bottom line," Rebecca added, "it comes down to communicating and having trust. We both know that neither of us is going to go out and buy frivolous things or something really big without discussing it with the other. We're both likely to look for a good deal."

"Who pays the bills?" Marlo asked.

"I pay them," Rebecca said, "but he makes the money, so I guess he ultimately pays them. Still, I'm the one who chases down all the paperwork."

The two share a strong desire to be charitable—but interestingly, that has actually caused occasional friction. "There's no problem with giving away money," Sanjay said, "but, frankly, we have probably given away more than we should have in terms of planning for the future. We'll go to a charitable event and think, *Gosh, we've been so blessed and lucky*—but that can sometimes lead us to ask ourselves later, *Do we have enough?* But the biggest financial argument we ever had was when I thought she might have been taken advantage of. We probably lost a bunch of money we didn't need to lose, but it wasn't her fault, even though it took me a little time to get over it. Those are probably the biggest sources of fights now."

PHIL: And if you do have a big fight, how long does it last, and does one of you pout or fall silent?

REBECCA: Big arguments never really end. I mean, he's still mad at me for buying him a ham sandwich fifteen years ago! Those fights are still there, like a splinter in your skin. They become almost a running joke.

SANJAY: We've had big arguments, for sure, and I think the longest they've lasted is two or three days. But I come from a pretty sedate household. I can probably count on one hand the number of times I heard my parents yelling when I was growing up, and it was jarring. So it's not really our style to have explosive arguments.

MARLO: So how does a typical Sanjay-Rebecca argument play out?

REBECCA: When the arguments happen, we've both learned to sit back, take a breath, look at the bigger picture, and value what we think. Plus, it's really hard for me to be mad at him for very long because he always makes me laugh.

SANJAY: Well, laughter is a funny thing, because it makes the person who's laughing feel good, but it also makes the person who's giving the laughter feel good. That's the idea.

PHIL: But what about when the fight isn't a laughing matter, Sanjay?

SANJAY: I am much more transparent now. Early in our marriage, I would hold things in and expect her to figure out why I was upset. At some point, I realized that was a waste of time. I should just get things off my chest.

PHIL: Why were you waiting?

SANJAY: I was being passive-aggressive. The way I saw it, if she didn't figure out why I was mad, I could stew even longer about it. I was feeling vindicated that she didn't even know why I was upset. But the other thing is, I don't have a lot of friends to talk to about this kind of stuff, and she does. *She* was the person I would probably talk to about this argument I was having if only she wasn't the person I was having the argument *with*! So I eventually realized it was pointless to let something fester, and I needed to make a judgment call: instead of me just living with my hurt, and her living with her hurt, I needed to fix it.

REBECCA: It helped that we started out as such strong friends. There have been times when I look at him and say, "Can you not be angry right now because I need to talk to my best friend to help me solve this problem." And that would help him say, "Okay, yes, we need to shift gears."

Sanjay is on the road a lot for his CNN work—covering everything from the 9/11 attacks to an indigenous tribe in an Amazon rainforest, to the 2010 earthquake in Haiti, where he famously performed emergency surgery on a twelve-year-old girl to remove cement shrapnel from her brain. He also gets a lot of celebrity attention, including being named one of *People* magazine's "sexiest men alive" in 2003 and being offered the post of U.S. surgeon general by President Obama in 2009. (Given his busy schedule—his medical career, family, and TV appearances—he declined the post.) Rebecca has supported his work by setting aside her family law practice after their second daughter was born to manage the home front.

"I'll bet that whole 'sexiest man alive' thing brought even more attention to Sanjay," Marlo said. "Do you ever have to deal with star-struck women coming on to him?"

"Yes, they're star-struck and they're powerful and they have money,"

Rebecca said. "And sometimes I think he has been taken advantage of—from people who want to disrupt our relationship so they can have a relationship with him. A couple of times he thought I was being unnecessarily suspicious, but it was more that I thought someone was trying to leverage his intelligence and his fame—and he wasn't recognizing it."

"And you were correct," Sanjay said.

"But he comes home to me every night, so I don't worry about someone else," Rebecca continued. "Sometimes I would say to Sanjay, 'Honey, this person is trying to weasel between us.' Like, women would send him photos of themselves with him and say, 'Don't we make a beautiful couple?'"

"Wow, I have to say, I've never heard anything that brazen—and I grew up in Hollywood!" Marlo said. "Sanjay, were you naïve about these things?"

"Probably," he said. "I don't see the warning signs until it's gotten to DEFCON status."

"I think jealousy takes so much energy," Phil said. "It's a terrible burden and a big distraction. I trust Marlo, and that hasn't always been true with women I cared for. It's liberating."

"I totally agree," Sanjay said. "I have friends who live with jealousy, and it can be all-encompassing. I've never had that. When I thought she was jealous or suspicious of me, I took it as more of an affront because I was working hard and never engaging in those sorts of things. I felt like somehow I had failed her—and what did I do to deserve that?"

"But it sounds like Rebecca is past worrying about such matters," Phil said.

"Well, that's because I'm secure in our relationship," Rebecca confirmed. "I know that even if something went wrong and we went our separate ways, he would still call me if he had a problem. Once, when we were dating, we broke up and he kept calling me. I said, 'Hey, this isn't a breakup if you keep calling!' We've always had that special connection."

PHIL: You're raising three children, Rebecca. That doesn't leave a lot of time for your professional life.

REBECCA: Well, I'm not practicing law now. That would be hard because it's an emotionally and physically demanding career.

MARLO: Are you and Sanjay on the same page about raising the kids?

REBECCA: Yes, we are. Of course, because Sanjay travels, I want him to be the good cop when he's home so the kids will always have happy memories and won't think, "When Daddy gets home, we're in trouble." He works so hard to make sure he can be home as much as possible. He operates every Monday, which means he's home every weekend for things like soccer games.

SANJAY: I love kids, and having a family was always something I dreamed of. We have a group of friends we travel with once or twice a year, and Rebecca and I get away for date nights.

PHIL: But if you're home with three kids and he's being named one of the sexiest men alive, that's got to be annoying.

REBECCA: Only because I didn't get voted sexiest woman with him! The truth is, we're so appreciative of our life and how fortunate we are. We try to remind our kids that this isn't how we grew up, by any means. And when they see him getting all this attention—people stopping us and wanting to take a picture—they know that the people he really wants to be with are us.

PHIL: You sound grateful.

SANJAY: We pinch ourselves every day. We've worked hard, but we know a lot of people who've worked hard and don't have what we have. If you can internalize that, it's a very powerful force. It keeps you sane, and it keeps your relationships grounded. Of all the things I want to give our girls, it's empathy for others.

MARLO: That comes across in your reporting—your naturally sympathetic nature. You can't fake a heart.

SANJAY: I do feel pretty deeply about things. That's something Rebecca and I have in common; she's on the board of UNICEF, I travel around the world doing stuff for organizations like that, and we're starting a fellowship at our alma mater. Some people have religion, some people have community; for us, it's that charitable philosophy.

"We've spoken with dozens of couples at this point," Marlo said, "but given the years that you devoted to family law, Rebecca, you're the only one who's actually done a kind of field study on the subject of marriage. Professionally speaking, what's the secret to a successful one?"

Rebecca took a moment to collect her thoughts. "As a family law attorney," she began, "I represented people in divorces, and the number one thing they felt was resentment. What I noticed is that resentment starts when all the other things go. Maybe the husband is working really hard and making all the money, and he resents that the wife is not contributing. Maybe she feels like she's drowning in crying babies and not getting any sleep and resents him for being on the road and getting eight hours of sleep. Those resentments can only be cured through communication. It's like when Sanjay said he'd sometimes want me to figure out why he was upset—I can't read his mind any more than he can read mine. Feelings have to be communicated. Sometimes he'll say, 'Hey, I'm working way too hard and I need you to notice and help me. I need something to look forward to, so can you get us a weekend away?' Or I'll tell him, 'I really need you to say, "Honey, I think you're doing a really good job right now."' Everybody needs that. Otherwise, you just have smoldering resentment."

"You know," Marlo said, "on movie sets we have something called an 'attaboy.' That's when somebody—could be an actor, could be the director, could be the food services guy—acknowledges the good work of a colleague. It's such a simple gesture, but it's so important. Every now and then I'll say to Phil, 'You know, I'm busting my tail getting everything done, so a little attaboy would really be nice any time now.'"

"That's so right," Rebecca said. "A lot of couples have that expectation that the other person automatically understands everything that's going on in your life because they are together so much. But nobody really knows what's going on inside your head."

PHIL: And so what's your advice to those couples?

REBECCA: It always comes back to that one word: respect.

SANJAY: Respect and trust. Maybe this is the medical part of my personality coming out, but it seems to me that everything in life is a risk-reward proposition. And marriage is far more reward than risk. Far more benefit than bad. For me, everything bad is offset by trust. When I don't know what to do—when I don't know the right answer to a situation—Bec can put herself in my shoes, which is a hard thing to do. I can always turn to her.

REBECCA: I also think it's important to be humble in your marriage, because humility and empathy give you perspective toward your partner and gratitude for all you have.

MARLO: Gratitude is a good word.

SANJAY: I agree. Nothing in life is perfect, and you can't let perfect be the enemy of the very, very good. We say that in the operating room a lot in the middle of surgery: Do we take out this last piece of a tumor, even though it's right up against something in the brain that is very important? If we do take it out, we could sacrifice all this incredible work we've just done in search of perfection.

MARLO: And you feel the same thing applies to marriage?

SANJAY: Absolutely. Why search for perfection when what you have is already so good?

Kelly Ripa and Mark Consuelos

MARRIED IN 1996

*"I told myself, No matter what he says,
do not have any expression on your face—
he might clam up. So my expression was always
flat—and this was before I got Botox."*

I t was a make-or-break moment for Kelly Ripa and Mark Consuelos—
the kind of confrontation that can either blow up a marriage or make
it invincible.

"We were newlyweds," Kelly told us, "and I think Mark felt he might
have rushed into things and made a mistake. We were having a big fight,
and he took my wedding ring and threw it out the window."

"Whoa!" Marlo said.

"Well, *that* was a big move," added Phil.

"He turned around to get my reaction," Kelly continued, "and I looked
at him and said, 'I'm still here.' I think he thought I might just go *poof!*
and vanish. But instead, I said, 'Okay, now what?' And in that moment,
he realized that, even though he had just done this horrible thing, I wasn't
that rattled. So what did I do? I said, 'I get it. I'm young and married and
scared, too. But this is forever. I'm with you. Now, let's go find that ring.'"

The memory was twenty-four years old—as old as the couple's marriage—but Mark still looked sheepish as he listened to his wife retell it.

"I was twenty-five years old," he said. "It wasn't that smart."

This remarkable story speaks to the true mettle of this couple's marriage. "It was a defining moment," Kelly told us. "I'm sure a lot of people would have said, 'This is outrageous. This is crazy behavior. I'm done.' But I understood where it was coming from. It was coming from a place of genuine fear. And I got that."

We spent a lazy summer afternoon with Kelly and Mark at their four-story brownstone on the east side of Manhattan. Throughout our conversation they were alternately funny and animated, serious and expressive, and always locked into the topic at hand—which was not at all surprising: they've been talking

Las Vegas, Nevada; May 1, 1996

about their marriage publicly for years, primarily on Kelly's talk show, *Live with Kelly and Ryan*, where Mark frequently fills in as a guest host (when he's not in Vancouver, filming his TV series, *Riverdale*).

As their fans well know, they're far from shy about sharing the details of their lives on Kelly's show. Their connection is no less intimate on social media, where they are very popular. They love to post photos of each other on Instagram, most of which make one thing clear: these two are still very much into each other, even though the photos sometimes incite finger-wagging. When Mark shared a picture of Kelly on vacation—in a teeny gold bikini—she was criticized for being too old to rock such a skimpy suit.

Mark swatted back: "My wife's commitment to exercise and a healthy diet is admirable," he wrote. "Yes, she's wearing a bikini at age forty-seven and will no doubt wear one for many years to come. If that offends you in some way, I suggest you get over it."

When they first met in 1995, Kelly was already a star on the long-running soap opera *All My Children*. Mark flew up to New York from Tampa in the hopes of landing a role on the show.

"He hates it when I tell this story, but this is how it was for me," recalled Kelly. "I had screen-tested a lot of guys for this role, and then one day the casting director said, 'I think I found our guy. He's green—he's never done anything—and he's in Tampa.' So she shows me his picture, and let me tell you, Mark today looks exactly the same as he did when he was twenty-four. I was dazzled. And that's not like me—I don't get dazzled."

"It wasn't a particularly good head shot either," Mark chimed in.

"That's how dazzling you are," said Phil.

"Mark had never done a screen test before," Kelly continued, "so they brought him in a day early to show him how it worked. I wasn't expecting to meet him that day, so I walked in with curlers in my hair and no make-up—a complete disaster."

"You had a pimple, too," teased Mark.

"Thanks for reminding me," Kelly shot back. "It was covered up with medicine that looked like toothpaste. So I walked into the room, and they said, 'Kelly, this is Mark Consuelos. You're going to screen-test him tomorrow.' And, in an attempt to be charming, I said the dumbest thing ever. I said, 'Are you sure you want to work here? I used to be handsome like you, and now look at me!'"

"Were you dazzled, too, Mark?" Phil asked.

"I thought she was adorable and sexy," Mark recalled, "but I had just gotten off a plane from Tampa and was screen-testing for a job that could change my life. My head was spinning."

Mark landed the part and slept on a friend's couch for the next six months until the role was permanent. During that time, the couple began going out with groups of people from work, which progressively grew smaller and smaller until it was just the two of them. "I was shy," Mark confessed.

He clearly got over his bashfulness, proposing to Kelly a year after they began dating. But the marriage almost didn't happen. One day in the run-up to the wedding, the two were taping an episode of *Live with Regis and Kathie Lee* when they began to quarrel in the studio. The fight was a biggie, and it continued as they stalked through Central Park, Mark trailing behind Kelly, pressing his case. The two ended up back at Mark's place, and whatever peace negotiations happened behind those closed doors apparently did the trick: the following day, the couple jetted off to Las Vegas and said their "I do's" at the legendary Chapel of the Bells on Las Vegas Boulevard.

Yet despite the pre-elopement combat, the newlywed ring-tossing, the public confessions of being human and imperfect, Mark and Kelly are a surprisingly traditional couple.

MARLO: How do you divide the day-to-day work of your marriage? For example, who controls the checkbook?

KELLY: Mark is the financial planner. He's responsible for every good financial thing that's ever happened to us. When we met, I said to him, "I've never met an actor who was good at math." And he said, "I'm a terrible actor."

MARLO: That's such a funny thing to say.

MARK: But that's my role, and she makes the home a home. If it were left to me, we would have nothing for the holidays.

KELLY: It's funny, because I think of us as being such a progressive couple. And yet, we're almost old-fashioned. Mark has made it possible that I've never had to leave New York to work. I've been able to maintain the nest. He's always been willing to travel to a set, sometimes even living in another country to work.

MARK: Some would say *you've* made the sacrifice.

KELLY: I don't know. Sometimes you missed the kids' milestones, and that was hard for you.

MARLO: Was this a decision you made together?

KELLY: In a way. There was a time when we were really agonizing over our future. *Who are we? What are we going to be?* Then the talk show opportunity came up, and Mark said I should do it, even though I thought it was out of my wheelhouse. He said it would let me do what I've always wanted to do, which was to raise my kids. The show allows me to work early in the morning and have the rest of the day to take the kids to their activities and be there for their ballet recitals. He made those sacrifices—though I think he wouldn't have known how to find a ballet class.

MARK: She's right. I don't even remember people's birthdays. Kelly remembers every birthday in our family. She'll remind me, "It's your dad's birthday. You should call."

KELLY: I think part of the beauty and the balance of marriage is to learn to adapt to each other. Like with Mark's schedule. He was raised in a military household, where everything ran with military precision. So when he says we need to be somewhere at 2 p.m., he means we get there at 1:57 p.m. and linger outside the front door for three minutes, and then we enter. When we were first dating, he once said he would be at my apartment at 7 p.m. I was so used to 7 p.m. meaning 9 p.m. that when he got there at seven, I wasn't dressed and had my hair in a towel. I said, "You're early," and he replied, "But we said seven." He actually thought I was being seductive, but I really wasn't. I was just getting out of the shower.

MARK: She was in a robe.

KELLY: So I had to learn that time actually *did* matter. Before that, I thought time was theoretical. That it was—

MARK: —a suggestion.

KELLY: And the fact that I was chronically late *and* left the top off the toothpaste—both of those things drove him crazy. Then I realized I was starting to do that deliberately to bug him. But one day I said to myself, "Okay, are we going to have a nice marriage, or are we going to be dramatic all the time? Just put the fucking cap back on the toothpaste, Kelly! It's not rocket science—just twist it on."

MARLO: Phil and I have similar stories—like him shaving even when he doesn't want to, because I think he looks more handsome when he's shaved. Or me not moving things around in his study in my attempt to tidy it up. These are all everyday examples of accommodation, so you don't drive the other person crazy.

KELLY: Right, and what's nice about marriage is that now, so many years later, we've settled into our happy place. I clean up after myself and I'm on time. I do it for him, but I also do it for myself now. And he does things that I know didn't always come naturally to him. At one point, he figured out that I love gardenias, so now he sends me gardenias once a week, just to let me know he's thinking of me. When he walks into our apartment, the first thing he'll say is, "It smells so good in here, like gardenias." And I'll say, "You're reaping the benefits of your own thoughtfulness."

MARK: It's a simple thing, and I know it makes her happy.

KELLY: But I remember the first time he sent them to me, I said, "These gardenias are so extraordinary," while inside I was thinking, *Now he's going to tell me he has a secret other family.*

MARLO: I love where your mind goes.

Although they both seem to be born to their roles as husband, wife, and parents, we were surprised to come across a quote from Mark that he'd given to a reporter not long before we sat down for this interview. "I'm just now getting this marriage thing," he'd said.

"Really?" Phil asked. "Just now, after twenty-four years?"

Mark smiled. "It goes back to raising two sons and a daughter," he said. "I see how fast our daughter gets things, while we men never really catch up in many ways. I'm a slow learner. It takes me a couple of times to go through a situation before I get it."

"When do things finally click for you?" Phil asked.

"Essentially when you realize that being selfish is a bad thing in a relationship," he said. "I still struggle with that."

Kelly sighed. "You have the weirdest perception of yourself!" she said. "To me, you've always seemed like the most adult person I've ever known."

Mark explained his "slow" learning by pointing to the quiet messages he picks up in his marriage. "Let's say we've been out at a party, and I've done something to upset her. I can always tell—I'll go to grab her hand and it'll be a dead hand. Like, 'I'm giving you my hand because I'm allowing you to save face in front of whoever—but I'm not really *holding* your hand.' At one point, I would have gotten defensive or said something stupid like, 'I'm sorry if you're upset.'"

"Which is the worst apology," Kelly said, "because it takes no responsibility for what you've said. When you're in a situation like that, even if you feel like you've done nothing wrong, you need to see it from the other person's perspective."

Kelly turned to us. "Okay, so he'll make a comment at a dinner party that embarrasses me. From his point of view, it got a laugh. But from my point of view, it hurt my feelings. Now, one thing Mark is really good about now—which he wasn't always—is instead of getting defensive, he'll say, 'I'm really sorry. I didn't mean to make you the butt of the joke.' It's a very kind, simple gesture."

Although this couple talks openly about the ways in which they're different, one thing about them is very much the same: they're both in a business that can invite uninvited trouble. We wondered whether the green-eyed monster ever came knocking at their door.

"Kelly's not a jealous person," Mark said.

"Which is good," Kelly replied, "but Mark can be jealous. I'm always shocked by that, because I would not consider myself someone who anybody would have to get jealous about."

"But jealousy is usually not about what the other person does," Marlo said. "Jealousy is your own thing."

"It is," Mark said. "It feels horrible, and you know you're wrong."

"Phil, did you ever get jealous?" Kelly asked.

"Oh, sure," Phil said. "She was making a movie with Kris Kristofferson, and they had this long love scene in it, and I have to say it made me very uncomfortable to watch it."

Marlo stepped in. "*Uncomfortable* is putting it mildly. He actually came to check on me in the middle of the night. It really took me by surprise. I was the executive producer of the film, and I specifically chose to shoot in Chicago so that Phil and I could be together. We had a house in Winnetka, but his company kept an apartment for him downtown in case of snowstorms. One morning I had a 4 a.m. call, so I'm in the apartment sound asleep—it's about three in the morning—and I hear this banging on the door and I think to myself, *God, I've got to be up in an hour. Who the hell is that?* And I open the door and there's Phil. The second I saw him, I thought, *Oh, for God's sake, he thinks Kris Kristofferson is here.*"

"That would be *my* move," Mark said.

"Yes, Mark would totally do that," Kelly said.

"I was so mad at him because I was going to miss a full hour of sleep," Marlo said, "and I was also aggravated that he would be suspicious of me. But I said, 'Come in, dear'—through clenched teeth. He walks in and goes, 'I just missed you.' And I thought, *Oh, please!*"

Kelly narrowed her eyes. "Phil, what would you have done if Kris Kristofferson had actually been there?" she asked.

"Well, let's just say there would have been an Irish-type activity," Phil said.

"With Mark, there would be crime scene tape," Kelly said. "Am I right?"

"Yes," Mark admitted. "It's the macho stuff—and it's so boring."

"Well, it was early in our relationship," Phil said. "Call me crazy, but I had no experience with seeing the woman I love in bed with another man."

Kelly laughed. "Mark did that a few times," she recalled. "He'd show up and try to catch me doing something. I remember one time I looked at him and said, 'Aren't you tired of catching me actually doing what I said I was doing?'"

We all looked at Mark.

MARK: Okay, so one time after we were married, I was doing a show in Boston and we didn't have cell phones then, and I couldn't get ahold of her all day. Then I got a really bad feeling. Unfortunately, there are flights to New York from Boston every hour—so I got on a flight and called her from the plane and asked her what she was doing that night—

KELLY: —and I said, "Believe it or not, I'm cleaning the toilets. I'm taking this opportunity, while I'm a single gal, to really spic-and-span this place up." Apparently, he thought that sounded very fishy.

MARK: So she said, "You sound funny," and I was like, "I guess it's just the phone."

KELLY: He wanted to catch me. So he gets home and tells the doorman to call up to the apartment and tell me there's a flower delivery. I'm excited because I'm thinking, *Oh my gosh, he's sending me flowers. This is so nice.* Meanwhile, I have a Johnny mop in one hand and I'm wearing a bathrobe. I am a disaster—not how I would want my husband to see me when he gets home from his movie set. So I open the door and it's him. He comes in—he doesn't even say hello to me. He's looking for something.

MARLO: He's sweeping the scene!

KELLY: Right. And I'm still looking for the flower guy! I said, "There's a guy coming up with flowers."

PHIL: So what did you discover, Mark?

MARK: That she was happy to see me. Look, it's a horrible feeling, right Phil? But wouldn't you say I'm less jealous these days?

KELLY: Oh, my gosh, yes.

Kelly and Mark have been parents almost as long as they've been spouses, so we wondered how they were dealing with their kids gradually leaving home. Their son Michael lives in Brooklyn and is a recent graduate of New York University, where his sister, Lola, just finished her freshman year. The youngest, Joaquin, is entering his senior year of high school.

"We have an almost empty nest," Kelly said, "and it's *really* empty because Mark lives in Vancouver nine months of the year for his series. I keep trying to get my in-laws to move in here because I feel like they're ready. They need to live in the city."

"Did your fame ever cause problems with your children?" Phil asked. "It certainly caused issues with mine."

Kelly laughed at a memory. "When the kids were really little," she said, "if someone asked them, 'What does your mom do for a living?' my oldest son would say, 'She works for Regis Philbin.' So people thought I was either his assistant, his aide, or his manager. Then when they put TVs in the back of taxis and played promos of our show, my younger one started saying, 'My mom works in taxi cabs.'"

Phil shook his head. "It wasn't always so funny for me," he said. "I once commented on the air, 'Jimmy won't eat anything green,' and the next day, a kid in his class said, 'Hey, Jim, why don't you eat your peas?' He came home that day and took my head off. I never mentioned my kids after that."

"You're smarter than me," Kelly said. "I put my foot in my mouth all the time."

MARLO: And yet your instincts—as both spouses and parents—seem to be spot-on. You must have had pretty good role models. Were your parents' marriages strong?

KELLY: Very strong. Between the two of us, our parents have been married more than 110 years.

PHIL: Wow. So you saw very good examples. Mark, you're Italian, Mexican, and Spanish, and men of those backgrounds are traditionally domineering. What about your dad?

MARK: He has always been a great husband to my mother—loving and protective.

PHIL: And your mother is—

KELLY: —she's no shrinking violet.

MARK: No, no, she's tough—nobody dominates. My mom took care of finances down to the penny. And because my dad was in the military, he instilled a strict atmosphere in the home.

KELLY: The surprising thing is that even though we grew up in different parts of the world—he was born in Spain, I'm from New Jersey—we had very similar values, and our parents were similar. Both of our moms left their careers to raise their kids. So in the beginning, I had tremendous working-mother guilt—just tremendous. It was my mother-in-law, surprisingly, who really helped me through that.

PHIL: What did she say?

KELLY: She said, "You're making this sacrifice early for your family so that later on you'll have the freedom to choose what you all do. This is part of how women live now." It was harder for women like her to be working mothers because they were expected to drop everything and put their careers to the side.

PHIL: What about you, Mark? Was your original expectation that Kelly would be a stay-at-home mom?

MARK: I knew she'd be a wonderful mom, but I didn't expect her to stay home and take that role at all. She was very independent and had lived in the city for five or six years before I got there. But I was a traditional guy. I remember we had a conversation early on when I said—and today it sounds super macho and misogynistic—"Listen, there's room for only one man in this relationship, and it's going to be me."

KELLY: And I said, "I'm a woman of this generation, and I've been on my own for a long time, so you're going to have to forgive me if it takes me a minute to keep up with the clock that you're rolling back."

MARLO: That's so great. You should write that down for your daughter.

It was obvious when talking with these two that their love of their parents runs deep. But what was especially touching was their love of each other's parents.

"From the very beginning," Mark told us, "Kelly and I have called both sets of parents 'Mom and Dad.'"

"My dad never had a son," Kelly added, "and he secretly always wanted one. He has said it a thousand times: Mark is the son he didn't raise but always wanted. If my dad needs 'grown man' advice, he calls my husband and they talk it out."

That mutual support helped the couple through a particularly rough patch for the family—when both of their mothers were diagnosed with cancer, and both of their fathers developed heart issues.

"Our parents were falling like dominos," Mark explained. "Thank God they're all fine now."

"How did you deal with that?" Marlo asked.

"Want to hear something really funny?" Kelly said. "Mark was with my mom when she was diagnosed. They came home from the doctor at 10:30 in the morning. This was more than twenty years ago. I had just had our son Michael, so I was still on maternity leave. We kept a bottle of Scotch in the house, just in case anybody successful ever came over and asked for it. So there's Mark and my mom, opening up that bottle and each having a tumbler full. I had never seen my mom drink before, let alone in the morning."

"But you were crying," Mark recalled. "You were devastated."

"I was sobbing. I called my sister and she said, 'I can't talk right now. Dad collapsed and I'm on my way to the hospital. He needs bypass surgery.'"

"Wait a minute—your mother and your father, on the same day?" Marlo asked.

"The same exact day," Kelly said. "And I said to Mark, 'Oh, my God, we are cursed. We have to get a priest here. We need holy water. We have to burn candles.' I couldn't believe it."

Mark revealed that when illness befell his parents, Kelly swept in as if they were her own. "She was so wonderful," he recalled. "When my mom was fighting her cancer, Kelly took her into our home. She lived with us for seven or eight months, and Kelly went to the chemo and radiation appointments with her, and she even bathed her. And when my dad came to

New York for his heart doctor, she went with him and sat there and took notes for him. I was out of town."

MARLO: Phil dove in that way when my father died. He brought my mom in from L.A. and she lived with us for three months—she was a mess and I was a mess. He entertained us every night, inviting people over, taking us out. He really brought us through it. I've always felt that marriage is the cushion of life. God bless you, Kelly, for being there for Mark's parents.

KELLY: Stuff is stuff. But when it's your parents who are vulnerable and you suddenly go into this caretaking role, it's somehow scarier.

PHIL: You worried about them dying.

KELLY: We never said the words out loud. I mean, this is a long time ago, but think about how young and terrified we were. But we owed it to them to take care of them the way they'd taken care of us. I just didn't want to screw up.

MARK: But my parents didn't raise you, and you still did it.

PHIL: This is such a wonderful testament to family.

KELLY: You might say that. But when we got married, we eloped. We didn't tell our parents. And my mom gave me the best advice any mother could give her daughter. She said, "Be good to your mother-in-law. Treat her as you would treat me—but nicer." And she meant it. My mom was very close to her mother-in-law, and we lived with our grandparents growing up. We think of family as the whole family, not just the married couple.

So I took mom's advice about Mark's mom, and it made things easy for me. It wasn't like there was this other woman in my marriage. It was like I gained another mom I could confide in, somebody who knew Mark from the beginning and could say what really drove him crazy.

As expressive as Kelly and Mark are with each other, they confess that it sometimes takes work to intuit what the other is thinking.

"Are you always this comfortable sharing your feelings?" Marlo asked.

"Well, now that Mark is a grown-up..." Kelly teased.

"...an actualized grown-up..." Mark added.

"...a full grown-up," Kelly finalized, "he's very good at sharing his feelings. But when we were young, it was hard for him."

"How did you get through that?" Phil asked Kelly.

"Patience," Kelly replied. "I told myself, *No matter what he says, do not have any expression on your face. If you have an expression, he might clam up and feel ashamed or judged in some way.* So no matter what he said, my expression was always flat—and this was before I got Botox. I didn't even know Botox existed, but I mastered the art of having no expression at all."

"God, you're funny," Marlo said.

"Because you don't want the person to think they're being judged," Kelly said. "You want your spouse to feel safe and know he has a confidant, somebody who's going to walk through the fire with him. And P.S., anytime he would say 'I have to tell you something and I don't want you to get upset,' my brain would always go to a dark and crazy place. I would think, *He's about to tell me he disposed of a body once.* But instead, he would say something like, 'Listen, remember how I told you I was going to go to the auto race with my dad? Well, I'm not. I'm going with a group of guys instead.'

"The point is," Kelly concluded, "early in a marriage, it's easy to let little things become big things—whether it's financial strain or career strain or you have kids and you're sleep-deprived. But Mark taught me to walk away and take a breath. That's when you figure out that it's not a marriage-defining moment."

"I taught you that?" Mark asked.

"Yes," Kelly said. "And when I think about some of the stuff we argued about—things that made me say, 'That's it! We're getting divorced!'—he'd laugh and say, 'Oh, okay. I'll see you in divorce court.' And I think if he had ever said to me, seriously, 'Okay, then we'll get divorced—fine,' I would have lost one of the greatest parts of my life over some tiny thing I couldn't even remember."

It was a touching observation that spoke directly to how Kelly and Mark coexist: they laugh and fight, they praise and zing each other—and it's all good.

Just before we turned off our tape recorder, Mark recalled a moment from just that afternoon.

"We took a walk today," he said. "I like to meet her in the park and walk her to her workout. We were talking about meeting with you two and how proud we are of our marriage. And it isn't so much that people would think we have a successful and loving marriage. It's that we're proud of getting through the bad stuff. Because there's really no such thing as the perfect marriage. Anytime you see a couple who seems truly happy, you can bet they've gone through some crazy, crazy stuff together and they've survived. That's something to be proud of."

Kelly smiled at her husband. "That's right," she said. "Marriage is like a roller coaster ride. There are these great highs where you've got this tickling in your stomach and it feels amazing. Then you sink down to the depths and get scared. But I think the reason we're enjoying our lives now is because, when all of our friends were going out on the town and taking trips to tropical islands, we had small babies and were exhausted and not being kind or nurturing to each other. That could have easily frayed our marriage. But we hung in there and got through it."

"You two are good to talk to," Marlo said.

"We feel the same way about you," Kelly responded. "It's always nice to be with a couple who like each other. Early on in our friendship circles, there were couples who made Mark and me unhappy when we were around them. We would get into an argument as soon as we got in the taxi. At first, we didn't understand it. Then we realized they were in an unhappy marriage, and we were wearing their energy.

"So, yeah," she concluded, "couples who are in a strong and loving marriage are always better to hang out with. Happiness is contagious."

Ted Danson and
Mary Steenburgen

MARRIED IN 1995

"I thought, *Oh, he's probably a super slick guy.* But slick guys don't say 'gosh-a-rooney' after making love."

I f first physical impressions dictate the life or death of a relationship, it's a wonder that Mary Steenburgen and Ted Danson ever got to a second date. For many women, the hairdo might have killed it.

The year was 1994, and both actors were about to be cast in *Pontiac Moon*, a quirky dramedy about a married couple living in small-town California—he an oddball science teacher with a yen for adventure, she an agoraphobic with a panic disorder. The film's producers were sold on Ted but still considering Mary, so they invited the two of them to dinner at Postrio, Wolfgang Puck's trendy eatery in San Francisco. At the time, the restaurant was a magnet for Hollywooders visiting the city, and it featured a grand central staircase straight out of *Gone with the Wind*. The purpose of the date was simple: to see if these two actors got along.

"Ted was already cast," Mary recalled, "and the only person who was a question mark was me—and I knew it. I had been up all night at a wedding and had to get on a plane to go there and find out if we had chemistry. So

I walk into the restaurant, and there's Ted, who was doing another movie in San Francisco, and he had these . . . what do you call them?"

"Hair extensions," Ted said. "My hair was longer than yours."

"Right," Mary said. "So I say, 'Oh, your hair is so long,' and he says, 'Oh no, no, these are extensions.' And then he started showing me these little beads and everything. And I'm like, 'Okay . . .' and he says, 'Come on, we're right over here.'"

So there was Ted, escorting his potential leading lady down those see-and-be-seen steps to their waiting table, his long locks swaying with every step.

"I remember walking behind him as we went to the table," Mary said, "and he's tossing his fake hair."

"I felt like Fabio," Ted recalled. "I was in love with my fake hair."

"And I'm thinking, *I have to have chemistry with Fabio.* Anyway, it was hilarious—but I guess it worked out. The chemistry still is there."

"My hair, not so much," Ted added.

"The hair, not so much," echoed Mary. "Thank God."

Mary landed the role, and she and Ted went on to make the film, which explored the life of a complicated relationship—something that was not unfamiliar to either of the stars. At the time, Mary—an in-demand actress who'd won an Oscar at age twenty-seven for her role in *Melvin and Howard*—had recently broken off with a boyfriend, just three years after her decade-long marriage to actor Malcolm McDowell had ended in an amicable divorce; and she was caring for their two children, twelve-year-old Lilly and ten-year-old Charlie.

"I had just told all of my friends, 'Guess what—I'm not good at relationships,'" Mary told us. "'I look like I might be, but, in fact, I'm not. I have two beautiful children and I'm done. I'm not putting myself through this anymore.'"

Then came Ted—the strapping hunk who began his career as eye candy on afternoon soap operas and commercials before launching to fame as

Sam "Mayday" Malone of the long-running series *Cheers*. By the time he met Mary, he had accomplished the often-difficult leap from the small to the big screen in *Three Men and a Baby*, but off-camera, his life was, to use his phrase, "a mess and a half." His 1993 divorce from his wife of fifteen years—producer Cassandra Coates, the mother of his two daughters, Kate and Alexis—played out painfully in the press. It had been his second marriage.

The bust-up occurred amid a very public affair with the actress and comedian-turned-*View* host Whoopi Goldberg. To make matters worse, his blackface routine at a 1993 Friars Club roast in Goldberg's honor touched off a frenzy of bad press.

But by the time Mary and Ted met, all of that was in the past. To find out more about their quarter-century marriage, we met up with them—Mary as luminous as ever, and Ted strikingly handsome in his matching white shirt and hair—at their home in Santa Monica, a charming bungalow that was carved into a hillside in 1922.

The couple's mini Australian Shepherd, Arthur, happily greeted our arrival, followed by Ted and Mary, who offered up big hugs hello. Their Craftsman-style home has a living roof ("it doesn't reflect heat up into the sky like most roofs," Mary explained) and a bohemian interior ("we don't use decorators, we just do our own thing"), and their own thing was warm and inviting.

They led us into their farmhouse-styled kitchen, a cheerfully lit space lined with bookshelves. The farm table, with its bright yellow glasses and napkins and an abundance of cheese and crackers, was all set for an illuminating conversation. We stepped right into that light with the number one question that was on our minds: Why had *this* marriage, Ted's third and Mary's second, clicked when the others hadn't?

TED: Well, I mean, the truth is, who knows why this works? It's divine on one level—we'll get to that—but I got married [to actress Randy Gosch] while I was in college. We were twenty-two years old and good friends, but it certainly wasn't a marriage, so we got divorced in 1975.

PHIL: Then, two years later, you married again, to Casey, the mother of your two daughters.

TED: Yes, and that lasted fifteen years. There was still a huge level of unconsciousness on my part. So when Mary and I got together, my life was incredibly messy. Underneath there was a lot of work going on. I was trying to wake up and stop being a liar.

MARLO: What were you lying about?

TED: Everything. I was not hugely faithful—let's leave it at that. But I wanted to stop being a liar. I wanted to be creative. So, I did all of this work on myself. I don't think we would have been in the same place at the same time if I hadn't started to grow up. But by the time we met I was convinced I was incapable of having a relationship that I wouldn't mess up.

MARLO: And what was it about Mary that made you think differently?

TED: When you are cast in a part together, you have an excuse to look at somebody in the eye. So I shared my life with her on that first night. It was very clear nothing was possibly going to happen because of how nutty I was, and because Mary wasn't looking to be in a relationship. Jump in here, Mary. I don't want to do a monologue.

MARY: No, you're doing great.

TED: All right. So, we were playing these 1960s eccentrics in the movie, and while it was clear that Mary and I were not going to have a relationship, I felt we should to do something fun and kind of old-fashioned romantic, because that's what the film was like. So, one weekend we took a canoe ride. We were in Mendocino, and there's this big tidal river called the Mendocino River—

MARY: —the Big River.

TED: The Big River—and we got into a canoe that had an outrigger. Just a beautiful canoe. Mary was in the front, and I was in the back, effortlessly paddling. You learn a lot in a canoe, I think, and there was very little conversation, except when it was right. Sea otters, blue herons. It was magically beautiful and peaceful, and we were totally in sync.

MARY: But you kept wanting to turn the canoe around.

TED: For our wedding, part of our vows was a poem Mary wrote about that canoe ride. It was kind of like a charter for our marriage, about finding the truth in each other's eyes. But Mary has always been the person who says, "Let's go around the next bend." I'm usually the one saying, "I think we shouldn't—we're fine." She always gets me to go around the next curve in life.

And yet even as the couple approached that first bend in the river, Mary had her own reservations about Ted, mostly because they were so unalike.

"I got really scared because we lived so differently," Mary explained. "He took private planes, I lived in an old farmhouse in Ojai and had a relatively small life—except I would go off occasionally to do a movie. His life was exploding, and I have always been a little shy about being out there and being talked about. I don't need that. I love being in front of the camera, but I don't like my life being out there, and his was *all* out there."

"Your children must have factored into your fear, as well," Phil said.

"They did. I was a single parent, and I didn't want to leave my kids. I'm so protective of them, and I didn't want to make their lives somehow not work for them. It was such a crazy time for me, and everything got filtered through my children—whether I dated someone, whether I didn't. I just wasn't looking for any of that."

"And I was a mess," Ted offered.

"You were a hot mess," Mary agreed. "But then I started noticing that, whenever we were all going out as a cast—to dinner or something—if he wasn't there, I was a little disappointed. So, it kind of snuck up on me, and soon it became more and more undeniable that I wanted to be around him. Also, the more I got to know him, the more I saw—in spite of everything that was going on in his life—what a fine human being he is. And he was so different from what I expected."

"In what way?" Phil asked.

"I saw him as Sam Malone. I sort of bought into that image, and I should have known better, because I'm an actor. I started to think, *Oh, he's probably a super slick guy.* But I was wrong, because slick guys don't say 'gosh-a-rooney' after making love."

Marlo laughed. "Well, your secret's safe with us, Ted," she said. "So, Mary, what did you learn about Ted that surprised you?"

"So many things," Mary said. "He was raised with the Hopi Navajo people and ranchers' kids outside of Flagstaff, Arizona. He spent his mornings riding bareback on a horse across the desert with his friend Raymond, who was Hopi. He had the most exotic American childhood, and once I started meeting his family and seeing all the pieces that made up this person, it was like, Wow, he's so *not* who I thought he was. He was so much more deeply spiritual, and a much deeper thinker."

"Your relationship sounds idyllic," Phil noted.

"Hey, we're madly in love," Ted said. "I feel so blessed on every level—from as spiritual as you can get to the most shallow. We celebrate how lucky we are a lot."

"You both use the word 'spiritual,'" Marlo commented. "How does that play out in your relationship?"

"We hike together," Mary began. "We usually go for forty-five minutes and sometimes with our dog—but only if it's not going to be too arduous for him; he's thirteen. But we love trees, and there are so many beautiful ones in our area. We also meditate together—transcendental meditation, TM. We both study that. And without being Buddhists, we both have a sense of spirituality that involves honoring our ancestors and the people who came before us—our parents, and even the people we don't know who led to our lives. That's just how we think about things."

Ted and Mary's home includes a room in which they meditate and celebrate their ancestors with family photographs and other collected mementos of their lives. A few years ago the couple purchased the house next door as a haven for their visiting four children and three grandchildren.

"Keeping everyone together like that is such a big gesture," Phil noted. "A common problem for second marriages and blended families is when the new partner doesn't embrace the kids of the other. And that can kill the relationship. One of the great blessings Marlo brought to my life was to embrace my children and bring my sister Kathy and her kids into our family circle."

"For me," Mary said, "Ted's tenderness toward my children—and now our grandchildren—is reason alone to love him."

Ted smiled. "When we were writing our marriage vows," he said, "it was clear what we wanted to say to each other. And then suddenly we realized, 'Oh, wait—first we need to make vows to our children, who will be standing up with us for the ceremony.'"

"What else did you say in your vows?" Marlo asked.

Mary answered: "Our vow was, 'I promise to treat you with love and respect and be the best friend I can be to you for the rest of your life.'"

"And, boy, have we," Ted interjected. "And in Mary's case it was a big leap sometimes, because I was a handful."

MARLO: Once you were married, did you consciously make some change in yourself as a way of keeping your vows?

TED: My changes came before I met Mary. I had a mentor who walked me through a lot of my stuff that I was going through, and my family was very sweet and pitched in. I was starting to get a good sense of who I am—why I was the way I was—and that empowered me. So, no, it wasn't, "Oh, I want to be with you so I'll need to accommodate or change something about me." It felt more like I had woken up and the gift of my life was standing right there.

MARLO: Once you got involved with Mary, did you ever notice yourself back-sliding into your old ways?

TED: I remember one moment early on, before we were engaged, that I started to do a version of push-pull. It was an old habit. This wasn't about lying or anything, but instead of moving forward with the relationship, I was going back and forth. And when I looked at Mary, none of this was registering on her face. She didn't even nibble at it, because she didn't play that game. And I thought, *This person doesn't even know this stupid dance. So I guess I don't have to do that anymore.*

PHIL: Still, I'm sure you've had moments of conflict over the years.

TED: Good Lord, we've had bumps and ups and downs, and we're okay with a little drama in our life. But 90 percent of the time, we want to have fun and be happy.

MARY: Our motto is: the only drama we like is drama that we're getting paid for.

PHIL: So what happens when you do butt heads?

TED: We can be in the middle of an argument, and I can trust that if I look at my stuff, she will look at her stuff, too—and vice versa. If you don't trust the other person to say, "Oh, I see what I'm doing, let's work this out"—if you're both not being responsible for your own actions in life—then you're in trouble.

MARY: That's really a huge thing, and it's rare, too. Of course, it feels a lot better to point over there and say, "*You're* wrong, and this is what *you've* done to me, and *I'm* a victim." That feels so much better than saying, "Okay, here's my half. I'm going to own up to it."

MARLO: How did you learn to do that?

TED: For both of us it was right before we met.

MARY: I was married to Malcolm McDowell, and I adore him still. It was a very imperfect marriage in which both of us were equally imperfect. I would want to know him even if I had never had children with him, because he's one of the great, hilarious, adorable characters I've ever met in life. But going through our divorce was painful, as we kept trying to sort things out. And I knew that I wouldn't be any good in life if I didn't look at my half of it. So we both went to each other at one point and said, "This is how I screwed up. Sorry." We owned it. So, by the time I met Ted I had already done that.

PHIL: And did you teach him to do that, too?

MARY: No, no. He had been going through the same thing. We had both learned that that language does exist, and we both knew it was the truth. Even when we're not practicing it, somewhere deep inside we're thinking, *Oh boy, I'm not being totally clean right now.*

TED: When we're in love and in tune and communicative and laughing, it is truly divine. I cannot overstate how that feels between the two of us.

But in a fight, that flow stops. It is so disturbing it's like a jolt. It's like stepping off a cliff.

PHIL: When that happens, do you get angry?

TED: Actually, I get angry at Mary only when it's my fault. When I see clearly that it's Mary's stuff and not mine, then I can be compassionate. "I get it. I love you. I'm fine."

MARY: But we have had some humdingers.

MARLO: And how do you come back from those?

TED: Well, if I'm not telling the truth, we'll keep going until I get there. Once I do, Mary will see that. I mean, I'll be apologizing as soon as the fight starts, but that's not good enough. I will do every kind of defensive move until I see genuinely what is at stake.

MARY: Also, remember: I like him. I respect him. And I don't want to be mean to him in life. I can be mad at him now and then, but I also have a gratitude that I get to spend my life with someone I like this much. But we're both actors, and the fighting can be dangerous, because we're both good enough actors that we're each thinking, *Is that real or not real?* I mean, during a fight I have said things like, "You're mean. You're mean like a junk-yard dog—"

TED: Junk. Yard. Dog.

MARY: —but, the truth is, we both hate it.

TED: And our fighting is almost always about *you can be better than that*, without saying that. But the thing is, you have to have something in the bank to get you through these moments. If I walk away in the middle of a fight and a voice in my head is saying, "Do you really think that your wife is not crazy about you—that she doesn't love you?" I have to say, "No, of course she loves me." So, there's something good about having a history of knowing she loves you.

MARLO: That's a great dialogue to have with yourself.

TED: Well, it's all about finally telling the truth that I don't want to tell, especially if I'm angry. I grew up with a mother who was unbelievable about the giving, the caring, the loving, the nurturing. But anything negative—a negative thought, a selfish, petty angry thought—was intolerable. She would almost get sick instead of dealing with her anger.

PHIL: So, stepping up to your own anger was hard for you?

TED: Huge. It still is.

MARY: For both of us, and for very different reasons. We both came from families where the anger was fully loaded and scary. And before I met him, that was one of the things I recognized in myself. I learned when I first went to therapy—on day one—how, as a kid, I had not been able to express anger, and that there was no place for it in my life.

When she was eight years old and growing up in Arkansas, Mary's father, a freight train conductor, was diagnosed with heart disease. Back in 1961, such patients were instructed to give up everything, from hunting and fishing to making love. "I remember my dad's doctor looking at me and saying, 'Your daddy needs you to be a good girl and keep everything quiet,'" Mary explained, "and, basically, the eight-year-old in me said, 'Okay, I get it. I can't make noise or make a mistake, otherwise, my dad is going to die.'"

"And that was backed up with eight heart attacks," Ted added.

"My God," Phil said, "the pressure must have been awful. You're always looking at your dad to see if he's breathing."

"A hundred percent of the time," Mary confirmed. "He'd have heart attack after heart attack, and I actually began naming them, because I knew exactly what I had done to cause each one. Like one time, it was because I'd gotten a B in school. So that was my childhood. The good news is, my world became safe in books. In books, people died but life went on. So I could vent just by reading."

"I read a lot as a kid, too," Marlo said. "I loved Nancy Drew—she was so powerful and smart. She was a detective!"

"My hero was Pippi Longstocking," Mary said, breaking into a big smile. "She was wild and redheaded and fought the bad guys and wore shoes too big for herself so she could wiggle her toes. I loved all of that because she was the opposite of what I was being."

"Right," Marlo said. "But you were suppressing an awful lot of emotional baggage—especially anger."

"Yes," Mary said. "I remember one day my therapist said, 'Well, no wonder you became an actress. That's your safe place.' And suddenly I saw it all. You know, in a lot of families with illness, the children adjust in ways that adults don't realize. When couples get divorced, everybody knows to say to the kids, 'It's not your fault.' But nobody says that to a kid whose father had a heart attack—that getting a B in school didn't make that happen. So, learning how to be a fully actualized human being—one who could actually experience things in a way that wasn't just sweet southern smiles—was a huge thing for me. And I think for a while after that, I got angry too quickly."

"So your therapist turned on a switch for you," Phil said.

"The switch was maladjusted," Mary replied. "I've learned to be centered with it. And, yeah, I do tell Ted whenever I'm mad at him."

"Yes, you do," Ted said.

PHIL: So you both worked through the anger issues. What about the part that involves telling the truth?

TED: That's the hard-work part. That's uncomfortable.

MARLO: When is it the most uncomfortable?

TED: When it's not going to feel good to the other person. Or when it's going to make me look bad. Or when I've done something that I know I shouldn't have done. At those moments, I feel like, "I can't ride in on my white horse and be wonderful and noble. I'm an asshole and I just proved it, and now I'm going to have to share this with Mary."

PHIL: And why do you have to share it with Mary?

TED: Because we have an agreement to not have secrets. It's not that I need to share it in order to get her blessing or permission. I need to share it so I don't have this little secret inside of me. For instance, Mary has a stronger sense—and rightfully so—of privacy than I do.

MARY: Not from Ted, but from the world.

TED: And there are times when I don't protect Mary or behave in the way that allows her that sense of privacy, without feeling jeopardized by me giving Joe Blow my number and being friends to the world and ha-ha-everything-is-fine to everyone. There are times when I do things that do not honor that privacy. So, I need a clean slate. I need to not be having secrets.

MARLO: Did you have secrets in the beginning?

TED: No, no.

MARY: That's what was unique about the relationship for each of us. I had never *not* had secrets. I'm sure there are people who would read this and think, *That's weird.* But for us, we'd both had enough of secrets. We had both lived that way and it caused us to feel alone in life. So, when I met him, I just realized: I'm not going to try to make him think I'm a better person than I am. I'm going to let him see exactly how small I can be and how dumb I can be at times. I'm not going to try to gloss myself up for him.

PHIL: How did you know to do that?

MARY: Well, it was painful to spend part of my childhood feeling responsible for the life and death of my dad, and part of the way I did that was to try to be perfect. I figured if I was perfect he'd stop having heart attacks. His heart wouldn't break in two. By the time I met Ted I had played that game throughout my life—and failed at being perfect, always. But with Ted it was like—he knows my warts. He knows exactly how smart or not smart or kind or not kind or how impatient a person I am. He knows all of that.

TED: And a secret for me can be when I'm feeling angry and sad. It's not that I've done something wrong or behaved badly. It's that I have a feeling or an emotion that I deemed inappropriate for this moment, and Mary can immediately see that in my eyes.

Several times during our conversation, we returned to the ways our now-grown children continue to influence our lives together; and how, for couples who come together at midlife, it can be like a tangle of wires behind the computer. Mary reminded us of a line from the 1989 film

Parenthood, which she starred in with Steve Martin, who played her husband, and Jason Robards, who played Martin's dad.

"I wish I could quote it perfectly," Mary said, "but the line talked about how, as a parent, you never cross the goal line, spike the football, and do your touchdown dance. Then Jason says to his son, 'It's like your Aunt Edna's ass—it goes on forever and it's just as frightening.'"

"That's really funny," Marlo said. "And it's the truth—you're a parent all your life."

"Yes, it's true," Mary said. "Just today we spent the morning dealing with, you know, an issue with one of our children and trying to put our best heads together to figure out how to handle it. And we're sixty-six and seventy-one years old."

In addition to being parents, Mary and Ted also had to learn to navigate the bumpy landscape of being stepparents. In both cases, they followed the same rule: don't try so hard.

"There is no book that tells you how to do it," Mary explained, "so the one thing I figured out right away is that they already have a mom—and it's not me. So what did they need from me? That's when I realized that everybody needs a cheerleader, right? There's never too many of those in your life, so that's what I'll be. I never set their boundaries, disciplined them, or tried to teach them right from wrong. They have parents who do that."

Ted was on the same page as his wife. "I think that's really wise, to offer yourself as a friend," he said. "'I'm not going to discipline you and I'm not going to judge you. What I'm going to do is hang out with you and be there for you.' And that's what you have to do: absolutely, genuinely be there."

"Also," Mary added, "I fell in love. I fell in love with my stepdaughters."

"And me, with yours," Ted said.

"Yeah, and he with mine."

Phil leaned back in his chair. "As I listen to these stories," he said, "I think back to raising my kids. After my divorce, I suddenly had four sons all on my own, and I didn't know what to do with them. Do I help Kevin with his homework, then Jimmy, Dan, and Mike? And then I said to myself, 'I don't have the time to do all of that.' And as a result I was very impatient. The first line I wrote in my memoir in 1978—a hundred years ago—was: If I could start all over as a parent, and I wish I could, I would let my children know when they pleased me: Hidden in the Irish culture is a feeling that you don't want to keep patting your kids on the back or they will grow up spoiled. Life is tough. And as a result of this, I yelled at my kids a lot. I raised my voice, and I feel bad about that."

The room grew quiet for a moment, and then Phil added, "Anyway, my kids still talk to me."

"He's a great dad," Marlo said. "His kids know they are loved."

A few days after meeting with Mary and Ted, we called them with some follow-up questions. They were in their car together, running an errand. It was sweet to hear them living the life they'd told us about—a husband and wife on an ordinary day, doing one of a million ordinary things that make a marriage. At one point we asked Ted to expound a little on the spirituality of his marriage.

"When I say 'spiritual,'" he explained, "I'm using it as a loose term that describes being truly, truly in love and in the moment. That feels spiritual to me. Without getting goopy, if I was to disappear tomorrow, I would disappear knowing that I'd experienced one of the great things about being a human."

"And that feeling is?" Marlo asked.

"Feeling like you're both totally one and complete," Ted said. "That, to me, is heaven on earth."

Judith and Milton Viorst

MARRIED IN 1960

"I am a pain in the ass and he can be a
major pain in the ass, which he has been for
almost sixty years. Who the hell would
have guessed we would work it out?"

A double bed is the key to a happy marriage. That is Judith Viorst's advice for keeping a marriage together. "It's very hard to stay mad all night in a double bed because a hand is always brushing against a breast, or a knee is pushing against a thigh," she said.

"Sometimes it's by accident, sometimes it's intentional," added her husband Milton.

"You can pretend, but you can't get away from each other," Judy continued. "It's very hard to turn your back and sulk, because your tushies are touching."

Meet the Viorsts. They are not a comedy team, though sitting across from them, it's hard not to think that. She's the author of dozens of funny and intuitive books, including the 1972 children's classic *Alexander and the Terrible, Horrible, No Good, Very Bad Day*. He's a scholar and policy wonk whose writing is geared more toward grown-ups. But put them in the

Washington, D.C.; January 30, 1960

same room and it's quickly apparent that you're witnessing a standoff that's been going on for more than sixty years.

Take, for instance, that double-bed rule, which isn't just a funny sound bite—it's a real strategy that has been in effect since the couple's honeymoon in 1960. "We went off to this nice ski resort in Mont-Tremblant, Canada," Milton explained, "because I was a skier and Judy graciously agreed to indulge my hobby. They put us in a room with two single beds, and I found that quite objectionable. I said, 'No!' in front of all these skiers. 'You have to give us a double bed!'"

"So embarrassing," Judy said. "What was worse about it was that our room was not in the hotel—it was in a separate little section. So it was a major spectacle with these guys carrying this double bed through the snow."

"To the sex maniacs!" Marlo said.

"To the sex maniacs, exactly!" Judy agreed, with a laugh.

As it happens, it wasn't the first honeymoon for either of them. They met when they were teenagers attending Rutgers University and working summer jobs as waiters in neighboring hotel restaurants on the Jersey Shore.

"After we finished serving dinner and cleared the tables, we would meet for what I thought was a little cuddling," Judy said. "I thought he was very attractive but much too fresh and disrespectful."

"I've been getting bad-mouthed on that for fifty-nine years," Milton said.

Following their summer flirtation, Judy decided they'd be better off as intellectual buddies. They'd meet for coffee and have deep conversations. Milton won a Fulbright scholarship and headed to France, and Judy thought they'd reconnect after his year abroad. Instead, they both ended up marrying other people.

"We never said goodbye; we just disappeared from each other's lives," Judy said. "Until 1959, when he had the nerve to call me at one in the morning in New York. He said, 'Do you happen to be awake?' At one in the morning! 'Do you happen to be awake?'—which is so Milton."

By then, they were both in their late twenties and separated from their spouses. Judy was living in Greenwich Village; Milton was traveling through New York and staying in a sweltering YMCA, unable to sleep. "I'd been out with friends a couple of weeks before," he said, "and the gossip across the table was that Judy was getting divorced. I said, 'Hey, wow, that's interesting.'"

Milton went over that very night. *Wow, what a second chance*, Judy thought as she opened the door to him. Deep into the early morning hours they walked around nearby Washington Square Park and talked about the future, and what they both wanted out of life.

"Had you been remorseful in your own private way that you'd never stayed together?" Phil asked.

"Yes and no," Judy said. "I was used to being treated a certain Jewish princessy way, and he wasn't doing that. But by the time I was twenty-eight, I really didn't need that anymore. I had grown out of that."

"What about him?" Marlo asked. "Had the years changed him, too?"

"He had improved by then," Judy said. "He was still devastatingly attractive and smart, but nicer. And both of us were dying to be parents—we talked about that on our first date after that night. It was like, after hello, we said to each other, 'Do you want children?' Because neither of us was going to waste our time on a man or a woman who did not want children. I had never wanted children—ever—and then after my marriage broke up, I realized that I didn't want children with *him*. It was a very big deal for me to have children, and I didn't realize it until I broke up with my first husband."

Milton couldn't put his finger on why having a family was so important to him, especially given that his parents' marriage hadn't been particularly positive.

MILTON: There was always a lot of arguing. My father was a petty gambler and it was the Depression, so there wasn't a lot of money around. Maybe marriage was part of my emancipation from my parents—rather than emulating them—because I never thought of myself as emulating my father. In fact, I'm still mad at him.

MARLO: For what? Gambling?

MILTON: No, not gambling. Because he was not a good father. I have often said to my friends that I don't envy other men their wealth, their beautiful women, their success, their whatever—but I do envy them their fathers.

MARLO: So, you became a good dad.

MILTON: I think so. You would have to check with my children about that.

JUDY: A wonderful father.

PHIL: I ended up with four sons all by myself.

JUDY: You had custody of them?

PHIL: It's just how it happened. We were Catholic and had five kids in six years. When our marriage broke up, their mother took them back to Albuquerque, which was her hometown, and one by one, the boys came back to me in Chicago, and I'd meet their planes at O'Hare. Big hugs. I took them to a house I had purchased—I didn't know how many I was going to get back. I did not get my daughter; she stayed with her mother. But I got my four sons, the oldest of whom was a freshman in high school, the youngest in fourth grade.

MILTON: That was a challenge.

PHIL: Yeah, and I was scared. I didn't know what to do with them.

MARLO: What fascinated me about Phil as a father was when I started living in his house, he knew the footfall of each of his sons. The staircase was near our bedroom, and I'd hear him say, 'Kevin?' 'Yeah, Dad.' A little while later, 'Mike?' 'Yeah, Dad.' It just amazed me. He was like a papa bear. It was one of those things that made me love him. That, and his sweetness as a man.

PHIL: That's my dad in me. He was a very sweet man—fun and easy. He used to love to tap dance—he'd entertain the babysitters with a little soft shoe and some lighthearted jokes. He was a good man. I'm sorry he didn't live long enough to see the big part of my career. He died in his fifties. Chesterfields.

Before they could make it official, of course, Judy and Milton had to settle affairs with their previous spouses. In Judy's case, that meant traveling to Juarez, Mexico, to get a divorce from her first husband. This triggered no small amount of anxiety in the bride-to-be.

"I called up Milton and said, 'I can't get married to you because I can't go through another divorce,'" Judy recalled. "'It's too horrible. How can you be so sure you're not going to get divorced again?' He was very calm about it. He said, 'When you come back from Mexico, don't go directly to New York. Come through Washington and we'll discuss it.' And by the end of the day he had bought me my dress to get married in."

Judy and Milton wed in a quiet ceremony not long after that fateful night in Greenwich Village. They had three sons and raised them in Washington, D.C., where Milton was based as a journalist. Throughout the ensuing six decades, Judy has often chronicled the family's life in humorous newspaper and magazine columns, poetry collections, adult advice books, and many other children's books in addition to the Alexander series. She has also joyously tracked her own decade-by-decade journey in books with such telling titles as *How Did I Get to Be Forty?*, *Suddenly Sixty*, and *Unexpectedly Eighty*.

But through it all, she's never pulled a punch, particularly about the art of marriage. One of her earlier poems—pointedly titled "True Love"—includes these lines:

> *When he is late for dinner and I know he must be either having*
> *an affair or lying dead in the middle of the street,*
> *I always hope he's dead.*

What's often easy to forget is that, apart from being flat-out funny, Judy is also a student of psychoanalysis who has produced a rich body of journalism on the subject. This becomes evident when she turns her analytic eye to her own marriage.

"I think getting along in a marriage involves a lot of conversations between you and yourself," Judy reflected, "in which you think about a problem and how you can solve it—like 'How can you not want to kill him?'"

As a foreign correspondent for *The Washington Post*, *The New Yorker*, *New York Times Magazine*, and *The Atlantic*, Milton traveled all over the world. Upon his return home, he would dump his bags in the front hall and leave them there.

Judy is obsessive about order.

"For years, I said to myself: 'Judy, three days—you are not saying anything until the third day after he arrives. He's got to go through his mail, he's got to get over jet lag, you're going to shut up.' Finally, on the third day, I would say, 'Honey, would you please put your stuff away?' I basically gave him three days while the halo was circling around my head, deciding how to handle this in a way that didn't irritate the hell out of both of us the minute he walked in from a trip. It was still annoying to me, but it made life so much easier."

"Gradually, we have acquired a certain respect for each other's idiosyncrasies," Milton summarized. "Men and women always say, 'My spouse doesn't understand me,' and there's a considerable amount of truth to that—we do trigger resistance in each other in many ways. But I think that we've gotten to the point where we understand where the triggers are. We're not always great at it, but we're a hell of a lot better than we were fifty years ago."

Judy echoes Milton's thoughts—in her own words.

"I am a pain in the ass and he can be a major pain in the ass, which he has been for almost sixty years," Judy said. "Who the hell would have guessed we would work it out?"

But they have worked it out, despite an unending stream of classic marital confrontations. Traveling together, for instance, was a particularly steep hill for the couple to climb. Milton liked to wait until the last second to leave for the airport. Not Judy.

"We used to go to Europe every year," Judy said, "and two days before we were getting on a plane—two days!—I would say, 'So when are we leaving for the airport?' I know I'm crazy on this. This is not a joke. I mean, I am something of a joke among my friends. If I am two minutes late, they figure I've been run over by a car and I'm unconscious or else I would be calling them and telling them I'm two minutes late. So, literally two days before we would leave for de Gaulle airport, I'd say, 'What time are you willing to leave?' and he would say, 'Make me an offer.'"

MARLO: Make me an offer. That's hilarious!

JUDY: And then we would negotiate—we would negotiate with a lot of emotion.

MARLO: Phil and I used to have horrible fights over the amount of luggage I take. I admit it. I know it's insane. We go for two days and I have three bags.

JUDY: I totally respect that.

MARLO: I have six pairs of shoes. I may want to hike, I'll need high heels, and I'll need flats for cobblestones. And he's wearing the shoes he'll have on for the whole trip. Meanwhile, I have four sweaters. Who knows what the temperature is going to be, right? He would nag me about it, all the way in the car. Then when we would get to the airport he would say to the baggage guy, "We're only going for three days. Can you imagine all these bags?" Like the baggage guy cares. But I think he was trying to embarrass me out of taking so much.

PHIL: Finally, after twenty years or so, I didn't mention the bags anymore.

JUDY: Phil, did you have a conversation with yourself that made you stop doing it?

PHIL: I wonder. After a while you begin to realize that this isn't going to change, so you're just wearing yourself out.

MILTON: When you're negotiating with yourself, you're not allowed to figure out who is going to win this battle or lose this battle.

MARLO: It's taken us years to be able to deal with the differences between us, and not see them as critical of the entire marriage. We are both sure of the love each of us has for the other—and I think, *Well, that should be in the bank.* So if a criticism arises, or something happens that one of us doesn't like, we have to be able to say to ourselves, "Okay, I'll take a nickel out." The whole bank account doesn't have to get drained.

JUDY: That's a good way to think about it.

MARLO: You've got to have something in the bank. You can call it benefit of the doubt or whatever.

MILTON: You polish it off a little bit. You modify it. You can never really give it up. Deep down, I still disagree about what time we ought to get to the airport. And Judy has polished off a lot of things, too.

PHIL: It seems to me you've brought a lot of insight into the marriage that many people don't think about. You both seem to analyze your behavior a lot.

MILTON: First of all, I think about it much more now than I used to. Second of all, I think we all—to one degree or another—think about it every day. This is not just something we do Mondays and Thursdays. That's not the way marriage works.

MARLO: I think you just hit on it. It's a daily job, and you're building something—even though you don't always realize that you're doing that. You don't consciously say, "Hey, look, we're building this bridge," but sooner or later you become aware that this marriage is a real living, breathing thing.

In the early days of the Viorsts' marriage, building that bridge wasn't all that easy. In some cases, their marital friction was baked in on account of their childhoods.

"One of the great things in my life was my emancipation from my family," Milton said. "I was an only child, and the one thing my mother would always say was, 'You're the only thing we have.'"

"'You're the only thing we have?'" said Phil. "Oh, my. That's kind of a rough thing to say to her little boy, isn't it?"

"We could sit here for another hour and talk about that one," Milton said. "She said those words when I finished college, when I went to Europe for a year, when I went into the service, and when I moved to Washington. I could've spent the rest of my life in Paterson, New Jersey. I still remember standing on the train platform with my mother, and she was crying and saying, 'You're the only thing we have—and now you're going to Washington.' And for me, this was a moment of great joy, of great opportunity."

Judy jumped in. "He was holding on to his direction, and doing what he wanted to do. He wouldn't let his mother control him or manipulate him, and that made him a free man. But it made it hard for me, because I knew there were certain tools that were just not available to me. Crying and pleading were not going to move his heart because he had learned that this was how you get controlled. It took me a few years to work all of this out in my head—to understand that Milton's imperviousness to whining and tears had actually been his salvation. These were important, liberating values for him. But it made things harder for me."

Judy was not always so empathetic about Milton's quirks. Before they had children, she revealed, she'd sometimes be so desperately at the end of her rope with him that she'd pack up and leave the house.

"Every time I got mad at Milton, I would move to a hotel," she said matter-of-factly.

"Wow," Marlo said. "That's serious."

"It was only a block away," Milton said.

"So one night, I got mad at him and went to the hotel," she continued, "and the next thing I knew, he had tracked me down, checked in, and moved in with me. It was very hot weather and the hotel had air-conditioning, which our place did not."

"So in other words..." Phil said.

"I had walked out on my husband, and he had come to live with me in the hotel."

Judy could always be persuaded to come home after these walkouts—such was Milton's gift at negotiation—but no matter how fiercely they fought, divorce was never on the table. That said, their fights could get loud.

"I used to run around the house closing the windows so people wouldn't hear us yelling and screaming," Judy said. "I don't know, somewhere in the past ten or fifteen years, we lost interest in having fights. We just let it go. The area of things we want to fight about has gotten very narrow."

"What kinds of things did you argue about?" Marlo asked.

"Everything," Judy said. "I mean, I couldn't believe I married a man who, when I said, 'I think we'll have a yellow refrigerator,' had an opinion about it. He said, 'I don't know if I want yellow.' He's got an opinion on the goddamn refrigerator? Well, it turns out he has an opinion on everything, so that opened a lot of doors."

"And closed a lot of windows," Marlo said. "This is fun. Give us one more example of a Viorst face-off."

"Well," said Judy, "one of our sublimely stupid arguments that will never go away is about food. Milton came from a very poor family, so he does not like to throw anything out unless it has turned green and is radiating poison throughout the house."

"Till it hurts your eyes," Milton chimed in.

"I mean, our kids come over here," Judy continued, "and the first thing they do is open up the refrigerator, and they smell everything and look at the sell-by dates because they do not trust their father. So what I do is wait until he is out of the house and then I go through the refrigerator, and very often I carry the food right out to the trash can, even if it's snowing, and I cover it up with things. Sometimes he finds it and puts it back in the refrigerator. He's crazy on this subject, and he's never going to change. So I do this behind his back so he can't catch me, which is most of the time. I mean, it is so pathetic."

And yet for all their domestic warfare, ask Judy and Milton their underlying philosophy of marriage, and they are surprisingly in alliance.

"Judy's position is that there are three things involved: the two spouses and the marriage itself," Milton said. "They're all separate and they all have to be addressed."

"And the third one—the marriage—is the thing you are creating together," Judy added. "You're not always winning or losing, and you're not giving up. You're *feeding* the marriage. You're *giving in* to the marriage. And that makes—"

"—that makes it an independent institution," finished Milton. "You have to think in terms of nourishing the institution, and that's hard to do."

"So basically, nourishing the marriage makes the man and the woman less selfish," Marlo said.

"That's exactly right," said Milton. "Because if you want to feed the marriage, you're going to have to give in. You're going to have to modify. You're going to have to negotiate. There's no other way. Otherwise, it's me-me and you-you and no marriage."

PHIL: I completely get that. For example, the older I get, the more I don't like to shave. I think it's a waste of time. But I know she hates it. We'll be going out somewhere, and I'll run downstairs and she'll look at me disappointed, and I'll realize, "I may as well just go back and shave." That's an accommodation I make.

MARLO: I just think it makes a man look so unkempt.

MILTON: Well, we've acquired this new thing. We'll get up in the morning at the same time, and I'll go into the bathroom to brush my teeth and take a lot of pills, and then I'll go downstairs to make the coffee—— because I'm regarded as a superior coffee-maker. And then Judy will look at me and say, "You're still wearing your fucking pajamas."

JUDY: The bottoms.

MILTON: The bottoms. And her position is, "You look like an old man walking around like that."

MARLO: Exactly.

MILTON: So lately I have been trying—the past few weeks, at least—to make sure I've put my pants on.

MARLO: That's just what I say to Phil. "You look like an old man with your whiskers sticking out. That's what old people do. And I'm not going to let you turn into an old man." It's as simple as that.

JUDY: And why should they? They're cute guys. Why should we let them turn into old men?

Shaving etiquette and morning fashion tips aside, what advice would this very smart, very practical couple offer a young couple considering a life together?

"There's no single way to go about it," Milton said, "and it's not going to be easy. But if you want to get married and think you have the capacity to do it, don't kid yourself that it's going to be something you'll dance your way through, or that the degrees of edginess don't still exist. But you do get better at it. As Judy says about our marriage, we now let a lot of things ride that, once upon a time, we didn't let ride.

MARLO: In other words, some things can be left unresolved, and that's okay.

JUDY: Yes—and I think that's such a valuable concept. You can't resolve everything. Walk around it, step around it, let it go.

MARLO: He's never going to be me and I'm never going to be him.

MILTON: That's exactly right.

JUDY: Annoying as that is.

MARLO: Phil and I broke up for three months before we got married. Both of us just said, "This is too hard. It's not possible." I was working in Los Angeles and couldn't live in Chicago. He said he couldn't live and work in L.A. There was the traveling, the compromises of it all, my work, his work, and the pressure of his kids. In that three months, he went out with other women. I went back to an old boyfriend, but I was miserable. It was apparent I didn't want to live without him. And then, he called me in the middle of the night—kind of like your 1 a.m. phone call from Milton. I picked up the phone and . . . Is it okay if I say what you said to me?

PHIL: Sure.

MARLO: He said, "I never thought anybody could be this irreplaceable."

JUDY: Wow. That's a very good line, Phil. A really nice line.

MARLO: It still makes me cry. And then we made a lot of adjustments and compromises to have a life together. We picked New York, even though neither of us lived there. Sometimes when people are struggling about whether they should marry somebody and whether it's too much trouble, I say, "You know what? Break up for a while. If you break up, you'll really get perspective on how much he or she means to you. That's when you see whether this is the right person or not."

There's no question that Judy and Milton Viorst are the right people for each other. Their accommodations for the marriage never stop, even as they continue their ever-bartering Bickersons routine, with their inexhaustible arsenal of zingers. Their brains are always tuned in to the marriage's frequency.

"Milton has always been the person our friends could depend on," Judy explained, "the one you call in the middle of the night and say, 'I need you here now,' or 'I need a ride to the hospital,' or 'Help me—there's a rat running around my house.' He is going to put his clothes on and come any time of the day or night."

But not anymore, Milton explained, unless Judy does the driving. That's because his eyesight is fading.

"There are a whole new set of burdens that have been imposed upon her by my growing inability to take care of the things I used to take care of all the time," Milton said quietly. "Sometimes she gets a little pesky about it, like, 'Don't bring up the ladder to change that light bulb—you'll fall off and have a terrible accident.' That's legitimate. I also used to love to drive around Europe, but I can't do that anymore. That is a vacancy that had to be filled, and she has filled it cheerfully and efficiently."

MARLO: What you're talking about is the ability to fill a gap.

MILTON: Yes. And I am absolutely aware of it and grateful for it.

PHIL: We know a couple who are having trouble. The wife is very impatient with her husband's deficiencies because they don't know how to make those allowances.

JUDY: Age-related?

PHIL: He's only a couple years older than she is, but she's got the genes of an Amazon woman and he doesn't. He's not in such great shape, and he drinks a little more than she would like him to, so she blames it on that. But she's very impatient that he can no longer do what he used to do, and driving is one of them. It's an adjustment, and it reminds us of our own mortality.

MARLO: And that we don't want our spouse to be deteriorating, because that means we would lose him. It's not just about the eyesight going. It's about fear.

JUDY: Well, I have absolutely forbidden him to die before me. I will not accept that.

MARLO: I see. So you're going to jump off the roof together?

JUDY: We can die together or I'm willing to pre-decease him. But he is not going to die before me. That's just unacceptable.

MILTON: I keep saying there may be a few things out of our control, and that may be one of them.

MARLO: Last question to Judy. You're famously funny—and cynical, and brutally honest—when you write about the human condition, especially matters of the heart. When you look back at your sixty years together with this man, how do you feel about the institution of marriage?

JUDY: Well, I'm certainly, passionately in favor of marriage. And if there was something even further than marriage—like an *M* you had to wear on your forehead—I'd want to have that *M* on my forehead. I mean, I think you go in all the way—for better and for worse. Yes, there are going to be a lot of "for worses," and unless you're incredibly lucky and find a soul mate from the start, there's going to be a huge amount of hard work.

MARLO: Yep, but the important thing is—is it worth it?

JUDY: It's worth it.

> There's you, and you, and then there's this third thing
> Which is the marriage. To it may you bring
> The finest strivings of the human heart.
> The "I," the "me," the "mine," the self apart
> Must yield some portion of its separateness
> And say a risky but unguarded yes
> To this third thing, this marriage you create.

—Judith Viorst, to her son and daughter-in-law on their wedding day

Al Roker and Deborah Roberts

MARRIED IN 1995

"I'm the type of guy who needs time to explain
what I'm feeling. On TV I can ad lib like—boom,
boom, boom! But when it's just us, I'm on
some kind of delay. I need time."

Approaching the home of Al Roker and Deborah Roberts, you almost expect to see Gene Kelly dancing down the sidewalk ahead of you. Tucked into a shady, tree-lined street on Manhattan's Upper East Side, the stately four-story townhouse—and its neighboring brownstones—could easily have been the product of MGM set designers charged with re-creating that ol' New York charm.

"It was built in 1860," Al told us proudly of his home.

"You were here in the beginning, right?" Deborah teased her husband.

"Yep," Al shot back cheerfully. "I watched them build it."

From its giant mahogany doors ("That's what sold me," Al confessed.) to the shiny parquet floors to the lovely garden patio out back—perfect for barbecues—the house is truly a family home. In fact, Al said, it is his dream home.

The problem is, it wasn't Deborah's. At least not at first.

Having grown up in Queens, Al had long considered owning a brown-stone in Manhattan as the definition of "making it." Deborah, on the other hand, was raised in the quieter climes of Perry, Georgia, and had always imagined a New York of sleek high-rises and ever-ready doormen. And so, the move to this house—a relocation they made in 2001, when their daughter, Leila, was just three years old, and their son, Nick, was almost due—came only after a bit of discussion, and some soul-searching on Deborah's part.

"We had been living in a really nice art-deco building," Deborah said. "That was our first apartment as a couple—it's where we lived when Leila was born—and I'm a very sentimental person. So I had to deal with some angry feelings when we first came here."

The story of how this family came to live in this home is also the story of Al and Deborah's marriage: a tale of different people with different backgrounds finding common ground through candor and compromise.

The day we met with this powerhouse couple, we were first greeted at the door by Al and their seven-year-old Havanese rescue dog, Pepper, who said hello with a few enthusiastic barks. Al led us into a soft, yellow living room, where a wedding album was open on a table, ready for us to choose a photo for these pages. It was our first indication of Al's warm and generous spirit—what a courteous man he is.

Moments after we sat down, Deborah rushed breathlessly up the stairs from the street level, having just returned from an appointment, brimming with energy and excitement. She eased into a chair next to Al, and we were ready to begin.

MARLO: Your debate over moving into this beautiful home is the perfect example of the conflicts couples face, and it always comes down to one thing: Who will win this particular battle?

DEBORAH: Right. And he won. I let him win it, but I was sort of resentful after the move.

New York, New York; September 16, 1995

MARLO: So, how did you get past the resentment?

DEBORAH: It took some time. I began looking at it from a different perspective, like I was beginning a new adventure with my family. Also, September 11 happened when we were at the other apartment, and many of us changed our lives and our thinking afterwards. That kind of pulled me closer to Al.

AL: And she did that in a very caring way. Because here's the other thing that was happening: my dad was dying of lung cancer at that point, and he was fading pretty quickly. I was in a rough state emotionally.

DEBORAH: Yes, you were. So I let go of some of the resentment and shifted my focus to caring more about him and us as a family, and not so much about the dwelling. I was sad about leaving the old place, but I eventually chose not to be resentful.

PHIL: That's an important thing to recognize: that couples often choose a way to feel about something—meaning, that we have more control over conflict than we sometimes realize.

DEBORAH: Yes. Also, I was pregnant by the time we moved—our son was born while we lived here—so that helped. It was clear that we were going to start to make some new memories. At one point we had a conversation about this, and Al said, "You know, you have a hard time letting go." And I acknowledged that.

AL: I'll give you a perfect example of that. Back when we lived at the old place, we used to go to this small Italian restaurant, Mediterraneo, with a little wood-burning pizza oven. This was before Nick was born, and we'd go with Leila...

DEBORAH: It's the restaurant she went to as a baby.

AL: Right—she would go with us, and the owner knew us. Anyway, a couple years later, after Nick was born, I said to Deborah, "Let's go back to Mediterraneo tonight, just the two of us. It'll be fun." So we go there, and it turns out they had purchased the store next door, knocked out the wall, and expanded the place. We're sitting there talking, and I can see that she looks like she's about to cry. And, sure enough...

DEBORAH: I burst into tears.

AL: Bursts into tears.

MARLO: Oh, you *are* sentimental!

DEBORAH: I'm very sentimental.

AL: And I was like, "Why are you crying? It's the same menu."

DEBORAH: When he suggested that we go, I was thinking, *Good, I'll grab some of those old warm feelings again.* But it was a different place. It wasn't as intimate, and the waiters we knew were gone. I'd wanted a little taste of the old place, and it didn't feel that way. So, yeah, I am very sentimental. We talked about it afterwards, and he was upset because he thought he was doing a nice thing. Instead, I got there and started crying, and it became a horrible nightmare.

MARLO: I once had a therapist who said, "If you ever go back to revisit a place of great romance, don't expect it to have the same magic. Reality can never live up to the glow of a golden memory."

DEBORAH: Yeah. It will never live up to that again.

If it seems like Deborah and Al are good at communicating, that's because they are. Between the two of them, they talk to millions of people every day. Al spent the first twenty years of his career as a journeyman weather anchor, delivering rain-or-shine forecasts to TV viewers in Syracuse; Washington, D.C.; Cleveland; and his native New York City. Then in 1995, his career skyrocketed when he landed at NBC's iconic *Today* show, replacing Willard Scott as the program's jovial weather guru and perpetually friendly costar. He's held that post ever since, along with becoming an integral part of the *Today* show family.

Deborah similarly bounced around television during her early years, reporting on the day's news across the American South—Georgia, Tennessee, and Florida. In 1990, her profile went national when she stepped in as a correspondent for the TV newsmagazine *Dateline NBC*. But it was her move to ABC in 1995 that cemented her reputation as a serious newswoman with a diverse portfolio. In her time there, she's been equally comfortable settling in at the anchor desk of the evening news or letting her hair down as guest host of the popular talk show *The View*.

It's also worth noting that Deborah has anchored *Good Morning America*, the perennial rival to her husband's show.

While they don't bring that professional rivalry home with them after a long day at the studio, Al and Deborah pull no punches when they talk about their relationship, and they're forthright about the ways in which their styles can clash.

"We never do major yelling," Deborah noted. "We're a little more passive-aggressive than that. I'll get quiet so that he thinks, *Oh, she's got that look on her face—I know she's pissed.* And then usually one of us will comment, 'Okay, I just need to say this…' That's when we sort it out and say what we're really feeling. But the thing is, I like to jump right in and talk it through. He'll say, 'Give me a minute, give me a minute.'"

Al cut in. "That's because I'm the type of guy who needs time to explain what I'm feeling," he said. "Put me on TV and I can ad lib like this—boom, boom, boom! But when it's just us, it takes me longer, like I'm on some kind of delay. I need time to figure out why I'm ticked off. She'll say to me, 'Why don't you just say it?' Well, sometimes I can't put it into words at that exact moment. It takes me longer to figure out why I'm upset."

"I have the same problem," Phil confessed. "But what's so interesting to me, Al, is that much of your work on TV is without a script. I was like that, too. I never used a teleprompter; I just bounced off what was happening around me. The most you have is a weather map, and everything else is off the top of your head. That makes me feel a kind of brotherhood with you—although I don't know whether that helps a marriage or not, because it can lead you to talk too much—"

"—without anybody interrupting you," Marlo interrupted.

"Right," Phil continued, "and not giving your partner a chance to speak."

DEBORAH: You know, it's so funny that you bring this up, Phil, because this is almost like a metaphor for our marriage. He's more of an ad-lib, off-the-cuff kind of guy—a little joke here, a little comment there—and that's one of the things that makes him really fun and desirable and lovely. But it can also be irritating. I mostly work with scripts, and in life I like that kind of order. So one of the things I've had to learn to do with Al is go off script more with him. Everything may not be perfect or the way I want it to be; but learning to ad lib a little bit in the marriage has helped me to become a better person, a better partner.

MARLO: That's so great. In what way, specifically?

DEBORAH: Sometimes when we have problems, it's because he feels he's displeased me—and Al really likes to make people happy, to do the right thing, to get things done. And if he feels he doesn't please me, it makes him feel bad. It took me a long time to figure this out, but it's actually at the core of marriage: you want the person to feel good about himself and feel good about making you happy. That's something I've had to learn to adjust to.

MARLO: And to not be such a perfectionist?

DEBORAH: Right. And to ad lib a little with him. To go off script.

MARLO: That's a challenging assignment for two newscasters—to learn to adjust to each other's style.

DEBORAH: It is. And when Phil pointed that out, how Al works without a script, it got me thinking that that's how he functions every day, and that I function in the opposite way—and sometimes that gets in our way.

PHIL: It's so refreshing to hear how self-aware you both are. Do you go to couples therapy?

DEBORAH: Off and on—it depends on the situation. Even before we got married, therapy was a good thing.

AL: Sometimes it's helpful to have a referee, because you can get bogged down wanting to be right or trying to get your point across, and you don't quite know how.

DEBORAH: Or not realizing what the other person is feeling, and then you're sitting there in therapy and talking it out and suddenly you realize, "Wow, so *that's* what it is!"

PHIL: It's also a sign that you care—that you give a damn about the marriage.

MARLO: And the other person.

As with many couples, Deborah and Al trace their different approaches to life—and to their marriage—to their pasts. "He's from Queens, I'm from small-town Georgia," Deborah noted. "He had been married before, I had not been." They both come from large families—Al is the oldest of six children, Deborah the seventh of nine—and described having parental models who were not at all similar.

"My parents didn't graduate high school," Deborah noted. "They were factory workers who were just scraping by. They didn't have the same glue as Al's parents—they had kind of a troubled marriage, and at one point the divorce word was being spoken. But, you know, for a struggling black couple in the post-segregated South, it was kind of a luxury to be able to do something like that. It wasn't like they were yelling or fighting all the time—they just didn't have that connectivity. So I think they made a decision to try to figure it out for the sake of their family and their kids."

Al's parents couldn't have been any more different. "They were a romantic couple," he explained. "My dad was a bus driver, and at the end of each run he'd find a phone booth and call my mother, just to check in. 'What's going on? How are things?' Then he'd get back on the bus, drive to the other end of the route, get off the bus, and make another phone call to her. That's what I grew up seeing."

"That's loyalty," Phil noted.

"Right," Al said, "and I try to emulate that. I like the phone. Deborah is not a big phone person."

"That's not true," Deborah noted, "but I don't like the check-in. If you're calling just to say, 'So, what's up?' no, I do not like that. And it's mostly because I'm busy at work in a way that's different from him. He's already got his busy stuff out of the way by eleven in the morning, while mine is just ramping up. It used to drive me crazy. I'd say to Al, 'Just give me the headline, so when you call I'll know if it's important. Is something going on with the kids?' Because sometimes he'll hem and haw, and I'll have to say, 'Are you calling to tell me something or are you calling just to chat?'"

MARLO: I wish I had the problem that Phil called me too much.

DEBORAH: A lot of my girlfriends say that. "My husband never calls me."

AL: She actually mentioned this on *The View* when she was filling in as a host. A couple of the women said, "Well, jeez, have him call me then."

MARLO: Here's an idea, Al—you call Phil and tell him, "Call Marlo!"

DEBORAH: Yes, that's what we'll do from now on.

AL: There you go, Deborah. I'll call Phil instead of calling you!

Their joking aside, what Deborah has come to understand—through therapy and talking with her girlfriends—is that Al's phone calls have meaning for him. "One friend said to me, 'Did you ever think that maybe he just feels comfortable when he hears your voice, because that tells him that all is right with his world?'" Deborah explained. "And I thought, *That's very sweet. I'd never thought about it that way. And if it means something to him, then it should mean something to me.* So I have learned to take a breath and say, 'Sweetie, I've got some stuff going on, but what's going on with you? Great. I'm glad to hear from you. Got to go. Talk to you later. Love you.' That makes all the difference in the world to him, and it doesn't kill me for two minutes to be nice and sweet."

While the calls may be an occasional source of friction in the marriage, Al has another recurring habit—but this one's completely welcome.

"Al is a big note writer," Deborah explained, smiling fondly at her husband. "If we've had some disagreement and gone to bed without sorting it out, the next morning I might very well find a note on my pillow, or by the coffee maker, with him saying, 'Listen, I couldn't quite get out what I was feeling, and I didn't realize it until I thought about it overnight. I'm really sorry. Let's talk.' He's really, really sweet about that. I've kept a lot of those notes, and one day I hope to publish a book of them."

It was one of those notes, in fact, that brought Deborah and Al together. But to tell a love story right, we need to start at the beginning.

The date was September 20, 1990—Deborah's birthday—and both Al and Deborah were filling in for regular hosts on the *Today* show: Al for Willard Scott, Deborah for Deborah Norville.

"I didn't want to tell anyone that it was my birthday because I was a little embarrassed," Deborah remembered. "But I somehow mentioned it to Al, because he had such a sunny persona." Al was delighted to learn that it was Deborah's birthday, and he offered to take her to a celebratory lunch a few days later. She accepted the invitation.

"He was really lovely," Deborah recalled, "just this sweet guy. So we hit it off from the beginning, with emails and IMs or whatever. I could talk to him about work. I would tell him these terrible stories about somebody in my office who was trying to thwart a project I was working on, and he would really listen to me. And so, I just kind of found him to be like a real nice friend."

Friend—the dreaded word for any guy in pursuit. But Deborah had her reasons for keeping Al at arm's length. For one thing, he was still in the process of ending his first marriage, and Deborah was clear that she didn't want to get involved with someone in the middle of a divorce. For another, she simply wasn't interested in him as boyfriend material—he wasn't her "type."

But Al was playing the long game, and in 1992, he saw his opening: Deborah was leaving the city to cover the Summer Olympics in Barcelona, and she asked Al to keep an eye on her apartment. He said sure.

"So I go over there," Al recalled. "I guess most guys would probably go into the bedroom to look around—"

"—okay, that's creepy," Deborah interrupted.

"But I go into the kitchen, because I like to cook," Al continued. "I open the pantry, and there's nothing in there but cobwebs. I open the fridge, and there's almost nothing in there either. Then I open the oven, because I want to see how messy a cook she is—and there's still cardboard on the oven rack. That's when I realize: she's never even used this oven. She's never cooked."

Al got busy: By the time Deborah had returned from Barcelona, he had stocked her pantry and fridge and left flowers for her on her kitchen table—along with a note welcoming her home and asking her for a date.

He got his wish: Deborah said yes.

MARLO: What changed your mind?

DEBORAH: At this point we had known each other a couple years and I had been dating other people off and on. I knew he was interested in me, but I wasn't interested in him that way. But when I came home and saw this, I thought, *What a sweet guy!* Meanwhile, these other relationships had been flaming out for various reasons, and I realized that there was this really nice guy right in front of me. Maybe I ought to give him a shot and go out on a date.

AL: Have pity on him.

DEBORAH: Yeah. And so we did.

MARLO: Like, have him come over and cook for you.

DEBORAH: Exactly. Exactly. I consciously thought, *Maybe you're just ruling him out because you don't see him physically as your type—and maybe you should rethink that.* And so something clicked in my head after that. We went out a couple times and I began to realize that this was a guy who loves his mom, cherishes his family, is a good dad, is a good guy at the network, and maybe I ought to give him a shot to see if this might work out. So we started to really date.

MARLO: And so you got past the fact that he wasn't your physical type.

DEBORAH: I thought that maybe he just hadn't found the right happiness in his life. I knew he wasn't happy in his previous marriage, but maybe that was because he hadn't found that person who made him feel alive and good about himself, and that once he did, he'd figure it out himself.

Deborah and Al married on September 16, 1995, at the St. Thomas Episcopal Church in New York City. The nuptials were star-studded—among the guests were Katie Couric, Barbara Walters, and Mayor Rudy Giuliani—and the date of the big day permitted Deborah to meet a self-imposed deadline.

"I always swore I was going to be married by the time I was thirty-five," she said, "so when we finally decided we were serious, I said, 'Okay, let's get going—the clock is ticking!'"

"Made it by four days," Al tossed in.

"Married on the 16th and my birthday is the 20th," Deborah finished. "I turned thirty-five on our honeymoon."

Their timing may have been perfect, but the marriage required work from the very beginning, in no small part because they were blending two families. When Al and Deborah began dating, his daughter from his first marriage, Courtney, was just five years old and didn't completely understand who this new woman was in her daddy's life. Now she was eight, and still not crazy about her stepmom.

"It wasn't easy," Deborah recalled. "Kids always want their parents to be together, no matter what the circumstances are; and girls in particular resent another woman in their father's life. So she didn't like me, and I would get mad at Al about that. It was like he was stuck in the middle, trying to make sure that everybody was happy."

"What kind of effort were you making with her?" Phil asked.

"I was trying very hard, maybe too hard, to be the stepmom with the mostest," Deborah explained. "Anytime she came to visit there was always a little tension. So when I would travel, I'd always try to bring her back something fun, and she was never really grateful for it. So I would get upset. At one point, Al probably told me just to back off a little, but I was also frustrated with him because I felt like it was a war of wills."

"Did you pull Courtney aside and speak with her, Al?" Phil asked.

"Yes," Al said. "I'd say, 'Look, Deborah is really terrific to you, and you've got to respect her.' And she would kind of ebb and flow. I think, intrinsically, she knew that Deborah was really good to her, but kids have a natural inclination to be loyal to their mom. As Courtney has gotten older, I think she's come to realize that Deborah has been nothing but supportive of her."

Deborah agreed, acknowledging that the relationship took decades to thaw. She attributed that change, to some degree, to Leila's and Nicky's births, and her deep desire to see all of them as a tight-knit family.

"It's still complicated sometimes," Deborah admitted, "but I would say we now have a beautiful relationship. I think we all kind of grew up a little bit."

MARLO: Some of what you're talking about is jealousy—that Courtney may have been jealous of the attention her dad was paying to his new wife. But what about jealousy between the two of you as a couple? Phil and I have had our own jealousies. I once did a movie with Kris Kristofferson where we had this love scene that was about four minutes long and...

AL: That must have taken a long time to film.

PHIL: It was the longest damn love scene I've ever seen in my life.

DEBORAH: That *is* a long time to sit through. I get that, Phil.

MARLO: So, how do you deal with your jealousies? You're both famous, you're both in demand...

DEBORAH: Well, it's something that we've had to work through. It's tough because the way Al works is very different from the way I work. He works in a very intimate environment—they all travel together, he forms a lot of tight bonds with people on his set. I don't do that. I travel with producers, and it's rare that I form those kinds of bonds.

PHIL: But you bring up an interesting point. One would think that the fact that you're in the same industry would be a plus in your marriage. But do you ever feel like your similar careers work against the marriage?

AL: Yes, actually. There was a point when *Good Morning America* wanted Deborah to be their news person. She was pregnant at the time—right before Leila was born—and we decided, "Well, somebody has to be home with the baby," so she turned them down.

MARLO: Wow.

DEBORAH: And I paid for it.

AL: She paid for it. She took a big hit in her career. She was almost pushed out.

DEBORAH: They don't like you to say no. They remember that.

AL: And it was difficult. Really difficult. I was on this upsurge in my career, and here she's taking a hit in hers because she's the mom. At the time I didn't realize how much of a psychic wound that was for her.

MARLO: Why did you make that decision?

DEBORAH: I just decided that I had to sacrifice.

PHIL: That's probably because you had a loyal mom, right?

DEBORAH: That's exactly right, Phil. You hit on something. My mom was always there for me. I just wanted my kids, at the end of the day, to look at me as a mom who was there. So I gave up the big job, and I was angry at Al for a long time because I felt like he had it kind of easy. If he came home and just changed the baby's diaper, everybody thought he was great. If they saw him in the grocery store with Leila, it was, "Oh, my gosh, he's such a devoted father!" And meanwhile, I have taken this hit in my career, I'm sleep-deprived, I'm doing all this other stuff...

MARLO: So, how do you reconcile those feelings? This is so important, Deborah, because it's what so many women have gone through.

DEBORAH: I harbored anger for a long time. I'm not saying that every time I saw him I was angry, but underneath the surface there was some resentment. I didn't understand what I was feeling for a while—not until Michelle Obama talked openly about being married to Barack back when he was a community organizer, and he was always gone and she was home with her kids and angry.

At a certain point, I think I realized I needed to be responsible for my own happiness—I couldn't make him responsible for it. At the end of the day I've got to do that. And, of course, as I enjoyed a little more success at work, it became sweeter. I won an Emmy when one of the children was a baby, and that was nice. I felt validated at work again.

Al began to take responsibility for his happiness, too, by confronting a lifetime of weight issues. In 2002, he underwent gastric bypass surgery, ultimately losing one hundred pounds (plus ninety more in later years) while gaining a whole new fan following. But the decision was anything but a publicity stunt.

"My dad was sick," Al recalled, "and he was just a couple of weeks from leaving us. So he basically said to me, 'Listen, I'm worried about you because I'm not going to be around to help you raise my grandkids. We've gone around and around about this, and I'm really worried about you. You've got to do something about your weight.'"

"Do you think you were another reason he lost the weight, Deborah?" Marlo asked.

"I would think so, yes," she said. "I mean, ultimately he had to make the decision himself. But weight had become a third party in our marriage, and I used to ride him about it. And he did have various levels of success over that first period of our lives. But once we started thinking about having a family, he knew that he needed to try to get himself healthy."

"So how do you feel now, Al?" Phil asked.

"I feel great," Al said. "And Deborah has been a big part of that. Like last weekend I did the Five Borough Bike Tour. I wasn't going to do it because it was raining, but Deborah said, 'You can do it.' And so I went out and did it."

"And, hello? You also ran the marathon," Deborah boasted for her husband.

"Well, I wasn't quite *running* the marathon," Al countered. "It took six hours."

"It was a good shuffle," Deborah said.

PHIL: One of the things Marlo and I talked a lot about when we began working on this book was what couples get from each other that they can't get from anyone else. In our case, it's our ability to lift each other up when we need lifting. What about you two?

AL: I think we're each other's best support, too. I can be very vulnerable, and she's really the only person I can tell everything to—whether it's professionally or personally, even things about our kids. I saw a greeting card the other day that made me laugh. It said, "It's okay to think that your toddler is an asshole." That made me laugh because some things about the kids drive me nuts, and Deborah has helped me see that it's okay to feel that and still love your kids. These are things I don't think any therapist would know about me, but Deborah does. There have also been times when I've had to lean on Deborah—times when I've lost my way. And she's taught me that I can't be afraid to say I need help.

MARLO: What about you, Deborah? What do you get from Al?

DEBORAH: His investment in my happiness as a person. That's something that isn't easy to find. Al knows all the warts, all the black holes. He knows what makes me tick and what baggage I'm carrying from childhood. And I think that's because he truly cares about my happiness and is invested in it. He once looked at me and said, "I just feel like I drive you crazy, that I annoy you so much," and he wasn't laughing when he said it. And, yes, there was a time in our marriage when we were going through a real rough patch and I was probably showing him a sour side because I was this tired woman who was a wife and a mother and trying to have a career. And then you know what? I realized: He's a person, too. And he cares about me. And he loves me. So show him the same compassion back.

PHIL: That's such a huge epiphany.

DEBORAH: It's funny, I went on a trip last week—I was gone for four days—and when I got to where I was going, I opened up my suitcase, and there were four notes in there, one for me to open on each day.

MARLO: Oh, my goodness.

DEBORAH: I know. Or one time I was talking about a book that I was interested in, and the next day, he's got it on the bed, wrapped up like a gift with a note that says, "I thought you might want to read this." When he's a kinder person to me, I'm a kinder person to him, and that makes for a kinder and happier marriage.

We had gone into this conversation expecting to find two seasoned professionals who would know how to field every question we asked them with easy charm and ever-ready answers. After all, this is their daily bread.

But instead, what we found—topic after topic—was that Deborah and Al discussed their quarter-century marriage with a kind of intense introspection and deep feeling that belied their comfortable on-screen personas. No wonder America has grown to love them. We did, too.

To My Love

My Love—

My one regret is I'm not here tonight on your birthday.

I love you and I love the smile on your face from last Saturday. It is something I will cherish forever, as I do you.

HAPPY BIRTHDAY—
I love you

♡ Al

Deb—
Now I can really breathe.

You are home.
Sometimes you need time apart to realize how much you miss someone.

I love you—

Al

With Lots & lots of Love On Your Birthday

Mariska Hargitay and Peter Hermann

MARRIED IN 2004

"We were dating, and I was crazy about Peter.
It was all magic, magic, magic and then . . .
we had different expectations."

The place was absolute chaos. Everywhere we looked, there were signs of disruption—plastic work pails, uncovered steel slabs, and broken walls that fill you with a sense of dread and make your head throb with the thought, "How will this ever get finished in my lifetime?"

Yet even as we dodged power tools and stepped over buckets, we sensed the excitement from actors Mariska Hargitay and Peter Hermann, as they took us on a grand tour of the next big project in their ever-evolving life together. They were combining two wonderful apartments on Manhattan's Upper West side into one huge, fabulous space, with several rooms leading out onto terraces with breathtaking views of the city.

"I mean, this whole thing fell out of the sky," Mariska enthused, gesturing to the high ceilings of her new home. "It's just luck, luck, luck—a real blessing!"

Santa Barbara, California; August 28, 2004

Although the construction work was still under way, somehow the couple had magically carved out a living space at one end of the apartment that was so homey we momentarily forgot the wreckage on the other side of the wall. As they welcomed us into it, we felt swept into a delightful vortex of energy, as their three kids, August, Amaya, and Andrew—and Kaia, their mixed-breed rescue dog—darted in and out happily.

"I'm a real nester," Mariska said, "and I just wanted the kids to have a home when they start school. But, yeah, it's been a lot of work between me and my assistant for the past month to get this part of the apartment together."

"And I put all the boxes away," Peter added.

It was only when we sat down and began to talk that we realized that their marriage was not all that different from the home we were sitting in: a place of constant renovation, expansion, and change.

Like Marlo, Mariska grew up in Los Angeles; but ever since 1999, when she was cast as Lt. Olivia Benson, the crusading detective on *Law & Order: SVU*, New York has been her primary base. She and Peter, who grew up in Germany and Connecticut, met on the show during its third season, on an episode auspiciously titled "Monogamy." He still occasionally guest stars on *SVU* as a defense attorney and is also a lead on the romantic-comedy series *Younger*.

In a business that values longevity as a badge of honor, Mariska has actually earned two badges. Four days after we met with her and Peter, *SVU* surpassed *Gunsmoke* as the longest-running prime-time drama series in American television history—and Olivia Benson became the longest-running character in that exclusive club. For her work on the show, Mariska has been nominated for eight Emmy Awards, winning in 2006.

MARLO: You've been doing Olivia for twenty-one years. What an achievement.

MARISKA: I'm still taking it in.

PHIL: Nobody runs that long. That's hall of fame stuff.

MARLO: Phil, you did it for twenty-nine years.

PETER: You did your show for twenty-nine years?

PHIL: Well, we started as a local show in Dayton, Ohio, in 1967.

MARLO: He did six thousand hours.

MARISKA: Well, if Phil can do twenty-nine years, I'm going to have to put in another eight.

PHIL: Peter, have you ever done scenes with Mariska on *SVU*?

PETER: On the first one I did, yes. And actually, the first scene Mariska and I shot was in the courtroom and—

MARISKA: —I remember it so differently.

MARLO: This is all couples. Not even President Carter and Rosalynn agreed on where they met.

MARISKA: Well, listen, he could be right. But my side of the story is this: We were in a very small scene in the interrogation room. Peter was on the other side of the table. I saw him, and I almost passed out. That had never happened before on a set. Normally, I'm the greeter, the welcomer—my job is to make everyone feel comfortable. But I was nervous. I didn't know what to say. Somebody had told me he was German, so I turned to him and said, "So, you're a Kraut." He took a beat, and he looked at me and said, "That's funny." But deadpan, not smiling.

PETER: I didn't like it.

MARISKA: He didn't like it. And I thought, *Wow. Okay. Wrong opening line.*

PETER: But I actually like that I answered honestly. Because somewhere deep inside me, I thought, *Well, if we're going to go down this road, we might as well start off being honest.*

MARLO: Go down what road? She said she almost fainted when she saw you. Did you have that kind of visceral reaction, too?

PETER: I knew very quickly that we had dealings with each other, business with each other. And it was very telling that at the end of that episode I didn't want to leave.

MARISKA: You came into my dressing room. Nobody does that. And then we talked for like three hours about God. That's where the conversation went.

PHIL: Are you both very religious?

MARISKA: I was raised Catholic. I wouldn't say I'm very religious, but it's something I take seriously and is a huge part of my life. Our first date was church.

PETER: It was a Presbyterian church. The sermon was on the role of beauty, what that means, and what true beauty is. I think I kept the program.

MARISKA: We should listen to it. Because I didn't hear a word he said.

PETER: Mariska just wept. I remember thinking, *Oh, my God, she's so moved by the sermon. That's so beautiful. We have such an incredible connection.*

MARISKA: I knew I was going to marry him that day. As a woman, you hear your whole life that you'll know, you'll know, you'll know. And I always thought, *What does that mean?* And then as I sat in that church, I just knew that this was my husband. This was it. We were getting married. I knew it and I wept the whole time.

Peter is classically tall and dashing, and we wondered if perhaps he reminded Mariska of her dad, Mickey Hargitay, a bodybuilder who won the Mr. Universe title in 1955 and went on to become a screen actor. Mariska was raised by him and her stepmother after the tragic death of her mother, actress Jayne Mansfield, in a car accident.

"No," Mariska said, "but ironically he reminded me of my grandfather."

"What was he like?" Phil asked.

"My grandfather was tall and gentle," Mariska recalled, "and he knew so much. You could ask him anything and he'd have the answer. And I loved the way he dealt with my grandmother, who was such a strong and fiery woman. He was also kind. Peter reminded me of that."

Peter laughed. "That's one of the least sexy things you can ever hear as a guy," he said. " 'You remind me of my grandfather.' But I thought, 'Okay, I'll take it.' "

By the time Mariska met Peter, she was in her late thirties and already an established star. That decision—to be self-reliant and not search for a husband to take care of her—was something her father had instilled in her.

"My dad always said to me—which I love now and am more grateful for as I get older—'Who are you? Where are you going? And who is coming with you?' It was all about who I wanted to be in this world and what my contribution was going to be.

"I identified with my father because he was so strong," Mariska allowed. "He was a champion, so he talked a lot about doing your best and not being a hack. I always say to our kids when they play sports or do ballet or go up a climbing wall, 'Give it your best or else you're a hack.' It really is all about grit. 'What do you want out of life?'"

PHIL: Everything about how you two came together seems preordained: you met on the show, you had an instant connection, you went to church on the first date. Did things ever get not-so-perfect?

MARISKA: We broke up a few times before we got married.

PETER: We thought it would be a good idea to get all the breaking up out of the way before the marriage.

PHIL: And you broke up because...?

MARISKA: Well, we were dating, and I was crazy about Peter. It was all magic, magic, magic and then... we had different expectations.

PETER: We saw the world differently. You end up opening your heart fairly wide when you marry someone, so I was proceeding with great care, sort of inching my way forward.

MARISKA: We were going down a path, and it all seemed to slow down a bit. And then it just ground to a halt. I remember it was Thanksgiving, and he came to my house. I had all these people over, it was beautiful and a very big deal—and he was the first to leave. I thought, *Wait, what? Are you in or are you out? I'm in, but I'm only in if we're both in.* I was in love and ready to really move forward, but—

PETER: It was an inelegant way of saying that I needed some more time.

MARISKA: And so we broke up. We didn't speak for two months, maybe three. And it was very hard. I was brokenhearted. And this is true: On the day that I woke up and thought I might be okay—that I was over him and could continue life as I knew it—all of a sudden I got a letter from Peter. It was an unbelievably beautiful letter that explained a lot. And then he asked me out for Valentine's Day.

Email was already a common form of communication in the early aughts, so it said something that Peter had chosen to express himself in a hand-written letter.

"There was this process going on," he explained, "that involved learning what it meant to actually open yourself up to somebody. There were certainly fireworks going off, but for me, the next step after the fireworks was full alert. I think that's the best way of saying it."

"You're a serious guy," Marlo said. "I admire that."

"It's a serious endeavor," Peter said.

"It *is* a serious endeavor," Mariska echoed, "and this is what I love about Peter. He's so thoughtful and there's nothing surfacey about it. If you ask him a question, there's no skating over the top. But I will say that we were in different places, and I love how seriously he took it. I'm a much more instinctual human being."

"You go by your gut, and he goes by his head," Phil said.

"Yes," Mariska said. "He's more cerebral in that way. And part of the story—" At this point she turned to Peter, "Is it okay if I tell them about the book? Because that was so beautiful." Peter nodded.

MARISKA: So we went out to dinner on Valentine's Day, and we both gave each other the exact same gift.

MARLO: Whoa!

MARISKA: It was so crazy. We both gave each other a book by Andy Goldsworthy, who was our favorite artist. It's called *Time*.

PETER: Andy Goldsworthy is a sculptor who sculpts in nature. He does things like take a boulder in a meadow in Scotland and, for hours and hours, rub it red with cranberries. So you've got this red boulder in a bright green meadow, and he photographs it, and then the rain washes it away. Or he'll sew together a mile of leaves. Incredible.

MARISKA: We'd seen a documentary on him called *Rivers and Tides*. It was about making art for the sake of the moment, having no attachment to it. So when we went to this restaurant in Tribeca, I was so excited to give him this book for Valentine's Day. And then I saw him pull out the same book and give it to me. I just started crying. And, again, I just knew.

MARLO: I would cry sitting at the next table, watching. Peter, what did you feel?

PETER: Calm. It was like more and more news was arriving that this was something to be greatly at peace about.

MARLO: I was just going to say, Peter, that you're touching on something about love that I learned when my father died. We were very close, and he died suddenly from heart failure. He was on a book tour, everything was fine, and I got called in the middle of the night that my father was dead. It was just a terrible shock.

PETER: How old were you?

MARLO: He was seventy-nine and I was forty-something. I was just destroyed. So, I went to a therapist I'd gone to years before, and I said, "I can't stop crying. I get up in the middle of the night and just go in the other room to cry. Is this abnormal?" And he said, no, this is why many people are afraid to love: because the other side of love is loss. And I realized then that if you really open up and give your heart to someone, you could lose your heart for all kinds of reasons. That person could betray you. That person could leave you. That person could die. So, this is why people are afraid to commit. This is why people don't give all of themselves. Because they figured out that the flip-side of loving is possible loss. It takes courage to love.

PETER: I think it's e. e. cummings—he has these beautiful, beautiful lines of poetry: "losing through you what seemed myself, i find selves unimaginably mine."

MARLO: That's lovely.

PETER: It's funny, we just took a school tour today with our son, and there was construction on the school campus. And so the headmaster wove that into what he said about the school. He said that (a) the school is under construction because, (b) we are *all* still under construction. It was elegantly done. I say this because when Mariska and I met, where she was in her life and her career felt to me much more complete than where I was in mine. That's one of the reasons I sort of battened down the hatches—I was afraid that I would get absorbed, that I would tumble into this beautiful, enormously incandescent life and somehow become unmoored.

PHIL: And that's why you'd backed up a bit?

PETER: Yes. I had to make sure that my feet were very solidly on the ground. And interestingly, that began the process of *losing through you what seemed myself, i find selves unimaginably mine.* We're absolutely two distinct people, and yet we are both also *one* thing that we weren't eighteen years ago when we met. It was good for me to pay attention to that on the way in.

MARISKA: We were both very moved today by this idea of the school being under construction, and I think that's because I feel like I've always been under construction. Knowing this, I still ask, what was that *thing*? Why was I crying in church about him? It can't be physical. Yes, you're attractive, but I don't cry over handsome people, so what was that thing that I knew? *Grace.* That God had put me here. I'm constantly reminded—and there have been these reminders all along the way— that this is right. Stay in. Do the work. The payoff is huge.

PETER: I made the decision to ask Mariska to marry me at her fortieth birthday party. It was really remarkable because I saw a more complete you than I had ever seen. All of your friends came—like *all of them*— which also speaks to how you nurture deep friendships. There was just so much love, and I saw what this person I had very significant feelings for looked like in the habitat she was meant to be in. In the climate, in the soil, in the air she is meant to be in. I saw how the flower opens in love. And I thought, *Wow, I want to be with her forever.*

MARLO: Was it spontaneous?

PETER: Can we call it "slowly spontaneous"? I knew we were in love, but in terms of the actual decision, that night it became, *How do I ask the question?* Her birthday was in January, and in April I asked her to marry me.

The ceremony was held on August 28, 2004, at the Unitarian Historical Chapel in Santa Barbara, with two hundred guests in attendance. During their honeymoon in Hawaii, Peter contemplated the new reality of being married. "It was about three days after the wedding and we were driving in a car, and I thought, *I don't know why everyone thinks this is so hard. What are you talking about? We're killing this!* It was so funny."

"Oh, that is so great!" Marlo said, laughing.

After the first year of marriage—"the rosy period," as Mariska called it—their differences began to emerge. Mariska is more of an extrovert who enjoys going out and being with friends, while Peter is more introverted. But even in that case, they resolved the standoff the way they do everything else—by communicating with each other. They still fight, of course, like all spouses, but as Peter noted, humor plays a vital role.

"At some point after a fight, one of us will test the waters with a joke—about the very thing we were fighting about. It's like one of us says, 'I'm not saying I was wrong, and I'm not still insisting I was entirely right, but can we at least inch our way back toward the place where we laugh at stuff together?' Once that happens, it's a pretty good sign that things are on their way to getting patched up. It's by no means a guarantee—the other person of course has the right to stay mad—but it's a good sign."

And sometimes, they both say, when they're lucky, the laughter is there right away. "Like the other night, when we really had it out," Peter recalled, "and the next morning I was still fuming. I was so determined to be mad at her the whole day. And then we looked at each other and just started laughing. Suddenly, all the air went out of the fight.

"And that's the point," he continued to Mariska. "I never thought that I would laugh this much in my marriage. That is such a fundamental ingredient of who you are, this insistence on joy. And I think what sustains our marriage is that I know you love me in spite of who I am, and that is the definition of grace. We like to think that God is crazy about us because of who we are, but I think the real beauty of grace is that we are loved in spite of who we are."

This introspective, in-the-trenches kind of dialogue has been their practice since the very beginning. They are both innately curious people (Peter called curiosity "the greatest state of mind, ever") who genuinely want to ask each other honest questions and give honest answers, without fear of judgment or animosity. Phrases like "Tell me how you feel" and "Help me understand," Mariska noted, are far more constructive than getting angry and stalking off to opposite corners.

They also share the firm belief that marriage is not something to try on like a new coat and then cast aside if the fit isn't perfect.

"Marriage is marketed to us as a fairly quick road to happy-ever-after," Peter offered. "'This will give you fulfillment!' But if the ad campaign was more honest, it would be: 'This will make you better and *out of that* will come happiness.' Happiness is not the primary goal, but it will happen if you're in it for the long run."

"So the short-term goal is 'I'm looking for happiness?'" Phil asked.

"Yes," Peter said. "And if a couple years later the person's barometer of happiness hasn't risen, they'll say, 'I'm out. I went into this thing to get some happiness—that's my spouse's job—and they're just not making me happy.' But what if the barometer was something more long-term? 'Am I kinder than I was three years ago? Am I more generous? Am I more patient?'"

"Am I more open?" Mariska added.

"Right," Peter said, sliding forward in his seat. "Now, the answer might be, 'No, I'm not, I'm a thousand times worse than I was three years ago. But at least I'm aware that I totally fall short in all those departments, so let's try for year four.' If the barometer is solely happiness, you can get into trouble quickly. But I don't want to say any of this without adding that I am deeply, profoundly happy in my marriage."

"And I'm in the marriage that I wanted to have," Mariska added. "When we got married, we talked about a lot of this. We talked about the climate of marriage, the love climate, the climate that is required to raise children in. And there have been so many times when I've believed that we have the right climate, because we've worked on it. Yes, there have been a lot of challenging times, but we somehow—graciously, elegantly, inelegantly—got out of them."

MARLO: Well, the climate here is lovely.

MARISKA: Will you stay for dinner?

MARLO: No, thank you. That's very sweet.

PETER: She sets a mean table.

PHIL: I can see that—all those flowers.

MARLO: And cheese and crackers and olives.

MARISKA: I make sure that the table is set every night for dinner. It's like an event for me—a moment of celebration and ritual and gathering. That's another thing I want to tell my children: *This is important.* When friends come over and you prepare the table, they'll say, "Oh, my God, this is so pretty and special, and I feel special." Life is so hard, and here we have this little moment of beauty in the day, and the love and care and connection that comes with it.

PETER: I'm always amazed at how rapturously in love we can be in this moment, where we feel so deeply blessed to be together. "Out of all the people in the universe, what a gift that it would be you!" And then a minute later you can have some disagreement about directions in the car, or wallpaper, or something that was left out on the counter, and suddenly you're like, "Why, out of all the people in the universe, did I have to end up with you?"

This is why I say, in terms of arguments, one thing that is always a mistake—and this is difficult, because it feels so right in the moment—is being cruel in what you say. If you have the zinger, *don't* say it. Especially when you remember that you're the one who lives deepest in the other person's heart, and that you can hurt them the most.

PHIL: And so what happens when you blurt out a zinger without thinking?

PETER: Then you say, as quickly as you can, "I am so sorry I said that." And as quickly as you can might be the next day. Or in a week. But just own it. "I meant to hurt you because I was so mad." *Not*, "I was mad because you did dah, dah, dah." Also, it's not "I'm sorry *if* I hurt you," because that's the most bullshit excuse there ever was. Just "I'm sorry."

MARLO: And I did it intentionally.

PETER: And I did it intentionally.

PHIL: But don't we do this less as the years go by? I know that Marlo and I have become more aware of things that can be hurtful.

MARISKA: Yes, we gain wisdom. But as Peter said before, it takes so much to really be open and vulnerable to someone else. This idea of becoming one takes a long time.

PETER: And early on, there were many parts of us that still weren't married.

MARISKA: Right. We would look at the marriage and say, "Okay, we're killing it *here*, but we're not great *here*." And a handful of times in our marriage, things really came to a head, and we had conversations where we really laid it all out without knowing the outcome. And it was scary; we'd feel like it was all in doubt, or like something would be a deal-breaker...

PETER:... and the cliff was morseling away beneath our feet...

MARISKA: And every single time we would come back that much stronger. The strength that came from those moments always surprises us.

Witnessing Peter and Mariska probe deeper into the heart of their marriage was like watching Olympic pair skaters, moving perfectly in step with music of their own choosing, always in sync as they glide together, then apart, then back together again.

"Interestingly," Peter observed, "as you grow more into one in a marriage, you paradoxically become aware that this other person is an entirely separate human being, and not just a canvas onto which you work out your own neuroses. You get a very clear look at your own point of view, and that can be entirely separate from that person. Those moments—if you can get through them—are incredible building blocks."

Mariska nodded. "That's what brings us happiness," she said. "Yesterday we had one of those moments. The light was perfect and the kids were playing and we sat there and said, 'This is as good as it gets. We're home. We're safe. We're relaxed.' It was this perfect moment of peace and contentment."

"And you acknowledged it out loud?" Marlo asked.

"We did," Mariska said.

Peter jumped in. "We were home, all in the same room, the dog was fed, there was sunlight, the door was open, a breeze was coming in, and we were like, *Yes*."

"We're having more and more of those," Mariska said, looking at Peter. "Part of it is age and wisdom and experience. But it's also just clarity. And a growing trust. We're both getting better, as partners and parents. And I think that we figured out a way to talk to each other."

"And one other thing that is remarkable," Peter added, "is how long it takes to get to know the person you're with.

"Well, look at how many years you were that other person," Marlo said. "You were Peter longer than you've been married. That's a lot of person in there who needed to get evened out, figured out, and rounded off."

Toward the end of our conversation, the discussion turned again to the ever-changing dynamic of the marital bond, and how the fireworks of those early days eventually give way to the familiar. Peter recalled something he'd just read on the subject.

"There was a piece in the *New York Times* two days ago," he said. "It was by Pico Iyer and it was all about learning to fall in love with the mundane, the ordinary. It talked about the beginnings of relationships that are all about newness and the pyrotechnics of discovery. And then comes the challenge of learning to fall in love with the familiar. It reminded me of an essay Joni Mitchell once wrote. Quoting from an article she'd read in *Esquire*, she said, 'If you want endless repetition, see a lot of different people. If you want infinite variety, stay with one.'"

"That's marvelous," Marlo said.

"So good," Peter agreed. "Then she went on to say that when you date, you make all of your best moves and tell all of your best stories, and that routine is basically a method for falling in love with yourself over and over again. You can't do that with a longtime partner because he or she knows all that old material."

"So what she's saying," Phil said, "is that if you actually want to discover newness, then dig down into a relationship with one person. So with that as your grounding philosophy, what would you tell a young couple who was thinking about getting married?"

"As much as you can," Peter answered, "stay deeply curious about each other. There's a poet named Jack Gilbert who wrote this beautiful line in a poem called 'Don Giovanni on His Way to Hell.' *To speak to her without habit.* I think that's something to aspire to."

Despite our earlier demurral, Mariska went into the kitchen and brought us each a plate of delicious food. It had been a wonderful evening, and our conversation had been too good to simply end right there—and we all knew it.

Two days later we received an email from Peter that included the Jack Gilbert poem he had mentioned to us. We were struck by the line he'd mentioned and how it reflected the profound and moving connection we'd witnessed between him and Mariska.

"*...to speak to her without habit. / This I have done with my life, and am content.*"

Patricia Cornwell
and Staci Gruber

MARRIED IN 2006

"I'm an equal opportunity employer. I was married
to a man and now I'm married to a woman. It's only fair.
I don't want anybody to feel left out."

W hen she walked into the room, I felt an electrical disturbance, like the air moved. It's very rare that happens with people. I knew then that I could not let her get away from me. I had to know this woman."

Those words could be spoken by the protagonist of any romance novel—a recollection of the breathless, knee-buckling feeling of falling in love at first sight. But in truth, this was not the confession of some fictional character, but rather the real-life testimony of a woman who creates fictional characters for a living.

And what's more interesting is that she doesn't even write romance books. Her beat is corpses, mayhem, and murder.

Patricia Cornwell has sold more than one hundred million books, an astounding body of work that has been translated into thirty-six languages. Dominating her gritty crime oeuvre are two dozen blockbusters (including *Postmortem*, *Flesh and Blood*, and *Body of Evidence*) featuring Dr. Kay

Truro, Massachusetts; February 24, 2006

Scarpetta, the tough and relentless medical examiner–turned–forensic sleuth who bounces from the mean streets to the morgue to get to the bottom of whatever grisly doings Cornwell has decided to whip up this time.

As of the most recent book, Dr. Scarpetta has been married twice—and so has Cornwell. From 1980 to 1988, Patricia was wed to Charles L. Cornwell, her college English professor who was seventeen years her senior. In 2006, she exchanged vows with Dr. Staci Gruber, an associate professor of psychiatry at Harvard Medical School.

"I'm an equal opportunity employer," Patricia told us with a laugh. "I was married to a man and now I'm married to a woman. It's only fair. I don't want anybody to feel left out."

We knew we had to sit down with this power couple (or "power-houses who butt heads occasionally," as Patricia put it), and as it happens, they were in Manhattan on business one midsummer day and agreed to stop by our place for an afternoon chat. We opened the door, and in walked Staci, a pioneering neuroscientist with bright red hair who could easily be mistaken for a family member of our pal Ron Howard. Behind her was Patricia, whose appearance surprised us. We hadn't expected her to be quite so pretty and delicate looking—this was the mistress of murder, after all!

Our conversation with these two turned out to be fun and easy, mostly because *they're* fun and easy. We began with the story of how the two connected, and it turned out to be quite a yarn—all about a magnetic attraction that was equal parts brainy and romantic.

It was the summer of 2004, and after a couple of decades writing Scarpetta novels, Patricia became intrigued to learn more about the human brain—*why* people murder instead of how the mystery is solved. This is a writer who will go to almost any lengths to satisfy her curiosity, immersing herself in her research to learn everything she can. That's why her books are so compelling. For instance, she told us, when she began her career as a police reporter, she couldn't stop thinking about where the body went after it was removed from the crime scene. That's how she ended up working at a Virginia morgue for six years. Watching autopsies being conducted on human corpses was hard for her to stomach, but she knew that in order to tell a good story, she had to do her homework.

"If you're a journalist and you're going into a war zone, you're going to see and smell a lot of things you don't like," Patricia explained. "If you can't do it, you can't do the job."

That same fearless search for knowledge was what led her to visit Harvard's McLean Hospital, world-renowned for exploring the cause and treatment of mental illness—a topic she was researching for her next book,

Predator. And it was on this visit to Staci's lab that Patricia felt that "electrical disturbance."

PATRICIA: I felt it before she even said anything. It was like her energy—that's what caught my attention. There's a connection. It doesn't necessarily mean you're going to date that person, but it means you're going to do something, or they're going to kill you.

STACI: I will never forget that day, actually, because I was very impressed with the questions that she asked. These were not the typical types of queries that most people make when they come to the lab. She was extraordinary, just in her questions.

PHIL: Was that why she was there in the first place—to interview you?

STACI: At McLean Hospital, we often have VIPs and philanthropists come through my department, and we're asked to do these dog-and-pony shows. We meet with these people, and they are frequently interesting and compelling. Sometimes afterwards, they might say, "Hey, would you like to do *x-y-z*"—go out, go to dinner, that sort of thing—and the answer is always "Absolutely not." Very politely and diplomatically, but no.

MARLO: So Patricia isn't going to let Staci get away, and Staci doesn't do after-hours dates with VIPs. So what happened?

PATRICIA: At the end of the tour, I said to the P.R. person taking me around, "I don't remember the name of that red-haired neuroscience person, but I have a few more questions for her." It's the oldest trick in the book.

The gambit worked. Staci had returned to her office to get ready to leave for the day; she had plans that evening. But then the call came from the public affairs person telling her that Patricia had more questions. Staci agreed to let her come to her office. They talked more, and Patricia asked whether she'd like to continue the discussion over dinner.

"For whatever reason—I don't know why—I thought, *Yes, I would,*"

Staci said. But once she saw that Patricia had arrived at the hospital in a flashy stretch limousine—which had already attracted the attention of her colleagues—she refused to get in. She told Patricia to go back to her hotel and that she would pick her up in her car to go to dinner.

"Why did you not want to get into the limo?" Marlo asked.

"Look, I'm a Jew from New York and New Jersey," Staci said. "We don't trust anybody."

"That's a riot," Marlo said.

"And I thought," Patricia said, *"Why is it okay for me to get into your car when I don't know you, but it's not okay for you to get into my limousine?"*

Patricia complied, however, and returned to her hotel alone. The limo was just one example of Patricia's extravagance at the time. For her 2002 book *Portrait of a Killer: Jack the Ripper—Case Closed*, she'd spent nearly $7 million of her own money to try to prove the identity of the infamous nineteenth-century serial killer. And over the years, she's owned several lavish homes, a Bentley, a Ferrari, and four helicopters (though not all at once). She was used to living large.

But in her hotel in Boston that evening, she had a small problem: she and Staci hadn't exchanged phone numbers. Patricia was registered at the hotel under an alias to ward off fans. If Staci asked for her at the desk, she'd be told she wasn't there. So, Patricia sat in the lobby, semi-hiding.

"I walked in and went up to the desk," Staci said, "and then I turned around, and there she was, right behind this big bowl of apples, just sitting and waiting."

"That must have impressed you," Marlo said.

"I was surprised, actually," Staci said. "Almost as surprised as she was that I wouldn't get into the limousine."

For the next three days, Patricia and Staci spent every evening together.

STACI: That first night I took her to dinner, and we talked and talked—

PATRICIA: —until about 3 a.m. sitting in the car in front of my hotel.

MARLO: Did you feel that chemical reaction too, Staci?

STACI: There was certainly something there that was absolutely compelling—this bizarre connection when you don't want to stop talking, which I think is rather magical. She was very sweet and kind. At one point she said, "Let's go upstairs and chat." I said no, and we just kept driving around.

PATRICIA: Like a sixteen-year-old boy on a date.

STACI: We went out the next night and did sort of the same thing. On the third night, I took her to my house and we stayed up through the night. We just talked. Then I drove her back and she got her plane.

MARLO: When did you both realize that something was going on here?

PATRICIA: For me it was when I was leaving. But I didn't know how she felt. I thought she might just want to be friends.

PHIL: You didn't discuss sexual orientation?

PATRICIA: We did eventually, didn't we? But it took me a while to figure it out, because she was being very careful with pronouns when we began discussing past relationships. I kept trying to figure out if she was talking about a he or a she. People do that when they're not sure how you'll react to it.

MARLO: Were you out by then, Patricia?

PATRICIA: Well, if you look it up, I was. You knew, didn't you, Staci?

STACI: I had heard. But you're never sure, so I didn't want to assume anything. I think we danced around it a lot that first night. The second night was a little different, with the intention question.

PHIL: I think it's remarkable when people make that immediate connection. That happened to Marlo and me. We met when she was a guest on my show. Something happened between us, and I had no idea what it was—it had never happened to me before.

MARLO: I lived in Los Angeles and, at the time, his show didn't air there, so I didn't really know him or his show. I was in the green room getting ready with my makeup person, and he walked in as he was putting on his jacket. I swear to God, I thought I would just faint. I was completely, chemically attracted to him. Period. The end.

PATRICIA: Wow.

After Patricia returned back home to New York, her conversations with Staci continued over the phone. Gradually, their feelings for each other emerged; and along with those feelings, they began to share their stories.

Patricia grew up in a deeply Christian environment in the small town of Montreat, North Carolina—or "Billy Grahamville," as she called it. And she wasn't being just metaphorical: evangelist Billy Graham and his wife, Ruth, actually lived nearby and became close family friends. Until she went off to school at nearby Davidson College, where she majored in English, Patricia didn't even know what being gay meant.

"Nobody talked about anything in that town," she explained. "Nobody talked about sex. You didn't cuss, you didn't drink. You couldn't even have cooking sherry in the house."

She was twenty-three when she married her college professor. After their divorce eight years later, she kept his name. They remain friends.

"Was he eventually shocked to learn that you liked women?" Marlo asked.

"No, he'd heard about it before," Patricia said. "It had been in the news for years. His first comment was actually, 'I didn't make you this way, did I?'"

"Wow," said Marlo. "Talk about making it all about him. What did you say?"

"I said, 'No, not even you have that power. I'm sorry.'"

When the time came for Patricia and Staci's first official date, Patricia arrived in Boston in a helicopter and piloted Staci back to New York. She had gotten her pilot's license in 1999 because a beloved character in the Scarpetta series, computer genius and vigilante Lucy Farinelli, flew a chopper—and how could Patricia write authentically about the experience without learning to fly?

To Staci, this was almost surreal. "So she says, 'I'll come get you in the helicopter,'" she recalled, "and she says it like it's any average day. And I'm like every other person who thinks, *Oh, sure, that's fine.*"

"But it's the coolest thing ever, right?" Patricia said.

"It was a lot of fun going back and forth," Staci remembered. "And she's a tremendous pilot."

The more time Patricia spent in Boston, the more she became concerned about Staci's lack of security at her home. In addition to fans seeking her out, Patricia had a stalker. So she insisted that Staci have an alarm system installed, along with cameras, a privacy hedge, and a gate.

MARLO: Staci, how did that make you feel when she did that?

STACI: You know, it *was* an unusual thing for her to come in and say, "Look, here's what you need to have." But I thought, *Okay*.

PATRICIA: Furthermore, "I'm paying for it and we're doing it now."

STACI: And I said, "You can't pay for this. I'm paying for this. We're not going to do it this way." And it worked out okay.

PHIL: But it actually makes sense that Patricia would be concerned about security. By now, she knows every crime that can possibly happen.

PATRICIA: I do, and I wanted to make sure it didn't happen to us.

MARLO: But this was her house, not your house.

PATRICIA: Yes. But I wanted her to be safe.

PHIL: I remember reading a quote of yours that was so smart. You said that bad people know everything there is to know about crime and forensics, so why shouldn't good people know everything, too?

PATRICIA: But forensics are for cleaning up after you've screwed up—meaning, you or someone you love has died. You don't ever want forensics, because that means something awful happened. Better to prevent the crime to begin with.

Almost every couple we spoke with mentioned the accommodations they made for their spouses. For Patricia, that meant leaving behind homes in New York, Florida, and Hilton Head and moving to Boston. "I could work up there on a book and get to know Staci better," she recalled. But if anyone has earned the award for the most *unusual* accommodations, it would have to be Staci:

Patricia was a motorcycle enthusiast, so Staci learned how to ride one, too. She also got licensed to carry a firearm.

And when Patricia dreaded going to the morgue for research, Staci went with her and stood in front of her, just in case the body was too gruesome to observe.

"A date to the morgue—how romantic!" Marlo said, laughing. "But wait a minute, Patricia. You're actually squeamish at morgues? How is that possible? You worked in one, and you write about dead bodies all the time."

"I had to do the research," Patricia said, "but there's nothing nice about it. I don't like anything dead. I wouldn't even go to funerals."

About two months after their high-flying romance began, Patricia told Staci they were invited to Kennebunkport for the weekend to stay with former First Lady Barbara Bush and President George H. W. Bush. Patricia had become friends with them through Ruth and Billy Graham. After they arrived in Kennebunkport, Barbara graciously led them upstairs—one floor above where she and George slept—where she promptly put them in separate bedrooms.

"And then she said, 'Don't you even think about visiting,'" Patricia recalled.

"Oh, God, my mother would have done the same thing," Marlo said.

But there was an additional problem: Staci's room adjoined a male guest's bedroom through a common bathroom.

"So here's the thing," Staci recalled. "She puts us in separate bedrooms. Whatever. I just found it so funny that we couldn't stay together, but it's okay for me to share a bathroom with some dude I never met."

Patricia, wary as ever, didn't like the idea of the communal loo. "What if the guy went in the wrong door?" she noted. "He could have climbed into bed with Staci!" So rather than stay up all night worrying about it, Patricia grabbed a chair and propped it against the bathroom door that led to the gentleman's bedroom.

Staci sighed. "Picture that. She puts this chair against the door, and now this poor schmuck can't get into the bathroom from his bedroom. He's got to go into the hallway."

"I'm sorry," Patricia countered. "I didn't want him to go into your room!"

"Now, don't think she's controlling or anything," Staci ribbed.

"Meanwhile," Patricia added, "Big George, as I called him, could not have been more sweet and lovely. I knew them for many, many years. They were both good people."

"I really liked Barbara," Marlo said. "She was a good person. After my dad died, she came to St. Jude, and she cut the ribbon on our new research building. And she spoke about how if Robin—her little daughter who died of leukemia at age three—had only been born later, she would have been cured by St. Jude. It broke your heart."

After dating for a year and a half, Patricia called Staci's office one day with a proposal—sort of.

PATRICIA: I basically told her we were getting married. There was no asking.

STACI: I said, "Is there something I don't know about? Do we have to?"

PATRICIA: I said, "I want to get married. I want to make this legal. This is not a romantic question—it's a legal question. We should do this."

STACI: Actually, what she said was, "Can you just get that set up?" Literally. Sort of like dinner reservations, or maybe a flight.

MARLO: That's so funny.

PATRICIA: Well, look, I'd been married before and it was a big thing—the dress and the bridesmaids and the church and three hundred people or whatever. I thought that was going to last forever. He'd been my professor since I was nineteen years old. I didn't want any of the hoopla this time. I didn't care about that at all. I said, "I just want us to be together."

STACI: Right. "Let's just get married. Can we get that done?"

PATRICIA: The point was, this was who I wanted to spend my life with. I'm not good at setting things up, and Staci is. Furthermore, I didn't tell my lawyers, and there was no pre-nup. Certain people got very angry when they heard about it later.

STACI: They were furious.

PHIL: I think that makes your commitment all the more meaningful, actually. When Marlo and I were about to get married, both of our business managers said we should get pre-nups, and we both said, "No, that's kind of betting against ourselves, isn't it? We're not going to do that. This is going to last, but if it doesn't, we'll be fair. I'll take mine, you'll take yours."

PATRICIA: That's the thing. While there might be a disparity in what I earn and what she earns, she's added value to my life, including economically. She's smart with money and I'm not. I would never want to quibble about something anyway.

And so, Patricia and Staci eloped on February 24, 2006. As planned, they had a hoopla-free ceremony at the house of a justice of the peace in Truro, Massachusetts, who was so excited and nervous that she forgot to put on her robe. She also forgot to present them with their complimentary bottle of champagne.

No guests were in attendance—"It wasn't a wedding," Staci noted, "it was a ceremony"—but that didn't keep her from being tremendously moved.

"Standing in that living room and taking those vows, I felt surprisingly emotional," she recalled. "All of a sudden, it sort of hit me what it meant. I won't ever forget that. I thought, *Oh, thank God no one else is here with us.* I almost cried again just now."

They didn't tell anyone about their nuptials for the better part of two years. Once it came out—via a tabloid—some of their friends were disappointed not to have been involved, but Patricia and Staci have no regrets about keeping it personal. It was their day.

But as personal as it was to them, Patricia and Staci are part of a long overdue national movement to recognize their right to marry. That battle was won in 2015, when the United States Supreme Court ruled that that right is guaranteed to same-sex couples by the Constitution.

PHIL: Do you have any particular advice for other same-sex couples?
PATRICIA: Yes, I do. The hardest thing is getting over shame, because a lot of people like me grew up where this was absolutely verboten, so there must be something wrong with you. You still hear that today, and it's

daunting. It's awful. So I would say to remember that shame is something that is inflicted on you by the outside. It is not real. It is not you. And there's nothing shameful about love.

STACI: Right. Don't let yourself be judged by someone else's metric. It does not apply to you. That may be their own stuff, not yours. Just remember who and what you are, both to yourself and to each other. You can't allow someone else's small-mindedness to define who you are—with your partner or without.

MARLO: Did you experience similar shame when you were younger, Staci?

STACI: Well, I'm an only child, and only grandchild. No other siblings or anything—just a very small family. My mother's closest friend when I was a kid happened to be gay, and I didn't necessarily think there was anything wrong or bad about it at all. I was raised to believe that all sorts of things were perfectly fine no matter what color you were or what your sexual orientation was. It didn't necessarily matter—until it's you, and then it's a little different, if you know what I mean.

MARLO: No, explain that.

STACI: Well, this is only on me—I can never speak for anybody else—but I think that I always felt like I was a bit of a disappointment to my family. I dated plenty of boys—I never had any trouble in that department—but I worried that I would somehow disappoint my family.

MARLO: In what way?

STACI: That I wasn't necessarily going to follow a traditional trajectory. Because it's hard, it's very hard, not to want to come home and actually say, "That's not the person I want to be with. I want to be with *this* person."

PHIL: You mentioned love, Patricia. We're living in a pretty cynical world these days. Love is hard to define.

PATRICIA: Right, and real love is not to be confused with just sexual attraction, although generally the two do go together. You tend to fall for what you're attracted to. So if you love somebody, you need to be comfortable with yourself. That's a big one, because if you're not comfortable with yourself, you're not going to have something that's going to work very well. Don't you think?

STACI: That's right. That's exactly right.

Marriage has not slowed either spouse's career. Staci forges ahead in her clinical research, which includes the MIND program (Marijuana Investigations for Neuroscientific Discovery), a double-blind, randomized study that looks at the long-term therapeutic effects of a cannabis-based product on people with anxiety. Patricia has supported that effort, contributing $1.5 million through her foundation.

"I'm very supportive of it because I've seen it," Patricia explained. "She comes home and tells me the stories about the patients, and it's a miraculous thing."

"I've spent a lot of time with medical cannabis patients," added Staci, "and my feeling is we can help people live better and more satisfying lives. The program has skyrocketed. But it never would have been anything without Patricia's interest or investment and belief. I think it's so wonderful she believes in me."

Staci, meanwhile, returns the favor by providing empathetic support when Patricia's writing isn't going well—when the words just won't come or a plot line isn't working.

"She understands the anguish," Patricia said, looking directly at Staci. "I can say things to you that I just wouldn't share with someone else. You know, like, 'I feel really dark today.' Or 'I don't like this.' Or 'I feel awful.' How many times have I called you when I'm finishing a Scarpetta book and start crying, telling you it's no good? 'Nobody's going to like this! I don't know what I'm doing anymore. I'm not cut out for this—I don't know how to write a book!'"

"Actors feel that way, too," Marlo said. "That's the artist's temperament."

Patricia nodded. "You can be at the top of the heap as a talk-show host," she said, "or an actress, a scientist, a writer, and still have moments of the most abject fear and darkness."

Ever the scientist, Staci boiled it all down. "Honestly," she noted, "it's so important to underscore the idea that, whether or not it's an 'artist's temperament,' it's just being a human."

PHIL: I'm sitting here listening to you two, and I can't help but be impressed with your connection. You've been together fourteen years and you're as taken with each other as a couple who just met.

PATRICIA: I think one of the most deadly things in a relationship is when people bore each other. You need to make sure that, even though you might like somebody physically in the very beginning—and you get so excited—you'd better have something up here in your head along with spiritual values. There may be things that still surprise you, so pay attention.

STACI: And keep listening. If you don't listen and you assume you know everything, you'll never learn anything about your person and yourself and your relationship together.

PATRICIA: Right. I think what both of us have learned over the years is that, even if you've been with someone a long time, don't be so sure that you know everything about them.

MARLO: That's so funny. No matter how much I convince myself that I know exactly what Phil is going to do in any given situation, he does something completely different. And I realize that I don't know as much about him as I thought I did.

PATRICIA: And he probably doesn't know what the hell you're going to do in a situation, either.

MARLO: So maybe that's the secret to a long marriage: you never know what's coming next.

STACI: And you have to give yourself up to the fact that you don't have any control. You can listen, you can wish, and you can hope. But you can't control.

PATRICIA: Exactly. I like to say, "You can't hold the wind, so, don't try." No one belongs to you, so continue to explore, like a planet you're visiting.

STACI: Isn't that what it's all about? I was a whole person before Patricia, and she was definitely a whole person before me. We don't need each other for anything. We *want* each other. We want to be together because we're better together in the world. And I think that's important.

PATRICIA: We're a work in progress. We're a work of art that's not done. We're still being chipped out of the marble.

Letty Cottin Pogrebin
and Bert Pogrebin

MARRIED IN 1963

"She goes into her bag and takes out this teeny
menorah. She's standing there wearing her negligee,
and lighting these little candles. And I'm thinking,
My God, I'm married to a religious fanatic."

We could find Letty and Bert Pogrebin's apartment in the dark. Not that we'd actually go there in the dark—Central Park lies between us, and no one walks in the park at night. But you get what we mean.

We've been friends with these two for more than four decades, and their warm and lively home is well-known to us—the wood-paneled living room, the two-story-high ceilings, the massive fireplace, and the walls completely covered with beautiful paintings and colorful posters. Our favorite is a Ben Shaun illustration with a caption that reads, YOU HAVE NOT CONVERTED A MAN BECAUSE YOU HAVE SILENCED HIM. So perfect for this couple.

And, of course, countless photos of their three children—twins Abigail and Robin, born in 1965; and son David, born in 1968—and six grandchildren fill every bit of open space.

New York, New York; December 8, 1963

Marlo and Letty have been close friends since 1972 B.P. (before Phil).
Marlo had just embarked on her children's project *Free to Be . . . You and Me*,
and she brought Letty in as a consultant. Already a veteran of the publishing business and one of the founding editors of *Ms.* magazine, Letty lent
her passion and wisdom to *Free to Be*, and along with Marlo, Pat Carbine,
and Gloria Steinem, co-founded the Ms. Foundation for Women.

"She was the first woman I knew who included her birth name in her
married name," Marlo recalled. "She was born knowing who she was. We
think alike, and most important, we dream alike."

When Phil met Letty's husband, Bert, a labor and employment lawyer, they also clicked as best buds; and each summer, we spend a long weekend at their lake house in the Berkshires with the Aldas—three days of food, music, laughs, and more food. We have also been ringing in the New Year together for thirty years, along with six other close couples. Through those decades, some of our friends have changed partners once or twice. But not the Pogies. Their marriage of fifty-seven years is the real thing, and it has been an inspiration to us.

We've long known how committed Letty is to her faith—Judaism—and we've learned a lot from her about Jewish customs and rituals. But what we never asked either of them in all these years is what kind of role Judaism plays in their marriage. So that's where we began.

PHIL: Letty, your devotion to the Jewish faith has always been one of your defining traits, and that's impressed me, especially in a time when people are falling away from religion. How were you raised? Were your parents this serious?

LETTY: Yes, they were. But I think it's important to distinguish being a serious Jew from being a practicing Jew. I ride on the Sabbath, I use money on the Sabbath, I break a lot of rules. I consider myself a serious Jew in that the ethos of Judaism is my guide—the values and the mind-set of the Jewish faith, and what I feel our role is on this earth. So in that sense, yes, it's very much a controlling factor in my life.

PHIL: And you, Bert?

BERT: I was brought up without religion in my family, and our marriage has continued with her being as religious as she is and my being not religious at all. She'll go to synagogue on Friday night if she has a free evening, and I'll meet her after for dinner. I do go every Yom Kippur. I pledged to do that years ago.

MARLO: Did you try to get him to go with you on Fridays?

LETTY: No, never. I'm perfectly happy that way. I love the fact that I never have to clear it with him, and I never have to drag him along against his will. It's my thing.

PHIL: And yet Judaism remains a big part of your family life, yes?

LETTY: Yes. I always did Shabbat at this table when the kids were growing up. You can see there are kiddush cups everywhere, and behind you is a wall of Hanukkah menorahs. Ritual means a lot to me, religious or otherwise. Feminine ritual, Jewish ritual, invented rituals, rituals that mark life-span moments of importance. That's who I am, and Bert accepts it.

MARLO: Funny that you mention the menorah. Didn't you once tell us a story about your honeymoon—

BERT: Yes. We were in Caneel Bay in the Caribbean. It was our first night after the wedding, and the water was lapping against the shore. Very romantic. It was during Hanukkah, and she goes into her bag and takes out this teeny menorah. She's standing there at the mantelpiece, wearing her negligee, and lighting these little candles. And I'm thinking, *My God, I'm married to a religious fanatic.*

MARLO: I love that story.

LETTY: The menorah was so tiny it actually took birthday cake candles, which I brought along. I also had eight Hanukkah presents for him, wrapped up in this suitcase. We had known each other for only six months, and we had never lived through a Hanukkah together. So he was horrified that I cared enough to bring Hanukkah to Caneel Bay.

Both Letty and Bert say that their stance on religion—like their approach to marriage—is informed by their parents' relationships with God and with each other. Letty, who grew up in Queens, New York, went to Hebrew school through high school. "I was very well-educated, Jewishly," she said with pride. "I was one of the first girls to be bat mitzvahed in Conservative Judaism, so I'm very grounded in my religion."

Bert, on the other hand, grew up in what he called a "radical left-wing household," where God was decidedly not in the picture. His parents, he said, shared the same politics, but it was his mother for whom progressive causes were a true passion. She was an avowed Communist, which made Bert what was then called "a red diaper baby." And just like any child of radical parents, he was taught his politics early.

"When we moved to a new town in New Jersey in 1947, the movie theater there was segregated," Bert remembered. "And my mother would make us sit in the 'black section.' I would say, 'Ma, they don't want us there,' and she'd say, 'Just go sit.'"

And there was the time when his high school American studies class was reading *Time* magazine and his mother had him instead bring in *The Nation*, which covered progressive political news and views.

"My parents raised me to be very skeptical of authority and of whatever the official government line was," Bert noted. "That put me in good stead in terms of my dealings with the world at large, like Vietnam and Iraq. Those kinds of things played out according to my mother's scenario. She wasn't right about a lot of things, but she was right about certain things."

"So she was a standup person," Marlo said.

"Yes," Bert replied.

"Like your wife," Marlo added.

Letty smiled. "That's why he never had trouble with me," she said. "I was never going to be as much of a transgressive woman."

And yet the irony, Bert pointed out, was that these two strong women in his life never quite hit it off.

"I thought my mother would just love Letty," he said, "but they didn't get along very well."

"She couldn't accept me," Letty added. "My daughter's theory is that I was too much like her and too much what she wanted to be herself."

Neither of their parents had strong marriages, they told us. "When Bert and I got together we bonded over a whole lot of things, like politics and music and everything else," Letty said. "But we also bonded because we both had parents whose marriages we did not want."

"In what way?" Phil asked.

"I don't remember my parents ever being happy," Letty said. "They were always arguing, and had completely different ways of life. If I had the marriage my parents had, I would have been divorced in one year. It's a wonder they ever got together in the first place."

"Why didn't they split up?" Marlo asked.

"Because, at that time it was considered a *shanda*—Yiddish for shame or disgrace—to be divorced," Letty explained. "They'd already been divorced from their first spouses, so they were damned if they were ever going to get divorced again."

For Letty, her parents' fear of being exposed as having been divorced—and what they did to hide that, even from her—left lasting scars.

"I grew up with so many secrets and so much betrayal," she revealed. "My parents lied to me about everything. I didn't know they had been married before. I didn't know that my sister wasn't my whole sister. I didn't know I had another sister. I didn't know so many basic things about my family history."

"Why would your parents do that?" Marlo asked.

"Because they were too embarrassed to be in the world as divorced people," Letty said. "They were Jews who could not stand the *shanda*. So, they moved from where they had lived and lied about everything in their life in order to not have to answer for having been divorced."

"That must have been a horrifying discovery for you," Phil said. "So how did you model your own marriage with such an unhealthy example in your past?"

"You know what you don't want," Letty replied. "And Bert and I don't really argue about things, so there's not a whole lot of challenge there."

That was no exaggeration. In all the years we've known the Pogies, we've never seen them fight—not even bicker. We asked them about that.

BERT: It's hard to believe, but it has been idyllic. I mean, I think our fights are the most mundane.

LETTY: Like, "Where is that paper we need for the taxes?" "I thought *you* had it." That kind of thing. That's about as much as we argue.

MARLO: So, in other words, you've never had to come back and reset from a disagreement.

LETTY: Never.

BERT: No.

LETTY: Which is why we don't usually talk about our marriage, because you can't learn anything from us.

BERT: I guess, in a way, our kids suffer from having grown up in a house where they never saw their parents fight. So, when they have a fight with their own spouses, they worry if something is wrong, because it's not the way it's supposed to be. I think they take disputes much more seriously, because they have no context for it.

One thing Letty and Bert clearly taught their children was that their marriage was very personal to them. Over the years, they made a habit of celebrating their birthdays and anniversaries on their own, taking vacations by themselves, and going out to dinner on Friday nights.

"We had three little children under the age of three, and we occasionally needed to nourish the marriage," Letty said. "So we'd find time just for ourselves. The marriage is a *presence* for us—I guess that's the way to put it—so on Friday nights, we would go out, knowing we had a night of our own. On the rest of our nights, there was just chaos in this house, with people running around and doing homework. And when they were little, we had bath times and story times and all of that."

"Didn't one of your kids once complain about the two of you doing things without them?" Marlo asked.

"Yes," Letty said. "We explained it to them that we took them on vacation every year, and that the other nights of the week were all theirs, but that we needed our time together."

"The way I remember it," Marlo said, "is that when the twins were about twelve, they came to you and said, 'Mommy, we really feel left out when you and Daddy go off together and celebrate your birthdays or anniversary,' and you said, 'We love you more than anything in the world, but you are not our marriage.'"

"Yes, that sounds like me," Letty responded.

"Oh, it's accurate," Marlo said. "I never forgot it. You also said it was a gift you were giving them for their own marriages someday."

"It's true," said Letty. "I grew up expecting my parents to get divorced any second, and everything under my feet was shaky. Our kids never had that feeling. And, yes, I think that's a gift to give a child, because I remember what it felt like not to have that security."

Creating space for intimacy, of course, is a challenge for many couples, especially when you have three young children born just three years apart. We asked them how they kept their marriage warm with so many little people inhabiting the house.

"Sex was very difficult for me when the children were home, at least until I knew they were really asleep," Letty confessed. "I once walked in on my parents, and I was terrified. I thought he was killing her."

Bert chuckled. "I used to say to her that we could be in Rome and in bed and she would say, 'Wait, the children will hear,'" he said.

"The good thing is, the kids were very good sleepers," Letty added. "That was another key to our success."

"But to be honest," Bert concluded, "they were abnormally good children. They didn't take up a lot of energy, and we never fought about how to parent them. There was none of that, 'You deal with them,' or 'Wait till your father comes home.'"

"Even when they were teenagers?" Phil asked. "I know that was a tough time for me. Did you both agree on what to tell them about things like money and sex?"

"We agreed on everything," Letty answered. "Our feeling was that, by the time our children were going out at night, if they didn't have their values, we had fucked up totally. So we said, 'You're on your own, and we're not going to give you a curfew—but you have to call us and tell us when you change locations.' I think that's one of the greatest things we did, because we didn't worry about their values—all we really worried about was their safety."

Letty and Bert met on Letty's twenty-fourth birthday, in July 1963. Bert was twenty-nine. At the time, Letty was focused on her career as a publishing executive and had no interest in getting married. "I was Holly Golightly, only happy," she recalled. "I was making a lot of money, I had a garden apartment, a motor scooter, a dog and a duck and a rabbit. And

I had just come back from a tour visiting my agents in seven European cities."

Jetlagged from the trip but determined not to spend her birthday alone, Letty accepted an invitation from a man she was dating to spend the day on Fire Island with a group of seven lawyers who had rented a house there. Bert was among them.

"At one point we played volleyball, and he made me laugh so hard," she recalled. "I remember thinking, *I really like this guy. He's so clever.* Luckily, I was wearing a yellow bikini, which I knew attracted his attention. So on the ferry home—even though I was with the guy who brought me—I slipped my business card to Bert and said, 'I'm in charge of four departments at a publishing company and I might need a lawyer.' Which is ridiculous. I had no labor law problems whatsoever."

PHIL: But you knew what he did for a living.

LETTY: I knew what he did for a living. And it never occurred to me to question you, Bert, about why you didn't think it weird that I didn't give my card to any of the other lawyers.

BERT: I knew you were coming on to me. I mean, it was such a bullshit thing that some publishing house needed a labor lawyer. I'm dealing with manufacturers and plants that hire working people, and she's from this publishing house and giving me her card. So, that was pretty clear.

MARLO: And what did you do with the card?

BERT: I put it away and called about two weeks later.

LETTY: No, you called me on Thursday. I know this because I was looking at the calendar and saying, "Is he going to call me?" Because in those days you did not call men—at least I didn't. He was at the San Gennaro Festival in Little Italy.

BERT: Right. I went over to her house in the Village, and this jazz musician, Charlie Mingus, was in her shower at the time.

LETTY: You took that so well, I just knew that you were different.

MARLO: So, what happened?

BERT: We went to some club for drinks.

LETTY: Tell them what you did at the table.

BERT: So, at one point I was gesturing flamboyantly with my hands—as I'm wont to do—and I knocked over everybody's drink. But being so self-involved, I continued talking, which Letty saw as a positive. She could have easily said, "This arrogant, self-centered guy—he's not for me." But she saw that as a—

LETTY: —I saw it as a person who cared about what he was saying at that moment. He was telling an interesting story, and he cared enough about it that he didn't get all ridiculous, like, "Oh my God, I've just humiliated myself by knocking over the drinks." He is a what-you-see-is-who-he-is kind of person.

BERT: And she was a very hot number, as far as I was concerned. I mean, she was very attractive, and I had visions of her in that yellow bikini, so she was a high priority for me. But I never moved that quickly in social things, and Letty started asking me, "When are we going to see each other again?" I said, "Probably a week from now." She said, "Why a week? If I like somebody, I see them a lot." And then when we got engaged, she said, "When do you think we'll get married?" I said, "Probably a year from now." She said, "Why a year? We could get married in December." This was October.

MARLO: That is so Letty! So how did you two know so quickly? I mean, this is a pretty big leap for a woman who didn't really need or want to get married.

LETTY: Honest to God, I had a lot of men in my life—which he knows— and I didn't need it. I had what I needed.

MARLO: So what was it?

LETTY: I don't know. I just *knew*...

BERT: We were old, for one thing. She was, what, twenty-five?

LETTY: I was twenty-four and a half when we got married. Exactly.

BERT: And I was twenty-nine. I had been out of law school and on the dating scene for five years, and the idea of getting married was not on my radar. I had this crummy little studio apartment that I lived in, and she had a really nice, grown-up apartment. So I thought it would please her if I told her I was thinking about getting a really good apartment, too. And she said, "For yourself?" I said, "Yeah, but you'll come over." And she just stalked off. It was such anger that—

LETTY: —I got on my scooter and I was out of there.

MARLO: So she was ready to take the next step and you weren't.

BERT: She wasn't in my future that way. I wasn't really thinking in terms of—

MARLO: She knew right away and wanted to get on with it, but you didn't want to rush it. So that's why she scooted off. She was basically saying, "Why are we waiting?"

Letty eventually won the waiting game: the two were engaged three months after their first date and married before the year was out. Letty's mother had died when she was just fifteen years old, so her father was in charge of the nuptials—or what Bert calls their "big, terrible wedding."

"He really did it on the cheap," Bert said. "We were so excited about getting married that nobody paid attention to the details."

"Give us an example," Phil said.

"Letty chose to get married in this humongous synagogue, which seated thousands," Bert began. "I don't know how many people were invited, but a lot. And then we had this reception in the basement of this place. So she's this hot-shot publicist who throws publication parties for people like the Marx brothers, and here we had this, this..."

"Downscale," Letty suggested.

"...this downscale thing," Bert continued. "I think her sister's husband provided the music. He played the piano—that was our wedding gift—and her uncle, who was essentially the janitor of the synagogue, saw the opportunity to sing, which he'd always wanted to do. So he croaked out these songs in Hebrew during the wedding."

"And his son-in-law was our photographer," Letty added.

Downscale or not, Letty experienced a moment of transformation during the ceremony that she's never forgotten.

"I'll tell you one thing that I don't tell everybody," she said, "but you asked about my faith: I had an experience going down the aisle that I never had before and I never had again. I was literally off the ground."

"As in happy?" Phil asked.

"I'm not saying happy/not happy," Letty explained. "I'm saying I wasn't touching the floor. I felt like I was rolling down the aisle, not walking. I've never had that feeling again, but I remember it to this day."

"Did you see that as a kind of religious moment?" Marlo asked.

"Well, I wanted to get married in that synagogue," Letty began, "even though it was humongous and we didn't have any more than a couple hundred people. I wanted to get married there because my mother had walked my sister down that aisle in 1946. She died in 1955 and I got married in '63. So I wanted to be in the space where she had been. I wanted to walk down the aisle where she had walked. My father was on one side of me, and nobody was on the other side, but I just felt I was in the right place, rolling down the aisle, rolling down the aisle, above the ground."

Bert watched his wife relive the memory, and his face softened.

"You know, once we got married, I had no second thoughts," he recalled. "Her confidence in the marriage was, to me, very reassuring."

"Still, you barely knew each other," Marlo said. "That didn't cause any problems?"

Letty shook her head. "I felt I knew him forever," she said.

PHIL: And here you are, fifty-seven years later. So what's the magic ingredient?

LETTY: It's so cliché to say mutual respect, but it's true. We had one rule that we articulated a hundred years ago, and that is that we would never say anything in the heat of an argument that we could not live with after. We said we understood that we had the power to hurt each other more than anyone in the world had the power to hurt us, and that we would not do that. Also, you know how most people say they won't go to sleep angry? If we had a disagreement over anything that annoyed us, we went to sleep with it and we woke up the next morning and it was gone.

PHIL: A lot of couples have told us that. Apparently, that's what happens.

LETTY: It *is* what happens. But some people are constantly picking at it—they won't let you go to sleep until you admit this and confess that and apologize. Especially when the argument begins with, like, "You left the cap off the toothpaste," and then it suddenly becomes, "You *always* leave the cap off. You don't give a shit about anything."

MARLO: One of Phil's and my rules is we can't say "always" and we can't say "never."

LETTY: That's a good one.

MARLO: Always and never. They're real killers. Because it makes you feel like you're consistently wrong.

LETTY: Like the whole marriage was a fake.

MARLO: Right.

BERT: With our kids, we modeled our values by the way we lived. They saw this involvement with the feminist movement, which has its own set of values and is all about equity and fairness and dignity for women. I remember one time with our son David, a camp director came to sell us on a camp, and afterwards David said, "I'm not going to that camp. It's sexist." I said, "Why do you say that?" And he said, "Didn't you hear him say it has a manmade lake?"

PHIL: That's great.

Letty has spent much of her career on the front lines of the feminist movement and has written extensively about that and other progressive causes. In addition to her work with *Ms.*, she is the author of eleven books, including the 1970 classic *How to Make It in a Man's World.* When we asked her about the roots of her feminism, she pointed without hesitation to what she saw as the constraints society and marriage placed on her mother.

"I wanted to free women so they didn't have to be what my mother had to be," Letty said. "She had so much more to offer."

Bert was totally on board with Letty's feminism when he first met her, in part because his dad had set a strong example.

"My father did a lot of work in the house," he recalled. "He was never like, 'This is woman's work.' There was no job that he didn't take part in, and I saw no division of labor along those lines in our house."

"So, your father could fry an egg?" Phil asked.

"Yeah," Bert said. "My mother actually wasn't that good at that. She was a good baker but not a good fryer."

"That's kind of like us," Marlo noted. "Phil, you're a way better cook than I am."

"You think so?" Phil said.

"I've always loved your steaks and eggs," Letty answered.

"He makes the best breakfasts and he's the best griller," Marlo confirmed.

"And Marlo makes great Italian food," Phil said. "Just like her mother."

After more than half a century together, the couple revealed, they've never had a worry about infidelity. "Our life together has been so rich and sexually satisfying that there was never any reason to go out of the house for it," Bert said. All the same, Letty laid down the rules—clearly and early.

"I knew that I could not survive an infidelity," she said. "Because of my parents' lies, I needed total trust. And so, when Bert and I got engaged, I said, 'I just want you to know that if you do it *once*, this marriage is over—because I can make it on my own. You don't get a second chance.'"

Letty glanced at Bert. "You know, his sister told me years and years and years later that I had inadvertently said exactly what he needed to hear," she noted. "That's because his mother had cheated on his father, and here I was saying I will never do that—and that I will not tolerate it."

"That's amazing," said Marlo. "It fits like a puzzle."

"And to have that worry not be a factor in the marriage is a tremendous relief," Phil added.

"Bert says that all the time," Letty agreed.

"Jealousy can be so corrosive," Bert concluded.

In 2009, Letty was diagnosed with breast cancer. We had lived through that time with them, and we vividly recall how they coped with such a terrifying body blow. "It was the first time, I think, that we ever had to worry about something really ending this thing," Bert reminded us.

"You'd had such an idyllic life," Marlo said, "and then without warning you've got an earthquake."

"We didn't suddenly have to become different people," Letty said, "we just had a mountain to climb. It was like, 'Okay, it's been smooth, smooth, smooth—but now we're going to climb this mountain together. And then we'll go down the other side, and just keep going.'"

Letty's treatment was relatively uncomplicated—no mastectomy, no chemotherapy, "just a lumpectomy and radiation," she said. And, not surprisingly, she turned the experience into another book: *How to Be a Friend to a Friend Who's Sick*, which was released in 2013.

"I had to go to Sloan Kettering Cancer Center every day," Letty recalled, "and I was sitting in the waiting room thinking about how some of my friends really didn't know how to relate to me at all. Have you ever had that experience, when some people disappoint you? They just say the wrong thing, or disappear, or get all bollixed up."

"I remember I offered to go with you to your appointments," Marlo recalled, "and you said, 'No, I'm going by myself—I'll walk through the park.'"

"And that's what I did," Letty said. "I didn't want anyone else along because I didn't want to have to talk to anyone, or explain anything, or see people sitting in the waiting room waiting for me. When you're sick, everything is about waiting: you're waiting for prescriptions, for lab results, for doctors to call you back. I remember sitting in the waiting room and thinking that I would like to read a book about friendship and illness. When I got home, I Googled and Googled and Googled and there was no book like that. So I wrote one."

Classic Letty.

As they talked about Letty's health crisis—as defining a moment as any couple can encounter—it was hard not to see the reason these two have stayed intact as a couple for more than half a century: They are grounded. They are in sync. And they are very much in love.

"Letty is usually unflappable about most things," Bert said, "so I use that for reassurance. People often say they have to work at marriage, but I've never felt we had to work at ours. I mean, the issues that came along, like feminism, were not destructive, they were constructive; they appealed to me as a lawyer because they were about basic equity and fairness in a relationship. If anything, they made us closer."

Letty nodded as she listened to her husband. Then she turned to us.

"Every time I have to toast him—whether it's a birthday or an anniversary or just some beautiful moment—I fall apart," she said. "Because I can't thank him enough for just being who he is, and who we are together. I cherish him. I cherish what we have. We have never taken ourselves for granted."

We've heard many of those toasts over the years, and we have to confess: we fall apart, too.

Deepak and Rita Chopra

MARRIED IN 1970

"I have no interest in being a public person like him. To be honest, I'm sitting here only because Mr. Phil Donahue called me."

When you enter the Greenwich Village apartment of Deepak and Rita Chopra, the aroma of incense wafts over you, and you instantly feel calmer. That therapeutic scent is just the beginning of the Chopra Experience: this place is, literally, an experimental residential environment designed to keep your head clear and your body healthy.

"It's a wellness building," said Rita, dressed in a pretty burgundy kaftan with mirrored work and casting a little sunshine on an otherwise gray Manhattan afternoon. "Deepak is involved with this company that wanted to demonstrate how you can control the environment, including with building materials. Deepak is on the advisory board, along with Leonardo DiCaprio, who used to live upstairs. He's also very much into wellness environments."

A computer monitors the air quality of the 3,663-square-foot, three-bedroom condo and controls the lighting that automatically adjusts to the body's circadian rhythms in order to enhance sleep patterns. There

New Delhi; February 8, 1970

is antimicrobial coating on all high-touch surfaces to minimize common diseases, and even a special shield to protect residents from electromagnetic fields. We couldn't help but feel we were going to seed in our own unshielded apartment.

"The floors encourage you to stand upright," Deepak offered enthusiastically, explaining that the sound-dampening Siberian oak flooring is supported on springs, like a Posturepedic bed. The entire apartment is soundproof, keeping the bustle and sirens of New York City at bay.

And, by the way, the showers have vitamin-filtered water. Technicians come by every so often to replace the vitamin C capsules in the showerheads, Rita told us.

All this, and their home is also very homey and very comfortable, with plenty of decorative touches from the Chopras' native India throughout—enchanting rugs, brass planters, and colorful scarves. After letting us try out his antigravity chair—a soft recliner that elevates your legs above your heart, ensuring proper circulation and reduced strain on your vertebrae—Deepak escorted us to a large marble dining table, where we all sat down to talk. The polished stone, he told us, was originally used in the building of pavements at Independence Mall in Philadelphia in the 1950s. But tourists were slipping on it, so the pavements were replaced and the used marble was sold. How great that a little piece of Americana would wind up in the dining room of a couple who came from the other side of the planet.

The wellness atmosphere of the Chopra home stands as a living symbol of a lifetime devoted to finding health and inner serenity in a noisy and often maddening world—a philosophy that took Deepak to the height of his fame. It's safe to say that until he popularized the concept of combining Western medicine with Eastern ideas in the 1980s, the term "mind-body"—that is, connecting the state of the body with the state of the mind—didn't exist in mainstream Western culture. Now it's everywhere—and has been for decades.

It took Deepak's self-help books about alternative medicine, the power of meditation, and the body's ability to rejuvenate itself to make the concept commonplace. "Today there's not a single medical school in the country, or a hospital that's prestigious, that doesn't have an integrated medicine center," he told us. And he's right.

But living in a bubble designed to promote well-being doesn't necessarily protect you from the environmental challenges of fifty years of marriage, electromagnetic fields or not. So we wanted to know how this unusually mellow couple kept the spark alive, how two people from a culture steeped in spirituality handled tension, and how they shared the burdens of child-rearing and life management in the face of one spouse's worldwide acclaim.

Even though they are natives of India—they both hail from New Delhi—theirs was not an arranged marriage, as many in their country are. It was the late 1960s, and Deepak was a medical student at the All India Institute of Medical Sciences, the top school in the country; and Rita, who was studying for her bachelor's degree in English literature at a women's college in New Delhi, was spending time at the hospital with a very sick aunt.

"This was a normal thing to do in India," Rita said. "You never leave a relative alone in a hospital. My aunt was on a ventilator, and she didn't have a good prognosis. So I used to go after class to sit with her, read her a book, and stroke her hand. And Deepak used to hang around there for some reason—in the room—and that's how we got to know each other."

"Rita's aunt was a patient of mine," Deepak added, "so we got friendly."

These frequent encounters, according to both of them, qualified as "seeing each other"; and when Deepak got the call to go to the United States to help fill "a big shortage of American doctors" who were serving in the Vietnam War, his mother pushed the budding couple to marry.

"She said she would not allow her son to go to America alone because some American woman would steal him," Rita said. "So we got married."

"This is the opposite of the jealous mother who insists that no woman is good enough for her son the doctor," Phil observed.

"Well, she was very clear she did not want him to come to America alone," Rita said. "I had graduated college and was ready to start a new life, so I thought, *Why not?* America. Who knows? And we had no idea where we were going."

Deepak was scheduled to complete his medical training in June 1970; the couple was married in February of that year. Rita was twenty-one, and he was twenty-three.

Their first taste of the States was Plainfield, New Jersey, where Deepak finished his internship at the Muhlenberg Hospital. After a year, the couple moved to Boston, where they would live for the next twenty-three years—and where Deepak would eventually start his career as a global leader in the field of mind-body health.

That first year in Boston wasn't easy, both of them confessed. While Deepak applied for his residency, Rita became pregnant with the first of the couple's two children. That happy event had an unexpected development: "I had to send Rita back to India to have our first child," Deepak said.

"Wait, Rita, you traveled all the way back home to give birth?" Marlo said. "Why not stay in Boston?"

"We couldn't afford it," Rita said. Turns out the couple's insurance considered her pregnancy a "pre-existing condition" and wouldn't cover the birth.

"My late father, who was a physician, he was shocked," said Deepak. "He said, 'My son is a doctor in the United States, but he can't afford to have a baby!'"

Rita nodded and sighed. "It was actually less expensive to buy an airline ticket to India—$400 through Kuwait—than to go through delivery in the Boston hospitals," she explained. "So, I went back to India and had the baby. When Mallika was six weeks old, I brought her back from India in a little basket."

By the time their second child, a son named Gotham, arrived four years later, Deepak was an established physician, though the couple was struggling financially. In addition to his regular position, he worked part time in emergency rooms for $5 or less an hour.

"If I worked all day," Deepak said, "I got $222 a month; and if I worked the night shift, too, I made another $40. So basically, we barely managed to pay our rent in our first three years in Boston."

Eventually, Rita made the decision to become a stay-at-home mom. She briefly considered going back to school, but she didn't have the family support system she would have had back in India. "It was just too complicated to drop off the kids, pick up the kids. We were not used to that," she said. "In India, yes, you have a lot of help with family at home, but in the U.S., I didn't have family and I didn't know the system, so I stayed home."

Rita didn't exactly admit to being lonely, but she did say that Boston was unsettlingly low-key. "I had never lived in such a quiet place before," she recalled, "and there was just nobody to communicate with." Indeed, with Deepak's first paycheck, the couple bought a television, "just to hear some sounds," Rita said—and one of those sounds was a familiar one.

"She started watching Phil Donahue," Deepak said.

Phil grinned.

"It's true!" Rita said with a laugh. "Phil Donahue! I would get so nervous that there was nobody to talk to, so the TV helped a lot. And then the second thing we bought was a Volkswagen Beetle to drive around in."

Up until now, the Chopras' story isn't all that unusual: He's a young immigrant doctor from India with a wife and two small children at home. She's managing the family on a limited budget and adjusting to a new life in a new culture. Nothing so revolutionary here, right?

Then their world changed. Seismically. One night in 1980, after ten years of marriage, Deepak heard about a seminar in nearby Cambridge that taught meditation. He had never before expressed an interest in the traditional arts of his Indian heritage, including meditation, whose earliest roots can be traced to the Indian subcontinent five thousand years earlier. The irony of Deepak's chance encounter with meditation is almost impossible to fathom: here is a man whose random curiosity about an interesting topic led him to a lecture he could have just as easily skipped, little knowing that what he learned that night would inspire him to revolutionize his life and what the world understood about medicine and the human mind.

Deepak Chopra was far from meditative as a young doctor. "I was smoking a pack of cigarettes a day and drinking alcohol," he said. "I did what everybody else did. I wanted to fit in. I hadn't been doing that in India."

When Rita heard that her husband was attending the meditation seminar, she jumped at the chance to accompany him. "I said, 'Okay if you're going, I'm going with you.' There was no way I was going to be left behind. So we learned how to meditate together."

The lesson set the couple on a life-altering course that would eventually touch millions around the world.

"It's almost like a miracle," Rita reflected. "The day Deepak and I started meditating, he stopped smoking cigarettes, he stopped drinking alcohol—he hasn't touched it since 1980. And I became a vegetarian, and I've never eaten meat again. It was like a switch that went off. Did it. Done."

Yet despite the serenity of the meditative life, Rita was growing restless. All the soothing mantras in the world couldn't compete with the tiny voice in her head reminding her how much she missed her family back in India, and the support they provided. That discontent had been sneaking up on her, but it was the weather—and a leaking chimney in their aging home in Winchester, a small suburb eight miles north of Boston—that was the final straw.

"The winters are very long in Massachusetts," Rita explained, "and one day I noticed that the chimney on the roof had started leaking. I just sat there looking at it, and then I turned to Deepak and said, 'I can't live here. I'm going to India. I'm going home. I need to be with my parents and my in-laws.'"

"Just like that?" Phil asked.

"Yes," Rita said. "I packed up both the kids and went back home to India. I said, 'I just can't deal with a leaking roof.' So, yeah, it was a little challenging."

This dramatic development might have devastated most any other husband, but Deepak took it in stride.

PHIL: You were all alone. Did you ever wonder, "Is she coming back?"

DEEPAK: No. We knew why she went back—it was so she could get help.

PHIL: And she was staying with your parents.

DEEPAK: And she was staying with my parents. That is the tradition—the wife stays with her in-laws.

PHIL: Did you at least stay in touch somehow, like calling each other on the phone?

DEEPAK: No. In those days it was very hard to call. You had to book a call person-to-person, and then you spent half your time standing in a phone booth saying, "Can you hear me? Can you hear me?"

MARLO: Well, you must have missed her and the babies.

DEEPAK: I did. But I also knew I had to stay in Boston and make a living for us. I was working twelve hours in a regular training residency, and they basically don't pay you enough. I also needed to be certified as an internist, and then I would work in an emergency room at night. So, all of this was very important.

MARLO: And you'd had enough, Rita?

RITA: Yes. A New England winter is not pleasant.

MARLO: That was actually very independent of you, just to pack up and move.

RITA: I said, "I am done with dealing with winter. I'm going home." And home was India. Home was Delhi.

MARLO: So, you came back when the weather was better?

RITA: Yes, we came back three months later, and the weather was better. The kids were too small at the time to go to school, but I eventually put them into a Montessori school in the Boston area and began to get adjusted.

DEEPAK: We were living in a little neighborhood called Jamaica Plain in Boston, and it was a very run-down area. All of our neighbors were either laborers or foreign doctors trying to get training.

PHIL: But you knew you had to stay. You were in medicine mecca, after all.

DEEPAK: Yes, I knew that. I had my eyes on Harvard, which I finally made it to. After two years, I got into all of the prestigious medical institutions. Every single prestigious institution in the Boston mecca, I've been there and trained there.

The hours and days and years Deepak had put in to his training began to pay off, not only in terms of his salary but in his ever-expanding knowledge of the people he treated. Many of his patients told him stories—about their ailments, about their lives—and he gradually began to suspect that these stories held the key to making them well.

"I started to write down what they told me," Deepak said, "and I began to have this faint idea that if you listen to a story—instead of just paying attention to what the diagnosis is—you'll find out what's going on."

"Explain that," Phil said.

"Well, you could have two patients who have the same illness but different outcomes," Deepak said. "Same disease, same diagnosis, same physician—but one person dies and the other recovers. I was convinced that what was happening in the internal life of these people was very important—that it wasn't just the physical thing. So I started submitting case reports to medical journals, and they got rejected every time."

Indeed, the professional medical community concluded that what Deepak was exploring was not science, but pseudoscience. But instead of beating his head against the tradition-hardened wall of Western medicine, he assembled the stories he'd collected into a book manuscript and self-published it. He ordered one hundred copies of the book—*Creating Health: The Mind-Body Connection*—and gave them away after his appearances at meditation events. Somehow a copy ended up in the window of a local bookstore, and it was bought by a child as a gift for his mother, Muriel Nellis—who happened to be a literary agent.

"Muriel called me out of the blue," Deepak remembered, "and she said, 'This book should be with a real publisher.' I said, 'I tried, but no one would publish it.' She said, 'How much did you pay to get it printed?' I said, 'Five thousand dollars.' She said, 'I'll get you a five-thousand-dollar advance.' And that's what she did."

The book swiftly became a national bestseller (and it still remains in print). Before long, Deepak received a call from Jacqueline Onassis, who was then a book editor at Doubleday.

"How many times do you get a call from Jackie Onassis?" Deepak said, still sounding star-struck. "She said, 'What are you doing with a Boston publisher? You should be in New York.' So I came to New York and had breakfast with her at the Peninsula Hotel. I eventually switched to a New York publisher, as she suggested—not with her, by the way—and before I knew it I was working with Stephen Hawking's editor. But I maintained a friendship with her. I still have the handwritten letters she wrote to me."

Suddenly, "Deepak Chopra" was a very big name. His exploration of the mind-body connection suited the zeitgeist of the flowering New Age era; but beyond that, there was a growing body of evidence that perhaps his ideas were scientific after all.

Deepak's increasing fame created envy in the Boston medical establishment, he noted, which continued to refuse to support him. But in the early 1990s, the Sharp Hospital System in San Diego decided to open a mind-body medicine department, and they offered Deepak the job of executive director.

"I said to Rita, 'We're going to California.' She said 'When'? I said 'To-morrow.' She said 'Fine.' So we went to California."

"Hold on," Marlo said. "Rita, you agreed to just pick up and move to California? What made you think that was a good idea for the family?"

"By that time our daughter was at Brown University," Rita explained, "and our son was working with Al Gore on his vice-presidential cam-paign. So I said 'Let's try something new.' I knew the weather would be better, and fortunately by that time we were financially okay. I kept the house in Boston, so we could travel back and forth. San Diego is a beautiful place. We found a home in La Jolla overlooking the gorgeous Pacific Ocean."

That was in 1993, the same year a pivotal interview with Deepak on *The Oprah Winfrey Show* brought him a robust new following. In 1996, he opened the Chopra Center for Wellbeing near San Diego and turned Deepak Chopra into a lifestyle brand—one that would add some seventy self-improvement books to his credit, not to mention those integrative medicine units in hospitals and medical schools around the world.

From the conviction in his voice—and his very focus—it is clear that Deepak is following a calling to help others, and he has done so on an enormous scale. Still, we couldn't help but wonder what Rita thought about all of this.

"Was Deepak's sudden fame an adjustment for you?" Marlo asked.

"In the sense that Deepak has a public life?" Rita said. "No. I'm not involved in his public life at all. I go wherever he goes, but I have no interest in being a public person like him. To be honest, I'm sitting here only because Mr. Phil Donahue called me. I agreed to be part of this book only because of that."

Thank goodness they bought that TV in Boston!

Rita continued. "For me, my life is being a mother, being a grand-mother. And that's why I always love going back to California, because I can be with my grandkids and my kids. I can help them out. My daughter will say, 'Mom, can you come pick up the grandkids from school?' It's a two-hour drive and I'm happy to do it."

We turned to Deepak.

DEEPAK: Our marriage works because we are not selfish. Rita doesn't think about herself. I do—I think about myself and my career—although I'm getting over that now that I'm seventy-two. But she's never thought about herself.

RITA: I'm happy. The role of the mother and grandmother and wife is enough. It feels so natural. This is my choice. Deepak has never said "Don't do this" or "Don't come here." We take trips with supporters of the Chopra Foundation. We go to Israel, we go to Jordan, we go to Italy—just recently we went to see his Holiness the Dalai Lama in India! I enjoy doing this. Yes, sometimes I don't enjoy a trip.

DEEPAK: I'm going to Detroit—she has no interest.

MARLO: When he's traveling so much and working so hard, do you ever think, "I need to have him here?"

RITA: No. I'm very happy by myself and totally independent. I can do everything myself. I mean, if he's here, it's good. But if he's not here, it's good also.

MARLO: So, how do you keep your love spark alive?

DEEPAK: We speak to each other every day. It doesn't matter where I am in the world, I'll call her in the morning and I'll call her before I go to bed.

RITA: And there are other kinds of communication.

DEEPAK: We're also very close to our kids and our grandkids. We have WhatsApp, so everybody talks to everybody all the time.

Meditation continues to be a central activity in the couple's lives: Deepak meditates and practices yoga three hours a day; Rita meditates daily, too. "Your body tells you, 'Okay, you need some quiet time,'" she said. "'Turn off all the sound—turn off the TVs, put away your iPad. You need some silence.'"

Which led us to the obvious question: Despite the meditation, the yoga, the perfection of the soundproof living environment, there has to be some stress—and, along with it, the occasionally noisy argument, right? It's a question we knew we were going to ask, but we never anticipated their answer.

MARLO: Do you ever fight?

DEEPAK: No.

RITA: No.

MARLO: Never fight.

DEEPAK: No.

MARLO: Never ever?

DEEPAK: No. In the early days we had some arguments.

MARLO: And how did you fight back then? Were you the loud one?

RITA: I used to start crying. I didn't argue or raise my voice or anything like that. I'd just start crying.

MARLO: So what did you do when she'd start to cry?

DEEPAK: I'd say I was sorry.

MARLO: Right away?

DEEPAK: Right away.

RITA: I mean, I'm very clear that I'm always right.

DEEPAK: And I let her be right.

MARLO: You do? Why is that?

DEEPAK: Because I care for her. And most of the things people argue about are not even important. Half the time they don't even remember what they're arguing about.

PHIL: Almost every couple we've spoken to argues at some point. You two are pretty remarkable this way.

MARLO: Well, not everybody has crying as a workable tool.

RITA: Yes, that's true. And remember, we're not in each other's way all the time. He does his own thing, I do my own thing—I go to the theater, go to a museum, hang out with friends. He never tells me what to do, and I never tell him what to do. I mean, if he wants to spend his day doing podcasts, more power to him. I'm happy by myself.

Were we surprised to learn that Deepak and Rita have somehow escaped the normal friction that most couples encounter regularly? Yes, we were. But the more we listened to them, the more we realized that the bottom line with this unique and uniquely suited couple is pretty basic: they are both fulfilled. He's fulfilled with meaningful work, and she's fulfilled with family and friends. They spend plenty of time in each other's company— they enjoy dining out and taking vacations together—but they are also entirely at ease in their own space. And they aren't looking for the highs that so many of us constantly seek.

"I think one of the things that we find different in America is that people are always about, you know, the excitement," Deepak said. "That's not a part of our culture. It's not just about me, it's not just about you. It's about everybody in the family."

But most important, their marriage works. They have designed it to suit them. As Deepak wrote in his 1996 book *The Path to Love*, "Love allows your beloved the freedom to be unlike you. Love imposes no demands. Love expands beyond the limits of two people." A half-century ago, they forged their own path to love, and they are still traveling it—side by side, and at peace.

And so, if they could pass on one bit of guidance to other couples who envy their supremely serene partnership, what would that advice be?

"Don't set up artificial expectations and expect every day is going to be date night," Rita said. "Learn to accept the other person with all their faults and all their good qualities. Just be accepting. Accept, don't expect."

We turned to Deepak, who, true to form, chose not to disagree with his wife.

"She's never tried to change me and I've never tried to change her," he said. "And I think that's it—allow your spouse to be the person they are. Totally."

It all sounds so easy, and for a moment we had our doubts. But when we left the Chopra's peaceful home and stepped back into the reality of noisy, smelly, insanely unmeditative New York City—and unsuccessfully tried to grab a cab—we noticed the difference right away.

"We should get some incense," Phil said.

"There's that candle shop on the way home," Marlo agreed.

Rodney and Holly Robinson Peete

MARRIED IN 1995

*"When girls would call or try to come over,
I'd say, 'He is now officially unavailable.' I'd say,
'Rodney Peete, Mr. Gregarious, the guy
giving all the parties—he's dead.'"*

Quarterback Rodney Peete was used to being protected by a gigantic offensive line that topped a collective fifteen hundred pounds—but he had never seen protection like this.

It was the nineties, and Peete, then the Philadelphia Eagles' quarterback, was coming off a very bad day on the field. Eagles fans were not happy with his performance in the game, and the switchboard at Philly radio station WIP was lit up like Times Square.

"Everybody was coming down on me," Rodney recalled, "and sports talk radio in Philadelphia is vicious—way worse than New York or Boston. They were just blasting me."

Then a rabid female fan called in and blasted back at Rodney's critics. But she was no ordinary fan. She was Holly Robinson Peete—Rodney's

Brentwood, California; June 10, 1995

wife—*pretending* she was just a fan. She tried to disguise her voice, but even though she is a professional actress, she got busted.

"The problem was that she was being way too specific," Rodney said, smiling. "Holly was a real football fan and understood the game. So we would analyze plays together. I'd say things like, 'So, this receiver ran three wrong routes and couldn't catch anything,' and she understood it all. So when she went on the radio, she was defending me in so much detail that these guys figured out it was Holly."

Oops.

"They didn't call me out on air," Holly recalled, laughing, "but to this day, when I go back to Philly, the guys at the radio station always kid me about it."

In sickness and in health—and in the end zone, too. That could have been the Peetes' wedding vows twenty-five years ago. Football has always been very much a part of their bond.

Holly's fierce loyalty to Rodney—and his to her—would help them drive their marriage down the field triumphantly, even as they endured the kind of body slams many couples never have to face—from constant separations to a devastating medical diagnosis of one of their four children. The former taught them about patience; the latter taught them about hope.

"You have to get yourself right before you can help anybody else," Rodney told us. "A coach I once had—who had been a Marine—started every day by telling each player, 'You've got to get The Man right.' In other words, before you can be effective with anybody else—or any*thing* else—you've got to get yourself right."

"And not everybody wants to get The Man right," Holly added. "So you have to strive to be the best version of yourself to make a marriage work. Because if you're not the best you, you're not going to contribute to this perfect union."

The early days of the Peetes' love story have all the makings of a movie romance: beautiful, successful actress meets big, handsome NFL quarterback, rejects the notion of being just another member of his harem, only to discover that her independence is like catnip to him. He eventually wins her over, shreds his little black book, and surprises her by proposing in front of the live studio audience at her hit TV show ("You're the best thing that's ever happened to me in my life," he tells her on air). When they marry, the Reverend Jesse Jackson, a family friend, presides over the ceremony, and the bride surprises the groom by bringing in the marching band from USC, his alma mater.

On the day of their wedding, Rodney and Holly were twenty-nine and thirty-one years old, respectively. She had starred on Fox's hit police drama *21 Jump Street* and was currently a lead on ABC's *Hanging with Mr. Cooper*. Rodney, the son of NFL coach Willie Peete, had been the starting quarterback for the Trojans, where he was a Heisman Trophy runner-up before embarking on a sixteen-year NFL career.

"So you were not babies when you walked down the aisle," Marlo said. "That's good."

"No, no, we weren't," Rodney said. "And thank God for that. Had we met in our early twenties, we wouldn't be here today as one of your long-married couples. As Holly likes to say, I was 'monogamously challenged.'"

"How did you figure that out, Holly?" Marlo asked.

"Well, come on, he was an NFL quarterback!" Phil tossed in.

"Exactly!" said Rodney. "You've got to experience the whole thing, right Phil? Holly was dating someone, and I was dating *everyone*—that's another way she puts it."

"So it sounds like you weren't all that impressed by his job, Holly," Phil suggested.

"I was very *unimpressed* with the whole idea of dating a quarterback," Holly confirmed. "But my dad, who loves football, was a fan of Rodney's and had talked to me about him. That's the only reason he was on my radar."

While the couple may have seemed mismatched at the start—his randiness, her wariness—their actual first meeting was memorable.

"I was at an R&B dinner club where we sat at this big table of ten people," Rodney recalled. "I knew who Holly was—I was a big fan of *21 Jump Street* and especially of her. And while we were sitting there, I got to know her a bit and became more attracted to her. And then she began eating like crazy. She wasn't going to just eat salad and nibble on fruit—she ordered a big plate of French fries and doused it with ketchup and then poured on the hot sauce. And I thought, *Okay, this is a girl who likes to let her hair down.*"

Holly glanced at Marlo. "But, *you* know that's how a woman acts when she's not really into a guy, right, Marlo?" she said. "I never would have eaten French fries with hot sauce around a guy I liked. You just don't do that."

"So you were genuinely not interested?" Marlo said.

"I mean, I thought Rodney was cute," Holly admitted, "but I was dating someone at the time, even though he wasn't right for me. I'd gone to Sarah Lawrence and had spent my junior year in Paris. I wanted to travel to faraway places, and when I told this guy that I wanted him to go to Vietnam with me, he said, 'Isn't there still a war going on over there?' He wasn't the sharpest tool in the shed."

There at the club, Rodney picked up on the vibe that Holly wasn't all that into him; and not long after that night, she took off on a three-week getaway.

HOLLY: I went on my *Eat, Pray, Love* trip to Indonesia. One day after I came back, my friend Lela said to me, "I really like Rodney Peete, and I hate the guy you're dating. So let's put on our Daisy Dukes and go to this party at Rodney's house"—which turned out to be only a five-minute drive from my house.

PHIL: Daisy Dukes?

HOLLY: Short jean shorts. This was in the early nineties, when they were the big thing. You put on those Daisy Dukes and some heels, you're ready to go.

RODNEY: She just *knew* that people were going to stare.

HOLLY: So we're at the party, and there were, like, five football players and twenty-five to thirty girls.

RODNEY: Well, that's a little exaggeration...

HOLLY: Okay, so it was a lot of girls and very few guys. We grabbed some brisket off the barbecue, ate, and took off. About half an hour later, there was a knock at my door. I opened it up and there was Rodney with all those teeth just smiling at me. I said, "Don't you have a party going on over at your house?" and he said, "When you left, the party was over."

MARLO: What a great line!

HOLLY: That's when I decided to give him a shot, and we basically haven't been apart since. We've had a couple of ups and downs, but we've never really broken up.

PHIL: So how did you get past the fact that he was, as you say, monogamously challenged?

HOLLY: Remember that song "Clean Up Woman"? That's what I had to be. When girls would call or try to come over, I'd say, "He is now officially unavailable." I'd say, "Rodney Peete, Mr. Gregarious, the guy giving all the parties—he's dead."

PHIL: And did you sign on to that, Rodney?

RODNEY: Yes, I did, because I really liked her. It was uncomfortable at times, because my world included a lot of male friends who liked to hang out at my place.

HOLLY: The party was always happening at Rodney's house. I remember one time I had to go out of town and I asked Rodney to babysit my dog, Christy.

RODNEY: I was cool with her dog, which was another reason she liked me.

HOLLY: So I dropped off Christy at his house and went off to do my thing. I came back four days later to one of those impromptu parties at Rodney's, with lots of girls. When I walked in, Christy came charging at me, like "Mommy, Mommy, Mommy!" Right? And this girl grabs my dog and says, "Come back here, Christy!" And then she says to me, "Don't worry, she doesn't bite." I was like, "Bitch, that's *my* dog. I know she doesn't bite!" And I'm also thinking: *So Rodney Peete has been letting these girls touch my dog.*

PHIL: That's like messing with your child.

HOLLY: Exactly. I took Christy home, but I told Rodney, "Look, you have to make up your mind what you want here, because there's not going to be any gray area for me. I am a self-sustaining woman. I work. And if you want a typical NFL wife—someone who goes to the NFL city you're playing in and takes care of her man all day long—I am not going to be that person." I was not going to police him all the time, so the little parties had to stop.

PHIL: You laid down the law.

RODNEY: Up until then, I had been the kind of guy who never really broke things off with girlfriends, so I had a lot of, you know, friends with benefits.

HOLLY: He always left the door a little bit ajar, if you know what I mean. And that was not working for me.

MARLO: So, Rodney, were you ready to shut that door for good?

RODNEY: Yes, I was. Deep down inside, I did not want the woman I would eventually marry to have an identity that was attached to mine. I wanted her to have her own world and her own career and not be someone just waiting for me to come home. It excited me that Holly could pick up at any time and leave. She didn't need me.

Holly was indeed independent—she had been around famous people her whole life. She'd grown up in Philadelphia; her mom, Dolores, was a teacher, and her father, Matt Robinson, was a producer and writer who played the original Gordon on *Sesame Street*. Holly actually made her first TV appearance at age six, walking down the street with Big Bird. "The people who came through our house in Philly—Dick Gregory, the Reverend Jesse Jackson, the Reverend Ralph Abernathy, Bill Cosby—it was quite amazing," she recalled.

So once she and Rodney started dating seriously, she was not awestruck by his fame, nor by his distinction as an African American starting quarterback, which was a rarity.

"I just wanted to see if we could make this work," Holly said. "Then, in 1993, when he was playing for the Detroit Lions, the NFL started doing occasional games abroad, and the Lions were invited to go to London to play the Cowboys. Rodney asked me if I'd like to go, even though I was his girlfriend, not his wife."

"That made a difference?" Phil asked.

"Yes," Rodney said. "The girlfriends and the wives didn't mix well together."

Holly laughed. "It was like, '*No ho's allowed,*'" she explained. "But I was Holly Robinson, who was on a TV series. The wives were looking at me sideways. They weren't very friendly or open-armed."

"Well, you were from a different world," Marlo said, "and that can be intimidating."

"Maybe so," Holly said. "I did have a little bit of heat on me. So the Lions put us in this tiny London hotel room—just a bed and a TV and a small bathroom—and I thought, *Well, this will be a real litmus test for this relationship—can we survive seven days in this tiny room?*"

"It was the Lions," Rodney said. "They were cheap."

One morning in London, Holly said, she got up to discover that Rodney had spread a large stack of one-hundred-dollar bills on a table—$5,000 total.

"Why did you do that?" Phil asked. "To show her how much money you were making?"

"No," Rodney said. "It was because she'd begun teaching me about fashion and other cultural things. I loved that she spoke French, and I made her speak it to me all the time. So I found out that she loved Manolo Blahnik shoes, and the headquarters were in London. So I went over there and got the manager's business card, and I put it next to the money, along with a note that said, 'Go buy whatever you want.'"

"Now, *that* is a present!" Marlo said. "How sweet of you!"

"It was pretty impressive," said Holly. "Just so thoughtful."

As far as Holly was concerned, Rodney passed the litmus test that week in London, and the relationship was "off and running." As the Clean Up Woman, she had a little housekeeping to do with some of Rodney's buddies ("He had to divorce *them*, too," she said), telling them he was no longer available to party or go clubbing every weekend. This provoked the usual barbs from them—"You're getting soft, man. I can't believe you're whipped!"—but for Rodney, it was worth the sacrifice.

"I knew Holly was the one," he said softly. "The dating world can be fun, but at the end of the day, I wanted to meet someone and get married and have kids. I knew what kind of woman I wanted, and Holly checked a lot of those boxes. And she understood a lot of things about life, and that impressed me."

Marlo turned to Holly. "Did you know all along that he would eventually come around?" she asked.

"I think I knew when he didn't put up a fight as I was kicking all of those girls out of his life," Holly said. "I mean, I was going through drawers, checking phone records. He understood early on what I needed to do to feel comfortable, and he allowed me to do it. I thought, *Wow, he must be pretty serious.* And I knew I didn't ever want to get divorced. My parents had had a terrible divorce when I was six or seven. I wanted to be married my whole life."

PHIL: What about your parents' marriage, Rodney?

RODNEY: Fifty-four years, and they're still going strong. My dad was a football coach, starting in college and then eventually in the pros, so I grew up in that world.

PHIL: He must have been so proud of you when you did so well at USC and then went on to the NFL. And Holly is perfect as the wife of an NFL quarterback. You can't be a shy little bird in that role.

RODNEY: But a lot of guys want that. They're like, *This is my time. You stay home and be quiet and don't invade my space.*

HOLLY: But to Phil's point, when you are the quarterback's wife, you have to be kind of a first lady. You have to take care of the receivers' wives, the offensive line wives.

RODNEY: And you've got to be Switzerland, too—neutral!

HOLLY: Exactly. You have to be on your game. The life of a quarterback's wife is not easy, especially in Philadelphia, my hometown. They try to run the quarterback out of town—and my relatives were some of the worst. On the evening of our wedding, Rodney was traded from the Cowboys to the Eagles, their arch-enemies. My dad was so happy to have a son-in-law who was going to be the Eagles quarterback, but for my relatives in Philadelphia, it was a slippery slope.

That wasn't the only tough part of Holly's assignment as an NFL wife. She became increasingly worried about injuries, especially when Rodney showed signs of pain.

"He would never talk about what was happening on the field," Holly noted, "so I'd say, 'Hey, what's wrong with your thumb?' And he'd go, 'Oh, I jammed it and it's a little sore.' Then I'd look on ESPN and find out that he was out for three weeks with a broken thumb."

We turned to Rodney. "She had so much on her plate already," he explained, "and I didn't want to burden her. So I downplayed everything, which only made it worse."

Part of Holly's full plate was the couple's new family. They had their first two children, twins Rodney Jr. (known as R.J.) and Ryan Elizabeth, in 1997, and three months after their birth, Holly was back taping on a new series, *For Your Love*, in Los Angeles. Like most working moms, she was performing a balancing act: she'd work three weeks on the show and then use her hiatus week to bring the twins back to Philly to see their dad play.

Everything was moving according to plan—and then came a shock: at age three, R.J. was diagnosed with autism.

"It was a giant kick in the gut," Holly recalled. "To this day, I'm still not sure how we survived that. When we got the diagnosis, I started reading books on the subject and dog-earing pages for Rodney, highlighting passages for him to read. But he wouldn't even look at them."

"Why not?" Marlo asked.

"Because he was in denial," Holly said. "We didn't even know what autism was. This developmental pediatrician told us everything that our son was *never* going to be able to do: He won't speak. He won't go to mainstream schools. He won't play sports. It was the most horrible thing. And then we started blaming each other. Meanwhile, R.J.'s twin sister, Ryan, was hitting all of her milestones."

"There were no signs of anything with her?" Phil asked.

"No, there weren't," Holly said. "But the crazy thing is, when we took him in to get a diagnosis, we brought her with us and she was doing the same thing he was doing—flapping and twirling and not making eye contact. So they came back with a diagnosis that both kids were on the spectrum. We were like, 'What? No way!' What we didn't realize until later was that Ryan was mimicking R.J. to let him know that she was with him. It was like she was saying, 'If *you're* going down, *I'm* going down.' As it turns out, she was *not* on the spectrum. She's a normal, typical kid."

MARLO: What a sensitive thing for a sister to do.

HOLLY: It was—but the whole thing was rough.

RODNEY: It was rough. You go in and someone spends two hours with your kid and then gives you a lifelong sentence of a diagnosis. You're going to tell me all the things my son will never do? No.

HOLLY: But I started wondering if Rodney would be my husband forever. I felt like he was not getting on board with what we needed to do. By then he was playing for the Raiders, and I would go to Oakland and look under his bed, and there would be a whole package of literature I'd sent him—with all these passages highlighted—not even opened. I knew I had to roll up my sleeves and become a gangster for this kid. I couldn't worry about, "Oh, he's not the son I dreamed of," or, "He's not going to win the Heisman Trophy or play in the NFL." These were the things that, in my mind, Rodney was obsessing about, even though he really wasn't.

PHIL: It's hard when your kid acts differently from other kids. It can be embarrassing to many parents.

HOLLY: Right. Whenever R.J. would come to games, the other players' kids would run around and get autographs and connect, but R.J.

would twirl around in the corner, flapping his hands and not talking to anybody. It was devastating. At Raiders camp, when R.J. was three or four, he pooped in the Jacuzzi. They had to drain the whole thing. It was so humiliating. If I could go back, I would have been more patient with Rodney because a dad's processing of his son's autism is different than it is for a mom.

MARLO: But it's great that you still brought him to games.

HOLLY: It was tough. And Rodney's denial was eating up time. There was a small window of time that R.J. had to get his brain right in order to present himself to the world, and Rodney was not moving fast enough for me. I thought, *He's holding me back from doing everything I can to get this kid ready for life.* It was a very frustrating place to be.

Until that point, Holly noted, she and Rodney had been strong partners and advocates for each other when it came to their livelihoods. But now R.J. needed to be their priority, and Holly needed Rodney's undivided attention.

"So she basically gave me an ultimatum," Rodney said. "She told me, 'You've got to get on board going forward.' I was stuck in my own selfish world. *Why me? What did I do wrong? This is not what I pictured for my firstborn son.* I wanted R.J. to experience everything I had growing up. So I thought, *Okay, I'm an athlete—I'm going to do this the way my dad did. I am going to coach the autism out of R.J., and I can do this myself.* But I was not equipped with the right tools to do that."

"Of course not," Marlo said. "Who would be? So what did you do?"

"Well, we had gotten him into all of these therapies," Rodney explained, "but you've got to continue the work at home. It's 24/7, but I wasn't willing to learn. I remember one embarrassing moment in a big group session when the therapist asked me to engage with my son and he did not engage back. No eye contact. No laughter. No playing. And then the therapist got on the floor with him and began engaging him, and R.J. immediately lit up and responded. My first reaction was that Holly had set me up to fail. But she was like, 'Look, this is how he is going to get better, and unless you're with us on this, we can't last.' And that's when I realized that I was about to lose my family over my stubbornness and ignorance."

Holly cut in. "It was an about-face for Rodney," she said, "and it happened on a dime. It was the most amazing thing. Thank God."

"That kind of situation can break couples up," Phil said.

"It can," Rodney said. "In our advocacy work for autism, we often meet parents who aren't together anymore."

The Peetes became overnight activists, launching the HollyRod Foundation, which offers support and information for families affected by autism and Parkinson's disease. They also created a reality show that ran for four seasons—first as *For Peete's Sake* on OWN, and then as *Meet the Peetes* on the Hallmark Channel—that spotlighted the day-to-day life of the family, including the twins (now twenty-two) and the Peetes' other two sons, Robinson and Roman. Pointedly, the show did not shy away from depicting the challenges of raising a child with autism.

"Did you do the show especially for R.J.?" Marlo asked.

"Yes we did," Holly said. "Because when he was growing up, autism wasn't represented on TV. I wanted to show a family rallying around this kid and showing what he'd accomplished."

"And what about that pediatrician's first diagnosis?" Phil asked. "That wasn't true?"

"No, not at all," Holly said. "I went on TV and said, 'Never let some doctor tell you what your three-year-old is going to become.' And had we not been the bulldog mom and Johnny-come-lately dad, we might have succumbed to that hopelessness."

MARLO: This was a gigantic boulder in the middle of your marriage. Did you guys ever find time for each other?

RODNEY: Our time together diminished, because we were so focused on R.J.

HOLLY: It was stressful. There were vacations we couldn't take, because R.J. struggled everywhere we went. There was a period when we neglected each other in our attempts to get this kid as right as possible.

PHIL: So how did you find your way back to each other?

HOLLY: We've done a lot of couples therapy and a lot of advocacy. Starting the foundation and meeting other parents who we were affecting really helped. Parents would come up to us and say, "R.J.'s story changed our kid's life." We realized we were doing something right, and it bonded us.

RODNEY: We had a family meeting and decided to go public with what we were dealing with. I did not want R.J. to be a poster child for autism, but at the end of the day it was the best decision we made.

PHIL: Tell us about R.J. today.

RODNEY: Uh-oh, here come the waterworks...

HOLLY: Phil, you're still doing those waterworks things! Well, R.J. now works for the L.A. Dodgers as a clubhouse attendant. They love him. I often post on social media, thanking the Dodgers for giving my son a job, and they'll say, "No, thank *you* for R.J. Do you know what he brings to the clubhouse?" He never had friends growing up, and now he has a whole dugout full of friends. And that is so powerful. He is driving a car. He is communicating and connecting. He has his dream job.

RODNEY: Makes his own money. Does his own banking. He lives with us and he's happy.

HOLLY: If he walked in here right now, he'd make eye contact and shake your hand. But he still has issues—he can't talk to women yet. He's gorgeous, and my biggest fear is that some skanky girl will take advantage of him.

MARLO: Or break his heart.

HOLLY: I don't want anyone to mess with him. But he's such a success story. When they introduce him on the jumbotron at Dodger Stadium, he's smiling from ear to ear.

MARLO: My God, that's fantastic. They didn't just give R.J. a job. They gave him hope.

HOLLY: I think R.J. also gives us hope for our relationship. The kid we were worried would push us apart—

RODNEY: —has brought us back together. And still does.

After getting their family's life back on track, the Peetes had one more significant tackle to clear: the end of Rodney's playing days.

"When the lights went out on his NFL career in 2005, I thought I was prepared for this momentous letdown in his life," Holly recalled, "but this time I was in denial."

"I was, too," Rodney said. "You don't want it to end because it's something you've done since you were eight years old. And then on top of that, it ends at thirty-eight, when everybody else is in the prime of their working life. You think, *Okay, I just had a wonderful life doing what I always wanted to do. Now that's over. Where am I going to find that same feeling?*"

"That rush," Phil said.

"Yes," Rodney said. "Where am I going to get that rush from? There's no handbook for an NFL player retiring. I went straight from playing to being hired by Fox to do *Best Damn Sports Show*, but I wasn't happy. I thought the show would fill the void left by the NFL, and I spent a lot of time chasing that rush."

On top of struggling with his transition, Holly revealed, Rodney was in immense pain from all those years getting battered on the gridiron. "He got used to taking painkillers, and he drank. Meanwhile, I was working on TV shows, often in different cities from him. My mom would say to me, 'Can't you see that he has to stop taking those pills?' And I would blame it on the pain he was in. But it all blew up after he retired. I couldn't understand why he couldn't just stop the pills and the drinking on a dime."

"I tried to fight through the pain," Rodney said, "because in football you just learn to live with it. And now we find out that the opioids they gave you for the pain were just so terrible and detrimental to your body. But they'd give them out like candy."

"You'd been king of the world, Rodney," Phil said. "How did you not go crazy?"

"I *did* go crazy," Rodney said. "There were definitely dark times with me trying to manage my own pain—physical, emotional, and mental. I was drinking and taking pills and chewing tobacco. It was like one of those dreams where you're falling and you can't stop."

"And if he was in denial," Holly said, "I was enabling him, for years."

But the enabling and the substance abuse eventually stopped, Rodney revealed, and things began to change.

"And now you work as a sportscaster," Phil noted, "which you obviously enjoy. Do you think getting off the pills and alcohol is what got you to this place?"

"Yes," Rodney said. "I enjoy the people I work with, I enjoy going in every day. I am finally able to say that the football chapter of my life is over and I can focus on family, longevity, and health. But I would not have overcome a lot of things if Holly had not been willing to work with me. She has been my biggest champion."

"What about you?" Marlo asked Holly. "Did a doctor ever tell you that you need to take care of yourself, too?"

"Not a doctor," Holly said, "but friends who were worried about how hard I was working to prop up Rodney would say, 'You've got to look out for yourself, because if you crumble, the whole empire falls.' And Rodney ultimately took the enormous step of going to a treatment program, which was a big deal."

Rodney nodded. "It was mostly about learning how to make better choices and understanding the effect it had on not only me but my family," he said. "Getting off the pills, stopping the drinking, losing weight—all those things made me feel good about myself and they give you clarity about where you want to go."

Rodney wasn't alone in his career trauma. Seven years after his retirement from the NFL, Holly endured a difficult moment in her own.

"I was on a talk show called *The Talk*," she began. "It was like *The View*, but not political. I went on that baby and—I have to say this because I am a very honest person—I was good."

"Very good," Rodney interjected. "She connects with everybody."

"I could talk about things and be funny," Holly continued. "I could do it all. And the network people would come into my dressing room and tell me, 'You're killing it. You're crushing it.' Until, I think, I crushed it a little too hard. There was a lot of jealousy, and I was let go. The network would not release any kind of statement about why I was fired. It was publicly humiliating to have to go through that. I don't think I've really gotten over it yet, but Rodney helped me through it. He was my savior."

PHIL: With all that you've been through, how did you manage to keep your marriage so strong?

HOLLY: Well, there's something we do that we call "Same Page Love"—and that's about the two of us getting on the same page. We take the time to sit down and talk what we're feeling. But you've got to sit back and allow the other person to talk without jumping in. And give them a time limit—maybe it's fifteen minutes. Okay, now you're on the clock. Then you talk and listen, and that's when the Same Page Love happens.

MARLO: Didn't you two also come up with something a little more physical—something called "The 20-Second Hug"?

HOLLY: Oh, my gosh, yes. How did you know that?

MARLO: I read it somewhere. Tell us about it.

HOLLY: Rodney came up with the idea.

RODNEY: It's literally a twenty-second hug. If I call for one, she's got to give it to me. And vice versa.

PHIL: No matter what?

RODNEY: No matter what.

HOLLY: And no matter when. Sometimes they're so painful! But even if you're really pissed at your partner, you've still got to hold that hug for a full twenty seconds. You can't pull away. There's all this energy going on—and even if I want to just fucking kill him, you've got to stay put.

MARLO: How did you come to think of that?

HOLLY: When we were going through some bad shit.

RODNEY: What happens is that even though you're angry, you start feeling what it means to be together.

PHIL: It's a memory thing.

MARLO: It's a physical thing.

HOLLY: It's pheromonal.

RODNEY: It's a connection.

John and Justine Leguizamo

MARRIED IN 2003

"I'm thinking, *Oh, my God, she cares about
my feelings.* She's not saying, 'You're an asshole,'
or 'You're an idiot.' She's just listening
to me and I just felt really heard."

On stage, actor-writer-comedian John Leguizamo is a lot of things—funny, smart, passionate. But one quality supersedes all the others in the life and career of this gifted artist, and that's bravery.

It takes bravery to assimilate as a child in a country that wasn't always welcoming to his ethnicity.

It takes bravery to write and perform raw, funny, and emotionally bare one-man shows about the Latino experience, and give them unforgiving names like *Mambo Mouth*, *Spic-O-Rama*, and *Sexaholix: A Love Story*.

And it takes bravery to lecture audiences about the misassumptions of his people's heritage, and leave them not only howling but chastened.

Here's this from John's award-winning show *Latin History for Morons*, which he debuted on Broadway in 2017, then took on tour across the country:

I'm going to un-moronize you and de-stupidify you! So let's start by looking at Latin DNA. We are at least 40 percent Indian,

25 percent black, 25 percent white, 25 percent Jewish, 25 percent Lebanese and 40 percent I-don't-know-what-the-fuck. That's a grand total of 180 percent. We Latinos are a bastardly people, and the reason we're such bastards is because those white European conquistadors came here in the 1500s without women. And these horny sons-of-bitches were sexing up all our fine native homeys like NBA players at a Kardashian pool party.

Edgy, right? But no one speaks more articulately to John's bravery than his most loyal fan, his closest friend, the mother of their two children, and his partner since 1999, Justine.

"It's one thing to do these shows in New York," she said. "That requires bravery all by itself—to get on stage anywhere and talk about these issues. But to do it in Texas, in Florida, to get up in front of those people who will sometimes yell angry things or walk out of the theater—that's brave. And he never flinches. That's because he knows what he's doing is right. He believes in what he's saying because he's lived with it all his life."

According to Justine, it was bravery in a different aspect of his life—their relationship—that sealed the deal for her. She'd never wanted to get married, and while John was okay with that, it didn't stop him from inviting Justine's entire family, along with his own, to his place for Thanksgiving shortly after the two began seeing each other. There were fifty guests in all—the Latin Leguizamos from Queens and the Jewish Maurers of New York's Upper West Side. And John played the host fearlessly.

"We'd been dating only a couple months," Justine recalled, "but I started to feel like I could trust him. Not only did I realize that he was ready to make a commitment to me, but also that he was a very brave man. That became important to me."

Justine ran a hand through her soft blond hair. "I feel like I'm very brave, too," she said, "so we have that in common. That's why, when I

John and Justine Leguizamo

saw him so early in our relationship welcoming his girlfriend's family, I thought, *He's not afraid of what life has in store for us.*"

That life has been very good to them. Twenty-seven years after first setting eyes on each other, Justine and John are still very much soul mates. They have two children—Allegra Sky, born in 1999, and Lucas Ryder, born in 2000, both now in college—and for the past ten years the family has lived in a smartly renovated brownstone in Greenwich Village. We ventured downtown for an afternoon chat at that home, but finding their building took some work. We were looking for the two-digit street address Justine had given us on the phone, but the number on the building she'd described was "1854." We walked past it three times before Justine finally popped her head out the front door.

"Don't worry, you're at the right place," she hollered.

"Why is the number different from what you told us?" Marlo asked.

"That's the year it was built—1854," Justine answered with a laugh. "Everyone makes the same mistake."

"It was built in 1854?" Phil asked reflexively. "That was nine years before Lincoln delivered the Gettysburg address."

This is why people don't play Trivial Pursuit with Phil Donahue.

Justine escorted us inside their home, where we were greeted by John, whose light mustache lent a bit of gravitas to his otherwise boyish face. Justine stood by his side, her hand looped in the crook of her husband's arm. Together, they looked like the little figurines on top of a very hip wedding cake.

"We love our block," John told us as he showed us around. "We have a really strong community here. Justine is part of the Greenwich Village Society for Historic Preservation. She protects the neighborhood from people who are tearing down old buildings. New York University knocked down Edgar Allan Poe's home and the Eugene O'Neill Playhouse. Imagine that—it's a place of learning, and they still tore down these original American authors. They just don't care about history."

John is not just engaging in activist spin here—learning has always been important to him. Marlo had interviewed him almost twenty years earlier for her book *The Right Words at the Right Time*, and even back then he admitted to being a voracious reader and natural autodidact.

"I wasn't born in this country, so English is just my stepmother tongue," he'd told Marlo. "But because I pursued this theater thing, I read tons of stuff I never would have read. I got my knowledge and vocabulary from all these great plays and period pieces."

It was one of those "theater things"—a movie, to be precise—that brought this unlikely couple together.

A native of Bogotá, Columbia, John had immigrated to the United States with his family at age four. He grew up on the streets of Queens—a "Fresh Air Fund kid," he called himself—where he perfected the craft of cracking wise as a way of keeping the neighborhood bullies at bay. "I learned to be funny so I wouldn't get hit."

He honed those comics skills in his high school, where he was the reliable class clown. One day, his math teacher pulled him aside and said the words that would change his life: "Instead of being obnoxious in class all the time, why don't you rechannel your hostility into something productive, like becoming a standup comic?" John took that advice seriously. He looked up "theater" in the Yellow Pages and came across the name Sylvia Leigh's Showcase Theater. ("I picked that one because 'showcase' sounded kind of snazzy," he said.) That was the beginning of his career—one that would ultimately span television, film, and concert stages.

Justine's trajectory couldn't have been more different. The granddaughter of Jewish Russian immigrants and daughter of Brooklynites, she was raised on New York's affluent Upper West Side, where she attended the progressive Fieldston School and fell into that lifestyle with ease. "At Fieldston, the people I grew up with were mostly from backgrounds similar to mine," she remembered. "We were upper-middle-class, Jewish families who went to summer camp, traveled a lot, and were college-bound. Education and social justice were important to us, and that was pretty much our main focus in school and at home. There were also bar mitzvahs every week, and I did all of that. Everyone I knew was just like me, so it was a pretty small world."

Their paths finally crossed in 1993 on the set of *Carlito's Way*, a gritty crime drama starring Al Pacino. John had been cast as a hot-tempered young gangster from the Bronx, and Justine was working with the wardrobe department.

JUSTINE: So John was cast in the movie and I was a costume production assistant, and we actually met at his fitting. I knew who he was because he'd already done *Mambo Mouth* and *Spic-O-Rama*...

JOHN: Both one-man shows.

JUSTINE: So I asked the costume designers if I could go to the fitting and help them.

PHIL: That's pretty intimate.

JOHN: It was kismet—I mean, she made it happen, in a way.

MARLO: Did he have his clothes on the whole time?

JUSTINE: No—and that was part of it!

JOHN: Well, she wasn't *inside* the fitting room—that would've been really uncomfortable. But it was the first time I saw her, and it was electric. She was the finest woman I'd ever seen—incredibly sexy and beautiful—but there was also, I don't know, some sort of connection there.

PHIL: Was it electric for you, too, Justine?

JUSTINE: Absolutely. I knew immediately that we should be together.

PHIL: From that first fitting?

JUSTINE: I really did. I mean, look, who can say? All I know is that I'd never felt that way before. Something just connected.

MARLO: You had been married once before, John. So when you met Justine, were you already divorced or just separated?

JOHN: So many questions! Am I being deposed? Where's the subpoena?

JUSTINE: No, he was engaged.

MARLO: I'm sorry, what?

JOHN: I was engaged when Justine and I met.

JUSTINE: We knew each other a long time before we started dating.

JOHN: By then, I'd had my starter marriage and was happily divorced.

MARLO: I see. And you were married for only two years that first time?

JUSTINE: If that.

This was not a comedy routine. The fact is, despite Cupid's arrows flying around that fitting room, the timing couldn't have been worse. At the time, John was engaged to an actress, whom he married the following year. But in 1996, he and his wife parted ways, freeing John to circle back to the woman who had stolen his heart as he tried on costumes.

Although Justine knew in her gut that they were made to be together, taking that trip down the aisle wasn't really important to her.

"I just didn't feel like I wanted to be married," she said. "It didn't mean anything to me. I knew I wanted to have children; I knew that my whole life. It's just that I didn't see the point of getting married, so I wasn't interested."

"And I thought that was really sexy," John admitted. "I thought, *Oh, yeah, I like that.*"

And so this very-much-in-love couple decided to do everything that married couples do—minus the getting-married part. They set up house. They had children. They shared a life.

So what made this otherwise happy pair decide to make it official?

"For me, it was September 11," Justine recalled, "After 9/11 there was all this talk that you couldn't travel together if you didn't have the same names. That really jolted me into reality. I began to think how scary it would be if we all needed to get somewhere and we couldn't go together. Getting married seemed like it would make things easier."

But the frightening events of September 11 also caused Justine and John to take stock of their lives.

"September 11th made you rethink your values," John said. "So we got married, got a country house, and changed life a little bit by focusing more on the moments—the important moments—and not chasing whatever it is you think is going to bring you happiness."

"By values, you mean family?" Phil asked.

"Yes," John said. "Family, friends, the things that really matter in the end."

Their cozy wedding—about twenty guests at their upstate New York lake house—was intimate and familial. Justine wore a floor-length gown with a rhinestone tiara ("A real Jewish princess!" Marlo laughed), and the ceremony combined traditions from both of their faiths, including the Jewish ritual of standing beneath the chuppah and stamping on a glass and the Christian practice of lighting a candle. Their daughter was the flower girl, their son was the ring-bearer—she was three, he was two—and the officiant was a representative from the Ethical Culture Society.

Their mixed-faith ceremony was an interesting choice, given that neither John nor Justine is particularly devout. John calls himself a "lapsed Catholic," explaining that he was raised in a household in flux—first Catholic and then Seventh-Day Adventist, before the family became evangelists. "All of Latin America converted to evangelism," he explained, "because the Catholic Church never really had a Latin pope, and then when they finally got one, it was too late. But when I was growing up, my parents weren't religious at all—unless they got mad, and then it was, *¡Ay dios mio!* They would use the words 'God' and 'Joseph and Mary,' but only when they were angry or upset. They didn't pray or anything."

Justine, meanwhile, was "raised sort of Jewish, but barely," she said. "I haven't been to temple since I was ten or twelve years old."

MARLO: Have your different faiths ever run up against each other?

JOHN: No, and I think one of the reasons we're still together is because none of that was a problem for us. I believe in a higher power and the collective universe, but organized religion is not my thing or her thing. But we love all of our traditions. I love doing the Passover Seder and Hanukkah with the menorah, and she loves doing Christmas and Easter. We have more holidays to celebrate, and more reasons to have family over.

PHIL: How did your parents feel about you not marrying a Latin, John? Was that a problem?

JOHN: No, no, Latin people don't have issues with that. We love everybody, and want everybody to love everybody.

PHIL: How about your folks, Justine?

JUSTINE: They never said a word about it. I think they were so relieved that I had found someone. I don't know that they ever thought I would.

I've always been extremely independent, so when they saw how much I loved John and what a wonderful man he is, they were fine about it.

JOHN: They were beautiful, man. They accepted me right away, and I loved them too.

PHIL: Did your parents have a problem with you and John having children out of wedlock?

JUSTINE: If they did, they kept it to themselves. By the time I had my kids, I was thirty years old, so they were used to me and my independence. They probably thought to themselves, *What good would it do to object?* But honestly, maybe they didn't even think it was an issue.

Time and again throughout our conversation, Justine mentioned her fierce independent streak.

"My father raised me to be independent, too," Marlo said, "and that's one of the reasons I took my time getting married. Who instilled the independent spirit in you?"

"My mother," Justine said. "She always reinforced to me that we don't need to abide by the rules of society just because they're there. Instead, she said, we need to follow them only if they make sense to us. She's now eighty, but she had an unusual way of living her life—she was sort of a Bohemian."

When it came to modeling what a marriage looked like, Justine said, her parents set an extraordinary example: Her mom traveled the world to far-flung places like Morocco, Kenya, and Tahiti for months at a time—often with a friend, sometimes with Justine and her sister, occasionally by herself. "People didn't really understand it," she explained, "but it made sense to her and it made sense to us."

"That's wild," Phil said. "And your father didn't mind that?"

"If he did mind, he probably knew he couldn't do anything about it," Justine said. "I think he loved her independent spirit. I don't know that it was necessarily easy for him, but he understood that it was something she needed to do, and he wanted her to be happy. My parents were amazing—I was very lucky."

MARLO: Your father is a wonderful example of marital accommodations. Tell us some of yours.

JOHN: Easy now, Marlo—calm yourself! You're opening up a Pandora's box here! Are you doing that on purpose?

JUSTINE: That's a good question, actually. John, I would like to know what you—

JOHN: —no, no! You go first. Ladies first.

JUSTINE: Fine. I mean, look, I married an actor—his life was no surprise to me. I knew him for years before we got married, so I understood that he was going to be traveling a lot and that there would be no clear schedule. That was just going to be how our life was. And I have to say, I thought about it a lot before we made a commitment to spend our lives together, because it made me nervous and I knew it would not be easy.

MARLO: An actor's life is never easy on a spouse. When we'd been married for about twelve years, I did an eight-month tour of *Six Degrees of Separation*, and it was hard.

PHIL: It was easier when she was playing closer to Chicago, which wasn't often.

MARLO: So most nights, my only company was a Snickers and an Amstel Light from the mini-bar.

JUSTINE: You're right. It isn't an easy life. But we have found a way. We've managed. I mean, we've been together a long time and raised the kids and gotten through this life. But, yes, it's complicated and it's unusual.

JOHN: We're like circus folk. But I've been an actor for so long that I'm used to being uprooted all the time and having no control over geography or time or destiny. So you just surrender to it. But what I didn't understand were the sacrifices she was making. All of this is hard on a marriage, and hard on raising a family.

MARLO: Did you take your kids with you?

JOHN: We tried at first, but it was really difficult to travel.

JUSTINE: From zero to five, they were with us when we were on tour or on location. Then we stopped taking them. And then I stopped going.

MARLO: Why?

JOHN: Well, we originally thought they would travel with us forever, like we were all gypsies. But eventually we learned that we were sending the wrong signal to the kids by pulling them out of school whenever we felt like it. All of a sudden you're telling them that school doesn't matter, and you can never come back from that and tell them school *does* matter. So, we learned, okay, they've got to stay in school no matter what, even if I have to go away for a while. It's better that they stay in something that's organized and a little more functional.

MARLO: Was that hard on your marriage?

JOHN: Yeah. But we tried to keep it to a two-week maximum. So I'd come back every two weeks, because she couldn't travel with me.

JUSTINE: I don't remember any of that.

JOHN: But that was...

JUSTINE: We tried, but there were times when we didn't see each other for months at a time. Was it hard on the marriage? I mean, yeah, I guess. Marriage isn't easy.

Even as they successfully navigated John's career responsibilities, their dissimilar upbringings required additional compromises. We asked them about that, and inadvertently stirred things up.

"Do you ever feel like there's a culture clash in your home?" Marlo asked.

"Well, we came from very different socioeconomic backgrounds," John offered, "but I think opposites attract for a reason. That's such a natural thing."

"But there are challenges coming from different cultures," Justine countered. "Like, I always thought, *Of course the kids will go to private school.* It wouldn't have even occurred to me to do anything else. I think public schools are great—we have one of the best in the world two blocks away from us—it's just, I wouldn't know how to do it. But John really wanted them to go to public school."

"Because that's all I knew," John said.

"To see the real world," Phil offered.

"It *is* the real world," John said. "Everybody is of color and it's so much fun. Sometimes it was tough for me, but it was also riveting. I learned so much in school from the people, not from the teachers. Our black and Latin cultures are always fun and exciting. I loved it."

"I don't know that you voiced those feelings to me at that time," Justine said.

"I did," John replied.

"Oh, you did. I guess I didn't listen. I didn't hear it."

"No, you heard it. We had arguments."

It was interesting to watch this dynamic play out in real time. Here Justine had forgotten what was no doubt a major disagreement between the two—what schools the kids would go to—or John was misremembering it. Either way, that brought us to the question of how they fight.

PHIL: Do you have a temper, John? You're Latin—don't tell me you don't have a temper.

JOHN [*to Justine*]: Do I have a temper?

JUSTINE: Yeah, you do.

JOHN: Okay, I have a little bit of a temper, but not often.

PHIL: Well, I'm an Irish guy married to an Italian-Lebanese, and these are not quiet groups. So what about the Jewish princess here?

JOHN: She has a temper.

MARLO: Okay, so we've got two healthy tempers here. How does that work out?

JOHN: Well, I believe you shouldn't say things you can't take back. Even when I'm enraged, I try hard not to do that. She's not as good with that part of it.

JUSTINE: I'm more mean.

JOHN: She'll say anything.

JUSTINE: It's true, though. It's very rare that he really loses control. And when I say rare, I mean, like, less than five times in the whole time I've known him.

JOHN: I guess it's because I'm an actor. I've learned how to be as fully angry as I can be without breaking things or hitting anybody, do you know what I mean? I learned to be angry without offending. I may be full of rage and yell, but I'll also demand articulately what I need.

JUSTINE: And I have less of that skill, maybe. I don't get mad that often, but I tend to lose control of my emotions more than John does.

MARLO: And who comes back from the fight first?

JUSTINE: John.

JOHN: In the beginning, it was always me saying, "Come on, let's try to fix this up. Let's not go to bed mad. Let's let it all out and go back to talking." That was me all the time. But she's gotten much better at trying to make amends, trying to apologize.

JUSTINE: I don't have as much of a problem apologizing as I used to. It's now easier for me to say I'm sorry. Maybe not in that moment, or even that day—sometimes it takes until the next day. But I don't have a problem anymore apologizing for anything. I think getting rid of that kind of pride is so important.

JOHN: Pride is a poison.

JUSTINE: It doesn't help anything.

For those keeping score, in the end, John made the accommodation: both children went to private schools.

"I tried to weigh all the factors," he remembered. "Coming from where we are now—with this new sort of income—I thought it might be uncomfortable for the kids. I had nothing at their age, and all the kids I went to school with had nothing, so we were all pretty equal. But what happens if you have all of this—everything what we have now—and then you go to a school where kids don't have enough? How is that going to feel for them? And then there was the idea of them going into a public school system with a celebrity name, and wondering if that was going to cause problems or steal the focus from them."

"I get that," Phil said. "My boys didn't like it when I came to their hockey games. I'd stand way in the back with a baseball cap on so I could watch them play. I respected their privacy."

"And they'd be embarrassed," Marlo added. "*Phil Donahue,* for God's sake! He was on TV every day. When they were growing up, it was like having a yacht in their front yard."

"With klieg lights!" said John.

The more we dug in with Justine and John about their marriage, the more apparent it became that it is built on a bedrock of trust. That's not any easy thing for any couple to claim, especially one challenged by frequent and often long separations. We asked Justine if she ever worried about what John was up to during those long periods when he was on the road. She just smiled.

"I am not a jealous person," she said. "I don't have it. It's not in me. But more important, I feel so safe in my marriage knowing that he's incredibly committed to our family. Never for a second do I worry what he's doing when he's on location or on tour—none of that matters—because I know that his ultimate commitment is to me and my children and his mother and our cousins and our life together. I know where his allegiances are, and I feel very grateful for that."

"And likewise," John concurred. "I know Justine is incredibly committed to the marriage and the kids and what we have and what we built together. I have total confidence in that. If you asked me to name the one beautiful thing about Justine, it's that she always tries. She's willing to put in the effort for our marriage. She doesn't even have to succeed at it—she's willing to just try. I love that about her."

MARLO: That kind of faith in your spouse can make you feel very safe.

JOHN: You know, we had a date early on at the Angelika movie theater. All the hipsters went to the Angelika—everybody who was cool—and Justine and I decided to meet there to see some indie film. I'm a pathologically early person, so I was there about forty-five minutes before the movie began. Well, she was late and I flipped out. Then she started crying. Do you remember any of this, Justine? We were standing on the corner, and I was very upset—though I was trying not to be too upset because it was early in the relationship. But the thing is, she was okay with me being this hot-headed about a stupid little thing. And I'm thinking, *Oh, my God, she cares about my feelings.* She's not saying, "You're an asshole," or "You're an idiot," or "What the hell is wrong with you? Are you crazy? I'm only twenty minutes late." Instead, she's just listening to me and we're talking about it. We didn't even go to the movie. We just kept standing there, talking, as she tried to calm me down. And, I don't know, man, I just felt really heard. I felt really respected. And it made me fall in love with her even more.

Ron and Cheryl Howard

MARRIED IN 1975

"With redheads it's not just temper. It's also
emotional—it can be high-strung and neurotic and,
'Oh my gosh, someone lock them up!'"

O h, look, there's a barge! My grandson would go crazy. He loves
boats."

We were sitting in the sunroom of the Cape Cod–style house
that Cheryl Howard shares with her husband of forty-five years, movie
director Ron Howard. Just seconds earlier, she had been reminiscing
about those long-ago days when she and Ron first met. They were in high
school—she was a tomboy, he was a former child actor—and they fell in
love on their first teen date.

But in mid-sentence, Cheryl had spotted the barge through the room's
large bay window, and now we were all gazing out at the water and watching it slowly drift by. That's what's so winning about Cheryl: she's an in-
the-moment kind of person.

"The tide comes and goes twice a day," Ron said, "along with the birds
and all sorts of wildlife. It's very dynamic." It was clear that, even after
living in this home for three-and-a-half years, they were still marveling

Burbank, California; June 7, 1975

at the surrounding natural wonders. These two are empty nesters, after all, though their children and grandchildren remain an active part of their lives.

The moment we'd arrived, we were charmed by the tranquility of the surroundings. The couple's two large dogs—Puddin', a big white Great Pyrenees, and a collie named Cooper—were lazily napping in the courtyard, signaling that this classic Connecticut house, which was built by a sea captain in 1911, was a peaceful place to be.

We were greeted at the door by both Ron and Cheryl. Behind them, four rescue cats roamed about as if they owned the place. Ron looked just as we expected him to look, with that sweet Opie smile and his signature baseball cap on his head. What was unexpected were the warm hugs and kisses from Cheryl. It was like a reunion with an old friend we'd never met.

Once we settled into our chairs in the sunroom, we asked them why they decided to move into this new home, when their previous home was just five miles away. They'd lived there for twenty years, Ron told us, but with the kids now gone, it was time to downsize.

"So I'm on an airplane coming home from London," Ron recalled, "and Cheryl is on another plane coming back from a trip to Romania. I was writing in my journal—I always do that on flights—about our house, and how it no longer made sense for us. On one hand, Cheryl had built it—it was an expression of her creativity, and I loved it. But it cost too much and somebody else could get more out of the property. So I wrote all of these things down and added, 'I don't think I have to bring it up now. Let's wait another year or so and see what happens.'"

When Ron got home, he prepared for Cheryl's return. "We hadn't seen each other for a while," he continued, "so I got the fire going—it was winter—poured some wine, turned on the music, and waited for Cheryl to come home. She finally comes in, sees the wine, sees the fire, hears the music, looks at me, and says, 'Oh, that's really wonderful, but I've got to talk to you. I think we have to sell the place. I thought about it on the plane.'"

"You're kidding!" Marlo said. "What did you say?"

"I told her, 'I literally just wrote about this in my journal!'" Ron said. "It was like an O. Henry story. She thought it was going to be hard for me to let go of it, and I thought it was going to be hard for her to let go of it."

O. Henry or not, the telling thing about this story is Ron and Cheryl's synchronicity. They have worked hard to be on the same wavelength. When they're not hammering things out on their own, they seek counsel from professional therapists who have taught them skills to survive marital impasses. "It's an ever-evolving thing," Ron said, "and it always comes back to one important question: How much value do you place on the relationship, and what are you willing to do to make it continue to work?"

"Trust is very important, too," Cheryl added. "We work hard to sustain it, to keep it."

You can't help but feel at ease with these two—we've had Ron in our homes most of our lives. He barnstormed into American households in 1960 as the precious red-headed moppet Opie Taylor on the *Andy Griffith Show*—a role he held from ages five to fourteen. When the show ended, he maintained a steady presence on the big and small screens—*The Wild Country, Gunsmoke, American Graffiti*—before returning to our living rooms in 1974 as perpetual teen Richie Cunningham in the iconic TV series *Happy Days*. Since 1977, he has established himself as one of the nation's preeminent film directors, churning out more than two dozen memorable movies, including *Apollo 13, Splash, Cocoon,* and *A Beautiful Mind*—the latter earning him an Academy Award.

"You started doing *Happy Days* as a single, nineteen-year-old man," Phil said, "but by the time you left the series six years later, you two were already celebrating your fifth wedding anniversary. You were both so young. How did you meet?"

"We met in our junior year of high school," Ron began. "We were both in Miss McBride's English class, and I was on the school's basketball team. At the time, I was working on a TV show with Henry Fonda called *The Smith Family*. I was starting to date a little, but I wasn't finding it very exciting or rewarding. It seemed like a lot of awkwardness. But I had my eye on this redhead here. One day, I was getting ready to leave school to do the show, gathering my homework assignments, and she said, 'Are you going to play basketball today?' I said, 'Yeah, I'm going to go to work and then I'll come back and keep practicing.' But she talked to me, so that was big."

CHERYL: And that was it. Then I left. I was shy.

PHIL: Did you pursue her?

RON: Yeah. I would get off work and go driving around, trying to figure out where she lived. I guess you would characterize that as stalking today. I'd listen to James Taylor's "Fire and Rain" and try to see if she was walking home from school. I never connected with her that way, but one thing led to another, and after just enough of these little casual conversations, I finally got up the nerve to call her up and ask her out for a date.

MARLO: So, you obviously liked him. Otherwise you wouldn't have said...

CHERYL: Well, I was Southern Baptist. My dad was raised Southern Baptist—he and my mother were divorced and I lived with him—and Ron was in a business I couldn't understand and didn't care for because I was my dad's daughter. But, yes, he just seemed so nice and shy.

RON: And right away, from our first date, that was it. We went to a movie—a rerelease of *It's a Mad, Mad, Mad, Mad World*—then went out for pizza afterwards.

CHERYL: And by the way, it was a G-rated movie, which was a lucky move because, again, I was raised pretty strict. He also had a Volkswagen.

RON: A 1970 VW Bug, which we still have, actually.

CHERYL: If he'd had a hot Mustang, I wouldn't have liked it. I would've thought he was a jerk.

RON: But it was a great first date. And it wasn't because anything really spectacular happened. We just really hit it off. I remember going home, walking in the door, and saying to my parents, "Now that's a date!" and going up to my room. I can only imagine what they were thinking, *What did this girl offer up that made this such a fabulous date?*

MARLO: And how old were you again?

CHERYL: We were both sixteen.

MARLO: Did you say "I love you" to each other?

CHERYL: Ron would say that, but I would respond, "You're just infatuated. We won't fall in love for probably another twenty years."

RON: Her dad had programmed her not to fall in love.

PHIL: Is that true, Cheryl?

CHERYL: I was very much like my dad.

PHIL: So you assumed that you were too young to feel what you were feeling.

CHERYL: Yes. But I couldn't help myself. I fell in love with him. He just seemed so sweet and shy. And he's cute, too. And, oh, I'm going to cry. I've got menopause, so just ignore me if I cry.

Ron had one other thing going for him that immediately attracted Cheryl: for a former child star, he was decidedly un-Hollywood—and that was something that might sit better with her father.

"My dad owned an apartment building," she explained, "and he paid me $3 an hour to paint, wallpaper, and cut grass. That was good pay for a fourteen-year-old. However, the building also had quite a few actors who didn't pay their rent regularly. My dad was from Louisiana and my mom was from a farm family in Wisconsin, so showbiz was not a part of our lives. Dating an actor—one who might struggle to pay rent—was not exactly what they imagined for their daughter. But, hey, I could paint, wallpaper, and cut grass, so I really don't know what they had to worry about."

For all his modesty, Ron admits to having been a very grown-up kid. "I was one of those guys who was kind of mature before his time," he told us. "There was an annoying expectation that as a successful child actor I would be some kind of a hellion—that I would have a hot rod and be a partier. But that wouldn't have gone over very well in my family. My dad was pretty strict. But it was also a cliché that I didn't particularly want to embrace. I knew early on that I wanted to have a long career and take responsibility for projects."

But most important, there was a certain something between the two teenagers that was undeniable. "It was chemistry," Ron said. "It all comes down to that, whether you're sixteen or sixty-six. I was so impressed with her from that first date because I had an immediate respect for this life energy that she had. She was very self-sufficient. She was living with her father and kind of like the lady of the house, looking after things and taking on a lot more responsibility than most girls her age would have to."

Indeed, even in their teens, both Ron and Cheryl were pursing robust lives. Cheryl was going to night school to study aerodynamics—her father was a pilot who taught her to fly solo when she was sixteen—and Ron was eager to turn his acting career into something more meaningful for him.

"And Ron loved his life," Cheryl added. "We both would get excited about things that we were doing."

While Ron and Cheryl's courtship and marriage were storybook perfect, Ron's parents' journey to the altar was decidedly wilder. "They got married in a very romantic, crazy way," Ron shared. His father, Rance, was a Kansas farm boy. His mother, Jean, was a butcher's daughter from Duncan, Oklahoma. They met at the University of Oklahoma where they studied acting. She was twenty and he, nineteen. As Ron tells it, Rance and Jean joined a children's theater troupe that would go around the country in a bus—plus one truck—and perform *Snow White* and *Cinderella*. While on the road, the couple decided to get married in Kentucky because there was no waiting period there. Jean wore Cinderella's dress minus the sequins so it wouldn't be too gaudy. The four dwarfs who performed in *Snow White* acted as groomsmen.

"They only had four dwarves in the company," Ron explained. "They couldn't afford seven."

"And the dwarves were drunk," said Cheryl.

"The dwarves were *always* drunk," Ron confirmed. "But my parents had a long marriage. I had good role models." (Rance and Jean were both prolific and respected character actors. He died in 2017 at the age of eighty-nine; she died in 2000 at age seventy-three.)

Cheryl's father, meanwhile, was cut from an entirely different cloth. An aerospace engineer, a math teacher at night, and a competitive aerobatic pilot toward the end of his life, he was also a mountain climber—the first Caucasian to ascend Mount Fuji in the winter and survive, Cheryl said. Her mother, who died at the age of sixty-nine, was from a German farm family in Wisconsin that was, in Cheryl's words, very traditional.

"I never saw my grandmother sit down," she noted. "She was serving the family, serving my grandfather. My mother left home when she was fourteen to work as a nanny."

Her parents divorced after thirteen years of marriage. "They both loved life and were curious about it," Cheryl observed, "but my dad was a very traditional man, and my mom needed someone who was much more nurturing of her creativity."

And so before she and Ron got married, Cheryl compiled a list of pros and cons. "Marriage is serious business," she explained. "I said no twice because I wanted to finish college."

"Tell me something from your con list," Marlo said.

"Well, one was that we had very different backgrounds," she said. "I actually didn't care for show business, and I knew I would have to be the one to adjust, since it was his passion. That's one of the big things about marriage—that you are willing to get out of your comfort level and help your partner."

"She was far more analytical about what marriage meant," Ron added. "I just knew I wanted to be married to her. I felt a tremendous level of comfort and respect and satisfaction from the relationship, and I really trusted that. 'My parents are married,' I said, 'and that seems to work. So let's get married.'"

MARLO: So you got married.

CHERYL: We got married. We were engaged for two months and married at the local church. We were that simple, and yep, in love for sure. It sounds a little saccharin, I know, but it's how it was—and is. Lucky me.

MARLO: Lucky him, too. Still, how did you know that you could trust a man who was in show business?

CHERYL: He's a special guy. And I fell for him despite the fact he was in a crazy business. And you know what? It wasn't hard to trust him. His dad was trustworthy. His brother. His mom—this is her ring I'm wearing. Oh, I'm crying again. It's the menopause.

PHIL: And you could trust her, too, Ron?

RON: Yes—and that says something because, as a child actor, you have trust issues growing up. You don't know who sincerely likes you for who you are. You tend to question who you can believe. I had a select group of friends, and I always felt this tremendous sense of trust with Cheryl. And I think one reason the relationship has lasted so long is that the trust that we have is something that we really value.

PHIL: Was having children a part of the equation?

RON: We didn't get married to have a family; we got married to be a couple. And I knew she was very ambitious. At that point psychology was her goal. I fully expected that to be her professional focus, and I wanted to support that as much as possible. But it shifted after we got married into other areas, including writing, and then eventually our own family.

CHERYL: One reason I started writing was to be with Ron. It's true that I was working toward a career in psychology. But if I had followed through, our family would have been separated for months every time Ron had a project. To be honest, I don't believe our relationship, or our family, would have had the same depth of affection that we have today. We all needed that time together.

MARLO: So you were on location with him all the time?

CHERYL: Yes. I even once cooked for his crew on location for eleven days.

MARLO: Really? What movie was that?

RON: *Grand Theft Auto.* It was my first directing job, and she came to the rescue. The crew was rebelling at the shitty food and she said, "I think I can do something about that."

CHERYL: By then they were all eating at McDonald's. It was a mutiny. So I said, "I'll come and cook. I can do better than McDonald's."

RON: And she did. One day the crew got leg of lamb for lunch.

PHIL: So, you became an active part of his professional world.

RON: She wasn't interested in it as a career, but she could do all these jobs.

CHERYL: I was the production bookkeeper, a boom girl, a script girl. I grew to love the people of show business through these productions.

MARLO: Money is often an issue for young couples, but you two had a cushion from Ron's acting career, right?

RON: Yeah. I did have some money.

CHERYL: He had $300,000. And what do we do? What did *I* do?

RON: She said—

CHERYL: —I said, "This is not my money. I had nothing to do with this."

MARLO: Really?

RON: Yes. She said, "If anything ever happens to us, that $300,000 is separate."

MARLO: And it wasn't like today's pre-nups—it was just your theory.

CHERYL: Right. I said, "Anything going from here on we split it in half—it's both of ours." But if Ron and I were, say, in a plane crash before we had children, I felt it was only right that the first $300,000 of our worth be given back to Ron's brother and his parents instead of being split between our families. It was a sum I felt I had no part in earning—typical alley pride. In those days, Ron and I were not even aware of pre-nups. Did they even exist?

MARLO: And Ron agreed to this?

CHERYL: I remember he was a little exasperated at the time with my insistence—we were pretty young and neither of us had ever dealt with lawyers—but I still believe it was the right thing to insist on. And I did say, "This is what I want," right?

RON: Yes. And I said, "Okay, fine."

PHIL: When Cheryl took up writing, what impact did that have on the marriage?

RON: I went out of my way to support her ambitions. She always supported me and my ambitions and dreams, and I wanted to support hers.

While it's tempting to define Cheryl and Ron as "soul mates," the term they choose to use is "being on the same page." And why not? They've worked hard at that.

"I'll tell you," Ron said, "our marriage counselors have really helped us at various times. Knowing that there are professionals out there who are good listeners and not necessarily referees can help you gain a perspective and, more important, reboot and recalibrate your communication with each other. Because, to me, that's where things begin to break down and ill feelings grow—when you're not willing to have the difficult conversations in a constructive way."

That observation jogged a memory for Marlo. "You know, going to a therapist is a very generous thing to do with each other," she said. "I was seeing a therapist in Los Angeles before we got married. Phil lived in Chicago. In the beginning, we were having difficulties, so my therapist said, 'Why don't you bring him in one day and we'll sit down together?' Now, keep in mind, Phil doesn't know this guy from Adam, and he immediately felt it was two against one—so that's not the greatest way to start. Well, Phil and I get into an argument in front of this therapist and Phil gets mad, leaves, and slams the door."

Ron and Cheryl turned to Phil.

"Guilty as charged," Phil murmured.

"So after he leaves," Marlo continued, "my therapist says to me, 'This guy is not for you.' Phil and I went home after that and made love, and that was the end of that. Years later we ran into that therapist and he said to me, "You guys kill me. You still love each other, but you don't resolve everything, do you?" I said, "We really don't." And, you know, you really *can't* resolve everything.

RON: It's foolish to think you're going to resolve everything. Yes, there are things that you have to get on the same page about, and it's important to understand what those things are—but then give yourselves the space to not sweat the other stuff so much. To me, the area where things begin to break down and ill feelings grow is when people aren't willing to have difficult conversations in a constructive way. Over the years, we've learned some tricks to fix that.

MARLO: Oh, good. Can you share a few?

RON: One of them is to record a conversation. Like, if you're having friction and it's getting a little nasty and tense, the advice we got was to stop talking about it then and schedule a time to continue the conversation. And then you record it. I remember once we were recording, and I honestly felt like I wasn't getting a word in edgewise and she was dominating everything. But when I heard the playback, I realized that it was about 50/50. So the great thing about recording these talks is that you're having a real conversation. It's not about hurting anybody's feelings—it's about actually talking things through and going on the record.

CHERYL: And it puts you both on notice.

RON: Also, you become just a little bit more polite on tape.

CHERYL: Right, for some reason your tone changes.

RON: You're not going to slam your fist down or do any of that destructive stuff that really prevents problem-solving. After a while, you begin to realize, wow, you can actually solve your differences and figure them out. You can have an impasse, but you begin to trust that you can figure things out and there's going to be give-and-take.

PHIL: This is great. Give us another trick.

CHERYL: Fewer words.

PHIL: What does that mean?

RON: Try to distill your feelings down to fairly simple ideas. Don't go on and on and on.

MARLO: Oh, I know that one—because, sometimes, somebody among us likes to go into lecture mode.

CHERYL: Yes. Someone here, too.

MARLO: But when Phil lectures, he starts way back at the beginning of mankind.

CHERYL: We can relate to this. So what you do is designate two minutes for each person. Also, it's important not to have these conversations when you're at your hottest. We'll say, "Okay, let's table this for four days," and then we'll go our separate ways and write our notes about what we're feeling, so that we'll remember what the issue was—and it's usually an issue that we have faced time and time again.

RON: That's a good point because, usually, if I'm mad on Tuesday, I don't even remember what was bothering me by Sunday. But the bottom line is: you're talking. For a long time I was really terrified of deep disagreement. I felt like if she knew that I was really upset it might lead to some sort of schism that would have a detrimental, maybe even lethal, effect. I built this thing up in my mind that you couldn't argue—you wouldn't *dare* argue.

CHERYL: Or disagree even.

RON: Or even express disagreement. But after about twenty years—pretty deep into our relationship—I realized, "Okay, I can really say this upsets me and it doesn't mean we're going to kill the marriage. It just means we've got something to work on."

"This may sound like ten-cent psychology," Marlo said, "but I know from watching Rusty Hamer and the other child actors on my dad's show [*Make Room for Daddy*] that they had to be responsible in such an adult way. They were certainly more mature than I was at that age. They had to show up, know their lines, and be ready to perform in front of an audience. They had these big responsibilities and they were only six years old. How old were you when you started, Ron?"

"I was five."

"There you go," Marlo said. "You were raised to be a good boy and not talk about what upset you."

PHIL: You're both natural redheads, and redheads are notorious for their tempers. Do either of you live up to that stereotype?

RON: Well, we both do, but Cheryl definitely has a sharper temper. I'm more of a slow-burn type—a very slow, slow burn—but I feel things deeply and have a lot of opinions.

CHERYL: We're not yellers. If he ever yells at me or I yell at him, we're a mess. We're wimps that way. But with redheads it's not just temper. It's also emotional—it can be charismatic, it can be fun, but it can also be high-strung and neurotic and, "Oh my gosh, someone lock them up!"

PHIL: And so when you get into a red-headed standoff, how do you resolve it?

CHERYL: We agree to disagree, which is probably something we'll grapple with until we die. But face it, sometimes you just don't agree on something, and it's better to move on and not hold it against the other. And even if you do make a decision, it's not always a compromise that everybody is happy with. It's not always 50/50.

RON: Right. Sometimes you have to say, "Okay, I'm going to give you a 60/40 or even a 90/10, but if you're on the 10 side of it, you need to say—"

CHERYL: "—I'm giving you 90 this time—"

RON: "—but I just want you to know this is a big one."

PHIL: Boy, you two have this down to a science.

CHERYL: Well, it's a system we're pretty good at. I mean, the whole reason we moved to Connecticut was because Ron gave a 90/10. We're here, right?

MARLO: So you were the one pressing to move to Connecticut, Cheryl? Why did you want to leave L.A.?

CHERYL: I felt it was very difficult for me to parent there. People were giving my five-year-old daughter scripts.

RON: We could see that was having an impact on the kids and our friends' kids.

CHERYL: If a film Ron made did great, he was king. If he didn't do so well, he was a goat. Is that a healthy perspective?

RON: And we didn't want our children to feel that they were inoculated into the business, so we moved to a place where show business was not king.

CHERYL: Our deal was: if he had four bombs in a row, then we had to go back to L.A.

RON: And so far we're still here.

Our conversation with these two showed no signs of flagging—this is a couple who really enjoys talking about marriage, and we were enjoying talking about it with them—but it drew to an obvious close in the sweetest of ways: with the sounds of giggling, as grandchildren began streaming into the house.

As Ron and Cheryl escorted us to the door, the warm breeze of family swept into the old sea captain's house.

"Before we leave," Phil said, "one last question: What would you tell a young couple today who are considering taking the plunge?"

As always, Cheryl was quick on the draw.

"Work at it. Give it your best effort. Take chances," she said. "And don't hide in technology. I know, interacting can sometimes be uncomfortable, but as you push through that and truly get to know each other, you can build a history together—and that history is so wonderful."

Ron picked up on his wife's thought. "You get into a relationship because you believe in the idea of it. You want to have a family. It's fulfilling and rewarding. If you open yourself up not to what you can get out of the relationship, but to what *both of you* can get out of the life you're going to build, then things get exciting, because it's exponential. Support and trust, give-and-take—all of that creates a history."

As Ron spoke, Cheryl appeared moved. "It's about making each other feel safe," she said. "I know, I probably stuck my foot in my mouth about ten times today. But he'll never know... I mean, he doesn't even... I mean, how great is that? It's the best."

And then the tears came again. But this time it wasn't the menopause. It was just good old-fashioned appreciation for all that they have.

Judy Woodruff
and Al Hunt

MARRIED IN 1980

*"You fall in love and it's the magic of all that.
But when the rough times come, it's
the deeper values that count—like honesty,
integrity, and respect. And, yes, love."*

Couples have no idea what fate has in store for them when they stand at the altar and make that age-old promise to stay together "till death do us part." It's a blank check written in blind faith. But it's also a vital assurance that each will be the most dependable partner they will ever have in the most important relationship of their lives.

Judy Woodruff and Al Hunt could never have imagined the gale-force headwinds life would deliver on them. Many marriages would have buckled under the weight of such challenges, but in the end, the trials they encountered and the heartbreak they endured only made their partnership stronger, even as they frequently doubted their own inner strength.

And somehow, this couple lived their personal crisis privately, despite having the most public of jobs.

Judy, of course, is the longtime TV anchorwoman and political correspondent for, first, NBC News in 1976; then PBS in 1983 on the popular

The MacNeil/Lehrer NewsHour; then CNN in 1993, as host of various news shows. In 2006, she returned to PBS, where she would share the anchor desk of the famously sensible *PBS NewsHour* with broadcast veteran Gwen Ifill. Upon Ifill's death in 2016, Judy assumed the post of sole anchor.

Al is a longtime print journalist, joining *The Wall Street Journal's* Washington bureau in 1969 to cover Congress and national politics—as a reporter, columnist, and bureau chief—for thirty-five years before joining the upstart *Bloomberg News* in 2005. Along the way he's been a regular on daytime, nighttime, and Sunday political talks show and still finds time to teach a course about political journalism at the Annenberg School for Communications at the University of Pennsylvania.

Both husband and wife are household names in households that take news and opinion seriously.

When we walked into their stylish condo in the leafy neighborhood of Cleveland Park, about five miles from most of "official Washington," Judy wasn't yet home from her 7 p.m. *NewsHour* broadcast. But Al was there with a warm smile and a cold glass of wine, the latter much appreciated on a typically muggy Washington evening. Marlo noted right away that Al and Phil have something in common besides an undying love of the news: they've both managed to hang on to enviable heads of healthy, white hair.

The condo is their downsized home not far from the big family house where they raised their three children—Jeffrey, Benjamin, and Lauren. They'd moved here just three-and-a-half years earlier; and as with most empty nesters, it wasn't easy at first for them to pull up roots and relocate.

But now they're thrilled they did—and who wouldn't be? It's a gorgeous space with wraparound windows that look out onto the lush green trees and legendary white buildings of D.C., the National Cathedral standing tallest among them. But not too tall: there is a rule in the nation's capital that no building can rise higher than the Washington Monument (which, if you look real hard, you can see from Judy and Al's living room).

Washington, D.C.; April 5, 1980

We settled into their easy club chairs in the living room and talked about—what else?—the news. Somewhere between immigration and the trade deficit, Judy arrived, appearing far too calm for someone who'd just come from a long and stressful TV day. She carried packages of groceries, which she took into the kitchen, then seasoned, chopped, and warmed, and set out on the large dining room table, all the while asking us if we needed anything. Just your everyday superwoman.

Politics has practically defined Judy and Al's life; indeed, they met while covering a presidential campaign. Twice.

The year was 1976, and Jimmy Carter had a lock on the Democratic nomination. Both Al and Judy were in Steubenville, Ohio, covering Carter's campaign. Judy was twenty-nine years old and an NBC reporter based in Atlanta; Al, four years her senior and divorced, was on the beat for *The Wall Street Journal*. In between events, Al was on a pay phone speaking with his editor in New York.

"We were arguing over when my next story should run," he recalled for us, "and in those days pay phones were rectangular booths with partitions between them, so you couldn't really see the top part of the person on the phone next to you. But you could see the lower half. I noticed a press pass dangling down, and then I saw the legs. And I just kept staring..."

"The legs you could see," Phil checked.

"The legs I could see," Al confirmed. "She's still got them. So I kept staring at these legs, and finally I said to my editor, 'Hey, Ed, whenever the story runs is fine,' and then I hung up fast because the legs had left and gone the other way. I dashed onto the press bus and I saw Sam Donaldson, who was covering Carter for ABC—this is a story you can't really tell in 2019—and I said to Sam, 'Who was that blonde with the great legs?' Sam said to me, 'That's Judy Woodruff, an NBC reporter in Atlanta.' So I sort of had a crush on her."

A few weeks later, the two crossed paths again, this time in Carter's hometown of Plains, Georgia. In keeping with the candidate's homespun spirit, the brain trust at the Carter camp decided to arrange a softball game between campaign staffers and the press corps on a scorching local ball field. Al and Judy were both in the lineup.

"The press thought this was a great idea because we'd have more access to the candidate and his staff," Judy told us. "Of course, what we didn't know is that the Carter team had Secret Service agents playing as ringers—you know, these bulked-up guys who were all in great shape—making up two-thirds of their team. Meanwhile, our side was shriveled, staying up late, drinking too much, hung over."

The press corps lost the game, of course, but Al scored a personal victory, formally meeting the blonde with the great legs who had eluded him in Ohio.

"I had secretly been smitten since Steubenville," he said, "so I came up and introduced myself. She didn't seem terribly impressed, but I sure was."

The couple would not reconnect until March of the following year. By then, Carter was president and Judy had made a significant career leap. Having proved herself both resourceful and ambitious during the campaign—and after breaking a few stories during the transition—she convinced the higher-ups at NBC to transfer her to the nation's capital.

"I thought I had died and gone to heaven," she told us, adding that she lived at the famed Watergate Hotel for a few months before getting her own apartment in Washington's Georgetown neighborhood. One night, Judy was having dinner at Clyde's with colleague Bob Jamieson, who was also covering the White House for NBC, when guess who sat down just two tables away from Judy.

"I was with Edie Wilkie," Al recalled, "who was married to Don Edwards, a congressman from California. She was a friend, and for months I'd been telling her I had this incredible crush on Judy Woodruff. She would always say, 'Why don't you ask her out?' and I would answer, 'I don't know if she's with someone,' or 'She just got here from Atlanta.' I guess I kept making excuses. Now we were suddenly sitting two tables way from her. Edie said, 'Go, go talk to her!' So I went up to Judy and said, 'Hi, how are you?' She said, 'Well, I'm fine, but I'm a little lonely up here.'"

"I said *homesick*. I didn't say *lonely*," Judy corrected.

"Homesick, yes," Al said. "So I came back to my table and told Edie what Judy said, and she commented, 'That was your cue.' And I'm like, 'Oh, I don't know.'"

The next morning, Al found a message on his desk that read, "Call Judy Woodruff."

"I thought to myself, *You old devil, you. You must have made an impression!*" Al said. "So I called her."

Only thing is, Judy had *not* called Al—it was Edie who'd left the message, forcing Al to place the unsolicited returned call. Even though the ploy worked, Al noted, "Judy was not smitten with me at all—at least not at first."

"I had recently broken up with somebody," Judy explained, "so I was not anxious to get back into a relationship. But I thought he was pretty cool. So we started dating, and then we broke up for a while, and then we got back together again."

MARLO: Breaking up is often helpful. Phil and I broke up once, too, before we got married, and it gave us time to get our heads together. Had you broken up because you were traveling a lot?
JUDY: I just thought we were getting too serious.
AL: I was devastated.
JUDY: It was only a two-week breakup.
AL: Right, only two weeks. I finally called her and said, "I've got a house on the Cape. Why don't you come up for a week?" And she agreed.
MARLO: Boy, that was some breakup. Two weeks.
AL: Yes.

This time things seemed to stick. Judy bought a house in Cleveland Park, and Al moved in at the end of 1977. They got engaged in November of 1979 and married in April of 1980. Newspeople to the core, they coordinated the date of their nuptials with the political calendar, as they were both covering the 1980 presidential campaign.

"We got married on April 5," Al said, "because it was equidistant between the New York and Pennsylvania primaries."

"It was the right equidistance," Judy added, "because you live and die by the primaries in presidential cycles."

Given the couple's passion for their profession—not to mention both of their high profiles—we wondered whether, in those early days, they ever felt competitive with each other for a scoop. Al insisted that he'd never considered Judy a rival. She agreed—with one exception: when they were covering Ronald Reagan in Santa Barbara.

JUDY: I remember once trying to get an interview with Reagan's budget director, David Stockman, and one day he called the house. I picked up the phone, and when he identified himself, I said, "Oh, Director Stockman, I've really been wanting to talk to you." He said, "Well, I'm actually calling for Al." Turns out Al was doing a series of off-the-record conversations.

AL: Background, to run later.

JUDY: Right, background. So I had to actually leave the room while Al was talking to him.

PHIL: That's a little awkward. Were you upset about that?

JUDY: Yes. I was not happy because he didn't want to talk to me on the record. He said, "I just don't have anything to say." He was ready to talk, but only on background.

MARLO: And did you bring this up to Al?

JUDY: Yes. I told him at the time I was not happy.

AL: You did, you did.

JUDY: But that was unusual. That stands out. Usually we were able to work around things like that. He's been very supportive of my work.

MARLO: Give us an example.

AL: All right, this is a story. She decided to leave NBC to go work for *The MacNeil/Lehrer NewsHour*, which was launching in the fall. NBC offered her a very lucrative contract to stay, but she was more interested in the challenge of *MacNeil/Lehrer*. Well, NBC did not like the idea of someone leaving, so they planted a story with Liz Smith at the *New York Daily News* saying that NBC had pushed Judy Woodruff out the door. Somebody told us about that, and the editor of the *Daily News*, Jim Wieghart, was an old friend of mine. I'd never done this before in my life, but I called Jim and I said, "That goddamned thing is wrong. It's just dead wrong. I could even send you a contract if you wanted to see that, Jim." And he said, "No, I don't want to see it, but I'll kill the item." I mean, that was pretty pushy.

MARLO: I think it was great you did that. It was professionally fair and maritally loyal!

AL: Yes, but it also was pretty pushy. I didn't think to ask her permission. I just went ahead and did it.

JUDY: I probably would have said, "Don't do it." I was young and naïve at that point.

AL: Yes, you were in your thirties. But it was just wrong.

JUDY: Anyway, that's what I meant. He's always been a big advocate, and I know he's got my back, always.

Their mutual support of one another, both personally and professionally, is something they came to themselves, given that neither Al's nor Judy's parents' unions were ideal models of a balanced marriage. Both say they had fathers who were inarguably alpha, resulting in family dynamics that were less than positive.

"My mother stayed at home and my father was a pediatrician," Al explained. "He was very loving but dominant. I remember once when I was fifteen, I came downstairs and told my dad that I was sick, and he said, 'You can stay home if you cut the grass.' Most kids of pediatricians will identify with that."

Judy's father likewise called the shots in her family. "He was in the Army for twenty-five years and he was domineering," she said. "My mother was so dependent on him she didn't even drive a car. It was a challenging marriage—there was a lot of tension in it."

"Her mother was a saint and her father was not," Al chimed in.

The couple's first child, Jeffrey, arrived in 1981, a year after the wedding. Although two more kids joined the brood—Ben came along five years later; and in 1989, Judy and Al adopted Lauren from South Korea, when she was just four months old—it was that first birth that would ultimately lead to "the hardest thing in our whole marriage."

Jeffrey was born with spina bifida, a birth defect in which the spinal cord does not form properly. The condition ranges from severe to mild; and while Jeffrey's was diagnosed as mild, it required surgery when he was just ten months old—the insertion of a shunt to drain the buildup of spinal fluid—to assure that he would be able to lead a productive life, which he did. He had some learning challenges through his teen years, but he was a good student, as well as an avid skier, biker, and swimmer.

Then in 1998, when Jeffrey was sixteen—after attending two of Washington's top private prep schools and getting ready to go to college—a second surgery was required to replace the shunt. Although the procedure was relatively routine, the first effort didn't work. The second attempt was tragic.

"The surgeon botched it," Al said flatly. "He came up with a different way to do it, and he screwed it. He went down the wrong channel."

In a single moment, a dark thundercloud broke open over the family—for Judy, for Al, and for their kids, especially for Jeffrey. Instead of going to summer camp or working part time in medical research, as he'd been doing, Jeffrey lay in a coma for six weeks, only to awaken with a host of disabilities. He was transferred to the prestigious Kennedy Krieger Institute, which was affiliated with the Johns Hopkins University School of Medicine in Baltimore, where he was operated on by a pediatric neurosurgeon named Ben Carson.

"This is the same Ben Carson who eventually became secretary of Housing and Urban Development?" Phil asked.

"Yes," Al said. "He was a great surgeon. We'd been sent to Carson by Guy McKhann, a Hopkins legend who founded the department of neurology. Guy became practically a rabbi for us over there, medically and personally—what a gift. One night at dinner, he told us that for most couples who go through this, the marriage doesn't survive because it adds such incredible tension to whatever else you might be going through. And it really did. We lived over at the hospital for four or five months—we took turns. We both kept working, so I'd go on Tuesday and Judy would come Wednesday, and so on. Meanwhile, we were both worried about the kids at home. It was an incredibly tough time."

Indeed, concern about the well-being of the other two children amplified the couple's stress. Ben was eleven and Lauren was nine when their older brother was in the hospital. "We tried not to bother them with our worry about Jeffrey and just charged ahead," Judy remembered. "That's a challenge for any family with one child who has an issue, because you pour so much of your attention into that child. I was conscious of not paying enough attention to them; and in retrospect, twenty-one years later, I don't think we grieved enough, which is really important."

"What do you mean by 'grieved enough?'" Phil asked.

"We didn't take the time to say, 'Oh, my God, this is really, really hard.' We were determined to get through it—pushing ahead with all the best intentions—but you also have to process the grief. This is something we have realized only in the past few years."

"But you couldn't fall apart," Phil said. "You had so many people depending on you, at home and at work."

"I know, I know," Judy remembered. "We had careers and we had kids; and when I was at work, I thought I needed to be with them."

As we listened to these two recount the most turbulent moments of their marriage, it was clear why both are stellar journalists. They were not by any means dispassionate as they told their story—indeed, both of their faces were pained as they recalled that point in their lives—but they did not skimp on the details, and, more touching, they did not avoid discussing the mistakes they believe they might have made.

MARLO: Did you go to therapy at the time to get some help with this?

AL: We didn't.

JUDY: We didn't. We just plowed through. We have been through therapy since, candidly. I mean, we had to. Our whole family has been in therapy.

AL: But it definitely affected the children.

JUDY: Especially his younger brother, Benjamin.

PHIL: In what way?

AL: He had a very delayed reaction. At the time, the doctors over at Hopkins gave us a piece written decades earlier by [renowned psychiatrist] David Hamburg on the effect that severely injured kids have on siblings. We read it and concluded that Benjamin showed no signs of being affected at all. But it turns out his reaction was delayed.

PHIL: Why?

JUDY: Because he was emulating us, copying the way we weren't breaking down. He was eleven. And he was also trying to fill the shoes of his older brother who had health challenges.

MARLO: That's heartbreaking. How about you two as a couple? Were you able to carve out time for yourselves to do any normal couple things, like going out to dinner, going to the movies, or something that would release the anxiety?

AL: We probably didn't do enough things by ourselves.

JUDY: But we did do a lot of things as a family, because we were so conscious of keeping all five of us together. So, yeah, the couple part of us probably suffered for a long time. We felt guilty about leaving the children.

MARLO: Still, you survived as a couple. That says something about the two of you and your marriage.

AL: I don't ever want to say it strengthened our marriage, because it just bothers me to say that, but, yes, we got through it. We enabled Jeffrey to have a life. It's not as good a life as we hoped it would be when he was growing up. But it's a lot better than anyone thought it would be twenty years ago.

As a result of the bungled operation, Jeffrey is in a wheelchair and suffers from impaired speech, loss of short-term memory, loss of the use of one arm, and vision issues, with one eye permanently closed. At one point in those early days, Judy considered leaving her job at CNN in order to care for her boy. She ended up taking six weeks off, returning only on a part-time basis.

"I was just ripped apart inside over what had happened to him," she said. "It was so unspeakable that I thought, *Maybe I should just stop. I can't do my job and this. I should just stop and be there for him.* Guy McKhann told me not do that. He said, 'There's only so much you can do.'"

McKhann had given Judy and Al exactly the right counsel, they told us.

"It was a hard thing to hear," Judy remembered, "but he was advising us to leave things up to the specialists—the physical and occupational therapists, the speech and recreational therapists, the MDs, the doctors and the nurses. 'They'll get him through this,' he told us, 'but you need to keep doing what you're doing because you have a long life ahead of you, and so does he.' And it was very good advice because I was just—I mean, I was devastated. *We* were devastated."

"He was a good doctor," Marlo observed. "He was taking care of Jeffrey and you, too."

"Oh, he's a great doctor," Al agreed. "I still talk to him. He's eighty-seven years old and he remains important in our lives. He was important for Jeffrey and important for us."

"One of the things I've learned at St. Jude," Marlo added, "is that the medical teams treat the whole family. They're treating the sick child, of course, but also the child's parents, siblings, everybody, in order to keep the family whole."

Judy and Al never blamed each other for what happened to Jeffrey, as some couples might do, but when any recriminations began to set in, they were more likely to be hard on themselves—particularly Judy.

"I blame myself more than anything else," Judy reflected. "I had asked the surgeon a lot of questions about this procedure beforehand. I'd taken notes. We'd called other doctors. I got the names of people from the Spina Bifida Association and asked them to check out the procedure. But afterwards, I kept thinking, *Why didn't I do more due diligence?*"

Still, this is a couple who knows how to do their research and get the things they need—the very tools of journalism—and as a result, they were able to rechannel any negative energy they might have been feeling into pursuing the best possible care for their eldest child.

"We're both type-A personalities, and we both have lots of drive," said Judy, "so we decided that the only alternative for us was to create as positive and uplifting an environment as we could—meaning, we were going to find the best caregivers for Jeffrey, the best programs, the best treatment, the best speech therapist, the best physical therapist. We put a lot of energy into that for a long time. Jeffrey took a year off after the injury, but then he went back to high school and he finished."

At first, Jeffrey went on to Montgomery Community College, near home, for four years. Then when his younger brother applied to colleges out of state, Jeffrey announced to his parents that he wanted to go away to college, too.

"We said, 'By golly, we're going to find you one!'" Judy recalled. "We looked all over the country. There were very few schools that could take somebody with that level of physical disability, but we found one in North Carolina—St. Andrews Presbyterian School in Laurinburg, North Carolina. We got him in, and he went there for almost five years."

At the time of our visit with Judy and Al, Jeffrey was thirty-seven and, at his insistence, living on his own in an assisted-living program in Westminster, Maryland, close enough for frequent visits home and to the family's weekend house on the Chesapeake Bay. "He told us, 'I don't want to live at home,'" Al said.

"If he said tomorrow, 'I want to live at home,'" Judy explained, "we would say definitely, and we would figure it out. Of course, we would have to hire someone..."

"And that would weigh on his siblings," Al added, "because ultimately, they would have responsibility. But Jeffrey doesn't want to do that. He wants to be independent."

Judy leaned forward. "We spent thousands and thousands of hours, literally, to give Jeffrey a better life," she said. "I think we succeeded to the surprise of some experts. He graduated from college in 2010, he's working part time, he's living in a good place, and he brings much joy to our family. But we still worry that we robbed Benjamin and Lauren of some of those hours."

The moon over Washington was now visible from Judy and Al's living room, signaling to us that it was time to wrap up. This had been one of the longest conversations we'd conducted for this book, and certainly one of the most powerful. Yet it was also profoundly hopeful. What this couple—this family—had endured for more than two decades was enough to shatter any marriage, but neither Judy nor Al permitted that to happen. Theirs was a battle they'd vowed to wage together from the first day they became husband and wife, and that is precisely what they did.

"We haven't brought up the subject of love tonight," Marlo said, "but it sure is all around—in your love for Jeffrey and your other children, and obviously in your love for each other."

Al smiled wistfully. "I not only loved Judy through this," he began, "but I so respected and admired how she was doing everything—as a mother, as a professional, as a wife—and it was just extraordinary. When you stop and think of this terrible hand we'd been dealt, you want to get bitter and angry about it. But what she could do with Jeffrey was remarkable. I would watch her when she came home after a hard day of work and, I mean, I think I'm pretty good with him, but she was really unbelievable."

Al took a thoughtful pause and leaned forward. "When you first get married, you're young and in love and everything seems great," he said. "But marriage is harder than you think. So when you go through those rough times—and we've had some really rough times—you couldn't get through it without someone you love."

Judy smiled. "Yes, that's right," she said. "You fall in love and it's the magic of all that. But when the rough times come, it's the deeper values that count—the eternal values, like honesty, integrity, and respect. And, yes, love."

On our cab ride back to our hotel, we caught a glimpse of the city's proudest monument, illuminated against the dark sky. It was the man for whom that monument—and this city—was named, who famously inspired his troops at Valley Forge by reading aloud the words of patriot Thomas Paine: "The harder the conflict, the more glorious the triumph."

In all that they've built and all that they've shared, the marriage of Judy Woodruff and Al Hunt is triumphant.

Bob Woodward
and Elsa Walsh

MARRIED IN 1989

"I was in the chain of command at the Post, *and we both knew that was risky. But it was worth the risk— and it really helped to be head over heels in love."*

T
he first time Elsa Walsh knew how *The Washington Post* investigative reporter Bob Woodward felt about her was when he told her who Deep Throat was. No one on the planet—other than Woodward's fellow reporter Carl Bernstein and their legendary editor Ben Bradlee—knew for sure the identity of the informant who exposed President Richard Nixon in the explosive Watergate scandal that eventually brought an end to his administration.

Walsh kept the secret for twenty-four years, until Mark Felt, the former number two man at the FBI, revealed in 2005 that he had been the mole.

But the point is, Bob had told her.

Now *that's* love.

MARLO: That's such a huge thing. The whole world wanted to know who Deep Throat was. I'm surprised you even had the guts to ask him about it.

Georgetown, Washington, D.C.; November 25, 1989

ELSA: We were just talking about it this weekend. I said to him, "Why did you tell me? I'm sure I wasn't the first person to ask."

PHIL: And the answer was...

BOB: Because look at her. Be around her. You know it when you see it.

ELSA: So that was the first time I knew. The second time was when he got me a dog. He knew I loved dogs, and he wasn't a big pet person. But he and his daughter Tali went to a pet store one weekend and came back and said, "Now close your eyes, we have a surprise for you." And they brought in this little Lhasa Apso. And I thought—

MARLO: —he really likes me.

ELSA: He really likes me.

Some call Bob Woodward a living legend, others call him the most feared man in Washington. Phil calls him King Kong. But whatever the moniker, we had not come to the nation's capital to talk with one man about an eighteen-and-a-half-minute gap in an old White House tape. We were there to sit down with a smart and thoughtful couple to discuss their thirty-year marriage.

Elsa and Bob live in an elegant Colonial house in the city's storied Georgetown neighborhood. Bob bought it in 1976; Elsa moved in bit by bit, and then for good in 1982. We were greeted at the door by Bob, with the couple's miniature poodle, Maggie, bouncing happily behind him. His warm hug hello was not so much Kong as it was gentle bear. Elsa soon appeared, lovely, light, and full of grace, and showed us into the dining room, where Marlo set up our mics. Elsa prepared a tray of light snacks (we were all heading to dinner afterwards), while Phil and Bob had already begun dissecting the world's problems, one by one.

As if it needed retelling, Bob's rise to fame is a classic story of grit and chance. He began his career as a journalist in 1970 at a small weekly news-paper, the *Montgomery Sentinel*, in suburban Washington before being hired as a police reporter by *The Washington Post* in 1971. The following year, he was handed a ho-hum courtroom assignment to cover a break-in at the Democratic National Committee headquarters in the Watergate office complex. The story had legs, and the ensuing investigative sleuthing by Bob and his colleague Carl Bernstein ultimately launched them into the stratosphere of journalism. Their backbreaking reporting not only served to unseat an American president but also helped earn *The Washington Post* the 1973 Pulitzer Prize for Public Service, inspiring future generations of journalists to devote their careers to unmasking corruption.

Bob's meticulous work led to another Pulitzer in 2002, for the paper's coverage of the 9/11 attacks. At the time of our interview, he'd written eighteen books—all bestsellers—about politics, presidents, the Supreme Court, national intelligence, and the life and death of John Belushi.

Elsa is also a journalist—most recently as a staff writer for *The New Yorker*—and an author. Her 1995 book, *Divided Lives: The Public and Private Struggles of Three American Women*, explored the careers of three women who seemed to have it all, and how they struggled to keep it: television journalist Meredith Vieira; first lady of West Virginia Rachael Worby; and Dr. Alison Estabrook, chief of breast surgery at Mount Sinai–Roosevelt Hospital in New York City.

Elsa and Bob met the way millions of couples meet every year: at the office. It was 1980, and Elsa was a rookie reporter at *The Washington Post*, having recently arrived from San Francisco, where she was an intern at *Newsweek*. Sally Quinn, a feature writer at the *Post* and the wife of executive editor Ben Bradlee, brought Elsa into the newsroom to meet the editors, one of whom was the taller half of the famed Woodward and Bernstein.

Elsa was twenty-two years old; Bob was thirty-seven. The age difference did not escape them.

"I mean, now, I would be arrested," Bob reflected.

"Our daughter says, 'Oh, Dad, you're like Hugh Hefner,'" Elsa added with a laugh.

"But you were smitten right away," Marlo said.

"Smitten is an understatement," Bob replied. "But it helped our relationship that there was risk in it—it made it more valuable. I was in the chain of command at the *Post*, she was working there, and we both knew that having a secret dating-love affair was risky. But it was worth the risk—and it really helped to be head over heels in love, physically and emotionally."

Their mutual attraction was undeniable, but given the work environment, they knew they had to keep things under cover. Not an easy task in a newsroom staffed by some of the best investigative reporters in the country. Elsa, for one, did not like the secrecy that was required early in their relationship, but she understood it. Although neither of them was married and Elsa wasn't technically working for Bob, he was in the paper's hierarchy, and journalism being a fairly dishy biz, "it was like a hotbed of gossip all the time," she said.

Even if the couple were found out, the fallout wouldn't have been anywhere close to the scandal that had erupted a decade earlier, when *Post* poobah Ben Bradlee—who was married—carried on a secret office affair with the much younger and single newsroom novice Sally Quinn. Tongues wagged all over Washington, and Bradlee ultimately divorced his wife and wed his paramour.

In a way, Bob noted with a smile, "they paved the way for us."

True journalist that he is, Bob is more accustomed to asking questions than answering them, and during our conversation it was clear that he'd prepared his own checklist of topics to discuss. In the middle of talking about how he and Elsa met, he interrupted himself.

"If I may skip ahead—way ahead," he said. "We've both thought about your question 'What makes a marriage work?' And something that works in our marriage is what I would call 'accelerated awakening.'"

"Awakening?" Phil asked.

"Awakening about who she is," Bob said. "We were in the car yesterday, coming back from our house on the river in Maryland, and a very, very close friend of Elsa's—who was going through a lot of stress—called on the phone. So I listened—I had no alternative for about forty minutes— and this was the accelerated awakening: Elsa has the power of empathy, of listening. The power of questioning. It's like when I come back from an interview. She'll say to me, 'What did he say? What happened? What does it mean?' It's like a mini-interrogation."

"And how do you respond when she does that?" Phil asked.

"I sometimes bristle at it," Bob said, "but I've come to realize that it helps me understand what I'm working on and what's going on. So when I listened to this conversation yesterday, it was like, *aha*, this is what happens between the two of us most days we're together. It's like Elsa is a therapist—a therapist who doesn't have a license but practices anyway."

"And he's my primary patient," Elsa concurred.

"And I'm the primary patient," Bob said. "So I just listened to Elsa respond to one of the most stressful matters in this person's life, and she was like, 'Okay, I'm here to listen.'"

"So what's the 'accelerated' part mean?" Marlo asked.

"Because this grows over time," Bob said. "It's the affection. It's the concern. It's the questions. 'What did she say next?' 'What happened?' It's totally like a therapist would do, or your best friend. And I think this is what happens in any marriage. You know its value, but you don't think about it every minute. So in this short period of time, I realized, *What a gift.*"

What Bob was describing is that delicious moment of discovery when we have a new appreciation for who our spouse is and what that person brings to the relationship.

That Elsa and Bob have made their marriage work is actually surprising, given that neither of their own parents' marriages were easy models. Elsa was born to a large Irish family—she has a brother and four sisters—and both of her parents were immigrants. Her mom and dad remained married for more than half a century—"fifty or sixty years," Elsa said—but despite that longevity, Elsa noted, there was a certain imbalance.

"My mom was an extraordinarily resilient person," Elsa said, "and my father was not. He was bipolar and handsome, and my mom was always this safe harbor of love and acceptance for him. They had a lot of fun, but he could be difficult. So when I think about what I learned from my mother about marriage, it's that once you're in it, you stay in it, and there's no looking back."

For a while, Elsa never wanted to get married. She came of age in the late 1960s and early 1970s, at the dawn of a new era of feminist empowerment.

"You always like to think of yourself as being sort of an independent operator," Elsa mused, "but when I look back on it, all of the great icons at that time—Gloria Steinem and *That Girl*—weren't getting married. These women were being strong and fun and adventurous. And so, as much as I would like to say that my not wanting to get married had something to do with my own originality, I don't think it did. In retrospect, it was that I wanted to be part of that movement."

While Elsa's earliest model of marriage was imperfect, Bob's was flat-out heartbreaking.

BOB: My family was not stable at all. My parents were divorced when I was quite young—about twelve or thirteen—and I don't know... should I tell the story of my father coming to me?

ELSA: You can, yeah.

BOB: My mother had been in the hospital—she'd had a nervous break-down. They did not have a marriage that was working, obviously. So my father came to tell me that my mother was out of the hospital and was marrying Tom Barnes, who was his best friend. My parents had gotten divorced in the process, and my mother and Tom had moved to Arlington Heights, which was twenty miles away. I'll never forget thinking to myself, *Ah, you're in this alone in your life. You can have a mother and a father and a friend, but you're in it alone.*

MARLO: Because your family had fractured?

BOB: Yeah. And the surprise of it all.

ELSA: That his mother didn't tell him herself.

BOB: You're twelve years old and you think your mom is going to love you enough to not leave the marriage and marry somebody else, let alone your father's best friend. It was so painful, but also kind of, "Ah, okay, I'm in this alone and I've got to figure it out."

PHIL: That's rough.

BOB: Yeah, it was. And then after college, I was in the navy because I had signed up for naval ROTC. I had married a woman who was my high school sweetheart, as they say. She was an academic—a very smart and lovely person—and when I was off in the navy, our marriage just fell apart. So this was kind of a second act of, *Oh, okay, you're in this alone.* And then after Nixon resigned, I was in a romance and got married a second time, and we had Tali, who is now forty-three or forty-four.

ELSA: Forty-two.

BOB: That didn't last, and she left with Tali. So that was the third act of, *Oh, okay, you're in this alone.* So, when my mother died and I wanted to get married, I was embarrassed to propose to you because I felt I had these two earlier failed marriages, and you were wonderful.

MARLO: You got past the embarrassment.

BOB: We were married about six months later.

ELSA: We were already living like we were married anyway. We had dated for two years and lived together for seven years.

BOB: And after all those years of living together, one day she said to me, "I'm wasting all that money on an apartment I never live in. I'm getting rid of it and here are my clothes." And I thought, *Wow, that's great,* because there's nothing stronger than having someone say, "I have been living with you but I'm moving in."

PHIL: So, Elsa, when Bob asked you to marry him, was it unexpected?

ELSA: It was unexpected. We were out at our house in Maryland, sitting in the little sunroom and talking about his mom, who had died, and he said, "Nothing would make me happier than if you would marry me." And instead of feeling shocked, I was so excited, I couldn't believe it. I had never felt such a great sense of pure pleasure as I did that day. And ever since then, I have loved being married to Bob. I love the idea of saying to each other, and to other people, that we're in this together.

BOB: And that's what's so interesting. Here we are with totally different backgrounds, and she's also feeling, "Ah, I'm not in this alone."

ELSA: No, I'm not. I don't want to be in it alone. I don't want to.

BOB: And that realization is liberating and empowering, because until that moment, the stakes were, People are going to desert you.

MARLO: But you somehow knew that she wasn't going to be one of those people. What an interesting man you've become. After all those years of people deserting you, making you feel alone, you somehow knew that Elsa wouldn't do that.

BOB: Right. Because she said so, and she acted so. We were talking recently about how you know when people are going to fail you, or you are going to fail yourself, and I mentioned the book *Lord Jim,* and the part when the steamer hits rough seas and Jim jumps into a lifeboat along with the captain and abandons the passengers. And remember what you said?

ELSA: Yes. I said, "I don't jump."

Elsa and Bob married in a private ceremony on November 25, 1989, at the Grand Hotel in Georgetown. A couple hundred people attended the dinner afterwards, including Carl Bernstein, *Post* CEO Katharine Graham, and author Tom Clancy. At the time, Bob's daughter, Tali—who was Elsa's maid of honor—was thirteen years old; and Elsa had no strong desire to have children of her own. That outlook changed, however, just a few years after the wedding, when Elsa began working on her book, *Divided Lives*.

"I was trying to figure out my own life at the time," Elsa recalled, "and what the next stage was for me. I thought I was never going to get married, and I changed my mind about that. So then I began thinking, *Well, should we have a child?* I'm a very deliberate person—probably too much so—and Bob would always say to me, 'Well, who are the women who are happiest? Who are the people who have marriages that last, and why?' And he actually said to me, 'Why don't you go out and talk to people? Why don't you write the book?' "

"And did writing the book help you want to become a mother?" Marlo asked.

"Very much so," Elsa said. "I interviewed a lot of women for it and had narrowed it down to about twelve, and then seven, and then three. And in the selection of the women there was still that debate going on in my own mind, 'Could a person be happy and not have a child? Or could you have a child and have a really active career, and a good marriage, and still do all those things you wanted to do?' And at the end of doing all the research, I decided that actually I wanted to have a child."

Tali's younger sister, Diana, was born in 1996, two weeks shy of Elsa's thirty-ninth birthday. "It turned out to be the most wonderful, most fun, most important thing that I—we—ever did," she said. Amazingly, Elsa noted, she never experienced one phenomenon that practically every new bride faces: a mother pushing her to have babies—that is, grandchildren—for her.

"My mom never once asked me if I was going to get married or if I was going to have a child," Elsa recalled with a warm smile. "She was a totally accepting person, which is one of the greatest gifts you can give your child. I once asked her 'Why didn't you tell me? Why didn't you ask me?' And she said, 'I thought that was something you had to learn yourself.' "

Researching and writing *Divided Lives* not only helped Elsa reconcile the baby question; it ostensibly became a guidebook for other parts of life.

BOB: She came up with, not quite a formula, but a list of ingredients that make up a balanced life for a woman.

ELSA: If you look at a woman's life—her sense of self, her sense of place, her work, her friends, her family—and if she devotes equal time to work and play, I think those are the happiest and most satisfied people. A sense of place has always been really important to me. Creating a home, creating a nest for yourself.

BOB: Or even an office—somewhere to go and sit. An attic.

ELSA: Right, like a room of one's own. Time with your friends is also really important. I guess that's often the first thing that goes for women when they start working and having kids. And your sense of who you are when you're by yourself. I like to be by myself a lot, which is probably a good thing in our marriage.

PHIL: Do you like to be by yourself, too, Bob?

BOB: No.

PHIL: So what do you do when she's having alone time?

ELSA: You rattle around.

BOB: Well, I rattle around, but it's not just your physical presence I'm thinking about. It's your sense of everything. You're very stabilizing and comforting to me. And you always encourage my work. If I say, "I have to work," you never say, "Oh, you can't work" or "We've got to go to dinner" or "We've got to go out." You've always got plenty to do yourself.

PHIL: So while you're rattling, what exactly do you do?

BOB: I order pizza and I waste time. The disorder of life takes over.

"So how do you deal with the disorders of life?" Marlo asked Bob. "Do you each handle challenges in different or similar ways?"

Elsa turned to Bob. "You're more of a catastrophic thinker than I am," she said.

"So, he buckles a little bit?" Marlo asked.

"Yes," Elsa said. "He sometimes goes to the worst-case scenario, and I try to go to the best-case scenario. But in the end, it's a double management job. I involve him, but I keep him calm and explain to him, 'We're going to handle this, and it's not going to be as bad as you think.' I kind of revert to my mother, which is, 'Everything's going to be fine.' I think one of the things that we've always felt is that we're a team, professionally and personally. There's probably been no other person who comes anywhere close to him as being my advisor and my encourager, who says to me 'Take a leap, do that thing you want to do, try something hard.' Or even, 'If you don't want to do anything at all, that's fine too.'"

PHIL: It's obvious that you're very much on the same page with each other. When *aren't* you on the same page—and how do you handle that?

ELSA: Bob and I are very different people from each other. One of the most important things to do in a marriage is embrace that. Bob's a much stronger person than I am. You're steadier than me...

BOB: And you taught me the ability to just move on. If I'm being grumpy about something, instead of having a little courtroom hearing about it, she lets it go and gives me a free pass, even if I don't really deserve it.

ELSA: I think very early on in our marriage, we always tried to assume good intentions. It's the idea that when someone is being a jerk, it's not that they're being a jerk *to you*. It's just that they're being a jerk, and it's not directed. It may be an annoying thing, but it's not an annoying thing directed at me.

MARLO: Explain that a little.

ELSA: Well, I remember once being really mad at Bob about something. We had this pool house with a pergola, and some of the wood had rotted on it. Bob is amazing at maintenance; I like to do all the fluffy stuff, but the only reason our houses are standing is because he's so responsible. And so he'd noticed the rotting wood. We were going to get it repaired and I went out there one day and the whole thing was taken down. All of the wood was in the driveway.

PHIL: It fell down?

ELSA: No. It was taken down.

BOB: At my direction.

ELSA: He'd had it taken down without discussing it with me. I said, "When are we putting that back up?" He said, "I didn't think we were. They told me it was going to cost $50,000 to build it again." That was a lot.

MARLO: But the thing is, he did this without discussing it with you.

ELSA: Yes. And then he got upset that I was upset and said, "Okay, if it means that much to you, we can put it back." But then I was upset with myself for having gotten so upset. Now, I had done a fair amount of cognitive behavioral therapy at that point in my life, and I had an appointment with the therapist and I mentioned this to him. He said, "Well, why do you think he wanted to take it down?" And I said, "Because it was rotting." He said, "Do you think he was doing that to bother you?" I said, "No, but he didn't ask me." He said, "Well, most people would be happy that they had a husband who would take care of these problems. I don't think he was doing this to irritate you. So stop the heart palpitations about this." He reminded me that, in fact, Bob's intentions were good.

BOB: And then you told me that, exactly as you had talked about it. And I thought how wonderful it was for her to be so honest and to share that with me.

ELSA: This cognitive behavioral therapy deals a lot with anxiety, and it effectively says that we have a distorted way of thinking about things. There are different magnified levels, and when people are in states of high anxiety, they're usually in catastrophic thinking mode—you know, "This is the worst thing that's ever happened in my life!" So what the therapist does is teach you how to identify that distorted thinking. Most people go to a Number Five, when in reality, the situation is usually about a Number One or a Two. So, let's say you're in your bedroom and you hear a huge crash in the middle of the night. You might think, *Oh, my God, someone has broken into my house. They're going to kill me!* The cognitive behavioral therapist will say, "Well, how likely is that? It's much more likely that a branch fell down outside." It trains you to see the One or the Two, rather than the Five.

PHIL: So how do you practice this with each other? Give us an example.

BOB: Well, maybe a month ago, something was bugging me. I was remembering the 2016 Trump campaign, and I felt, for good reason, that I didn't work hard enough on getting his tax returns. We had talked about it at the time, but I was still feeling bad about it. Elsa said, "Well, what you did was reasonable and you're not carrying the world on your back, old boy." And I said, "Well, I really feel like I let myself down." We all should have done more, including myself. And I was churning and gnawing on it. And Elsa said, "Well, that's not your job, and there are always reasons for not doing something, and they're all reasonable."

MARLO: Did that work?

BOB: I don't think it got me down to a One or a Two, but it got me to a Three.

PHIL: Well, that was an improvement.

Toward the end of our conversation, Bob and Elsa revealed a private ritual of theirs, one that has endured almost as long as the mystery of Deep Throat: every year, Bob writes a letter to Elsa, recapping their life together.

"The letters are about what happened during the year," Bob explained. "What was our place in it? What did we do? What was memorable?" In addition to doing the kind of detailed reporting Bob is known for, the letters also confirm how their relationship has grown, and provide insight for the coming year.

For her part, Elsa creates photo books that are the "visual version of his letter," she said. At one point, she even snapped a photo of us setting up our microphones for this conversation. It was fun to know that our time together on this day would be included among the memories that Elsa and Bob collected for the year.

"There's one of these photo books for every year of our thirty years together," Bob said, thumbing through the pages of a recent one. "Look, there's Diana with her boyfriend, Dylan."

"And there are those two Italian chefs from New York," Elsa added, smiling.

MARLO: One of the things we've thought about a lot throughout this project is that we all enter into marriage with a kind of blind faith, without an emergency escape hatch. Or as Kyra Sedgwick noted, you can't go into it with a Plan B. You two seem to fit that model.

ELSA: Marriage is the most important decision you make in your life, so you should be pretty careful about it in choosing. One thing Bob often says is, "What can I do to make you happy?" And I'll say, "That's not your job. That's my job. I appreciate you wanting to make me happy, but I need to make my own self happy."

PHIL: And so if you were advising a pair of newlyweds about what to remember as they embarked on their life together, what would you tell them?

ELSA: Assume good intentions. Keep your promise. Don't leave the house angry.

PHIL: Don't leave the house angry. That's a new one. You usually hear, "Don't go to bed angry." Do you subscribe to that?

ELSA: I try to, but it's not always easy. We actually don't argue very often, which is good for me. I don't like arguing.

BOB: And sometimes having discussions isn't worth it.

PHIL: Because you know where it's going. You know the ending.

ELSA: Right. And sometimes that can get you madder. But I have one other thing I'd want to tell a young couple, and that is, once you've gotten married, it's so much easier to work on being married, and staying married, than it is to work on getting divorced. It takes a lot of effort to get out of a relationship, but if you put that effort back *into* the relationship, it would make life so much more satisfying. I don't understand the impetus toward disruption.

MARLO: When you say, "Keep your promise," you're talking about the commitment to making the marriage work, right?

ELSA: Yes. And for me, that promise was so different from my original idea—that you don't need to get married. But the truth is, getting married is like a seatbelt. You don't need your seatbelt 99 percent of the time, but it does hold you in firm when you need it.

PHIL: What about you, Bob. What would your advice be?

BOB: Well, I had two bad experiences and then the most important experience of my life with Elsa, so somebody who is batting .330 doesn't get to give advice. But I will say that there are certain expectations Elsa and I have of each other that we actually fulfill. And in no way have we ever made the other feel they're in this alone. There is a kind of a code that Elsa and I have for this, and that code is, "I love you."

MARLO: Is that a code you say when things are hard?

BOB: No.

ELSA: No. We say it all the time. Each morning, when he gets up before me, and he's down here having coffee, I come down and give him a kiss and say, "I love you."

BOB: And I say, "I love you." Or going to bed at night I say, "I love you. I love you." It means that there's no volcano churning under the surface. It means nothing's at a Four or Five in our lives. It just means we love each other.

You provided me with many gifts this year.
I believe they will last forever…
My heart is larger, I hope, even giant, because of you.
The day we met all the barriers came down.

—Bob, in his year-end letter to his wife, Elsa, 12/31/18

Charlotte and John Henderson

MARRIED IN 1939

"Charlotte was kind of shy, so she didn't want a big wedding. I remember the day as though it were yesterday. I had a new 1936 Model Ford."

W e honestly thought we were done.

It was early December 2019, and we were on the final lap of our adventure in marriage journalism. All of our interviews had been conducted, and we were just putting the final touches on our manuscript, when we boarded a flight for a fast trip to the west coast for a St. Jude event.

Somewhere over the Midwest, Marlo received an email on her iPhone. She read it carefully and turned to Phil.

"You're not going to believe this," she whispered, "but Guinness World Records has found the oldest living married couple. And they've been married for *eighty years*."

"Eighty years?" Phil said. "How old are they?"

"Their combined age is almost 212," Marlo responded. "Their names are Charlotte and John Henderson, and they live in Austin, Texas. What a shame we didn't know about them sooner."

We went back to our reading, and then seconds later turned to each other again.

"Are you thinking what I'm thinking?" Marlo said.

"What a great way to end our book," Phil said. "Let's make a little side trip to Texas on our way home."

And that's how we found ourselves, two days later, at Longhorn Village, a quiet and lovely retirement community in Texas Hill Country, just eleven miles northwest of Austin.

The Hendersons' residence is an assisted-living facility tucked between two lakes and surrounded by lush greenery. Nestled at the end of a long driveway, it looks like a charming southern hotel; and the large lobby was filled with fine furniture and, at this time of year, festive Christmas decor.

As it turns out, we weren't just visitors to Longhorn—we were its two newest residents. That's because, when we asked the proprietor where in town we could stay for the evening, she told us—with perfect Texas hospitality—"Well, don't waste your money on some fancy hotel. Bring your bags in and be our guests!"

It was 3 a.m. when we arrived (we seem to be magnets for plane delays), so we were very happy to accept the gracious invitation and settle in for the night. In the morning, we invited Charlotte and John into our roomy two-bedroom suite, which overlooked the beautiful property.

The couple offered warm handshakes.

"Good morning, Mr. and Mrs. Henderson," we said respectfully. "We're so pleased to meet you,"

"You can call me John," John said.

"You can call me Charlotte," Charlotte echoed.

Charlotte was in a wheelchair that was pushed by an attendant—and why shouldn't she be? She took her first steps just around the time Babe Ruth hit his first career home run—she's earned the right to put her feet up.

John is more ambulatory than his wife; but for longer distances, he uses wheels, too. The only difference is that his chair was motorized, and he

Houston, Texas; December 22, 1939

operated it with youthful exuberance. That's fitting, given that motor vehicles have always been a part of this man's life. In fact, a used car was what brought this couple together.

It was the early 1930s when John plunked down $26 for a 1925 Dodge Roadster. The car was stylish and dark green, which John remembers vividly.

"I painted it myself," he told us. "I bought a quart of green paint at Western Auto, then got a brush, and I brushed that whole thing green," John voice is surprisingly boyish for a man of 107. He speaks slowly, to be sure, but his words are charmingly accented with a twang that's as thick as a barbecued Texas rib eye.

"I loved that little Roadster," recalled Charlotte, 105, obviously relishing the sweet memory. "It was most unusual for a boy to have a car."

"That's right," John confirmed. "I was one of, I would say, a hundred students who had an automobile."

"Did it have rumble seats in the back?" Phil asked.

"No, no," John said, "no rumble seats. It was just a two-seater with soft leather upholstery that was a little bit before its time. It was actually the last Dodge car built with the old Dodge shift. Low was up here, second was back here, high was up there," he added, reflexively reaching out for a stick shift that was long gone.

John told us that he enjoyed cruising around the University of Texas campus, where he was a student and football star. Indeed, today he is the oldest living former UT football letterman. He played guard, both offense and defense, and he still faithfully roots for his team, attending at least one Longhorn game every season.

"In those days I could park anywhere on the campus I wanted to," he recalled. "I'd climb into the car, pick Charlotte up, drop her off at her class, and then head to mine."

It was in one of those classrooms that John first had the pleasure of meeting the young and pretty Charlotte Curtis, an Iowa native who had relocated to Texas with her family after the death of her father. Charlotte and John were in the same zoology class; and, lucky for them, the alphabetically assigned seating in the lecture hall put the *H*'s behind the *C*'s, placing Charlotte's desk directly in front of John's.

CHARLOTTE: He would look over my shoulder and say something to me, so that's how we got acquainted.

MARLO: It sounds like you were fated to be together. Did you immediately find him cute? I mean, he was this handsome football star...

CHARLOTTE: Handsome? Well, he might not be *perfectly* handsome, but he was fine for me.

JOHN: I don't know, I saw myself on TV the other day, and I didn't think I looked that old.

PHIL: What about you, John? Were you swept off your feet when your first laid eyes on Charlotte?

JOHN: Well, yeah, she was the closest to me in class, and she was a good-looking chick, too. Back in those days, the girls all wore high-heeled shoes—and didn't you wear a hat?

CHARLOTTE: Sometimes we wore hats, yes. And dresses. Just completely different then from the way it is now.

MARLO: So you began dating. Where would you go?

JOHN: You know, somebody recently asked me what we did on our first date, and I didn't have the slightest idea.

CHARLOTTE: Well, he liked to dance. He didn't do anything fancy—you know, twirling or things like that. But I didn't either, so it worked out perfectly.

JOHN: I liked to foxtrot.

CHARLOTTE: That's right, the foxtrot.

MARLO: Did you date other boys, too, Charlotte, or just—

CHARLOTTE: No, no. Only John.

MARLO: And what about you, John?

JOHN: Charlotte was the only one I had a date with. But, as a matter of fact, I think my roommate had a date with Charlotte before I did. Hubbell. Didn't you have a date with Hubbell?

CHARLOTTE: I didn't have a date with Hubbell. You always thought I did, but I never had a date with him. I knew Hubbell and I liked him, but never did we have a date.

JOHN: Well, I don't know. Hubbell and Fred Beasley and I roomed together. And I think maybe Hubbell told me that he had a date with Charlotte.

PHIL: I guess even after eighty years, some things don't get resolved.

John was born in 1912, the same year the *Titanic* set sail. World War I hadn't yet started, and women didn't have the right to vote. After graduating high school, John came to Austin to attend college. He lived in a rooming house across the street from a gymnasium and next door to a family that kept chickens and a cow in their backyard.

Charlotte and John Henderson, married eighty years, set the Guinness World Record as the oldest living married couple on August 28, 2019, with an aggregate age of 211 years and 175 days.

"Chickens on one side and a gymnasium on the other," John said with a broad Texas grin. "Imagine that!"

By the time Charlotte met John, she'd already lived through more than her fair share of tragedy. In addition to losing her father at a young age, her sister Larraine's husband, Ernest, had died in a terrifying way. He was an army pilot, and in December 1929, he was on a routine flight from Georgia to Alabama with three other airmen when their plane caught fire. The crew made an emergency decision to evacuate the burning aircraft—at five hundred feet. While the three other men survived the jump, Ernest's parachute failed to open and he died on impact. He left behind Charlotte's sister and an infant daughter.

As John recounted the story, Charlotte watched him attentively. "I always like to hear him talk," she said.

"But anyway," John continued, "that's how Charlotte's family got here to Texas, and I think she liked me pretty well. Her mother always called me Hendy. She knew we were going to do well in our later life, and sure enough it turned out that way."

Despite his future mother-in-law's blessing, however, it would take a while for wedding bells to toll.

"The whole reason we waited so long to get married is because it took me five years to talk her into it," John revealed.

"Really?" Marlo said. "Why, Charlotte? At that time, most mothers were pushing their daughters to marry. Wasn't yours?"

"No," Charlotte said. "She wanted me to have an education, and that was just perfect for me. We lived in a good area that was convenient for me—I walked to school. So, no, she didn't mind that I waited until I was ready."

Money was also an issue for Charlotte and John. They met in 1934, when the Great Depression was in full swing, and gangsters like John Dillinger wreaked havoc across the nation. It was a volatile, desperate time in America, with nationwide unemployment higher than 20 percent.

"Everybody was in the same boat," John remembered. "It was the Depression, and everyone we knew didn't have much of anything. That was just the way it was, so we got along fine. We just took life one step at a time."

So after graduation, the couple decided to hold off on the nuptials and "put a little money in the bank," as John put it. He coached high school football and made a profit selling the Dodge Roadster for $75, while Charlotte worked as a schoolteacher and lived with her family.

The couple finally tied the knot by eloping to Houston on December 22, 1939. John was twenty-seven, Charlotte was twenty-five. They had a small ceremony with just two witnesses.

"Charlotte was kind of shy," John noted, "so she didn't want a big wedding. One of the witnesses was the son of the minister who married us, and the other was a friend of Charlotte's brother from Austin. I remember the day as though it were yesterday. I had a new 1936 Model Ford and it was black. Henry Ford said he would sell you a car in any color you wanted, as long as it was black."

"I read about that once," Phil said with a laugh. "That was the joke in the ad. So it sounds to me like pretty much every chapter of your life is marked by some automobile or another."

"Yup," John said proudly. "As a matter of fact, I had a Model T Ford when I was in high school. So I've had a jalopy of some kind from the time I could drive until today."

The couple honeymooned in San Antonio, staying at the St. Anthony, a luxury hotel known for its elegant mahogany furnishings and telephones in every room. The Henderson's room cost them $7.50 a night. Charlotte saved the receipt.

But when they returned from their honeymoon, Charlotte had to give up her teaching job at the private Kinkaid School in Houston. The reason? Back then, women in Texas were prohibited from working after marriage.

"Mrs. Kinkaid didn't want me to get married," Charlotte explained. "She said, 'What will the children do?' I said, 'They won't have any trouble at all.' She said, 'Well, with your name changed, *you* will.' I said, 'Well, I can resign and you can get another teacher if you like.' She said, 'Oh, no, I don't want you to do that.' But Mrs. Kinkaid was very particular about this. So I said, 'Well, I'll finish out the year.' And that's what I did. I finished out the year and only substituted after that."

"I find that outrageous," Marlo said. "Why should you resign just because you were getting married?"

"That's what they did in those days," John said.

John and Charlotte settled in Baytown, Texas, a marshy grassland just north of Galveston Bay. John prospered there, enjoying a thirty-four-year career in the oil trade as the head of business services at Humble Oil & Refining Company, which later merged with Exxon.

The couple never had children and expressed no sign of regret about that. "We just accepted what the Lord gave us," John noted, "so we didn't have any."

Throughout their marriage, they told us, they enjoyed an active social life: he played poker, she played bridge, they bowled a bit, and did most of their traveling on cruise ships. They'd even gone on the *Mississippi Queen*—the very same paddleboat on which we once floated in our early time together.

Not surprisingly, Charlotte and John have outlived all of their friends and siblings. Is it genes, diet, exercise, or luck to be well-functioning supercentenarians? Could be a combination. Over the years, the couple often had a cocktail or wine before dinner. Charlotte never smoked, and John quit in 1950. He had bypass surgery in 1999, but he still walks a couple of miles every morning. Charlotte has never had a serious medical challenge.

When it was time for John to retire, the couple relocated to a place of familiarity.

"In all the time we were married," John recalled, "we said that when I retired, we were going to move back to Austin. But when Longhorn

Village came along, we decided that this was the place for us. So that's where we ended up. We were the first couple to move in here."

Guinness record or not, we didn't give the Hendersons a pass on the battery of questions we asked our other couples. So we gave John and Charlotte a lightning round.

MARLO: No couple can survive eighty years without a healthy fight or two. Charlotte, you've been living with this guy since the premiere of *Gone with the Wind*. Surely he must occasionally drive you crazy.

CHARLOTTE: No, no. I don't believe he could drive me crazy.

PHIL: What about you, John? Was there ever a moment when you just couldn't see eye-to-eye with Charlotte?

JOHN: Oh, it would have been something trivial, I'm sure. But that was so seldom with us. Maybe we had a moment or two when I realized we just weren't going to settle something right then and there, so I probably left the room and got out of the house to cool off. But we never let it last. That's the main thing. We always got through the problem.

PHIL: Some couples can't do that. Some just get on each other's nerves once in a while.

JOHN: Well, yeah, but there's a remedy for that.

PHIL: Which is?

JOHN: Never go to bed with a chip on your shoulder. If you can do that, you wake up in the morning and you're ready to move forward. I always say, "Try to make tomorrow a better day than today." It's a give-and-take situation with us. I can't insist on my way all the time, and Charlotte can't insist on hers. So if we ever disagree, we try to smooth things over as soon as possible. We let each one have their say and work it out. You can't carry that chip on your shoulder.

MARLO: Does he share the household responsibilities, Charlotte?

CHARLOTTE: Yes, he's good help, but I wouldn't say he ever took over.

MARLO: So you're the chief cook.

CHARLOTTE: Yes, I like to cook.

JOHN: And I did a lot of the cooking on the weekends—barbecuing chickens out in the yard.

MARLO: That's very Texas of you. I've noticed that Charlotte is wearing a diamond wedding ring and you're wearing your football ring. Why no wedding band, John?

JOHN: Never thought of it.

MARLO: And you didn't make him wear one, Charlotte?

CHARLOTTE: No, I didn't even think about it.

MARLO: So this is why you get along so well. You don't make demands on each other.

JOHN: That's right.

MARLO: So that's the secret to your record-breaking marriage, right there.

CHARLOTTE: Yes. And to have all the fun you can.

PHIL: I know it's bad manners to talk politics in these parts, but by my count, John, you've lived through nineteen presidential administrations. Do you have a favorite president?

JOHN: Well, I thought Roosevelt did a good job. I remember voting for FDR when I was at the university. But I just drifted away from politics. I never got into politics, really.

PHIL: Smart choice. It's probably the reason you've lived so long.

No matter how we tried to stir things up with these two, they were having no part of it. They took those vows in earnest eighty years ago, so why waste time bickering? In Charlotte's words, it's all about "the fun."

That included going back to the St. Anthony hotel for their fiftieth anniversary. These days it's a high-end property offering rooms that can go as high as $1,000 a night. When John called to make the reservation, he mentioned what they'd paid in 1939.

"They didn't charge us $7.50," he said, "but they did give us a suite and a bottle of champagne."

Since their move to Austin a decade or so ago, John and Charlotte have made new friends and have stayed close to their nieces and nephews.

John and his great-nephew, Jason Free, thirty-three, share the same birth date—Christmas Eve—and celebrate together every year.

We called Jason to thank him for helping to connect us with John and Charlotte, and he was just as sweet as they are. At one point he recounted one of his favorite memories of the couple.

"I was about sixteen or seventeen," he said, "and I was visiting their home. Charlotte was out shopping or something, and John and I were in the house talking. Suddenly, we heard the garage door open, and John jumped up from his chair. 'Oh, Charlotte's home!' he said, and then he ran out to the garage to greet her."

So maybe the big secret to Charlotte and John Henderson's long marriage is in the small stuff.

"You just have to be kind to each other," John told us. "You have to respect each other. And it goes on and on like that."

And maybe it's jumping up from your chair when the other one comes home.

Epilogue

This is a big book—and that was a surprise to us, once we put it all together. We hadn't expected it to have quite so many pages—but then, we hadn't expected the couples we interviewed to be so open and real and willing to dig in on such a deeply personal subject as marriage.

And that was just the first surprise. The next was how much we talked about our own marriage. That wasn't the plan. After we became husband and wife in 1980, a lot of people seemed to want to look under the hood of our marriage (to borrow a metaphor from Bryan Cranston), and we decided that wasn't for us. We weren't being obstinate; we felt that we had no authority to weigh in, and we thought it wise to keep personal things personal.

But when you sit down on a double date, as we did forty times over the past year with the remarkable couples who populate these pages, an interesting thing happens. Everyone talks. Everyone remembers. Everyone *feels*. And before you know it, you're all telling stories—in this case, the stories of the most intimate journey any of us has ever taken.

That happened time and again throughout the creation of this book. One perfect example: we'd kind of forgotten that story about our trip to Rome in 1977—pre-marriage—when an unexpected business opportunity for Marlo back in New York threatened our first private time together, an escape that was crucial to the future of our relationship. But when our conversation with Billy and Janice Crystal turned to the topic of how you build trust, that conflict in Rome—and the way we confronted it—came rushing back to us.

Even more unexpected than drawing back the curtain on our marriage were the little nuggets of gold we took home with us after we packed up our equipment. Halfway through the project, we found ourselves repeating bits of wisdom to each other that we'd picked up during our interviews with our couples.

One night we were going around and around in endless circles about some issue that was bothering us, and Phil said, "You know what? Let's kick this can down the road." Thank you, James Carville.

And often we reminded each other that Bob Woodward and Elsa Walsh say "I love you" to each other every morning. We're trying.

But the biggest revelation for us was the kind of book this collection became. Starting out, we thought we would be putting together a helpful and hopeful "how to" book—a straightforward compendium of the do's and don'ts of marriage, courtesy of dozens of celebrated and thoughtful people. But almost immediately it became clear to us that this wasn't a "how to" book at all. It was a "what" book. *What* were the experiences these people lived through—and came through—that have torn many couples apart but, for them, tightened their hold on each other?

Our takeaways were endless. We learned about grit and determination from Chip and Joanna Gaines. About supporting each other's dreams from Alan and Arlene Alda. About social purpose and personal forgiveness from Jesse and Jackie Jackson. About creating compatibility from chaos from John McEnroe and Patty Smyth. About building hope from heartbreak from Judy Woodruff and Al Hunt. About the curative rewards of laughter from Melissa McCarthy and Ben Falcone. About courage and resilience from Kelly Ripa and Mark Consuelos—even as their marriage suddenly, and quite literally, went out the window.

And we were reminded again of the importance of marriage by Neil Patrick Harris and David Burtka—and Lily Tomlin and Jane Wagner, and Elton John and David Furnish, and Patricia Cornwell and Staci Gruber—when they revealed to us how they passionately embraced their chance to marry and build a family, claiming precious rights they'd grown up believing would never be available to them.

So this is why you're holding such a big book in your hands. There was much for us to learn and much for us to share with you. And our biggest lesson is: there is no one secret to a lasting marriage, there are a million secrets. So keep looking for them. Because the longer you look, the more you'll discover reasons to stay in it. As Jamie Lee Curtis so perfectly said: "What's the secret to a long marriage? Don't leave."

Thank you for celebrating our fortieth anniversary with us. And for all of you with someone special of your own, let us offer you this closing toast.

May you continue to greet each day as a new adventure—one filled with friends and family, laughter and love, bickering and bonding, and, yes, all the missing toothpaste caps you can tolerate.

May you fall into your bed at night—tushies touching or not—and always dream the same dreams.

And may you forever honor the most beautiful and audacious promise you will ever make: to be together, as long as you both shall live.

Acknowledgments

Typically, a marriage is the union of two people, a powerful and personal bond that travels from one heart to the other with, hopefully, little interference. Publishing, however, is a seriously polygamous business, one that depends on the loyalty, love, and occasional meddling of a whole mess of spouses.

And so, this book would not have been possible without the assistance of many significant others, each of whom brought their own brand of marital commitment to the union.

Thank you to Judith Curr, Shannon Welch, and the entire team at HarperOne, who said an instant "I do!" to us when we first proposed the idea for this book, and who continued to renew that vow for a full year, helping us turn a collected 1,252 years of marriage into forty beautiful little wedding albums.

Our deepest gratitude to Kim Schefler and Robert Levine, who arranged this marriage with precision and care, and who guided us every step along the way. Thanks also to Susie Arons, who lent her expertise to ensuring that this book would have the perfect reception.

Our sincerest appreciation to our talented wedding photography crew: Charlie Pratt of Impressive Printing, for brilliantly recapturing the magic of all those special days, some of them more than half a century old; and Paul Williams, for helping us assemble those pictures picture-perfectly. A giant toss of the bouquet to Seth Dixon and Jere Parobek for our fortieth anniversary photo, which graces the cover of this book; and a toast of bubbly to Steven Rice, Eric Barnard, Kim Chandler, and Lonnie Richards, who lovingly styled this bride and groom for that special portrait.

High-fives and hugs to our able—and inexhaustible—team of wedding planners, Jill DeVincens, Phyllis Iovane Mainiero, Todd Trantham, and Ken Haywood, for catering to our every request, soothing our pre-wedding jitters, and making damn sure that we got to the church on time. And loads of thanks to Dan Sallick, Julian Schlossberg, David Slavin, and Tony Thomas, who were the first readers of our manuscript, and, like good spouses everywhere, showered us with praise while gently telling us the things we needed to fix.

We couldn't have thrown a single grain of rice without the skill and passion of bridesmaids Julie Besonen and Alison Gwinn, and groomsmen Donald Liebenson and Buzz McClain, who helped us turn our romantic adventure into the most royal of weddings. And thanks, too, to Greg Fagan, Lori Oliwenstein, and Stephen Randall, for joining the procession halfway through the service and becoming irreplaceable members of the wedding party.

And thank you most of all to our Best Man, Bruce Kluger, whose keen eye, buoyant humor, and good heart were fundamental in helping us usher this baby down the aisle.

About the Authors

MARLO THOMAS is an award-winning actress, author, and activist whose body of work continues to impact American culture. She has been honored with four Emmy Awards, the George Foster Peabody Award, a Golden Globe, and a Grammy and has been inducted into the Broadcasting Hall of Fame. In November 2014, President Barack Obama awarded Marlo the Presidential Medal of Freedom, the highest honor a civilian can receive.

Marlo burst onto the scene as television's *That Girl*, which broke new ground for independent women everywhere and which she also conceived and produced. Her pioneering spirit continued with her creation of *Free to Be . . . You and Me*, which became a platinum album, bestselling book, Emmy Award–winning television special, and theatrical production. She has also produced and starred in numerous movies for television, including her portrayal of a mentally ill woman in *Nobody's Child*, for which she won the Emmy for Best Dramatic Actress. She continues to win critical acclaim on stage, most recently in Elaine May's 2012 Broadway comedy-drama, *Relatively Speaking*, and in Tony Award–winning playwright Joe DiPietro's 2015 dark comedy, *Clever Little Lies*.

Marlo has produced seven bestselling books (three of them #1 *New York Times* bestsellers), including *Free to Be You and Me*; *Free to Be a Family*; *The Right Words at the Right Time* (Volumes 1 and 2); *Thanks and Giving: All Year Long* (which became a Grammy-winning CD); her memoir, *Growing Up Laughing*; and *It Ain't Over Till It's Over*.

Marlo is the National Outreach Director for St. Jude Children's Research Hospital, which was founded by her father, Danny Thomas. In 2004, along with her siblings, she created the annual St. Jude Thanks and Giving campaign, a national holiday fundraising program that has raised more than $1 billion to date. In 2014, in recognition of her commitment to the hospital, St. Jude christened its newest building the Marlo Thomas Center for Global Education and Collaboration.

PHIL DONAHUE is a journalist, writer, producer, and media pioneer who revolutionized the talk-show format, ushering in a new era of broadcast television. In 1967, Phil debuted his first TV talk show in Dayton, Ohio, interviewing world leaders, newsmakers, celebrities, and people from all walks of life. Three years later, the program entered nationwide syndication, launching the first coast-to-coast audience participation talk show in the country and making "Donahue" a household name and an American institution. The *Donahue* show was honored with twenty Daytime Emmy Awards, including ten Emmys for Outstanding Host and ten for Best Talk Show. In 1996, the Daytime Emmys presented Phil with a Lifetime Achievement Award for his contributions to television journalism. As one of the few voices who opposed the 2003 American invasion of Iraq, Phil produced and codirected the 2006 film *Body of War*, which was chosen as Best Documentary by the National Board of Review of Motion Pictures and was honored with the People's Choice Award at the Toronto International Film Festival.

Phil has been inducted into the Academy of Television Arts & Sciences Hall of Fame and is a recipient of the George Foster Peabody Award.